YOUNG STUDENTS

Learning Library®

VOLUME 1

Aardvark—American History

NEWFIELD
PUBLICATIONS

MIDDLETOWN · CONNECTICUT

Young Students Learning Library is a federally registered
trademark of Newfield Publications, Inc.

Copyright © 1992 by Newfield Publications, Inc.; 1974, 1972
by Funk & Wagnalls, Inc. & Newfield Publications, Inc.

ISBN 0-8374-0471-1

Editorial Staff

ACKNOWLEDGMENTS

PHOTO CREDITS

STATE OF ALABAMA BUREAU OF PUBLICITY AND INFORMATION page 81(bottom right); 83(top left). JOHN T. ALLEN page 38(top left). ANGLO/CHINESE EDUCATIONAL INSTITUTE page 12(top). ASSOCIATED PRESS page 62(top). AUSTRALIAN NEWS & INFORMATION BUREAU page 53(bottom right). BETTMANN ARCHIVE page 52(top left); 84(bottom left); 85(bottom left); 94(bottom left); 119(top left); 123(bottom left); BRITISH MUSEUM page 115(top right). BUREAU OF INDIAN AFFAIRS page 85(bottom right); 95(bottom right); 100(top left). J. ALLEN CASH page 74(bottom center). CHILDRENS TELEVISION WORKSHOP page 29(top left). COCA COLA page 38(bottom left). DAVE COLLINS page 48(top left). COLONIAL WILLIAMSBURG page 111(bottom right); 113(top right). COLOUR LIBRARY INTERNATIONAL page 113(bottom right). CONNECTICUT HISTORICAL SOCIETY page 124(top). ARMANDO CURCIO EDITORE page 17(bottom right); 20(top); 21(both pics); 24(bottom left); 28(top left); 31(top left); 32(top); 32(bottom left); 34(center left); 36(bottom left); 41(center right); 44(bottom right); 51(top right); 53(top right); 65(bottom left); 69(center); 77(bottom center); 75(top right); 89(bottom center); 90(bottom); 93(bottom right); 104(top left); 106(bottom); 122(bottom); 125(bottom); 126(top left); 127(top). WALT DISNEY PRODUCTIONS page 28(center); DERBY MUSEUM & ART GALLERY page 93(top left). EDITORIAL PHOTOCOLOR ARCHIVES page 101(top left). FOX-RANK page 28(bottom left). GOODYEAR TIRE & RUBBER COMPANY page 79(bottom left). GREEK TOURIST OFFICE page 26(top left). ROBERT HARDING PICTURE LIBRARY page 77(top left). DAVID HARRIS page 108(top); MICHAEL HOLFORD page 99(top). IMITOR page 108(bottom left). IMPERIAL WAR MUSEUM page 119(top center). INTERNATIONAL HARVESTER COMPANY page 52(center, bottom left, bottom right). JAPAN AIRLINES page 75(top right). LIBRARY OF CONGRESS page 33(top right); 98(bottom left); 105(top left). WILLIAM McQUITTY page 20(bottom right). MANSELL COLLECTION page 111(top right); 118(right center); 118(bottom left). NATIONAL FILM ARCHIVE page 28(top center). NATIONAL MOTOR MUSEUM page 37(bottom right). NATIONAL SCIENCE PHOTOS page 92(P Bowman)(left). NAVAL PHOTO CENTER, WASHINGTON page 59(top right). NASA page 40(top left); 95(top right); 119(bottom right). THE PHILIPS COLLECTION, WASHINGTON page 19(top). PHOTO RESEARCHERS INC. page 102(bottom); (T. McHugh). PHOTOSOURCE page 119(center left); PHOTRI INC. page 109(top right); POPPERFOTO page 120(bottom left); 121(both pics). REDIFFUSION page 65(bottom). ROLLS ROYCE (1971) LTD page 69(top left). SATOUR page 46(top right); 48(bottom). SHELL page 88(top left); SIMON FRASER/SCIENCE PHOTO LIBRARY page 23(top right). SPECTRUM COLOUR LIBRARY page 17(top left); 82(bottom right). TATE GALLERY page 19(bottom right). UNITED STATES AIRFORCE OFFICIAL PHOTOGRAPH page 62(bottom left). UNITED STATES CAPITOL HISTORICAL SOCIETY page 123(top right). UNITED STATES NAVY, OFFICIAL PHOTOGRAPH page 60(top left & bottom left). UNIVERSAL CITY STUDIOS page 27(bottom left). UNIVERSITY OF ILLINOIS AT CHICAGO page 33(center right). JEAN VERTUT page 19(center). JOHN WATNEY page 101(bottom right). ZEFA page 10; 25(top right); 35(top); 39(top left); 42(left center); 46(bottom left); 48(top right); 49(bottom); 54(top left); 56(top left); 59 (top right); 64(top right); 72(left); 80(top left); 87(top left); 88(bottom left); 89(top right); 91(bottom left); 107(top right).

FOREWORD

Growing up in a rapidly changing world is a challenge for every child. THE YOUNG STUDENTS LEARNING LIBRARY has been written especially for children to enable them to keep pace with the world in which they live.

Children have inquistive minds. THE YOUNG STUDENTS LEARNING LIBRARY answers their questions and, at the same time, builds learning skills that last a lifetime. THE YOUNG STUDENTS LEARNING LIBRARY is ideal for use at school or at home. Many of the subjects contained in THE YOUNG STUDENTS LEARNING LIBRARY support actual lessons children learn in school. Plus, THE YOUNG STUDENTS LEARNING LIBRARY is filled with topics that naturally fascinate young people—airplanes, dinosaurs, the human body.

In this 22-volume set, children are introduced to people, places, and events that have shaped their world. The latest information on such topics as AIDS, acid rain, waste disposal, computer technology, fiber optics, and terrorism is written in easy-to-comprehend language. Biographical sketches tell children about famous people who have influenced their lives. Such personalities include: Blaise Pascal, the 17th-century vanguard of computer technology; Susan B. Anthony, champion of women's rights; George Washington Carver, great 19th-century botanist; Mother Teresa, Nobel Peace Prize recipient; Sandra Day O'Connor, first woman Justice of the Supreme Court; and Mikhail Gorbachev, modern-day leader of the Soviet Union and Nobel Peace Price recipient.

Children will find THE YOUNG STUDENTS LEARNING LIBRARY an invaluable reference tool as well as a stimulating and enjoyable reading adventure.

INTRODUCTION

Welcome to *The Young Students Learning Library.* In today's world of rapidly expanding information and discovery, it is crucial for young people to begin as early as possible to understand the dimensions of the world in which they live.

This comprehensive 22-volume library, developed specifically for the needs of elementary-school-age children, makes learning a vitally interactive part of your family life.

More than 3,000 entries are presented in this encyclopedia. Subjects represent basic concepts underlying current elementary school curricula as well as children's outside interests.

Children will find these books accessible, stimulating, activity-orientied, and most important, especially for primary-grade youngsters, non-threatening. Potentially difficult or unfamilir terms are defined or explained in context. The following special features of this series make this accessibility possible:

READING LEVEL

Parents and educators agree that a child's interest level often exceeds his or her reading level. Therefore, a prime goal of this series is to provide interesting, factual, and readable materials for a wide range of readers. Information is presented on many levels of comprehension to meet the needs of students throughout their elementary and junior high school years. Articles begin with the simplest information and gradually become more detailed as the text progresses. Charts, up-to-date maps, and more than 5,000 colorful pic-

tures and two-page picture spreads offer the youngest reader a satisfying and stimulating survey of important topics. For the older reader, in-depth coverage offers a more expanded view of a subject. Entries devote considerable attention to biographical and geographical subjects, science and technology, historical and contemporary personalities, countries of the world, U.S. states, and Canadian provinces. While most children will be completely comfortable using this series on their own, younger children will always benefit from the assistance of a parent.

LEARN BY DOING

The activity-oriented Learn By Doing sections are an integral part of this series. Through hands-on involvement, the concepts presented in each book become real and meaningful. The variety of activities suggested in Learn By Doing sections make *The Young Students Learning Library* an interactive learning tool, expand a child's understanding of a subject, and stimulate creative thinking. The Learn By Doing activities provide numerous suggestions and step-by-step instructions for completing class projects and have been designed to generate questions and discussions that will produce long-lasting learning. Each Learn By Doing activity is designated by a ■ at the beginning and end of the feature. The entries having Learn By Doing activities are also identified by asterisks (*) in the index contained in volume 22.

NUGGETS

High points of a topic are presented in capsule form through the Nugget. Printed in bold type in the margin, each Nugget is designated by a wide color-bar for eye-catching appeal. Nuggets contain additional information related to an article and provide children with contrasts, records, trivia, and special examples for selected entries. In addition, the Nugget will make learning more inviting for readers who like to browse. While a reader is flipping pages, the Nugget can grab his or her attention and stimulate a taste for more information.

FULL-COLOR MAPS

New and up-to-date maps of the 50 U.S. states and Canadian provinces have been especially created for this series by Rand McNally. These colorful maps, representing geographical and historical information feature major cities as well as the physical features of states, provinces, and countries. The information provided through the maps—like the entries in each volume—has been carefully selected to correlate with school curricula, making *The Young Students Learning Library* a most practical learning tool.

HOW TO READ THE MAPS

Each map features:
- A scale bar and a north arrow,
- Major rivers, lakes and mountain ranges,
- A prominent star indicating each state capital,
- Major national parks,
- Boundaries of surrounding states, including state names and very major cities.

In addition to the foregoing, *The Young Students Learning Library* includes the following important elements:

- More than 3,000 articles arranged in alphabetical order, letter by letter, except when a comma appears in the title. For example, **CAT, WILD,** appears before **CATACOMBS**, but **HORSEPOWER** appears before **HORSE RACING**.
- An interlacing chain of cross-references that guide the young student to related information. At the ends of articles, they appear as ALSO READ: followed by one or more article titles. In alphabetical order, where a subject might be expected to appear but instead has been incorporated into another article, a slightly different form of cross-reference has been used; for example, **ACCIDENT PREVENTION** see SAFETY, or **ADENOIDS** see BREATHING.
- Traditional measurements along with the metric equivalents are located throughout each volume.
- An index, located in Volume 22, provides more than 20,000 entries. Complete directions for the best use of the index appear at its start in the last volume.
- Tables of information and fact boxes with each U.S. Presi-

dent, U.S. state, Canadian province, and nations that highlight important data about each.

- Glossaries of terms commonly used in relation to the subject of an article. For examples, see **BOXING, CATTLE** or **MUSIC.**

Designed for use at home or in school, *The Young Students Learning Library* provides children with a basic information and activities source for their pleasure and enlightenment. Regular use of this set will develop an exciting and rewarding foundation for every child's future.

CONTENTS

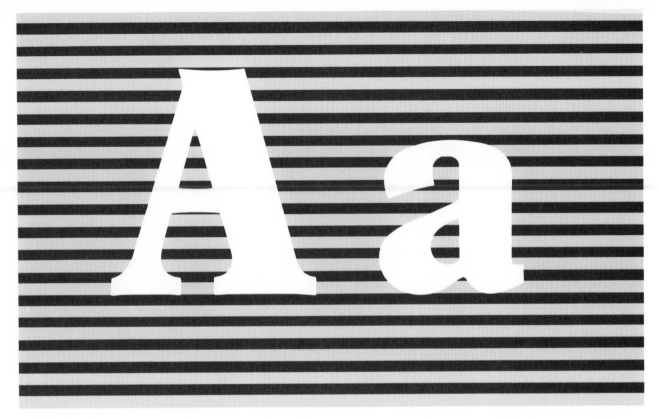

AARDVARK The aardvark is a strange animal of Africa. It is so unusual that scientists place it in an order of mammals by itself—order Tubulidentata, which means "tube-toothed." Its teeth have no roots or strong enamel. But the aardvark does not really need strong teeth because it eats only termites and ants.

The aardvark grows up to 6 feet (1.8 m) long, including its thick tail. Very few bristly hairs can be seen on its pinkish-gray skin, although some aardvarks have long, full coats of hair. The aardvark's narrow head is topped by large rabbit-like ears. Its ears can pick up the faint sounds made by termites in their nests. The aardvark uses its strong front claws to tear open the hard mud-mound nests of termites. The insects attack the aardvark, but not even their sharp pincers can go through its tough skin. The aardvark catches the termites with its long, sticky tongue. The aardvark

also uses its claws to dig a home underground. It digs a deep burrow, where it hides from enemies and sleeps during the day, coming out to hunt for food at night. If attacked, it lies on its back and uses its claws to defend itself.

Dutch settlers in South Africa gave it the name aardvark, which means "earth pig." It is also called "ant bear." Aardvarks live throughout Africa south of the Sahara.

ALSO READ: ANTEATER, MAMMAL.

If caught away from its burrow, the aardvark digs a hole for itself at astonishing speed, earth and stones flying out from its powerful front feet to a height of some 14 feet (4 m).

▼ *The aardvark is a mammal that lives in the dry parts of Africa. It uses its long tongue to catch termites.*

◄ *African camel riders, from the Sahel region.* (See AFRICA.)

ABACUS An abacus is a device that helps a person count and do arithmetic problems. As you can see in the diagram, an abacus uses beads to keep track of the numbers. The beads slide along rods. Each rod has seven beads—five on the left and two on the right of the center strip. Before starting to solve a problem, the beads should be pushed away from the center strip, because that is where the numbers are counted.

The more rows of beads on an abacus, the larger the numbers you can count. Each row stands for a different *power of ten*. Powers of ten are 1, 10, 100, 1,000, and so on, adding as many zeros as you like.

The five beads on the left in every row each stand for *one* of the unit of that row. The two beads on the right are each *five* of the unit. Numbers are formed by bringing the beads from their starting position to the center strip. To count a number on an

▼ *These pictures show some western abacuses with three rows of beads. But some abacuses have more rows. You can tell that no adding is being done on the top abacus. No beads are touching the center strip. A real abacus does not have the numbers written on the beads as this one does. Each abacus in the six lower drawings shows a different number—(a) 3; (b) 7; (d) 73; and (e) 98. Can you work out what numbers abacus (c) and abacus (f) show?*

▲ *Chinese schoolchildren are still taught to use the abacus.*

abacus, you push enough beads into the center to equal your number. To subtract a number, you push the right number of beads away from the center.

■ **LEARN BY DOING**

You can make an abacus. You will need a picture frame, string, beads, and thumbtacks. Many abacuses have 13 rows of beads. But you can make a smaller one, with only five rows, and still count up to 166,665. To make a five-row abacus, first cut five pieces of string the same length—long enough to cross the picture frame plus 3 inches (7.6 cm) for tying knots. Tie a knot one-fourth of the way down each piece of string. Make the knots fat, so no beads can pass them. The knots will be the center strip in your abacus. Now carefully put five evenly spaced thumbtacks on each side of the picture frame. Slide five beads onto one string at the end that is farther from the knot. Put two beads onto the short end. Tie the ends of the string to the first thumbtack on either side of the frame, with the group of five

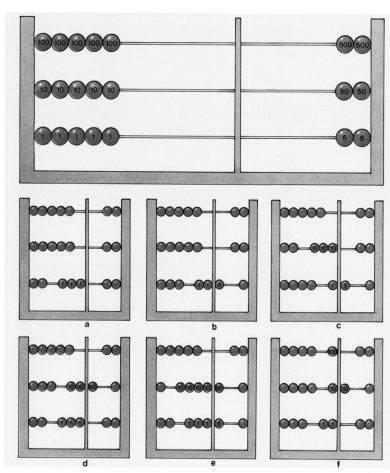

beads at the left. Then load the other four strings with beads and tie them to the other four pairs of tacks.

Hold your abacus flat, with the groups of five beads toward your left, and you are ready to try a simple problem. First, count 3 on your abacus. Push three beads on the bottom row to the right until they touch the center strip (the knot). Now add 5. Do this by pushing one right-hand bead on the bottom row to the left until it touches the center strip, too. You have just completed an addition problem. What is the total? Now try subtracting 6 from the total. What answer do you get? (Remember, to subtract, you push the right number of beads *away* from the center strip.) Next, add 210 to the number on your abacus. You can read this number in three parts—two hundreds (200), one ten (10), and no ones (0). If you work carefully, the total that your abacus shows will be 212. You will find you can solve difficult problems with the help of your abacus. ■

Bead abacuses like this were used in ancient China. The ancient Egyptians, Greeks, and Romans used a kind of abacus that had pebbles or other movable counters. Today, the abacus has largely been replaced by the electronic calculator, but it is still used for calculating in the Middle East and in parts of Asia. It is also especially useful for teaching blind children to calculate.

ALSO READ: ARITHMETIC, CALCULATOR, COMPUTER.

ABBREVIATION To abbreviate means to make shorter. Words and phrases are often shortened to save time and space in speaking and writing. Abbreviations, acronyms, and contractions are some ways of shortening language.

Abbreviations are letters that stand for common, well-known words and

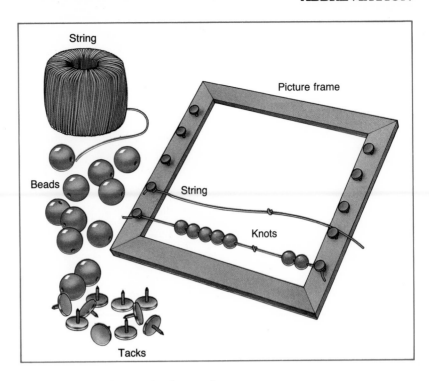

String
Picture frame
Beads
String
Knots
Tacks

phrases. Sometimes, the letters have periods after them to show that other letters have been left out. There are no basic rules for forming abbreviations. Perhaps somebody just decided to shorten a word or phrase in a certain way. It soon became accepted and understood. Sometimes just the beginning of the word is used, such as *doz.* for "dozen" or *max.* for "maximum." Other abbreviations use the first and last letters, such as *Rd.* for "Road" or *Dr.* for "Doctor." And still others use just the first letter: for example, *m* stands for "meter."

Some abbreviations do not look like the words they stand for. Such abbreviations usually come from ancient Latin or Greek words or from modern foreign languages. *A.M.* means "before noon." It is an abbreviation of the Latin *ante meridiem.* The shortened form for *pound* is *lb.*, from the Latin word *libra*, which was a unit of weight. *R.S.V.P.* (on an invitation) means "Please reply." It stands for the French words, *Répondez, s'il vous plaît.*

Abbreviated words can be confusing. Several words may share the same abbreviation. The letters *St.* can mean either "Street" or "Saint." And

Many of the words we use today are abbreviations. We seldom stop to think that bus is short for omnibus, flu for influenza, zoo for zoological gardens, and cello for violoncello.

SOME COMMON ABBREVIATIONS

A.A. Alcoholics Anonymous
AAA American Automobile Association
abbr. abbreviation
ABC American Broadcasting Company
A.D. *anno Domini,* "in the year of our Lord"
adj. adjective
adv. adverb; advertisement
AFL-CIO American Federation of Labor and Congress of Industrial Organizations
Ala., AL Alabama
Alas., AK Alaska
A.M., a.m. *ante meridiem,* "before noon"
anon. anonymous, "author unknown"
AP Associated Press
Apr. April
Ariz., AZ Arizona
Ark., AR Arkansas
assn. association
asst. assistant
atty. Attorney
Aug. August
Ave. Avenue
A.W.O.L. absent without leave
b. born
BBC British Broadcasting Corporation
B.C. before Christ; British Columbia
bldg. building
Blvd. Boulevard
bros. brothers
c. *circa,* about
C Celsius; centigrade
Calif., CA California
CBC Canadian Broadcasting Corporation
CBS Columbia Broadcasting System
cc cubic centimeter
cm centimeter
Co. Company; County
c/o in care of
C.O.D. cash on delivery
Colo., CO Colorado
conj. conjunction
Conn., CT Connecticut
cont. continued
Corp. Corporation
CPA Certified Public Accountant
CST Central Standard Time
d. died
D.A. District Attorney
DAR Daughters of the American Revolution
D.A.V. Disabled American Veterans
D.C., DC District of Columbia
D.D.S. Doctor of Dental Surgery
Dec. December
Del., DE Delaware
Dem. Democrat
Dr. Doctor; Drive
DST Daylight Saving Time
E. east
e.g. *exempli gratia,* "for example"
Eng. English; England
EST Eastern Standard Time
etc. *et cetera,* "and so forth"
F Fahrenheit
FDIC Federal Deposit Insurance Corporation
Feb. February
Fla., FL Florida
Fr. Father; French; France

Fri. Friday
ft. foot; feet
Ft. Fort
g gram
Ga., GA Georgia
Gov. Governor
H.I., HI Hawaii
Hon. Honorable
HRH His (Her) Royal Highness
I. Island
Ia., IA Iowa
ibid. *ibidem,* in the same place
Id., ID Idaho
i.e. *id est,* "that is," "in other words"
ill., illus. illustration
Ill., IL Illinois
in. inch; inches
Inc. Incorporated
Ind., IN Indiana
IOU I owe you
IQ intelligence quotient
Jan. January
Jr. Junior
Kans., KS Kansas
kg kilogram
km kilometer
Ky., KY Kentucky
l liter
La., LA Louisiana
m meter
Mar. March
Mass., MA Massachusetts
M.D. Doctor of Medicine
Md., MD Maryland
Me., ME Maine
Mich., MI Michigan
Minn., MN Minnesota
Miss., MS Mississippi
ml milliliter
Mlle. Mademoiselle
mm millimeter
Mo., MO Missouri
Mon. Monday
Mont., MT Montana
mpg miles per gallon
mph miles per hour
Mr. Mister
Mrs. Mistress (used for a married woman)
Ms. written form of address for any woman
MST Mountain Standard Time
Mt. Mount; Mountain
n. noun
N. north
NASA National Aeronautics and Space Administration
NATO North Atlantic Treaty Organization
NBC National Broadcasting Company
N.C., NC North Carolina
N.Dak., ND North Dakota
Nebr., NB Nebraska
Nev., NV Nevada
N.H., NH New Hampshire
N.J., NJ New Jersey
N.Mex., NM New Mexico
no. number
Nov. November
N.Y., NY New York
O., OH Ohio
Oct. October
Okla., OK Oklahoma

Ore., OR Oregon
p. page
Pa., Penn., PA Pennsylvania
pat. patent
PBS Public Broadcasting Service
P.D. police department; postal district
Pfc. Private first class
pl. plural
Pl. Place
P.M., p.m. *post meridiem,* "after noon"; *post mortem,* "after death"
P.O. post office
POW prisoner of war
pp. pages
prep. preposition
pron. pronoun
P.S. *post scriptum,* "postscript"; Public School
PST Pacific Standard Time
R. River
Rd. Road
Rep. Republican
Rev. Reverend; Revelations
R.I., RI Rhode Island
rpm revolutions per minute
R.R. railroad
R.S.V.P. *Répondez, s'il vous plaît,* "please reply"
S. south
SAC Strategic Air Command
Sat. Saturday
S.C., SC South Carolina
S.Dak., SD South Dakota
Sept. September
sing. singular
S.P.C.A. Society for the Prevention of Cruelty to Animals
sq. square
Sr. Senior
S.S. steamship
St. Saint; Street
Sun. Sunday
Tenn., TN Tennessee
Terr. Terrace; Territory
Tex., TX Texas
Thur., Thurs. Thursday
TNT trinitrotoluene
Tues. Tuesday
U., UT Utah
UHF ultra-high frequency
UN United Nations
UNICEF United Nations Children's Fund
UPI United Press International
U.S. United States
U.S.A. United States of America
U.S.S.R. Union of Soviet Socialist Republics
v. verb
Va., VA Virginia
VHF very high frequency
VI Virgin Islands
VIP very important person
Vt., VT Vermont
W. west
Wash., WA Washington
Wed. Wednesday
Wis., WI Wisconsin
W.Va., WV West Virginia
Wyo., WY Wyoming
YMCA Young Men's Christian Association
YWCA Young Women's Christian Association

Fr. may mean "Father," "France," or "French." It is up to the reader to decide what an abbreviation means by looking at the rest of the sentence.

An *acronym* is an abbreviation that is actually a word, because it can be easily pronounced. *NATO*, for example, is an acronym for *North Atlantic Treaty Organization. NASA* stands for *National Aeronautics and Space Administration.*

A *contraction* is a shortened phrase that, when written, has an apostrophe to show that letters are missing. Contractions, such as "isn't" and "won't," are used more often in speaking than in writing.

■ LEARN BY DOING

You probably know more abbreviations than you think you do. Find out. Print one letter of the alphabet on each of 26 small pieces of paper. Mix them up in a bag and draw five pieces of paper. How many different abbreviations can you make from the five letters you drew? Have a contest with a friend and see who can make the most abbreviations. ■

In the list of common abbreviations with this article, the regular shortened form of a state's name is followed by the official two-letter U.S. Postal Service abbreviation. For example, Minn. and MN are shown for Minnesota.

ALSO READ: WRITTEN LANGUAGE.

ABOLITION Slaves were first brought to North America during the 1600's. Even then, there were people who thought that slavery was wrong. These people were part of the *anti-slavery* movement, which grew both in Europe and in the United States. By the 1800's, a growing number of people in the United States were outraged about slavery. These people refused to obey laws that helped slave owners. They hid runaway slaves.

They gave speeches and wrote books and newspaper articles against slavery. They decided that slavery had to be *abolished* (ended) as quickly as possible. These people were called *abolitionists.*

One of the most famous abolitionists was William Lloyd Garrison. From 1831 to the end of the Civil War in 1865, he published an anti-slavery newspaper called *The Liberator.* Another important abolitionist was Frederick Douglass, a black journalist. His newspaper, *The North Star,* urged blacks and whites to help slaves escape from the South. Charles Lenox Remond, a black abolitionist speaker, traveled through the country, speaking against slavery wherever people would listen.

Harriet Beecher Stowe wrote *Uncle Tom's Cabin* in 1852. This novel told a dramatic tale of how slaves were forced to live. It told about beatings and about how slave families were separated when the mother or father was sold to another slave owner. The book made many people examine their own attitudes toward slavery.

Some people did not like the abolitionists. People threw stones and rotten eggs at William Lloyd Garrison when he made speeches against slavery. An angry mob in Boston once dragged him through the streets. Another abolitionist editor, Elijah P. Lovejoy, was murdered by a mob.

Some people thought that speaking and writing against slavery was not enough. John Brown tried to convince the slaves to start a revolution. In 1859, he and some followers captured the U.S. arsenal, a place where guns and ammunition were kept, at Harpers Ferry, Virginia (now in West Virginia). He hoped the raid would be a signal to all slaves to fight for their freedom. But many of his followers were killed by soldiers. Brown was captured and hanged for treason.

People who were afraid of abolitionists lived all over the U.S. They thought abolitionists caused trouble

▲ *Charles Lenox Remond, a respected black speaker for abolition.*

In the days before the Civil War, about 50,000 slaves escaped from the South to the North. Most of them traveled by the Underground Railroad—a system for helping slaves to travel from one safe hiding place to another. The Underground Railroad was centered in Pennsylvania and Ohio.

▲ *The abominable snowman is also known as the yeti. The British mountaineer Eric Shipton photographed 'yeti' tracks which he found in snow near Mount Everest in 1951.*

Some aborigines believed that they could kill an enemy by pointing a sharpened bone at him, while singing a death chant. They believed that an invisible bone splinter flew into the victim's body without leaving a mark on the skin. Often the victim died out of sheer terror unless a witch doctor could be found to magic away the invisible piece of bone.

and did not try to find a workable solution to the problem. Some Southerners tried to silence the abolitionists, even in Congress. But those who spoke out boldly against slavery finally won their battle. On January 1, 1863, President Abraham Lincoln made his Emancipation Proclamation, freeing the slaves in the Confederate States. The Thirteenth Amendment was added to the U.S. Constitution in 1865, and slaves were freed in all of the United States.

ALSO READ: BROWN, JOHN; CIVIL WAR; DOUGLASS, FREDERICK; EMANCIPATION PROCLAMATION; SLAVERY; STOWE, HARRIET BEECHER; UNDERGROUND RAILROAD.

ABOMINABLE SNOWMAN

The abominable snowman is a creature some people believe lives high in the Himalaya Mountains of Asia. The people of Tibet call the snowman the *yeti*. Local stories tell of a large, hairy beast with arms that hang to its knees. It walks upright, on its back legs, and has a humanlike face. The yeti is supposed to leave the snowy regions from time to time, and come down to attack villagers. However, no one has yet proved that the yeti exists.

Many people have seen large, strange footprints in the snow of the Himalayas. Some people believe these are the yeti's prints. Others think they are footprints of a running bear, whose hind feet may land partly on the prints made by its front feet. These two sets of prints may, together, look like a large human print. Other large prints are probably formed when snow melts around a group of several small animal footprints. Since the 1890's, several explorers of the Himalayas have seen huge footprints of a large, unknown creature. The Tibetans have pieces of hair and dried scalp, which they claim are from the yeti. But scientists know these pieces are from bears, yaks, antelopes, and other animals.

Sir Edmund Hillary, an explorer, led an expedition to the Himalayas in 1960, to search for the creature. No abominable snowman was found. It does not seem likely that a large ape, or similar animal, could live in such high and snowy regions, where food is scarce. Yet, there are stories of similar strange creatures in other parts of the world. Some people claim to have seen a hairy, humanlike animal in the forests of the northwestern United States. They call it *Bigfoot*, for its large "footprints." But, as with the abominable snowman, no one has proved that this creature really exists. People enjoy stories about legendary animals, such as the abominable snowman and Bigfoot, even though such stories rarely turn out to be true.

ALSO READ: ANIMALS OF MYTH AND LEGEND; HILLARY, SIR EDMUND; HIMALAYA MOUNTAINS.

ABORIGINE The first people to live in any region are called *aborigines*. The term comes from the Latin words, *ab origine*, which mean "from the beginning."

The name *aborigine* or *aboriginal* is most often given to the earliest known people of Australia. These people were living in Australia when Europeans began to explore that continent in the 1700's. Scientists call these aborigines *Australoids*. They moved to Australia from Southeast Asia 12,000 years ago.

Between 150,000 and 300,000 aborigines lived in Australia when Europeans settled there in 1788. Now there are only 40,000 pure aborigines. Many were killed by diseases brought by white settlers, who sometimes took away their land. Most aborigines now live among nonaborigines, often working on cattle and sheep ranches and in factories and offices. Others have kept their old tribal ways of life,

▲ *An Australian aborigine boomerang and shield.*

living on reservations in the Northern Territory, Queensland, and Western Australia. The aborigines have sought the return of some of their tribal lands. Their hunting weapons are the *boomerang*, the *waddy* (a war club), and the *woomera* (a throwing stick with a three-pronged spear in front). They are expert at tracking and finding food in the wilderness.

The aborigines have always lived close to nature. They know the secret ways of animals and plants, and their colorful rock paintings are full of beauty and magical meaning. Aborigines believe that ancestral spirits live in certain places. One of these tribal "spirit homes" is Ayers Rock, now protected as an aborigine monument.

ALSO READ: AUSTRALIA.

ABRASIVES If you want to make a rough piece of wood smooth, what do you do? You rub it with sandpaper. The tiny, hard bits of sand in the sandpaper are *abrasives*. They wear away the roughness of the wood, which is softer.

Abrasives are materials used to smooth, polish, grind, or cut other substances. Most abrasives are minerals. The hardest of all minerals is diamond, so this makes the best abrasive. But diamond is very expensive. Sandpaper is made of bits of quartz, which costs a lot less.

Some abrasives are formed naturally in the earth. Quartz, diamond, sand, and pumice are all natural abrasives. Carborundum is a manufactured abrasive. It is made from a mixture of clay and powdered coke heated in a furnace. Carborundum is so hard that it can easily scratch glass, and for this reason it is used to polish gemstones.

Big blocks of abrasive material have been used since ancient times to make grindstones, to sharpen knives, and to mill grain. Another use for abrasives is to clean buildings. A jet of sand and metal particles is blown by compressed air to scrub away the soot and grime on the walls. This is known as "sandblasting." The tips, or cutting edges, of drills are covered with tiny pieces of tough abrasive. An oil well drill can cut through rock be-

▲ *An Australian aborigine. At one time all the people of Australia were aborigines. But now there are only about 40,000 full-blooded aborigines in the country.*

ABSORPTION

Toothpaste usually contains a mild abrasive—generally fine powdered chalk. The oldest abrasive is sand. It was used to polish stone weapons as early as 25,000 B.C. Diamond, the hardest known substance, was used as an abrasive in India by 700 B.C.

Dark objects absorb more light and heat than light objects do. This explains why people in hot countries usually wear white clothes. The heat tends to bounce off them. It also explains why houses in hot countries tend to be painted in light colors.

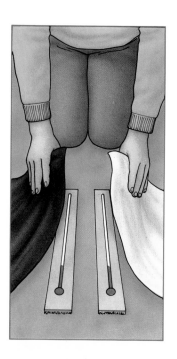

cause of the tiny abrasive diamonds in its cutting edge.

■ LEARN BY DOING

If you build models, then you have probably used sandpaper. Have you noticed how sandpaper comes in different grades? Get a piece of board. Sand sections of it with three different grades of sandpaper. Compare each section carefully. What did you find? ■

ABSORPTION   Liquid spilled on a table top can be soaked up by a sponge, a napkin, or a paper towel. This soaking up is absorption. Many things can be soaked up, or absorbed, by other substances or objects. Gas, liquid, light, heat, and even sound can be absorbed.

Let a glass of *cold* water stand in sunlight. You will see small air bubbles form on the sides of the glass. The bubbles rise through the water to the surface. These bubbles are air that was absorbed in the water. The air was forced out as the water warmed up because warm water cannot hold so much air as cold water can.

Absorption is an important process for living things. Fish breathe the air that is absorbed in water. In humans and other animals, digested food is absorbed by the blood through the vessels of the small intestine and then carried to all parts of the body where it is used for energy. Plants absorb water from the soil. The water keeps them alive and healthy. What happens if you put a partly wilted flower in a glass of water?

■ LEARN BY DOING

Light and heat can be absorbed too. Dark objects are better heat and light absorbers than light-colored ones. You can prove this with a simple experiment. On a cold, sunny day, put two thermometers on the ground. Be sure they show the same temperature. Put a black cloth over

one and a white one over the other. Which thermometer shows the highest temperature after half an hour? ■

ALSO READ: COLOR, DIGESTION, GAS, HEAT AND COLD, LIGHT, LIQUID, PLANT, SOUND.

ABSTRACT ART   You probably know that "subtract" means "take away." *Abstract* means "to take what is important away from what is not." Abstract art shows what is important in a scene and leaves out unimportant details.

Look at the picture of the horse on the next page. It was painted on the wall of a cave near Lascaux, France, thousands of years ago. It is a simple painting. The cave artist left out details. He arranged the horse to fit the picture, not as it really looked wandering around outside his cave. The picture is *not* "realistic," just like life. It is *abstract art*.

In the 1880's in France, some artists began to make painting less realistic. Why? For one thing, the camera had been invented. A photograph could be made to get an exact likeness of something or someone. So the French painters began new ways of painting. "Looking like something" became less important. Two French painters, Paul Cézanne and Georges Seurat, found that people could see the shapes of nature more easily if the shapes were painted simply, without all the details used in realistic art.

Some years later another artist, Pablo Picasso, began to paint abstractly, too. Only he went much further. He would change nature to what he thought a picture should be. He tried in his paintings to show more than the appearance of an object, to seek new meaning. Sculpture too could be abstract. Artists ignored the exact form of a real-life object. The feel and texture and shape of a sculpture were more important to abstract artists than showing exact form.

▲ Arrival of the Circus *by Paul Klee.*

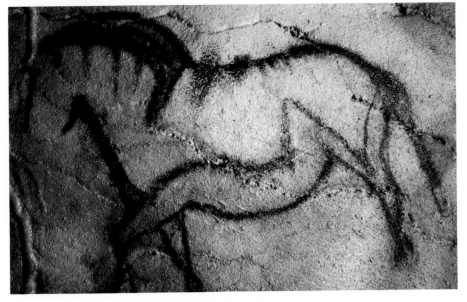

◀ *A Stone Age painting of a horse in a cave at Lascaux, France.*

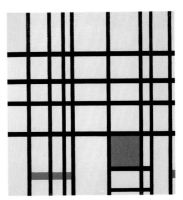

▲ *Piet Mondrian's* Composition in Red, Yellow and Blue.

■ LEARN BY DOING

Look at Paul Klee's painting of a circus arriving in town. See the circus parade with a dog leading it? The painter uses no perspective in this picture, so things that might be farther away don't look smaller. Instead, the picture is in layers. Nearly everyone in the painting is wearing a funny hat. Why? Many things are happening at the same time, as in a real circus. Look for details, such as the boy holding a balloon over his head. Banners often mean fun and excitement. How many do you see here? See how Klee has "framed" his picture with dark paint in a smudgy way. Is the picture a dream of long ago?

How would your community look if a circus were arriving? Make a picture of it on a big piece of paper. Is your painting an abstract one, rather than a realistic one?

Do you see the horse in the Jackson

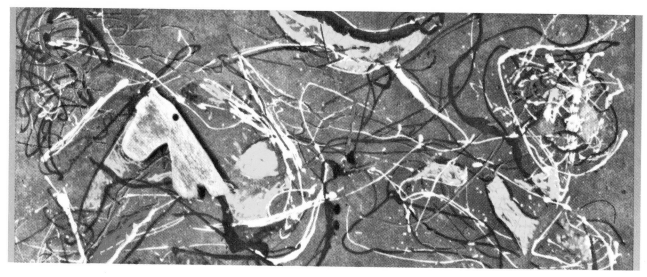

▲ *Jackson Pollock's* The Wooden Horse.

Pollock painting, *The Wooden Horse*? What does the rest of the picture look like to you? Could those tangled lines be paths the horse followed? The yellow splotches could be places where the horse rested. Do the red lines show a really fast ride? Think what fun it would be to take off along those trails. See if you can paint a picture story of an exciting horseback ride.

Look at Marcel Duchamp's sculpture—a bicycle wheel mounted on a kitchen stool. He called these sculptures "ready-mades." Can you put together your own ready-made? ■

Of course, you may see Pollock's painting in a very different way. That is the fun of abstract art. You can see it in a new way every time you look at it. Abstract art can be more exciting than a realistic painting or sculpture which looks exactly like the real scene or object every time you see it. A photograph shows you a scene. An abstract painting can show you more.

ALSO READ: CÉZANNE, PAUL; MODERN ART; PICASSO, PABLO; REALISM; SCULPTURE.

ABU SIMBEL   Abu Simbel is the site of two ancient temples on the Nile River in Egypt. The temples were carved into a sandstone cliff about 1250 B.C. by order of Ramses II, an Egyptian pharaoh (king).

The Great Temple reached over 180 feet (55 m) into the side of the cliff. The entrance was guarded by four statues of Ramses II. Each statue was 67 feet (20 m) high. Ramses II wished to honor the sun god. The pharaoh had the temple built so that the sun's early-morning rays shone through the halls and touched the carved figure of the sun god deep inside. The smaller temple had six figures, each 33 feet (10.2 m) high, at

▼ *A drawing of Marcel Duchamp's* Bicycle Wheel, *1913. Duchamp fixed the wheel to a kitchen stool. The original no longer exists.*

▶ *The giant statues of the Temple of Abu Simbel used to stand beside the Nile River. When the Aswan Dam was built they were moved to higher ground.*

its entrance. Four were of Ramses II and two were of his queen, Nefertari.

Egypt planned a great dam on the Nile River in the 1960's. But the plan called for the valley of the temples to be flooded. Egypt asked the United Nations to help save the temples before the dam was built. More than 50 nations helped fund the project. The temples were cut into huge blocks. The blocks were moved to high, safe ground and put together again. Egypt finished the Aswan High Dam in 1968, and a lake now covers the old site.

ALSO READ: EGYPT, ANCIENT; NILE RIVER.

ACADEMY AWARD The Academy of Motion Picture Arts and Sciences was founded in 1927 by Louis B. Mayer and other leaders of the Hollywood film world. The Academy is made up of several thousand people in every area of movie making. Its main purpose is to help improve the art and science of film making. The Academy also honors outstanding film achievements with its Academy Awards. The Academy members vote on who should win.

Once each year in Hollywood, California, small gold statues are awarded for the best performances by actors and actresses in leading and supporting roles and for best direction, music, costume design, photography, writing, sound recording, and other areas of production. An award is also given for the best movie of the year. Each award is a statue of a man, nicknamed "Oscar."

The first movie to win an Oscar was *Wings* in 1928. The first film to capture all five major awards (Best Picture, Best Actor, Best Actress, Best Director, and Best Screenplay) was *It Happened One Night*, starring Claudette Colbert and Clark Gable, which did so in 1934. Today, the Oscar ceremony is a much publicized

event. Winning can mean box office success as well as artistic acclaim.

ALSO READ: ACTORS AND ACTING, MOTION PICTURES.

ACANTHUS see GREEK ART.

ACCELERATION see MOTION.

ACCELERATOR see PARTICLE ACCELERATOR.

ACCIDENT PREVENTION see SAFETY.

ACCORDION An accordion is a musical instrument that works like a reed-organ. The accordion hangs by straps from the player's shoulders.

The first accordion-like instrument was made by Friedrich Buschmann in Germany in 1822. An Austrian, Cyril Demian, soon made some improvements, and gave the instrument its name. About the same time, Charles Wheatstone of England invented the concertina, which is like the accordion.

The accordion is mainly a bellows. The player stretches the bellows to let in air. He then closes, or squeezes, the bellows, and the air is forced out through metal parts called *tongues* or *reeds*. These tongues are of different sizes, so they produce different musical notes. The piano accordion has, attached to the bellows on the right side, a keyboard like that of a piano. The accordionist plays the melody on the keyboard. On the left are buttons which he presses to produce bass notes and chords.

Pioneers traveling West in the 1800's enjoyed accordion music.

ALSO READ: MUSICAL INSTRUMENTS, ORGAN.

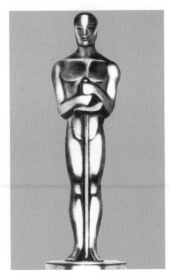

▲ *Oscar, the little statue given as an Academy Award, stands 13½ inches (34 cm) high.*

In 1931, the Academy Award statue was accidentally nicknamed "Oscar" by Academy librarian Margaret Herrick. When she first saw the statue, she said, "Why, it looks like my Uncle Oscar!" A newspaperman heard her remark and printed it in his newspaper.

▲ *An accordion is like an organ. The player squeezes the bellows in and out while playing a melody on the keys.*

ACCOUNTING AND BOOK-KEEPING

Business people must keep records of the money they take in and the money they spend. The work of keeping such records is called *bookkeeping*. The work of deciding how the records should be set up is called *accounting*. An *accountant* also finds out whether or not a business is doing well. If a business takes in more money than it spends, it makes a profit. If it spends more than it takes in, it suffers a loss.

The owner of a small clothing store can keep accounting records without much trouble. But a giant oil company or a big bank has many difficult accounting problems. The company must know how much money is to be paid by its *debtors* (people who owe the company money) and how much it owes other companies (*creditors*) for supplies. It must know how much the company's buildings and machines are worth, and how much the company has lost in *depreciation*, or wear and tear, of its equipment. Big companies employ many accountants.

After a company's accountants finish their yearly count, their work must be *audited*. Experts from outside the company double-check the records to be sure the accounts are correct. These experts are called *auditors*.

■ LEARN BY DOING

You can practice bookkeeping by keeping records of your own money. Suppose your weekly allowance is 3 dollars and 75 cents. Your grandmother gives you 5 dollars as a gift. A piece of candy costs you 50 cents, and a balsa-wood glider costs 2 dollars and 95 cents. You also want to go to the movies on Saturday.

Make a chart with three columns on a lined sheet of paper. Mark the first column "Received," the second column "Spent," and the third column "Balance" (meaning the money you have left). What numbers go in what columns? How much money will you be able to save if the movies cost you two dollars? ■

This is a simple bookkeeping system. It is a record of money received, or *income*, and money paid out, or *expenses*. Today, many bookkeeping and accounting records are made by computers. But people still have to provide the information the machines need to do the jobs.

ALSO READ: CALCULATOR, ECONOMICS, MONEY.

ACHILLES see TROJAN WAR.

ACID RAIN Rain is always slightly acid. This is because the Earth's atmosphere naturally contains substances such as carbon dioxide and sulfur dioxide, which dissolve in moisture to form weak acids. When we burn fossil fuels, such as coal and oil, either in factories or automobile engines, extra amounts of chemicals are added to the atmosphere. Some of these chemicals can form acids. When clouds gather, the rain that falls has a higher than normal acid content. It is called *acid rain*.

Dirt put into the air in one part of the world can affect other places, thousands of miles away. If a factory in one country gives off too much dirt, acid rain may fall somewhere else. Scientists are not in agreement

Acid rain is not new. People have known about it for quite a long time. In 1858 the British chemist Robert Angus Smith presented a paper to the Chemical Society. In it he spoke of how "the stones and bricks of buildings crumble more readily in large towns where much more coal is burned, than elsewhere." He said that this was caused by "the slow but constant action of the acid rain." This was the first time that the term "acid rain" was used.

on exactly what harm is done by acid rain. Trees and soil and fish may suffer, and so may buildings, since acid eats into stone.

Acid rain, like other kinds of air pollution, can be checked in several ways. Low-sulfur fuels can be burnt. Automobiles that burn lead-free gasoline are cleaner than automobiles that do not. The smokestacks of power stations can be fitted with equipment to clean smoke and gases before they are released into the air.

ALSO READ: ACIDS AND BASES, AIR POLLUTION, RAIN AND SNOW, WATER CYCLE.

ACIDS AND BASES Have you ever tasted an unripe apple? It has a sour taste. Lemons are sour. Vinegar is sour, too. What makes things taste sour? The answer is, they all have acid in them. There are many kinds of acid. Some are very strong and can eat their way through almost anything. *Sulfuric acid*, for example, can *corrode* (eat into) most metals and it will quickly burn into flesh or other living matter. *Nitric acid* and *hydrochloric acid* are two other strong acids. These strong acids are among the most important of all chemicals used in industry.

But not all acids are strong and dangerous. Yogurt, for example, contains acid, and so does aspirin. Our own bodies make many acids to digest food and build new tissue.

Bases are substances that are the opposite of acids. Some bases are strong and corrosive too. Substances such as caustic soda and lime are strong bases. Caustic soda is often used for cleaning the insides of stoves because it has a powerful action in removing grease. Weak bases include baking soda and magnesium hydroxide, the white powder or liquid we take to cure an upset acid stomach.

Another name for a base is an *alkali*, although strictly speaking an al-

kali is a base that can dissolve in water.

When an acid and a base are mixed together in the right quantities they *neutralize* each other—cancel each other out in some ways. If we mix hydrochloric acid and caustic soda, for example, both very strong and dangerous substances, the result is harmless common salt and water. Acids and bases always react together to give some kind of salt and water.

Some substances change color when they are put into an acid or base. One of these is a dye called *litmus*. Litmus paper turns red if dipped into anything acid. It turns blue if dipped into a base. So litmus makes a good test for acids and bases.

▲ *Most scientists agree that acid rain can cause a large amount of damage to trees. Experts think that the terrible destruction in this forest was caused by acid rain.*

If wine ferments for too long, acetic acid forms. This acid turns the wine into vinegar. Any fruit or vegetable can be fermented to make vinegar.

◀ *Acid tests are useful in distinguishing between some rocks and minerals. When a few drops of hydrochloric acid are placed on limestone, the rock fizzes. This does not happen when the acid is put on dolomite, a rock which may be confused with limestone.*

Strong acids will dissolve most metals, but they do not affect gold. One way of testing whether something is gold or an imitation is to test it with acid. This is the origin of the phrase "to give something the acid test." Gold is dissolved in the laboratory by a mixture of hydrochloric and nitric acids: this is called *aqua regia* (Latin for royal water).

▲ *These acrobats need great skill. They are doing expert stunts on a moving ladder.*

Acids and Health Our bodies need acids to keep healthy. Protein foods such as meat, fish, soybeans, and wheat flour provide *amino acids* that help build body tissue. Humans also need *ascorbic acid* (found in oranges, potatoes, and tomatoes, for example) otherwise they may suffer from a disease called scurvy. Pellagra, a skin complaint, is caused by a lack of *nicotinic acid* in the diet. Liver, bran, and wholewheat are foods containing large amounts of this acid.

■ **LEARN BY DOING**

You can make your own indicator to test for acids and bases. Chop up a few of the outer leaves of a red cabbage. Put them in a pan with enough water to cover them. Boil the water until it turns purple, probably about 20 minutes. Remove the cabbage leaves by straining the liquid into a container.

When the liquid has cooled, put some of it into a jar and add a little lemon juice. The color changes from purple to red. Next, put some of the indicator into another jar. Add a little baking soda. This time the liquid changes to greenish blue. Why?

You are now ready to test some of the liquids around your home to see if they are acid or base. For example, put a drop of liquid soap into some of the indicator. Does it change color? Now add some vinegar to the same liquid. What happens now? Is liquid soap an acid or a base? What happens when a substance you test is neutral? ■

Acids and Bases are Useful A small amount of acid gives flavor to our food. We add vinegar, a mild acid, to pickles, lettuce, and other foods to give them a slightly sour taste.

Acids are used in very many industrial processes. They are used to make other chemicals, for cleaning metals, and to etch (mark) glass and other materials.

FOUR IMPORTANT ACIDS

Sulfuric Acid
Chemical name H_2SO_4
Uses: fertilizers, purifying metals, dyes, medicines
Burns the skin

Hydrochloric Acid
Chemical name HCl
Uses: in chemical plants and laboratories
Burns the skin

Nitric Acid
Chemical name HNO_3
Uses: explosives, medicines, dyes, fertilizers
Burns the skin

Citric Acid
Chemical Name $C_6H_8O_7$
Uses: in the preparation of lemon-flavored drinks
A natural acid in citrus fruits

Bases are useful too. Windows sparkle when washed with water containing ammonia, a common base. Car tires, the pages of this book, and some of the clothes you are wearing were made with the help of bases.

ALSO READ: CHEMISTRY, FIRST AID, POISON, TASTE.

ACNE see SKIN.

ACOUSTICS see SOUND.

ACROBATICS The word *acrobat* comes from two Greek words that mean "one who walks on tip-toes" and "one who climbs high." Persons who can move quickly, perform gymnastics, and keep their balance high above the ground are acrobats. Acrobats were greatly admired in ancient China, Egypt, Greece, and Crete. Tightrope walkers were honored in ancient Rome. At fairs during the Middle Ages, tumblers performed somersaults, back-flips, and other tricks to entertain large groups of people.

Most of us have swung on a rope, or climbed a tree. But just being able to climb or swing does not make someone an acrobat. An acrobat must have strong muscles and good control of them (called *coordination*). He or she must be in top physical condition, and must spend many years training to be an acrobat. A good way to begin acrobatics is to practice routines on a trampoline.

Circus Acrobats   The most dangerous and spectacular forms of acrobatics are seen in circuses. *Aerialists*, or high-trapeze artists, have been thrilling audiences for many years. Perhaps you've heard an old song called "The Daring Young Man on the Flying Trapeze." A *trapeze* is a small swinging bar suspended by two ropes. Most trapeze performers use trapezes that are very high above the ground. Performers climb up to their high equipment on a rope ladder. Some performers are so strong they can go up a rope hand-over-hand, without using their legs.

Trapeze artists usually work in teams. An act may begin with the artists standing on two high platforms. One flyer (the "catcher") begins to swing from his trapeze. A partner swings from the opposite platform. The first flyer changes his position on the swinging bar, so that he hangs by his knees, arms outstretched. His partner—with perfect timing—lets go of her trapeze, dives through the air, and is grabbed by the catcher's hands in midair. A third flyer may join in, to do a triple somersault through the air between the other two performers. All of the act is done with split-second timing, and to the sound of gasps from the spellbound audience below.

Acrobats called *tightrope walkers* do more than walk across a rope (actually a heavy wire cable). When they do

▲ *Trampolines are used by both acrobats and gymnasts. Bouncing up and down on a trampoline is good fun and exercise for everyone.*

walk on the rope, they wear special shoes with soft soles. But they also do handstands and somersaults. Some ride bikes and even motorcycles on the narrow cable. A famous acrobat called Blondin tightrope-walked across Niagara Falls blindfolded, on stilts, and carrying a man on his back!

Another kind of acrobatics is performed by *high-wire* artists. One of the most famous high-wire acts, called the "Great Wallendas," performed a spectacular "human pyramid," without a safety net beneath them. Four members of the family balanced on a wire with a long rod placed across their shoulders. Two others stood on that rod with another rod on their shoulders. On the very tip-top stood a lone girl far above the crowd.

Acrobatic Safety   Circus acrobats are always trying to develop new acts. Their urge to do new stunts sometimes leads them to try dangerous tricks. Most circuses now have large rope safety nets stretched out beneath the acrobats. If a performer loses his balance or his grip, he falls into the net.

ALSO READ: CIRCUS, GYMNASTICS.

Karl Wallenda was head of the famous family of acrobats until his death in 1978. In July, 1970, he walked across Tallulah Gorge in Georgia, on a wire 750 feet (229 m) above the gorge. He walked the 821-foot (250-m) wire in 20 minutes, stopping twice to stand on his head.

▲ *The Parthenon is the greatest of the temples that stand on the Acropolis at Athens. The Acropolis complex was rebuilt after it was destroyed by Persians in 479 B.C.*

Lord Elgin was British ambassador to Greece in the early 1800's. He removed ancient marble sculptures from the Acropolis and sent them to London to prevent their destruction in war. Now called the Elgin marbles, they are in the British Museum.

▼ *The "Porch of the Maidens" on the Erechtheum, another famous temple on the Acropolis.*

ACROPOLIS In the Greek city of Athens stands a hill 500 feet (152 m) high. This hill is the Acropolis. The word "acropolis" means "upper city." The ancient Greeks used hills as forts, because fighting uphill was hard for enemies, and as religious centers. Handsome buildings called *temples* were built on these hills to honor the gods and goddesses of the Greeks. Many cities in ancient Greece had an acropolis, but the most famous one is in Athens.

Over 400 years before Christ, several magnificent marble temples were built on the Athens Acropolis in honor of the goddess Athena. The great gatehouse of the Acropolis, called the *Propylaea*, was the Athenians' favorite building.

The most famous temple is the *Parthenon*, designed by Phidias, one of the most noted architects of all time. The Parthenon is one of the most beautiful buildings ever built. Inside it stood a tall gilded statue of Athena, which was lost long ago.

Another temple, the *Erechtheum*, is known for its Porch of the Maidens. The six maidens are *caryatides*, statues of women that hold up the roof of the porch.

Many parts of the original Acropolis temples were destroyed by time and war. In recent times, those that remain have been restored.

ALSO READ: ATHENS; GODS AND GODDESSES; GREECE, ANCIENT; GREEK ART.

ACTORS AND ACTING Everyone is an actor sometimes. Playing "make-believe" is acting. So is dressing up in old clothes. Trying to get out of doing something unpleasant by saying you are sick is acting, too.

An actor pretends to be someone else. He or she *impersonates a character* (person) in a story or play, usually watched by other people who make up the *audience*. To impersonate means to study the character, or *role*, that an actor will play, and then act in such a way that an audience believes the actor is that character.

No one knows when people first started acting, but it is a very ancient art. It probably began with hunting and victory dances, such as the dances of the American Indians. Many religious rites or events were acted out. Telling a story was most important in these ceremonies.

The History of Acting The Greeks were writing plays and performing them in outdoor theaters by the fourth century B.C. Later, the Romans copied the Greeks. Actors became very important. Many of them did not have to pay taxes or fight wars. Mime, or pantomime, which is acting without speaking, became popular. Mime actors use their bodies and faces, rather than their voices, to tell a story.

Foolish plays produced in Rome made acting less serious. Many actors quit. The Romans then trained slaves to act. But people began to think of acting as a bad thing.

During the Middle Ages in Europe, *minstrels* and *troubadours* (singers and poets) and jugglers wandered from place to place, entertaining people. In some churchyards and marketplaces, actors performed in *miracle* or *mystery plays*, which dealt with saints and Biblical events. In the 1500's, *morality plays*, in which characters stood for good and evil, attracted large audiences.

James Burbage built the first theater in England, in 1576. Many companies of actors were formed during the reign of Elizabeth I. William Shakespeare was a famous playwright and actor of that time. Many people, even the ladies and gentlemen of the royal court, came to the theaters.

The Puritans closed down the theaters in England in 1642, because they thought plays were sinful. But theaters reopened when King Charles II came to the throne in 1660. Plays were popular again by the end of the century. Women began to act on the English stage for the first time. Boys had played women's parts in Shakespeare's time.

Plays have remained popular ever since then. Today, actors and actresses have many opportunities for careers on the stage, in television, and in movies.

Acting in the Theater Some of the greatest actors in theater history are Richard Burbage (James's son), David Garrick, Adrienne Lecouvreur, Sarah Siddons, Henry Irving, Sarah Bernhardt, Laurence Olivier, Eleanora Duse, Katharine Cornell, and the Barrymore family. Many world-famous actors have performed

in New York City, the center of professional theater in the United States. Touring companies, college and high school acting groups, summer theaters, community theaters, and children's theaters are located all over the United States.

An actor uses talent, education, experience, and imagination to create a role for the stage. He must use both his voice and his body when he acts. To be a successful actor, he must study and practice. He must observe other people and understand their emotions. He must learn the *motivations* (reasons) for people's behavior, so that his acting is believable.

Acting in the Movies Many movie actors and actresses are more famous than kings and presidents, because millions of people all over the world watch movies. Hollywood, California, the capital of the movie industry, created the star system. A *star* is an actor or actress who is considered to be an outstanding performer, and who has leading roles in movies. Actors such as Charlie Chaplin, Clark Gable, Elizabeth Taylor, and Dustin Hoffman became world-famous because of their movies.

Working in movies is different

▲ *Marcel Marceau, the French actor, is one of the world's great* mimes. *Mimes are actors who show what they mean by gestures and facial expressions instead of using spoken words.*

Throughout history actors have been treated in different ways. In ancient Greece they enjoyed honors and privileges. In ancient Rome they were once banished from the city!

◄ *Special effects play an important part in modern movies. Actors must learn to work with the technical wizards. This is a scene from* Back to the Future.

▲ *Some children become famous actors. Shirley Temple was a popular child star of the 1930's. She starred in this movie with Gary Cooper.*

► *The Marx brothers (Groucho, Chico, Gummo, Harpo, and Zeppo) were Jewish-American comic actors. Groucho, Chico, and Harpo became the most famous. The three are shown here in a scene from their movie* A Day at the Races.

▲ *A scene from the musical* My Fair Lady. *The movie was based on the stage play* Pygmalion *by George Bernard Shaw.*

► *Walt Disney (1901-66) with a life-size Mickey Mouse. Disney invented this famous cartoon character.*

from working in the theater. A theater actor performs in a whole play in front of people. In a movie, he works in bits and pieces in front of a camera. He may perform the last scenes first, and weeks later do the first scene. He must sometimes travel to distant places, or go on location, to film some sections of a movie.

Television and Radio Acting for television is somewhat different from stage acting. The television screen is small, so TV actors tend to make much smaller movements and gestures.

Radio actors and comedians were popular in the 1930's and 1940's. Jack Benny, Fred Allen, and Orson Welles were made famous by radio. *Soap operas*, stories that continue from day to day, began on radio, later switching to television. After television arrived, radio lost some of its popular appeal.

Acting Styles There are two basic styles of acting. To be a good actor, it is probably best to combine the two styles. The first style uses *external techniques* alone. An actor uses gestures, movements, and vocal and facial expression to create a believable character. A skillful actor can make his audience feel emotions through his movements and voice, even when he does not feel all the emotion himself. This kind of acting can sometimes seem faked when done by a poor actor.

The second style of acting uses *internal techniques*. The most famous of these techniques is called the *Stanislavski method*, named after the Russian actor and director Konstantin Stanislavski. This is sometimes called "method" acting. Stanislavski taught that an actor can make his part believable only when he really feels the emotions of his character. If an actor is playing an unhappy person, he tries to feel sad himself. An unskilled actor may get careless using this method. He may not speak clearly, or he may not respond properly to another actor's words.

■ **LEARN BY DOING**

With some friends, why not try some acting? One game that is fun is "paper bag theater." Divide the group into two teams. Each group puts into a paper bag five or six things, such as a comb, a handkerchief, a doll, a seashell, and so on. Each group trades its bag with the other. From its bagful of surprises, each group makes up a play using all the items in the bag and then, after

Big Bird, a character on television's Sesame Street. *The actor is disguised, but the character is well-loved by children.*

about an hour, presents their play to the other group. You'll be amazed at the plays and the acting started by a few things in a paper bag. ■

Becoming an Actor To become a good actor, a person must train his body, voice, and mind to express what a character is really like. *Mimicry* (imitating) of voices, mannerisms, and movement is good training. Acting in school plays is fun, and useful too. To become a professional actor, the student usually goes to a special school. Many colleges and universities have classes in acting and drama. There are also many acting schools in large cities, such as the Actor's Studio in New York City. While an actor studies his craft, he usually continues to *audition* (try out) for plays or movies, hoping some day he will get an important leading role.

Rewards of Acting Very few actors are successful enough to earn worldwide fame and large sums of money. All actors appreciate awards for their talents. One of the best-known awards is the Academy Award, or *Oscar*. It is presented every year by the Academy of Motion Picture Arts and Sciences, for best performances in movies. The best television actors win *Emmy* awards presented by the Academy of Television Arts and Sciences. Stage actors are given awards, too. Most famous is the Antoinette Perry Award, called the *Tony*.

ALSO READ: ACADEMY AWARD; DRAMA; MOTION PICTURES; PANTOMIME; SHAKESPEARE, WILLIAM; THEATER.

ACUPUNCTURE Sticking needles into people can actually relieve pain rather than making it worse. This was discovered more than five thousand years ago by the Chinese. The medical treatment based on this principal is called *acupuncture*.

In ancient China, as in other countries, doctors believed that illness was caused by some kind of upset in the natural balance of the human body. Doctors in medieval Europe thought they could cure this balance by "bleeding," or draining off some of the sick person's blood. In China, doctors believed that by sticking needles into certain points on the body, natural health could be restored.

Ancient drawings show the points on the body where needles may be inserted.

How acupuncture works is a mystery that not even the Chinese fully

Medical students in China are taught ancient techniques, such as acupuncture, alongside modern medicine. Western observers have been startled to watch operations carried out on patients who, instead of being given a pain-killing anesthetic, had been prepared for surgery by the insertion of acupuncture needles. The patients appeared perfectly happy to be needled in this way.

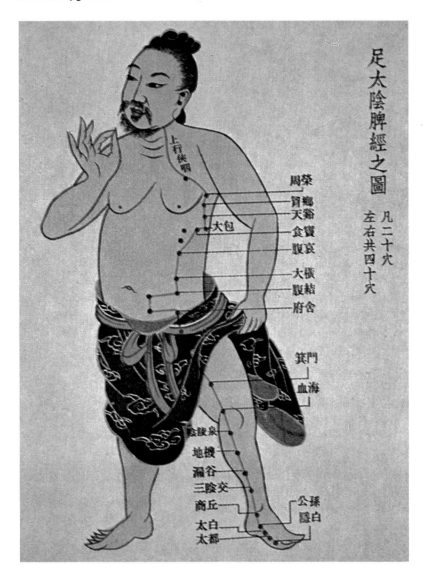

足太陰脾經之圖

凡二十穴

左右共四十穴

上行俠咽

周榮
胷鄉
天谿
食竇
腹哀
大橫
腹結
府舍

大包

箕門

血海

陰陵泉
地機
漏谷
三陰交
商丘
太白
太都

公孫
隱白

▲ *Acupuncture—the practice of inserting needles in the body—has been used in Chinese medicine for thousands of years. This picture shows some of the points on the body where the needles are placed.*

understand. It is said to help patients suffering from many different conditions, including malaria fever, narcotics addiction, arthritis, back pain, and headaches. The needles used are up to 9 inches (24 cm) long. Acupuncture is now practiced in other countries outside China and is becoming very popular in the United States. It is not necessary in the United States for somebody to be a qualified doctor to perform acupuncture.

ALSO READ: ANESTHETIC, CHINA, MEDICINE.

ADAMS, JOHN (1735–1826)
The second president of the United

States was John Adams. His family were farmers in Massachusetts, where his great-great-grandfather, Henry Adams, had settled in 1636.

John Adams first studied at Harvard College to become a minister. But he decided to study law instead. He became known throughout Massachusetts as an honest, courageous, and able lawyer. He was a leader in the American colonies' fight for independence from Great Britain. In 1774, he went to the First Continental Congress. He signed the Declaration of Independence at the Second Congress, in 1776. He worked hard to convince the colonies to accept the Declaration. Adams went to France and the Netherlands during the American Revolution, to urge those countries to support the colonists. John Adams, Benjamin Franklin, and John Jay worked on the peace treaty with Britain, in 1783. Adams served as George Washington's Vice President after the Revolution. He was a leader of the Federalist Party.

When Adams became President in 1797, France was at war with several European countries. U.S. ships were being attacked at sea. Many Americans, led by Thomas Jefferson, supported the French Revolution; they wanted to give aid to France. The Federalists, however, led by Alexander Hamilton, wanted to restore the French king and urged a war against France. Adams himself wanted to keep the United States neutral.

U.S. diplomats were sent to France to work out a peace treaty. Negotiations ended in anger after three French diplomats tried to bribe the U.S. (in what is known as the XYZ Affair). French and U.S. warships fought several battles until President Adams and French Foreign Minister Talleyrand signed a treaty in 1799.

Although the treaty kept the U.S. out of war, it made President Adams very unpopular, especially with the Federalists. Another cause of his un-

JOHN ADAMS
SECOND PRESIDENT   MARCH 4, 1797–MARCH 4, 1801

Born: October 30, 1735, Braintree, Massachusetts (now Quincy)
Parents: John and Susanna Boylston Adams
Education: Harvard College
Religion: Unitarian
Occupation: Lawyer
Political Party: Federalist
Married: 1764 to Abigail Smith (1744–1818)
Children: 3 sons, 2 daughters (1 died in infancy)
Died: July 4, 1826, Quincy, Massachusetts
Buried: First Unitarian Church, Quincy, Massachusetts

popularity was his support of the Alien and Sedition Acts. Adams was not reelected, and Thomas Jefferson became President in 1801.

John Adams was one of the most famous members of a noted American family. His second cousin was Samuel Adams, a leader of the American Revolution and, with John, one of those who signed the Declaration of Independence. Another interesting family member was John's wife, Abigail (1744–1818), probably the best-informed woman of her day. She is remembered for the intelligent, amusing letters she wrote to her husband during his stay in Europe. You can find out more about Abigail by reading her letters. The eldest son of John and Abigail, John Quincy Adams, was the sixth President of the United States.

ALSO READ: ADAMS, JOHN QUINCY; ADAMS, SAMUEL; CONTINENTAL CONGRESS; HAMILTON, ALEXANDER; JEFFERSON, THOMAS; PRESIDENCY.

ADAMS, JOHN QUINCY (1767–1848) The American Revolution began when John Quincy Adams was eight. He and his mother watched the Battle of Bunker Hill from a nearby field. Later, he went with his father, John Adams, on a government mission to France. They sailed safely through a line of enemy British ships, but they were shipwrecked in Spain. Riding mules, they took three months to reach Paris. When he was 14, John Quincy was an aide to the first U.S. diplomat to go to Russia. He later went with his father to the peace treaty conferences between the United States and Great Britain at the end of the American Revolution. John Quincy Adams was an experienced traveler and diplomat by the time he graduated from Harvard College in 1787.

Adams served as an ambassador for President George Washington, and then for his own father, who followed Washington as President. Then John Quincy, too, entered politics. He was elected to the Senate in 1803. But he angered his own political party, the Federalists, because he did not always vote the way they wanted him to. After five years, they elected a new Senator. President Madison then asked Adams to become a diplomat again and sent him to Europe. President Monroe made Adams his Secretary of State in 1817. Adams acquired Florida from Spain for the U.S. and helped write the Monroe Doctrine.

In the Presidential election of 1824, Adams was one of four candidates. Andrew Jackson received the most popular votes, but not enough electoral votes to win. The House of Representatives had to decide who

▲ *This is how the U.S. Capitol looked when John Adams was President. The building was not finished, and the city of Washington, D.C., was hardly begun.*

When John Adams became President in 1797 the population of the United States was only 4,900,000. He was the first President to live in the White House.

When John Quincy Adams was president, the Erie Canal was completed (1825). It linked New York with the Great Lakes and the boat trip took eight days.

Also during his presidency, in 1828, Webster's Dictionary was first published. It gained fame as the best English dictionary of its time.

JOHN QUINCY ADAMS

SIXTH PRESIDENT   MARCH 4, 1825–MARCH 4, 1829

Born: July 11, 1767, Braintree (now Quincy), Massachusetts
Parents: John and Abigail Smith Adams
Education: University of Leyden, the Netherlands; Harvard College
Religion: Unitarian
Occupation: Lawyer
Political Party: Federalist, then National Republican
Married: 1797 to Louisa Catherine Johnson (1775–1852)
Children: 3 sons, 1 daughter (died in infancy)
Died: February 23, 1848, Washington, D.C.
Buried: First Unitarian Church, Quincy, Massachusetts

▲ *Samuel Adams, American patriot and Revolutionary leader.*

would be President, and they picked Adams. Jackson's supporters in Congress argued constantly with President Adams. He had good ideas, but they were not accepted, because he was not popular. In 1828, Andrew Jackson was elected President.

Adams went back to Washington in 1831, this time as a congressman from Massachusetts. He served for 17 years. He believed that slavery was wrong and should be stopped. He spoke about it so often that slave owners called him the "Madman from Massachusetts." In 1848, he collapsed in the House of Representatives, and he died two days later.

ALSO READ: ADAMS, JOHN; JACKSON, ANDREW; PRESIDENCY.

ADAMS, SAMUEL (1722–1803) "A hot-headed radical!" "An arch traitor!" These were just two of many names the British called Samuel Adams of Boston in the years before the American Revolution. Sam went to Harvard College, like his younger cousin John Adams. Also, like John, Sam never stopped fighting for the independence of the American colonies from Great Britain.

Samuel Adams constantly gave speeches to tell the colonies they had

to be free from British rule. He urged the colonists to protest the Stamp Act and other examples of "taxation without representation." He helped organize groups of rebels, such as the Sons of Liberty. He led the Boston Tea Party. Adams and his friend Patrick Henry were both delegates to the Continental Congress. They urged the other delegates to demand immediate independence for the colonies. Samuel Adams voted for and signed the Declaration of Independence.

Adams served in the Continental Congress during the Revolution. Then he returned to Boston. He was governor of Massachusetts from 1794 to 1797. In American history, Samuel Adams is remembered as an important leader of the American Revolution.

ALSO READ: ADAMS, JOHN; BOSTON TEA PARTY; CONTINENTAL CONGRESS; DECLARATION OF INDEPENDENCE.

ADAPTATION   see EVOLUTION.

ADDAMS, JANE (1860–1935) "She belongs to all people." "She was everybody's friend." Jane Addams earned this praise from a lifetime spent helping people. She worked for the poor, for immigrants and minority groups, for women and children.

Born in Cedarville, Illinois, Jane graduated from nearby Rockford College. She had been born with a badly curved back. She wanted to be a doctor, but her poor health kept her from finishing medical school.

Her family sent her to Europe to recover. In London she visited a *settlement house*—a gathering place and education center for poor people. She decided to start such a place for the poor of Chicago. Hull House was the result. Jane and her friend, Ellen Starr, worked hard at Hull House. They set up various programs, from day nurseries to adult evening classes. Hull House became a model for the rest of the nation.

Jane Addams called social work the profession of helping people in need—in need of food, clothing, housing, education, work, or play. She helped women win the right to vote. Her work for world peace won her the Nobel Peace Prize when she was 71.

ALSO READ: SOCIAL WORK.

ADDICTION Using some drugs for a long time can make people need to keep on taking them. This need is called *addiction*. The drug users, or *addicts*, become addicted when they take habit-forming drugs often, for a long time. Their need for a drug is called a *habit*. Their habit makes them take larger and larger amounts of the drugs. People can become addicted to other habits, like drinking alcohol or smoking.

There are different kinds of addictive drugs. Some drugs, such as sleeping pills and "pep pills," act on the body's central nervous system. The addicts think they need such drugs, especially during times of stress. This need of the mind is called *mental dependence*. Other drugs, called *narcotics*, set up such a need that the addicts' bodies cannot do

without them. This kind of need is called *physical dependence*. If the drugs are taken away from an addict with a physical dependence, he or she experiences *withdrawal* symptoms. One of these symptoms is intense pain. People who use *heroin* and then stop must suffer through withdrawal. Heroin has medical usages, but it is so addictive that it is never prescribed.

Many drugs that cause physical or mental dependence are dangerous and illegal. There are four main kinds of drugs. (1) *Pain killers*, such as opium, morphine, and codeine, are given to patients by doctors to stop severe pain. But if people take these drugs over a period of time, they develop physical dependence. (2) *Depressants* slow, or relax, the central nervous system. Sleeping pills (*sedatives*) are depressants. (3) Other drugs called *stimulants* pep up the central nervous system. These include *amphetamines*, which are called "speed," and "crack." (4) *Hallucinogens* are the fourth main kind of drug. They are drugs that make a person see colors and objects and hear sounds that are not really there. LSD (lysergic acid diethylamide) and similar chemicals are the strongest and most dangerous hallucinogens. Drug users usually do not become physically addicted to hallucinogens, but the drugs often cause mental dependence.

Drug addiction and misuse have grown greatly in recent years. There has been a particularly large increase in the abuse of crack. Treatment of addicts has become a big community problem. Addicts hurt themselves by using drugs; they may die. Addicts may turn to crime to raise money to buy drugs.

Most ways of treating addicts start by *withdrawing* the drug. People addicted to "hard" drugs, such as heroin or cocaine, usually stay in treatment centers, to stop them from getting new supplies of drugs and to have help available during the pain of

▲ *Jane Addams, social reformer. She worked to improve life for the poor and sick, especially women and children.*

▲ *Hull House, where Jane Addams worked to give people a better life. It is now part of the University of Illinois at Chicago.*

withdrawal. Many scientists are trying to develop safe drugs that can be given as substitutes for hard drugs during the withdrawal period. It is very, very difficult to break an addiction and not many addicts are successful. Those who get past the withdrawal period need help for a long time after this.

The best way to prevent addiction is to keep people from getting harmful drugs, except when a doctor *prescribes* (gives) them. Mental health and drug-education programs give information on drugs to help young people avoid misusing drugs.

ALSO READ: DRUG ABUSE, NARCOTICS.

ADDITION see ARITHMETIC.

ADENAUER, KONRAD (1876–1967) Konrad Adenauer was the first Chancellor (chief minister of state) of West Germany. He was elected in 1949—at age 73—when Germany was divided and suffering from its defeat in World War II. Adenauer helped rebuild his war-torn country. Today, West Germany is one of the major industrial nations in the world.

Adenauer was born in Cologne, Germany. He became a lawyer and entered politics when he was 30 years old. He was elected mayor of Cologne in 1917. He remained active in politics until 1933, when Adolf Hitler's Nazi party took over Germany. The Nazis removed Adenauer from office because he spoke up against them. They imprisoned him twice during the war.

After World War II, Adenauer organized a new political party, the Christian Democratic Union. He also helped write a constitution for West Germany before he was elected Chancellor. As Chancellor, he helped improve West Germany's relations with the United States and other European

nations. Adenauer signed a "Treaty of Cooperation" with France in 1963. This treaty helped end the long hostility between Germany and France. Konrad Adenauer retired in 1963, knowing that West Germany was a strong and respected nation.

ALSO READ: GERMAN HISTORY; HITLER, ADOLF; WORLD WAR II.

ADENOIDS see BREATHING.

ADJECTIVE see PARTS OF SPEECH.

ADOLESCENCE Boys and girls usually look forward to becoming teenagers. These particular years of growing up are called *adolescence*, which is a time of many changes. The changes usually begin to take place in girls 10 to 13 and in boys 11 to 14. The changes of adolescence go on for several years.

Physical Changes The adolescent's body changes in many ways. Girls are turning into women and boys into men. Hair begins to grow on various parts of the body. Girls' hips become rounder and their breasts develop. Boys' voices deepen, and their muscles grow larger. In both girls and boys the sexual organs mature. These changes are part of *puberty*, the stage of growing up when people become physically able to reproduce.

At first, it seems that girls are growing faster than boys of the same age. But boys soon catch up and then become taller and heavier than most of the girls. Some teenagers start growing very fast and then slow down. Others develop slowly at first and later speed up.

Because so many changes are taking place in the body, adolescents often are very tired and need extra sleep. Other times, they seem to have a great deal of energy. Their bodies

▲ *Konrad Adenauer helped rebuild his country as West German Chancellor from 1949 to 1963.*

The German people fondly called Konrad Adenauer *Der Alte*, "the old one." He did much of his best work in his 70's.

▲ *Adolescence is a time of preparation for adulthood. This Jewish boy is being prepared for his bar mitzvah.*

are sometimes changing so fast that they become very clumsy. They may be embarrassed because they develop pimples on their faces.

But it helps the teenager to know that his or her friends are also going through these changes. Adolescence is a necessary part of growing up to become mature adult men and women.

Changes in Feelings   Just as a small child gives up his wagon and blocks for two-wheelers and mystery books, adolescents' interests change, too. Boys lose interest in their bicycles and look forward to driving cars. Girls no longer want to spend time making doll clothes, but become interested in their own clothes instead. Both boys and girls become interested in each other. They spend a lot of time together and learn many things about getting along with the opposite sex, which will help them later when they want to marry.

Adolescents' feelings may be confused because they are no longer a child but are not quite a grown-up. Sometimes they cry very easily and other times they act as though nothing can hurt them. Parents who are understanding (and remember their own adolescence) can help make things easier. Teenagers still need the love and help of their parents, but of a different kind. They need support and encouragement, but they must also be free to make many decisions themselves, even though some will be mistakes.

Adolescence is a time of adventure. Teenagers begin thinking about what kind of work they want to do as adults. They also begin preparing for this work in school. They make plans about whether or not to go to college. Sometimes they take part-time jobs. They learn to do more and more things for themselves, so that they do not have to depend so much on their parents. They want to think out answers for themselves. Many adolescents are very concerned with problems in their community and their nation, such as pollution and war and discrimination. They are well on their way to becoming responsible adults.

ALSO READ: AGING, GROWTH, HUMAN BODY, REPRODUCTION.

ADOPTION   Some children have no family because their parents are dead or are too sick or have too many problems to take care of them. Men and women who do not have children

It is estimated that 2 out of every 100 children in the United States are adopted. About half of these children are adopted by relatives.

Adoption is mentioned in many old legends and stories. The Bible tells how Moses was adopted by Pharaoh's daughter.

of their own may *adopt* children who have no families. To adopt means to become the legal parent of someone else's child. Often, if a person marries someone with children, he or she adopts those children. Sometimes a mother allows her new baby to be adopted because she cannot make a good home for the child and she wants him or her to be happy.

Adoption agencies have the job of making sure that the people who want to adopt children can give the children good, loving homes. These agencies try to keep brothers and sisters together.

A child cannot be adopted until an agency learns all about the child and the people who want to adopt him. The child usually lives with his new family for a while. If the agency thinks that the child will be happy with his new family, a court makes the adoption legal. Then the child really becomes part of his new family. His last name is changed to theirs. And his natural parents—those to whom he was born—cannot take him from his adopted family.

Adoption can ensure good homes for children who need special love and understanding. Sometimes these are older children, or children who have physical or emotional problems.

ALSO READ: CHILD CARE.

▼ *The Adriatic Sea is between Italy and Yugoslavia. This sea has been a route for travelers through many centuries.*

ADRIATIC SEA   Italy is shaped like a boot sticking southward into the Mediterranean Sea. The Adriatic Sea lies along the back of the boot. The Adriatic is actually a gulf of the Mediterranean Sea. (See the map with the article on EUROPE.)

The Adriatic was named after the ancient town of Adria, once a major Roman port. Roman sailing ships, bulging with cargo, crisscrossed the Adriatic. Many vessels sailed through the Strait of Otranto into the open waters of the Mediterranean and beyond. The place where Adria stood now lies 15 miles (24 km) from the sea, because mud has piled up at the mouth of the Po River and pushed back the sea.

The Adriatic's Italian coastline is low-lying and has few harbors. On the eastern side of the sea, the coasts of Yugoslavia and Albania have steep sides and good harbors. Many islands are near the Yugoslav shore. Wealthy Romans once built summer homes along this rugged coast. Today, there are tourist hotels and vineyards. Fishermen sail from the harbors to cast nets into the Adriatic for sardines. Venice, the city of canals, lies at the top of the Adriatic.

ALSO READ: MEDITERRANEAN SEA; ROME, ANCIENT; VENICE; YUGOSLAVIA.

ADVERB   see PARTS OF SPEECH.

ADVERTISING   Advertising is the business of trying to convince a *consumer* what to buy. A consumer is a buyer of products or a user of services. Business and industry provide more products and services than any one person can ever use.

One kind of product may be made by several different companies. So each company uses its own special name for a product. That special name is called the company's *brand name*. No other company can use that name. Coca-Cola and Kleenex are brand names.

Ads Are Persuaders Advertising gives useful information about which products to buy. But modern advertising does more than give news about products and services. Today's advertisements, or ads, try to get consumers to buy certain brands. Writers of advertising are so skillful they can sometimes persuade a consumer to wear a certain kind of clothing, eat a special kind of cereal, or see a movie. Consumers might never even want a product if they did not see or hear advertisements for it.

For example, you probably do not need the newest cereal in the supermarket. There are probably many cereal brands on your kitchen shelves. You may not have space on a shelf for another. But if you see ads about a new cereal that is extra-tasty and has a free prize in the box, you may want it.

Advertising must get attention. To be effective, it must be exciting, entertaining, or provide some pleasure. The secret of writing good advertising *copy* is to offer a good idea as well as a product. The idea is what the ad is really selling. One example is an ad that says eating a certain cereal will make a person do well in sports. That cereal brand may sell better if consumers think it offers strength and energy.

■ LEARN BY DOING

Suppose you are running a lemonade stand in your neighborhood. How would you advertise it?

First, you could decorate your stand with different colors of crepe paper. Next, you could paint a large, bright sign, so that people notice you.

Maybe you could write some handout posters. Your copy should say something about the lemonade to make people want to buy it. Think of how good a glass of lemonade is on a hot summer day.

If someone else has a lemonade stand on your block, he may take business away from you. If this happens, you can offer something he does not have, to win back business. You can advertise that your lemonade is made with fresh lemons instead of with a frozen mix. Many *advertisers* offer other things along with the products they are trying to sell, such as prizes or trading stamps. Perhaps you could find something to give away with your lemonade. How about a special offer? ■

The Media A communications *medium* is a means of carrying information to an audience. The plural form of medium is *media*. Some examples of media are television, films, newspapers, magazines, and radio. Advertising uses nearly all media.

▲ *An 1853 poster advertising buses. Before magazines and television, posters were important advertising media.*

▼ *A French advertisement from around 1900 for various forms of wheeled transport.*

▲ *Years ago big wooden Indians stood outside cigar stores to advertise tobacco. The models were carved and painted, and often held cigars in their hands.*

The red-and-white striped pole outside a barber shop was an old form of advertising. It was colored red (for blood) and white (for bandages) as a reminder of the days when the local barber was also the doctor and surgeon.

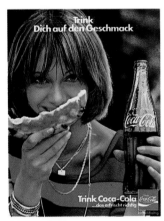

▲ *Advertisements can make a product well-known in many countries and in many languages.*

Many ads can be found in the *print* media, such as newspapers, magazines, catalogs, posters, and billboards. Newspapers and magazines depend on advertising to pay the cost of printing them. Payments that newspapers and magazines get from advertisers give publishers enough money to sell their newspapers or magazines for much less than it costs to print and mail them. Successful magazines make most of their money from the advertising they carry. Some newspapers and magazines have so much advertising that they can be given away, not sold.

Ads go wherever people can see them. *Outdoor advertising* is mounted above the windows and doors of buses and subways. Ads are sometimes painted on buildings. Big ads made of electric lights flash on and off at night in the downtown parts of cities.

Direct mail advertising uses letters and colorful brochures mailed to people's homes. The letters or brochures may ask people to subscribe to magazines, give money to charity, or attend a special sale.

Radio and television ads, called *commercials*, probably reach the most people. The amount of TV advertising increased with the arrival of cable and satellite TV. A special television program may be viewed by 100 million or more persons. Advertising on TV is expensive. For example, a few seconds ad time on a TV network costs thousands of dollars. But if 50 million persons see that ad, the advertiser pays only a tiny cost for each person who sees it. Because TV ads, especially at peak viewing times, are so expensive, not all companies can afford to advertise on TV.

When Did Advertising Begin? Town criers in ancient Greece called out what could be bought in the local marketplaces. Newsboys still hawk (advertise by shouting) papers in big cities as they walk down the street. The earliest billboards were in ancient Egypt. The Egyptians carved announcements on tall stones called *stelae*. Ads were first printed in 1480. William Caxton, one of the first English printers, nailed printed papers on church doors to advertise a religious book he was selling.

Many different newspapers and magazines appeared in Europe and America in the 1800's. Britain took the lead in advertising in the print media. But, by the 1860's, American manufacturers had seized the new opportunities offered by advertising. Special *advertising agencies* were set up to create ads.

Advertising agencies grew into big businesses with the coming of radio and television in the 20th century. An agency provides advertising to the media for anyone with a product or service to sell. In advertising, a customer is called a *client*. A client can be one person or a huge company. A client has an *account* with an ad agency. An account includes the entire job of producing the client's ads and getting them into the media. An agency and a client agree on the media that will carry the ads. A team then goes to work. Most ads—even television ads—need an illustrator, a copy writer, a designer, and often a photographer. Audio and video tapes are needed for radio and television ads.

ALSO READ: CONSUMER PROTECTION, PATENTS AND COPYRIGHTS, PROPAGANDA, PUBLIC RELATIONS.

AEGEAN SEA Lying between Greece and Turkey is the Aegean Sea. It is an arm of the Mediterranean Sea. Crete, the largest island belonging to Greece, lies at its south end. About 400 other islands are also in the Aegean. (See the map with the article on EUROPE.)

The Aegean Sea covers more than 69,000 square miles (178,700 square km). At its widest point, it is about

200 miles (322 km) across, and 400 miles (644 km) long. Most of the Aegean islands belong to Greece, and many are "dead" volcanoes. Tourists come to enjoy the historical sites, the warm sun and sandy beaches, while the local people fish in the sea, and grow grapes to produce wine and raisins.

The Aegean was the center of a rich ancient civilization, that lasted from about 3000 B.C. to 1200 B.C. The Minoans (named after the legendary King Minos of Crete) and the Myceneans were peoples of the Aegean region. Great cities were built around the sea's natural harbors. Trading ships carried bronze and gold. Adventurers went in search of fortunes. Many stories were told by the Greeks about these exciting times. The beautiful temples and palaces of the Aegean islands, some of which are still standing, remind visitors of this lost world.

ALSO READ: ANCIENT CIVILIZATIONS; GREECE, ANCIENT; MEDITERRANEAN SEA.

AEROSOL A fluffy white cloud in the blue sky overhead is one kind of aerosol. The unpleasant smog that stings your eyes and makes breathing difficult is an aerosol, too. An aerosol is a scattering of very tiny droplets of liquid, or bits of a solid, in a gas.

Clouds are droplets of water hanging in air. *Fog* is a cloud at ground level. Solid bits of carbon or ash in air form an aerosol called *smoke*. If smoke is mixed with fog, *smog* is the result. Clouds and smog are examples of natural aerosols.

Whipping cream, paint, and insect sprays can be bought in *aerosol cans*. A non-poisonous gas, called a *propellant*, is put in the can under such high pressure that it turns to a liquid. A useful product, such as paint, is mixed with the propellant. When a button on the can is pushed, the propellant sprays out, carrying the paint with it. The propellant turns back to gas and evaporates in the air.

Scientists now agree that aerosols are slowly helping to destroy the *ozone layer*. The ozone layer is a layer of gas about 12 miles (20 km) above Earth. It is this layer that protects us from most of the sun's dangerous ultraviolet rays. Chemicals named chlorofluorocarbons, or CFC's, used as propellants in most aerosols, drift slowly up into the air and begin to make holes in the layer—particularly over Antarctica.

Some aerosol manufacturers are producing cans in which the propellant is a less harmful gas. CFC gas is also used in refrigerators and to make the bubbles in foam plastic.

ALSO READ: AIR POLLUTION, ATMOSPHERE, CLOUD, GAS, OZONE LAYER.

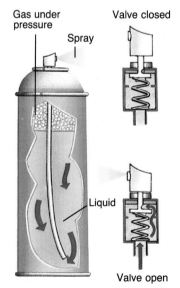

▲ *When you press down the nozzle of an aerosol can, it releases a spray of fine drops of liquid. Gas under pressure forces the liquid out of the nozzle.*

▲ *The U.S. Saturn 5 rocket blasting off. This multi-stage launcher was used by NASA for the Apollo moonlanding program.*

AEROSPACE The beginning of the Space Age in the 1950's added a new word to our vocabularies—*aerospace*. Scientists saw that the Earth's atmosphere and outer space together can be seen as one vast realm that includes everything from the surface of the Earth outward. This realm is *aerospace*.

The word also means the science of all flight within the realm of aerospace. This includes *aeronautics*, the science of navigating through air, and *astronautics*, the science of navigating through space. Craft that move through the air are *aircraft*. Craft that move through space are *spacecraft*. The Space Shuttle can be rocketed into space, and glide back to Earth. Soon there will be true *aerospace craft*, which will fly like airplanes in the atmosphere and like rocket-driven spacecraft in space. One of the achievements of aerospace science is the study of the planets at close range by spacecraft.

The human desire to explore space led to the aerospace industry. Hundreds of thousands of new jobs were created. It takes huge amounts of energy to launch craft into space. So engineers and technicians learned how to make large parts small—this is called "miniaturization"—so they could be used in space travel. Experts found how to guide robot spacecraft to faraway planets, and how to keep human beings alive in space. They learned how to put artificial satellites in orbit around the Earth.

Aerospace technology has become part of everyday life. Television programs from other continents, improved telephone calls across the ocean, more accurate maps, and better weather forecasts are some of the results. The space photographs we now see of Earth would not have been possible before aerospace research.

ALSO READ: ASTRONOMY, AVIATION, SPACE, SPACE RESEARCH, SPACE TRAVEL.

AESCHYLUS (525–456 B.C.) Aeschylus was the first great Greek writer of tragedy. He lived most of his life in Athens. As a young man, he helped defeat the Persians at the Battle of Marathon in 490 B.C.

Aeschylus wrote about 90 plays, of which only seven survive in full to-

▶ *Skylab was a manned science laboratory in space. Launched in 1974, it was visited by three crews of U.S. astronauts who carried out experiments in orbit.*

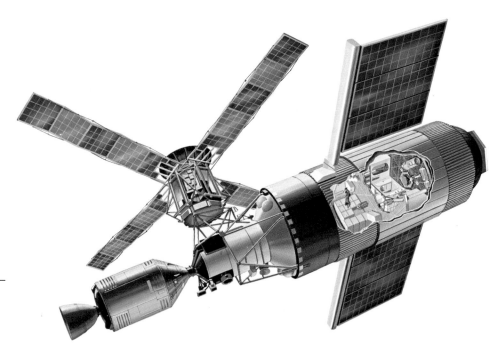

day. Many people consider them the first real tragic dramas in Western culture. Before his time, tragedies consisted of one actor who responded to questions from a chorus. Aeschylus added an actor, and later a third actor. (Though only two or three actors and the chorus were on the stage at one time, an actor sometimes took more than one role.) Also, Aeschylus instilled more life into the various roles and relationships between characters. He added costumes and decorated his stage scenery.

Today, his plays may seem slow and cumbersome to many, but they are filled with deep thoughts about human life. Some say that only William Shakespeare can rival him in richness of language and wisdom.

One of Aeschylus's better known plays is *The Persians*, which praises the Athenian victory over the Persians at the Battle of Salamis in 480 B.C. *Prometheus Bound* attacks the gods for their harsh treatment of man. Aeschylus's greatest work is the trilogy (three plays forming one drama) called the *Oresteia*. It is made up of *Agamemnon*, *The Libation Bearers*, and *The Eumenides*. In the *Oresteia*, Aeschylus deals with the importance of human suffering and the meaning of justice.

After his death, Aeschylus was honored at Athens by having his plays performed repeatedly.

ALSO READ: DRAMA; GREECE, ANCIENT.

AESOP (about 620–562 B.C.) A marvelous storyteller named Aesop lived long ago in Greece. Very little is known about him except that he was a young slave on the island of Samos. Legend says that he was an ugly man, perhaps deformed. But he had a brilliant mind, and he enjoyed telling stories in which animals acted like human beings. Each tale taught people a lesson. These tales are called *fables*.

One legend tells that Aesop was freed from slavery. He was sent to divide money among the people of Delphi, a Greek city. But he found that they were dishonest, and he refused to give them the money. The angry people of Delphi threw Aesop over a cliff to his death.

In those days, stories were shared mostly by word of mouth. Aesop's stories were not written down until at least 200 years after he died. Since then, they have been translated from Greek into almost every language in the world.

Many people have laughed at Aesop's fable of the race between the slow, patient tortoise and the swift, bragging hare. Perhaps you know the stories about the goose that laid the golden egg, the grasshopper and the ant, or the lion and the mouse. These are just four of *Aesop's Fables*, some of the best-loved stories of all time.

ALSO READ: FABLE.

AFGHANISTAN The landlocked mountain republic of Afghanistan is at the crossroads of Asia, surrounded by the nations of Iran, the Soviet Union, Pakistan, and China. Afghanistan's location has made it important throughout history. Main trade routes run through it, connecting Asia with the Western World. (See the map with the article on ASIA.) In early times, the Persians, Greeks, Arabs, and Mongols conquered the region. Tribal revolts and political assassinations have often disrupted Afghanistan. This helped bring about

▲ *In Aesop's fable of the hare and the tortoise, the slow-but-sure tortoise wins a race with the boastful hare.*

▲ *Aesop's shrewd tales may have earned him his freedom from slavery.*

Legend has it that Aeschylus was killed by a turtle that an eagle dropped while flying over his head. The eagle mistook Aeschylus's bald head for a rock!

AFGHANISTAN

Capital City: Kabul (1,200,000 people).

Area: 250.018 square miles (647,497,000 sq. km).

Population: 16,590,000.

Government: Republic.

Natural Resources: Natural gas, some coal, iron ore, and other minerals.

Export Products: Natural gas, cotton, karakul sheepskins, fruit.

Unit of Money: Afghani.

Official Language: Pashtu, Dari.

▲ *The largest statue of Buddha stands near the town of Bamian. This is in the north of Afghanistan.*

It comes as a surprise to most people to learn that Africa is almost as wide as it is long. From north to south it measures 4,400 miles (7,080 km) and from east to west 3,750 miles (6,035 km). The average height of the African continent is 2,460 feet (750 m) above sea level.

the country's troubled present, with a civil war between the communist government and rebel forces.

Afghanistan is about the size of Texas. No part of Afghanistan touches a sea. The high Hindu Kush Mountains separate Afghanistan into two sections. Nomads roam the rough mountain country, herding livestock. The Karakul lamb is one of the animals the nomads raise. The curly black Karakul fur is exported, to be made into Persian lamb coats. The low, dry land south of the mountains is a farm region where farmers use river water from the highlands to irrigate crops.

Afghanistan's ancient capital, Kabul, lies on the banks of the Kabul River. Kabul has wide modern streets through which automobiles travel. But the old part of Kabul has unpaved, narrow streets surrounded by high walls of mud-brick houses. Merchants sell fruits, nuts, spices, furs, and jewels in outdoor bazaars (marketplaces).

Transportation beyond the cities is poor in Afghanistan. There are no railroads and few paved roads. People cross the mountains only on foot or on animals. Camel caravans carry goods along rocky roads and through steep mountain passes, such as the famous Khyber Pass. Alexander the Great conquered Afghanistan about 330 B.C., and led his armies through the Khyber Pass to India.

The Afghan people did not know the ways of the outside world for hundreds of years. Most Afghans live far from cities in small, walled villages. Very few nomads or villagers can read or write. Most Afghans still strictly obey the old laws of Islam. Some tribespeople claim they are descended from the Mongol warriors of Genghis Khan.

Afghanistan was a kingdom until 1973, when military forces overthrew the king, Zahir Shah, and set up a republic. In 1978 the republican government, which had begun a democratic reform program, was itself overthrown by pro-Communist forces. The country's new leader, Babrak Karmal, was backed by the Soviets. But there was resistance to the government from tribespeople, and civil war broke out. The U.S. ambassador was killed.

In 1979 Soviet troops entered Afghanistan to prop up the Karmal government. Soviet tanks and helicopter gunships attacked Afghan villages. The Soviet army withdrew in 1989. But in 1991, the civil war was still going on, despite efforts by the United Nations to bring it to an end. During the conflict, Afghanistan's population shrank by as much as one third. At least one million people died, and four million fled to Iran or Pakistan.

ALSO READ: ASIA.

AFRICA Africa is a giant continent, more than three times bigger than the United States. Africa is divided in two by the equator, so the continent is partly in the Northern Hemisphere and partly in the Southern Hemisphere. A narrow bridge of land in the northeast connects Africa to the Sinai Peninsula of Asia. The rest of the continent is surrounded by water. The Mediterranean Sea separates Africa from Europe to the north. The Atlantic Ocean is to the west, and the Red Sea, the Gulf of Aden, and the Indian Ocean are to the east. Several islands—including one of the world's largest, Madagascar—lie off the African mainland.

The Land People used to imagine that most of Africa was a steaming jungle of twisted vines and tangled bushes. Jungles are actually found only in a small part of central Africa. The rest of the continent is mainly desert and grassland. Tropical forests and woodlands occupy about one-fifth of the total area of Africa. The various land regions are distributed over a great *plateau* (a high, fairly level land mass). The plateau rises sharply from the low coastal plains and stretches across most of the continent.

The largest desert in the world—the Sahara—is the main feature of the northern plateau. Two smaller deserts, the Kalahari and the Namib, are in the southern plateau. The deserts are mostly dry and barren, although the Sahara has a few green spots, called oases, where date palms and cereals grow. The rain forests of central Africa, near the equator, are just the opposite. These moist tropical lands are thick with fruit trees, oil palms, and hardwood trees such as ebony and mahogany. The trees often grow so high and thick that sunlight can barely reach the ground.

Between the desert regions and the rain forests are *savannas*—lonely stretches of grassland with scattered trees and shrubs. These lands make up almost half the area of Africa. The dry savannas near the deserts have short, stubby grass. But the savannas close to the rain forests have coarse "elephant grass," which can grow tall enough to hide a person, or even a large animal.

Much of Africa lies in the tropics, but highland regions throughout the continent have a cool and comfortable climate. The Atlas Mountains in the northwest are Africa's longest range. The smaller Drakensberg mountain chain lies along the southeastern tip. Mount Kilimanjaro and Mount Kenya are in the east-central highlands.

These mountains are close to the equator, but they are capped with snow all year. Also in the eastern ranges are Africa's largest lakes, including Lake Tanganyika, the longest fresh-water lake in the world. The waters of the eastern lakes help feed

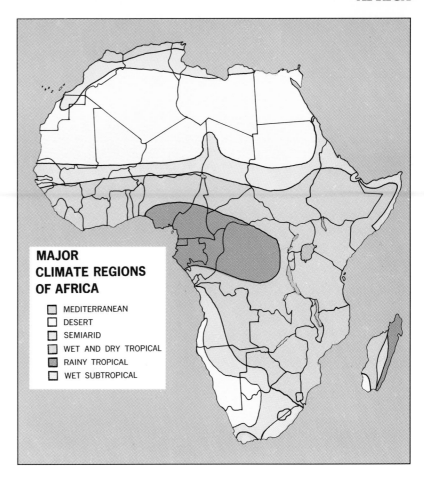

MAJOR
CLIMATE REGIONS
OF AFRICA

☐ MEDITERRANEAN
☐ DESERT
☐ SEMIARID
☐ WET AND DRY TROPICAL
▨ RAINY TROPICAL
☐ WET SUBTROPICAL

▼ *Africa is a continent rich in wildlife and natural splendors.*

AFRICAN NATIONS

Country	Year of Independence	Area in sq. miles	Area in sq. kilometers	Population	Capital
Algeria	1962	919,662	2,381,741	25,060,000	Algiers
Angola	1975	481,388	1,246,700	8,970,000	Luanda
Benin	1960	43,487	112,622	4,550,000	Porto Novo
Botswana	1966	231,822	600,372	1,220,000	Gaborone
Burkina faso	1960	105,877	274,200	7,700,000	Ouagadougou
Burundi	1962	10,747	27,834	5,230,000	Bujumbura
Cameroon	1960	183,582	475,442	10,870,000	Yaoundé
Cape Verde	1975	1,557	4,033	330,000	Praia
Central African Republic	1960	240,553	622,984	3,000,000	Bangui
Chad	1960	495,791	1,284,000	5,710,000	N'Djamena
Comoros	1975	838	2,171	459,000	Moroni
Congo	1960	132,057	342,000	2,030,000	Brazzaville
Djibouti	1977	8,495	22,000	330,000	Djibouti
Egypt	1922	386,690	1,001,449	54,780,000	Cairo
Equatorial Guinea	1968	10,831	28,051	390,000	Malabo
Ethiopia	c. 1000 B.C.	471,812	1,221,900	47,710,000	Addis Ababa
Gabon	1960	103,354	267,667	1,100,000	Libreville
Gambia	1970	4,361	11,295	840,000	Banjul
Ghana	1957	92,106	238,537	13,750,000	Accra
Guinea	1958	94,971	245,957	6,148,000	Conakry
Guinea-Bissau	1974	13,949	36,125	930,000	Bissau
Ivory Coast (Côte d'Ivoire)	1960	124,513	322,463	11,800,000	Abidjan
Kenya	1963	224,977	582,646	23,720,000	Nairobi
Lesotho	1951	11,721	30,355	1,680,000	Maseru
Liberia	1847	43,003	111,369	2,540,000	Monrovia
Libya	1951	679,411	1,759,540	4,270,000	Tripoli
Madagascar	1960	226,674	587,041	11,150,000	Antananarivo
Malawi	1964	45,750	118,484	8,060,000	Lilongwe
Mali	1960	478,801	1,204,000	8,450,000	Bamako
Mauritania	1960	397,984	1,030,700	1,800,000	Nouakchott
Mauritius	1968	805	2,085	1,048,000	Port Louis
Morocco	1956	172,426	446,550	25,400,000	Rabat
Mozambique	1975	302,351	783,030	15,260,000	Maputo
Namibia	1990	318,284	824,292	1,300,000	Windhoek
Niger	1960	489,227	1,267,000	7,400,000	Niamey
Nigeria	1960	356,695	923,768	115,150,000	Lagos
Réunion	FRENCH OVERSEAS DEPARTMENT	969	2,510	570,000	St. Denis
Rwanda	1962	10,170	26,338	7,270,000	Kigali
São Tomé and Príncipe	1975	373	965	110,000	São Tomé
Senegal	1960	75,756	196,192	7,700,000	Dakar
Seychelles	1976	108	280	80,000	Victoria
Sierra Leone	1961	27,701	71,740	4,300,000	Freetown
Somali Republic	1960	246,219	637,657	8,550,000	Mogadishu
South Africa	1931	471,479	1,221,037	35,600,000	Cape Town, Pretoria
Sudan	1956	967,570	2,505,813	25,000,000	Khartoum
Swaziland	1968	6,704	17,363	760,000	Mbabane
Tanzania	1964 (UNITED)	364,927	945,087	24,740,000	Dodoma
Togo	1960	21,623	56,000	3,400,000	Lomé
Tunisia	1956	63,175	163,610	7,900,000	Tunis
Uganda	1962	91,141	236,036	16,800,000	Kampala
Western Sahara	IN DISPUTE-OCCUPIED BY MOROCCO	102,703	265,980	95,000	El Aaiún
Zaire	1960	905,633	2,345,709	34,000,000	Kinshasa
Zambia	1964	290,607	752,614	7,700,000	Lusaka
Zimbabwe	1980	150,815	390,580	10,000,000	Harare

AFRICA

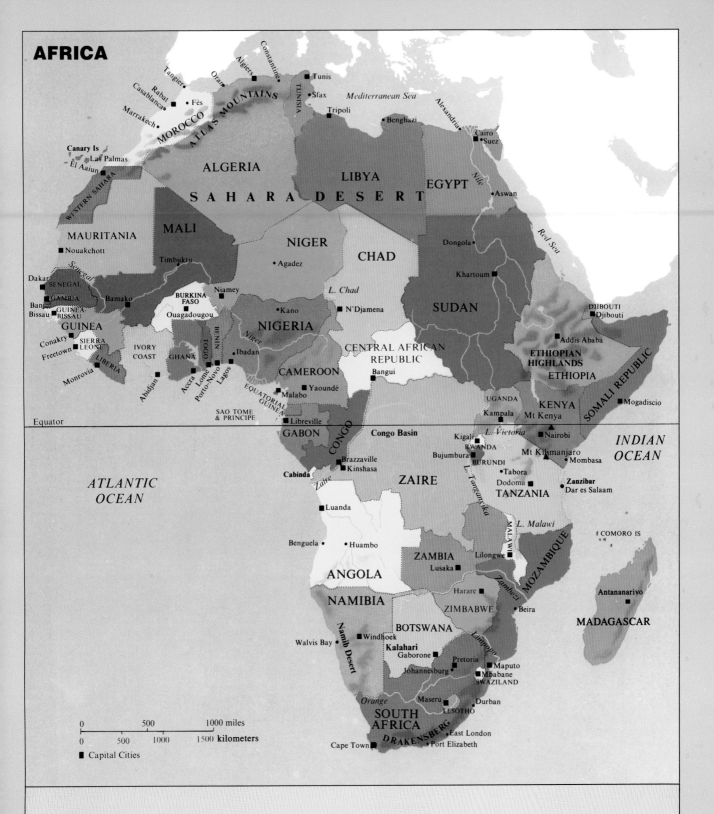

Total Population: 642,100,000.

Total Area: 11,700,000 square miles (30,300,000 sq. km).

Highest Point: Mount Kilimanjaro in Tanzania; 19,565 feet (5,963 m).

Mountain Ranges: Atlas, Drakensberg, Ruwenzori.

Lowest Point: Qattara Depression in northern Egypt; 440 feet (134 m) below sea level.

Longest River: Nile River; 4,160 miles (6,695 km).

Other Major Rivers: Zaire (Congo), Niger, Zambezi.

Largest Lake: Lake Victoria; 26,828 square miles (69,479 sq. km).

Largest City: Cairo (6,300,000 people).

Natural Wonders: Great Rift Valley, Victoria Falls, Sahara Desert (world's largest desert), Lake Tanganyika (world's longest lake).

▶ *Zebras, antelopes, and guinea fowl quench their thirst at a waterhole on the African savanna. In the distance are more antelopes and a lone giraffe.*

▼ *A finely carved ivory mask from West Africa.*

▼ *A Bushman hunter. Bushmen can find food, even in the most barren country and can survive where others would die of hunger and thirst.*

three great rivers—the Nile, the Zaire (Congo), and the Zambezi. Another important river, the Niger, drains the waters of west-central Africa. Steep waterfalls and rapids often occur at the places where these mighty rivers plunge from the high plateaus to the low coastal lands. The spectacular Victoria Falls, on the Zambezi River in southeastern Africa, drop about 335 feet (102 m).

Animal Life Some of the world's most famous animals come from Africa. Giraffes, elephants, zebras, antelopes, and rhinoceroses feed on the plentiful grasses and shrubs of the savannas. Fierce meat-eaters such as lions, leopards, and cheetahs also dwell in the grassy plains. Ostriches, the largest of all birds, are found in the sandy savanna lands near the Sahara. Many of these large animals are protected in special parks, because so many have been killed by hunters.

Crocodiles and hippopotamuses are common in warm rivers and swamps. The tropical rain forests are the home of gorillas, chimpanzees, monkeys, colorful birds, and a great variety of insects and snakes. The rock python

is a giant African snake that squeezes its prey to death and swallows it whole. An especially dreaded insect of the tropical lands is the blood-sucking tsetse fly. It carries the germs that cause sleeping sickness and other diseases.

People Africa has an enormous variety of people, with different customs and ways of life. Most Africans are farmers who live in villages in the grasslands and coastal areas. Many are nomads, who wander from place to place, herding cattle, sheep, or other livestock. Some live and work in modern cities. A few primitive tribes hunt and gather wild plant food. They live much as their ancestors lived for thousands of years.

Negroes (blacks) are the largest group of Africans. They live mainly in regions south of the Sahara Desert. The people of the various African tribes can be quite different in appearance. Many tribes take their names from the languages they speak. The *Bushmen*, a tribe of hunters of the Kalahari Desert, and the *Hottentots*, nomadic herding peoples of the southwest, are sometimes referred to as Negroid (Negro-like). Their yellowish-brown skin makes them different from most other blacks. The *Nilotes* include several tribes, such as the Dinkas, who live in the Nile River Basin. They are rather dark-skinned and are unusually tall and slender. The *Pygmies*, also called Negrillos, rarely grow taller than 4½ feet (1.4 m). They are hunters who live in the tropical rain forests.

North Africans are chiefly Caucasian (white) peoples. Most of them are Arabs and Berbers who dwell north of the Sahara. A few nomadic tribes, such as the *Bedouins*, roam this vast desert, living in tents and tending herds of camels, goats, and sheep. There are more than five million Africans of British, Dutch, French, Spanish, and Portuguese descent. Most of them live in South Africa, with small numbers in Zimbabwe, Kenya, or along the Mediterranean coast, where the climate is much like that of Europe. About a million Asians, mainly of Indian origin, live in eastern and southeastern Africa.

LANGUAGES. Africans speak more than 800 languages. Arabic is the chief tongue of northern Africa. Great numbers of eastern Africans speak Swahili. It is just one of 80 Bantu languages. Hausa is also widely spoken, especially in the west. The Bushmen and Hottentots speak a variety of Khoisan languages, which are quite unusual. They feature clicking sounds that are not found in any other language. English or French are widely spoken in many countries that were once European colonies. The Dutch of South Africa speak Afrikaans, a Germanic language developed by Dutch settlers in the 1600's.

RELIGION. The religions of Africa are as varied as the people. Many different groups have their own tribal religions. Most tribes believe in one god who created the universe and who controls human life. They may also worship their ancestors as minor gods, and believe in spirits that rep-

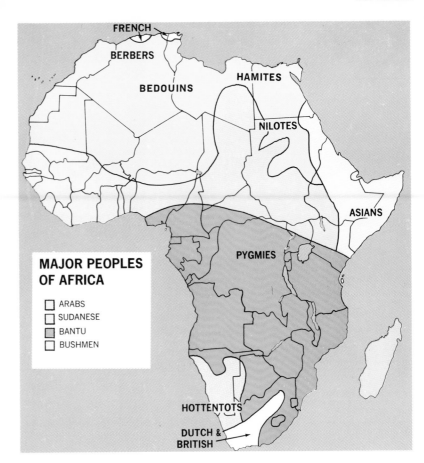

▲ The modern map of Africa overlies the ancient pattern of peoples and cultures. The borders of the modern states of Africa were largely fixed by the European colonial powers. The Bantu are the most widespread African people.

▲ Fishermen in Chad, in central Africa, get their nets ready to go fishing on Lake Chad.

47

▲ (Left picture) *A modern African woman.* (Right picture) *Traditional business is unchanged in an African market. Here traders still sell grain much as their ancestors did centuries ago.*

▼ *A Zulu woman in a colorful headdress. The Zulus are the largest single group of black African people in South Africa. They number over 4 million.*

resent parts of nature, such as trees, water, or the sun. Religious rituals are an important part of tribal life. They mark events such as births, marriages, and deaths. Magic ceremonies are often performed to heal the sick and to make the land more fertile.

About 145 million Africans, mainly in the north, are Muslims. Many African peoples were converted to Christianity by European missionaries in the 1800's. Large numbers of Egyptians and Ethiopians are members of the Coptic Orthodox Church. About 177,000 people, including several Negro groups, are Jewish.

History   Africa has a long and complex history. Fossil bones and other ancient remains found by archeologists show that the human race had its beginnings on the African continent millions of years ago. Rock paintings and tools of the Stone Age have also been discovered. But not much is known about the earliest peoples of Africa. The first highly developed civilization began in Egypt in the Nile Valley about 3,000 B.C. An important area of settlement after 1,000 B.C. was the Mediterranean coast of Africa. Phoenician and Greek invaders founded colonies there. As Egypt gradually became weaker, it was conquered about 725 B.C. by the Kushites, a black society on the Nile

River south of Egypt. The Kushites built the oldest and greatest civilization of black Africa. It lasted a thousand years. Both Egypt and the Mediterranean lands had become part of the Roman Empire by the middle of the first century A.D.

Still another group of invaders, the Muslims of Arabia, began to conquer northern Africa about the year 700. Muslim influence spread in time to west-central Africa, where there were several large black kingdoms. Camel caravans were sent across the Sahara to trade with kingdoms of Ghana, Mali, and Songhai. Northern African goods such as cloth and wheat were exchanged for gold and ivory. Arab traders brought their religion and culture to the coast of eastern Africa, and also captured black slaves.

The next great influence on African development came from Europe. The Portuguese set up trading posts on both the east and west coasts during the 1400's. At first they were interested only in African gold, ivory, and spices. But as colonies began to be established in the Americas, the Portuguese found that the slave trade was even more profitable. The British and French also set up coastal trading posts in the 1600's, and the Dutch started a colony at the Cape of Good Hope. The slave trade began to decline in the 1800's. But millions of black Africans had been captured and brought to the Americas by that time.

European explorers and missionaries penetrated the interior of Africa in the 1770's. Europeans became interested in colonizing Africa when this continent's vast natural resources were discovered. Great Britain, France, Germany, Belgium, Spain, Portugal, and Italy competed for control of Africa, beginning in about 1850. These nations had divided up almost all of Africa among themselves by 1914. Only Ethiopia and Liberia were independent countries.

Colonial rule brought great changes to Africa. Transportation was improved, industries were developed, and new cities were built. Missionaries set up schools and hospitals in remote places. But not all the changes brought about by the Europeans were good. Often the white settlers did not understand the Africans' ways, and they tried to do away with the cherished customs of tribal peoples. Many blacks were offered jobs in mines and factories, but they were not given the same rights and wages as white people. Europeans often took the best lands for themselves, leaving the less productive lands to the Africans. Even the borders of the colonial states were drawn without much regard for the identities and traditional boundaries of the Africans.

People in some parts of Africa began to demand the right of self-government in the late 1880's. The struggle for independence became stronger and more widespread after World War II. A new generation of black African leaders emerged, ready to lead new nations to independence. Most of the colonies gained their independence peacefully during the 1950's and 1960's. Many former French and British colonies kept trading and other links with France and Britain. Portugal was reluctant to give up its African possessions, and only wars in the 1970's finally led to their independence. By the 1980's only the

French-held island of Réunion remained dependent. In South Africa, the whites retained control of the government, but faced growing demands for change from the black majority.

Africa's new nations face many problems. Some enjoy rich natural resources, such as oil and other minerals. But many are poor. Drought, hunger, and civil war have brought hardship to millions of Africans. Ancient ways of life have altered dramatically, with the growth of cities and new industries.

However, enormous advances are being made. Education is now widespread, and each year more Africans are being trained as scientists, engineers, doctors, and business people. Women are playing a leading part in this educational revolution. Art, especially music and literature, is flourishing. In international affairs, including sports, Africa is emerging as a powerful force.

One problem is the difficulty of unifying groups of people with very different traditions and customs. The Organization of African Unity (OAU), established in 1963, promotes economic and political cooperation among African nations and tries to settle disputes peacefully.

For further information on:
Animals, *see* ANIMAL DISTRIBUTION,

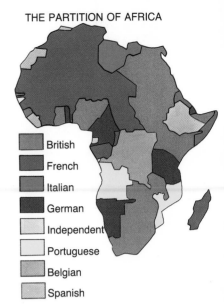

THE PARTITION OF AFRICA

- British
- French
- Italian
- German
- Independent
- Portuguese
- Belgian
- Spanish

▲ *A map showing how Africa was divided, or partitioned, between European states in the late 1800's.*

▼ *Modern buildings line the streets of Nairobi, the capital of Kenya, in east Africa.*

AGASSIZ, LOUIS

▲ *Louis Agassiz, Swiss-American naturalist, added greatly to our knowledge of fish and geology.*

People, on average, live much longer in developed countries than in the underdeveloped world. In Sweden, for example, 22 percent of the population is over 65. In Zimbabwe, only 3 percent of people reach that age. Half the population of Zimbabwe is under 15.

NATIONAL PARK, RARE ANIMAL.

Arts, *see* ART HISTORY, FOLK ART, MUSICAL INSTRUMENTS.

History, *see* ANCIENT CIVILIZATIONS; BOER WAR; CARTHAGE; DIAS, BARTHOLOMEU; EGYPT, ANCIENT; GAMA, VASCO DA; LIVINGSTONE, DAVID; RHODES, CECIL; SCHWEITZER, ALBERT; SLAVERY; SONGHAI EMPIRE; STANLEY, HENRY MORTON; WORLD WAR II.

Language, *see* ALPHABET, ARABIC, LANGUAGES.

People, *see* CIVILIZATION, HUMAN BEINGS, PYGMY.

Physical Features, *see* CONTINENT, EQUATOR, JUNGLE, MEDITERRANEAN SEA, NILE RIVER, RED SEA, SAHARA DESERT, ZAIRE RIVER.

Also read the article on each country shown in the table.

AGASSIZ, LOUIS (1807–1873) The ambitious son of a villager in Switzerland grew up to be one of the greatest naturalists of the 1800's. He was Jean Louis Agassiz. He gained his greatest fame for important work in *ichthyology*, the study of fish. He was a geologist who added to scientific understanding of glaciers and the ways continents form.

Even as a child in Switzerland, Agassiz was determined to be a great naturalist. He formed the habit of observing nature closely. This habit became the key to his life's work. He had to see nature at first hand, not just read about it in books. Once he risked his life to go into the center of a glacier to study it. Agassiz was a

teacher as well as a scientist. He had a warm personality and was popular.

When he came to America at the age of 39, Agassiz was already world famous. He became a professor at Harvard University, and he founded Harvard's Museum of Comparative Zoology.

ALSO READ: GEOLOGY, ZOOLOGY.

AGING On each birthday a person adds one year to his age. Growing older year by year is called *chronological* aging.

However, each person grows and ages at his own pace. Some babies take longer than others to learn to walk. Some children grow faster than others. Scientists believe that each person has a "biological clock" that sets his speed of aging. Most plants keep growing throughout their lives, but most animals do not. A human being is usually full grown by age 21.

Scientists divide human life into three periods—youth, middle age, and old age. In youth, the speed with which the body obeys orders from the mind, called *coordination*, is quickest. The muscles of young people move easily and usually do not stay stiff or tired for long after hard work or play. People's muscles tire more quickly in middle age.

As it ages, some parts of the body weaken, while others remain strong. Parts of the body wear out at different speeds. Some worn-out parts of the body can be replaced. For example, heart valves (that pump blood) can be replaced by artificial valves that work as well as natural ones. Hip joints can also be replaced by artificial bones.

Many older people with frail bodies may still have very active minds. The growth of the mind may be at a different rate from the aging of the rest of the body.

ALSO READ: ANIMAL, GROWTH, HUMAN BODY, PLANT.

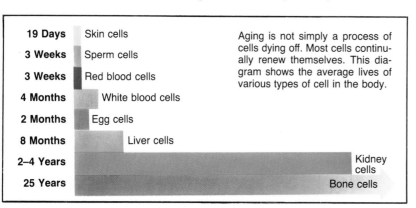

19 Days	Skin cells
3 Weeks	Sperm cells
3 Weeks	Red blood cells
4 Months	White blood cells
2 Months	Egg cells
8 Months	Liver cells
2–4 Years	Kidney cells
25 Years	Bone cells

Aging is not simply a process of cells dying off. Most cells continually renew themselves. This diagram shows the average lives of various types of cell in the body.

AGRICULTURE Life for human beings was difficult before they found out how to grow food. Prehistoric people lived in small groups, because it was difficult for a large number of people to find food. The groups roamed the countryside, constantly looking for animals to kill or wild plants to pick. If they could not spear or trap an animal, and if they did not find plants, they went hungry. Agriculture, often called the "mother of civilization," changed all that.

The word *agriculture* comes from two Latin words meaning "to plant and to care for the fields." But agriculture is far more than planting and raising crops. Agricultural scientists today study soil, climate, how plants grow, how to stop plant disease, and how to develop better plants. They also study farm animals. They try to find new ways to raise better animals, and to prevent and cure diseases. Farms, ranches, plantations, orchards, gardens, dairies, sheds for beehives, and a great many laboratories and factories are now parts of agriculture. The areas where most plants and animals are cared for are called *rural areas*. "Rural" is an adjective meaning "open country."

Agriculture employs more than half the people on Earth. But in the United States, only about 3 out of every 100 working people work full or part-time on farms. Many machines are used on North American farms, ranches, and plantations. Scientific methods are used in crop production and livestock care. Although they are a small group of people, U.S. farmers produce more food each year than all the people in the United States can eat.

Other parts of the world cannot run farms with so few people as the U.S. does. Three of the main reasons for this are the lack of good cropland, the cost of buying and using machines, and the slow change away from ancient ways of farming. About 60 out of every 100 people in Africa live in rural areas and work on the land. About 15 out of every 100 people in Europe are "farm folk." So are about 55 out of every 100 in Asia, and 40 out of every 100 in South America. Some of the cattle and sheep stations (ranches) in Australia cover thousands of square miles, and about 20 out of every 100 Australians live and work in farm areas.

The Start of Agriculture People living in the sunny, fertile lands between the Mediterranean Sea and the Persian Gulf are believed to have started agriculture more than 10,000 years ago. The first farmers discovered that wild seeds planted in plots, kept clean of weeds, and watered regularly produced reliable harvests. They lived near their plots to guard them from both human and animal robbers. So, instead of wandering, they settled down to live in huts by their fields, with nearby pits for storing crops. After a time these places became villages. Then roads were made between the villages, and peoples became acquainted.

The first animal to live side by side with people was probably the dog, which was used in hunting. Animals such as goats, sheep, and pigs were hunted, not kept on farms. The first farm animal to be tamed, or *domesticated*, was probably the goat. Soon sheep too were domesticated, then—hundreds of years apart—chickens,

▲ *A wall picture of ancient Egypt shows the time when all work in agriculture was done by hand, using animals and simple tools.*

In ancient Egypt farmers sowed seed in the fertile mud left after the Nile River's yearly flood. Today, canals drain the floodwater into basins. After about eight weeks, the basins are emptied and farmers plant crops in the rich silt the Nile water leaves behind.

AGRICULTURE

▲ *In early times, villages were formed where people joined together to care for the fields. Work was done with simple tools. (Top picture.) The scythe was used for mowing for many centuries. (Middle picture.) The harvester machine was invented in 1830. It picked up cut wheat automatically, while workers tied the bundles of grain by hand. (Lower picture.)*

pigs, cattle, donkeys, and finally horses. Domestication of these animals took place mostly along the shores of the Mediterranean, and farther east, on the grassy plains of Russia, called *steppes*, between the Black Sea and the Caspian Sea. These changes caused agriculture to split into three major divisions.

Kinds of Agriculture STOCK FARMING. Some families chose to tame and care for herds of animals. These were the herders. In the years of the American Wild West, herders, especially cattle ranchers and shepherds, often lived on the frontier. Until re-

cently, slow transportation forced dairy and poultry farmers to keep their animals close to the cities. Today, in Asia and Africa there are still peoples called *nomads* (wanderers) who live as herders. They move from place to place, seeking food and water for their herds.

ONE-CROP FARMING. The ancient Greeks discovered many uses for the fruit and wood of the olive tree. Some Greeks became specialists in growing olives and processing olive oil. Many Egyptian farmers specialized in growing and harvesting cotton. They learned how to harvest the puffy bolls of the cotton plant, remove the seeds, and weave the fibers into cloth. The efforts of the ancient Greeks and the Egyptians were the beginnings of another major branch of agriculture—one-crop farming.

Examples of one-crop agriculture in the U.S. today are the Midwest wheat farms, the southern cotton plantations, and the citrus groves of Florida and California. Each of these places, as well as many other farming areas in the world, has climate and soil that are very good for the one crop of the region.

DIVERSIFIED FARMING. Several different crops can be grown on one farm. *Diversified farming* was, and still

▲ *Small American farms are fast disappearing. They are being combined into large farms where big and powerful machinery can be used more easily, and crops and livestock tended more economically.*

52

AGRICULTURAL MARKETING IN THE UNITED STATES

If certain products were added up and divided among the 248 million people in the United States, here's an idea of how much each person would get.

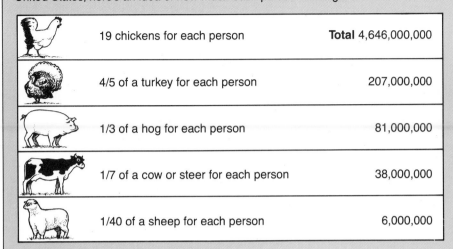

19 chickens for each person	**Total** 4,646,000,000	
4/5 of a turkey for each person	207,000,000	
1/3 of a hog for each person	81,000,000	
1/7 of a cow or steer for each person	38,000,000	
1/40 of a sheep for each person	6,000,000	

▲ *Women picking olives, which have ripened and fallen from the trees. Olives are an important crop in the warmer lands of Europe.*

THE COMBINE HARVESTER
1. Rotating blades
2. Cutting bar
3. Auger lifts stems.
4. Conveyer
5. Thresher
6. Sieve separates grain from stalks.
7. Fan
8. Conveyer for grain
9. Conveyer for straw
10. Storage tank for grain
11. Bale binder

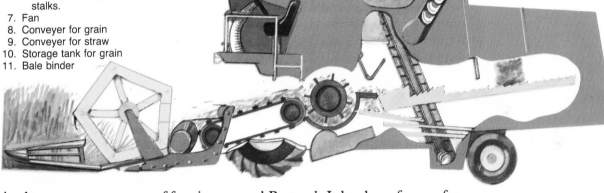

is, the most common type of farming. It got its start in America from European farmers such as those from Estremadura, in Spain. They brought their knowledge of this farming to the New World.

European Farming in America
Spanish soldiers conquered Mexico and Peru and first explored the southern and southwestern U.S. between 1521 and 1550. These Spaniards were called *conquistadors*, meaning "conquerors." Many of them grew up in Estremadura, one of the most beautiful areas of diversified farming in Europe. It is a region of many mountains, river valleys, and red-earth fields along the border between Spain

and Portugal. It has been famous for more than 2,000 years for its crops of wheat, olives, fruit, and cork, and for its herds of sheep, goats, and pigs.

The conquistadors quickly realized that the mountains, plains, and climate of Southern California, Arizona, and New Mexico were very much like the countryside and weather of their Spanish homeland. The first Spanish settlers in the Southwest planted the crops they had known in Estremadura—oranges, olives, figs, grapes, and wheat. They brought cattle, horses, and pigs from Spain, too.

▶ *Combine harvesters in an Australian wheatfield. With machines, today's farmers can produce bigger crops with less labor.*

▲ *In parts of the world ancient farm methods are still used. Here an Asian farmer plows a flooded rice field with the help of oxen.*

Machinery has completely changed the farmer's life. Before 1830, cutting an acre of wheat by hand took about 40 hours. Now a large combine-harvester can cut and thresh an acre of wheat in seven minutes.

Spanish settlers also moved into Florida, in the last half of the sixteenth century. The climate and soil of their new home reminded them of Andalusia, the region of Spain that is Estremadura's southern neighbor. So these settlers brought oranges from Andalusia and found that this fruit grew well in Florida. They learned about a New World plant food when they received the small, sweet nuts of the pine-nut tree from Indians. The Indians had used these *piniones* in soups, breads, and candies for a long time.

The French founded New Orleans and began other settlements along the Gulf of Mexico. They, like the Spanish, thought of their European homes when they began to farm. They brought pears and carrots from France to America.

Colonists in Massachusetts and Virginia found their land and climate much like that of their native England. So they brought familiar animals, such as sheep and cattle, and plants, such as apples, to America. These settlers also got help from the Indians, who taught them how to plant and raise corn, squash, and tobacco.

All these New World settlers were fortunate that their new homes were much like their old ones. Plants from

one part of the world cannot easily be grown in other parts. Plants do well in certain soils and climates. In different soils, or in different weather conditions, they may not grow at all.

Names for Agricultural Land The three most common names for agricultural property come from the regions where European methods of caring for the land began. The words *ranch*, *plantation*, and *farm* are really lessons in the history of both language and agriculture.

Ranch comes from the Spanish word *rancho*, which first meant "where the cattle graze." It was used by the Spanish people who pioneered the Rio Grande Valley of New Mexico in 1598. The word spread to Texas, Arizona, and California, and then moved eastward. Most ranches today are west of the Mississippi River, but many of them have no cattle at all. They include mink ranches, horse ranches, fruit ranches, and even rose ranches.

Plantation comes from a Latin word used in the Middle Ages in England to mean a rural estate where servants tended the crops and cared for livestock. Virginians began to develop large one-crop areas of tobacco or rice. Agricultural properties throughout the South were often called plantations, especially where planters owned slaves to do the hard work. Dairy herds, beef cattle, poultry, fruit, grains, beans, vegetables, and peanuts have now become important agricultural products in the South. Diversified farming has replaced much one-crop farming. Agriculturists in the South now prefer to be called farmers instead of planters.

Farm is an old English word that the Pilgrims brought to New England. The word originally meant "land that is rented." The man who worked a farm was not a serf or peasant, but paid an annual rent to the lord or knight who owned the land. If an agriculturist owned his own land, but was not a knight or lord, he was called a *franklin*.

Technology Comes to Agriculture

Abraham Lincoln was President in 1863. At that time, seven out of every ten Americans worked and lived on farms, plantations, and ranches. Nearly everybody owned a horse, and almost every home had a horsebarn and a horse pasture. Horse-power was the chief method of getting the job done. Horses plowed and tilled the fields, hauled the wagons, carriages, coaches, and harvesting machines, and trampled the kernels of grain free from the stalks on the threshing floors. Horses and mules were the great servants of American agriculture from 1600 until 1920. Slaves on Southern plantations also played a very important part in shaping modern American farming.

Tractors, trucks, and hundreds of planting, spraying, weeding, and harvesting machines took the place of horses and mules in the 1920's. Scientists discovered ways to grow two or three times as much crop on the same amount of land. These inventions and discoveries made it possible for a family to farm three, four, or five

times as much land as they could have with horses and mules. Fewer people were needed on farms. Machines and other materials needed for modern agriculture were expensive and complicated. Large properties and scientific training became necessary for successful farming. More and more farmers and ranches sold their lands and moved to town. Hired workers were laid off or went to cities for better jobs. In 1900 about 35 of every 100 people in the U.S. worked on farms. Today, only 3 of every 100 people are employed in agriculture.

A major division of the U.S. Government is the Department of Agriculture. Its director, the Secretary of Agriculture, is a member of the President's Cabinet. Working for the Department are thousands of scientists, engineers, economists, and other specialists in modern agriculture. Each state in the U.S. has its own department of agriculture. Many also have a state college of agriculture. The local advisers on agricultural affairs in each area, who have offices at each of the 3,000 county seats in the U.S., are called *county agents*.

Agriculture still faces big problems despite the great changes brought

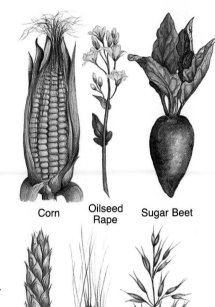

Corn   Oilseed Rape   Sugar Beet

Wheat   Barley   Oats

▲ *Farmers produce many crops. But certain plants are favored, because they provide basic foods. Here are six common farm crops.*

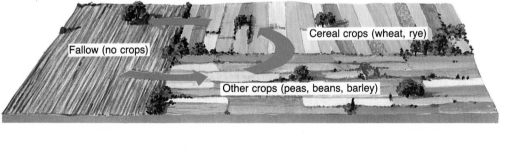

Cereal crops (wheat, rye)

Fallow (no crops)

Other crops (peas, beans, barley)

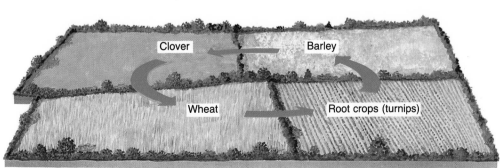

Clover   Barley

Wheat   Root crops (turnips)

◀ *Farmers know it is unwise to plant the same crops in the same fields year after year. This exhausts the soil and helps the buildup of plant diseases, so that poor yields result. Instead, farmers plan to grow crops in rotation, so that no field is seeded with the same crops two years running. Here are shown two examples: a three-year rotation, where the land is allowed to rest, or lie fallow, one year (top picture); and a four-year rotation (bottom picture), where a new crop is grown in each field every year.*

AIDS

▲ *A traditional farmland scene, with small fields and grazing dairy cattle. Such farms are common in parts of Europe as well as America.*

People have bred sheep, hogs, cattle, and poultry for thousands of years. Chickens now lay at least 250 eggs per year, which is 15 times more than wild hens lay. Cows now produce more than 1,000 gallons (4,000 l) of milk each year, which is about 20 times more than a wild cow produces.

about by machines and science. In the developed world, such as the United States and Europe, farmers can produce far more food than is needed by their own people. This extra food creates a *surplus*, which may be thrown away. Yet in other parts of the world, such as in the desert lands of Africa, millions of people are hungry. Here local agriculture is suffering from climatic change, and from a breakdown of old village ways as people leave the land.

By using sensible "intermediate" technology (some machines and fertilizers, but not so much that small farmers are driven out of business), countries like India have done much to feed their hungry people. Agricultural experts are working to find better ways of feeding everyone.

For further information on:
Conservation, *see* CONSERVATION, FERTILIZER, IRRIGATION, NATURAL RESOURCES, SOIL.
Crops, *see* CORN, FRUIT, RICE, VEGETABLES, WHEAT.
Farm Life, *see* FARM MACHINERY, WEATHER.
Livestock, *see* CATTLE, GOAT, HORSE, POULTRY, SHEEP, VETERINARY MEDICINE.

Processes, *see* DAIRY FARMING, FISHING INDUSTRY, FOOD, MEAT, PLANT BREEDING.

AIDS AIDS, short for Acquired Immune Deficiency Syndrome, is a deadly disease that was first reported in the late 1960's. It was not recognized as an epidemic until 1981. AIDS is caused by a virus that attacks the body's immune system—the body's defense force that protects us against infections. The virus is named HIV (Human Immune Deficiency Virus). People infected with the HIV virus may take several years to develop the symptoms of AIDS. If they do, they may fall victim to any number of infections that might not cause any disease in a normal person. The body's defense system cannot fight off the disease, and most AIDS patients die.

A person can become infected with the HIV virus when it enters his or her blood stream. The infection most commonly passes from person to person during intimate sexual contact or can also be passed when drug abusers share injection needles. An infected person can give a needle contaning virus-carrying blood to another drug abuser. The HIV virus is then injected into the second user's blood stream.

A person is very unlikely to catch AIDS by ordinary contact with another person who has AIDS—by working together, by sharing food or drink, even by kissing. Scientists in many countries are hard at work trying to find treatments for AIDS and a vaccine against the HIV virus.

ALSO READ: VIRUS

AIR Air is all around you. You cannot see it, smell it, or taste it. But you can feel the wind blow. You can see the wind move waves on the water, clouds in the sky, and tree branches. Wind is moving air.

Without air you could not breathe.

There could be no living plants or animals. Because sound travels through air, without air there would be silence. The movement of invisible air can support a large, heavy airplane. Air makes up a precious blanket of atmosphere wrapped around the Earth. Beyond this blanket lies airless space. Humans must carry their own air supplies to be able to live and work when they travel in spaceships through this airless space.

Air is a mixture of gases and water vapor. The most important gases in the air are nitrogen and oxygen. About 78 percent of the air is made up of nitrogen, and about 21 percent of oxygen. The remaining one percent is mostly argon, plus very tiny amounts of some other gases. Almost all living things use the oxygen in air. Fire cannot burn without oxygen.

When air expands, it becomes lighter. This fact allows a small electric heater to heat an entire room. The heater warms the air next to it. The warmed air becomes lighter and moves upward. Cool air moves into its place. The new air gets warm and also rises. Then it cools and moves down. The air keeps moving in circles, and the whole room is soon heated.

■ LEARN BY DOING

AIR CAN BE COMPRESSED. Get a small paper bag and blow into it until it swells up. Close the bag by twisting the end. Feel the bag. If the bag were just standing open, it would be filled with air. But by blowing into the bag, you have forced even more air into the same amount of space. The air from your lungs has been *compressed*, or squeezed together, in the bag, so the bag feels firm.

Now lay an empty bag on the edge of a table. Place a small book on top of it. Blow the bag full of air. The book will be lifted from the table. It is held up by the air in the bag. In the same way, air in tires holds a car off the ground. You are really riding on compressed air when you ride in a car.

AIR EXPANDS WHEN HEATED. Fasten a balloon containing a little air to the open top of each of two small-necked bottles. Place one bottle in a pan of hot water and the other in ice water. The air in the first bottle is heated by the hot water. The *molecules* (small particles) of air move faster and faster. The air *expands* and moves into the balloon. The balloon gets bigger. Air in the other bottle cools and takes up less space than before, so the balloon shrinks and looks nearly empty.

AIR IS EVERYWHERE. Pack a glass full of soil from a garden. Add water to the glass. Watch the bubbles of air rise through the water. A lawn is often dotted with earthworms after a rain. The rain has forced air out of the ground, so the worms must come to the surface to breathe. ■

ALSO READ: AIRPLANE, AIR PRESSURE, ATMOSPHERE, GAS, WATER CYCLE, WEATHER.

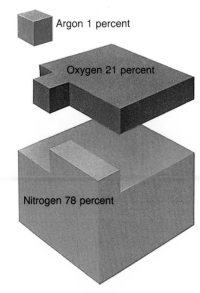

▲ *Air is made up of gases. As this diagram shows, nitrogen is the most common, making up 78 percent of the air.*

Air is heavier than you think. The average roomful of air weighs more than 100 pounds (45 kg).

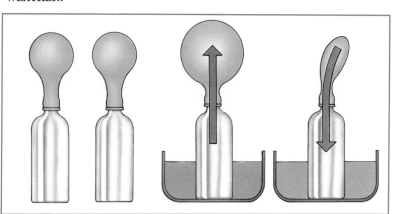

AIR CONDITIONING Air is seldom at the temperature comfortable for most people—about 70°F (21°C). So we have learned to build machines that change air temperature. Machines that raise the air temperature are heaters. Machines that lower the air temperature are air conditioners. The work that these machines do is called *air conditioning*.

■ LEARN BY DOING

You can make a simple *air conditioner*. You need an electric fan, a bowl of ice cubes, a thermometer, and an adult to help you. Put the fan on a table, and put the thermometer on the table about 15 inches (38 cm) in front of the fan. Note what temperature the thermometer shows. Now turn on the fan, but be careful. Do not go near the fan while it is running. You can feel a cool breeze when you stand in front of the fan. Wait five minutes and see what temperature the thermometer then shows. Next, place the bowl of ice on the table, just in front of the fan. Is the breeze even cooler? After five minutes, what temperature does the thermometer show? ■

Air conditioners have other jobs besides changing the air temperature. The amount of water vapor in the air is called *humidity*. Humidity is also important to comfort. A person's perspiration usually evaporates into the air. This makes the person feel cool. (Put a drop of rubbing alcohol on your arm and blow on it. What happens?) But in summer, the humidity is often high. The air has no room for evaporated perspiration. So air conditioners remove water from the air. Perspiration evaporates and a person feels cool.

One more important job for air conditioners is to filter, or clean, the air. Air is filled with dust, pollen, and many other substances. Air conditioner filters are made of fine threads of glass called *glass wool*. The air conditioner's fan blows the air through the filter, which catches the dust.

Many home air conditioners are small, and fit in windows. Larger buildings often have *central* air conditioning, and one big machine cools the entire building. Pipes carry cool air from the machine to all the rooms. And sometimes the same pipes that carry cool air in summer carry hot air in winter. Many modern automobiles too have a controlled air conditioning system. So do passenger airplanes, railroad cars, ships, and television studios (where there are very hot lights).

ALSO READ: GAS, HEATING, HUMIDITY, REFRIGERATION.

AIRCRAFT CARRIER An aircraft carrier is a huge ship with a military airport on its top deck. On board are workshops that repair airplanes; places to store ammunition, bombs, and fuel; and almost everything else that would be found at a military airport. Thousands of people live and work on board this floating town.

Most jet airplanes need a long runway on which to gain the speed needed to take off or to lose speed on landing. Airports on land usually have runways about 10,000 feet

▼ *A window air conditioner takes warm air from the outside and sends cool, clean air into a house. The blower sucks in warm air. The filter cleans out dust and dirt. The evaporator has cold coils, which cool the air and remove moisture from it. The condenser fan blows air over the condenser to make the gas in the coils turn to a cooling liquid. The compressor is a motor that squeezes and pumps the gas through the coils. The blower does its second task by blowing cool air into the room.*

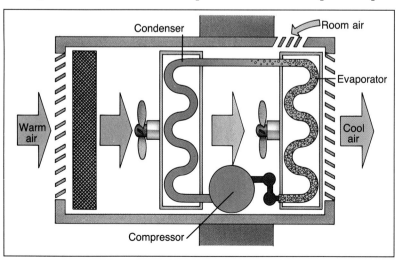

(3,000 m) long. Because there is not this much room on a carrier, planes are "thrown" into the air moving fast enough to fly. A carrier plane is launched much as a small model glider is catapulted into the air with a rubber band. Hooks on the airplane are attached to a powerful steam catapult or "slingshot" that runs down a track on the deck.

On landing, another hook on the tail of an airplane catches cables strung across the flight deck. The ends of the cables are attached to cylinders that move in a big pipe filled with oil. The cables relax or "give" when an airplane first catches them, but they bring it to a stop in about 125 feet (38 m). Some planes, such as vertical take-off "jump jets" and helicopters, can take off from and land on a carrier without these aids.

History   Aircraft carriers got their start on November 14, 1910. On that day Eugene Ely flew an airplane off a wooden platform on the cruiser USS *Birmingham*. Aircraft carriers were not important in World War I, because they were not practical. But in 1918 the British navy built the first true aircraft carrier, called HMS *Ar-*

▲ *Looking down on the flight decks of the U.S.S.* Enterprise. *The carrier has two flight decks, and can launch four jets at a time, as seen here. Other jets are moving into position for takeoff. A carrier task force can quickly display its formidable power in any trouble spot around the world.*

▼ *The U.S. Navy nuclear-powered carrier* Nimitz. *Built in 1971, this mighty ship can carry 90 airplanes and helicopters.*

gus. The first U.S. carrier was the USS *Langley* (1922).

Aircraft carriers became really important when Japan bombed Pearl Harbor, Hawaii, on December 7, 1941. The airplanes that carried the bombs came from Japanese aircraft carriers. This surprise attack came near to crippling the United States Navy stationed in the Pacific.

During three great naval battles (Midway Island and Coral Sea, fought in 1942, and Leyte Gulf,

▲ *The USS* Langley, *a converted coal-carrying ship, was the Navy's first aircraft carrier. It went into service in 1922, carrying biplanes (two-winged airplanes).*

▲ *Cables across the flight deck slow down a landing plane. A hook underneath the plane catches the cable.*

fought in 1944), planes from U.S. aircraft carriers destroyed almost all of the Japanese carrier fleet. U.S. carriers had assured an Allied victory in the Pacific during World War II.

Carriers Today After the war, aircraft carriers were enlarged and improved. Steam-powered catapults and angled flight decks permitted carriers to launch jet planes. Helicopters also proved effective as carrier-borne aircraft. The Soviet Union began to develop its carrier fleet from the 1960's. Today, the U.S. and the Soviet Union have the most powerful carriers in the world. Other nations, such as France and Britain, have small carriers.

The U.S. Navy has five nuclear-powered attack aircraft carriers: the *Enterprise, Nimitz, Eisenhower, Vinson,* and *Theodore Roosevelt.* The *Nimitz* is the world's largest warship in *displacement tonnage.* It displaces (occupies) 93,400 long tons (94,900 tonnes) of water when fully loaded. The *Nimitz* is 1,092 feet (333 m) long. The deck where the airplanes take off and land is 254 feet (77 m) wide. In combat or on patrol duty, *Nimitz*-class vessels carry about 6,300 crew members and 100 aircraft.

Other U.S. attack carriers are powered by oil. They include the *Kitty Hawk, John F. Kennedy,* and *Forrestal,* each of which carries about 4,900 persons and 85 airplanes. Another type of carrier is equipped with com-

plicated electronic devices to find and destroy enemy submarines. And there are also special carriers which carry marines, their helicopters and landing craft, and the jet planes to support them.

Military experts argue about which is more useful—aircraft carriers or land-based airplanes. Both are expensive. The people who favor carriers claim that carriers can be anywhere in the world in a short time. Land airfields overseas may not always be usable. But the floating airport—the carrier—is ready whenever it is needed. Moreover, aircraft carriers with nuclear power plants can run for as long as 13 years without refueling.

ALSO READ: AIRPORT, NAVY, SUBMARINE, WORLD WAR II.

AIR CUSHION VEHICLE (ACV) An air cushion vehicle, or *hovercraft,* is a machine that rides on a layer of *compressed air* that holds it off the ground or water. It may ride only a few inches or several feet above the surface, depending on the vehicle's design. The advantage of being off the surface is that there is less friction between the machine and the surface. Friction is a force that opposes movement when one object or surface is rubbed against another. It is caused, for example, by a car's wheels turning against the ground, or by a boat's hull moving through water. The more friction there is between a vehicle and the ground or water, the slower the vehicle travels.

You probably cannot push even a small car. You would fight the weight of the car and the friction of its wheels on the axles. But if a strong wind underneath the car lifted it straight up, even one inch, you could probably move the car as long as the air held it off the ground. All you would have to do is push the car through air, and the friction between the car and the air would be very little. The wind would be an *air cushion*. An air cushion can also be formed by a strong wind blowing down from the car, to lift if off the ground. Air cushion vehicles use large fans to create the strong wind.

Air cushion vehicles (ACVs) come in several designs. One works only over water. Another must follow a big track. Other ACVs can travel over any flat surface.

Scientists and inventors thought of these machines as early as 1716. But they did not have the materials or the powerful engines to make them work. The first ACVs that really "flew" were built in the early 1950's. Big fans made the air cushions that lifted the vehicles off the ground. Propellers or jet engine exhausts then drove them forward.

Modern ACVs usually look like boats. Several fans may work to push the air down, and as many as four large propellers push the machine forward. ACVs can travel over land or water at up to 80 miles an hour (130 km/hr). ACVs that follow tracks are faster, up to 150 miles an hour (240 km/hr).

Some ACVs have skirts made of a rubber-like material. These skirts are attached around the bottom of the machine. They hold the air cushion in place. An ACV with skirts can ride as high as 10 feet (3 m) above the surface. It can jump wide ditches and cross marshes. ACVs can travel over ice and snow, and over deserts.

Large hovercraft ferries that carry 175 passengers and 35 automobiles cross the English Channel between England and France. But so far ACVs have not proved as successful as was at first hoped.

ALSO READ: AIR PRESSURE, TRANSPORTATION.

AIR FORCE One job of an air force is to defend its country by using airplanes and missiles against the

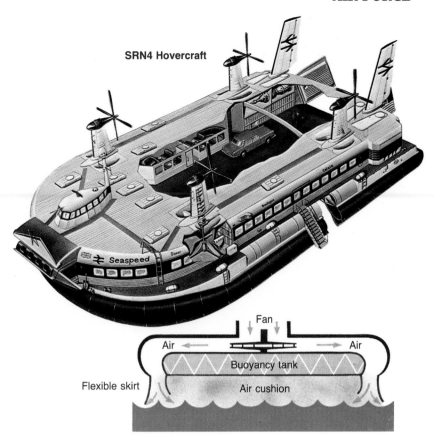

SRN4 Hovercraft

Fan

Air ← → Air

Buoyancy tank

Flexible skirt

Air cushion

▲ *A large ferry hovercraft. This kind of ground-effect craft skims over the water, supported by a cushion of air. The air is held in place by the craft's flexible skirt. Four propellers push the craft along.*

country's enemies. Air forces have other jobs, too. One is rescuing people who are hurt or lost. All air forces do many of the same jobs, although each country organizes its air force differently. Only the United States Air Force (USAF) is described here.

USAF Combat Commands The *Military Airlift Command* (MAC) is one of the four main combat commands of the USAF. MAC furnishes air transportation for the Army, Navy, and Air Force. It carries anything needed in a hurry. MAC has all kinds of aircraft, from small helicopters to the huge C-5A jet transport. The C-5A is almost as long as a football field and can carry tanks and trucks, or as many as 900 soldiers.

MAC also runs a rescue service. It has helicopters and special airplanes to pick up wounded soldiers and air crew shot down over enemy territory. The rescue service has bases in many countries. It has saved many civilians who got lost or had accidents on mountains or in canyons, forests,

The U.S. Air Force has about 4,000 combat airplanes, but a total of 600,000 people. At the end of World War II (1945), the Air Force had 80,000 airplanes and nearly $2\frac{1}{2}$ million people.

▲ *The B2* Stealth Bomber *is designed so that it is almost invisible to radar. The airplane has an unusual shape and is made of carbon fiber composites, which absorb radar rather than reflect it.*

During World War II, the Army Air Forces dropped over 2 million tons of bombs. It lost more than 20,000 airplanes, but destroyed at least 40,000 enemy aircraft.

deserts, or snowstorms. At the President's request, MAC flies medicines, doctors, food, and supplies to countries where there have been earthquakes, floods, and other disasters.

A special MAC squadron flies the President of the United States and his staff all over the world. The people in the squadron, from pilots to mechanics to clerks, are carefully picked. The squadron's aircraft range from small helicopters to big jet transports. The squadron is often called the *Air Force One Squadron,* because any airplane the President flies in is *Air Force One.*

The *Strategic Air Command* (SAC) is another major part of the USAF. SAC is set up to attack military bases and factories in an enemy's country in case of war. SAC's main weapons are bombers and guided missiles. The B-52 is the biggest bomber. It can carry atom bombs and cruise missiles. It can fly halfway around the world, at 650 miles an hour (1,050 km/hr), without refueling. Another bomber, smaller and faster, is the F-111. For long-range missions, bombers can be refueled while flying, by a *tanker airplane.* The tanker hooks up

with the bomber in flight and pumps fuel into its tanks.

SAC's intercontinental ballistic missiles (ICBMs) are kept in deep, concrete-lined holes in the ground, called *silos.* An ICBM carries an atom bomb in the nose. It can travel 7,000 miles (11,000 km) at 15,000 miles an hour (24,000 km/hr) and is very difficult to intercept. Atomic missiles can be fired only by direct order from the President of the United States. They have never been fired.

The *Aerospace Defense Command* (ADC) operates from a huge cave drilled out of a mountain, near Colorado Springs, Colorado. It has computers, radar, telephones, and radios to keep in touch with bases around the world. Its job is to protect the U.S. from enemy airplanes and missiles. ADC shares its cave with a group from Canada. Together, they make up the North American Air Defense Command (NORAD).

To shoot down enemy airplanes flying over Canada or the U.S., NORAD would use *fighter-interceptors* and *surface-to-air missiles* (SAMs). Fighter-interceptors are airplanes which can fly fast and high. The F-15 Eagle is a fighter-interceptor that carries *air-to-air guided missiles* (AAMs). Another form of defense is the surface-to-air missile, such as the Patriot, which is fired from the ground like a rocket.

The job of *Tactical Air Command* (TAC) is to help the Army in its ground operations. TAC has fighter-bombers to carry bombs, cannons, rockets, and guided missiles to shoot at enemy tanks, trucks, trains, and storage places for ammunition.

The Air Force also works, usually secretly, to find out what enemy countries are doing. This is called *reconnaissance*. Reconnaissance satellites circle the Earth and take pictures of enemy territory. Reconnaissance planes can fly 2,000 miles an hour (3,200 km/hr) at 80,000 feet (24,000 m)—twice as high as most airliners. Cameras in these planes photograph tiny details. Experts can even recognize different kinds of cars in such pictures!

Other USAF commands train the personnel of the Air Force, handle supplies, and support the combat commands. The USAF at present has about 7,000 combat planes and al-most 604,000 people. The people must be highly trained to take care of complicated airplanes, missiles, and radio and radar equipment.

History of the Air Force   The U.S. Air Force started August 1, 1907, as part of the Army Signal Corps, with one officer and two enlisted men. The division got its first plane in 1909, from the Wright brothers.

No American airplanes flew in combat during World War I. By the end of that war in 1918, the U.S. had 58,000 Air Service officers and men in France. Many of them had learned to fly in France and Britain.

From earliest days, Army pilots did not want to be controlled by Army ground forces. Most ground generals did not understand the airplane. They thought it should be used as a sort of long-range gun on the battle-field. The pilots believed airplanes should carry the war to an enemy's country and destroy its ability to make war. Military leaders were slow to recognize the importance of the airplane. U.S. General Billy Mitchell, assistant chief of the Air Service, argued for a large independent air force. His public criticism of the War and

AIR FORCE INSIGNIA

United States

Great Britain

Soviet Union

China (People's Republic)

◀ *The F-111 is a swing-wing bomber, which first saw service during the Vietnam War. The picture shows the aircraft's wings open, for slow-speed flight.*

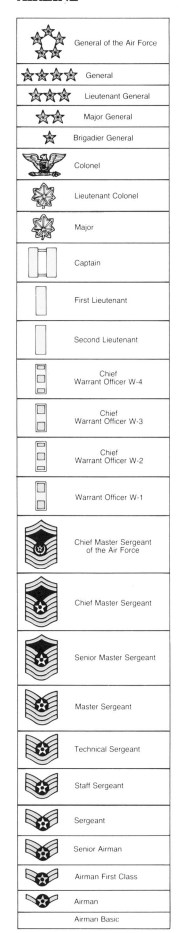

✮✮✮✮✮	General of the Air Force
✮✮✮✮	General
✮✮✮	Lieutenant General
✮✮	Major General
✮	Brigadier General
	Colonel
	Lieutenant Colonel
	Major
	Captain
	First Lieutenant
	Second Lieutenant
	Chief Warrant Officer W-4
	Chief Warrant Officer W-3
	Chief Warrant Officer W-2
	Warrant Officer W-1
	Chief Master Sergeant of the Air Force
	Chief Master Sergeant
	Senior Master Sergeant
	Master Sergeant
	Technical Sergeant
	Staff Sergeant
	Sergeant
	Senior Airman
	Airman First Class
	Airman
	Airman Basic

Navy Departments led to his court martial (military trial) in 1925.

In 1926, the U.S. Air Service was reformed as the Army Air Corps. The Army's first B-17 bomber, known as the Flying Fortress, was built in 1935. It played a major role in World War II. In 1941, the Army Air Forces (AAF) were organized under the command of General Henry H. "Hap" Arnold. Top strength of the AAF during the war was 2,400,000 members and almost 80,000 airplanes. In addition, the U.S. supplied thousands of planes to the Allies. In 1947, the U.S. Air Force was established as a separate military service. Since then, U.S. warplanes have lifted vital supplies to

▲ *The United States Air Force Academy is near Colorado Springs, Colorado. Opened in 1958, the Academy trains cadets wishing to become officers in the Air Force.*

West Berlin, flown combat missions in Korea, Vietnam, and Gulf Wars, and helped maintain the peace around the world.

ALSO READ: AIRPLANE, ARMY, MISSILE, NAVY, WORLD WAR II.

AIRLINE An airline is a system that carries passengers and cargo through the air. Persons, mail, and freight can be rapidly transported by

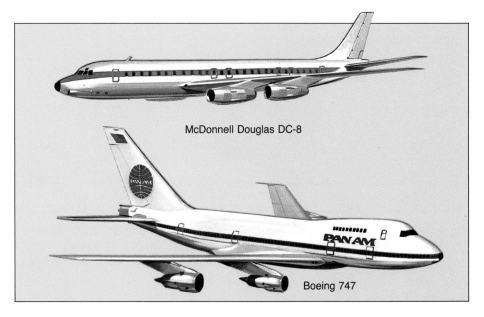

McDonnell Douglas DC-8

Boeing 747

airlines to almost any part of the world.

There are several kinds of airlines. The *commuter airlines* fly small planes that carry up to 20 people between small cities, or from small cities to larger ones. *Local airlines* fly between medium-sized cities or from medium-sized to large cities. Their planes may carry from 20 to 100 passengers. *Trunk airlines* usually fly between large cities within a country. Most of their airplanes are jets that carry from 100 to 300 people. *International flag carriers* fly big jets between the major cities of the world. These four kinds of airlines are called *scheduled air carriers*. They must fly at the times they advertise to the public, whether their airplanes are filled or not.

Cargo airlines carry freight instead of people. They fly fresh vegetables, fruits, and flowers to restaurants, grocery stores, and shops. They carry automobile parts, furniture, and animals for zoos. They deliver almost anything that needs to be delivered quickly and that requires careful handling. Cargo airlines use all kinds of airplanes, including the biggest jets.

Charter or *supplemental airlines* do not have schedules. They rent their airplanes and crews to clubs and other organizations, usually for vacation trips or meetings. The trips are usually planned six months before the flight, and all the passengers must go and come back together. Because a charter airline knows ahead of time that the airplane will be filled with passengers, the fare for each passenger is low. It is usually about half the cost of the same trip on a scheduled airline. Supplemental airlines fly the same big jets and have the same kinds of crews that the international scheduled airlines use.

Great changes have been made since the first airline flight. On January 1, 1914, a flying boat carried two passengers from Tampa to St. Petersburg in Florida. But air travel grew rapidly, especially after World War II. Today, millions of passengers are in the air, every year. They travel in comfort inside large airplanes such as the Boeing 747 which can carry more than 350 passengers for 6,000 miles (9,660 km) at 600 miles an hour (960 km/hr). It has a cocktail lounge and elevators to bring food up from the galley, or kitchen, to the cabin.

The first stewardess to serve on an airline was Ellen Church. She helped the passengers on a United Air Lines flight from San Francisco, California, to Cheyenne, Wyoming, on May 15, 1930.

▼ *On the flight deck of a modern airliner, the crew are aided by computers and other electronic instruments. The pilots sit side by side in the cockpit.*

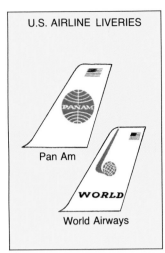

U.S. AIRLINE LIVERIES

Pan Am

WORLD

World Airways

▲ *Airlines are identified by a symbol on the vertical stabilizer.*

The first successful rocket-powered airplane was the German Me-163 *Komet* fighter. In 1944 it achieved a speed of over 500 mph (800 km/hr), with a very high rate of climb. But its fuel was used up in about 10 minutes.

▼ *The Wright brothers first flew in 1903. Their plane carried only one person at 30 miles an hour (about 50 km/hr). On its first flight, it flew just 120 feet (37 m).*

The People of an Airline The cockpit of an airliner is called the *flight deck*. The crew, or people who fly the airplane, includes the *captain*, the senior pilot who is in charge of the airplane, and usually another pilot called the *first officer*. The *flight engineer* is also a member of the flight crew. He is in charge of the mechanical operation of the airplane, which includes everything from the coffee makers to the engines. He watches all the meters and gauges in the cockpit and adjusts temperature, power, fuel, and other things to be sure everything is working right. On long overwater flights, the crew also includes a *navigator*. The navigator's job is to know where the airplane is at all times. He tells the pilot what route to follow and how long the trip should take.

The *cabin crew* of an airliner is made up of men and women called *flight attendants*. A Boeing 747 usually has about 15 flight attendants; smaller airplanes may have only two or three. Flight attendants serve food and are trained to take care of sick persons and to evacuate passengers quickly in case of an emergency. Many flight attendants speak several languages and can talk to passengers from different countries. Most of them have been to college. They are very important to airlines because not only do they help make the passengers' flight more pleasant, but they also make it safer.

The maintenance or engineering people take care of the airplanes on the ground. They are a very important part of the airline because they make sure that the airplanes are ready to fly safely.

Air travel has become so popular that every year the number of passengers who fly on world's scheduled airlines (not counting charter airlines and private planes) is larger than the total population of the United States.

ALSO READ: AIRPLANE, AIRPORT, AVIATION, TRANSPORTATION.

AIR MASS see WEATHER.

AIRPLANE On a lonely beach at Kitty Hawk, North Carolina, on December 17, 1903, a man flew an airplane for the first time. The man was Orville Wright. The flight was not far, only 120 feet (37 m). The airplane never got more than 20 feet (6 m) off the ground. Its top speed was only 30 miles an hour (50 km/hr). But, unlike earlier aircraft (such as balloons and gliders), it was an airplane—it flew under its own power and could be controlled by the pilot.

Aviation is today one of the world's largest industries. Orville and Wilbur Wright can be called the "fathers of aviation" because they were the first to design, build, and fly a successful engine-powered airplane.

The Wright brothers were good and careful mechanics. They tested small models of different types of wings before they built a full-size airplane. These models helped them understand the four basic forces that explain how an airplane flies.

Why an Airplane Flies The forces the Wrights discovered are called *lift*, *weight*, *thrust*, and *drag*. These forces work in the same way on a small model airplane, with a propeller driven by a rubber band, as they do on a giant transport plane driven by powerful jet engines.

Lift and weight are opposite forces. *Lift* makes an airplane go up, and *weight*—or *gravity*—makes it go

Thrust of engines — Lift of wings — Drag of air — Weight of aircraft

down. The lift must be stronger than the weight, if an airplane is to fly. Thrust and drag are also opposite forces. *Thrust* makes the airplane go forward or faster, and *drag* holds it back or slows it down. Thrust must be stronger than drag, for an airplane to take off.

To understand how these forces work on an airplane, you must look carefully at the airplane itself. The main parts of any airplane are the wings, the engine (or engines), the fuselage or cabin (the long part where the pilot and passengers or cargo ride), the landing gear (usually two large wheels or groups of wheels, and other parts to support an airplane on the ground), and the tail at the back.

LIFT. The movement of air around a wing creates lift. A wing of an airplane is curved on top and flat on the bottom. Air moving over the top must move faster than air moving under the bottom, because it has a longer distance to travel. The faster air travels, the less pressure it exerts. The air above the wing has a lower pressure than the air below. The higher pressure below forces the airplane up.

■ LEARN BY DOING

You can easily see how lift works. Tear a strip of paper, about 2 inches (5 cm) wide and 8 inches (20 cm) long, off a sheet of paper. Hold the strip at one end between your thumb and first finger so the long part hangs down over the back of your hand. Hold your hand near your mouth and blow across the top. The paper "wing" rises. If the paper were an airplane wing, the whole airplane would rise with it. ■

THRUST. The forward movement, or speed, of an airplane overcomes the drag of the air. A turning propeller pulls or pushes an airplane through air, much as a propeller pushes a motor boat through water. A jet engine works on the principle of

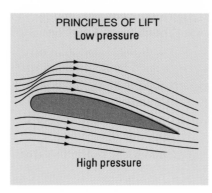

PRINCIPLES OF LIFT
Low pressure

High pressure

reaction—the action of hot gases moving out the back of an engine causes a reaction of an airplane moving forward. If more thrust is supplied by the engine, more lift is created and an airplane can climb, or, if it is flying level, it can go faster.

WEIGHT. The weight of an airplane is the weight of the machine, plus cargo, passengers, and fuel. This force, which must be overcome by lift, is called *gravity*.

DRAG. The drag, or resistance, is caused by the friction of air on every part of the airplane. An airplane is going as fast as it can when as much drag as possible is overcome by

▲ *Four forces act on a plane in flight: lift and thrust (which move it upward and forward), and drag and weight (which move it backward and downward).*

◄ *An airplane wing tends to lift, because the air pressure beneath it is higher than the air pressure above it.*

The airplane with the longest wingspan ever made was the Hughes Hercules flyingboat. It had a span of 320 feet (98 m) and weighed 190 tons (172 metric tons). In a test flight in 1947 its eight engines lifted it to a height of 70 feet (21 m) for a distance of 3,000 feet (914 m). It never flew again.

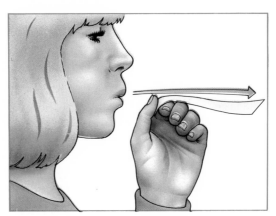

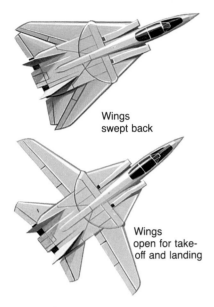

Wings
swept back

Wings
open for take-
off and landing

▲ *A high-speed plane flies faster if its wings are swept back. In a swing-wing design, the wings can be moved forward into the open position for take-off and landing.*

▲ *On a propeller-driven plane, the propellers pull the airplane forward against the drag of the air.*

thrust. Designers reduce the amount of drag by making the outside surfaces of the airplane as smooth and rounded as possible. The *landing gear* on most airplanes retracts, or pulls up, to reduce resistance during flight.

Other Parts of an Airplane An airplane's *tail* has *horizontal stabilizers* that look like tiny wings on the tail. It also has a *vertical stabilizer* that sticks straight up from the middle of the tail. These parts keep an airplane balanced in flight and are called *control surfaces*. The *elevators* are attached to the horizontal stabilizers. A pilot can move these up or down and apply more or less power to make an airplane climb or descend.

The rudder is attached to the vertical stabilizer but (unlike a boat's rudder) is not normally used to steer the airplane. The rudder is used to stabilize the airplane while two movable sections near the wing tips, called *ailerons*, are used to turn the airplane to the left or right. To turn to the right, the pilot raises the right aileron and lowers the left aileron. This tips the right wing down and raises the left wing. The airplane then banks to the right and makes a slow, smooth turn. Other wing sections, near the fuselage, are called *flaps*. Flaps can be turned down to make the curve of the wing top greater. The increased pressure difference increases lift.

Many important parts of an airplane can be seen only in the *cockpit* where a pilot sits. In the cockpit are all the controls and electronic devices that enable a pilot to fly the airplane safely. The *flight controls* consist of a wheel or control stick, and rudder pedals. The wheel, which looks much like an automobile steering wheel, controls the elevators and ailerons. To make a right turn, a pilot turns the wheel to the right and pushes the right rudder pedal. If he pushes the wheel forward, the airplane descends. The airplane climbs if he pulls the wheel back.

Even on a small airplane a pilot has a number of dials, gauges, switches, and lights on an instrument panel that looks much like an automobile dashboard. On large airplanes, instrument panels cover the front, sides, and ceiling of the cockpit. The instruments tell a pilot everything he or she must know about how fast the plane is going, the direction it is flying, how much fuel is left, and many other things. Radar equipment shows the aircraft's position on its planned course. Radio equipment permits pilots to talk to people on the ground and to other airplanes. Ground radar and navigation beacons help pilots avoid storms and navigate their airplanes. *Automatic pilots* take over control from pilots on long flights.

Types of Airplanes Three kinds of power systems are used today to furnish thrust. (1) Gasoline engines turn propellers that pull or push an airplane through the air. These airplanes are called *conventional aircraft*. They usually fly at speeds of 120 to 225 miles an hour (190–360 km/hr), but some can go faster. (2) Jet engines that turn propellers are called *turboprops*. Planes with such engines fly from 250 to 400 miles an hour (400–640 km/hr). (3) *Pure jet* engines push an airplane through the air at very high speeds—600 miles an hour (970 km/hr) or faster.

Most airplanes today are monoplanes, which means they have only one wing. In the early days of aviation, airplanes had two wings (biplanes) or three wings (triplanes). The extra wings added more lift, but also more drag. The lift was more than the drag, so the airplanes flew but could not go very fast. In very fast airplanes, the wings are often delta-shaped (like a triangle) or swept back in a V-shape.

ALSO READ: AIR FORCE, AIRLINE, AIRPORT, AVIATION, JET PROPULSION, TRANSPORTATION, WRIGHT BROTHERS.

Spoilers

Ailerons

▶ *The pilot has various controls to fly the airplane. Flaps and spoilers act like brakes. Ailerons are moved up and down to make the plane turn.*

Flaps

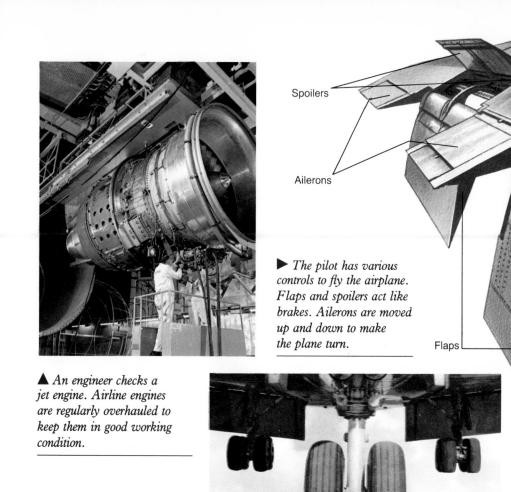

▲ *An engineer checks a jet engine. Airline engines are regularly overhauled to keep them in good working condition.*

▶ *The landing gear of a DC-8 airliner. The wheels are lowered and the flaps are pushed down to create drag. The two sets of center wheels hit the runway first, followed by the nose wheel. The airplane then slows to a stop.*

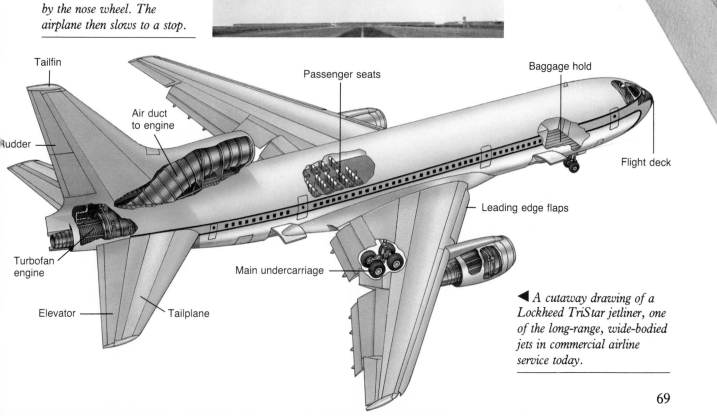

Tailfin

Passenger seats

Baggage hold

Air duct to engine

Rudder

Flight deck

Leading edge flaps

Turbofan engine

Main undercarriage

Elevator

Tailplane

◀ *A cutaway drawing of a Lockheed TriStar jetliner, one of the long-range, wide-bodied jets in commercial airline service today.*

Famous Airplanes—1903-1918

Wright brothers' first plane
(USA) 1903

Voisin-Farman
(France) 1907

Curtiss "June Bug"
(USA) 1908

"Henri Farman III"
(France) 1909

Wright "A"
(USA) 1909

Levavasseur "Antoinette"
(France) 1909

Bleriot #11
(France) 1909
(first to cross English Channel)

Curtiss (USA) 1910

Avro Biplane
(Britain) 1911

Curtiss "Triad"
(USA) 1911

Morane-Saulnier "L"
(France) 1913

Sopwith "Tabloid"
(Britain) 1913

Curtiss "America" flying boat
(USA) 1913

Vickers FE-6
(Britain) 1913

Sikorsky "Grand"
(Russia) 1913
(first multi-engine plane)

Farnborough BE-2
(Britain) 1913

Rumpler "Taube"
(Germany) 1913

Martin "TT"
(USA) 1914

Caudron G-III
(France) 1915

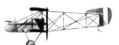

DeHavilland DH-2
(Britain) 1915

Nieuport 17
(France) 1916

Albatros D-1
(Germany) 1916

Avro 504-J
(Britain) 1916

Bristol F-2B
(Britain) 1917

Breguet 14
(France) 1917

Fokker DR-1
(Germany) 1917

SPAD 13 fighter
(France) 1917

Gotha bomber
(Germany) 1917

Sopwith "Camel"
(Britain) 1917

Junkers D-1
(Germany) 1918

Loening M-8
(USA) 1918

Fokker D-VII "Jasta"
(Germany) 1918

DeHavilland DH-4
(Britain-USA) 1918

Curtiss F-5L
(USA) 1918

Famous Airplanes—1919-first jets

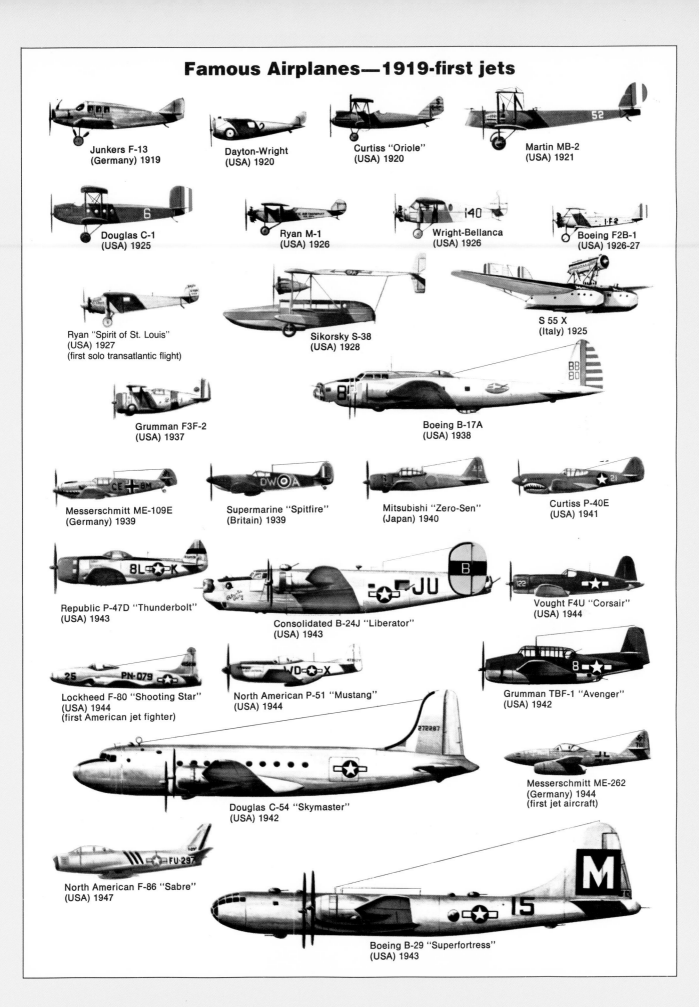

Junkers F-13
(Germany) 1919

Dayton-Wright
(USA) 1920

Curtiss "Oriole"
(USA) 1920

Martin MB-2
(USA) 1921

Douglas C-1
(USA) 1925

Ryan M-1
(USA) 1926

Wright-Bellanca
(USA) 1926

Boeing F2B-1
(USA) 1926-27

Ryan "Spirit of St. Louis"
(USA) 1927
(first solo transatlantic flight)

Sikorsky S-38
(USA) 1928

S 55 X
(Italy) 1925

Grumman F3F-2
(USA) 1937

Boeing B-17A
(USA) 1938

Messerschmitt ME-109E
(Germany) 1939

Supermarine "Spitfire"
(Britain) 1939

Mitsubishi "Zero-Sen"
(Japan) 1940

Curtiss P-40E
(USA) 1941

Republic P-47D "Thunderbolt"
(USA) 1943

Consolidated B-24J "Liberator"
(USA) 1943

Vought F4U "Corsair"
(USA) 1944

Lockheed F-80 "Shooting Star"
(USA) 1944
(first American jet fighter)

North American P-51 "Mustang"
(USA) 1944

Grumman TBF-1 "Avenger"
(USA) 1942

Douglas C-54 "Skymaster"
(USA) 1942

Messerschmitt ME-262
(Germany) 1944
(first jet aircraft)

North American F-86 "Sabre"
(USA) 1947

Boeing B-29 "Superfortress"
(USA) 1943

AIR POLLUTION A large city, even on a warm sunny day, may sometimes be covered by a hazy mist, or even by a dense gray cloud. The mist is dirty, or *polluted* air. The cloud is *smog*—a mixture of smoke and fog—an especially unpleasant kind of air pollution. Smog is harmful. It often causes shortness of breath, dizziness, watery eyes, and runny noses. Smog can also be dangerous if it is extra thick and lasts a long time. In the days when people burned coal for cooking and heating and in factory furnaces, cities were often shrouded in smoke.

Wind carries many substances through Earth's air. Among them are pollen from plants, sand from dry beaches, and dust from fields. These are natural substances. But humans add other substances to the air. Smoke pours from factory smokestacks. Chemical fumes rise from paper mills and metal-working plants. Garbage-dump incinerators spread black soot. Automobiles stream a blue, smelly haze that hangs over crowded cities. The air is polluted when it is filled with unnatural substances.

What Pollution Can Do Polluted air can destroy the balance of the exchange that goes on among plants, animals, and the oceans. Animals, including people, get the oxygen they need from the air they breathe. They exhale (breathe out) the gas carbon dioxide. Plants, even those that live in the oceans, all need carbon dioxide as much as people need oxygen. Carbon dioxide supplies the carbon that plants need to make food. Plants draw in carbon dioxide, then release oxygen. But *pollutants* such as soot, sulfur, lead, and automobile exhaust and factory fumes poison the air.

◀ *Smoke and gas are poured into the atmosphere by oilfields, factories, cities, automobiles, and power stations.*

Over a long period of time, these pollutants could poison all forms of life.

Air pollution causes other serious problems, too. Foul air damages crops. Air pollution wears away (*corrodes*) metals as though they had been put into acid. Layers of ash and soot from air settle on buildings and clothing, and cleaning costs rise. People cannot see clearly in heavy smog, so accidents happen more often. Fumes in the air even eat away buildings made of stone. Pollutants cause holes in glass and kill lawns and trees. Polluted air can also cause a health threat, especially to people with breathing problems.

Pollutants from industrial plants, such as steelworks and chemical factories, can be carried by the wind many hundreds of miles. The chemicals in this dirty air can fall back to Earth as another form of pollution, *acid rain*.

Take a Deep Breath Almost 1,000 tons (910 metric tons) of soot and ash land on every square mile (2.5 sq. km) of New York City each year. The 125 million cars that Americans own add large amounts of poisonous carbon monoxide (from their engines) to the air every day. Each year more factories are built, more fuel is burned to provide power and heat, more people drive cars.

The most serious fact about air pollution is that it endangers health. Eyes water and vision blurs. A person may not get the oxygen he needs when he breathes. He may choke on harmful gases instead. Old people, and people with heart or lung diseases, suffer most from polluted air.

People of all ages have become aware of the danger of air pollution today, and they are working to stop it. The United States Government formed the Environmental Protection Agency in 1970. This office studies pollution and works with people all over the U.S. to prevent further pollution of the air.

Automobile makers must now produce engines that give off less pollutants. To meet U.S. federal standards, most new cars have special pollution control devices, called *catalytic converters*. These clean up some of the poisonous gases from the car's engine. Automobile makers have begun to develop electric-powered cars, which do not cause air pollution. Jet airplanes have devices that cut down the dirty black clouds of jet fuel exhaust. Los Angeles has a city law to shut factories when there is danger of heavy smog. Many cities no longer allow people to burn trash or leaves.

The Greenhouse Effect Some scientists believe that one effect of the air pollution caused by human activities

▲ *This wind-power electricity generator in Denmark causes no air pollution.*

Air pollution throughout the United States is slowly increasing. But in dozens of U.S. cities the air is actually cleaner than it was 15 years ago. In 1970 the average city dweller breathed unsafe air for almost 70 days in the year. That figure is now down to less than 40 days.

DANGEROUS POLLUTANTS

SMOKE: People complained about smoke from coal fires as early as the 1200's.

SULFUR OXIDES: Come mostly from burning coal and oil. They combine with water to form sulfuric acid and so are a major cause of acid rain.

HYDROCARBONS: A dangerous hydrocarbon is carbon monoxide gas, from automobile engines' unburned fuel.

NITROGEN OXIDES: From automobiles, power plants, and factory boilers. They combine with hydrocarbons to form photochemicals—one of the causes of smog.

PARTICULATES: Such as dust, grit, and soot.

LEAD: From automobiles using old-style, unleaded gasoline.

RADIOACTIVE MATERIAL: Comes from nuclear waste and nuclear accidents.

OTHER DANGEROUS SUBSTANCES: Include ammonia, chloroform, vinyl chloride, ethylene oxide, asbestos, mercury, and benzene.

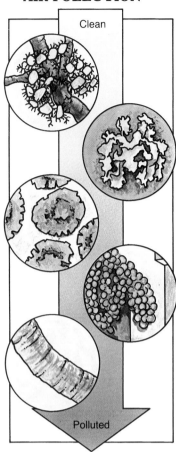

Clean

Polluted

▲ *Air pollution affects living things. Lichens thrive in clean air, but cannot live in polluted air.*

One of the main causes of air pollution is the gasoline engine. Automobile manufacturers are trying to reduce the pollution from vehicle exhausts, but the only real answer may be the development of new kinds of engines driven by steam, hydrogen, or electricity.

▶ *Chemicals in polluted air eat into the surface of stone buildings and statues. Historic buildings need to be protected if their stonework is to survive hundreds more years.*

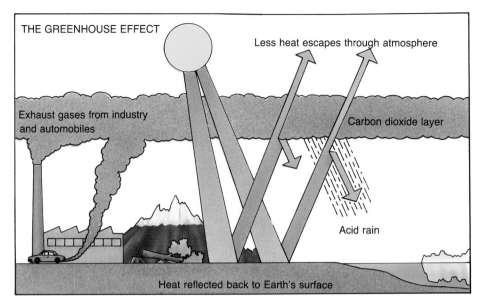

THE GREENHOUSE EFFECT

Less heat escapes through atmosphere

Exhaust gases from industry and automobiles

Carbon dioxide layer

Acid rain

Heat reflected back to Earth's surface

on Earth is to make the climate warmer. They call this the "greenhouse effect." This is how they think it works.

From the exhausts of automobiles and the smoke from factory smokestacks, carbon dioxide gas is released into the atmosphere. This gas forms a kind of blanket around Earth. Heat from the sun, which warms Earth, normally escapes into space. But as the amount of carbon dioxide in the atmosphere grows, more of this heat is trapped. The polluted atmosphere begins to act just like the glass in a greenhouse. As Earth warms up, more water vapor forms, and this too

prevents heat from escaping into space.

The "greenhouse effect" could have good results. It could make the cold, dry areas of Earth warmer and wetter, and better for agriculture. But it could also cause problems. Areas that are mild and fertile today could become too hot for the kind of agriculture carried on there today. Clouds could blot out the sunlight needed to ripen crops. If Earth got too warm, the glaciers and ice caps of polar regions would melt more freely. This extra water would run into the seas, and the rising sea level could flood low-lying land. No one knows for sure about the results of the "greenhouse effect." But most scientists agree that we must do our best to clean up the air, and prevent further pollution.

To solve the air pollution problem, scientists in the U.S., Europe, and Japan have begun to develop cleaner alternative energy sources, such as solar heat, wind, and wave power. They are concerned about the long term effect of air pollution on people and the environment.

■ LEARN BY DOING

Many newspapers print a *pollution index* each day. It usually shows whether the air was "good," "poor," or "unacceptable" during the day.

(The terms used in your paper may be different.) Follow the changes in the pollution index for your town. Make a chart with six columns. Label the columns "Day," "Sunny," "Cloudy," "Rain," "Wind Speed," and "Pollution Index." Fill in the chart each day for several weeks. Do you see a pattern developing? When is the pollution index "unacceptable"? When is it "good"? ■

ALSO READ: ACID RAIN, BREATHING, CONSERVATION, ECOLOGY, WATER POLLUTION.

AIRPORT An airport is a place where an airplane can take off and land safely. A simple airport may be just a piece of smooth ground. But ground gets muddy, so most airports, even far from cities, have runways. These are usually made of concrete or asphalt, like highways. But they are wider and thicker than highways. Runways are built following the most frequent wind directions. A small airport is usually owned by a person or a town. It is run by a *fixed-base operator* who provides the basic services needed at all airports. These include "parking lots" for the airplanes, taxiways (roads) to the main runway, fuel supplies, weather information and maps for the pilots, and mechanics to make repairs. Many fixed-base operators also give flying lessons.

Small airports can be as important as larger ones. Some small airports are the center of areas called *industrial air parks.* The airport itself is surrounded by factories and other businesses that need swift transportation. It helps the local community by serving manufacturers as well as privately owned aircraft.

The Large Airports Large airports in cities have two main types of customers—the airlines and the passengers. For the airlines, airports have maintenance services in huge build-

ings, called *hangars.* Airplanes can be parked in the hangars and worked on in any kind of weather, day or night, by expert mechanics. The mechanics make sure the airplanes are safe to fly. Communications services at airports include the control towers, where air traffic controllers watch the airports and tell pilots when to land or take off, and which of several runways to use. Landing and navigation aids, which are radio and radar stations, help pilots to find the airports and to land in bad weather. Airport weather services tell pilots what the weather is anywhere in the world, and what it will be like when they arrive at their destinations. Inflight food services furnish food for passengers in airplanes. Air cargo warehouses are big buildings where cargo is stored between flights.

An important job of the people who run airports is to keep airplanes safely going and coming in bad weather. Runways must be maintained so that rainwater quickly drains away. In winter snowplows keep the runways clear of snow. The light and radar aids on runways must always be ready to help pilots in darkness or fog. Airports often do such a

▲ *The departure lounge of a Japanese airport. Airport design aims to provide comfort and security for travelers.*

▼ *Landing lights on the airport runway guide incoming aircraft.*

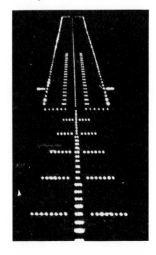

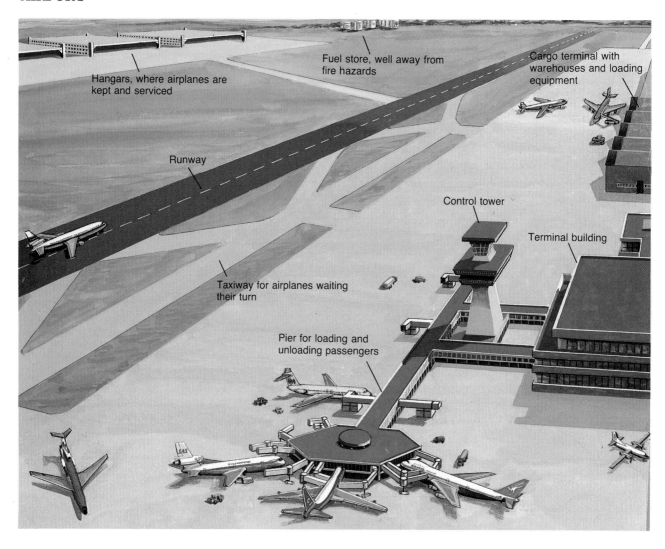

Hangars, where airplanes are kept and serviced

Fuel store, well away from fire hazards

Cargo terminal with warehouses and loading equipment

Runway

Control tower

Terminal building

Taxiway for airplanes waiting their turn

Pier for loading and unloading passengers

▲ *Typical layout of a modern airport.*

Two of the world's largest airports are in Saudi Arabia. They are named after kings. The King Abdul-Aziz airport, at Jeddah, opened in 1981. The even larger King Khaled airport, at Riyadh, opened in 1983. The Jeddah airport receives Muslim pilgrims journeying to Mecca, and its marble buildings are designed to look like Arab nomads' tents.

good job that airplanes keep flying after ground transportation has been almost halted by bad weather.

Each airline has ground services including people who check passengers' tickets, check in passengers' luggage, and announce arrivals and departures of planes. The skycaps who carry passengers' luggage, and the people who fill airplanes with fuel, are also part of the ground services. At large airports, passengers wait in lounges in the passenger terminal buildings before they get on the airplanes. They also go into these buildings when they get off at their destinations. The passenger terminal buildings have ticket counters, restrooms, telephones, barber shops, restaurants, drug stores, and various shops.

Some large airports are *international*

airports, where flights go to and from other countries. These airports have United States officials who check all arriving passengers to see if they are legally allowed to enter the U.S. and to see if passengers are bringing into the country things they should not. Flights across oceans use very large airplanes that need much runway space, so international airports are usually very large. Dulles International Airport, near Washington, D.C., is an example. It is about 4 miles (6 km) wide and 5 miles (8 km) long. It has four runways, the longest ones 11,500 feet (3,505 m) long, and 150 feet (45 m) wide.

International airports are very busy, because they handle not only overseas flights but domestic flights as well. Some have flights of more than 50 airlines arriving and leaving each

▲ *Electronic scanners check air passengers' baggage and bodies, to ensure safety in the air.*

day. The two busiest airports in the world are Chicago's O'Hare International and Atlanta's Hartsfield International. (On a busy day, an airplane lands or takes off about every 40 seconds.) These airports are followed by Los Angeles International, London's Heathrow, and New York's Kennedy International.

Take-offs and landings of jet airplanes have caused problems of noise control. New airports are being built away from populated areas.

ALSO READ: AIRLINE, AIRPLANE, AIR TRAFFIC CONTROL, AVIATION.

AIR PRESSURE Air is not very heavy. One cubic foot (.03 m3) of air at sea level, and at 32° F (0°C), weighs only one ounce (28 g), which is about the weight of eight pennies. So much air is in the *atmosphere* above and around us that it presses on us from all directions with a pressure, or weight, of almost 15 pounds per square inch (1.1 kg/cm2) at sea level. The air pressure on our bodies amounts to thousands of pounds. We are not generally aware of this great force because the fluid and air in our bodies are pushing out with an equal pressure.

The air above just one acre (4,047 sq. m) of ground weighs over 40,000 tons (36,287 metric tons). The weight of air is only half as much 4 miles (6 km) above Earth. At 15,000 feet (4,500 m) above Earth the air is thinner and contains less oxygen than at ground level. A pilot must wear an oxygen mask unless his plane is pressurized and has oxygen supplies. Passenger airplanes are pressurized, to keep the cabin pressure much like that of ground level.

An instrument called a *barometer* measures atmospheric pressure. Knowledge of air pressure is very useful in predicting the weather. High air pressure usually means fair weather. If air pressure is low, stormy weather is likely.

Air pressure can be put to work. When air is *compressed*, or squeezed together, in a small space, it rushes out through any opening with great force. A tool called a *pneumatic hammer*, or drill, uses the force of compressed air to drive the hammer deep into concrete, breaking it up.

■ LEARN BY DOING

Test the pressure of the air yourself, using a bowl of water, a glass, and a napkin. Fill a deep bowl with water. Crush a paper napkin and force it tightly into the bottom of the glass. Turn the glass upside down and push it straight down into the water. Now pull the glass straight out. Feel the napkin. It should be dry. The air that was inside the glass when it was

▲ *A vacuum is created inside a can when all the air inside is pumped out. The outside air pressure will then cause the can to crumple (bottom).*

◀ *A great deal of air can be compressed into small tanks. These divers are checking their air tanks. They will wear the tanks under water and breathe air from them.*

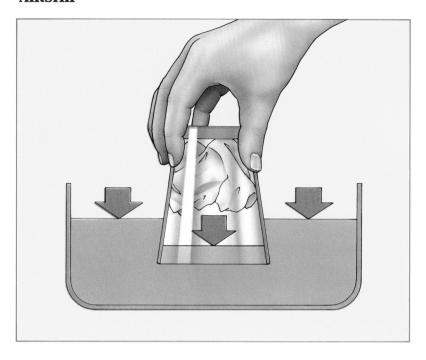

ship aloft. Rigid airships remain the same shape, even if there is no gas inside them. They are sometimes called *dirigibles*, from a French word for "steerable." They are also called *zeppelins*, after Count Ferdinand von Zeppelin of Germany, who designed the first rigid airships that worked well.

Non-rigid airships are called *blimps*. Blimps do not have a complete inside frame. They depend on the pressure of the gas inside to keep them inflated to their normal shape. They may have a number of separate gas sections so that a gas leak in one section will not cause the blimp to come down suddenly. Non-rigid airships are the kind most often seen today.

pushed into the water had enough pressure, or force, to keep water from filling the glass. ■

ALSO READ: AIR, AIRPLANE, ATMOSPHERE, WEATHER.

AIRSHIP You may have seen an occasional airship overhead—half-floating, half-gliding through the sky like a giant silver cigar. It is a huge "balloon" filled with lighter-than-air gas to make it rise. A balloon has no engines. It must travel wherever the wind takes it. In the 1800's inventors tried fitting engines into balloons. They made the first airships. An airship has engines to move it through the sky and controls to steer it by.

There are two main types of airships—*rigid* and *non-rigid*. Rigid airships have a "skeleton" or framework of aluminum or some other lightweight but strong material. The frame is covered with a tightly stretched skin of cloth or some other fabric. Lightweight metal is sometimes used instead of cloth to cover the frame. A number of bags of light gas are inside the frame. If one bag breaks or leaks, the others keep the

Development of the Airship Henri Giffard of France in 1852 flew a long sausage-shaped balloon filled with hydrogen, for 17 miles (27 km) at 5 miles an hour (8 km/hr). He used a 3½-horsepower steam engine to turn a big three-bladed propeller for power, and used a boat rudder to steer. Other airship pioneers tried other ways of developing power, including electricity. However, none of these early airships worked very well until the lightweight gasoline engine was invented. The Brazilian Alberto Santos-Dumont flew a number of gasoline-engined airships in the early 1900's.

Count von Zeppelin had four airships flying passengers between German cities by 1910. German zeppelins bombed London in World War I. However, British airplanes soon proved it was easy to shoot down the huge, slow airships.

The Age of the Airship The high point in airship history came in 1929, when the German *Graf Zeppelin* flew around the world in 21 days. It had a crew of 40 and carried 20 passengers. The huge silver airship was 776 feet (237 m) long, and flew 80 miles an

▼ The age of flight dawned in 1783 when two Frenchmen rose into the air in a hot-air balloon, invented by the Montgolfier brothers.

hour (129 km/hr). The *Graf Zeppelin* started its famous flight in Lakehurst, New Jersey. It landed only three times, first in Friedrichshafen, Germany, next in Tokyo, Japan. It then flew over the Pacific Ocean to Los Angeles, California. From there it returned to Lakehurst. The *Graf Zeppelin* flew safely for nine years, and carried a total of more than 18,000 passengers.

Encouraged by the success of the *Graf Zeppelin*, the Germans built the *Hindenburg*. The *Hindenburg* was the largest rigid airship ever built—803 feet (245 m) long and twice as fat as the *Graf Zeppelin*. It carried 78 passengers and 19 crew members. It made ten successful round trips between Germany and the United States in 1936. But, on May 6, 1937, the hydrogen gas inside it exploded and the *Hindenburg* crashed as it was landing at Lakehurst. Of the 97 people on board, 36 were killed and the rest were badly injured. This tragedy ended the age of the airship. The British had lost their *R-101* airship in 1930, and with the *Hindenburg* disaster Germany too abandoned lighter-than-air craft.

Many accidents to European airships were caused by explosions of the hydrogen gas used to lift them. Hydrogen burns easily. U.S. airships used helium, a gas almost as light as hydrogen, but which will not burn. The U.S. has most of the world's helium supply. Germany had none for its zeppelins and so had to use hydrogen.

Between 1920 and 1935, the U.S. Navy built three huge dirigibles—the *Shenandoah*, the *Macon*, and the *Akron*. The *Macon* and the *Akron* each carried five small airplanes that could take off and land from the airship in flight. All three airships eventually crashed: *Shenandoah* in 1925, *Akron* in 1932, *Macon* in 1935. They were not strong enough to fly in bad weather.

One type of airship that worked successfully was the U.S. Navy blimp. Ten of these were used in World War II on antisubmarine patrols and to escort 80,000 U.S. ships across the ocean.

Today, there is new interest in airships, and better ways of building them. Airships move so slowly and calmly that they are useful for shooting television pictures from above, for a "bird's eye view" of important news events. In the future, airships could provide cheap transportation and also popular sightseeing flights. The age of the airship could return.

ALSO READ: AVIATION, BALLOON.

▲ *The* Hindenburg *exploded while landing at Lakehurst, New Jersey, in 1937. This tragedy halted airship development.*

The German Airship Transportation Company was the world's first airline. From 1910 to 1914, it carried more than 35,000 passengers between various cities in Germany. Though there were some accidents, not one person was killed.

◄ *Blimps contain no solid structure. This is the blimp* Mayflower *built by Goodyear.*

▲ *Air-traffic controllers make sure that airplanes take off and land safely, and warn the pilots by radio if two planes get near one another. From the airport control tower, they watch all local air traffic on their radar screens.*

Most airplanes nowadays have automatic landing equipment. The pilot sets the speed for touchdown and a computer does the rest. It adjusts all the controls and throttles automatically.

AIR TRAFFIC CONTROL The traffic police of the air is air traffic control (ATC). This control system directs airplanes somewhat as the police direct cars. It keeps airplanes from running into each other by telling them when to turn, how high and fast to fly, and when to land. Air highways in some areas are almost as crowded with airplanes as highways on the ground are crowded with automobiles. Different kinds of airplanes fly at different speeds, too. Some small airplanes fly at about 120 miles an hour (190 km/hr). Airliners can fly at 600 miles an hour (960 km/hr). Some military airplanes fly more than 1,200 miles an hour (1,900 km/hr). Dozens of airplanes may be flying over an area at the same time. All have to share the sky in safety.

Radar is a device that allows air traffic controllers to "observe" an airplane as a blip of light on a screen. The blip moves as the airplane moves. Two-way radio lets the controllers talk to the pilot of a plane. Air traffic controllers use these two main ways to keep track of all air traffic in their area.

The highways of the sky are called *airways*. The airways are run from *air route traffic control centers*. The control centers are in big buildings equipped

with radar screens, powerful radios, computers, and many telephones. Each controller is in charge of all the airplanes flying in one *sector*, or area. When an airplane is about to leave this sector, the controller "hands it over" (by radio) to the controller of the next sector. The controller then tells the pilot to tune his radio to the new controller's frequency.

ATC provides *separation* between airplanes to keep traffic moving smoothly, quickly, and safely. This separation is like keeping all trucks and cars in separate lanes on a highway. Airplanes must be kept apart in three directions—up and down, side to side, and forward and behind.

When one airplane is flying above another, it must stay at least 1,000 feet higher (300 m). Controllers help keep these distances by assigning *altitudes*, or *flight levels*, to each airplane. Above 18,000 feet (5,400 m)—where the big, fast passenger jets fly—airplanes are kept 2,000 feet (600 m) apart. When they are side by side, airplanes must keep at a safe distance away from each other. Also, airplanes must usually be kept at least ten minutes' flying time from the airplanes in front and behind that are at the same altitude. In order to speed traffic, controllers may at times reduce the forward-and-behind distance to five minutes when they can see all the airplanes in their sectors on their radar screens.

Powerful radar stations along the airways send up *signal patterns* in the shape of a cone, with the small end at ground level. There are enough radar stations along the continental United States airways, so that the cones overlap above 24,000 feet (7,200 m) and all high-flying aircraft can be seen. At lower altitudes, planes may fly in spaces that the controllers cannot see on their radar screens. So pilots must make *position reports* over their radios. The pilots tell the controllers at what time they are over the stations, and their altitudes and speeds. A pilot is told to slow down, or hold, if his plane gets too close to an airplane in front of him. To *hold* means to circle the station until the traffic ahead is cleared.

Traffic jams happen at big airports, where different kinds of airplanes are coming in to land from all directions. As soon as they are within 30 miles (50 km) of an airport, all planes must call the *airport traffic control tower*. The control tower takes over from the air route traffic control center. The tower has special radar equipment that can detect all airplanes at all altitudes. The controller in the tower tells each pilot when to land and which runway to use.

The control tower is also in charge of the radar and radio landing aids at the airport. These are called *precision approach radar* (PAR) and *instrument landing systems* (ILS). A trained pilot can safely land an airplane by using them, just by looking at the instruments in the airplane cockpit. In bad weather or at night, a pilot may not be able to see the runway until he is only 100 feet (30 m) above it. But with PAR and ILS, he can still land safely. In fact, the most modern planes can land themselves, without a pilot, in an emergency.

Air traffic control works the same way all over the world. Air traffic control in the United States is run by the Federal Aviation Administration (FAA), which is part of the U.S. Department of Transportation.

ALABAMA When Alabama was Indian country, the Alibamu tribe lived along one of its rivers. The name *Alibamu* meant "I clear land." These Indians made clearings in the forest. In the clearings, they raised corn, squash, and beans. White settlers gradually turned *Alibamu* into *Alabama*. The state later took this name.

Alabama is in the Deep South. It is bordered on the west by the state of Mississippi, on the east by Georgia,

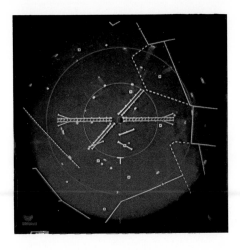

on the north by Tennessee, and on the south by Florida and the Gulf of Mexico.

The Land Nature has divided the state into two natural parts. One part, northeastern Alabama, is high and hilly. It belongs to the great Appalachian Highland. Trails used for hiking and riding twist through the hills. There are waterfalls and caves to visit and lakes for fishing and swimming. Beautiful flowers and shrubs brighten the woods. Farms here have always been small because the land is not very good.

The rest of Alabama is part of the Gulf Coastal Plain. The plain is low. In some places, it is almost flat. In others, it is gently rolling. More than half of Alabama is in the coastal plain. Not all of this part is good for farming. Some land is swampy. Some has poor soil. Pine woods cover much of the poorer land. Bald cypress trees grow in the swamps, with gray streamers of Spanish moss hanging from their branches.

Alabama's coastal plain has much good soil. The very best lies in the Black Belt. This strip curves through central Alabama. It is one of the most fertile areas in the world. The soil that gave the belt its name is dark because thickly growing plants decayed in it for thousands of years. Summers are long and hot in Alabama. Winters are mild. There is usually plenty of rain. Farmers like the climate.

◀ *Radar shows the ground controllers where every plane is, and in which direction it is heading. Each plane shows as dots of light, or blips, on the radar screen.*

▼ *In Alabama, the owners of cotton plantations often had very large houses. This one in Mobile was built in 1830. It is now a museum.*

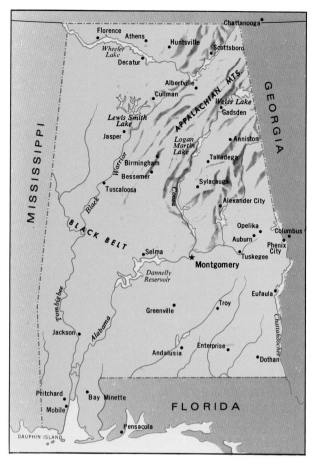

ALABAMA

Capital
Montgomery (194,300 people)

Area
51,609 square miles (133,657 sq. km)
Rank: 29th

Population
4,102,000 people. Rank: 22nd

Statehood
December 14, 1819 (22nd state admitted)

Principal river
Mobile River (formed by Tombigbee and
Alabama rivers)

Highest point
Cheaha Mountain 2,407 feet (734 m)

Largest city
Birmingham (280,000 people)

Famous people
George Washington Carver, Hellen Keller.

Motto
Andemus Jura Nostra Defendere ("We Dare
Defend Our Rights")

Song
"Alabama"

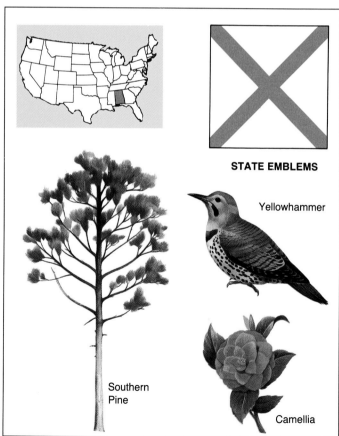

STATE EMBLEMS

Yellowhammer

Southern
Pine

Camellia

▲ *An impressive display of rockets at the Huntsville
Space Center, Alabama.*

History Among the Indians of Alabama were the Creeks, Chickasaws, Choctaws, and Cherokees. The Indians saw first Spaniards, then Frenchmen and Englishmen arrive in their territory. After the American Revolution, the land was given up by the British and became part of the United States. The government made the Indians give up their hunting grounds. Most of them were moved to reservations.

New settlers, spurred by the end of Indian troubles, poured into the region. The whites were mainly farmers; the blacks were their slaves. In 1817, the Territory of Alabama was formed; two years later it became a state.

White men who could not afford to buy fertile bottomlands settled in the uplands. They made a poor living cultivating the stony fields. Wealthy white men established large farms called *plantations* in the bottomlands. The plantation owners, planters, grew cotton in the rich soil. They raised so much that Alabama became known as the "Cotton State." The slave-owning planters grew richer and dominated Alabama. The black men, women, and children who worked in the fields earned nothing.

Alabama left the Union in 1861 and joined the Confederate States of America. Alabama's capital, Montgomery, was also the capital of the Confederacy until the Confederate government moved to Richmond, Virginia. The Civil War ended in defeat for the Confederate States. All slaves were freed. Workers had to be paid. Although they were offered very little, most blacks went back to the cotton fields because they had no other way to earn a living.

It was bad for Alabama to rely on just cotton. The black field hands never made a good living raising it. Neither did white farmers whose farms were small. And in some years, cotton did not sell very well. Such years were hard for everyone, even

▲ *Beautiful gardens abound in Alabama. This one is part of Bellingrath Gardens near Mobile.*

the plantation owners. By planting only one crop, they allowed cotton to wear out the soil.

An insect, the boll weevil, helped save Alabama and the rest of the South. It destroyed so much cotton every year that farmers began raising a number of other crops. Alabama no longer depends on cotton. In the town square of Enterprise, Alabama, stands a monument honoring the boll weevil!

During the 1880's, business owners began building factories in Alabama. The wages they paid were not high. But factories gave some Alabamians a better living than they could earn on farms. As manufacturing grew, wages were raised.

The poorest people of the state were the blacks. But they, too, made progress. Black leaders appeared in Alabama. One was Booker T. Washington. Born a Virginia slave, he built Tuskegee Institute for the education of blacks. At the institute is the workshop of the Missouri-born black scientist, George Washington Carver.

People from Alabama have contributed much to the world. William Gorgas, a U.S. Army doctor, helped stop yellow fever, a disease that almost prevented the building of the

Since Alabama became a state in 1819 it has had five different capitals: St. Stephens, Huntsville, Cahaba, Tuscaloosa, and Montgomery.

▲ *Alabama's Capitol Building in Montgomery.*

Panama Canal. Helen Keller, who as a baby was made deaf and blind by a serious illness, learned to communicate with others. The example of her courage has helped many handicapped people. Georgia-born Martin Luther King, Jr., went from being a minister in Montgomery to winner of the Nobel Peace Prize for his work in civil rights. And scientists at an Alabama university discovered a new chemical element, francium.

Alabamians at Work The nickname "Cotton State" no longer fits Alabama. Farmers earn more from broiler chickens, cattle, eggs, and milk products than from cotton and all other field crops put together. Much cotton is still grown, but today more land is planted in corn than in cotton. Soybeans, peanuts, and pecans are also major crops.

Agriculture has today lost its first place to manufacturing. Metal production is the leading type of manufacturing. The Birmingham area is the biggest iron-and-steel center in the South. On top of Red Mountain, overlooking Birmingham, is a tall statue of Vulcan, the Roman god of fire and metalworking. Other products are textiles, chemicals, paper goods, and food.

Manufacturing is aided by Alabama's raw materials. Coal is burned to make iron and steel and to produce electricity, too. Stone is used for building and for making cement. Gas-

oline, oil, and other products come from petroleum. Timber is made into lumber and paper.

Fishing is important to Alabama. Alabamians haul in several million dollars' worth of seafood every year. Crabs and oysters are taken from Mobile Bay. Boats go out into the Gulf of Mexico for shrimp, sardines, and other fish. Mobile Bay is also a major seaport. Goods from all over the South are shipped around the world from Mobile.

The Space Age brought a new kind of work to Alabama. In 1960 the National Aeronautics and Space Administration (NASA) opened a flight center at Huntsville. Scientists and engineers came there to work on rockets for space flight. They developed the mighty Saturn 5 Rocket that sent Americans to the moon.

ALSO READ: CARVER, GEORGE WASHINGTON; CIVIL RIGHTS; CIVIL WAR; KELLER, HELEN; KING, MARTIN LUTHER, JR.; WASHINGTON, BOOKER T.

ALAMO "Remember the Alamo!" was the Texans' battle cry during their fight for independence from Mexico. Often called the "Cradle of Texas Liberty," the fort of the Alamo in San Antonio was built as the Mission San Antonio de Valero in 1718 by Spanish missionaries. The mission-fortress was later nicknamed "Alamo," the Spanish word for "cottonwood," because of the cottonwoods around it.

San Antonio was part of Mexico in 1835. But Americans living there decided to rebel. A small group of Texas volunteers, led by William Travis, took over the Alamo in late December. Davy Crockett and Jim Bowie, the famous frontiersmen, were among them.

The Mexican General Santa Anna surrounded the Alamo with over 4,000 troops on February 23, 1836.

▼ *Remember the Alamo! In 1836, Texans fought for their freedom from Mexico at the old mission fort called the Alamo.*

All the 150 fighting men in the fort, plus 32 volunteers, refused to surrender. Against such overwhelming odds, they held out for 13 days until the last man was killed. The only survivors were two women and two children.

This heroic resistance aroused all Texans. Sam Houston led Texas forces to victory against General Santa Anna six weeks later, and Texas won its independence. Many years later, the Alamo was restored as an historic site and memorial.

ALSO READ: BOWIE, JIM; CROCKETT, DAVY; HOUSTON, SAM; TEXAS.

ALARIC (about A.D. 370–410) A group of people called the *Goths* lived in the fourth century. The Goths were divided into two branches, the eastern *Ostrogoths* and the western *Visigoths*. Alaric was king of the Visigoths.

Alaric was born on the island of Peuce in the Danube River, now in Romania. The Roman emperor gave him an army in 394. The next year the Visigoths elected Alaric king. He wanted more power. He tried first, unsuccessfully, to conquer Greece,

---

▼ *Alaric was the warrior king of the ancient Visigoths.*

and then turned against Rome.

The Visigoths entered Italy several times to attack Rome. In 408 and 409 Rome paid a large ransom to save itself. In 410, Alaric made a third try. The Romans refused to give him the land and power he demanded. So he marched his army into Rome, unconquered for almost 800 years.

Alaric, however, did not stay long in Rome. He still wanted land where his people could settle in peace. He led them south, planning to go on to Africa. But a storm destroyed their ships. They had to stop in southern Italy, where Alaric, their leader, died.

ALSO READ: ROME, ANCIENT.

ALASKA The name of the largest state in the United States comes from a word used long ago in the Aleutian Islands. These islands lie off the southwestern part of Alaska. Aleuts called the mainland *alakshak*, meaning a land bigger than the islands. And Alaska is a "great land"—over twice the size of the second largest state, Texas.

The Land Alaska can best be described in terms of three main parts.

TUNDRA. The cold, almost treeless plains called *tundra* lie along the western and northern coasts. In winter, the tundra is covered with ice and snow. Flowering plants and mosses appear when summer sunshine melts the ice. But ice underneath the surface does not melt, so the water does not drain off. The land is swampy all summer. The tundra slopes down to the Arctic Ocean north of Brooks Range mountains. Here the tundra is much colder in winter than it is on the west coast.

INTERIOR. The interior part of Alaska lies between two mountain ranges. On the north is Brooks Range. The Alaska Range is on the south. The interior stretches from the western tundra to the border of Can-

---

Although Alaska has very few people—only about one person to each square mile (2.6 sq. km)—its population has increased rapidly over the years. In 1940 the population of the state was 75,524; in 1960, 226,167; today there are more than half a million Alaskans.

▲ *An Eskimo woman busy making a hat for a hatmaking contest in Nanupitchuk, Alaska.*

Juneau, Alaska's capital since 1900, was settled in 1881 by gold miners and named for Joe Juneau, who made Alaska's first big gold discovery in 1880.

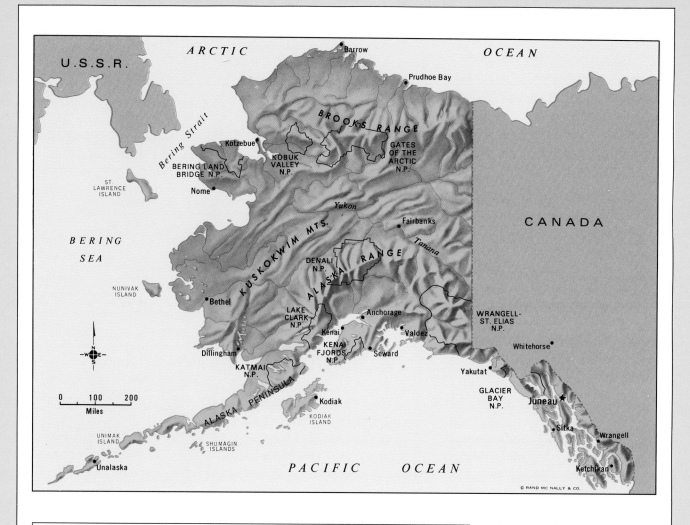

ARCTIC OCEAN

U.S.S.R.

Barrow
Prudhoe Bay

Bering Strait

BROOKS RANGE

Kotzebue

BERING LAND
BRIDGE N.P.

KOBUK
VALLEY
N.P.

GATES
OF THE
ARCTIC
N.P.

ST.
LAWRENCE
ISLAND

Nome

Yukon

Fairbanks

CANADA

BERING
SEA

KUSKOKWIM MTS.

Tanana

DENALI
N.P.

ALASKA RANGE

NUNIVAK
ISLAND

Bethel

LAKE
CLARK
N.P.

Anchorage

Kenai

KENAI
FJORDS
N.P.

Valdez

WRANGELL-
ST. ELIAS
N.P.

Whitehorse

Dillingham

Seward

Yakutat

KATMAI
N.P.

GLACIER
BAY
N.P.

Juneau

N
W · E
S

0   100   200
Miles

ALASKA PENINSULA

Kodiak

Sitka

Wrangell

UNIMAK
ISLAND

KODIAK
ISLAND

SHUMAGIN
ISLANDS

PACIFIC OCEAN

Ketchikan

Unalaska

© RAND MCNALLY & CO.

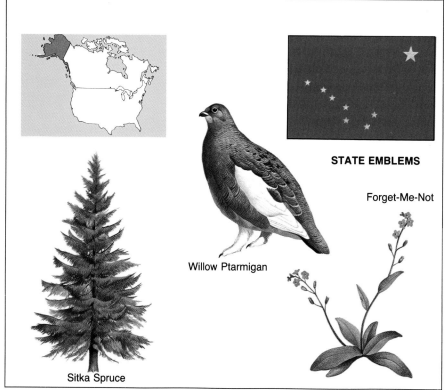

STATE EMBLEMS

Forget-Me-Not

Willow Ptarmigan

Sitka Spruce

ALASKA

Capital
Juneau (26,000 people)

Area
586,659 square miles
(1,518,659 sq. km) Rank: 1st

Population
524,000 people Rank: 49th

Statehood
January 3, 1959
(49th state admitted)

Principal river
Yukon River (1,265 miles/
2,036 km in Alaska)

Highest point
Mount McKinley 20,320
feet (6,193 m)

Largest city
Anchorage (227,000 people)

Motto
"North to the Future."

Song
"Alaska's Flag."

Famous people
Carl Eielson, Joe Juneau

ada. It is mostly the Yukon River basin.

Interior Alaska is colder in winter and warmer in summer than land nearer the ocean. Ocean temperature does not change so much as land temperature from summer to winter. Water is warmer than land in winter. It is cooler than land in summer. So winter winds from the ocean warm the land near the coast. And summer ocean winds cool the nearby land. Interior Alaska is not "protected" by the ocean, so its temperature changes much more from summer to winter.

SOUTH. Most of southern Alaska lies near the water. It follows the long southern coast. Southern Alaska may be divided into three sections.

The *southwest* consists of the Alaska Peninsula and many islands. Mount Katmai, a volcano, is near the northern end of the peninsula. This volcano has one of the largest craters in the world. The Valley of Ten Thousand Smokes was formed when Katmai erupted in 1912. Steam rises from thousands of holes that dot the valley floor.

At the eastern end of southern Alaska is the *panhandle*. This narrow strip has the Pacific Ocean on one side and the Coast Mountains on the other. Canada lies beyond the mountains. Green forests and blue water make the panhandle beautiful. It is a land of mild winters, cool summers, and much rain. The capital, Juneau, is in this region. A new state capital is under construction, at Willow.

Between the southwest and the panhandle is *south-central* Alaska. Winters are mild here, too. The Alaska Range keeps out icy winds from the north. And winds blowing over the warm Alaska Current in the ocean raise winter temperatures.

Summers are cool and short in south-central Alaska, but summer daylight is long. (Summer periods of daylight lengthen as you go north.) The extra hours of sunshine make northern crops grow fast. Huge cabbages, turnips, and potatoes grow in the Matanuska Valley. Over half of the crops raised in Alaska come from this one valley.

The People The population is small for such a large state. About one-sixth of the people are Eskimos, Indians, and Aleuts. Around 4 out of

Alaska is by far the largest state in the United States. It is more than twice the size of Texas, the second largest state. There is less than one person per square mile (2.6 sq. km).

ALASKA

▶ *A pipeline being built through the forest in Alaska to carry oil from the Arctic oil fields.*

▼ *Kodiak bears are very large brown bears of Alaska, and are found on Kodiak Island. These bears eat salmon from the cold rivers.*

every 10 Alaskans live in or near the city of Anchorage, which is by far the biggest city in the state.

History Alaska was the "front porch" of the Americas 30,000 years ago. At that time, there was probably a land or ice bridge connecting Asia and North America. The Bering Strait flows over it today. The first people to reach the New World crossed from Asia to Alaska. They were the ancestors of modern American Indians and Eskimos.

Most of the people moved southward. But some stayed in Alaska. When the first white men arrived in the early 1700's, the Tlingit and Haida Indians lived in the southeast, the Aleuts on the Alaska Peninsula and Aleutian Islands, and Eskimos in the far north and west. Russian fur traders from eastern Siberia sailed across the short Bering Strait to Alaska. They called the region *Russian America*.

The Russians came in search of furs. They fought the Eskimo and Indian hunters and killed a great many of them. Russia's czar (emperor) was in Moscow, half a world away. He found that he could not control his fur traders. Something else also worried him—Britain might capture Russian America. The land was too far away for the czar to defend.

He sold Russian America to the

United States in 1867. The price was 7,200,000 dollars—less than 2 cents an acre! Alaska was truly a bargain. But many Americans did not think so at the time. They said that Secretary of State William H. Seward had wasted government money buying an "icebox." Many people called Alaska "Seward's Folly."

For the next 45 years, Alaska was neglected by the U.S. Government, which could not control the men who sailed there to get furs, fish, copper, and gold. Some U.S. companies built fish canneries in the 1890's. Alaska's gold rush from 1899 to 1902 brought thousands of prospectors and settlers to the Nome and Fairbanks regions. Finally, in 1912, Congress established Alaska as a U.S. territory, with criminal and civil laws. A U.S. farming colony was set up in the Matanuska Valley in the 1930's; the Alaska Highway was built in 1942. Alaska became a state in 1959.

Alaskans at Work This state differs from the other 49 in several ways. Because it is so far north, little farming is done. Nearly 97 percent of Alaska's land is owned by the U.S. Government. Many people who live in Alaska are members of the armed forces.

Manufacturing is the leading industry in Alaska. Food items, especially canned and frozen fish and crabs, head the list. Lumber and other wood products are second on the list of manufactured goods.

For many years, gold was Alaska's major mineral resource. However, with the discovery of oil on the Kenai Peninsula in 1957, large-scale drilling activity began throughout the state. In 1968, huge oil and natural gas reserves were found near Prudhoe Bay on Alaska's Arctic coast. The Alaska pipeline was built to carry the oil 800 miles (1,287 km) from the Arctic region to the ice-free port of Valdez on the south coast. In 1977, oil began flowing through the pipeline. There has been an increase in environmental worries about Alaska following a huge oil spill from the *Exxon Valdez.*

Alaska's second most valuable resource is sand and gravel, which is used in highway construction. Coal, silver, platinum, and uranium are also mined. The state's mineral wealth has brought much economic growth and an influx of newcomers.

ALSO READ: ALEUT INDIANS; ARCTIC; ESKIMOS; INDIANS, AMERICAN.

ALBANIA North of Greece is Albania, the smallest Communist nation in Europe. Green valleys with many farming villages lie between rugged mountains. The larger towns can be reached by car. But pack animals are the only means of transportation to many villages. In the mountains, the climate is moderate. In summer it is hot on the beautiful beaches along the Adriatic Sea. (See the map with the article on EUROPE.)

Many women wear traditional baggy trousers and veils. Men often wear white felt caps, homespun breeches, and beautifully embroidered jackets.

Foreign conquerors ruled Albania for many centuries. They came from the Italian peninsula, the Balkans, and the Middle East. Albania's national hero, Scanderbeg, fought fierce battles against the Turks in the

fifteenth century. But the Turks conquered Albania in 1468 after Scanderbeg died. They made the country part of their territory, the Ottoman Empire. The Turks ruled Albania for more than 400 years. Most Albanians adopted the Turks' religion, Islam. Others were Orthodox Christians and Roman Catholics.

In 1912 the Albanians finally overthrew the Turks and became independent. But Italian soldiers occupied Albania for four years during World War II. German troops later replaced the Italians. The Communist Party, led by Enver Hoxha, took over in 1946. Albania ended close relations with the U.S.S.R. in 1961 and was a loyal ally of China until 1978. In 1990, demonstrations forced

▲ *Most towns in Albania are small. Transportation is difficult in this mountainous land.*

ALBANIA

Capital City: Tirana (270,000 people).
Area: 11,100 square miles (28,748 sq. km).
Population: 3,200,000.
Government: Communist republic.
Natural Resources: Oil, natural gas, coal, water power.
Export Products: Oil, bitumen, chrome, copper, fruit, and vegetables
Unit of Money: Lek.
Official Language: Albanian.

Alberta supplies about three-fourths of Canada's oil. It is known that there are enormous quantities of oil locked in the Athabasca tar sands in the northeast of the province. Experts believe that there could be as much oil in this one area as is known to exist in the rest of the world.

the Communist government to agree to free elections, which were held in 1991.

Albania is a poor country. Most Albanians are farmers. They raise tobacco, livestock, grain, fruits, and vegetables. Few own their land. Most farms are owned by the government. Albania is rich in mineral resources, notably oil, coal, copper, iron, and chromium, but they have not been fully developed. In 1991, many Albanians started trying to leave the country to escape economic problems.

ALSO READ: COMMUNISM, EUROPE, OTTOMAN EMPIRE.

ALBATROSS   see SEABIRDS.

ALBERTA   Alberta is a western, or prairie, province of Canada. In both area (about the size of Texas) and population, it is the fourth largest of the ten Canadian provinces. Its principal cities are Edmonton (the capital), Calgary, Lethbridge, Red Deer, and Medicine Hat (named for the cap worn by an Indian medicine man). The province is named after a daughter of Queen Victoria.

The eastern side of Alberta has gently rolling prairie. The land builds up through foothills to the towering Rocky Mountains that form the province's border with British Columbia. Mt. Columbia, the highest of Alberta's peaks, is 12,294 feet (3,747 m) high. The southern part consists of treeless plains, and is one of the few

sections of Canada with so little rainfall that it requires irrigation to keep its farmlands blooming. The central part is known as the *parklands*, because of its many small lakes, rivers, and forests. A feature of the province's winter climate is a warm wind called a *chinook*, which may change the temperature from 40°F below zero (−40°C) to 40°F (4°C) above in two hours. Alberta has more sunshine than any other Canadian province.

History   Some of the oldest traces of life in Canada are found in Alberta. The Drumheller Valley is famous as a dinosaur burial ground. Millions of years ago the region must have been a tropical jungle. Later, Alberta was covered by a polar ice cap. As the ice retreated, hardy Indian settlers arrived from Alaska. Their descendants, the Sarcee and Blackfoot tribes of the Athabascan-speaking and Algonkian-speaking families, still live in Alberta. Only 2 percent of Alberta's people are Indians. The rest are descendants of European immigrants. The first Europeans to arrive in the Canadian West were adventurers and fur traders from the Hudson's Bay Company of England. Today, about 45 percent of Alberta's people are of British origin or ancestry.

Alberta became part of the new Dominion of Canada in 1870. The Royal Canadian Mounted Police established outposts and forts, and the railway soon arrived from the East. Cattle ranching began. The land was ideal for growing a new type of wheat called *Marquis*. In 1905, Alberta became a province. It has a lieutenant-governor, like other Canadian provinces, an elected law-making assembly, and an executive council.

Industries   Coal, oil, and natural gas are found in Alberta in abundance. One-third of all Albertans earn their living from oil production and mining. Alberta's oil resources are vast: a

▶ *People who love nature would be happy here. This is part of Banff National Park in Alberta.*

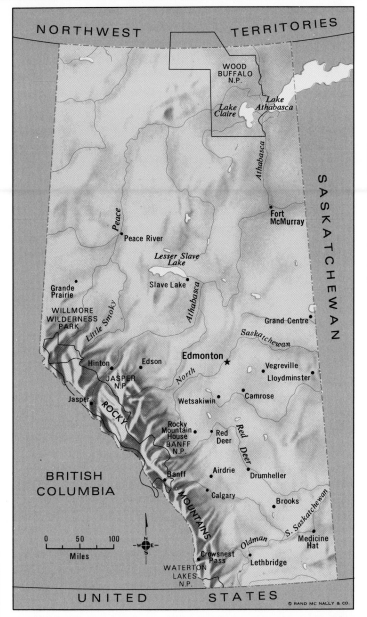

ALBERTA

Capital
Edmonton (785,000 people)

Area
255,285 square miles (661,137 sq. km)

Population
2,375,278 people

Entry into Confederation
September 1, 1905.

Principal river
Saskatchewan 1,205 miles (1,939 km)

Highest point
Mount Columbia 12,294 feet (3,811 m)

Largest city
Edmonton (6th largest Canadian city)

Famous people
Alexander Mackenzie, James Gladstone, Joe Clark

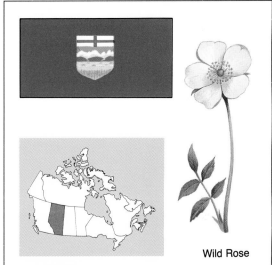

Wild Rose

◀ *The skyline of Calgary, one of Alberta's major cities. Notable landmarks are the Petro Canada Center and Calgary Tower.*

In some countries albino animals are sacred. White cattle are worshiped in India and white elephants in Thailand.

deposit near Lake Athabasca in the north is thought to contain the world's largest single reserve. Alberta petroleum is sent to much of Canada and the western United States. The province also has a large lumber industry.

Ranching and farming are important, though 7 out of 10 Albertans nowadays are town-dwellers. Alberta is Canada's major supplier of meat. Calgary is the cowboy capital of Canada, and every July plays host to the world's largest "stampede," or rodeo, with hundreds of contests of bronco-busting, steer-riding, and chuck-wagon races. Wheat and other grain crops are grown.

Many of the beautiful areas of Alberta have been set aside as national parks. One of the most popular is Banff National Park. Wood Buffalo Park in the north, at 17,300 square miles (44,800 sq. km), is the largest national park in the world. It is the home of the biggest herds of bison in North America, and is the nesting ground of the rare whooping cranes, which migrate to Alberta from southern Texas each year.

ALSO READ: CANADA, NATIONAL PARK.

ALBINO Animals, including human beings, are sometimes born with no coloring matter in their skin, hair, or eyes. They are albinos. White hair, pink eyes, and pinkish skin mark the albino.

Coloring matter in normal people and animals is called *pigment*. Pigments carry many colors: the yellow of a canary's wings, the stripes of zebras, the green of a cat's eyes. *Melanin*, a dark pigment, is the main coloring material of skin. A blonde person has less melanin than a black person. An albino's skin and eyes have no melanin. They look pink because blood vessels show through. Human albinos must wear dark glasses in the sun, because their eyes

have no pigment for protection from strong light. An albino's hair is snow white. Look at the squirrel in the photograph. Notice its eye color.

Not all albino animals are pure white. *Partial* albinos are more common. Most white horses, for example, have some coloring, perhaps blue eyes or a dark patch of skin. Certain black-and-yellow butterflies sometimes have white offspring, but with black markings on their wings. Rare white tigers have darkish stripes.

Albinos inherit their colorless condition from their ancestors, through *genes*, tiny parts of body cells. Genes control what a living thing inherits from its parents. An albino parent may produce normal young, and the young may later produce albinos. It may not happen again for many, many generations.

Plants can also produce albinos. They lack chlorophyll, a green material that makes food for the plant. Without food, albino plants quickly die.

ALSO READ: GENETICS, PHOTOSYNTHESIS, SKIN.

ALCHEMY From about the third century B.C. to the 1700's, the study of metals and elements was a strange blend of science, magic, and religion known as *alchemy*. It was the forerunner of the modern science of chemistry. Alchemy was practiced by the ancient Chinese, Egyptians, Greeks, and Romans. Greek alchemists first introduced the belief that all matter is a mixture of four basic elements—air, earth, fire, and water. They thought that every form of matter could be made by mixing these four elements in the right amounts. From the Greeks and Romans, the study of alchemy reached the Arabs, probably about the eighth century. Later in the Middle Ages it reached Europe.

The people who practiced alchemy had three main goals. First they

▲ *This albino (all-white) squirrel lacks the natural color of its relatives. Its eyes appear red from tiny blood vessels, normally masked by eye coloration.*

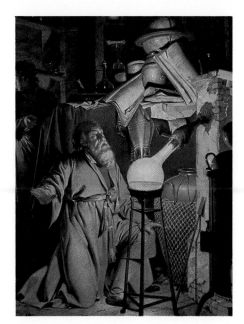

▲ *The German alchemist Hennig Brand discovered phosphorus in 1669. However, like all other alchemists, he failed in his attempt to change base metal into gold.*

see that many of the claims made by the alchemists were not based on scientific facts. But even though many of the alchemists' ideas were wrong, some of their discoveries helped pave the way for the development of modern chemistry.

ALSO READ: CHEMISTRY, ELEMENT, METAL, SCIENCE.

ALCOHOL   see DISTILLATION.

ALCOHOLIC BEVERAGE   People probably made the first alcoholic beverage by accident, thousands of years ago. Someone might have kept some grape juice standing too long, before drinking it. When the person drank the juice, it probably tasted sour and made him feel dizzy.

What this person discovered was a chemical process called *fermentation.* Fermentation occurs when microorganisms, such as bacteria, yeast, and mold, are added to certain plant and animal substances. The two major products of fermentation are carbon dioxide, a gas, and alcohol, a colorless liquid. When the grape juice was left to stand too long, yeast spores fell into it from the air and grew in the juice. The juice fermented into an alcoholic beverage which has come to be called *wine.*

The manufacture of alcoholic beverages is one of the biggest industries today. Among the beverages made are beer, wine, whisky, gin, rum, and bourbon. Beer is made from cereal grains, and wine is made from fruits. Whisky is made from barley, gin is made from fermented grain flavored with juniper berries, and bourbon is made from corn. Fermented molasses produces rum.

Some people can drink alcoholic beverages in modest amounts without serious or long-lasting damage to their health. There are other people, however, who should never drink alcohol

wanted to change inexpensive common or "base" metals, such as lead, into gold, the "perfect" (and most valuable) metal. Second, they wanted to find a medicine that would cure all diseases. And third, they wanted to make a substance that would make old people young and allow them to live forever. Alchemists believed that there was a magical substance, called the *philosophers' stone*, that could do these three things. Many strange recipes were invented in an effort to make this "stone." Some alchemists cooked "witches' brews," using ingredients such as hairs, bats' wings, and spiders. Of course, these brews never succeeded in curing sick people. Nor did the alchemists ever find a way to make gold from other metals. But some of their experiments led to the discovery of new elements, such as phosphorus, used today to make matches and fertilizers. Alchemists also invented some useful medicines.

At the end of the 1700's, the practice of alchemy began to fade. People no longer believed that the philosophers' stone existed. They began to

Drunk driving is a crime. Organizations such as MADD (Mothers Against Drunk Drivers) and SADD (Students Against Driving Drunk) are helping to make motorists aware that they should never drink and drive.

▲ *Beer is a popular alcoholic beverage. Beer ferments in wooden vats as part of the brewing process.*

Edwin Aldrin had made a spaceflight before the historic 1969 moonlanding. In November, 1966 he partnered James A. Lovell aboard Gemini 12. During a 59-orbit mission, Aldrin spent over five hours working outside the spacecraft.

because they are victims of *alcoholism*, a serious health problem in the United States. There are about 10 million alcoholics in the U.S. Alcoholics are people who cannot stop themselves from drinking alcohol. They become *addicted* to alcohol.

Alcohol acts as a *depressant* on the body. A depressant dulls the centers of the brain that control speech, emotions, judgment, and coordination of movement. The depressant effects of alcohol become dangerous when a person drives an automobile after drinking alcoholic beverages. Alcohol may interfere with a driver's judgment, blur vision, and destroy muscle coordination. The U.S. National Highway Traffic Safety Administration has found that about two out of five drivers who are in car accidents that kill people have been drinking before driving.

Alcoholics Anonymous (A.A.) is an organization that has helped thousands of alcoholics conquer their addiction. A.A. helps alcoholics help one another solve their problems.

ALSO READ: ADDICTION, DISTILLATION, FERMENTATION, YEAST.

ALCOTT, LOUISA MAY (1832–1888) *Little Women*, the story of a New England family during the Civil War, was written by Louisa May Alcott. She wrote the story about her own family. She was Jo, and her real-life sisters, May, Elizabeth, and Anna, were the other March sisters—Meg, Beth, and Amy.

Louisa May Alcott was born in Pennsylvania, but she lived most of her life in Massachusetts. "Orchard House" in Concord, Massachusetts, where she sometimes wrote, can be seen today. Ralph Waldo Emerson and Henry David Thoreau, famous writers, were the Alcotts' friends. They sometimes taught Louisa and her sisters.

Louisa's father, Amos Bronson Alcott, was a writer and teacher, too. He had ideas about education that most people of that time did not accept. For example, he believed girls should have a good education. He did not earn much. So Louisa tried all kinds of ways to earn money, including writing.

Louisa worked as a nurse during the Civil War. The letters she wrote about her experiences were made into a book and in 1869 she published *Little Women*, which was a great success. Money she earned from *Little Women* gave her a chance to spend time working in the women's suffrage movement (for voting) and in the temperance movement (against drinking alcoholic beverages).

Some of Louisa May Alcott's other well-loved books are *Little Men*, *Jo's Boys*, and *Under the Lilacs*.

ALSO READ: EMERSON, RALPH WALDO; THOREAU, HENRY DAVID.

ALDRIN, EDWIN (born 1930) Astronaut Edwin "Buzz" Aldrin was the second person to walk on the moon. He was the pilot of *Eagle*, the Apollo 11 lunar module that carried Neil Armstrong and him to the surface of the moon on July 20, 1969. This was the first moonlanding.

Born in Glen Ridge, New Jersey, Aldrin is the only son of a United States Army officer. Aldrin graduated

▼ *Louisa May Alcott (below, right) wrote* Little Women. *It was the story of the four March sisters—Meg, Jo, Beth, and Amy (below).*

third in his class at West Point, the U.S. Military Academy. He joined the Air Force and became a jet pilot in the Korean War.

Buzz Aldrin studied space travel at the Massachusetts Institute of Technology, where he earned a doctor of science degree in astronautics. He became an expert in rendezvous and docking—the meeting and joining together of two craft moving through space. Aldrin's knowledge of rendezvous and docking techniques contributed to the success of the Apollo program.

Aldrin began astronaut training in 1964. His first space trip was in November 1966, on the Gemini 12 mission in Earth orbit, during which he worked in space outside his spacecraft for 5½ hours.

ALSO READ: ARMSTRONG, NEIL; ASTRONAUT; COLLINS, MICHAEL; MOON; SPACE TRAVEL.

ALEUT INDIANS The Aleutian Islands, off the Alaskan Coast, are the home of the Aleut Indians. The Aleuts call the islands the "birthplace of the winds" because strong, hurricane-like winds often blow there. Some Aleuts also live in the Pribilof Islands, other islands nearby, and the Alaskan peninsula.

For centuries, the hardy Aleuts relied for their living on the Pacific Ocean. Their boats, called *kayaks* and *umiaks*, were made of animal skins sewn together by Aleut women and stretched over a frame made of bone. There are no trees on the islands from which to make a wooden boat. The Aleuts used poison-tipped harpoons to kill seals, whales, and fish. They used seal oil and whale blubber as fuel. The Aleuts' homes were holes dug in the ground and covered with sod, driftwood, and whale bones.

The Aleuts are closely related to the Eskimos of Alaska. But the Aleuts spoke a language of their own, and had some different customs. The

Aleuts' ancestors wore long garments made of bird skin, with feathers turned to the inside for warmth. They also wore light raincoats with pointed hoods, made from strips of seal intestines and decorated with bird feathers. The Aleut women once sewed beautiful, colorful clothing, using tiny sewing needles made of bird bones.

About 30,000 Aleut Indians were living on the Aleutian Islands and the Alaskan mainland when Russian traders first arrived in 1741. Great numbers of the Aleuts were killed in massacres, or died from diseases, such as smallpox and tuberculosis, brought by the white people. Marriages between whites and Indians also reduced the number of full-blooded Aleuts. The old ways and customs of the Aleuts mostly vanished. Many of the Indians today have Russian names and are members of the Russian Orthodox Church. There are now only about 1,000 full-blooded Aleuts and about 5,500 of mixed blood.

ALSO READ: ALASKA; INDIANS, AMERICAN; ESKIMO.

▲ *Edwin "Buzz" Aldrin, the second astronaut to walk on the moon.*

▼ *Aleut women on Attu Island in the Pacific Ocean weave some of the finest baskets in the world.*

The empire of Alexander the Great.

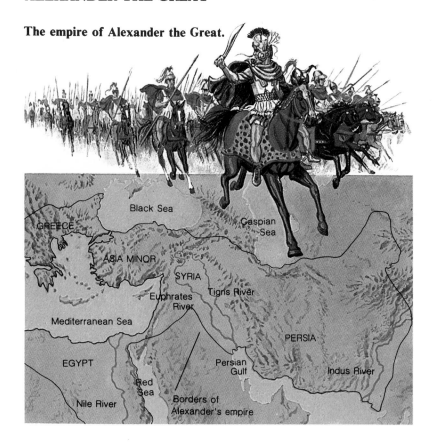

Black Sea

GREECE

Caspian Sea

ASIA MINOR

SYRIA

Euphrates River

Tigris River

Mediterranean Sea

PERSIA

EGYPT

Persian Gulf

Indus River

Red Sea

Nile River

Borders of Alexander's empire

▲ *Alexander the Great and his conquering armies brought a vast empire under Macedonian control. Egypt and Persia both fell to this brilliant general.*

When Alexander was a boy he tamed the great and spirited horse Bucephalus, a horse that no one else dared to ride. This famous horse carried Alexander as far as India, where it died. Alexander built a city and named it Bucephalo after his beloved steed.

ALEXANDER THE GREAT
(356–323 B.C.) Alexander the Great was a mighty king and conqueror. He was one of the greatest military geniuses the world has ever known.

He was born in Pella, Macedonia. Alexander grew to be a handsome, brilliant man. Aristotle, the famous philosopher, came from Greece to teach him geography, politics, literature, medicine, and science. Alexander's father, King Philip II of Macedon, taught him to plan and win battles.

The young prince became king when he was 20. He then began the series of marches that continued until he ruled almost all of the then-known world. On his great war horse, Bucephalus, he first took over Greece. He went on to conquer southeastern Europe, Asia Minor, Egypt, and India. On his way he crushed the Persian Empire, and was made king of Egypt and Asia. He and his troops traveled over 11,000 miles (17,700

km). He spread Greek customs and ideas wherever he went.

In India his men refused to go farther. They were tired and frightened, and wanted to go home. Worn out, Alexander agreed to turn back. He died of fever in Babylon, at the early age of 33.

ALSO READ: ANCIENT CIVILIZATIONS, MACEDONIA.

ALFRED THE GREAT (849?–899)
Alfred was the king of Wessex, the southernmost of four kingdoms that became England. He is remembered as "the Great" because he led his people, the West Saxons, against the Danes—who had invaded Wessex—and defeated them.

Alfred became king in 871, after his father and three brothers had all ruled and died. Alfred, as a prince, had helped fight off the invading Danes. As king, he led an army against them. The mightiest Danish invasion came in 877, when King Guthrum landed in Wessex with his army. Alfred lost a battle to Guthrum, and went into hiding. While in hiding, Alfred made new plans for battle, and he defeated the Danes in 878.

Alfred built ships and towers along the coast to fight off the Danish invaders, should they break the peace. The Danes did so, in 886. Alfred once again defeated them, and also took over London. He drove the Danes from southern England in 897.

Alfred believed in the importance of education. He helped translate several books from Latin into Anglo-Saxon (Old English). He asked teachers from Wales and the European continent to come to his kingdom to teach. He also set up a school, and encouraged the development of arts and industries.

ALSO READ: ANGLO-SAXONS, ENGLISH HISTORY, VIKINGS.

ALGAE The slimy green scum that often floats on shallow lakes or ponds is a kind of algae, the simplest of plants. *Algae* is the plural form of the word *alga*. The plural form is usually used. There are many kinds of algae. These plants grow on land in damp places as well as water. Sometimes they grow attached to rocks or stones along the shore or way out at sea and are called *seaweeds*. They grow on other plants, on wood, turtles, water fleas, and even within plants and animals. Much of the green stuff in an aquarium is algae.

Some algae are so small that a thousand of them will fit on the head of a pin. Others are large, stretching for hundreds of feet. Certain small, fresh- and salt-water algae, called *diatoms*, are single cells with "glassy" outer walls made of silica. Diatoms are found in plankton and are the major food of many water aminals.

Algae Groups All algae contain a pigment called *chlorophyll*, which gives plants their green color. But some algae contain other pigments that hide the green color. Although algae are plants, some of them can move about. They do this by sliding, twisting, gliding, or by floating with currents.

Most algae can be put in one of four groups according to their color—blue-green, green, brown, and red.

Blue-green algae, such as pond scum, are cells with no definite *nuclei* (cell centers). Cells of green algae have definite nuclei. Green algae grow in fresh and salt water, or in any place that is light, moist, and cool. Green algae make up the largest of the four main kinds of algae. *Kelp*, a seaweed, is a brown alga. Kelp is sometimes attached to rocks near the shore. Some forms of brown algae are so small that they can be seen only with a microscope. Others are more than 200 feet (61 m) long. Red algae can be found in oceans, especially in warm seas. Coral reefs are formed partly from red algae.

Useful Algae Algae are food for fish and other animals. Even humans use algae as food. A single tablespoon of the alga called *chlorella* has as much protein as an ounce of steak. Chlorella also contains vitamins, fats, and starches. As yet, it has not been made to taste good on its own, but it is a nourishing food.

The Japanese have made soup, noodles, tea, bread, and ice cream from kelp and other kinds of algae. The bread is pale green. So is the ice cream. But all these foods taste good. Algae are also used in food in the United States. Puddings thicken because of a product called *agar*, which comes from algae. You can also make algae cookies, using chlorella.

Why should people eat algae? For one thing, we may need new foods before very long. The number of people is growing faster than the food supply in many parts of the world. Science must find new foods. Some of these new foods may come from the plentiful supply of algae.

ALSO READ: CELL, FOOD WEB, PLANT, PLANT KINGDOM.

▲ *Alfred the Great, King of Wessex, led the English against the Danes.*

▼ *In the sea live many-celled algae called seaweeds. In fresh water are found pondweeds, such as* Spirogyra.

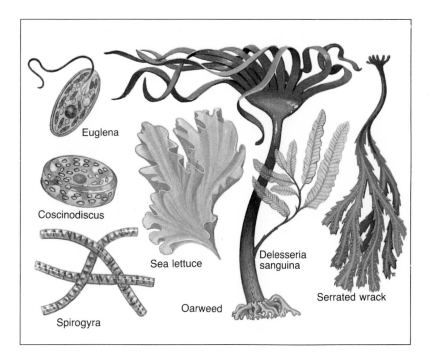

Euglena

Coscinodiscus

Spirogyra

Sea lettuce

Oarweed

Delesseria sanguina

Serrated wrack

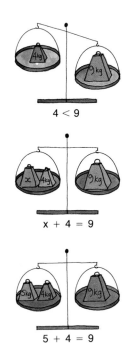

4 < 9

x + 4 = 9

5 + 4 = 9

▲ *An equation in algebra is like a balance scale. Four is less than nine. But if 9 kg are put on one pan and 4 kg plus 5 kg on the other, the scales will balance. In other words, 9 = 4 + 5.*

▲ *Horatio Alger, Jr., wrote the Ragged Dick series which tell the stories of hardworking boys who lived a century ago. Alger's books about their adventures and success sold millions of copies.*

ALGEBRA Here are three math problems.

(1) What number would you add to 5 to get 7? $5 + \Box = 7$.

(2) What number would you multiply by 3 to get 6? $\Box \times 3 = 6$.

(3) What number would you subtract from 5 to get 3? $5 - \Box = 3$.

In each of these examples, the correct number is 2. In (1), $5 + \boxed{2} = 7$; in (2), $\boxed{2} \times 3 = 6$; and in (3), $5 - \boxed{2} = 3$. Although you may not have known it, you were doing problems in algebra.

Several symbols, $+$, $\times$, $-$, $\Box$, and $=$, are used in these problems. Symbols are a quick, easy way of getting across an idea. Algebra is a branch of mathematics which uses symbols.

Two of these symbols are very important. One is the symbol $=$. This symbol means "is equal to." It means that everything on the left of the symbol "is equal to" everything on the right of it. When the symbol $=$ is used, the group of symbols and numbers is called an *equation.*

The other important symbol is $\Box$. When you first considered the problem, you did not know what number went in the box. The correct number was *unknown* to you. The symbol $\Box$ in the examples is called an *unknown* for this reason. The problem was to find the *unknown number.* The symbol for an unknown is not usually a box. It is usually a letter, such as x, t, or v. Problem (1) written with a letter instead of a box would look like this:

$$5 + x = 7.$$

The mathematician knows that x stands for an unknown number. To solve the problem, you have to find a number to use for x that will make the equation true. So algebra can also be the study of rules that help you find an unknown number.

■ **LEARN BY DOING**

How Algebra Is Used Here is an example of how algebra can be used to help you solve mathematical problems. Suppose you are an athlete, planning a training session. You plan to run for 30 minutes. You can run one lap of the running track in 5 minutes. If you keep up the same speed, how many laps will you run in in your training session?

The unknown number is x (the number of laps). The equation to work it out is $x = 30 \div 5$: the number of laps (x) is equal to the total running time (30 minutes) divided by your time for each lap (5 minutes). How many laps will you run in the planned training sesson? ■

This is a simple example, but algebra problems can be more difficult. Scientists often use algebraic equations in their work. The unknown might be how much fuel to put in a rocket, or how many seeds to plant in a cornfield.

History of Algebra One of the oldest pieces of writing ever found is about algebra. The writing was carved on stone thousands of years ago by an Egyptian named Ahmes. The equation written on the stone is $\frac{x}{7} + x = 19$.

It took a long time for the study of algebra to progress. Greeks, Indians, Persians, and others knew a little about algebra. The Arabs learned more about algebra than any other people. An Arab mathematician wrote a book in 825, called *Hisab al-jabr w' almuqabalah*, meaning "the science of equations." We get our word "algebra" from the *al-jabr w'* in the title. The Persian poet Omar Khayyam wrote a book on algebra in the late 11th century.

A Frenchman, François Vieta (1540–1603), is known as the "father of modern algebra." He collected all the known writings on algebra, and added many new ways to prove that algebraic equations are true. Since Vieta's time, algebra has grown and changed. Mathematicians today use many different kinds of algebra to solve many different kinds of problems.

ALSO READ: ARITHMETIC, MATHEMATICS, NUMBER.

ALGER, HORATIO, JR. (1832–1899) "Poor but honest boy works hard to win fame and fortune." This "rags-to-riches" idea made Horatio Alger, Jr., one of America's most popular writers of novels in the 1800's.

Alger was born in Revere, Massachusetts. His family expected him to follow in his father's footsteps as a Unitarian minister. But he had plans of his own. After graduation from Harvard, Horatio traveled, and then worked as a private teacher and as a newspaperman. He returned to Massachusetts after several years, and gave in to his family's wishes. He became a Unitarian minister in 1864. Two years later, he moved to New York City and became the chaplain of the Newsboys' Lodging House, a home for orphans and runaway boys. The ideas for the stories that later made Alger famous came from the young people at the home. His first successful book was *Ragged Dick*, published in 1867. His stories showed that anyone could make good if he or she tried hard enough.

ALSO READ: CHILDREN'S LITERATURE.

◀ *Ancient Roman buildings are part of the historic heritage of Algeria.*

ALGERIA The African nation of Algeria covers a very large area. It is the second largest country in Africa—only Sudan has a larger area—and is one-fourth the size of the United States. It is bordered by seven other countries and the Mediterranean Sea. The Sahara Desert covers most of Algeria. Few people live in the vast region of rocky plains and great sand dunes, where rain may not fall for years. There are valuable mineral resources beneath the desert. (See the map with the article on AFRICA.)

The people of the Sahara are nomads, wandering from oasis to oasis, caring for their goats and camels and living in animal-skin tents. But most Algerians are crowded into the more fertile narrow strip of land along the Mediterranean Sea. Algiers is the

In Algeria, 47 percent of the population is under 15 years of age. Four percent is over 65. About 25 percent of Algerians can read and write.

ALGERIA

Capital City: Algiers (1,500,000 people).
Area: 919,662 square miles (2,381,741 sq. km).
Population: 25,000,000.
Government: Republic.
Natural Resources: Oil, natural gas, minerals.
Export Products: Oil, natural gas, metal ores, fruit.
Unit of Money: Dinar.
Official Language: Arabic.

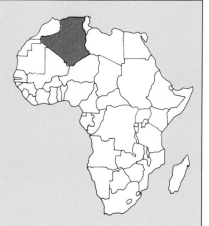

▲ *A warrior, dressed in eagle feather warbonnet, of the Blackfoot, an Algonkian-speaking tribe of Great Plains Indians.*

Ethan Allen, one of the Green Mountain Boys in the American Revolution, told the Continental Congress that he was fighting for the independence of Vermont, not for the United States. Vermont declared its independence in 1779, but the Congress refused to let the state go. Ethan Allen then told the British that he wanted the state to be made a part of Canada. This was also refused.

largest city and port, and the nation's capital.

The first known settlers of the region were the ancient Berbers. However, Arabs conquered the land about a thousand years ago, and most Algerians are now Arabo-Berbers, who speak Arabic and follow the religion of Islam. A few Algerian Berbers still cling to their old language and customs.

Many nations have controlled Algeria. It was called Numidia under ancient Roman rule. Arabs seized the country later on, then the Turks in the 1500's. The French captured Algeria in 1830, to stop pirates who hid there. The French stayed and slowly gained control of the whole country. The Algerians grew unhappy with French control, especially after World War II. They began to rebel in 1954. The Algerians and the French fought for eight years and more than 250,000 people died before Algeria won independence in 1962.

Algeria is now a republic. Beneath its desert sands lies oil, and this provides much of the country's wealth. Algeria also has reserves of natural gas and other minerals. Social and economic reforms are bringing great changes to the lives of the Algerian people.

ALSO READ: AFRICA, BARBARY COAST, SAHARA DESERT.

ALGONKIAN Algonkian is a family of languages used by a large number of North American Indian tribes. The name is also spelled *Algonquian*. Algonkian-speaking Indians moved from Alaska to eastern Canada and the northern United States sometime before 3000 B.C. Each tribe adapted to its new surroundings. Tribes in Canada and New England hunted deer and moose, wore buckskins, and lived in bark-covered tepees or wigwams. New England tribes also learned to

tap the sweet sap from sugar maple trees. Those in marshy regions near the Great Lakes gathered wild rice.

Algonkian-speaking people along the eastern seaboard met the first white settlers who sailed ships from Europe to the New World. The Indians taught the colonists how to plant corn, pumpkins, and squash; bake clams; make canoes; use seaweed for fertilizer, and even how to smoke tobacco. Without the Indians' help, the colonists would not have survived.

Algonkian-speaking tribes in the northeast included the Delaware, Wampanoag, Illinois, Narraganset, Mahican, and Powhatan. Other Algonkian-speaking Indians lived in the Great Plains. They included the Arapaho, Blackfoot, and Cheyenne. The Naskapi, Cree, Ojibwa, Montagnais, and Algonkin tribes roamed eastern Canada. The Algonkin tribe, which gave its name to this language family, lived along the Ottawa River. They are now often called Ottawa Indians.

You may not realize it, but you already know some Algonkian words. The English colonists borrowed *racoon*, *pecan*, and *squash* from Algonkian-speaking Indians, for example. Many American place names come from Algonkian words, too. Examples are Manhattan, Chicago, Illinois, Massachusetts, Mississippi, and Wisconsin.

ALSO READ: INDIANS, AMERICAN.

ALIMENTARY CANAL see DIGESTION.

ALLEN, ETHAN (1738–1789) Ethan Allen was a hero of the American Revolution. He was born on a Connecticut farm, and planned to enter Yale College. But his father died when Ethan was 16. He had to go to work to support his family.

▲ *Ethan Allen, a hero of the American Revolution, demanding the surrender of Fort Ticonderoga at the start of the Revolutionary War.*

He served with the citizens' army (militia) during the French and Indian War (1754–1763). He moved to what is now Vermont when he was 31. He later helped to form the Green Mountain Boys, and he became their leader. These brave frontiersmen defended their farms from New Yorkers, who considered the region part of New York. When the Revolutionary War began in 1775, Allen and Colonel Benedict Arnold led the Green Mountain Boys in the daring capture of Fort Ticonderoga from the British. Allen joined a small group who tried to seize Montreal later that year. He was captured by the British and spent nearly three years in jail in England. After his release in 1778, he wrote the hair-raising autobiography, *Narrative of Colonel Ethan Allen's Captivity*.

Allen tried to convince Congress to make Vermont a state after the Revolution. But not until two years after his death in 1789 was Vermont admitted to the Union.

ALSO READ: AMERICAN REVOLUTION, VERMONT.

ALLERGY You probably have an allergy, if playing with a dog seems to make you sneeze, or if you feel itchy after eating chocolate. You are "sensitive" to something—your body does not like it.

The human body has a built-in safety device that sets off an alarm signal if something harmful, such as a germ, enters the body. When it gets the signal, the blood begins to release disease-fighting substances called *antibodies*. In some people, the alarm signal goes off in response to something that to others is not harmful at all—such as dog hairs or chocolate. When this happens, antibodies increase the production of substances called *histamines*, which cause an allergic reaction, such as sneezing, itching, or vomiting.

A substance to which a person is allergic is called an *allergen*. It might be something a person swallows, breathes in, or touches. One of the most common allergies is *hay fever*, which is caused by pollen in the air. There is a lot of interest also in allergies to food and food additives.

Once a doctor has discovered what the allergen is, the doctor may tell the patient to avoid exposure to it, or he may give him a drug called an *antihistamine*. This drug counteracts the histamines in the body and thus stops the allergic reaction.

A doctor can also treat an allergy by giving the patient injections (shots). These shots contain tiny amounts of the allergen itself—so tiny that the body does not react. Then, over a period of time, increasing amounts are injected. The body gets used to the allergen and no longer reacts when coming in contact with it. This procedure must be used with care and is not suitable for some allergies.

Doctors can treat, and sometimes cure, allergies, although they still do not understand everything about them. Much remains to be learned about why some people have them, while others do not.

ALSO READ: ANTIGEN AND ANTIBODY, BLOOD, DISEASE.

About one person in seven in the United States has an allergy that needs medical attention. Allergies tend to run in families. If both parents have an allergy, each of their children has about a 75 percent chance of developing one.

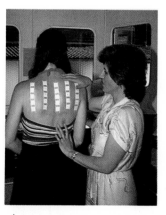

▲ *Sometimes a person shows an allergic reaction, but does not know what has caused it. To find out, doctors may test different allergens on the patient's skin.*

Crocodile

Alligator

▲ *One way to tell a crocodile from an alligator: when a crocodile closes its jaws, the fourth tooth of the lower jaw can still be seen. In alligators and their relatives, the tooth fits into a hole in the upper jaw and cannot be seen.*

ALLIGATORS AND CROCO-DILES Biologists believe that alligators and crocodiles have lived in rivers and swamps in many of the warm parts of the world for about 135 million years. They are found today in Asia, Africa, Australia, and North and South America.

Alike but Different Alligators and crocodiles look alike in many ways. But there are differences, apart from their different names. Ancient Romans saw one of these animals basking in the North African sun and called it *crocodilus*, meaning "worm of the pebbles." The English word "crocodile" came from this name. Spaniards saw a similar reptile in the New World and called it *el lagarto*, meaning "the lizard." From this, came the word "alligator."

Crocodiles generally grow to be longer than alligators, although both start out life as tiny babies—a few inches long—hatched from eggs. Crocodiles 30 feet (9 m) long have been seen, but alligators are rarely longer than 15 feet (4.5 m). Crocodiles are found in both fresh and salt water, while alligators prefer fresh water. Crocodiles have more green in their body color than alligators do.

In spite of their differences, alligators and crocodiles both belong to the same order of reptiles, *Crocodylia.* Members of this order are called *crocodilians.* Other crocodilians are the gavial of southern Asia, a close relative of the crocodile, and the long-snouted caiman, a Latin American cousin of the alligator.

Crocodilians have a tough, leathery skin covering an armor of bony plates. Temperature is very important to a crocodilian because, like all reptiles, it is a cold-blooded animal. It dies if its body becomes too hot or too cold. So it usually crawls up from its mudbank in the morning, basks in the warm sun until its body temperature rises.

On land, the crocodilian walks with its body high off the ground, dragging its long, powerful tail. Its rear legs are longer than its front ones. In the water, the animal swims by swishing its tail from side to side. The tail is also used as a weapon, for defense.

A crocodilian is well suited for a life spent hunting in the water. Its eyes and nostrils are on top of its head, so it can see and breathe when the rest of its body lies hidden underwater. It closes its nostrils to seal off its nose when it dives.

Crocodilians prey on birds, fish, and small mammals. The largest crocodilians are strong enough to drag

▶ *The American crocodile lives in salt water. It is darker and greener than the alligator. The American crocodile is rare.*

a cow or a horse into the water, and some kinds of crocodilians will attack people. Sharp teeth grip and hold the prey. New teeth grow in if some rip out. One animal was reported to have grown 45 sets of teeth by the time it grew to 13 feet (4 m) in length. Crocodilian teeth are sharp, but they are not strong enough to chew prey. The animal swallows its prey whole or tears it up by twisting it into pieces. The muscles that close the jaws are extremely strong, allowing the crocodilian to snap its mouth shut quickly. The muscles that open the jaws are weaker.

The Alligators There are two species of alligators, the *Chinese alligator* found in the Yangtze River and the larger *American alligator*. The American alligator lives in the southern United States, mostly in swamps in Louisiana, Georgia, South Carolina, and the Everglades of Florida.

Crocodilians, notably alligators, make a wide variety of sounds, from grunts and hisses to roars that can be heard a mile away. Alligators were once common, but so many were killed for their hides or for sport that they became scarce and were listed as an endangered species. But alligators have now increased so rapidly in Florida and other coastal areas that limited hunting of them is permitted.

Food for an alligator can be anything that it can outswim, ambush, or overpower. In the stomach of one dead alligator, a zoologist found several pieces of wood, a fishing sinker, and a crumpled can. The alligator had swallowed these objects to help grind the coarse food it could not chew.

Like other reptiles, crocodilians lay eggs. Most female crocodilians bury their eggs in sand or in a pile of leaves. The American alligator, however, builds a mound of plants up to 4 feet (1.2 m) high. The female lays from 30 to 70 hard-shelled eggs that hatch in nine weeks. The mother remains near the nest to guard the eggs. After the

eggs hatch, she helps her young find their way out of the nest to begin life in the water. Most of the young alligators stay with their mother until the next spring.

In Central and South America live relatives of the alligators, the caimans, also called *jacares*. The *black caiman* is the largest, reaching a length of 12 feet (3.7 m). The smallest is the *dwarf caiman*, rarely more than 4 feet (1.2 m) long.

The Crocodiles Some American crocodiles share southern Florida swamps with the American alligator. But the crocodile is quite rare in the U.S. Most American crocodiles live in South America.

The *American crocodile* is up to 14 feet (4.3 m) long. Like the American alligator, it eats fish and small animals. It will attack a person only in self-defense. The most dangerous crocodile is the *Nile crocodile*. It lives in African rivers and lakes, and was regarded as sacred in ancient Egypt. The *estuarine crocodile* is found mostly in coastal swamps and in the mouths, or estuaries, of large rivers, but often swims to sea. This habit probably explains why the species is found over such a wide range—from India southward to northern Australia. Both Nile and estuarine crocodiles can be 20 feet (6 m) long.

The smaller *marsh crocodile*, or *mugger*, is found in India and Sri Lanka. The *gavial* of northern India has a very slender snout that looks like the handle of a frying pan. The gavial may grow up to 20 feet (6 m) in length. It feeds mainly on fish that it catches by snaps of its long jaws.

ALSO READ: DINOSAUR, LIZARD, REPTILE.

▲ *In the United States alligators were once hunted for their hides. A bigger threat to them now is water pollution.*

An alligator can break a person's arm with one snap of its jaws. But the muscles that *open* the creature's jaws are so weak that a man can hold the alligator's mouth shut with only one hand.

ALLOY

▲ *This strange face was made in bronze in prehistoric times. Bronze was probably the first alloy made.*

▼ *The metals that go into a stainless steel fork.*

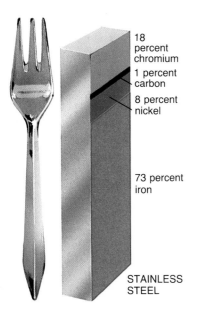

- 18 percent chromium
- 1 percent carbon
- 8 percent nickel
- 73 percent iron

STAINLESS STEEL

ALLOY You might think that a bright new penny is copper. But a penny is not all copper. It is an alloy of copper, tin, and zinc. A mixture of two or more metals, or a metal and a non-metallic element, is an alloy.

Fewer than 80 pure metals exist naturally, but thousands of alloys can be made from them. The first alloy was *bronze*, which was made as long ago as 3000 B.C. Bronze was probably first discovered by accident, when copper and tin melted together and hardened. Alloys are still usually made by heating the metals until they melt and turn into liquids. The liquids are then mixed and allowed to cool. The solid that forms after cooling is the alloy.

Alloys are used for many purposes. They are used most often to make objects less expensive or more useful than objects composed of pure metals. Pure gold is beautiful, but a ring of pure gold bends and scratches easily. A ring of less expensive gold alloy is much stronger. A reddish-yellow ring is probably made of an alloy of gold and copper. A white or silvery gold ring may be an alloy of gold and nickel, called *white gold*.

Steel is one of the most useful alloys made today. It is a mixture of iron and other metals or non-metals, such as carbon and manganese. Other substances can be added to make the exact kinds of steel needed for special purposes. One example is the special steel alloy used to make steel sinks.

Pure steel would rust very quickly, so an alloy of steel, chromium, and nickel is used. Rust cannot form easily on a *stainless* steel sink. A smooth ride in a car is possible because of the springs between the passengers and the wheels. The springs would break if they were not very strong. An alloy of steel and vanadium makes them strong. Other parts of a car are also made of steel and other alloys.

Many different alloys of steel are used in building large buildings and ships. As metal scientists, or *metallurgists*, learn more about metals, they are developing many other alloys that can do some jobs better than steel. One example is carboloy—an alloy of carbon, cobalt, and tungsten—that is used to make cutting tools.

Alloys are very important in building airplanes. A plane made of pure steel would be very strong, but it would be so heavy that it would need immensely powerful engines. Aluminum is a very light metal, but an airplane of pure aluminum would not be strong enough. An alloy of aluminum, copper, manganese, and magnesium is often used to build airplanes, because it is both strong and light. This alloy was discovered by a German metallurgist in 1910. Alloys are also very important in building high-speed jets, missiles, and space rockets. Such craft must be able to resist heat, cold, and the stresses of supersonic flight.

ALSO READ: IRON AND STEEL, METAL.

SOME COMMON OBJECTS AND THEIR ALLOY MAKE-UP	
Object	Metals in alloy (Metal shown first has largest amount in object)
Brass door knob	Copper and zinc
Aluminum pots and pans	Aluminum, copper, and manganese
Dime	Copper and nickel
14-carat yellow gold ring	Gold and copper
Stainless steel knives and forks	Stainless steel, which is made up of steel (iron and carbon), chromium, and nickel.

104

ALMANAC An almanac is a book full of all kinds of useful information. Most almanacs have a calendar and facts about countries, governments, history, and geography. They may also have weather information for cities and countries all over the world, and tables that tell the movements of the sun, planets, and stars.

People have written almanacs for thousands of years. The first ones, made in ancient Persia, contained astrologers' predictions. The word "almanac" probably comes from the Arabic *almanakh*, for "calendar." One of the most famous American almanacs was *Poor Richard's Almanac*, written by Benjamin Franklin. The book contained poetry, proverbs, astronomy, and weather information. Today most almanacs, such as *The World Almanac*, *The U.S. Fact Book*, and *The Statesman's Year Book*, contain general information and tell the reader about events that happened during the past year. Some organizations, such as the United Nations, publish special almanacs that give facts about many countries. Farmers and sailors still use almanacs to tell when the sun will rise and set or tides will rise and fall.

■ **LEARN BY DOING**

You might enjoy making your own almanac, based on events at home or at school. You could predict when the first snow will fall, or when you will go on vacation. Other entries might show game scores of your favorite team; birthdays of family, friends, and pets; or notes on books, movies, and hobbies. ■

ALSO READ: ASTROLOGY; FRANKLIN, BENJAMIN; REFERENCE BOOKS.

ALPHABET All written languages are made up of marks called *symbols*. In most languages today, these symbols are *letters* that stand for the sounds of the language. An alphabet is a list of these letter symbols, arranged in a particular order. The word "alphabet" comes from *alpha* and *beta*, the first two symbols, or letters, of the Greek alphabet. Our English alphabet of 26 letters is sometimes known as the ABC's.

Humans first tried to write down language when they made pictures of objects by scratching or painting them on surfaces. Some of these pictures told a story or gave a message. For instance, simple pictures of a person, a boat, and the sun rising in the sky might have meant, "I will make a trip down the river tomorrow morning."

People later began to use pictures to stand for words rather than for stories or ideas. Little by little, these pictures became simple shapes or marks that symbolized the separate *syllables* of words.

The earliest alphabets were probably developed sometime before 1000 B.C. The Phoenicians, who lived in the fertile regions east of the Mediterranean Sea, used an alphabet that may have come from earlier Egyptian *hieroglyphics*, a system of picture writing. But the symbols of the Phoenician alphabet were not picture ideas. The symbols became letters, each of which stood for a separate *consonant* sound of language. It was the first real alphabet.

The Phoenicians were great sailors and traders and they carried their alphabet on westward voyages to Europe and Africa. Other peoples wrote their own alphabets, using the Phoenicians' idea of setting symbols down in regular order, naming them, and having each one represent certain sounds. But the Phoenicians' alphabet had no *vowels*. Can you figure out this line from a well-known nursery rhyme written without vowels?

TH CW JMPD VR TH MN

The Greeks used the Phoenician letters, but made many changes.

Poor Richard, 1743.
AN
Almanack
For the Year of Christ
1743,
Being the Third after LEAP YEAR.

And makes since the Creation Years
By the Account of the Eastern Greeks 7251
By the Latin Church, when ☉ ent. ♈ 6942
By the Computation of *W. W.* 5752
By the *Roman* Chronology 5692
By the *Jewish* Rabbies 5504
Wherein is contained,
The Lunations, Eclipses, Judgment of the Weather, Spring Tides, Planets Motions & mutual Aspects, Sun and Moon's Rising and Setting, Length of Days, Time of High Water, Fairs, Courts, and observable Days.
Fitted to the Latitude of Forty Degrees, and a Meridian of Five Hours West from *London*, but may without sensible Error, serve all the adjacent Places, even from *Newfoundland* to *South-Carolina*.

By *RICHARD SAUNDERS*, Philom.
PHILADELPHIA
Printed and sold by *B. FRANKLIN*, at the New Printing-Office near the Market.

▲ *The title page of* Poor Richard's Almanac, *published by Benjamin Franklin. Some people read this almanac for its funny stories. Others wanted to find out things about the future.*

Did you know that the 26 letters of our alphabet can be arranged in 620,448,401,733,239,439, 369,000 different ways?

The oldest letter in our alphabet is O. It has remained the same since it was first used by the Phoenicians over 3,000 years ago. The newest letters in the English alphabet are V and J. They were not in use in Shakespeare's time, the late 1500's.

PHOENICIAN	ANCIENT GREEK	MODERN ENGLISH
𐤀 𐤀	A	A
𐤁 𐤁	B	B
𐤂	Γ	C G
𐤃 𐤃	Δ	D
𐤄 𐤄	E F	E F
Y	Z	Z
𐤆 𐤆	H	H
𐤇 𐤇	Θ	
𐤈	I	I J
𐤉 𐤉	K	K
𐤊 𐤊	Λ	L
𐤋 𐤋	M N	M N
𐤌 𐤌	Ξ O	X O P
O O	Π	
𐤐 𐤐	Ϙ	Q R
𐤑 𐤑	Ρ Σ	S
ϙϙϙ	Τ	T
𐤓	Υ Φ	U V
W	Χ Ψ	W
Χ	Ω	Y

▲ *The first alphabet, with letters standing for sounds, was the Phoenician alphabet. You can see that modern English and ancient Greek alphabets have some letters in common.*

▼ *Letters from the Etruscan alphabet. Etruria was an ancient kingdom in Italy.*

They were the first to develop an alphabet with vowel sounds. With these new vowel letters, one could write the nursery rhyme line as,

THE COW JUMPED OVER THE MOON

This Greek practice was later copied by Etruscans, whose alphabet was in turn copied by the Romans. The Romans created their own symbols. A modern form of the Roman, or *Latin*, alphabet is now used most often in the Western world. Our own ABC's are Roman letters. Roman letters are also used for some of the languages of Africa, which did not have written forms of their own.

Early alphabets had only *capital*, or *upper-case*, letters. Later, to save space, small, or *lower-case*, letters were made. Being more rounded, these letters were easier to write, too.

Several other alphabets are used in the world today besides the modernized Latin symbols. Greeks still use the Greek alphabet. But modern Greek uses sounds and rules for writing and speaking different from those in ancient times. Russians and other Slavic peoples use the *Cyrillic* alphabet, based on old Greek. The alphabets of modern *Hebrew* and modern *Arabic* developed from Aramaic, a language spoken and written in Palestine during the time of Christ. Modern Hebrew is spoken today in Israel. *Early Hebrew*, a much older language, was used to write the Old Testament of the Bible.

Chinese is the only major language of the modern world whose writing is not alphabetical. Its symbols, known as *characters*, stand for words instead of sounds. However, in modern China, a uniform written language based on sounds, is being developed. Japanese writing is based on old Chinese characters, but some symbols represent syllables instead of words.

Without a written alphabet, you could never read a book, or write a letter to a friend, or use a computer. And when your mother sent you to the store, you would have to remember everything very carefully, because you could not make a list!

■ LEARN BY DOING

You can have fun by making up your own alphabet to stand for the sounds of the English language. You can start anywhere and make up your own order. What will you do with the sound "a"? Will your letter be long and pointed like an arrow, or rounded like an acorn? Or will you just make a funny little squiggle? What about the "b" sound? Could this look like a ball or a boat, or will it just be one special shape that always means "b"?

Write down, then say, the words "car," and "kite." Does your alphabet need two different letters for these sounds ("c" and "k")? Can you use one letter for both? What will you do when "c" sounds like "s," as in "cereal"? Would one letter be enough there? What about the "a" sounds in "father" and "face"? Some alphabets use one letter for each sound of the language. Other alphabets use one letter for more than one sound. Will your alphabet use one letter or two to show the "a" sounds of "father" and "face"? Think of other sounds for

which you might want separate letters. How many letters will your alphabet use? ∎

ALSO READ: ARABIC, BRAILLE, CHINESE, HIEROGLYPHICS, WRITTEN LANGUAGE.

ALPS MOUNTAINS The Alps form the largest mountain system in Europe. They curve for 700 miles (1,127 km) from the French Riviera coast, along the French-Italian border, through Switzerland and Austria, and into Yugoslavia. Mont Blanc, 15,771 feet (4,807 m) high, is the highest peak in France and the highest in the Alps. (See the map with the article on EUROPE.)

Have you read the book *Heidi* by Johanna Spyri? Heidi lived in Switzerland with her grandfather and his goats in a high pasture called an *alp*. This Swiss word gave the mountains their name. Many of the people in the Alps today still live in villages in the meadows between peaks. Farmers herd cows and goats high in the mountains in summer, bringing the animals down to shelter in winter. Skilled craftsmen make watches, clocks, toys, and wood carvings.

Mountaineers come to challenge the rocky peaks of the Alps. Snow collects on the mountain slopes, and every winter thousands of people flock to the Alps to ski and enjoy other winter sports. Tourists are also attracted year-round to the lovely scenery of the Alps. Waterfalls pour hundreds of feet down the sides of the mountains. Melted snow flows into deep, blue lakes and into large rivers such as the Danube, Rhine, Rhône, and the Po. Roads and railroads pass beneath the Alps through tunnels, such as the Simplon. Other roads wind over passes, such as the Brenner and Simplon passes.

ALSO READ: EUROPE, GLACIER, MOUNTAIN, SWITZERLAND.

AMAZON Greek myths told of a group of fierce women warriors called Amazons. The myths say that these warlike women lived near the Black Sea in Asia Minor, in what is now Turkey. Theirs was a land ruled by women. When the Amazons captured a man, they made him a slave. They taught their girl children to hunt and fight. They sent away their boy babies. The Amazons were ruled by Queen Hippolyta.

Hercules, a hero of Greek mythology, ventured among the Amazons to take Hippolyta's girdle, or belt. She gave it to him, but they argued, and Hercules killed Hippolyta.

ALSO READ: HERCULES, MYTHOLOGY.

▲ *The Alps have many high mountains including Mont Blanc, the Matterhorn and the Jungfrau.*

▼ *According to legend, Amazons were a race of warrior women who were ruled by a queen and raised only girl children. They fought the Greeks during the Trojan War.*

▶ *The Amazon River winds through thick forest on its way to the Atlantic Ocean. A small number of Amazonian Indians still live by hunting fish with spears.*

The Amazon pours out so much fresh water into the Atlantic Ocean that more than 100 miles (160 km) out at sea from the great river's mouth the ocean's water is still fresh. The Amazon is so wide that the water pouring from its mouth is one-fifth of all the moving fresh water on Earth.

▼ *This fly was trapped in resin millions of years ago when the resin fossilized. The fly was preserved in amber.*

AMAZON RIVER The Amazon River and its tributaries (smaller rivers) make up the largest river system in the world. The Amazon begins high in the Andes Mountains and empties into the Atlantic Ocean, almost 4,000 miles (6,440 km) away. As the Amazon flows east across most of northern Brazil, it is fed by rivers from Peru, Venezuela, Colombia, Ecuador, and Bolivia. (See the map with the article on SOUTH AMERICA.) Only the Nile, in Africa, of all the rivers in the world, is longer than the Amazon. But the Amazon carries more water than any other river.

Francisco de Orellana, a Spaniard, first explored the Amazon in 1541. He later told how he and his men battled with female warriors. He gave the river its name because he thought they were the Amazons, the famous fighting women of Greek mythology.

Regular steamship service up the Amazon began in the 19th century, and settlements developed along the river banks. Today, even though new roads have opened up the country, and people have moved in to settle the land, much of the Amazon region remains unexplored. Most of the Amazon basin (land drained by the river) is a vast, dense jungle—the largest and most valuable rain forest in the world. The basin is about three-fourths the size of the United States. It is the home of animals, such as alligators, anacondas, monkeys,

and sloths, many kinds of insects, and many interesting plants. The flesh-eating piranha fish live in the river. A total area more than twice the size of New Jersey of the Amazon rain forest is destroyed every year. This is mostly to make room for new agriculture. Most scientists think that this destruction is an ecological disaster.

Until the settlers came, the Amazon forest was home to scattered Indian tribes. Few Indians now follow their old way of life, as the modern world has brought change and industry to the Amazon basin.

ALSO READ: AMAZONS; BRAZIL; INDIANS, AMERICAN; JUNGLE; RIVER; SOUTH AMERICA.

AMBASSADOR see FOREIGN SERVICE.

AMBER A piece of amber looks very much like a stone, but it is actually a fossil substance that formed from the sticky, gummy resin of pine trees millions of years ago. The resin was buried, and it hardened after many years in the ground.

Amber is usually golden or reddish-brown. It is almost transparent. In some pieces you can see the bodies of insects that were trapped in the sticky resin before it hardened. Amber is often used to make jewelry today.

ALSO READ: ELECTRICITY, FOSSIL.

AMBULANCE An ambulance, with its lights flashing and its siren wailing, may someday save your life. An ambulance is a "moving hospital." It is a car designed to give first aid to people who are injured in accidents, or who suddenly become very sick. Ambulances carry injured and sick people to hospitals.

The first ambulances were made to follow armies. Before then, wounded soldiers were either carried from the battlefield by their comrades or left lying where they fell until the fighting stopped. Napoleon's personal surgeon, Baron Dominique Jean Larrey, introduced the first ambulances to the French army in 1792. They were light carriages, each pulled by a single horse. They quickly took the wounded from the battlefield.

Ambulances drawn either by horses or mules carried wounded soldiers during the American Civil War. A plan for an ambulance corps was proposed in Congress in 1862. But Congress did not give its approval until 1865, when the war was ending. So the corps played little part in the war.

Many hospitals in the United States began to develop ambulance services after the Civil War. Cincinnati General Hospital was one of the first. Bellevue Hospital in New York also started an ambulance service. Michael Reese Hospital in Chicago was probably the first U.S. hospital to use motor-driven ambulances, in 1899. Since about 1950, helicopters have often been used as ambulances and have saved many lives.

Ambulances played an important part in both the World Wars of the present century. They were used on the battlefield, and also in cities to aid victims of bombing.

Large ambulances today are equipped to handle various kinds of medical emergencies. They carry bandages, drugs, oxygen masks, splints, *resuscitators* (breathing machines), and more. Ambulance attendants with medical training, called *paramedics*, are ready to give emergency treatment as the ambulance speeds to the hospital's emergency room. There are also airplanes specially converted to serve as air ambulances.

ALSO READ: HOSPITAL.

▲ *In an ambulance paramedics take care of the patient on the way to the hospital. This ambulance is attending an accident on an expressway.*

AMENDMENT see CONSTITUTION, UNITED STATES.

AMERICA The United States is often called "America," but this name really belongs to two great continents of the Western Hemisphere— North America and South America. Part of North America, the seven countries from Guatemala to Panama, is called Central America.

The two continents stretch 9,500 miles (15,288 km) from north to south. They vary in width from just 30 miles (48 km) in Panama to more than 4,000 miles (6,440 km) across Alaska and Canada. Millions of years ago, the two continents were separate. Then volcanoes spilled lava that formed the narrow, connecting link known as Central America.

The Americas were explored thousands of years ago by groups of Asian people. Some of them were the ancestors of the Indians and Eskimos of today. For centuries, Europeans did not know that the Americas existed. Vikings visited eastern Canada about A.D. 1000, but their settlements died out. In 1492, Columbus reached the Caribbean islands but thought he was in Asia. A later explorer, Magellan, sailed around the southern tip of the

Potatoes, tobacco, corn, tomatoes, lobsters, and other foods were brought back to Europe from America. In return, Europeans introduced pigs, cattle, horses, poultry, and cereal grains. These exchanges greatly shaped the habits of both Old and New Worlds.

Americas and across the Pacific. Europeans then realized that these lands were two new continents.

An Italian merchant named Amerigo Vespucci persuaded Spanish and Portuguese sea captains to take him along when they visited South America. He returned to Europe and wrote colorful letters claiming he had discovered a new world. One of these letters reached a German geography professor who named the Brazil area *America* (from Amerigo), in honor of Vespucci. The name became popular, and later became the name of both continents.

■ LEARN BY DOING

Imagine you could travel back in time. It would be exciting to discover a new world. Which of the first explorers of America would you choose to be? Maybe an Indian, journeying across the land bridge from Asia? How about Leif Ericson, or Columbus, or Amerigo Vespucci? You could write a history of your adventure. ■

ALSO READ: CENTRAL AMERICA; EXPLORATION; INDIANS, AMERICAN; NORTH AMERICA; SOUTH AMERICA; VIKINGS.

AMERICAN COLONIES The discovery and exploration of North America caused great excitement among seafaring people of Europe. They looked upon America as a New World, as a "land of opportunity." Most of all, they saw it as a source of marvelous treasures. Many of the leading European nations were eager to get the valuable furs, important minerals, and other useful natural resources of North America, so they could grow rich and powerful. They dreamed especially of discovering huge fortunes in gold, silver, and precious gems.

The Spanish were first in the rush to claim some of the riches of North America. They established the first permanent North American fort at St. Augustine, Florida, in 1565. English colonies were not started until after 1600. The French made a claim to Canada and most of the Mississippi Valley. The Dutch got hold of the lands along the Hudson River, and the Swedes took over the region of the Delaware River.

Britain was the most successful of all the nations competing for America's vast wealth. The colonists from France and Spain were interested mainly in trading with the Indians and taking gold and furs back to Europe. But the British colonists were determined to set up permanent homes in the New World. In time, Britain gained control of a large area of land along the Atlantic coast—including the regions that had first

THE THIRTEEN COLONIES (1770)

been claimed by the Dutch and Swedes. Britain had established 13 permanent colonies by 1733. In the North were the *New England colonies*—Massachusetts, Connecticut, New Hampshire, and Rhode Island. The *middle colonies* were New York, Delaware, Pennsylvania, and New Jersey. The *southern colonies* were Virginia, Maryland, North Carolina, South Carolina, and Georgia. These colonies later became the 13 original United States of America.

The Early Settlements A large group of men and boys landed at Virginia in the spring of 1607. They founded the Jamestown Colony, the first permanent British settlement in the New World. A second group of people, the Pilgrims, sailed on the *Mayflower* from Plymouth, England, to the coast of Massachusetts in 1620. There they set up the Plymouth Colony. Puritans came from Britain ten years later to found the Massachusetts Bay Colony, with settlements in Boston and Salem.

Many hardships and dangers awaited these Europeans who first made the long ocean voyage to the New World. America of the 1600's was a vast wilderness. The colonists had to get used to this strange New World. They had to give up many of their Old World habits of living. Even the kinds of food they were used to eating were no longer available to them.

The Indians often lent a helping hand to the colonists. Indians had already explored most of the land, and they knew the best ways to travel the waters and cross the mountains. They showed the colonists where to find minerals and other important resources. They also knew all about the kinds of foods that could be found. The Massachusetts colonists had never even heard of such vegetables as corn, squash, and sweet potatoes. The Indians showed them how to grow these crops and to prepare foods

such as samp, corn pone, hominy, succotash, and popcorn.

But many Indian tribes were not so friendly to the newcomers. They were angry because the white men had forced them out of their homes and hunting grounds. They fought back with all their might. Men and boys in Virginia and Massachusetts had to learn to defend their homes and families from Indian attacks.

Not all the early settlers were prepared for the tough and dangerous life in Colonial America. The Jamestown colonists suffered from the burning heat of summer and the damp cold of winter. They worked hard. Many died of starvation and disease. But luckily, most of the early colonists were brave and hardy folk. They were ready to face all hardships in the struggle to build a new life in the land of opportunity. Many Europeans hoped to make new lives in the New World, so the settlement of America grew quickly after the founding of the earliest colonies. By 1700, the whole eastern coast was peppered with towns.

The People of the Colonies Most colonial settlers were English, but

▲ *Sir Walter Raleigh attempted to establish a colony in Virginia.*

▲ *In the 1500's, the Iroquois Indians of North America united together to protect themselves against the threat of invasion by white settlers.*

Colony	Date Founded	Founder	Reason for settlement	Statehood
Virginia	1607	Capt. John Smith	Profit and trade	June 25, 1788
Massachusetts	1620	William Bradford	Freedom to be Puritans	Feb. 6, 1788
New York	1626	Peter Minuit	Profit and trade	July 26, 1788
New Hampshire	1630	John Mason	Left Massachusetts because rules were too strict	June 21, 1788
Maryland	1634	George Calvert	Freedom to be Roman Catholics	Apr. 28, 1788
Connecticut	1636	Thomas Hooker	Left Massachusetts because rules were too strict	Jan. 9, 1788
Rhode Island	1636	Roger Williams	Thrown out of Massachusetts because he did not conform to Puritan thinking	May 29, 1790
Delaware	1638	Peter Minuit	Profit and trade	Dec. 7, 1787
North Carolina	1653	Eight Lords Proprietors	Profit and trade	Nov. 21, 1789
New Jersey	1664	John Berkeley and George Carteret	Profit and trade	Dec. 18, 1787
South Carolina	1670	Eight Lords Proprietors	Profit and trade	May 23, 1788
Pennsylvania	1682	William Penn	Freedom to be Quakers	Dec. 12, 1787
Georgia	1733	James Oglethorpe	Colonization	Jan. 2, 1788

▲ *This splendid doll was made in colonial times. It is dressed in a plaid cotton dress and straw hat.*

many others were French, Irish, Scottish, Dutch, German, and Swedish. They all had one thing in common—they wanted to make new lives for themselves. Some were drawn to the New World by the promise of work, because in their home countries they were not able to make a good living. Others were excited by the chance to get some land to call their own. The New World offered lands that were cheap, or even free. Still others fled Europe because they were not allowed to worship as they wished there. They hoped to find freedom of religion in the New World colonies. The Pilgrims and the Puritans had been the first religious groups to come to America for this reason. Others were the Quakers, Roman Catholics, and French Protestants known as Huguenots.

Some Europeans who wanted to settle in the New World were poor people who did not have enough money to make the trip. So they offered themselves as *indentured servants* to wealthy colonists. An indentured servant agreed to work for his master for a certain number of years. In return, the master agreed to pay for the servant's trip and to provide him with room and board for the period of his service. But not all indentured servants came to America by choice. Some were criminals who had been forced to leave their countries. A few were black people brought from Africa by white Europeans. Many more blacks were captured in Africa and sold into slavery. Most of the slaves were brought to the southern colonies, to work on the farms. Other slaves were taken to the North and put to work in the homes or shops.

Everyday Life Each one of the three regions—New England, the middle colonies, and the southern colonies—had special conditions that made it different from the others. So people in each region developed different ways of living and working.

All the colonies depended on farming. The South was best suited for large-scale farming. The soil was rich and the climate was warm. Many southern colonists lived on huge plantations where tobacco and rice were grown for export to Britain. Every southern plantation was a tiny village.

The plantation owner, or planter, was mayor, judge, sheriff, preacher, doctor, lawyer, and storekeeper for the community. He and his family often lived in a great mansion. His black slaves lived in small shacks away from the main house. Most of them spent their days at hard labor in the fields. Some were put to work as servants in the planter's home.

Each plantation had its own carpenter, cooper (barrel-maker), blacksmith, cobbler (shoemaker), tanner, and other craftsmen who provided the basic needs of everyday life. From the plentiful plantation trees came the wood for the carpenter and the cooper. The blacksmith used wood for charcoal, which is needed to make ironware. Cotton and flax were grown and made into thread for weaving cloth. Cattle supplied milk and meat, as well as skins for the tanner and leather for the cobbler. Sheep's wool was woven or knitted to make clothing and bedding. Some planters were so rich they did not have to wear homemade clothing. They ordered fine silk gowns, satin breeches, and other fancy clothes from Britain.

The land in New England was rocky, the soil was poor, and the farms were small. Most towns were two rows of wooden or stone houses facing a *common* (a piece of land shared by the community) on which livestock grazed. Unlike the plantation family, the New England family did not raise crops for export to Britain. Each family grew only enough food for itself. The New Englander hardly ever bought ready-made British goods. People made all their own tools, clothing, and furniture. The North was blessed with rich forests, so there was plenty of lumber. New England woodworkers made especially fine furniture.

The main profit of the northern colonies came not from the land, but from the sea. Fishing, shipbuilding, shipping, and whaling were all important industries. Trading ships made

voyages along the Atlantic coast, bringing goods to the other colonies. They also crossed the Atlantic and traded with Europe, Africa, and the West Indies. Whaling ships sailed out of Nantucket, New Bedford, and other New England ports. Voyages sometimes lasted two or three years. One lasted eleven years!

The middle colonies were known as the 'bread" colonies. Their most important export was wheat. They also kept livestock and produced beef, pork, and lamb. Most of the farms were run by single families. But in the Hudson River Valley were large estates where wealthy landowners lived as comfortably as the planters of the South. The rich merchants of the cities also lived in splendid style.

Transportation The early colonists traveled by foot over the Indian paths and wilderness trails, or they rode horseback. For many years, there were no roads outside cities. People found it easier to travel by water than by land. Vessels sailed regularly up and down the coast from port to port. Inland, large rivers, such as the Hudson, were heavily traveled.

Overland travel became easier as city streets were paved with cobblestones and wilderness trails were made into dirt roads. In 1732, a stage-

▲ *The kitchen was the center of family life in most colonial homes. Every kitchen had a fireplace. With its crane and spit, the fireplace was used for cooking as well as heating. This is the kitchen at Wythe House in Colonial Williamsburg.*

▼ *Bacon's Castle, Virginia, was built in 1655. The Virginia Company was given a charter by King James I in 1606, and English colonists settled in Virginia a year later.*

In 1606 the east coast of North America was an almost unbroken wilderness. There were no Europeans except for a small group of Spaniards at St. Augustine, Florida. By 1750, less than 150 years later, there were over 1½ million men, women and children living in the 13 colonies.

▲ *American colonists had to do many jobs for themselves. Here, a man dressed in colonial clothes shows the art of flaxbreaking. The flaxbreak separates linen fiber from its woody core to prepare the fiber for spinning into thread.*

coach journeyed between New York and Philadelphia in record time—one week. Wealthy colonists imported splendid coaches from Europe. These coaches must have been a grand sight, painted with shiny gold and red paint, and drawn by four prancing horses.

But colonists who walked in the cities did not always have such a grand time. City streets were often used as garbage dumps. Hogs and other animals ran free in New York's streets, looking for food among the garbage. Rich people were able to buy *sedans* to avoid all this. The sedan was an enclosed chair with two poles attached to each side. Servants or slaves carried the chair, with its rider, on their shoulders.

School and Church Colonial children helped their parents with everyday chores. But schooling was also an important part of daily life for many children. The three R's—"Reading, 'Riting, and 'Rithmetic"—were the basic lessons taught by every school teacher, whether he or she was teaching in a public school or was hired as a private tutor. America's first public schools were in New England. The schools were free, but only boys could attend. Girls were rarely sent to public schools in colonial times. But both boys and girls could attend a "dame" school, run by a woman who taught in her home. The children learned their three R's seated around the kitchen fire. They made their own pens by carving sharp points from goose quills. They boiled bark to make a syrup that they used as ink.

On southern plantations, the planter's children were tutored by a schoolmaster who lived with the family for several months of the year. Some boys—and a few girls—were sent to private schools in Europe. The first free school in the South was the grammar school at the College of William and Mary, in Williamsburg, Virginia.

Going to church was another important part of colonial life. The

church was not only a place of worship—it was also the center of community life. People in the South enjoyed staying around the church after the services were over. Adults gathered in groups to chat, while boys and girls played tag or hopscotch or flew kites. But the mood in New England churches on Sunday was quite different. The Puritans believed that people should be quiet and serious on the Sabbath. Children were not allowed to shout and play. Every Sunday morning, after the drum roll that announced the beginning of church services, every man, woman, and child had to be in his or her seat at the meeting house. Sermons often lasted three hours in the morning and another three hours in the afternoon.

Recreation Life in colonial times offered many pleasures as well as duties. Fox hunting, horse racing, and week-long house parties made life gay. New England parties were happy occasions that often combined work and play. Neighbors gathered together to husk corn, make quilts, and even build houses.

Like today's Americans, the early colonists especially enjoyed their holidays. Thanksgiving was first observed by the early settlers at Plymouth. But the colonists did not celebrate Christmas as this holiday is celebrated today. For the Puritans believed that it was wrong to be joyful about religion. Christmas did not become a real holiday until the middle of the 1800's. An important holiday in colonial times was the king's birthday.

In time, however, the links with the old homeland, Britain, became strained. The American colonists wanted more freedom to govern their own affairs. This desire grew stronger and stronger, until the colonists declared their break with British rule. A total of 169 years had passed between the time of the first permanent colony, at Jamestown in 1607, and the Declaration of Independence from Britain in 1776. After the 13 colonies won their right to be an independent nation, a happy day on the American calendar was Independence Day, the Fourth of July.

ALSO READ: AGRICULTURE; AMERICAN HISTORY; AMERICAN REVOLUTION; DECLARATION OF INDEPENDENCE; JAMESTOWN; MAYFLOWER; MAYFLOWER COMPACT; PILGRIM SETTLERS; PURITAN; RALEIGH, SIR WALTER; and the articles on each state shown on the table.

AMERICAN HISTORY

Britain did not start to colonize the east coast of North America until more than a century after Columbus and other explorers had begun their explorations of the Western Hemisphere. The first permanent British settlement in the New World was started in 1607 at Jamestown in Virginia. The Virginia Colony was governed by the British governor and the House of Burgesses. The people elected the *burgesses* (representatives) to this assembly beginning in 1619. The Virginia House of Burgesses was the first representative assembly in America.

A second British settlement was started when the Pilgrims landed at Plymouth, Massachusetts, in 1620. The Pilgrims had left home because they were not allowed to worship God in their own way. They were part of a large group of people called *Puritans*, who wanted to "purify" the Church of England. Another group of Puritans founded the Massachusetts Bay Colony at Boston and Salem in 1630. The British had set up 13 colonies along the Atlantic Coast, from Maine to Georgia, by 1733.

Many North American Indians were friendly to the settlers and helped them learn the ways of the new land. But often bloody fights broke out between the colonists and the Indians. The Indians fought be- cause the colonists were taking over their lands.

The Roots of Revolution Wars fought by Spain, France, and Britain caused fighting in several parts of America during most of the 1700's. In America these were called the French and Indian Wars. Both the French and the British had Indians fighting for them. France lost the French and Indian Wars, and by 1763 Great Britain had gained nearly all French land in America, including Canada. The British needed money to pay their war debts. So Parliament decided to tax the colonies. The angry American colonists felt the taxes were unfair, because they had no representatives in Parliament. But even though they protested, King George III and Parliament would not end the taxes. Colonists who took the side of the king were called *Loyalists* or *Tories*. Other colonists wanted independence from Britain. They were called *Patriots*. Still others—probably a majority— had a "wait and see" attitude.

The Patriots felt that Britain was taking away rights that they deserved as free citizens. They could not get enough help from the British Parlia-

▲ *An Indian chief drawn in about 1585. As settlers moved westward and took over the most fertile land, they came into conflict with the Indians.*

▼ *A model of the "Santa Maria," the ship in which Christopher Columbus made his first Atlantic crossing in 1492.*

▲ *Two of the many different North American shelters: a bark tepee built by Cree Indians, and a Creek Indian house of branches.*

▲ *Early Puritan settlers in North America. They went there from England so that they could worship God in the way they wanted.*

▲ *Covered wagons, drawn by oxen or horses, carried pioneers westward. Settlers survived through their skills as hunters and farmers.*

ment, or from the king and his ministers. The colonists, therefore, defied the British government. This was particularly true in Massachusetts and in the city of Boston, beginning about 1761. Resistance had spread to other large cities by 1765. It continued to grow for ten years.

The Fight for Independence One night in April, 1775, the Patriots learned that British troops planned to capture guns and ammunition stored by the colonists in Concord, Massachusetts. Leaders of the Patriots were in danger of arrest, so Paul Revere and other Minutemen rode for miles through the darkness to warn them. The American Revolution began the next day at the Battles of Lexington and Concord.

The fighting lasted for almost seven years, during which George Washington was the commander in chief of the Continental Army. He kept the soldiers of the ill-equipped colonial army together until they won the war in 1781. In the peace treaty, signed in 1783, Great Britain recognized the independence of the United States of America, and turned over to the new country all British lands east of the Mississippi.

A national flag for the new United States was approved on June 14, 1777, during the Revolution. This first flag, the original Stars and Stripes, had one star for each state and 13 stripes to stand for the first 13 colonies.

The new nation needed laws to guide and protect its people. A first attempt at setting up a system of national law was made in the Articles of Confederation, which became law in 1781. But the system did not work, and a new Constitution of the United States was created in 1787. Adopted in 1789, it is still the basic law of the land today. Under the Constitution, a President is elected by the people every four years. The country called on George Washington again. He was

elected the first President and took office on April 30, 1789.

The Union Expands Not all Americans were content to live in the settled areas of the eastern coast. Looking for land to farm, some began to move west toward the Ohio River even before the Revolution. The land between the Appalachian Mountains and the Mississippi River was quickly settled. It was soon divided up into states, which joined the Union. By 1800, three more states—Vermont, Kentucky, and Tennessee—had joined the original 13.

The size of the country was more than doubled in 1803 by the Louisiana Purchase. The U.S., under the leadership of President Thomas Jefferson, paid France 15 million dollars for a huge tract of land that extended from the Mississippi River west to the Rocky Mountains, and from New Orleans all the way to Canada. Two young army officers, Meriwether Lewis and William Clark, explored this new land for the U.S. Government. Lewis and Clark traveled beyond the Rockies to the Pacific Ocean. Their glowing reports of the western frontier made many Americans decide to move west.

The United States and Britain went to war again in 1812, fighting over the freedom of U.S. ships at sea. U.S. troops burned government buildings at York (now Toronto) in Canada. In August, 1814, the British burned the U.S. Capitol, some other buildings, and the President's House in return. President James Madison had the house painted white to cover the scars and smoke stains. The home of the President of the United States has been called the "White House" since that time.

The U.S. continued to grow in size and political power after the War of 1812. Spain sold Florida to the U.S. in 1819. Settlements were founded beyond the Mississippi by pioneers who traveled to the West in wagon trains. Many Americans settled in Texas, which belonged to Mexico at that time. They fought with the Mexicans over laws and boundaries. In San Antonio, in 1836, an entire group of Texan Americans was killed by Mexican soldiers in the Battle of the Alamo. Angry Texans crying, 'Remember the Alamo!" defeated the Mexicans a few weeks later. The Texans then went on to win their independence from Mexico. Texas was *annexed*, or added, to the Union as a state in 1845. The U.S. and Mexico fought over this annexation in the Mexican War from 1846 to 1848. The U.S. won. Mexico agreed to sell much of its western land, including California, to the U.S.

In 1849, gold was discovered in the new U.S. land of California. Many people, called 'Forty-Niners," went west in the search for gold. Other travelers to the West went to make new lives for themselves and their families. The trip westward was long and dangerous. The Oregon Trail, which many of these pioneers took,

was more than 2,000 miles (3,220 km) long. Indian attacks troubled almost every wagon train.

The Civil War In the first half of the 1800's, debate between the North and the South on the question of slavery became more and more bitter. Slaves brought from Africa had been used on the large plantations in the South since colonial times. When cotton became a popular crop, more and more slaves were needed. The South's prosperity was based on the slavery system. In the North, slavery was not profitable and most Northern states had laws against it. A large group of Northerners believed that slavery should not be allowed in new territories. They wanted to *abolish* (get rid of) slavery in the whole country. They were known as *abolitionists*. States' rights became a major issue. The Southern states saw less and less reason for staying in the Union.

In 1860—the year Abraham Lincoln was elected President—several southern states *seceded from* (left) the

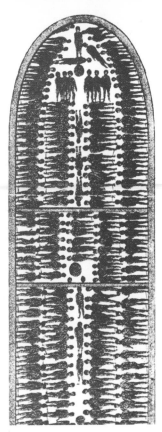

▲ *Slave ships packed like this sailed from Africa to the United States in the early 1800's.*

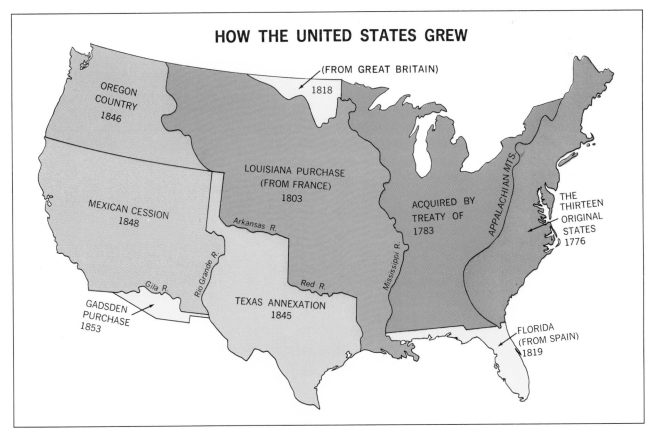

HOW THE UNITED STATES GREW

OREGON COUNTRY 1846

(FROM GREAT BRITAIN) 1818

MEXICAN CESSION 1848

LOUISIANA PURCHASE (FROM FRANCE) 1803

Arkansas R.

ACQUIRED BY TREATY OF 1783

APPALACHIAN MTS.

THE THIRTEEN ORIGINAL STATES 1776

Gila R.

Rio Grande R.

Red R.

Mississippi R.

GADSDEN PURCHASE 1853

TEXAS ANNEXATION 1845

FLORIDA (FROM SPAIN) 1819

▲ *A new nation's victory. The British surrender to the American forces at Yorktown.*

▶ *First President of the new republic, George Washington.*

▲ *A nation divided by war between North and South.*

▼ *The first telephone call on the new New York to Chicago line in 1892.*

▼ *Henry Ford and other automakers sent a nation off on a new craze—the automobile.*

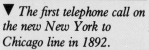

▲ *America takes wing. And the Wright brothers write a new page in history.*

AMERICAN HISTORY TIMETABLE

Peopling a wilderness
Over 25,000 years ago the first people to settle North America travel across the land bridge linking the continent to Asia

1400's–1600's
First European exploration
First English settlement, at Jamestown, 1607
Pilgrims sail to Massachusetts, 1620
New York founded, 1624

1630–1760's
The colonies grow
From 1650 to 1750 the population of the colonies increases from 52,000 to 1,600,000.

1775–1789
A new nation is born
Declaration of Independence, 1776
Revolutionary War ends with British surrender at Yorktown, 1781

1803–1900
A century of expansion
Louisana Purchase, 1803, doubles the size of the country
War with Mexico 1846–48
California Gold Rush 1849
Alaska purchase, from Russia, 1867
First railroad link across the country, 1869
Civil War, 1861–65, followed by the years of Reconstruction
Many immigrants from Europe settle in the United States, 1840–1900

1870–1920
Industrial growth
Invention speeds the nation's progress:
electric light, 1879; telephone, 1892; first airplane flight, 1903; Ford Model T, 1908. United States at war; World War I, 1917–18

1920–1945
Prosperity, depression, war
After 1920's Boom comes Depression of 1930. New Deal helps restore confidence
World War II, and United States at war following Pearl Harbor, 1941

1945–today
A world power
Atomic age, 1945
Korean War 1950–53
Supreme court rules against segregation, 1954
First U.S. space satellite, 1958
Vietnam War, 1968–73
Moonlanding, Apollo 11 1969

▲ *Uncle Sam called volunteers to fight in World War I.*

▼ *World War II saw the attack by the Japanese on Pearl Harbor.*

▲ *Lean years between world wars: the economic depression of the 1930's.*

▲ *The nation was divided over the rights and wrongs of the Vietnam War.*

▶ *President Kennedy vowed to send Americans to the moon, opening a new era in exploration.*

When the Civil War began, President Lincoln hoped that he would need only 75,000 volunteers for a few months to put down the uprising. In the end, four million men fought in a cruel war that lasted for four long years.

Union and formed a new government. They called themselves the Confederate States of America. They chose Jefferson Davis as their president. The Civil War began on April 12, 1861, when Confederate soldiers fired on a U.S. fort, Fort Sumter, in the harbor of Charleston, South Carolina.

Abraham Lincoln remained President of the U.S. throughout the four-year war. General Ulysses S. Grant was the most famous of the commanders of the Union forces. Robert E. Lee was the commanding general of the Confederate army. In this war, brother often fought against brother, and friend against friend. After the North won this long and bloody war, two things were settled—slavery was abolished, and it was clear that no state could leave the Union. Just five days after the Civil War ended, President Lincoln was assassinated in Ford's Theater in Washington, D.C. by John Wilkes Booth, an actor who was a strong supporter of the South.

The Railroad Helps Settle the West
The U.S. went through a period of prosperity for the next 20 years, mostly due to the growth of transportation. Railroads were built, running all the way to the Pacific coast. This

opened up the West for further settlement. Cattle raising, land development, lumbering, and silver mining made the western lands prosperous.

But the new settlers, miners, and ranchers posed a serious threat to the Indians. The American Indians were fighting not only for their lives, but for their way of life. They were being driven from their ancient hunting grounds, from the homelands that had been theirs for generations. One tribe that fought the hardest was the Apache. The Apache War raged in New Mexico, Arizona, and Texas. It lasted almost 40 years, and was probably the bloodiest Indian war. Other serious Indian wars were the Sioux War in North and South Dakota, Minnesota, and Montana; the Nez Percé War in the Pacific Northwest; and the Modoc War in California.

In the East, where manufacturing had become the most important business, another kind of fight was going on. The long struggle between factory owners and workers had started. Labor unions were seeking better working conditions, higher pay, and shorter hours for workers.

By 1890 there was scarcely any frontier (completely unsettled land) left. The nation stretched from the Atlantic to the Pacific. Forty-five states had been formed by the time the 20th century started. Three more states came into the Union in the next 12 years. The admission of huge Alaska and distant Hawaii in 1959 brought the number to 50 states.

A World Power Another war took place before the end of the 1800's. The Spanish-American War, fought with Spain in 1898 over Cuba's independence, began when a U.S. battleship, the *Maine*, was blown up in the harbor of Havana, Cuba. America won this brief conflict, and the world began to realize that the young country was becoming a power to reckon with. Under President Theodore Roosevelt, the U.S. dug the Panama

▼ *During the Depression years of the 1930's hunger and unemployment brought hardship to many Americans.*

◄ *U.S. Navy warships crippled by Japanese bombing. The attack on Pearl Harbor brought the United States into World War II in 1941.*

Canal, which made it possible for ships to go from the Atlantic to the Pacific without going around stormy Cape Horn at the southern tip of South America.

World War I started in Europe in 1914. Germany fought against France and Britain. America did not want to enter this war at first. But events forced the country to fight. President Woodrow Wilson and Congress declared war on Germany in April, 1917. With fresh American troops helping out, Germany was defeated in 1918.

For more than ten years the world tried to recover from the debts and social changes brought about by the war. But finally there was a worldwide economic depression. The Depression began in the U.S. in 1929. Many people did not have jobs or money during this time, and they could not buy food or clothing. The government started many new building projects to make work so that people could earn at least some money. Highways, dams, bridges, and public buildings were constructed.

The U.S. was at peace with the rest of the world for 20 years after World War I. Then in 1939 World War II broke out in Europe. Germany, under Adolf Hitler and his Nazi party, aided by Italy, attacked and captured many European and North African countries. The U.S. still did not want to enter another world war. But the

Japanese, who were allies of the Germans and Italians, bombed the American naval base at Pearl Harbor, Hawaii, on December 7, 1941. Congress declared war on Japan, Germany, and Italy. Not until the Germans surrendered in May, 1945, was the war over in Europe. Japan did not surrender until August of that year, after the U.S. had dropped the first atom bombs on two Japanese cities.

One of the results of World War II was the organization of the United Nations. Nearly all the countries of the world belong to the UN. The representatives of the member nations work together to try to solve world problems. When war broke out between the North and South Koreans in 1950, the UN sent troops to defend the South Koreans from the North Korean Communists. The

The annual income of 250 million Americans is roughly equal to the total income of all the three billion people of Asia, Africa, and South America.

▼ *A U.S. soldier with a Vietnamese child. The Vietnam War was one of the great issues troubling the nation in the 1960's and early 1970's.*

Most people know the story of how Israel Putnam dropped his plow in the field and rode a day on horseback to Boston after hearing the news of the battle of Lexington. What is not so well known is that Putnam did volunteer and fight at Bunker Hill and elsewhere as a general in the American Revolution.

U.S. gave the largest share of troops and equipment.

In spite of its war efforts, the United States had become more and more prosperous. Americans enjoyed a higher standard of living than any other people on Earth. Industry grew steadily through the 1950's.

Because of its position as the world's strongest and richest nation, the United States plays a leading part in world affairs. Its main rival in foreign affairs is the U.S.S.R. In the 1950's and 1960's U.S. personnel were sent to help the South Vietnamese in their war against the Communist North Vietnamese. By 1965 U.S. troops were fighting in Vietnam. The Vietnam War led to discontent at home. A peace accord was signed in 1973, to conclude the longest and unhappiest overseas war fought by Americans.

On July 20, 1969 two U.S. astronauts became the first men to walk on the moon. They left on the moon a sign which read, "We came in peace for all mankind." The U.S. has continued to advance in space technology, despite setbacks to its manned shuttle program. U.S. achievements in communications, computers, laser science, and microbiology in particular have been considerable. U.S. doctors have pioneered advanced surgery, such as organ transplants. During the late 1980's, relations between the U.S. and the U.S.S.R. improved, and a start was made in mutual disarmament.

For further information on:

Government, *see* ARTICLES OF CONFEDERATION; CABINET, U.S.; CONSTITUTION, U.S.; FLAG; UNITED STATES GOVERNMENT.

Life, *see* AMERICAN COLONIES; BLACK AMERICANS; EXPLORATION; HISPANIC AMERICANS; INDIANS, AMERICAN; PIONEER LIFE.

Major Events, *see* AMERICAN REVOLUTION, CIVIL RIGHTS MOVEMENT, CIVIL WAR, DEPRESSION, FRENCH AND INDIAN WAR, GOLD RUSH, INDIAN WARS, KOREAN CONFLICT, MEXICAN WAR, RECONSTRUCTION, SPANISH-AMERICAN WAR, WAR OF 1812, WORLD WAR I, WORLD WAR II, VIETNAM WAR.

Also read articles on each state and each President.

AMERICAN INDIAN see INDIANS, AMERICAN.

AMERICAN REVOLUTION

"These United Colonies are, and of right ought to be Free and Independent States." So said the Second Continental Congress in the Declaration of Independence in 1776. Many events happened before the colonists were ready to take this stand. It took

▶ *"Give me liberty or give me death." Patrick Henry uttered these famous words before a convention of Virginians in 1775. They expressed the mood of an America ready to fight for freedom.*

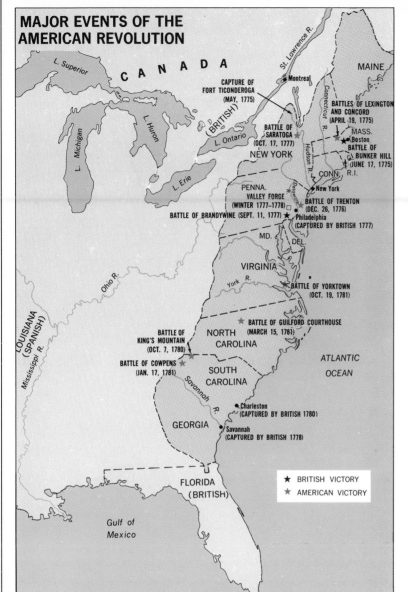

MAJOR EVENTS OF THE AMERICAN REVOLUTION

L. Superior

C A N A D A

MAINE

L. Michigan

L. Huron

L. Ontario

St. Lawrence R.

Montreal

CAPTURE OF
FORT TICONDEROGA
(MAY, 1775)

(BRITISH)

BATTLE OF
SARATOGA
(OCT. 17, 1777)

BATTLES OF LEXINGTON
AND CONCORD
(APRIL 19, 1775)

L. Erie

NEW YORK

Connecticut R.

MASS.
Boston
BATTLE OF
BUNKER HILL
(JUNE 17, 1775)

Hudson R.

CONN.
R.I.

PENNA.
VALLEY FORGE
(WINTER 1777–1778)

New York

Delaware R.

BATTLE OF TRENTON
(DEC. 26, 1776)

BATTLE OF BRANDYWINE (SEPT. 11, 1777)

Philadelphia
(CAPTURED BY BRITISH 1777)

MD.

DEL.

Ohio R.

VIRGINIA

LOUISIANA
(SPANISH)

Mississippi R.

York R.

BATTLE OF YORKTOWN
(OCT. 19, 1781)

BATTLE OF GUILFORD COURTHOUSE
(MARCH 15, 1781)

BATTLE OF
KING'S MOUNTAIN
(OCT. 7, 1780)

NORTH
CAROLINA

ATLANTIC
OCEAN

BATTLE OF COWPENS
(JAN. 17, 1781)

SOUTH
CAROLINA

Savannah R.

Charleston
(CAPTURED BY BRITISH 1780)

GEORGIA

Savannah
(CAPTURED BY BRITISH 1778)

★ BRITISH VICTORY
★ AMERICAN VICTORY

FLORIDA
(BRITISH)

Gulf of
Mexico

▲ *A group of patriotic Americans at the First Continental Congress in 1774. They came from far and wide to plan joint action against the British.*

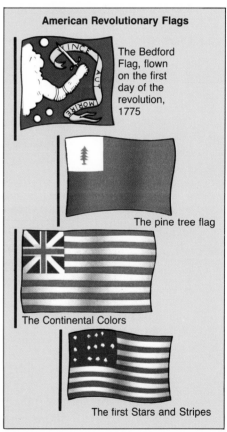

American Revolutionary Flags

The Bedford Flag, flown on the first day of the revolution, 1775

The pine tree flag

The Continental Colors

The first Stars and Stripes

◄ *The signing of the Declaration of Independence on July 4, 1776, was the highlight of the Revolution and the birth of a new nation. To all the world, it served notice of a new order—the rights of the people had now replaced the rights of kings.*

AMERICAN REVOLUTION

▶ *The Battle of Lexington, 1775. British troops fire their muskets at the fleeing Lexington militia.*

The chief weapon used in the American Revolution was the flintlock musket with a bayonet. Each soldier carried cartridges of paper, lead balls, and black powder in a box slung over his shoulder.

When the original 13 colonies declared their independence in 1776, the United States was only a fourth of its present size. By 1850 it was a nation of 31 states stretching from the Atlantic to the Pacific, an area of 3 million square miles (nearly 8 million sq. km).

a long and hard struggle to make these words come true.

The British won the French and Indian War in 1763. They needed money to pay for the war and govern Canada and the eastern Mississippi Valley, which they had taken from the French. Parliament decided to raise funds by increasing taxes in the American colonies. The Stamp Act of 1765 required that tax stamps had to be bought for wills, deeds, and other legal documents. Every newspaper, magazine, almanac, or calendar sold in the colonies also had to be stamped. Americans were not allowed to have anyone represent them (speak and vote for them) when tax laws were made in Parliament. "No taxation without representation," was the cry of the angry colonists. They wanted the right to make their own laws, not to be ruled by the Parliament in Britain.

Trouble in Boston Another act of Parliament that the colonists hated was the Quartering Act. The colonies had to provide housing and supplies for British soldiers in America. The people of Boston and New York,

where many troops were stationed, were especially upset by this law. A noisy crowd of men and boys gathered near Boston's Customs House on a cold March day in 1770. Some of the boys threw snowballs at a British sentry. The sentry called for other soldiers, and the crowd became angrier and angrier. Shots rang out. Three Americans lay dead and eight were wounded (two of the wounded died later). Crispus Attucks, a leader of the crowd and probably a runaway slave, was the first to die. This incident was called the *Boston Massacre*.

The Boston colonists were spurred to violence again three years later, in December of 1773. The British shipped tea to America. The tea tax was small, but the colonists were not allowed to vote on the tax. The protest known as the Boston Tea Party was held when the ships arrived in Boston Harbor with their cargo. Colonists disguised as Indians dumped 342 chests of tea into the harbor. The British promptly closed Boston Harbor. The British governor sailed home, leaving General Thomas Gage in command. The Quartering Act, which had been stopped, was started again. And if a British official were charged with a crime against a colonist, he was not tried locally, but was sent to Britain for trial.

The people of Boston and of Massachusetts were angry. So were many other colonists. The First Continental Congress met in Philadelphia in September, 1774. Every colony except Georgia was represented. The Congress formed the Continental Association, adopted a declaration of rights, and decided not to import British goods. The delegates agreed to meet again the following May if Parliament did not rewrite the unjust laws.

The Shot Heard 'Round the World
In April, 1775, General Gage marched his British troops from Boston, through Lexington, to Concord. Spies had told the British commander that guns and ammunition were stored in Concord. These spies also told Gage that two patriot leaders, Samuel Adams and John Hancock, were hiding in Lexington. Gage planned to capture the supplies and the rebels. But the Americans also had spies. When the red-coated British started their secret march, two Americans saddled their horses and sped through the darkness to warn the colonists at Lexington and Concord that the British were coming.

Those heroic riders were Paul Revere and William Dawes. They were aided by Dr. Samuel Prescott, who took the warning to Concord after Revere was captured.

Gage's 700 or 800 redcoats met a band of Minutemen (farmers and shopkeepers who were ready at a minute's notice) lined up on Lexington's village green. No one knows who fired the first shot. But, in the shooting that followed, eight Americans were killed and the rest scattered. The British marched on to Concord. British troops did not find Adams, Hancock, or the supplies, because Dr. Prescott had warned the colonists in Concord.

The British dumped several barrels of flour and set fire to some buildings at Concord before starting back to Boston. The redcoats found their return route blocked by angry Minutemen. Aroused by the news of the Americans killed at Lexington, hundreds of farmers and merchants swarmed toward Concord. The British fought off an attack on Concord's North Bridge. But their return march became a nightmarish retreat. Rifles and muskets were fired from behind every stone wall, building, or brushpile that could hide a Minuteman. By the time the redcoats finally reached the safety of their barracks, 273 of

The Revolutionary War was a small war compared with modern ones. Large numbers of men were never involved. There were never more than 20,000 men in the American army. Estimates of the number of American soldiers killed in the war vary between 5,000 and 12,000.

◀ *The Battle of Bunker Hill was one of the first battles of the war. During this fight, when ammunition was scarce, the American colonel, William Prescott, told his men, "Don't shoot until you see the whites of their eyes."*

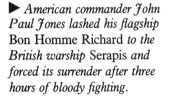

▲ *In this famous painting by Emanuel Leutze, George Washington is shown crossing the Delaware River on Christmas night, 1776, to attack Hessian soldiers in New Jersey.*

► *American commander John Paul Jones lashed his flagship* Bon Homme Richard *to the British warship* Serapis *and forced its surrender after three hours of bloody fighting.*

companies of Virginia volunteer soldiers. His name was George Washington.

The first major battle of the war—the Battle of Bunker Hill—was fought on June 17, 1775. It actually took place on nearby Breed's Hill. The British captured the hill, but more than twice as many British soldiers were killed or wounded as Americans. Many American colonists—called Loyalists—were still against breaking away from Britain, even though battles had been fought and men killed. This deep-seated struggle between American Patriots and Loyalists went on throughout the Revolution.

The Declaration Leads to Full-Scale War The Continental Congress continued to hope until the summer of 1776 that Great Britain would be fair to the colonies. Then a delegate from Virginia finally offered a resolution for full independence. Thomas Jefferson wrote the first draft of the document that declared the colonies were free. John Adams and Benjamin Franklin made small changes. Other minor changes were made by the Congress. The Declaration of Independence was adopted in Philadelphia, on July 4, 1776.

That summer, the British shifted the fighting from Boston to New

their number had been killed or wounded.

One month later, Ethan Allen and Benedict Arnold led the Green Mountain Boys in the capture of Fort Ticonderoga, the most important British fortress north of the Hudson River. News of their daring attack encouraged the delegates to the Second Continental Congress in Philadelphia. The Congress now had to deal with a real war, so they called for a real army. The Congress chose a wealthy planter from Virginia to command this Continental Army. He was well suited for the job. He had been a lieutenant colonel in Britain's wars with France, and he later led several

York. Washington's army was pushed from Long Island and Manhattan by troops led by Sir William Howe. Washington was forced to retreat into New Jersey and then into Pennsylvania. Washington and his men crossed the ice-packed Delaware River on Christmas night, 1776, in open boats and captured the garrison at Trenton, New Jersey. The troops at Trenton were German soldiers, called Hessians, whom the British paid to fight for them. The Americans won a small victory a few days later at Princeton, New Jersey. The British then began a major attempt to capture Philadelphia, the colonial capital. Philadelphia was taken from American hands in the fall of 1777. This was a staggering blow. The Continental Congress moved the capital to York, Pennsylvania, about 80 miles (129 km) west of Philadelphia.

The Tide Turns The British tried to cut the colonies in half by advancing south from Canada with another army commanded by General John Burgoyne. But they were forced to surrender at the Battle of Saratoga in New York. This American victory was the turning point of the war. The

French became allies of the Americans after Saratoga. French soldiers, ships, and money aided the American cause. Spain also helped, and the Netherlands loaned money for the fight.

But the American cause was in danger during the dreadful winter of 1777–1778. The British held Philadelphia. The government was in exile at York. And General Washington was camped in the snow at Valley Forge. His men were starving and frozen. The young French nobleman, the Marquis de Lafayette, was barely 20 when he joined General Washington and spent that winter at Valley Forge. Lafayette did not believe that men could survive such misery and hardship. Washington stated in one report that 3,000 men could not fight because they had no shoes or warm clothing.

Baron von Steuben, a friend of Benjamin Franklin, brought hope and encouragement to the Americans in the spring of 1778. Von Steuben, a former Prussian (German) officer, trained the Continental soldiers until they became better fighters, both in groups and as individuals.

The American Navy had had only

▲ *A group of war-weary Americans encamped at Valley Forge. Although supplies were short, many men braved the terrible winter of 1777-78. They stayed with George Washington to fight again.*

It has been estimated that the Revolutionary War cost the United States about a hundred million dollars.

AMERICAN REVOLUTION

When the United States bought the Louisiana territory from France in 1803, it doubled its size overnight and added an area which made up almost 13 present-day states. The purchase cost about three cents an acre for what proved to be some of the richest food-producing land in the world.

four ships when the Revolution began. Congress later had more built. Many small, privately owned ships were used as *privateers*, seizing British supply and merchant ships. They also transported arms from France. John Paul Jones was a hero of the war at sea. With his ship, the *Bon Homme Richard*, he captured the British warship *Serapis* in a spectacular battle in 1779.

George Rogers Clark of Virginia captured several British forts in the region of Illinois and Michigan in 1778 and 1779. Clark's victories over the British and their Indian allies helped the Americans gain more favorable terms when the peace treaty was signed. Britain was forced to give all lands east of the Mississippi River to the Americans.

The British turned their efforts to the southern colonies in 1780 and 1781. They captured Savannah, Georgia, and won at Charleston, South Carolina. But they lost at Kings Mountain and Cowpens. American heroes of the South included Francis Marion, the 'Swamp Fox," whose guerrilla-like (hit-and-run) warfare confused the British troops, and led to their defeat.

Surrender at Yorktown Lord Cornwallis marched his British troops north and occupied Yorktown, in

midsummer of 1781. He wanted to help the Royal Navy control Virginia, Maryland, and the Chesapeake Bay.

General Washington and the French leader, Count Rochambeau, cornered the British troops with the help of Lafayette and "Mad Anthony" Wayne. The French navy, led by Admiral de Grasse, blocked escape by sea. Lord Cornwallis surrendered at Yorktown on October 17, 1781.

John Adams, Benjamin Franklin, and John Jay started peace talks for the Americans in April, 1782. When the Treaty of Paris was signed in September, 1783, Great Britain granted independence to the Americans and recognized the new United States of America.

For further information on:
Background, *see* AMERICAN COLONIES, BOSTON MASSACRE, BOSTON TEA PARTY, CONTINENTAL CONGRESS, DECLARATION OF INDEPENDENCE, FRENCH AND INDIAN WAR.
Leaders for Independence, *see* ADAMS, SAMUEL; FRANKLIN, BENJAMIN; HANCOCK, JOHN; HENRY, PATRICK; JEFFERSON, THOMAS; PAINE, THOMAS; REVERE, PAUL.
Leaders in War *see* ALLEN, ETHAN; CLARK, GEORGE ROGERS; HALE, NATHAN; JONES, JOHN PAUL; LAFAYETTE, MARQUIS DE; MARION, FRANCIS; WASHINGTON, GEORGE.

▶ *Supported by the French, Washington's American army compelled the British forces of Cornwallis to surrender at Yorktown, Virginia in October, 1781. The peace treaty was signed in 1783.*

www.wadsworth.com

wadsworth.com is the World Wide Web site for Wadsworth Publishing Company and is your direct source to dozens of online resources.

At *wadsworth.com* you can find out about supplements, demonstration software, and student resources. You can also send e-mail to many of our authors and preview new publications and exciting new technologies.

wadsworth.com
Changing the way the world learns®

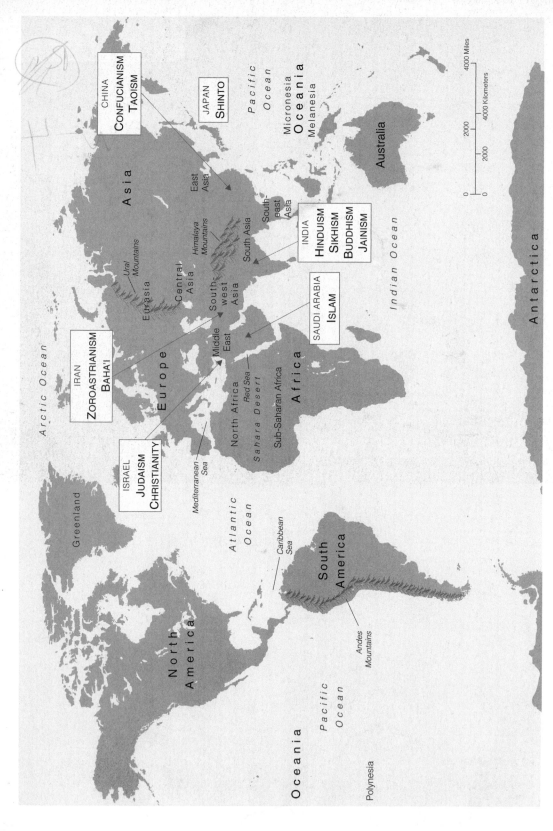

Geographical birthplaces of some of the living religious traditions.

SIXTH EDITION

WAYS
TO THE
CENTER

AN INTRODUCTION TO WORLD RELIGIONS

Denise Lardner Carmody
Santa Clara University

T. L. Brink
Crafton Hills College

THOMSON

WADSWORTH

Australia • Canada • Mexico • Singapore • Spain • United Kingdom • United States

Publisher: Holly J. Allen
Acquisitions Editor: Steve Wainwright
Assistant Editor: Lee McCracken and Barbara Hillaker
Editorial Assistant: John Gahbauer
Technology Project Manager: Julie Aguilar
Marketing Manager: Worth Hawes
Marketing Assistant: Andrew Keay
Advertising Project Manager: Bryan Vann
Project Manager, Editorial Production: Megan E. Hansen

Art Director: Maria Epes
Print/Media Buyer: Judy Inouye
Permissions Editor: Kiely Sisk
Production Service: Aaron Downey, Matrix Productions, Inc.
Copy Editor: Lauren Root
Cover Designer: Yvo Riezebos
Cover Image: © Jim Zuckerman/CORBIS
Compositor: International Typesetting and Composition
Printer: Transcontinental Printing/Louiseville

Printed in Canada
1 2 3 4 5 6 7 09 08 07 06 05

For more information about our products, contact us at:
Thomson Learning Academic Resource Center
1-800-423-0563
For permission to use material from this text or product, submit a request online at
http://www.thomsonrights.com.
Any additional questions about permissions can be submitted by email to thomsonrights@thomson.com.

Library of Congress Control Number: 2004117062

ISBN 0-534-52120-7

Thomson Higher Education
10 Davis Drive
Belmont, CA 94002-3098
USA

Asia (including India)
Thomson Learning
5 Shenton Way
#01-01 UIC Building
Singapore 068808

Australia/New Zealand
Thomson Learning Australia
102 Dodds Street
Southbank, Victoria 3006
Australia

Canada
Thomson Nelson
1120 Birchmount Road
Toronto, Ontario M1K 5G4
Canada

UK/Europe/Middle East/Africa
Thomson Learning
High Holborn House
50-51 Bedford Road
London WC1R 4LR
United Kingdom

Latin America
Thomson Learning
Seneca, 53
Colonia Polanco
11560 Mexico
D.F. Mexico

Spain (including Portugal)
Thomson Paraninfo
Calle Magallanes, 25
28015 Madrid, Spain

BRIEF CONTENTS

CONTENTS

CHAPTER **7**

Greek and Hellenistic Religion   201

CHAPTER **8**

Buddhism   221

CHAPTER **11**

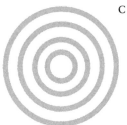

PREFACE

TO THE INSTRUCTOR

We want to be your partner in your students' educational endeavor. We have operated under the assumption that you have a unique depth of expertise in some areas of scholarship and a unique classroom (or online) style of teaching. Our goal is to complement your strengths by providing a foundational textbook. Every textbook strives for a balance between in-depth scholarship and readability. When we had to come down on one side or the other, we erred on the side of the student, choosing to be comprehensible rather than comprehensive. Our goal has been to create a foundation for understanding culture and history in general, and religious phenomena in particular. We must rely on your expertise as scholar and instructor to build on that foundation. Let's keep in touch so that we can improve the book and share learning resources. Most of our materials can be found in the public file cabinet at http://www.ureach.com/tlbrink.

There are also Blackboard, WebCT, and Etudes sites to which your students may gain access. Contact us at the following websites if you want a current list or if you have placed materials accessible to other students:
TL_Brink@redlands.edu
TLBrink@yahoo.com

A NOTE TO STUDENTS

We want you to read the book, but we want to emphasize the great value of our free and easily accessed online materials: drills, games, puzzles, and practice quizzes. The QUIA links are listed in the book, and the other materials can be found at several places on the Web, such as the public file cabinet at http:// www.ureach.com/tlbrink

These materials can be downloaded and distributed on other Web sites and media. If you place them on other Web sites for general access, let us know.

If you want to know about other Web locations, e-mail us:

TL_Brink@redlands.edu
TLBrink@yahoo.com

We hope that you will participate in our moderated forum at http://forums.delphiforums.com/rel101 and encourage your professor to do so. We are especially interested in your feedback so that the next edition of this text can be even better.

T. L. Brink
Denise Lardner Carmody

REACTIONS TO THIS COURSE				
STUDENT	GENDER	AGE	DENOMINATION	REACTION
J	Male	19	Mormon	"This class made it apparent to me just how important my religion is in my life. I was wondering whether if I should take two years off and go on a mission, but now I am certain that this is an experience I do not want to miss."
S	Female	24	Jehovah's Witness	"I was pretty quiet during most of the class but it made me think. About two years later, I just couldn't see the relevance of knocking on doors to tell people something they had already heard and did not want to hear again. I will probably go back to being a Roman Catholic."
T	Female	38	Presbyterian	"Since my divorce, I have had serious depression and loneliness. The Presbyterians were the ones that seemed the friendliest church, at least in my small town. I still don't agree with Calvinism, but I don't think that should stop me from joining them."
V	Female	19	Jewish	"My parents were Jewish, but we weren't strict or kosher. We made it to temple once or twice a year. Now, I don't want to ignore the value of my traditions."
Z	Male	26	Calvary Chapel	"I was raised Lutheran, my wife Methodist, but I really haven't heard anything there that I disagree with: doctrine, rituals or ethics."

> Some buildings are easily recognized as sacred rather than secular.

CHAPTER 1

WHAT IS RELIGION?

when?	where?	what?
ca. 1500 B.C.E.	India	Vedas
ca. 1360 B.C.E.	Egypt	Hymns of *Akhenaton*
1000–500 B.C.E.	Palestine	Redactions of Pentateuch
800–400 B.C.E.	India	Upanishads
750–550 B.C.E.	Palestine	Hebrew Prophets
ca. 550 B.C.E.	Persia	Oldest parts of Zoroastrian *Avesta*
ca. 500 B.C.E.	China	Oldest parts of Confucian Analects
400–250 B.C.E.	Palestine, India	*Job; Ecclesiastes, Bhagavad Gita*
ca. 350 B.C.E.	Greece, China	Plato's *Laws; Dao der Jing*
ca. 330 B.C.E.	Greece	Aristotle's *Metaphysics*
160–80 B.C.E.	India	Earliest Buddhist scriptures
50–90 C.E.	Roman Empire	New Testament Writings
413–426 C.E.	Rome	Augustine's *City of God*
ca. 500 C.E.	Babylon	Talmud
ca. 650 C.E.	Arabia	Canonization of the Qur'an
712–720 C.E.	Japan	Shinto *Chronicles*
ca. 1100 C.E.	Baghdad	Al-Ghazzali's *Revivification of the Sciences*
1175 C.E.	China	Neo-Confucian Synthesis
1190 C.E.	Cordoba	Maimonides' *Guide for the Perplexed*
1270 C.E.	Paris	Aquinas' *Summa Theologica*
1536 C.E.	Geneva	Calvin's *Institutes*
1581 C.E.	India	Compilation of Sikh Scripture, *Adi Granth*

DEFINITION OF RELIGION

We define **religion** *as*

> *a system of symbols, myths, doctrines, ethics, and rituals for the expression of ultimate relevance.*

Memorize that definition now. We will give you a more precise understanding of each of its component terms later, but your success in this course depends upon your ability to comprehend what religion is (and is not) and apply that definition to specific phenomena in order to figure out what is religious and what is something else.

Now let's see if you can apply that definition to a specific case. Picture yourself in New Delhi. You are outside Rajghat, the memorial to Mahatma Gandhi, the politician and holy man who led India to independence from British colonial rule. Before you, squatting on the broken sidewalk, are three small boys with wooden flutes. They are piping tunes toward round wicker baskets. When they lift the baskets' covers, three silver cobras slowly weave their way out. You watch for several minutes, fearful but entranced.

Come up with your own definition of religion. Is it too broad or too narrow? (or both, or neither)? Let's try these examples.

DEFINITION 1: *Religion is the acceptance of the existence of God.*

PROBLEM: This is too narrow, because some religions do not have one supreme Deity but may recognize many lesser gods.

DEFINITION 2: *Religion is a Sunday "get-together" to celebrate common values.*

PROBLEM: This definition is too narrow because some religious denominations meet on Saturday or Friday for their religious services.

PROBLEM: This definition is too broad because it would also include some nonreligious get-togethers, such as a Super Bowl party.

Contribute to this discussion at
http://forums.delphiforums.com/rel101

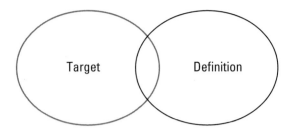

A good definition has maximum overlap with its target concept.

Is the music just a catchy tune to put the tourist in a generous mood, or does it have an established tradition in Indian religious rituals?

Is there something about the location (so close to the statue of Gandhi) that creates a religious context?

Of course, another issue is whether you can really *know* what is going on in other people's hearts and minds. All you can really do is observe what they do, listen to what they say, read what they have written. Anything beyond that is a matter of *inference*

Then the boys shove the cobras back into their baskets and approach you for their fee. A few rupees seem fair enough—you don't want to upset those cobras.

Come back to the classroom and visualize your professor putting forth this question:

"Did you just witness (and maybe even participate in) something religious?"

The right answer is not a docile "yes" or a defiant "no" (and it is certainly not a dubious "maybe"). The right answer in this sort of course is analogous to the right answer in the field of jurisprudence—the product of the deliberation is less important than the process. Here is the way to proceed: Identify the pertinent issues to be resolved in determining the appropriate answer to the question by raising some other questions.

Are the youthful snake charmers just merchants trying to put on a show for the tourists, or are they recognized spiritual functionaries in some religious denomination?

Are the snakes just performing animals (akin to circus seals or an organ grinder's monkey), or are they seen as symbols of something religious (or even incarnations of gods)?

Can we ever really *know* what another person is thinking? Or how committed he or she is to God? We observe what people say and do, and then *infer* something about their religious ideas and practices. Give an example of where you (or someone else) made an inference about religion based upon some observation that was made. Contribute to our discussion with an example.

WHAT WAS OBSERVED? (Describe a scene, event, or a person's behavior, or speech.)

WHO MADE THE INFERENCE? (Was it you or someone else who saw something and then came to a conclusion?)

WHAT INFERENCE WAS MADE? (What conclusion was reached as to motive, cause, affiliation, etc.?)

HOW APPROPRIATE WAS THE INFERENCE? IF IT WAS APPROPRIATE, WHAT FACTORS FACILITATED IT? IF NOT, WHAT MISLED THE CONCLUSION?

Contribute to this discussion at
http://forums.delphiforums.com/rel101

(reasoning from something directly observed to something else not directly observed).

These are the types of questions that would help you apply the definition of religion to the case at hand, but in order to answer those questions you would have to know a lot more about the culture and history of India. That is one of the central points of this course: any religion can only be understood within the context of the people who live it. A study of religion must become a study of society, culture, and history.

RELIGION VERSUS SCIENCE?

If you have already had a course in the physical sciences (e.g., physics), the life sciences (e.g., biology), or the social sciences (e.g., sociology), then you know something about how scientists go about trying to study and prove something. They use a method based upon objective and precise observation known as the empirical method. We are to believe a fact if it can be confirmed by a laboratory experiment or statistically analyzed survey. Truth is equated with verifiable factual data.

Although the sciences can often present useful perspectives on religious phenomena, we prefer to anchor our approach within the humanities—disciplines such as philosophy, art, and literature. Such an approach demands more self-awareness and personal engagement with materials than the scientific disciplines do. Pure science does not make great demands on a student's inner experiences of suffering or love. The humanities are disciplines that study our efforts at self-expression and self-understanding. The humanities involve more of such inner experiences because suffering and love shape so much of history and literature, yet even the humanities seldom deal with direct claims about ultimate relevance.

Only in the disciplines of philosophy and religion do we directly encounter systems about God, evil, and humanity's origin and end. Philosophy deals with such concepts principally in their rational forms, whereas religious studies meet them more directly in the myths, rituals, doctrines, behavior patterns, and institutions through which most human beings have been both drawn to the ultimate and yet are terrified of it. More than in any other discipline, the student in

> ### WHAT'S WRONG WITH THIS DISCUSSION?
>
> ERIC: I can't understand why you belong to the XYZ church. Their **beliefs** are just so ignorant.
>
> ASHLEY: But we base everything on the Bible.
>
> ERIC: That's just a book of **myths** and fairy tales.
>
> ASHLEY: But the Bible is **truth.**
>
> ERIC: That's just your **faith.** You can't **prove** that the Bible is **true.**
>
> ASHLEY: You can't **prove** that the Bible isn't **true,** and until you do I am going to **believe** it.
>
> *Eric and Ashley will get nowhere until they start using a little more care with terms like* truth, proof, faith, belief, *and* myths.

a religious studies course is confronted with imperative claims. The religions are not normally warehouses where you pay your money and take your choice. Rather, they are impassioned heralds of ways of life. More than most people initially like, the religions speak of death, ignorance, and human viciousness. However, they also speak of peace and joy, forgiveness and harmony.

To understand the key differences between the scientific and the religious perspectives, let's set up an appropriate terminology to be used with each. Only in that way can we overcome the inherent vagueness in the use of terms such as *truth, proof,* and *faith.* If we do not make these clarifications, some people will end up dismissing religion by saying, "Science deals with things you can prove, the truth, but religion is just faith." Both science and religion seek the truth, both have techniques for proof, and both involve faith. The difference between science and religion lies in the kinds of truth, proof, and faith.

Suppose I make the statement: "I believe that it is about 70 degrees in this room." Is that statement true? Scientific truth must be descriptive (i.e., describe something in the physical world). Scientific truth must be objective (i.e., be true whether I say it or someone else in the room says it, because it is the same temperature for both of us). The type of meaning involved is *cognitive* (i.e., it must involve precisely defined concepts). In other words, I am obligated to define what I mean by "70 degrees" (Fahrenheit? Celsius?). I would also have to describe the empirical procedures that would verify (prove) my claim: perhaps the use of a mercury thermometer. After making this measurement, I could discover if my initial statement was valid. But this type of belief is not something for which I would fight a "holy" war. Indeed, if someone else came up with a more precise measure of temperature, perhaps a digital thermometer with decimal gradations, I would be willing to change my belief if it were to show, say, 74 degrees. The faith we put in any given scientific finding is contingent upon the data at hand, and we should be willing to change our beliefs according to the discovery of new data in the next laboratory report.

Suppose I were to say: "I have faith in God." Are we dealing with the same type of truth, proof, and faith? Religion and the humanities in general are more subjective, not in the sense of being vague, or incapable of consensus, or beyond proof, but in the sense of depending upon the unique perspective of each individual. I may have faith in God, and someone else may not. Here is a different type of meaning and a different type of truth. We prefer to use the term **value** to describe religious truth. Values are prescriptive, **validity** is descriptive. The type of meaning involved is not mere cognitive definition, but **relevance**. Values cannot be comprehended as cognitive concepts but are based upon relevance to some person: there is no relevance without a promise of a value or a threat to a value. The kind of faith we have in God must not be some fragile belief that is contingent upon the next laboratory report. We cannot prove the existence of God empirically: no telescope or microscope can discover Him.

The kind of faith we have in God is one of **commitment.** Over 90 percent of Americans agree that God exists, but that does not end the religious debate. That only begins the greater discussion: How do we work out the details of living daily that commitment to God? This is not something that can be verified by the discovery of any fact; it can only be **vindicated**—that is, proved in the realm of relevance—by the creation of a life filled with values.

This book is based upon the assumption that there is a center, a common core of values to which all humans are inextricably drawn. The world's religions

SCIENCE VS. RELIGION		
DIMENSION	SCIENCE	RELIGION
Knowledge from	observation	revelation
Focus on	object	subject
Terms	descriptive	prescriptive
Form of meaning	cognition	relevance
Truth	validity	value
Proof	verification	vindication
Faith	belief	commitment
Realization	discovery	creation
Past	history	myth
Driving force	mechanism	dynamism

Practice using these terms correctly.
Download the drill
truth.exe
From the rel1 folder in the public filing cabinet at
http://www.ureach.com/tlbrink

are the journeys that people (in different times and places) have made toward that center.

Throughout history, individuals, families, and societies have had to make decisions about the religious doctrines and rituals to which they should commit. These decisions cannot be referred to the outcome of a laboratory experiment (as would be the verification of science). Let's take a look at one historical incident and how a people changed its religious commitments.

Go back about 1,300 years. The place was medieval England, the date was 627 C.E. (**common era,** what we used to call A.D.). The Christian monk Paulinus came to King Edwin in northern England and urged him to convert his people to Christianity. After some debate, one of Edwin's counselors stood up and said: "Your majesty, on a winter night like this, it sometimes happens that a little bird flies in that far window, to enjoy the warmth and light of our fire. After a short while it passes out again, returning to the dark and the cold. As I see it, our human life is much the same. We have but a brief time between two great darknesses. If this monk can show us warmth and light, we should follow him."

When we first hear the story of the little bird, it is not clear what the counselor is talking about. Is he saying that the monk is just a little bird who came in from the cold and if we just ignore him, he will fly out of the castle and return to a warmer climate? When the counselor then explains his symbolism, we see that the bird stands for a seeker of values. According to this homily, if Christ offers us warmth and light (symbols of spiritual values), then we must commit ourselves to His way.

So religion and science are different ways to approach human reality, with different forms of truth, proof, and faith. We do not suggest that each one of us must choose to be religious *or* scientific. The two operate in different spheres of human life. A religious person can respect the findings of science. A great scientist can be religious. All we are cautioning against is that we should not expect to use the methods and language of science to understand religion, nor should we attempt to use the language and methods of religion to answer questions best left to the laboratory.

RELIGION VERSUS OTHER VALUES

Religion deals with values, but not all values are religious. Religion deals with values that are relevant in the realm of the **ultimate.** Most of the things we find relevant to us on a daily basis are less than ultimate, although they are important and sometimes essential and urgent. Eating a good breakfast is relevant because it assures my health, and it may even be a pleasant experience. Brushing my teeth is not intrinsically pleasant, but it also assures my health and prevents some degree of social embarrassment. Investing my retirement fund wisely can increase my overall level of wealth, so that too is valuable. Anything that deals with health or wealth is useful, but it is not ultimately valuable. So let's use the term *utilitarian* to describe such values to distinguish them from religious values (those which are ultimately relevant). *Utilitarian* relevance involves instrumental values (those which can be rationally shown to lead to some other goal). The type of commitment appropriate to such utilitarian relevance should be only contingent. If other, more effective means can be found, we should adopt those other means.

The relevance of some values is not immediately apparent to the neutral observer. Why does the alcoholic live as if the most important thing in life is the next drink? Why do some gamblers throw away the rent money on the unlikely chance of winning the lottery? Why does an obsessive-compulsive patient waste most of the day washing hands to remove any possible trace of germs or filth? We would say that such values are **ulterior** and irrational. Indeed, they do not lead to other values but may even serve to inhibit other values such as health and wealth.

Let's go back to our initial example about seeing the snake charmers in India. Was it a religious ritual? Whether or not you perceived the snake charmers as involved in a religious ritual depends upon how they themselves perceived the relevance of their actions. Were they doing it out of fear that the snakes would curse them if they did not? If so, then most Westerners might regard this as superstitious behavior in the pursuit of inhibitory values: it would have ulterior relevance. Do the snake charmers see what they are doing merely as a way to earn a living and strike up pleasant contacts with foreigners? If so, then this is clearly utilitarian, an instrumental means for wealth and pleasure. If the snake charmers see what they are doing within some ultimate context (worshipping gods, preparing for the next life, expiating sin), then it has a religious aspect for them.

What type of relevance did you yourself find in that ritual? You participated by watching and throwing some coins. If you did this out of pure irrational fear, then the relevance was inhibitory. If you did it as payment for an entertaining show, then it was utilitarian, much as buying a ticket to a cinema. Only if you see how your presence and actions tie into ultimate issues of your life can you say that the experience was religious for you.

The great challenge of life is to figure out how to balance all of our different commitments. Should I rush home from mass on Sunday so I don't miss the opening kickoff? Should I contribute more to the temple even if it means that my daughter cannot go to her first-choice college? Every time we make a decision about how we spend our time or money, we are making a commitment. Life is not as simple as swearing off lottery tickets and soap operas so that we have more time to pray and money to put in the collection plate.

FORMS OF RELEVANCE			
DIMENSION	ULTIMATE	UTILITARIAN	ULTERIOR
Terms (prescriptive)	spiritual	technical	psychopathological
Truth (value)	intrinsic	instrumental	inhibitory
Proof (vindication)	transrational	rational	irrational
Faith (commitment)	absolute	contingent	rigid/fluid
Activity (proaction)	ritual	means	compulsion

COMPONENTS OF RELIGION

We opened with our definition of religion as a system of symbols, doctrines, myths, ethics, and rituals for the expression of ultimate relevance. Now let's look at each of those terms and see how they fit together.

A **symbol** is something that is used to represent something else. So is a sign. Symbols and signs present something to the senses, such as a visual icon, and the individual must then interpret what has been seen. If you are driving down the street and see a stop sign, you interpret the specific meaning conveyed: I had better stop or risk a traffic ticket. The relevance of signs is utilitarian because they promote safety and efficiency. Most corporate logos are signs; the Nike swoosh or McDonald's golden arches merely identify the brand. A symbol also points to something beyond itself, but in a more evocative way. A cross is a Christian symbol intended to evoke a memory of Jesus and his atonement for the sins of mankind. Religious symbols are intended to lift us out of the mundane, utilitarian basis of our existence and point us to the realm of the ultimate. Symbols are the foundation of other dimensions of religion.

Sometimes it is not possible for an outsider to understand how other people regard a certain icon: Is it mere sign or evocative symbol? Take your school's mascot (bronco, tiger, bulldog, etc.). If it merely serves to identify one team versus another, then it is only a sign. However, to the extent that it inspires a commitment among the loyal students, faculty, and alumni, it may be a powerful symbol. So, although we don't say that symbols are "believed," they are revered.

You are probably familiar with several definitions of the term *myth*. One definition we do not want to use in this course is the idea that a myth is the opposite of verified fact. We define **myth** as a story about the past told and retold in order to express certain values. History is also a story about the past that is told and retold. The difference is that history, like science, claims to be verifiable fact. The kind of faith we should place in a historical account is the mere belief that we would place in any scientific claim: a tentative faith subject to revision when more evidence comes in. Myths should not pretend factual claims but serve only to express certain values. The proof of a myth is not whether some archaeologist can unearth evidence verifying the claim but whether the values it conveys can be vindicated.

Let's take the case of the story of Adam and Eve in the book of *Genesis*. We take the position that this is a myth repeated for thousands of years because it expresses a truth (that is, a value) about the relationship of God to humans and the nature of sin. It might be hard to verify the claim that the *Genesis* story represents history. Even if historians, archaeologists, and paleontologists were able to come up with indisputable evidence that Eden never existed, most of us would still read *Genesis* and find it a relevant account of the human condition.

Are we saying that a story about the past is either history or myth (but not both)? Not at all! The **Bible** contains many myths and much history. Theologians may disagree among themselves about which myths are relevant to a contemporary understanding of God and the church. Historians may disagree about which

We suggest that the use of the terms *faith* and *belief* leads to confusion in the study of religions. In order to improve your writing, and thinking, about topics in religious studies, catch yourself when you are tempted to use the term *faith* and try to replace it with one of these: **denomination** (when referring to a religious *organization*), **doctrine** (when referring to a body of official *statements* about God, sin, and/or salvation), or **commitment** (when referring to the *strength* of a person's intention to follow a religion).

FUZZY	CLEAR
Rachel is a member of the Jewish *faith*.	Rachel is a member of the Jewish **denomination.**
The Trinity is an important element of Christian *faith*.	The Trinity is an important element of Christian **doctrine.**
Ali is very strong in his *faith*.	Ali is very strong in his religious **commitment.**

"By faith Abraham obeyed when he was called to go out to a place which he was to receive as an inheritance; and he went out, not knowing where he was to go." (*Hebrews* 11:8, Revised Standard Version of the Bible)

Abraham was righteous in the sight of God because of his faith. It is clear from the context of this passage that the type of faith that saved Abraham was neither that of belonging to a certain denomination, nor that of having the theologically correct doctrine, but that faith of having a strong **commitment** to obey God and do whatever He said.

We also suggest that the term **belief** be confined to "acceptance of factual statements" and that the terms **doctrine** and **commitment** be used for religious contexts. We "believe that" the Declaration of Independence was signed in 1776 (a factual statement), but we "believe in" freedom (in that we are committed to defending it).

The Gospel of John used the word "believe" over sixty times. Notice that the Evangelist usually says "believe in" or "believe on" rather than "believe that": "For God so loved the world that he gave his only Son, that whosoever believes in him should not perish but have eternal life." (*John* 3:16, Revised Standard Version)

---

biblical accounts can be verified by external evidence. For example, that a man named Jesus, son of Joseph, came from Nazareth and preached around Galilee and was executed in Jerusalem during the first century C.E. is generally accepted as historical fact. Whether you see his death as representing a myth about salvation will determine if you commit yourself to follow one of the denominations collectively known as Christian.

Symbols are often incorporated into myths as a way to alert us that we should evaluate these stories according to their relevance, not as valid accounts of historical events. Myths may also serve to explain the importance of symbols. For example, the cross is an important symbol in Christianity because it was the instrument for the crucifixion of Jesus.

Rituals are prescribed, formalized actions that dramatize religious symbols. Brushing my teeth is a prescribed action, but it is not a ritual, because it promotes dental health and reduces social embarrassment. Brushing my teeth has instrumental value, utilitarian relevance. Rituals are repeated in order to

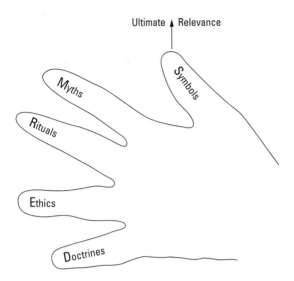

Ultimate ▲ Relevance

Myths

Symbols

Rituals

Ethics

Doctrines

Look at the skin "derms" on your fingertips

attain, or sustain, the individual's contact with ultimate relevance and to consolidate the cohesion of the community. Such rituals are usually performed in a sacred space: in a church or temple, in front of an altar, or the like. Rituals often have prescribed times for their performance: the Jewish sabbath meal on Friday night, an Aborigine subincision at the time a young male makes the transition to manhood, a Roman Catholic penance when certain sins have been committed. Rituals usually employ music, dance, and special costumes to make ritualistic occasions the more impressive. Rituals carry the danger of becoming overly aesthetic, ends in themselves, antagonistic to doctrinal clarity, and legislated in all their details.

Religious rituals are fundamentally different from magic. Here we are not talking about stage magicians who perform for our entertainment. Indeed, performers such as David Copperfield or Lance Burton describe themselves as illusionists rather than magicians. **Magic** is the attempt to manipulate spiritual forces. Religious rituals seek to worship spiritual forces. Magical rituals are undertaken in private and are usually secret, whereas religious rituals are celebrated in public. Religion tries to invite humans into the realm of the ultimate, whereas magic tries to keep people in the realm of the ulterior.

The origins of rituals are often explained in myths. Many rituals are reenactments of myths. The performance of rituals usually involves the use of symbols.

For example, each Sunday (prescribed time) Roman Catholics attend mass (a ritual) in a church (a sacred place). Just before the priest distributes a small wafer (a symbol) to devout participants, he retells the story (myth) of Jesus' last supper with his disciples. This explains the origin of the ritual and the importance of the symbol: the bread represents the body of Christ.

The primary purpose of myths and rituals is akin to that of symbols: to connote some profound understanding or evoke some commitment within the person who hears the myth or participates in the ritual. Symbols, myths, and rituals lack the precision found in signs, history, or actions undertaken as means to promote specific ends.

There are also more denotative, precise aspects to religion. An example would be **ethical** prescriptions. Since religions are concerned with values, and certain actions can have a direct impact on values, religions say what must be done and what must not be done. Do the duties of your caste, and do them gladly, says the Hindu book, the **Bhagavad Gita.** Honor your parents, says Confucius. Don't lie, steal, kill, or have sex outside marriage, say the rules at a Buddhist monastery. Don't worship idols, said Muhammad. Most of these sound similar to the Ten Commandments of the Old Testament.

Ethical behavior is more closely tied to reason than is usually the case with ritual behaviors. We may willingly perform a ritual simply because it is tradition, but most people want to know the reason behind a moral precept. Most ethical pronouncements based upon a religious foundation are **deontological,** emphasizing specific duties and/or rights. Duties may be seen as coming from God, and rights are often seen as coming from the natural order of things. On the abortion debate, for example, the pro-life side argues from the starting point that we as a society have a duty (coming from "Thou Shalt Not Kill") to protect the right to life of the unborn fetus. The pro-choice side argues from the starting point that we have a duty to protect the right of the woman to choose whether or not she will become a parent, based upon the natural principle that she should have autonomy over her own body.

Another rational basis for ethics is the **utilitarian** approach. To determine if a given action or policy should be regarded as good or bad, right or wrong, consider the outcomes for everyone concerned. Does an act (or rule) increase their welfare or reduce it? In practice, this approach to morality says that we have to think through the ramifications and balance the good against the evil. For example, should I drive my car to work or take public transportation? I have to balance the convenience of taking my own vehicle versus the adverse impact on others through increased congestion, pollution, and depletion of fossil fuels.

Ethics ties into both myths and rituals. Myths often justify certain ethical positions by telling powerful stories that demonstrate virtuous or evil behavior. People often turn to rituals when ethical rules have been violated. The Roman Catholic may go to confession and perform a penance. The ancient Hebrews dealt with collective sin by sacrificing an animal.

Yet another area in which religions strive for precision is the area of **doctrine**. Doctrinal positions involve statements about the nature of the Deity (God) or deities (gods), sin, salvation, and/or afterlife. We prefer to use the term *doctrine* instead of *beliefs* because these statements are not like historical events or laboratory results that we are called upon to believe. Doctrine is proven (vindicated) because it expresses a religion's value. The Christian doctrine of heaven and the Hindu doctrine of transmigration express the values that people who do their duty should be rewarded after this life. Doctrine can be vindicated through its ethical implications. Doctrine cannot be proven (verified) in the same way that empirical statements can be. You cannot verify the existence of God by a telescope or microscope. No historian or scientist has been able to verify (or disprove) the doctrine of reincarnation.

Many students new to the study of religion make two serious mistakes. One is to rely on the structure of their own religion to provide a template for understanding other religions. Since most students of the English-speaking world come from a Protestant Christian background (e.g., Baptist, Methodist, Presbyterian, Episcopalian, Lutheran), they tend to overemphasize the importance of one of these components (doctrine) and try to reduce world religions to mere doctrinal comparison. Most tribal and ancient religions (along with Judaism and Hinduism) deemphasize doctrine in favor of ritual and ethics. (A Jew does not define himself in terms of his religion as "believing" or "not believing" but as "practicing" or "not practicing," "observant" or "nonobservant") The different religions can be compared, however. (This process of comparison is known as a **homology**.)

COMPONENTS OF RELIGION		
	THOUGHTS	ACTIONS
Denotative (precise)	**Doctrines** Statements about deities, salvation, afterlife EXAMPLE: Jesus is the Son of God	**Ethics** Actions are deemed to be right or wrong, sinful, or moral EXAMPLE: Thou shalt not kill
Connotative (evocative)	**Myths** Stories about the past retold because of the values they portray EXAMPLE: Jesus had a last supper with his disciples	**Rituals** Actions prescribed as ceremonies EXAMPLE: Holy Communion

Usually, more similarities can be found than differences, and rarely are the differences in doctrine the most important. Usually, the most striking distinctions among religions can be attributed to differences in geography, culture, or historical events.

Another blind spot for most students is the tendency to conceive of a religion as a static system of doctrines, rituals, and ethics. Indeed, many Christian denominations base their claims to legitimacy or superiority on their perception that they are closer to "pure" original Christianity. However, since specific religions arise and develop within the context of human culture and the flow of history, religions change: doctrines and ethics may evolve, adapting to the changing times. Two thousand years ago, a main Jewish ritual was animal sacrifice. Then, in 70 C.E., the Romans destroyed the Jerusalem temple and the sacred site for this ritual was lost.

Myths, symbols, and rituals are especially susceptible to change via **syncretism** (the blending that takes place when different religions come into contact). Think of the two most important Christian holidays celebrated in North America: Christmas and Easter. Think of the symbols associated with those rituals.

Contribute to this discussion. Come up with an *analogy* for understanding religion. Tie in course terminology.

EXAMPLE: Religion is like an onion. A person's religion involves rituals, symbols, and myths that are at the very core of life. Each additional layer of life is influenced by the shape of that core. This understanding of religion is especially appropriate for comprehending the role of religion in the lives of fundamentalists, who take scripture literally and attempt to apply it to daily life.

Contribute to this discussion at
http://forums.delphiforums.com/rel101

First-century Christians did not have evergreen trees for Christmas or colored eggs for Easter. These symbols came from Teutonic and Celtic traditions Christianity assimilated as it moved north.

The study of the changing structure and form of religion is known as **morphology.** Remember a popular kids' TV show a few years back (somewhere between the Ninja Turtles and Pokemon) known as the *Mighty Morphin Power Rangers?* Remember how the heroes could quickly change their form? Religions can morph, maybe not as quickly as the Power Rangers, but a particular doctrine, ethical rule, symbol, ritual, or even myth may evolve in its relevance over time. So when we study what Buddha said 2,500 years ago in India, don't assume that his doctrine and monastic ethics completely comprehend the rituals followed by a twenty-first-century Japanese.

GOD OR GODS?

Many students assume that religion centers on a doctrine about God. This is another example of the North American and Christian tendency to reduce religion to doctrine. Because of the tendency to use the term *God* almost as a proper name for the supreme being described in the Old and New Testaments, we suggest that in this course the term *Deity* might be used to describe the one God of the Judeo-Christian-Islamic tradition.

The position that only one Deity exists is known as **monotheism.** This is a key element of doctrine in the religions coming out of the Middle East: Atonism,

Zoroastrianism, Judaism, Sabaeanism, Christianity, Islam, and Bahai. Some monotheists are **theistic** and regard the Deity as personal—as loving and merciful (and/or wrathful, when our sins have offended Him). Theists usually emphasize the importance of prayer and see it as essential to the ongoing intimate relationship between creature and Creator. Most evangelical Christians could be described as theistic.

Another understanding of monotheism is **deistic.** Deism is the view that a supreme god or deity set up the natural world but does not actively intervene on a regular basis. The deistic approach is that God is impersonal, worthy of worship but not interested in the details of the individual lives of humans. Many of the founders of the American Republic (e.g., Benjamin Franklin and Thomas Jefferson) could be described as deists.

A further twist on monotheism is **pantheism,** the doctrine that everything is God (or that nothing exists apart from the Deity). This doctrine was suggested by the **Upanishads** in India about 2,500 years ago. Pantheistic approaches assume that the Deity is *immanent* (in everyone and everything), whereas the more traditional monotheistic religions coming out of the Middle East view God as *transcendent* (apart from this world, a Creator who preexisted and stands outside His creation).

Polytheism is the doctrine that several deities exist. Most of the religions of the ancient world (e.g., those of the Egyptians, Mesopotamians, Canaanites, Greeks, Mayans, Aztecs, Incas) recognized several deities worthy of worship. These deities can take human form (i.e., be **anthropomorphic**) in terms of their bodies or characteristics, or they can take the form of animals (i.e., be **theriomorphic**). Some polytheistic religions view these deities as unequal in function or importance. Myths may explain that one deity conquered another or was selected to be the king of the gods. Among the Babylonians and the Aztecs, the deities of the conquering tribes and the defeated peoples alike were incorporated into structured hierarchy of deities known as the **pantheon,** but the deities of the victors remained superior. The Egyptians, Greeks, Teutons, and Vedic Aryans each had a different pantheon of deities.

Many tribal religions have an animistic doctrine. **Animism** is the doctrine that there are spirits in everything—not just in each person, but in animals, plants, places, and even natural phenomena. One

POSITION	VIEW OF DEITIES	WHERE FOUND
Animism	spirits are in everything	tribal cultures
Polytheism	several gods exist	ancient civilizations, Hindus
Pantheon	several gods, arranged in a hierarchy	Mayans, Aztecs, Greeks, Teutons, Vedic Aryans, Mesopotamians
Henotheism	several gods, some more important than others	Hindus
Monolatry	worship one deity	Akhenaton? Abraham?
Monotheism	only one deity exists	Judaism, Islam, Christianity
Theism	personal deity (deities) who answer prayer	some Christians, some Hindus
Deism	impersonal deity who does not actively intervene in world	Jefferson, Franklin
Pantheism	everything is God	Upanishadic Hinduism
Atheism	no deities exist	about 5% of U.S. population
Agnosticism	God's existence cannot be proved, so we must doubt	adolescence

debate within the history of religion has been whether an inevitable progression of doctrine has taken place throughout the ages. Did we all start off living in hunting and gathering tribes, with an animistic doctrine? As humans developed the herding of domesticated animals, settled agriculture, and cities, did polytheism arise? Did polytheism tend to structure its doctrine as civilizations grew, so that pantheons arose? The big question would be: How did these polytheistic pantheons lead to monotheism? One possible answer is **henotheism:** that one deity then emerged as most worthy of worship. Another step could have been the development of **monolatry:** the worship of one god (although the existence of other deities might be acknowledged). Scholars who have studied ancient religions disagree on whether the Egyptian pharaoh Akhenaton or the Hebrew patriarch Abraham should be regarded as true monotheists or merely monolatrous, advocating the worship of only one Deity while not clearly denying the existence of others.

Atheism is the position that no deities exist. Most atheists are committed to the scientific point of view and attempt to apply scientific standards of proof to religious doctrines, finding religious proofs inade-

quate. Another possible motive for the atheist position is the view that humans should confine their activities to the sphere of utilitarian relevance and that when religions try to lead people into the realm of the ultimate, the result is simply that the mass of people are led into superstition and ulterior relevance. In other words, some people may not want to acknowledge the existence of God because He would get in the way of their (sinful?) pursuit of pleasure. Although most people acknowledge some type of Deity (or higher power or spiritual dimension), between 5 percent and 10 percent of North Americans would describe themselves as atheists.

Many atheists are humanists. **Humanism** is the position that people are basically good and can work out their own salvation. This position may involve such an appreciation of human virtues and needs that it leads to a focus on human concerns, sometimes to the neglect of divinity or ultimate reality.

Atheistic humanists would say that religion is not necessary to make people good. Not all atheists are humanists. (As we shall see, psychoanalyst Sigmund Freud embraced atheism, yet contended that religion helped control the evil impulses in humans.) Not all humanists are atheists. Humanistic doctrine can be found among some deists and theists. However, religion lives from present attainment, reaching out to the infinite. Humanism can define itself so as to be compatible with such transcendence, but frequently it does not. Secular humanism expressly does not, taking its name from the this-worldly horizon that at best brackets divine transcendence.

A position slightly less extreme than that of the atheist is that of the agnostic. **Agnosticism** says that God's existence is not provable and therefore we should doubt; we can never know with certainty the monotheist claims for the existence of God or the certainty the atheist has in the nonexistence of God. Clearly the agnostic, like the atheist, attempts to apply the same standards of proof (empirical verification) to religious doctrine as are appropriately applied to the realm of science. Although the number of lifelong agnostics is probably small, many adolescents and young adults go through an agnostic phase as they begin to question their own religious traditions. Perhaps some adolescent agnostics will go on to become confirmed atheists as their doubts harden into rejection of religion. Others will find another, more relevant denomination to which they will convert. Most will probably reembrace the religion of their childhood as the the life tasks of matrimony and parenthood approach along the road of adulthood.

The purpose of this course is not to turn you into an atheist or agnostic, or to make you a convert to Buddhism or Catholicism, or to get you to return to the religion of your upbringing as a "born-again" adherent. However, we must ask you to suspend using your own doctrines as standards of judgment. In this way, you can begin to comprehend the complexities of other religions. In other words, if you are a committed evangelical Christian, you cannot simply dismiss other religions as wrong because they do not follow the Bible (or perhaps do not follow it in the way that you do). If you are an atheist or agnostic, you cannot simply dismiss all religions as unscientific superstition.

RELIGION VERSUS GOVERNMENT

Church and state are two of the strongest institutions in most societies. Sometimes they work together, supporting each other's efforts in controlling human behavior and promoting values that have been jointly agreed upon.

A **theocracy** is a government run by religion, or at least one in which the religious leaders have a great deal of influence over government policy. In most ancient civilizations, the king supported the religious institutions financially and enforced laws that were based upon ethics. In some societies, the performance of religious rituals was compelled by the government. A good example would be ancient Israel. Kings such as David and Solomon understood their duty as enforcers of God's laws of the Old Testament (Torah). One contemporary example of a theocracy would be the Vatican, a complex of buildings occupying several square blocks in Rome. By virtue of a treaty with Italy, the Vatican is recognized as a separate and sovereign country, complete with powers to conduct diplomatic relations with other nations. The chief executive of that country is the Pope of the Roman Catholic Church. Other contemporary examples would be the mullahs of Iran and the Taliban of Afghanistan, where revolutions brought religious-led factions into positions of political leadership. These theocrats used their political power, guided by their religious values, to demand that women dress and behave in ways deemed appropriate.

A pro-religious government may lack the unity between church and state seen in a theocracy, but such a nation is not neutral when it comes to different denominations (or sects). Such sectarian governments may "tolerate" the rights of other denominations to worship, but one denomination is clearly favored. If a sectarian government has a monarchy, a requirement of succession may be that a prince or princess belong to the state religion in order to assume the throne. The next king of England must be Anglican. The next king of Spain must be Catholic. Even a nonmonarchy-democracy such as Israel is clearly pro-religious, insofar as that state was created to be a homeland for the Jews. Prior to the American Revolution, most of the British colonies in North America were sectarian. In most colonies, the Anglican Church was established and supported by taxes. In some New England colonies it was the Congregational Church. In Rhode Island, it was the Baptists. The Quakers predominated in Pennsylvania, the Catholics in Maryland, and the Dutch Reformed Church in New York.

The U.S. Constitution outlined a different approach based upon the principle of neutrality. This approach

GOVERNMENT POSITIONS ON RELIGION

APPROACH	POLICY ON RELIGION	EXAMPLES
Theocracy	Religious leaders run or influence the government	Vatican, Taliban Ancient Israel, Iran since 1979
Pro-religious	Government supports certain denominations	England, Spain since 1939, Israel since 1948, American colonies before 1787
Secular	Government supports no denominations, but protects the rights of all denominations	U.S. since 1787
Anticlerical	Government opposes the power of religious leaders	Mexico 1917–2000, Spain 1931–1939
Anti-religious	Government suppresses worship by individuals	U.S.S.R. 1930s, China 1950s

Is the U.S. government too pro-religious or too anti-religious?
Join the discussion at
http://forums.delphiforums.com/rel101

was prompted by the realization that the different denominations probably could not agree on anything except that they all wanted to preserve their right to worship without government interference. The First Amendment affirms this diversity and promises to keep out of purely religious affairs. This amendment has been interpreted to mean that neither the federal, state, nor local governments could support denominations with tax monies. Throughout the 1790s, many of the new states were required to "disestablish" churches. The movement to oppose this constitutional requirement (and keep tax money supporting the churches) was known as *antidisestablishmentarianism* and eventually gave way to the nonsectarian position.

Secular is another term that describes this neutral approach. This may seem confusing, because the word *secular* looks like *sectarian,* but they have opposite meanings (secular = nonsectarian). Public institutions funded by the government are supposed to be secular. Crafton Hills College, for example, is one of California's 108 tax-supported community colleges. Many of the faculty, administrators, and students at Crafton are very religiously committed individuals, but the taxpayers and the government

expect faculty and administrators to do their jobs without advancing a religious agenda of any kind. Santa Clara University is a private university founded and still led by the Jesuit order of Roman Catholic priests. Many students and faculty members are non-Catholics, but all know that the university will expose them to certain Catholic doctrines, symbols, and rituals and that many decisions will be guided by Catholic ethics. Santa Clara is sectarian; Crafton is secular.

An **anticlerical** government is one that sees the power of the nation's largest religion as a threat. An anticlerical government may not try to prevent individuals from worshipping, but it may try to limit the church's wealth or the influence of church leaders. One example would be Mexico in the 1920s. As the agrarian revolution led by Pancho Villa and Emiliano Zapata hardened into the bureaucracy of the Institutional Revolutionary Party (PRI), there was an inevitable conflict with the Roman Catholic Church. The government confiscated church lands, limited the church's role in the educational system and told priests not to wear clerical garb in public. The result was the armed Cristero rebellion in western Mexico, in which the church recruited devout peasants to

Theocracies, such as Iran since 1979, give religious leaders major authority within the government. The U.S. model is secularism: a separation of church and state.

oppose these government measures. The PRI won that civil war, and for over seventy years a nation that was 95 percent Catholic was governed by a string of non-Catholic presidents (until 2000, when opposition leader Vicente Fox from the National Action Party, PAN, was elected, and for the first time Mexicans saw their president on television attending mass).

Another example of an anticlerical government comes from Spain in the 1930s. In 1931 a republic was declared, and in 1935 a leftist coalition of socialists, communists, anarchists, and syndicalists won the elections. Their reforms angered not only the wealthy but also the Roman Catholic Church. The following year, units of the Spanish Army (led by General Francisco Franco) rose up against the government under the banner of defending Catholicism. After three bloody years of civil war, Franco won, establishing a right-wing dictatorship and a pro-religious government.

Some revolutionary governments have gone even further in their opposition to religion. Communist governments have usually been suspicious of any other center of power in the nation, including religion. During the 1930s, the Soviet Union under Stalin became anti-religious, promoting atheism as an ideal and discouraging citizens from religious affiliation or worship. (In the 1940s, Stalin reversed his position, seeking to get the support of the Russian Orthodox Church in the war against Nazi Germany.) Similar anti-religious extremism was reached in the 1950s in Mao's China and the 1960s in Castro's Cuba. Today, both China and Cuba try to appear more tolerant of religion, but oppression may wax and wane as political needs shift.

SACRED WRITINGS

Tribal societies often preserve their myths by repeating the stories ritually in an oral tradition. After the invention of writing, many religions started to write down their myths and doctrines. (Examples would be the book of *Genesis* for the Hebrews and the *Rig Veda* for the Aryans in India.) Priests also wrote down guidelines for those performing rituals. (Examples would be the book of *Leviticus* for the Hebrews and the later **Vedas** for the Hindus). Then there were books that recorded laws (e.g., Hammurabi in Babylonia) and ethical behaviors (e.g., *Deuteronomy* for the Hebrews). **Scripture** is the name given to sacred writings. Each of the modern religions has a **canon** (an official list of the writings to be regarded as scripture). In Hinduism, the Vedas are the scriptural canon; in Judaism, the **Torah;** in Islam, the **Qur'an;** in Christianity, the books of the Bible. Writings that have not been admitted to the canon but that are nevertheless revered for their historical or inspirational value are sometimes called **apocryphal.** In Hinduism, these writings would include the Brahamanas, Aranyakas, Upanishads, and Bhagavad Gita (although some Hindus might base more of their own doctrines and rituals on these books than the Vedas). Islam regards the Christian Bible as apocryphal (having many useful myths, but not as scripturally authoritative as the Qur'an). The Jewish and Protestant **Apocrypha** includes fourteen books written by Jewish prophets after 400 B.C.E. but before the birth of Jesus. (After 1500 C.E., the Catholic Church decided to include these inter-testamental writings into the Catholic Old Testament canon.)

Hermeneutics involve the principles of interpretation of documents. Physically, a text is simply marks on a piece of paper or parchment, or some impressions in clay. These marks have to "speak" from the mind of the person who set them down to the minds of people like you who are trying to understand them. Thus, the languages and assumptions of both minds come into play, your own as much as the author's. You can assume that you and the author share a great deal, since you are both human, but you must be careful about how you use this assumption. Essentially, hermeneutics involve walking the tightrope between the sameness we have as members of one species and the differences we have as individuals, as people of different cultures, and as people of different historical eras.

Hermeneutical techniques include the study of literary style as well as the historical context of those who wrote a document. We cannot simply rely upon translations of texts into modern English. To become

expert in the interpretation of scripture, we would need to acquire a knowledge of the ancient languages in which scripture was written, both the vocabulary and the grammar. **Exegesis** is the attempt to arrive at the most relevant interpretation of a specific scriptural passage.

Fundamentalists are people who are strict about their religious doctrine and ethics. Fundamentalists usually emphasize a literal interpretation of scripture and its rigorous application in daily life. Fundamentalists are often concerned about the growth of secular humanism in modern society, because it represents a trend away from the importance of religion in institutions and the daily lives of individuals.

RELIGIOUS ROLES

All social organizations, including religious denominations, have various roles that their members may assume. Most adherents or followers of a given religious denomination are known as *laypersons,* in that they do not have leadership roles. Laypersons participate in rituals but do not lead the rituals. Laypersons

This shaman is from Tibet, but his role is similar to that of shamans in other tribal societies.

are supposed to accept the denomination's doctrine but probably will not get a chance to vote on it. Such decisions are made by the leadership.

In tribes that subsist largely by hunting and gathering, the major religious figure is the **shaman** (such as the medicine man in North American Indian tribes). Shamans are the intermediaries between the tribe and the world of the spirits and may have to arrange for a good hunt by negotiating with the keeper of the animals, by locating the herd, or by capturing the spirits of the game before the hunters capture their bodies. The shaman may have to guide the souls of the dead to an afterlife. Shamans have the primary duty of healing the sick through the use of herbs or through exorcism (casting out evil spirits).

In societies that have developed a pastoral or agricultural economy, the main religious figure is usually a **priest,** who officiates at regularly scheduled rituals. Most of these rituals are sacrifices in which an offering is made to the deities to propitiate human sin or

the violation of a taboo or to encourage a rich harvest. In the early civilizations calendars were developed, and rituals were scheduled at appropriate times.

Some contemporary Christian denominations use the term *priest* to describe their religious leaders: the Roman Catholics, Episcopalians, Mormons, and Eastern Orthodox. The sacrifice that is reenacted in the ritual of the mass is the Last Supper of Jesus (Eucharist). Brahmin priests are the highest caste of Hindu society. Priests were important in Jewish religion during the time of the Israelite kingdom, but for about two thousand years Jewish religious leaders have been known as **rabbis** ("teachers"), who are distinguished for their knowledge of the Jewish tradition. Most of the Protestant Christian denominations that arose during the period of the Reformation (sixteenth century C.E.) refer to their officials as *ministers* or *parsons* or preachers. A *pastor* is a priest or minister who is in charge of a particular locality (e.g., a Roman Catholic parish).

ROLE	FUNCTIONS	WHERE FOUND
Shaman, Medicine man, Witch doctor	Exorcism, Healing, Finding game, Making rain, Guiding souls to afterlife	Tribal cultures
Priest	Rituals of calendar and propitiation, confession	Ancient Civilizations, Hebrews and Israelites, Hindus, Mormons, Roman Catholics, Episcopalians, Eastern Orthodox
Prophet	Speaks for the one God	Hebrews and Israelites, Zoroastrianism, Islam, Mormonism, Japanese Buddhism
Diviner	Predicts future	Africans, Celts, Mayans, Aztecs, Chinese, Greeks, Mesopotamians
Psychic, Medium	Predicts future, Perceives distant events, Reads minds, Communicates with dead	Worldwide: usually outside of religions
Mystic	Seeks ecstatic union with God	Buddhism, Jainism, Neoplatonists, Gnostics, Upanishads, Daoism, Sufi Moslems, Hasidic and Cabbalist Jews, monastic Christians
Theologian	Uses reason to defend doctrines and ethics	Paul, Augustine, Anselm, Aquinas, Averroes, Maimonides, Al-Ghazzali, Calvin, Arminius
Teacher	Conveys doctrine and ethics	Jewish rabbis, Confucius
Lay person	No leadership role	Most people in most denominations

The higher levels of leadership in the Christian church are also denoted by special roles. A **bishop** is in charge of several priests or ministers within a geographic area (e.g., a Roman Catholic diocese or Mormon ward). An archbishop (or metropolitan or patriarch in the Eastern Orthodox churches) is in charge of several bishops. In the Roman Catholic Church, the **Pope** is the Bishop of Rome and is the head of the entire Church. He is not a prophet in the sense that he receives specific revelations from God, but the Church accepts the Pope's ability to speak authoritatively, infallibly (Ex Cathedra) on doctrinal issues. The Pope selects certain archbishops to be *car-dinals*, who meet in large councils to proclaim church doctrine and to select a new pope upon the death of the old one.

A **psychic** (or **medium**) is a person who claims abilities such as foretelling the future (augury, sooth-saying, omens, **divination**), perceiving objects despite distances or obstacles (**clairvoyance**), reading the mind of another person (**telepathy**), manipulating physical objects or energy fields without using one's muscles (**psychokinesis**, levitation), or contacting the spirits of the deceased (seances, channeling, necromancy). Although these psychic phenomena are comparable to magic, some religious leaders may claim some psychic abilities. For example, shamans may conduct the spirits of the departed to the happy hunting ground, scare away troublesome ghosts, determine the location of game herds, and the like.

Do not confuse psychics with **prophets.** Some prophets do foretell the future, but what separates them from mere diviners is that the prophet claims to speak the will of God. Noah, Abraham, Moses, and most of the authors of the books of the Old Testament are regarded as prophets in Judaism because they received special revelations from God. One of the first prophets outside the Judaic tradition was the Persian Zoroaster (about 600 B.C.E.). Muhammad is regarded as the last and greatest prophet in Islam. Some recent religions have founders who have been regarded as prophets (e.g., Joseph Smith of the Mormons). Usually, prophets are found within the monotheistic religions coming out of the ancient Middle East. One exception would be the Buddhist Nichiren (thirteenth century), who commanded that a temple be built.

Mystics seek to attain an altered state of consciousness that they understand as intimate union with the Deity. The usual technique employed is the use of meditation. We could describe what they are doing as stripping away all pretense of cognitive meaning, utilitarian relevance, and ulterior relevance from their lives. The strategy is to reduce their lives to just one factor: ultimate relevance.

When mystics contemplate, they attempt to focus their minds on the whole of a scene or experience, or to commune with the ultimate directly. Perhaps contemplation may be distinguished from meditation as something more holistic, more affective, and less intellectual.

Historically, mysticism began in the **Axial Age** (roughly 600 B.C.E–200 C.E.). Asian religions (Upanishadic Hinduism, Jainism, Buddhism, Daoism) urged liberation from the material and social ties of this world. In Western monotheistic religions, mysticism has usually been seen as a potential source of heresy. Nevertheless, Judaism had Cabala in medieval times and Hasidism since the eighteenth century; Islam has had the Sufis; and the Christians have canonized mystics as saints in the Roman Catholic and Eastern Orthodox traditions. With the exception of Quakerism, Protestantism has rejected mysticism.

Many Christian and Buddhist mystics have been part of the tradition of **monasticism:** monks and nuns

Give us an example. Take a scriptural passage and indicate how it portrays the role of *Jesus.* (You may use the New Testament, noncanonical gospels, Qur'an, Book of Mormon, or any other writing about Jesus.) Is he portrayed as a . . .

PRIEST: absolving guilt, performing ritual?

MYSTIC: seeking an ecstatic union with God (similar to Lao Tzu, Buddha)?

TEACHER: trying to apply religious tradition to specific ethical questions (similar to Confucius)?

PROPHET: bringing new messages from God (similar to Zoroaster, Isaiah, Nichiren, Muhammad)?

SHAMAN: healing, exorcising?

Contribute to this discussion at
http://forums.delphiforums.com/rel101

living in separate communities where they are freed from the everyday concerns of utilitarian relevance such as earning a living. These monks and nuns are usually required to be **celibate:** they must avoid marriage and sex outside of marriage. The requirement of celibacy has also been made of Roman Catholic priests for the last thousand years. The only religion to require celibacy for all of its followers was the Shaker sect, which had dozens of utopian farm communities throughout the northeastern part of the United States in the nineteenth century (but which has now died out).

The mystic differs from other religious figures such as the psychic, shaman, prophet, priest, and theologian. The psychic also claims to enjoy altered states of consciousness, but these are associated with specific occult abilities. Prophets claim to have received a conceptual message from the Deity, while mystics have a nonconceptual message. Priests try to preserve the rituals, doctrines, and authority of established denominations, while mystics often transcend them for a direct union with what is ultimately relevant.

Mysticism has been criticized by established religions as "beginning in 'mist,' centering in 'I,' and ending in 'schism.'" The mystic usually tries to transcend established doctrine, rituals, and authority.

Theologians attempt to use philosophy and rational elaboration in order to explain or argue religious doctrine. In other words, theologians attempt to link

ARGUMENTS ABOUT THE EXISTENCE OF GOD

ARGUMENT	PROPONENTS	SUBSTANCE
Cosmological	Aristotle (384–322) B.C.E. and Aquinas (1224–1274)	Since every earthly event is the effect of some other event, which in turn must be caused by some other event, the beginning of this causal chain must be a **first cause** that lies outside of earthly events: God exists as the first cause.
Teleological	Paul (1st century), Aquinas (1224–1274), and Paley (1743–1805)	All the wonders of nature, from the great planetary bodies to the intricate organs of the smallest forms of life, show evidence of complicated **design,** so there must exist a great designer that we call God.
Ontological	Anselm (1033–1109) and Descartes (1596–1650)	God is defined as a perfect being and therefore possesses all the qualities of perfection—is all-knowing, all-powerful, and good. Existence is also a quality of **perfection,** and therefore God also has that quality: God exists.
Moral	Kant (1724–1804)	We must **postulate** the existence of a good God who will compensate men for the performance of their moral duties.
Wager	Pascal (1623–1662)	If God exists, and we do not accept Him, we will spend eternity in Hell, whereas if we accept God, and He does not exist, we have only missed out on some sins; so bet that God does exist.
Mystical	Mystics	The universality of the mystical experience means that mystics are experiencing the same thing: God.
Theodicy	Atheists	The existence of **evil** and suffering in the world means that there cannot exist a God who is good, all-knowing, and all-powerful.

religion back to the realm of cognitive meaning. One role of theology is to clarify a denomination's doctrine for priesthood and laity alike. Some theologians are engaged in trying to defend the doctrines of their denominations against atheists or the doctrines of other sects. This branch of theology is known as **apologetics.** Some of the greatest theologians are

Paul, who distinguished Christian doctrine in the first century; Augustine, who blended Christianity with Plato; Aquinas, who blended Christianity with Aristotle; Maimonides, who blended Judaism with Plato; Averroes, who blended Islam with Aristotle; and Al-Ghazzali, who reconciled Islam, reason, and mysticism. Since the theologian champions the use

of reason in the development of religious doctrine,
few have been mystics seeking to transcend reason.
(However, Augustine and Al-Ghazzali did reconcile
mysticism and theology.)

Theologians have offered various proofs for the
existence of God. The **cosmological** argument says
that everything is caused by something else that must
have come before it—but how then could the first
cause get started? God must be the uncaused first
cause who stands outside the material world's causal
chain. The **teleological** argument is also known as the
design argument: since there is so much structure and
apparent purpose in the natural world, there must be
a God who set the planets in their orbits and designed
the organs of the body in all their intricacy. The
ontological argument is based upon a logical syllogism:
God is defined as a perfect being, and since existence
is one of the qualities of perfection, God must exist,
by His very definition! The philosopher Immanuel
Kant (1724–1804) presented a moral argument for
God: since moral actions must be rewarded, we must
postulate the existence of God.

There are also powerful rational arguments against
the existence of a supreme Deity. One of the best
is known as **theodicy:** the problem of evil. Let us

assume three characteristics about the Deity (and
most Christians would agree with these), that God is
omnipotent (all-powerful), omniscient (all-knowing),
and beneficent (good). The atheist now asks, "How
would such a God, if He did exist, permit suffering or
evil in the world?" Human disease, natural disasters,
and the existence of any evil would be impossible if
God really had all of those characteristics. Although
many atheists find this argument conclusive, many
theists respond that the time when humans experience evil and suffering (such as the death of a loved
one) is exactly when they are in the greatest need of
divine consolation. In this way, the existence of God
is vindicated.

SCHOLARLY APPROACHES

Throughout most of human history, the scholars who
have written about religious topics have been theologians dedicated to the defense of the doctrines of a
specific denomination. This was also true of those
scholars who studied comparative religion. About
1700 C.E., Jesuit Catholic priests translated the works
of Confucius and Daoism, but their main purpose

was to facilitate their missionary efforts in China. Then Europe experienced a period known as the **Enlightenment.** This intellectual movement of the eighteenth century embraced humanism and secularism and attempted to extend the rational method of philosophy and the empirical method of science to the study of all human endeavors, including religion. By the nineteenth century, European scholars were writing objective accounts of the history and doctrine of non-Christian religions (e.g., Thomas Carlyle, 1795–1881, on Islam), but few scholars attempted to develop a comprehensive view of religion itself. The twentieth century saw the rise of a scholarly approach to the study of religion that emphasized the role of the social sciences: history, psychology, sociology, and anthropology.

A cognitive view of religion takes the perspective that it represents a merely rational attempt to explain the universe. This view was advanced by several nineteenth-century British scholars who were little more than "armchair anthropologists." E. B. **Tylor** (1832–1917) argued that religion at its core was animistic and began in an attempt to explain ghosts. Sir James **Frazer** (1854–1941) thought that religion was merely the second stage in the development of human explanation—comprising magic (manipulation), religion (revelation), science (empiricism)—and would eventually disappear.

This cognitive view was dealt a blow by the fieldwork and functionalist theory of anthropologist Bronislaw **Malinowski** (1884–1942), who found that all peoples use the best technology available to them but turn to magic and religion when the problems they confront exceed that technology.

The last remnant of a cognitive theory of religion can be found in the structuralism of linguistics. Benjamin **Whorf** (1897–1941) argued that the structure of language determines the structure of our thoughts about things. Anthropologist Claude **Lévi-Strauss** (1908–) noted similar structures between the religions, languages, and clan organizations of tribes.

The idea that religion lies outside the sphere of the cognitive slowly gained favor among German scholars. Friedrich Max **Müller** (1823–1900) thought that religion has its origin in forms of confused speech in which metaphor was mistaken for objective description. Friedrich **Schleiermacher** (1768–1834) argued

that religion transcends reason and should be considered as an emotional response. Rudolf **Otto** (1869–1937) contended that the essence of religion was the human experience of the sacred, "the holy," and the profound emotions of awe and fear that accompanied this experience. Frenchman Lucien **Lévy-Bruhl** (1857–1939) argued that the emotional experience was different for primitives, who experienced a *participation mystique* in which there was no boundary between the individual and community or nature. A. **Ritschl** contended that facts and values occupied completely different spheres and that no set of facts could prove or disprove a value claim. H. **Vaihinger** distinguished between facts and "guiding fictions," and he grouped religion under the latter. Fictions cannot be verified the way that facts are (empirically or logically) but they can be vindicated in the sense that they are relevant to the way people guide their lives. American philosopher and psychologist William **James** (1842–1910) contended that religious doctrines and practices should be judged by their fruits (i.e., their results) rather than their roots (i.e., their origins).

Twentieth-century psychological theory has also examined the role of religion as a human phenomenon. Sigmund **Freud** (1856–1939), the founder of psychoanalysis, contended that humans were driven by unconscious sexual and aggressive drives and that religion was merely one of society's tools for controlling such drives. An atheist, Freud noted parallels between religious ritual and obsessive-compulsive and other neurotic behaviors. Like Frazer, Freud predicted that religion would disappear, to be replaced by science (i.e., psychoanalysis). One of Freud's early colleagues was the Swiss psychiatrist Carl **Jung** (1875–1961), who held a more optimistic view of human nature, especially of the creative and nurturing capacities of the unconscious. For Jung, religion (along with art and literature) was one of the fundamental ways in which people used archetypal symbols to contact the potential of the collective unconscious. Whereas Freud contended that psychotherapy would replace religion by the end of the twentieth century, Jung asserted that the only reason modern people need psychotherapy is because they have turned away from their religious roots.

Favorable views of religion were offered by humanistic psychologists such as Gordon **Allport** ("mature religion leads to personal growth and not

SCHOLARLY APPROACHES TO RELIGION

THEORIST	DATES	FOCUS	EXAMPLES	MAIN POINTS
Müller	1823–1900	myth	Teutons, Greeks	confused speech: myth begins as a confusion with metaphor
Tylor	1832–1917	ghosts	Africans	animism: religion begins with speculation about ghosts
Robertson-Smith	1846–1894	totems	Semites	ethics and rituals show importance of tribe
Durkheim	1858–1917	rites	Australia	rituals celebrate and strengthen social cohesion
Mauss	1873–1950	gifts	Native Americans	gift exchange defines relationships
Frazer	1854–1941	myth	Greeks	first magic, then religion, then science
Marx	1818–1883	class	19th century Europe	dialectical materialism: religion is the opiate of the masses
Fromm	1902–1980	class	20th century Europe, Mexico	humanistic materialism: religion a tool for exploitation or community
Otto	1869–1937	emotion		religion is an emotional encounter with the Holy: awe, fear
Freud	1856–1939	ritual, totem, taboo	patients	psychoanalysis: religion controls sex and aggression, but will die out
Jung	1875–1961	myth	patients	analytical psychology: religion fosters healthy contact with collective unconscious
James	1842–1910	mysticism	introspection, biographies	functionalism: judge religion by its fruits
Malinowski	1884–1942	magic	Pacific Islands	functionalism: people use best available technology before turning to magic or religion
van Gennep	1873–1957	ritual	Africa	rites of passage: rituals transition people through life events
Erikson	1902–1994	ritual	biographies	psychoanalysis: religion transitions people through developmental tasks
Lévi-Strauss	1908–	totems	Australia	structuralism: cognitive thought is projected onto myths and social structures
Eliade	1907–1986	yoga, shamanism		phenomenology: consider each religion in its own context

discrimination against other groups"), Erich **Fromm** ("religion can be used as a key to social progress and equality instead of oppression"), and Abraham **Maslow** ("the peak experience of mysticism represents the highest level of human functioning").

The founders of sociology and anthropology had much to say about religion. J. J. **Bachofen** viewed the transition from animism to female fertility deities to male tribal deities as reflecting the development of society from promiscuity to matriarchy to patriarchy. Emile **Durkheim** (1858–1917) and **Robertson-Smith** (1846–1894) emphasized religion's role in promoting social cohesion, especially in tribal societies. Religious ritual is a celebration by the tribe of the tribe.

The role of socioeconomic aspects of religion was noted by Marx and Weber. Karl **Marx** (1818–1883), who is also known as the ideological father of communism, viewed religion as just another social institution reflecting and reinforcing prevailing social class structure. An atheist, Marx contended that religion merely served as a tool for oppressing the masses, a kind of "opiate" that distracted them from the misery of their exploitation by promising them a better life in the next world. Marx predicted that religion would die out in the perfect communist society because the masses would no longer need otherworldly promises to distract them. Max **Weber** (1865–1920) argued the opposite relationship between religious ethics and economic systems: that doctrines and practices had nurtured the rise of economic systems. Specifically, Weber saw the rise of capitalism in northern Europe as reflecting the Protestant Ethic of hard work and saving. Marcel **Mauss** (1873–1950) focused on the exchange and transactions between members of the religious community (e.g., gifts) and between the worshippers and the deities (e.g., sacrifices and blessings).

The importance of religious ritual in the life cycle has been noted by anthropologists as well as psychologists. Anthropologists Arnold **van Gennep** (1873–1957) and Victor **Turner** looked at how religion helped individuals move through social roles and life events (e.g., childbirth, puberty, marriage, death) with rites of passage. Psychoanalyst Erik **Erikson** (1902–1994) agreed that such rituals were important in resolving life's developmental tasks and demonstrated this in case studies of sixteenth-century Protestant Reformer Martin Luther and India's twentieth-century leader Mahatma Gandhi.

An ongoing debate within these social science perspectives concerns **reductionism**, whether they fairly portray religion as a phenomenon in its own right or whether they reduce religion to physical, psychological or social phenomena. Freud, for example, would try to interpret any religious symbol as if it had arisen in the dream of one of his patients, as symbolic of something sexual that had been repressed. Marx would reduce any doctrine to a justification of the ruling powers, and any ethical constraints to an attempt to thwart revolutionary efforts. It is unclear how Marxists could explain away religious figures such as Gandhi or the movement for social justice in contemporary Catholicism, both of which are thorns in the side of the ruling political and economic hierarchies.

Opposed to the reductionistic approach has been the rise of the **phenomenological** approach of Geraldus van der Leeuw (1890–1950) and Mircea **Eliade** (1907–1986). While these scholars eagerly note homologies of ritual, symbol, and myth between diverse religious traditions, they also try to respect the unique perspective of each religion. The phenomenologists may find typical patterns (e.g., mysticism, sacrifice) but also unique configurations.

> Stonehenge, England, was a Celtic megalith.

CHAPTER 2

TRIBAL

RELIGIONS

ANCIENT AND TRIBAL RELIGIONS: 25 KEY DATES	
Date	**Event**
4.6 billion years ago	formation of the earth?
3.6 billion years ago	rise of life?
4 million years ago	advanced hominids in Africa
2 million years ago	stone tools
1.5 million years ago	*Homo Erectus;* more sophisticated tools
500,000 years ago	use of fire
100,000 years ago	*Homo Sapiens;* ritual burial
75,000 years ago	cave dwellers; clothing to survive northern winters
70,000 years ago	*Homo Sapiens* in Australia
30,000–25,000 B.C.E.	migrations across Bering Strait to New World
20,000 B.C.E.	colonization of Europe, Japan
15,000 B.C.E.	extensive cereal grain collecting
10,000 B.C.E.	humans migrate throughout South America
8,000 B.C.E.	full withdrawal of glaciers
7,500 B.C.E.	cereal grain agriculture; domestication of animals
8350–7350 B.C.E.	Jericho (first walled town, 10 acres)
6250–5400 B.C.E.	Catal Huyuk, Turkey (large city, 32 acres)
6000 B.C.E.	rice cultivation in Thailand; pottery and textiles in Catal
3500 B.C.E.	megaliths in Brittany, Iberian Peninsula; invention of the wheel
3000 B.C.E.	farming in central Africa
800 C.E.	Polynesians reach Easter Island and New Zealand
900–1500 C.E.	rise of African states
1200–1300 C.E.	Eskimos arrive in Greenland
1526–1870 C.E.	10 million slaves shipped from Africa
1880–1913 C.E.	Europeans partition Africa

We begin our study of the world religions by trying to understand prehistoric human beings. *Prehistoric* implies having no writing, because we moderns require writing for a critical, objective, factual, trustworthy account of what happened—a history. The ancient religious mentality was without written records. Therefore, these peoples and times are sometimes referred to as *preliterate.*

Another term describing these cultures is **oral**—those without writing. Obviously all cultures have been oral in the sense that living speech has been the first mode of communication. But peoples that develop writing change their cultures significantly. Writing starts to mediate relationships—official, personal, religious, economic—and education may become more reflective. And while oral peoples often have prodigious memories, they do not develop the written archives on which history in the modern academic sense depends. Thus their accounts tend to be somewhat *ahistorical,* all the more so when they remain entranced by mythic accounts of creation, the rise of their culture, and where their time will end.

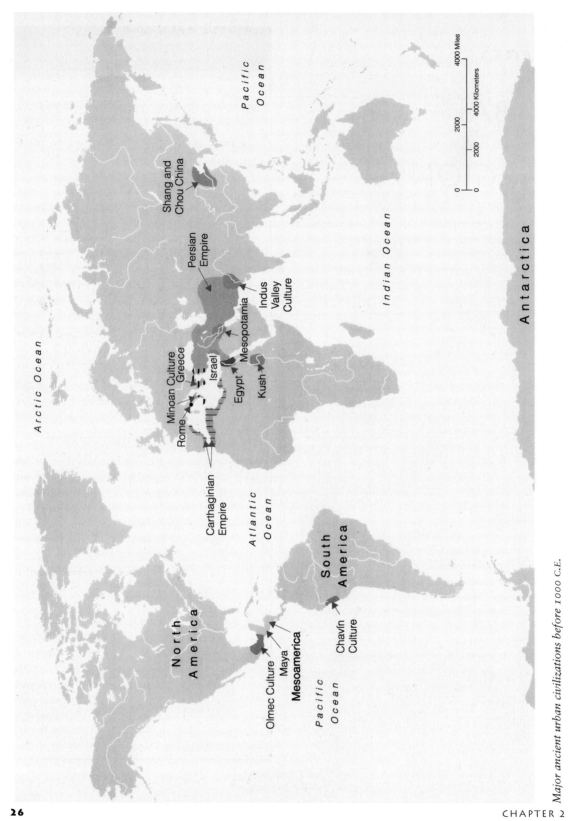

Major ancient urban civilizations before 1000 C.E.

Other terms used to describe these peoples would be *tribal, ancient,* and *primitive.* **Tribal** refers to the form of social organization used by these peoples: small groups of hunters and gatherers in an extended family or clan. The term **primitive** only means "first" or "early," but many people infer some pejorative connotation. To call a people or their culture "primitive" or "ancient" should not imply inferiority, except perhaps in terms of technology: they lacked electricity, machinery, or the domestication of animals beyond the dog. One term with a pejorative connotation that we prefer not to use is **pagan,** which missionaries used to label non-Christian religions in general, especially those pertaining to preliterate societies.

To feel sympathy for the earliest religionists, we must be convinced that they were as human as we are. From excavations in a Paleolithic cave at Shanidar in northern Iraq, archeologists have described the skeleton of a man whose arm had been severed in his youth. He would be at a disadvantage when it came to hunting or self-defense. He could not have dragged as much fuel or carried as much water. Life in his time was hand-to-mouth, and there was little extra food to go around. But this is not a case study of an individual person, but of his tribe. Why did they not allow this man to die? There must have been something about him, something more than the ability to hunt and gather. Maybe he sang, bringing cheer to the dark night. Maybe he loved children—was patient, kind, quick to tell stories. Maybe he was a great wit, or a great lover, or a great reader of signs. Or maybe he was just a good man in pain—a man whose smile broke your heart. Perhaps the best explanation is that there was something special about the family that kept him on, made sure he got food and clothing. He did not die by famine or by beast. He died in a cave-in, at home in his family circle.

This case illustrates something seen over and over again in the study of humans: they are social beings who live together and worship together. Hermits are the exception, rather than the rule. Such a valuing of humanity for itself, with little concern for pragmatic benefits, indicates that prehistoric people were more than our peers. Sometimes they were our betters, at least in terms of their capacity for selfless behavior.

EARLIEST RELIGION

How long have humans existed on this planet? The answer could range from 100,000 years to 6,000,000 years, depending upon the definition of *human* (e.g., *Homo sapiens,* or modern humans). On the basis of archeological evidence, religious behavior is probably as old as humanity itself. What we might call human beings capable of abstraction and calculation emerged at least with the Aurignacian era 32,000 years ago, and they possessed a reflective religion, complete with the components of myth, doctrine, and ethics as well as ritual.

A hundred years ago, there was a tendency to dismiss ancient religion as intellectually inferior, the result of "primitive stupidity" (*Urdummheit*). Bedeviled by the evolutionary perspective that had burst on the scene with Darwin in 1859, many people considered nonliterate peoples to be savages, more bestial than rational. But rational they were, and such remains as cave paintings and rock incisions lead us to conclude that they were thoroughly absorbed in making religious sense of their condition. The main economic activity was hunting and gathering, and these processes varied greatly according to geographical and historical peculiarities.

We find some common features worthy of our attention, however. For the first humans, the most absorbing issues were probably those relating to survival: birth, subsistence, and death. The first religious interest may not have dealt with an ultimate sphere totally apart from these utilitarian concerns of food, disease, and natural disaster. These issues tied into spiritual vulnerabilities: madness, loss of hope, and noncooperation. What makes this concern more than the merely utilitarian is that these ancient peoples reached beyond practical technology.

At this stage of human existence, the hard distinctions between nature and human beings that our culture maintains did not exist. Rather, the art of prehistoric caves suggests that animals and plants were intimate fellow creatures, close links to humans in the chain of life. What happened to plants in the spring might well illumine what would happen to human dead in the next turn of their cycle. So as the earliest people mourned their dead, treasured their frail offspring, or marveled at sexuality, they probably drew on a sense of the life chain, the continuum

Sydney Garden

of plants, animals, and themselves. We know that they anointed their dead with substances like red ochre, which resembles life-giving blood. (The red ochre might be a symbol of blood, of life-giving force; the ceremony of anointing would be the ritual.) From this we would infer that they probably saw hunting and gathering as sacred affairs, dealing with nature's awesome powers of life and death. Nature, then, was the great interest and educator of the earliest people. Much more than we moderns, they felt part of the seasonal cycles, dominated by sun and cold.

Much of the religion of early humanity, much of its worship, probably focused on generative powers and the Great Mother. Relics from a swath of land extending from Siberia to the Near East attest to the prehistoric use of figurines of pregnant women. From these symbols we might infer doctrines about female deities. In the same way, numerous relics attest to a concern with hunting rituals and animal fertility. In a cave near St. Girons in France, explorers found the head of a lion engraved on a stalactite. The presence

of numerous arrows suggests that the lion head functioned as a target in a hunting ritual. The famous "sorcerer" painting in the same cave depicts a figure presiding over such rituals. His legs are human, his eyes are those of an owl, and he has reindeer antlers, the paws of a bear, the tail of a horse, and prominent genitals. Some scholars suggest that he is a "Master of the Animals," who led a dance or ritual in which his people expressed their needs and hopes for the hunt.

So prehistoric peoples probably understood their world largely in terms of quite concrete, emotion-laden interactions with the life powers. From nonliterate peoples living today, we can hypothesize that the earliest peoples probably developed stories about the origin of the world and of themselves based on their observations of human and animal birth. Moreover, because they could create by making things, and so sensed their special powers of consciousness, prehistoric peoples may have developed the doctrine of a soul— a source of psychic or spiritual life.

New Guinea Masks

Our ancestors may have pondered life's mysteriousness in terms of the implications of hunting. Living off animal flesh, they both established a symbolic bond with the animal world and made a significant change in their own evolution: a gender-based division of labor in which the adult males went on hunting parties away from the camp, while the women and children stayed close to camp, gathering roots, fruits, nuts, and vegetables.

Just as hunting trained people to pay close attention to the characteristics of the game—where they fed, when they migrated south or north—so gathering trained people to pay close attention to the characteristics of plants. Gatherers, the majority of whom probably were women, had to know where to find the roots, nuts, berries, fruits, and other plant products that furnished the staple portion of the earliest peoples' diet (meat from hunting was not always available). Gatherers of plants experimented to find out which ones were good spices or had healing or hallucinogenic properties and which ones could be boiled or dried to produce dyes, decorative hangings, or good fuel for the fire.

COMMON THEMES IN TRIBAL RELIGION

Let us begin by describing some of the basic characteristics of the religious lives of recent nonliterate peoples.

THE SACRED

The **sacred** is that which is holy, *ultimately relevant,* more significant than ordinary reality, purer and deserving proper handling. Sacredness often elicits *piety* (devotion), as people experience the goodness of what is most ultimate and perhaps has been merciful to them. Awe, fear, and intoxication also may result from dealings with the sacred, as the exalted spirit either appreciates the blinding holiness and power of the sacred or loses its footing in the world. Cultures differ as to how they conceive of the sacred, but virtually all premodern cultures agreed that sacredness was the crux of reality. In modern times secularity has risen to challenge sacredness but also to tempt humanity to try to do without sacredness—a trend most religious people think unfortunate, if not disastrous.

The key to understanding the sacred is that it is perceived as being beyond the physical, material, everyday, utilitarian world with its laws of cause and effect, means and ends. It transcends the limits of cognitive signs and concepts and requires symbols to portray an emotional, transrational encounter with the core of reality, living in passionate connection with what is most real and valuable.

The experience of the sacred, in Rudolf Otto's celebrated description, involves the sense of a mystery that is both fearsome and fascinating. It has been most vivid in nature's manifestations of power, but it might also occur in initiation rites, ceremonial ecstasy, or other intense experiences. With modifications, we can glimpse the experience of the sacred in accounts of enlightenment and peak experiences. The visions of *Isaiah* (6:1–13), *Ezekiel* (1:1–29), and *Revelation* (1:1–29) show some of the biblical expressions of the sacred. In all these cases, we can see human imagination dazzled by the pure power that makes everything that is. This omnipresence of sacred power is perhaps our best thread through the labyrinth of the nonliterate religions.

Just about every aspect of human experience has at some time been held sacred. Thought and sex, trees and waters, stones and ancestors—all have been considered manifestations of power or holiness. The sacred may even focus on human hair and fingernails as symbols to be dealt with in a ritual or mythic context. We can say, therefore, that the sacred is the ultimate or deepest significance that any thing, place, or person can manifest if seen at the right angle. For instance, the beggar can seem to wear a coat of holiness. On the other end of the social scale, chieftains and kings have regularly been reverenced as sacred. In fact, the king has been not only a ruler by divine right but also frequently a sacrificial figure, killed for the sake of his people.

THE PROFANE

Profane is the term for the opposite of sacred; that which exists outside the shrine or realm of the holy; ordinary reality when taken without reference to its ultimate source or goal. The sacred stands in contrast to the profane, which is experienced as nonultimate, business-as-usual, perhaps even sullied. Most peoples have separated off certain times and places as special—holy, given over to divinity, deserving of respect or even awe.

Modern Western consciousness has increased humanity's general sense of profanity by removing many portions of reality from the divine influence. Thus the processes of nature, and many of the processes of the human mind and social consensus, now tend to be viewed as implying nothing sacred—nothing showing the direct imprint of the transcendent, other, holy reality traditionally called God. This may reflect the difference, if not antagonism, between **secular** outlooks, in terms of which virtually everything is profane, and religious outlooks, which suspect that everything positive is a gift of God and that with a properly contemplative or mystical spirit normal people could appreciate them as such. If there is one thing that tribal societies are not, it is secular. The social order and the religious order are closely intertwined.

ANIMISM

One frequent outcome of living in a sacralized world is the doctrine of **animism:** that everything has a soul—not just deities, demons, and humans, but animals, places, and even natural events (e.g., rainstorms, volcanic eruptions). Animism can be found in many tribal religions, and this often connects with doctrines about taboos and afterlife as well as indicating the specific duties of the shaman.

TABOO

A **taboo** describes something forbidden: usually an action or a place. This is a Polynesian word used to designate something one should avoid because of its sacral or dangerous character. Taboos are found in many nonliterate or tribal religious traditions, but we also find analogies in literate and city-based traditions. Thus, while it is clearly a taboo when Inuits (Eskimo) avoid contact with the seals in certain periods or when any tribal group segregates menstruating women, it is something quite the same when Jews establish kosher laws and Muslims, Buddhists, and some Christians prohibit any use of alcohol. Taboos defend against violations of nature's strange (never fully knowable) laws. Taboos keep the tribe distinctive, preserving a sense of cleanliness that it tends to equate with godliness.

To increase their chances of living in a good age, ancient hunters probably developed a code of behavior and a cluster of taboos that they attributed to their ancestors: "Live this way and you will prosper." In some cases, the taboos may have had some utilitarian payoff. There is some instrumental value in saying that there is a taboo against going through the poison oak bushes because it is the sacred garden of the forest spirit (who would retaliate by afflicting the violator with an itchy rash). The kosher dietary laws of the Hebrews prohibited eating animals that were scavengers (e.g., vultures, swine), and this practice may have had some public health benefits. Avoiding contact with the dead may have been explained because the spirit was in transition to a different realm, but once again a public health benefit may have ensued.

But the vindication of most ancient aversions and taboos was more irrational than rational and should be explained by the notion that the sacred demands purity. Many ancient peoples considered contact with

THEMES IN TRIBAL RELIGIONS

THEME	DESCRIPTION	EXAMPLE(S)
Sacred	some things are holy, more special than regular aspects of reality	all tribal societies
Profane	aspects of life that are not sacred	all tribal societies
Animism	people, animals, and things have souls	most tribal societies
Magic	manipulate spiritual forces in private rituals	most tribal societies
Exorcism	cast out evil spirits	most tribal societies
Rites of passage	rituals that occur during life stage transitions (such as puberty)	Aborigines, Indians, Africans, Melanesians, Polynesians
Sacrifice	giving something of value back to the spirits	Ainu (bear)
Shaman	religious functionary who deals with spirits, exorcises, heals	Aborigines, Indians, Eskimo
Healing	use herbs and massage to treat physical illness	most tribal societies
Divination	predicting the future	Africans, Indians, Celts
Totemism	animal symbols of ancestors	Aborigines, Indians, Polynesians
High god	creator father god who is now inactive	Aborigines, Indians, Africans
Ancestors	worship or reverence for departed family	Aborigines, Africans, Melanesians
Tricksters	clever figures in myths	Indians, Japanese, Africans, Celts, Teutons
Megaliths	stone ritual centers	Celts, Teutons

a menstruating woman to be polluting, but this may be the way that these people had for expressing the reverence for (and fear of) the great power of reproduction held by the female and blood as a symbol of life. Neither contact with the dead nor contact with a menstruating woman involved an ethical dimension: a matter of bad will, bad choice, or sin. Rather, it was a matter of being out of phase with the sacred.

RITES OF PASSAGE

Ritual refers to the conduct of ceremonies. In the non-literate context, it consists of the dances and dramatic presentations by which tribes have displayed their mythic histories and realities. All religious rituals are ceremonial actions designed to express a people's awe, fears, and hopes. Rituals allow people to participate in their myths and dramatize their doctrines.

A **rite of passage** is a ceremony in which a person moves from one life stage to another: birth, puberty, marriage, and death. These rituals of traditional peoples have carried the motif of further disclosures of tribal wisdom. The rites themselves tend to create what Van Gennep called a liminal state or free zone, different from ordinary existence, in which people may bond in fresh and deeper ways and their ordinary identities are laid aside in the threshold to a new stage of intimacy with the sacred. As the gods did at the beginning, so human beings have given birth, passed over to adulthood, married, and buried their dead.

At birth, the child is initiated into the tribe. It is more of a ritual for the tribe than the child, arousing the commitment of the adult extended family to the child.

Most impressive have been the rites for **puberty** (the passage from child to adult). Rites for young men regularly have stressed enduring suffering. Those for young women have stressed preparing for feminine tasks, as the particular society conceived of them. For both sexes, puberty has been a time to learn about sexuality, the tribal gods, and the discipline that adulthood demands. They are ordeals designed to toughen children into adults and to impart adult sacred lore. Men will get new identities as members of hunting and raiding parties; they will no longer stay behind in the camp with the women and children. This transformation may not take place exactly at puberty, but perhaps as early as age six or as late as the teens. Boys may undergo various bodily operations: tattooing, scarring, the loss of a tooth, but the most popular is circumcision (the removal of the foreskin of the penis).

Arnold Van Gennep and Victor Turner argued that rites of passage were necessary social events to usher the individual through frightening life stages and events. The last thirty years have seen the decline of many formal adolescent rituals in our secular society: fraternity hazing, the military draft, etc. I protested against the draft in the 1960's and was happy to see it replaced by the all-volunteer military, but now I wonder if something has been lost. Was military conscription a sort of puberty rite for males? Young men were taken from every social class, ethnicity and geographical region and placed into an adult role. Is the rise of urban youth gangs an attempt to fill the vacuum, and create new roles and rituals for gaining an adult male identity? Do you have any suggestions for rituals that our secular society could institute to function as puberty rites?

Contribute to this discussion at
http://forums.delphiforums.com/rel101

Marriage rituals are also important. The norms of marriage may differ: monogamy (one husband–one wife), polygamy (one husband–many wives), and more rarely, polyandry (one wife–several husbands), but rarest is **celibacy** (abstinence from sex and marriage). Adultery and divorce are rare in most tribes. This is not because individuals have taken such care in selecting the most compatible mate but because the boys have been trained to be the husbands that their wives will expect and because the girls have been trained to be the wives that their husbands will expect.

Funeral rites are intended to separate the dead from the living without offense. One must perform these rites most carefully, for they can influence the dead person's peace in the spirit world. Funerals keep the living in view, too, stirring up consoling memories and reminding the bereaved that all life is fleeting.

SACRIFICE

Sacrifice is a basic ritual in which the worshipper offers something to a deity or spirit. This offering may be in the form of a gift (Mauss's concept) or a penalty paid for breaking a taboo. The essential feature is that the worshipper gives up something in the utilitarian realm in hopes of pleasing the deity. In hunting cultures, the sacrifice is usually an animal slaughtered in honor of the deity (or part of a slaughtered animal dedicated to a deity and not eaten by the worshipper). Evidence of animal sacrifice is present in some of the oldest burial sites of Paleolithic religion. A frequent recipient of animals sacrificed by hunting cultures was the Master of the Animals: a deity who protected the animals yet also allowed hunters to succeed. It was seen as good etiquette to ask permission of the Master of the Animals before hunting and to give back a portion of the kill after the hunt.

In later, agricultural societies, grain, wine, beer, or humans might be substituted for the animals. Ritual cannibalism and head hunting had somewhat of a different rationale from human sacrifice. Head hunting was usually part of a rite of passage: a trophy from a young man's first raiding party. Cannibalism might involve eating part of an ancestor who died of natural causes, in order to assimilate his spirit or create a closer bond.

Asceticism is a related sacrificial path to the spiritual. It involves self-privation, abstinence from pleasurable

MAGIC

When taboos are broken, peoples may turn to religious or magical rituals. **Magic** is the attempt to manipulate spiritual forces, whereas the religious attitude is one of adoration of, and obedience to, the spirits. Religious rituals are usually performed in public, magical rituals in private. The main similarity between magic and religion is that they both acknowledge that reality has a dimension of spirits.

Both religion and magic can inhibit the utilitarian dimension of life to the extent that practical solutions are ignored. Fortunately, most people turn to technology first, then rely upon magic or religion to solve what is beyond the reach of technology (Malinowski's theory). Recall that it was Frazer who assumed that humankind first went through a phase of magic before turning to religion. Yet interest in magic and sorcery persists in all cultures. The greater the lack of access to technological solutions, the greater the interest in magical solutions.

Sorcery is one type of magic: the use of power gained from evil spirits. Sorcery is like "black" magic or "negative witchcraft" in seeking to use its powers for harm. It usually depends on a worldview in which impersonal powers can be brought to one's side or spiritual forces may be divided into those serving evil spirits and those serving good. Thus in some situations sorcery is connected with diabolism—the attempt to gain and serve satanic powers. In most cases, the goals of sorcery are petty, such as vengeance against a foe.

The term **witch** has several different connotations. It is usually reserved for a woman (men are referred to as *warlocks* or *wizards*). She may perform sorcery or magic with evil intent or may simply be a wise woman rooted in the pre-Christian traditions of European religion. Witches could be advocates of naturalistic methods of healing, childbearing, and worship. They could be people stigmatized as social deviants. When engaged in sorcery, witches tried to tap powers of animals or malign spirits. In societies that both acknowledged witchcraft and feared it as a source of black magic, people labeled as witches could be marked for death.

Here is a case study of a modern *brujo*, or wizard, who lived in Acapulco. His neighbors were government clerks, taxi drivers, and construction workers. He had no occupation other than to be on his front porch and maintain an eagle eye on his Colonia Jardin Palmas neighborhood. Neighbors did not like this man, but they were afraid to leave swept trash in front of his house or even to gossip about him. The women of the barrio would seek his talents to bring bad luck against their husband's mistresses.

Another neighbor paid him to work evil against a contractor who was bringing him to court. Whether the neighbors' denominational affiliation was Catholic, Pentecostal, or Jehovah's Witness did not seem to make a difference: when they needed to put a hex on someone (or needed a defense against a hex placed against them) they turned to *el Brujo*.

Also related to magic is the concept of fetishes. These can be thought of as excesses of the symbolic. A **fetish** is an object thought to have protective powers. Fetishes, like geomancy (determining the forces of local spirits), flourish in an animistic world, where one needs protection from powers that may be either malign in themselves or sent on malign errands by one's enemies. By giving the frightened person something specific upon which to fix hopes for defense, the fetish provides a measure of psychological comfort. Although the technologies of the sophisticated religious traditions certainly can bring forward other justifications, the beads of pious Muslims, the *mezuzah* of pious Jews, and the icons of pious Christians all draw much of their impact from the same psychodynamics that earlier peoples fixed on fetishes and amulets.

EXORCISM

Exorcism is the process of casting out evil spirits that have possessed a person. Exorcism depends on the notion that malevolent forces can take over at least portions of the body and psyche and that representatives of holy counterforces can intercede to cast the evil forces out. It is often hard to draw a distinction between exorcism and sorcery (indeed, if a sorcerer had placed a hex on someone, that person might have to see an exorcist for relief). Similarly, exorcism overlaps with healing, since there might be physical manifestations of the possession. The entire phenomenon involves interactions among psychic and somatic forces that make it hard to determine precisely what the undeniable phenomena of possession—swellings, cursings, supernormal strength, apparent hatred of everything holy, bestial sounds—represent. One possible explanation for what is going on here is hypnosis: the induction of an altered state of consciousness in which the patient is put into a relaxed and highly suggestible state. The patient then willingly (though not consciously) behaves as *if* she is possessed and then through posthypnotic suggestion, behaves as *if* she is cured.

Let's consider another case study from modern Acapulco, this one known as the Templo Espiritualista. About a mile from the tourist hotels that ring the bay is a Barrio Negro (African district). One small house made out of driftwood and cardboard held together by wire has a line of "patients" outside waiting for a consultation with a spirit doctor. They are afflicted by the *ojo malo* (evil eye) or *envidia blanca* (white envy). Inside the house, the women who run the temple make *tortillas* and sweep the floor. When a patient comes and asks for one of them specifically, she puts down the broom and dons a white robe, transforming herself into a powerful medium speaking with the voice of a spirit. She throws alcohol on the rough concrete floor. She then takes a candle burning brightly under a picture of Jesus and Mary and turns the floor into a circle of fire. The patient must jump in and out of the circle three times and will get a vision of the evil spirit. The patient is then sent to the market to bring some items—flowers, ammonia, more alcohol—and another ritual is performed. The spirit doctor may go around the patient's body chanting prayers and sucking out the evil spirits. Then she may pour the alcohol onto the flowers and light them, creating a great fragrant torch, and swat the bare back of the patient in order to drive away an evil spirit. The cost for this two-hour ritual: about $2.50 (plus the cost of materials).

HEALING

One technology lacking in ancient times was modern medicine: surgery, antibiotics, vaccinations. Tribal healers often used what they had: massage and herbal remedies. In some cases (e.g., aspirin, quinine) the forest herbs discovered by ancient healers have passed the modern rigors of controlled clinical trials. In other cases, the herbal remedies had been selected for no reason beyond symbolism (e.g., rhinoceros horn is assumed to treat erectile disorder in aging males). For nonliterate peoples, illness is as much a spiritual matter as a physical one.

Even when the herbal remedy has no direct medicinal value, the patient may get better. One reason for this is the placebo effect (the tendency of patients to get better just because they know that they are receiving treatment). A second explanation is that the disease has run its natural course (e.g., any treatment for a common cold will be followed by improvement in three to ten days).

Don Abel is a modern healer who lives in a village called Luces, about 15 kilometers up the coast from Acapulco. Although he claims to be over 80, Don Abel goes into the city each day to work as a janitor in a hotel. Each night he takes the bus out to his thatched roof home with his dozen small children and wife (in her mid-thirties). He arrives just as the sun goes down and finds a line of eager patients. He treats them by massage with special balms he has made out of herbs he has gathered himself in the mountains on his days off. A woman of about 50 with a painful bunion is his first patient this evening. Don Abel rubs the affected foot for almost twenty minutes with a concoction that has the look and texture of used crankcase oil but the smell of a pungent mountain plant. Then, for preventive reasons, he also applies the remedy to the other foot for an equal amount of time. The cost for the treatment: under three dollars (and the patient gets to carry home a week's supply of the ointment). The patient said that she had seen a podiatrist with no improvement but that if Don Abel did not get results, she would not be back. "This stuff smells too bad" she said.

DIVINATION

Divination is a noun; *to divine* is the verb. This is confusing because the word *divine* can also be an adjective referring to something that pertains to a deity (a divinity). The word *divination* has no direct connection with divinity or deity. Divination is similar to magic in that it is an occult, nontechnological solution to life's problems, but whereas magic tries to manipulate future events, **divination** is the mere attempt to predict those events. Divination can also refer to the art of discerning other things, such as the cause of sickness, the will of a god, and other practices by many tribal peoples. Diviners use innumerable methods in their work: studying the entrails of special animals, determining the flight of birds, reading the cracks in tortoise shells, shaking out yarrow stalks or chits in a basket, and the like.

Both ancient tribal peoples and we moderns prefer future events that we can foresee (if not control). Over a quarter of American adults have an interest in astrology. Psychic hotlines do enough business to spend millions on advertising. The difference between ancient and modern is mostly in the types of events we need to predict: the movements of the stock market versus movements of herds of buffalo. Perhaps moderns have more technological sources of information, such as weather reports. But modern mediums have additional techniques as well: ouija boards, divination baskets, tarot cards, and crystal balls.

CREATION MYTHS

Nonliterate peoples have usually described the sacred through myth and ritual. A **myth** is a storied form of explanation, usually traditional. Myths may discard the limits of ordinary experience and portray divine or ultimate realities acting beyond the constraints of space and time. A myth is an explanation of what has happened, and it is repeated because it expresses the tribe's identity and values. Peoples tell myths explaining how they came to be where and what they were. Of course, our present-day critical history distances itself from myth by rigorously controlling sources and arguments (the process of verification used in all sciences). Nonetheless, critical history could not have developed without the capacity of human beings to remember what had happened to them and its relevance.

There are several kinds of myths. Usually a people's most important myth concerns **cosmogony:** how the world was born. *Creation* is the subject of this most basic myth, which ritual frequently uses to integrate a people with the sacred. This sets the pattern for all the things in creation and tends to be renewed at the turning of each new year (often through rites of dissolution [orgy] and reformation), and it may be invoked

at any other new start, such as erecting a house, passing from childhood to adulthood, marrying, or passing from the living to the dead.

Etiological myths explain the origin of particular aspects of the natural or cultural world; **teleological** myths deal with the design of history, whereas **eschatological** myths deal with the end of time. Myths of judgment describe what will happen after death to reward the good and punish the wicked. Myths often are sung, danced, and ritualized. Overall, they make people's basic notions vivid, memorable, capable of empowering them to live with direction and commitment.

TRICKSTERS

Another important theme in many ancient myths is the **trickster.** Trickster figures are clownlike, clever and deceitful, living by their wits; their numbers include gods, demons, and even mortal humans and animals. Some of these myths take the form of legends, tall tales, or crude jokes. The trickster can be a hero or antihero, saintly or sinnerlike, both a cunning person and a dupe, a principle of both order and disorder, the founder of convention and yet its chief defier. This rascal may have an uncontrolled and insatiable appetite for food or sex. Tricksters perform gross, scatalogical pranks and will not control their bowels or bladder, making practical jokes and humbling the haughty. Tricksters entertain us as the personification of human impulsiveness, the psychoanalytic id.

Yet myths also show tricksters playing a part in the founding of the tribe's culture: wresting a victory against the chaotic forces of scheming demons and unfeeling natural disasters. The retelling of these myths may function as a safety valve—a way for a people to project their own animal appetites, mock

> Tricksters are mythological figures who use their wits to deceive and defeat their opponents. Tricksters are common in Native American, Celtic, Teutonic, African, and Japanese religion.
>
> Who would qualify as a trickster in contemporary, secular American culture?
>
> **Contribute to this discussion at**
> **http://forums.delphiforums.com/rel101**

law and order, and tame with humor the destructive potential in their instinctual makeup.

TOTEMS

Important myths for tribal and personal identity often center on **totems.** A totem is a symbol, usually an animal, plant, or other object that serves as the emblem of a clan. It suggests the symbiosis between human and animal life. A clan usually thinks of its totem as a helper as well as a symbol of its special qualities. Thus an eagle could be a messenger from heaven as well as a symbol of freedom and speed. A bear could be a source of wisdom about the ways of the forest as well as an emblem of strength. It would be natural to speak to the clan totem, venerate it in regular rites, and let it embody the whole animal economy on which one's people depended for food and clothing. The totem is venerated not just out of fear or greed but out of sincere respect for nature and ancestors.

THE HIGH GOD

The apparent locations of this life power were the sky and the earth. The sky, vaulted over everything, was in a position to observe and perhaps control everything, and it contained the sun and the rain; thus, it regularly attracted the mind's search for an ultimate principle. From the experience of human birthing, people seem to have given the earth a maternal modality very early — to have thought of it as a Great Mother. The sky is usually portrayed as masculine, a father who inseminates the mother.

A related myth is that of a father deity, "Great Spirit" or **high god.** His abode is in the sky. He had an important role in creation but is now inactive, distant, aloof, retired, or senile, so he may be lacking active worship. His present status may reflect a myth of a fall from heavenly grace and may necessitate calling upon lesser deities for daily rituals and concerns.

AFTERLIFE AND ANCESTORS

Most tribal peoples were more concerned about the difficulties of this life than the next. Salvation was seen in the context of the here and now, nature and tribe. One desired to have a full belly, healthy body, and many children and to know the spirits intimately. Yet do not conceive of this as the tribal equivalent of our modern material goals of success: accumulated unneeded luxuries and status symbols that "kept up with the Joneses" or kept a step ahead of the Smiths. Such competitive notions would be inconsistent with tribal and natural harmony, which were of far greater value.

Nevertheless, doctrines of afterlife were an important feature in nonliterate traditions. More than 500,000 years ago, in the Dragon Bone Hill caves of China near Beijing, people buried bodies in the hope of an afterlife. Some of the earliest peoples, then, tried to break death's stranglehold by imagining that something in them survived death. That something might be the part that traveled in dreams, that could fantasize and construct realities other than the physical. This hope was inspired by numerous *symbols:* the smoke that wood releases when it is destroyed by fire, the part of plants that makes them flower again after winter. These prehistoric peoples used their imagination and at least rudimentary reflection to project hopes that they could overcome their biological weakness and mortality.

Bones buried in the Mousterian period (70,000–50,000 B.C.E.) suggest the practice of burial with hopes for an afterlife. The problem in interpreting ancient artifacts (many of them much older than the Mousterian), though, is that without written texts or at least semididactic ("teaching") art, we can only imagine how the earliest people used such artifacts — what they thought when they laid the dead in the ground, why they sang and danced, and so on.

Conceptions of the human soul varied. In many tribes it was assumed that the soul departed the body during sleep, illness, or trance and certainly after death. Tylor looked at religion and assumed that it began in this doctrine, and the need for the tribe to continue the relationship with the lingering souls of the ancestors and also to protect itself against the ghosts of slain enemies. In this way, the dead had a semiphysical presence, making them more than just their children's memories.

Some immortal souls went back to the place where they first passed into the fetus. The dead person's second, mortal soul turned into a ghost and was capable of malicious acts. Consequently, the mourning ceremonies tried to mute any anger that the deceased might have borne against relatives and friends. After a stated time, the ghost was incapable of mischief because it departed for other haunts or faded away.

In some cultures, death was conceived as a transformation: from human to something in nature or the spirit world. The Pueblo had a singularly clear and happy conception of the afterlife. For them the dead would either join the *kachinas* ("spirits") or become rain clouds. Other tribes hoped for some reenactment of human life. The Hopi buried women in their wedding dresses, anticipating the women's passage to the next world.

Many hunting tribes also considered that the game animals had souls and established special rituals for the hunt and butchering of the animals so that the bones could be ritually treated. Indeed, some tribes understood there to be a **reincarnation** (rebirth in a new form) of one animal's soul going back to be recycled in a new body, or even a possibility of a movement from animal to human or vice versa, this connecting with the use of animal names or totems.

Even more common was the notion of reincarnation of human to human, and the Hopi buried dead infants in the hope that their souls would return in future children. Even more common was the notion of reincarnation of ancestor to descendent and the possibility of inheriting skills, powers, or personality traits. A child was named for a dead person in the hope that he or she inherited that person's soul and qualities. For that reason, the Caribou Inuit called a child who had inherited an ancestor's name "grandmother" or "grandfather."

Such conceptions of soul may have thought of death as a passageway, a threshold to a new level of existence. As one passed thresholds at birth and puberty, so one might pass a last threshold at death. In death one might even follow a circle that led the soul back to a new phase of earthly life—one's life force might animate another breathing creature, even another human body.

In many traditions there is a heaven, but the road to it is confusing. Many souls get lost along the way. One of the duties of the shaman could be to guide the souls of the departed and accompany them to the land of rest.

MEGALITHS

Megaliths were ritual centers, usually constructed out of stone. Many examples are found in northern Europe and played an important role in the worship rituals of the Celts and Teutons, but other examples can be found in Africa (e.g., ancient Zimbabwe) and even Australia (e.g., Ayer's Rock). *Megalith* means "great stone," and it brings to mind the prehistoric European cultures that left remains such as the famous cromlech (circle of huge stones) at Stonehenge in England. There was a megalithic cultural complex centered at Los Millares in southeastern Spain and covering Portugal, half of France, western England, and parts of Ireland, Denmark, and Sweden. In some cases, prehistoric peoples in these areas arranged either cromlechs or dolmens (immense capstones supported by several upright stones arranged to form a sort of enclosure or chamber) from slabs weighing as much as 300 tons. What was the point of all this labor?

Apparently the megalith was the major symbol for a ritual pertaining to the dead. For Neolithic peasants of the fifth and fourth millennia B.C.E., stone was the symbol of permanence—of resistance to change, decay, or death. Unlike peoples in central Europe and the Near East, who strictly separated themselves from the dead, the megalithic tribes of western Europe sought close communion with the deceased, probably because they regarded death as a state of security and strength. To these people, ancestors could be powerful helpers and great allies.

The megaliths represent burial vaults or ritual areas. At **Stonehenge,** for instance, the cromlech was in the middle of a field of funeral mounds. (Stonehenge was also a sophisticated instrument that could be used for making astronomical calculations.) At Carnac in Brittany, there was an avenue large enough for thousands to parade. Both sites likely were ceremonial centers or unenclosed temples—areas of sacred space for communing with ancestral stones. Practically the whole island of Neolithic Malta was a megalithic sanctuary system. There a great goddess presided as the guardian divinity over a cult of the dead. One necropolis, now called the Hypogeum, has yielded bones of more than 7,000 people. The northern European megaliths are older than the remains from the prehistoric Aegean, so western Europeans apparently developed their megalithic religion independently.

Moreover, megaliths later cropped up in a vast geographic area extending from Algeria to Korea and North America. Thus, huge stones probably prompted in many different peoples similar ideas about death, ancestors, permanence, and escape from time and

Megaliths were stone ritual centers in northern Europe, like these standing stones on the Isle of Lewis in Scotland.

decay. If most prehistoric peoples were moved to ponder their mortality more deeply because of agriculture, perhaps they tended to use stone to assist them in this contemplation.

Certain customs of European peasants in megalithic areas further confirm this hypothesis. As late as the early twentieth century, peasant women in parts of France slid along stones or rubbed themselves against stones to stimulate conception. For them, as for women who lived in their locales 5,000 years earlier, stone was a powerful and fertilizing force.

THE SHAMAN

The central figure of nonliterate religion is the **shaman.** He (or she) may have duties that could include healing, exorcising, divining, assisting the souls of the dead, or conducting puberty rites. Shamanism is so widespread that it cannot be explained by cultural diffusion from a single original center. Mircea Eliade viewed the shaman as a specialist in archaic techniques of ecstasy. For example, the Yanomamo shamans, living at the border of Venezuela and northern Brazil, indicate that their visions come from ingesting hallucinogenic snuff. The snuff induces visions of *hekura,* tiny humanoid figures who may be used for healing friends or making enemies sick.

How do shamans gain their tribe's confidence to do this? Some claim paranormal powers, including **clairvoyance** and *clairaudience* (seeing and hearing beyond the normal range). Others possess an impressive knowledge of herbs, drugs, tribal traditions, or special vocabulary. Probably the shamans' greatest success, though, comes from their mastery of techniques of suggestion, which are especially effective with peoples of vivid imagination.

The functions of shamans differ greatly by geographic location. Nepalese shamans may perform simple exorcisms and healing rituals using fetishes of rice and the blood of roosters. Native American shamans may have to make the rainfall in due season or determine the whereabouts of herds of game.

The shamans in China and Japan (typically female) sing songs and go into a trance as a way of being taken over, being temporarily inhabited or possessed. In China, the female shaman's song to her guiding spirit has often had a romantic tone, as though a beloved were pining for her lover. In Japan, the *kami,* or spirits, who come can be erotically intimate. In both places, the possessed shaman discerns what the spirits want or divines what the future will require. Additionally, the Japanese shamans used to band together and walk a regular beat through the local villages, offering personal advice and medical healing.

Not all shamanist figures have been exalted personalities or even all that sincere. Some have been charlatans who performed for applause or money, and some were more like sorcerers, soliciting the powers of evil to inflict harm. However, most shamans are probably sincere, committed to their roles and the accompanying worldview.

Etymologically, enthusiasm means "being filled with the god." Those modern societies that grant women little status tend to have a substantial number of female enthusiasts. Most likely, such women use their religious experience to gain a little respect and influence. So, too, with the powerless people prominent among other groups of ecstatics. In Acapulco, for example, most of the spirit doctors at the Templo Espiritualista were poor women of African and indigenous descent (the most marginalized segment of modern Mexican society).

The shaman is a special member of the tribe, recruited and trained for this special role. Specifically, tribes of Siberia and central Asia (which may represent the purest form of shamanism) often select their shamans for psychological features and capacities that render them apt for ecstasy—for going outside themselves. The typical candidate is sensitive, introverted, inclined to solitude, and perhaps given to fainting or hallucinations. By adolescence he (males predominate in Siberian shamanism) is thought to be more peculiar, brooding, or religious than his peers. If he has an emotional crisis or if something strange happens to him (such as getting very sick or being struck by lightning), elders will consider him appropriate for initiation into shamanism, which will entail learning tribal lore and ecstatic techniques and then passing an initiatory ordeal.

The initiatory ordeal (at least in Siberia) amounts to a ritualized experience of suffering, death, and resurrection. The candidate's body is symbolically dismembered; he dies and is transported to the realm of the gods. There his organs are replaced or renewed, sometimes with special stones or other tokens of his visit added. Depending on the symbols of his tribe, he may fly to heaven as a bird, climb a sacred pole or tree (the *axis mundi* connecting earth to heaven), or travel up the rainbow. Which organ is replaced seems to depend on what the shaman's tribe thinks is the organ that ultimately quickens human beings. (Bone and blood are popular choices.)

This experience takes place while the candidate is in ecstasy, outside his normal consciousness. If the initiation is public, the community gets a running narration of how it is going, with descriptions of the ascent, the celestial realm, the dismembering, and sample voices of the gods. A modern Westerner would probably call the proceedings hallucinatory, but nonliterate peoples tend to equate the real with the vividly experienced, so they consider it quite real. Furthermore, studies show shamans to be the healthiest members of their tribes psychologically, in the sense of being well adjusted to their society and the role to which it has assigned them. Performing his duties makes the shaman feel good and heals him of his ills, so whenever he is out of sorts, he will sing or drum and go out of himself to the gods.

When the candidate has passed his initiatory ordeal, he is usually accepted by his community and can start functioning as a shaman. His principal functions are healing, guiding the dead to the afterworld, and acting as a medium between the living and the dead. The universe is dualistic because it includes the human realm, where the shaman's body remains, and the spiritual realm, to which his spirit travels. The human being is dualistic because he or she has both a body and a spirit.

Ordinarily, a shaman goes into ecstasy to gain knowledge or power. He must find out from the gods what is ailing a patient or what the right medicine is. Similarly, to find where the game has gone, the shaman must be able to travel to the gods who keep the game. For example, to the coastal Inuits, this meant the shaman's swimming to the depths of the sea, where the goddess Sedna, who ruled the seals and the fish, had fenced them in. To guide the souls of the departed, the shaman must also be able to travel to the land of rest. If a tribal member suffers soul loss (which causes sickness), the shaman must be able to trace the soul and retrieve it.

Wherever he goes, the shaman reports on his progress. His functioning therefore recreates the community in two senses: (1) He helps his people reassert their view of the world, and (2) he gives them an entertaining account of his plunge to the bottom of the sea, his fight to get past Sedna's vicious watchdog, and so forth. When he returns from a mission, he often requires the community to renew itself. Sedna may be withholding the fish because someone has broken a taboo—a hunter may have mistreated a seal, two brothers may have had a violent fight, or spouses may have aborted a fetus. Such a violation of the tribe's ethic must be atoned for because it has ruptured their harmony with nature. Thus, the skillful shaman creates a forum in which his people can confess their guilt and express their regrets and fears. He tries to reconcile enemies and convince the whole tribe to reaffirm its ethical ideals.

The shaman may well touch psychic depths that technical, literate modern cultures have neglected. The way of the shaman may well have a lot to teach modern Western medicine, but the nonliterate shaman also has only a slippery hold on the distinction between imagination and reason and knows only a little bit, and that intuitively, about the distinctions that might separate the sacred, the psychic, the aesthetic, and the therapeutic.

We will now examine four traditions in depth— Australian, Inuit (formerly known as Eskimo), Native American, and African—and then consider briefly several other tribal traditions.

AUSTRALIAN ABORIGINES

Aborigine means "native." These inhabitants of the southern hemisphere were nomadic hunter-gatherers, having domesticated no animals other than the dog, no pottery, and no bows and arrows (hunting was done with the boomerang). They lived in the inland part of the Australian continent, now known as the "Outback." European settlement along the coastline followed Captain James Cook's exploratory voyage of 1770 and gradually disturbed the delicate ecology of aboriginal civilization. At the time of European contact, the Aborigines probably numbered about 350,000. Presently they number about a third of that, with less than half estimated to be of pure stock. In the semidesert northern region, they maintain much of their original culture, which is based on hunting and gathering and which was fairly uniform across the numerous tribes.

The primary impression that the Aborigines made on European observers was of living in a different set of aspirations. Their apparent listlessness seemed to grow more intense with age. A young man or woman who was manifestly alert and able to solve practical problems steadily became more "dreamlike." The first European observers did not know that this psychological makeup had a firm rationale. Were the native informants clearly to have spoken, they might have said something like the following: "In our religious ceremonies, we are initiated ever more deeply into the Dreamtime of the eternal ancestors. That is the world's own time, by which creation moves. Around us, at the places in the landscape that we memorialize, the ancestors exert the pull of this Dreamtime. Slowly, they return us all to our origins, to where we were before this life. How strange that you whites rush and bustle. You must not know the Dreamtime, must not want to return. Too bad. Life is for returning. We are as the ancestors have dreamed us."

The Aborigine doctrine was animistic but acknowledged a high god, now pretty much removed from active participation. Western knowledge of totemism begins with its discovery in Australia, although it differs somewhat from other totemic systems. The specific animal symbols may be assigned by the location of one's birth rather than one's ancestry, so siblings may belong to different totems (the tribe is nomadic). The clan founders symbolized by the totems are the eternal supernatural beings themselves.

Dreamtime is what the Aborigines call the Eden-like time of creation. In the beginning, many tribes say, these supernatural beings slept under the earth's crust. Time began when they were "born out of their eternity" and burst to the surface. According to the Unambal of northwestern Australia, in the beginning

Ungud lived in the earth as a snake, while in the sky resided Wallanganda, the Milky Way. During the night they created everything through a creative dream. Ungud transformed himself into the beings that he dreamed; Wallanganda threw out a spiritual force, shaped it into images, and projected them onto the rocks of the present landscape. Next, spirits arose, shaped as either animals or humans and based on Wallanganda's images. In turn, they shaped the rest of the earth: mountains, sand hills, plains, and so on. The ancestors were also responsible for the Aborigines' sacred songs and rituals, which were preserved with great care. The ancestors were restrained by a vague, superior force that could punish any crimes. Ancestors were also subject to age, sickness, and decay. Eventually they sank back into their first state of sleep, having produced the sun, moon, stars, death, labor, and pain.

Thus, Australians parceled divinity out among several supernatural figures. Central Australians say that human beings came into existence as semiembryonic masses that were joined together by the hundreds. The totemic ancestors then sliced these masses into individual infants. The traces of these masses left in the landscape became a principle of human life, for pregnant women would receive them and pass them on to the unborn. In other words, a soul could enter the fetus from a certain point in the landscape. It would be an immortal gift from one of the ancestors, the ancestor's own reincarnation. The newborn was thus a being of high dignity. Also, the newborn had strong links to a particular rock or tree, since from it had come the ancestor's spirit. But if humans were linked with eternal ancestors, why did they die? According to the Wotjubaluk of southeastern Australia, originally the moon raised the dead. Then an old man said, "Let them remain dead." So now only the moon itself returns to life.

Life begins when one's parent perceives the coming of the ancestor's spirit to the womb. This most often occurs in a dream but may be prompted by morning sickness or even birth pangs. During initiation into maturity, one partially reenters the Dreamtime—the time when he or she originated out of eternity. Adult life means returning deeper and deeper into this time through religious ceremonies. At death one crosses the final threshold and again becomes a sacred spirit in the sky.

Puberty rites took place in considerable secrecy on sacred ground. Often this sacred ground represented the world as it was in the beginning, for in the puberty ceremonies the participants relived the time of creation. The puberty rites of the Kamilaroi, for instance, reenacted the time when their god Baiame was on earth and founded their ceremonies; in this way the tribe reactualized his presence and regenerated the world. Accordingly, the Kamilaroi prepared the sacred ceremonial ground in terms of a cosmic symbolism. The dominant features were two circular enclosures. The large enclosure, about 23 meters in diameter, had a pole about 3 meters high with emu feathers on top. In the smaller circle were two young trees with their roots in the air. The Kamilaroi drew figures on the ground or modeled them in clay. The largest was a 5-meter representation of Baiame. Then they pantomimed the sacred history of Baiame's creative acts. For the adolescent initiates, this was their first exposure to the tribal lore about how things were in the beginning. For the adults who directed the ceremony, it was a renewal.

One tribe, the Kurnai, separated adolescent boys from their mothers matter of factly, but most tribes even today begin the ceremonies with much weeping and lamentation. Initiates may vary in age from 6 to 14, and they undergo various bodily operations. Most ceremonies follow a regular pattern of segregation of the initiates, instruction, bodily operations, revelation of some sacred objects and ceremonies, washing, and returning to ordinary life. The dominant symbolism of the entire ceremony is death and resurrection. The novice dies to the child's world of irresponsible ignorance and is reborn as a mature, spiritual being. Supposedly the mothers take the death motif literally. Thinking hostile supernatural beings have killed their sons, they mourn as at a funeral. When the boys return, the women treat them as new beings, quite different from what they were as children.

During the ceremony, the boys are covered with branches or rugs. They may not use words, only sounds and signs. When the bullroarer (a slat of wood tied to the end of a thong that roars when whirled) is sounded, the supernatural beings may knock out a tooth, pull out hair, or scar the body. **Circumcision** (removal of the foreskin) is the key act, however, because it is a direct slash at a life source.

Six months to three years after circumcision, many tribes perform a second operation called *subincision,* which involves slitting the underside of the penis and permanently opening the urethra. Some tribes give it overtones of bisexuality, likening the wound to a vulva. In that case, it may represent males' efforts to arrogate powers of mothering. Supporting this interpretation is the sociological fact that the boys pass from female to male control at this time. Other evidence indicates that subincision is a way to gather blood, which is needed for other ceremonials. From this perspective the act approximates menstruation.

Girls' initiations are tailored more for the individual, since they are triggered by the onset of menstruation. In seclusion older women teach the girl songs and myths relating to female dignity and duties. After this instruction, they lead the young woman to a lagoon for a ritual bath and then display her to the community as an adult. In some tribes, a girl's initiation includes defloration with a sort of dildo, followed by ritual intercourse with a group of men. No doubt this act has more than a sadistic or carnal motive, and its exact religious significance is unclear.

The female puberty rite is only the first rite in an Australian woman's life. Marriage, childbearing, menopause, and old age occasion further instruction in the nature of the sacred. As the revelations become more profound, the ceremonies become more secret. There is a pattern in the women's rituals similar to that in the men's—the reenactment of mythical events from the time of creation. In early times, women apparently played important parts in the men's rituals. Myths speak of female ancestors who were more powerful than male ancestors and of men stealing songs, powers, and artifacts that had belonged to the women. The bullroarer is one of the artifacts that the men supposedly stole. Women may have originally functioned in the male circumcision rites, for among some tribes today the initiate gives his foreskin to his sister, who wears it around her neck. In modern times, women have not been privy to male lore.

The principal figure in traditional Australian ritual life has been the **medicine man,** who derives his healing powers from visionary contacts with supernatural beings. Usually he possesses items that symbolize these powers: quartz crystals, pearl shells, stones, bones, or the like. During his puberty rites, after a tooth has been knocked out, he learns to go down into the ground and bring up quartz crystals. The initiators take him to a grave, where a dead man rubs him to make him clever. The dead man also gives him a personal totem, a tiger snake. By following the snake, the boy and his father find the living places of various gods. At the initiation's climax, they climb a thread to Baiame's place in the sky. Baiame looks like an old man with a long beard, and from his shoulders extend two great quartz crystals. Evidently, the medicine man is a sort of shaman whose healing powers derive from his ability to "travel to heaven" and that are represented by his quartz crystals, which are part of divinity itself, and by his animal spirit, the tiger snake, which helps him in his tasks.

Funeral rites had two functions—consoling the bereaved and helping the deceased to find his or her new station. The Aranda said that finding one's new station entailed the immortal soul's returning to the place where it first passed into the fetus. The dead person's second, mortal soul turned into a ghost and was capable of malicious acts. Consequently, the mourning ceremonies tried to mute any anger that the deceased might have borne against relatives and friends. After a stated time, the ghost was incapable of mischief, because it departed for other haunts or faded away.

INUITS (ESKIMO)

The Arctic peoples (Eskimo, Inuit, Aleuts) who stretched from Siberia to Alaska, to Canada, to Greenland were the most sparsely populated people on earth, numbering less than a hundred thousand in total. *Eskimo* was actually a term hung on them by a neighboring Indian tribe and means "meat eaters," which makes sense because they rely upon hunting and fishing. These people call themselves *Inuit,* which merely means "the men."

Inuit children learn to disregard egocentric or self-indulgent impulses. From their earliest years, they are part of a group dominated, regulated, and challenged by the wind, the river, the tundra, and above all the snow and ice. Inuit children see the harshness of life so clearly that the behavior demanded by their parents makes sense. Furthermore, the opportunities to express kindness and friendliness are all the more precious.

Creation myths vary by locality but frequently involve violent themes. The Inuit of northern Canada had a myth of Sedna, goddess of the sea and source of the sea animals. Originally, Sedna was a handsome girl who proudly spurned prospective suitors. One spring a bird flew in from across the ice and wooed her; his song described the soft bearskins she would rest on and the good food she would never lack were she to become his wife. However, the suitor never fulfilled his promise, and the new bride found herself in the most wretched conditions, bitterly lamenting her rejection of previous human suitors. To avenge her, Sedna's father killed the bird; but he and Sedna then became objects of the other birds' wrath. While Sedna and her father were fleeing from their attack, a heavy storm arose, and the father decided to surrender Sedna to the birds by throwing her overboard. She clung to the side of the boat, but he cut off her fingers. The first joints became whales, the second joints became seals, and the stumps became land animals. The storm subsided and Sedna returned to the boat with a fierce hatred for her father. While he was sleeping, she had her dogs gnaw off his feet and hands. He cursed her, the dogs, and himself, whereupon the earth opened and swallowed them all. Ever since, they have lived in the nether world, where Sedna is mistress of sea life.

In a Greenland version of this myth, Arnaquagsaq, the old woman living in the ocean depths, sits in her dwelling in front of a lamp and sends out the animals that the Inuit hunt. Sometimes, however, parasites settle on her head, and in her anger she keeps back the game. Then the shaman must brave the way to her and remove the parasites. To do this, he must cross a turning wheel of ice, negotiate a kettle of boiling water, skirt terrible guardian animals, and finally navigate a bridge as narrow as a knife's edge. He narrates this journey to the community, who follow the tale breathlessly in their mind's eye.

On the traditional Inuit earth lived the goblin people—dwarfs, giants, trolls, shadows, and the like—who could either help travelers or carry them off to torture. Below the earth was an underworld—a warm, comfortable place where the dead could enjoy what they liked in the afterlife. The sky was usually considered a good place, too, although western Greenlanders pictured it as being cold and deserted. When the northern lights appeared in the sky, the dead were thought to be playing football with a walrus head.

The Inuit were animistic, traditionally regarding rocks, animals, food, and even sleep as alive. Their whole world was alive, though only humans and animals had true souls. The basic image for those souls was either a shadow or a breath. The souls were miniatures of what they animated; thus, they were pictured as tiny humans, tiny caribou, and so on.

The most general Inuit religious conception, however, was Sila, a great spirit having some of the characteristics of a high god. Frequently, he spoke to small children. Since many of his messages warned of danger, children were directed to alert the shaman. When all was well, Sila dwelt in endless nothingness, apart from everything.

Normally, the shaman mediated between Sedna or Sila and the tribe. The hidden powers themselves chose the people who were to deal with them, often through revelations in dreams. Igjugarjuk, for instance, became a shaman because of strange visions he had at night, which marked him as a potential shaman. He was therefore given an instructor. In the dead of winter, his instructor left him without food or drink. His only provision was an exhortation to think of the Great Spirit. Five days later, the instructor returned and gave the shaman some lukewarm water. Again he exhorted him to think of the Great Spirit and left. Fifteen days later, the instructor gave Igjugarjuk another drink of water and a small piece of meat. After ten more days—a total of thirty days of nearly complete solitude and fasting—Igjugarjuk saw a helping spirit in the form of a woman. For five months after this he was kept on a strict diet and forbidden sexual intercourse, to consolidate his new power. Throughout his later career, he fasted whenever he wanted to see his spirit and gain her help. Other Inuit shamans have reported initiations involving being shot through the heart or drowned. One who was drowned described being tied to a pole and carried out onto a frozen lake. His instructor cut a hole in the ice and thrust him into it. In these accounts, we can see that the Inuit shaman's way to power is through an initiatory ordeal that often has had a death-resurrection motif.

Some shamans claim powers of divination. One shaman said that his brain flashed a sort of searchlight or luminous fire that enabled him to see in the dark, perceive coming events, or read others' secret thoughts. The Iglulik spoke of the shaman's ability to see himself as a skeleton, all of whose parts he could name in a special language. The skeleton represented elemental human stuff, that which could best resist sun, wind, weather, and even death. By going in spirit to his skeleton, the shaman stripped himself of perishable flesh and blood and readied himself to deal with the holy.

Traditional Inuit society focused on survival: gaining shelter against the cold and obtaining the seal, fish, or deer that furnished food and clothing. The basic social unit was the married couple; the male hunted and the female sewed. Both the hunting and the sewing took place in the midst of complex taboos. As interpreted by the shaman, these taboos formed a system for dealing with the spirits. Shamanist ecstasy, then, served social as well as individual ends. The shaman fasted, danced, or ingested tobacco to gain for the tribe access to the control center of the natural world.

Therefore, great precautions were taken to placate the spirits of the game and avoid their anger. For instance, the Inuit poured water on the snout of the ringed seal when they killed it, because it lived in salt water and was thirsty. The harpoon had to stand by the blubber lamp the first night after the kill so that the soul still in the harpoon head might stay warm. If one killed a bearded seal or bear, no one could work for three days; also, such a prize deserved presents—for example, sole skin for the bear, because bears walk so much. The Bering Sea Inuits spent a month preparing for their festival of the bearded seal, during which they returned to the sea the bladders of all seals caught in the preceding years. In honor of the whale, they held masked dances and gave gifts.

The Inuit of central Canada had taboos to separate land animals from sea animals. For instance, eating walrus and caribou meat on the same day was forbidden. Before seal hunting on ice could begin, the hunters had to smoke their weapons over fires of seaweed to remove the smell of the land. Similarly, all sewing of caribou skins had to cease on a particular day.

Such a *taboo* system posits a network of relations among the different forms of life. Because of those relations, many Inuits carried amulets or fetishes—bits of bone, feathers, or the like. An amulet represented a power bond between the wearer and the animal of origin. One might give a baby some owl claws so that the baby would have strong fists. A man would wear a piece of caribou ear to gain sharp hearing. Even soot was given to impart strength, since it is strong enough to extinguish fire.

Traditional Inuit marriage customs strike most Westerners as unusual at best and at worst reflecting an unfavorable status for women. Marriage began with the man "capturing" the woman (carrying her off more or less against her will). It was not sexually exclusive, for a man might offer his wife to a visiting friend, regularly arrange to share her with other men, take another man's wife on a hunt with him if his own were pregnant, and so on. Some groups practiced formal polygamy, and the general attitude was that sexual desire is just another appetite like hunger. In part, these marital arrangements usually reflected a shortage of women. Fathers prized male children, so many female infants were killed by strangling or exposure because raising them and providing a dowry loomed as too great a burden. In daily life, however, women were indispensable. They cooked the food and made all the clothing, often chewing for hours on an animal skin to soften it for sewing. Women went on dogsled trips, and some could handle the dogs better than men. Inuit men feared menstrual blood, so women were forbidden contact with game. For the same reason, men isolated women who were in labor. In fact, both birth and death were awesome events involving dangerous forces. A new mother was restricted in what she could eat, whom she could see, what clothing she could wear, and more. Only certain persons could touch the dead, and, if possible, a person died outdoors because if death occurred indoors, everything in the house had to be destroyed.

NATIVE AMERICANS

The native tribes of the North American continent and Caribbean islands were labeled *Indians* by Columbus who thought that he had reached India. The label has been replaced by the more appropriate *Native Americans*. These tribes in the present-day United States and Canada have a tremendous diversity of language, culture, and geography. Some tribes fished, others hunted the buffalo, others raised corn, while some merely gathered nuts, fruits, roots, and vegetables. However, a few generalizations can be made.

The Native American view of the **deities** ranged from a great-spirit high god, to animism, to a sort of pantheism that unified and deified all of humanity and nature. At the core was a doctrine of a primary holy sacred force. The Sioux called it *wakan;* the Algonquin, *orenda.* Other tribes gave this force other names. But shamans throughout the continent agreed that a holy force held all things together. Native North American life largely revolved around this force. It made nature alluring and intimidating, a source of benevolent influences that on occasion turned severe. Perhaps the key goal of most Native Americans was to maintain harmony with such holy natural power, to move in rhythm with its cosmic pulse. Harmony was the way to ensure the fertility of both tribe and field, to guarantee success in both hunting and war, to achieve a full life. By contrast, disharmony led to disaster: ruined crops, sickly children, defeat in war. As a deliberate exercise in disharmony, witchcraft caused a perceptible shudder.

For the Delaware tribe of North America, the four directions of the compass were sacred and merited prayers of thanksgiving. They thanked the east for the morning, when the light is bright and everyone feels good. They thanked the west for the end of the day, when the sun goes down and everyone can again feel good. To the north they owed thanks for the wind, whose cold coming reminds us that we have lived to see the leaves fall again. To the south they owed thanks for the warm winds that make the grass turn green.

Animist doctrine can be seen in the respect for animals and natural forces. For the Naskapi of Labrador, hunting was especially sacred, since it was their most important occupation. The Naskapi thought that the animals they hunted had emotions and purposes like their own and that in the beginning animals could talk like humans. So the Naskapi would sing and drum to them as to friends. Similarly, they would take great care not to mutilate certain bones of the elk or beaver that enclosed an inner soul, a spirit like the hunter's own. Indeed, they thought that at death the animals gathered in an animal realm, just as human spirits gathered in the human realm. Both realms were conceived as stages in a cycle of reincarnation (rebirth in a new form), and so both sets of spirits were bound together. If the hunters did not know the behavioral principles governing their sacred connections with the animals, all sorts of misfortune could ensue. The hunt would be fruitless, the people would be without food, sickness or even death might descend.

As hunting peoples have considered their pursuit of game sacred, so agricultural peoples have considered farming sacred. The Native Americans who raised corn (maize) reverenced it as the gift of the Corn Maiden and harvested it ceremonially. Other Native American tribes insisted on treating the earth especially gently in the spring, for then it was like a woman pregnant with new life. To plow it, even to walk or run on it without care, would have been to mistreat a full womb.

There are a variety of Native American creation myths. Earth Diver (an animal or bird who brings the earth up out of the water) is a common one, but the Zuni tell of numerous workers who disappeared once the world was organized. According to the creation myth of the Maidu of California, a turtle collaborated with a heavenly spirit called "Earth Initiate" to pull the land up out of the waters. The turtle wanted a place to rest from his ceaseless swimming, so he volunteered to dive down for some earth. Earth Initiate held a rope tied to the turtle's left arm. The turtle went down, stayed six years, and returned covered with green slime. Under his fingernails was some sand, which Earth Initiate rolled into a ball that swelled up and became the earth. In the slightly different version of the Yauelmani Yokuts of California, a duck and an eagle replace the turtle and Earth Initiate.

The Winnebago pictured creation as a process of pure divine thought. When the Father, the Earthmaker, came to consciousness, he cried because he did not know what to do. Noticing that his tears, which had fallen from heaven, had become the waters, he realized that by wishing he could make other things become, so he wished for light and earth, which became. Then he made a likeness of himself from earth, and when it did not answer him he made a mind and soul for it and breathed into it so that it could reply. Thus, in one myth, the Winnebago taught that the world was made by design and that humans were made in God's image to converse with him.

Less revered than creative deities are the culture heroes celebrated in myths, whose function was to socialize the tribe. Often they are twins to whom the people trace their arts and crafts. Another superhuman figure in many tribal myths is the spirit who owns

Indigenous tribal peoples of the Americas

the animals. Unless the people reverence this spirit, they will not have good hunting or fishing. A third power in North American mythology is the antihero called **Trickster.** Native American tribes frequently thought of animals, such as the coyote, as Trickster figures.

Puberty rites were the most important rituals for most tribes. For the Oglala Sioux, the pattern for the female puberty rite was set by a vision of a buffalo calf being cleansed by its mother. Out of this grew the traditional ways that young women were cleansed (as the Sioux thought necessary for their fertility power) so that they could bear children and raise them in a sacred manner, so that their fertility power would not conflict with the killing power of Sioux males (who were hunters and warriors).

Agricultural tribes developed rituals based upon the agricultural cycles. The Pueblos feared that the world itself would cease to function if they did not perform these rituals: the sun would not travel the sky, the mountains would not stand tall. Without thanks from, and exchanges with, humankind, the forces of the world would not abide humankind, they would not function. Native Americans and sun, then, kept a holy compact.

Much Native American ritual aimed at intimacy with a benevolent supernatural power. A good example of this is the **vision quest.** Many North American tribes strenuously sought a vision of a guiding spirit. (South American tribes accepted visions that came but tended not to pursue them.) The vision quest became a rite of passage, a threshold to maturity. Without a vision as a guiding experience, one could not walk with direction or live with full purpose. If a young man's vision quest failed, he might become a tribal marginal, forced to dress in women's clothing and barred from male roles.

Along the Great Lakes and Mississippi Valley, the vision quest was largely used to train boys. In the Plains, men used it throughout life whenever they felt the need. On the Pacific coast, it often took the form of spirit possession. When the vision quest was used as training, children as young as seven years learned to fast. Boys heard that they would amount to nothing if they did not see a spirit and obtain its guidance. Girls could quest until puberty, when a different kind of power came, the power of motherhood.

A young man would begin the vision quest with a steam bath, putting off all worldly thoughts. Then he would ascend the most commanding summit, strip to his moccasins and breechcloth. To demonstrate his commitment, he might cut off strips of flesh from his arm. When his vision came, it usually included a promise for his tribe, a glimpse of a tutelary animal (often a wolf or eagle), and a token (perhaps a feather or hair) that became his most prized possession. Finally, the youth would also receive his song—the particular chant that he alone could sing on important occasions. If he had other visions in the future, he could accumulate a "medicine bundle" of tokens. Often shamans who were great healers relied on such tokens to work cures.

An important variation on this vision theme was the Hopi representation of spirits through ceremonial masks. In that tribe, children up to eight or nine years old understood the *kachinas,* or masked dancers, to be real spirits in their midst. The crisis of the Hopi passage to adulthood occurred when the dancers dropped their masks, for then the young person had to accept that the reality of the *kachinas* was not physical but completely spiritual. The participants projected themselves into the spirit world and became what they were representing.

Largely through their visions, Native American shamans functioned as healers, exorcists, and diviners. As healers, they sucked from victims' bodies objects thought to be the tools of witches or ghosts. Shamans from the Navaho and other tribes of the Southwest stressed healing by ritual singing, while holy people of planting tribes specialized in spells for crop fertility. The Pueblos of New Mexico were agriculturalists who shifted from shamanist and rather individualistic ceremonies to more formalized priestly rituals. However, even their lengthy chants for healing and fertility retained ecstatic elements from a preagricultural, nomadic, and shamanist past.

Doctrines about the afterlife varied greatly from tribe to tribe. Among hunting tribes, the concept of the self or soul was not well defined. Human beings were thought to have several souls, one or more of which might live on after death. In fact, the Sioux were exceptional in not fearing the dead. Other tribes would have a child "adopt" a deceased relative to tame the relative's loosed soul. Reincarnation was a common assumption, and the Hopi buried dead infants in the hope that their souls would return in future children. The Pueblos had a singularly clear and happy conception of the afterlife. For them the dead would either join the *kachinas* or become rain clouds. More typical was the Hopis' muted hope—they buried women in their wedding dresses, anticipating the women's passage to the next world.

Despite the importance of these notions, most Native Americans were less concerned with salvation in a future heaven than with a good life in the present. Happiness or success was to enjoy the beautiful land, to have many children, and to know the spirits intimately. Our modern priorities of getting ahead would have meant little to a traditional Native American. Far more important than possessions was the power to see the spiritual side of life.

After separate tribes from different parts of the country and different traditions were herded together onto the reservation system, there arose some syncretistic sharing of traditions. In the nineteenth century, a pantribal movement called the **Ghost Dance** was a response to the Native Americans' oppression and subjugation by whites and temporarily lifted their hopes. The Ghost Dance was a cult based on trance and a spiritual message promising that if the participants renewed their old ways and danced the new dance, they would be immune to the white man's diseases and bullets, the ancestors would return, and with them the buffalo. In 1886, a Paiute named Wowoka rallied hundreds of Paiutes, Kiowas, and Cheyenne in Nevada. By 1890, the Sioux, who had lost 9 million acres of their best land, turned to the Ghost Dance as a last resort. Across the country, Native Americans sang of the **apocalyptic** message brought by a spotted eagle: The dead are returning; the nation is coming; the Father will return the elk, the deer, and the buffalo. But the whites killed Sitting Bull, and the movement ended in the tragedy of Wounded Knee, when cavalry soldiers panicked at the sight of unarmed Indians dancing and chanting.

Some tribes responded to the reservation system by using hallucinatory drugs. At the time of Columbus, Native Americans used perhaps a hundred different substances. The first and most widespread of these was tobacco. In the twentieth century one of the most interesting Native American religious movements was the **peyote** religion, introduced in the late nineteenth century by Apaches, who traded for peyote across the Mexican border. Slowly a body of rituals developed, many of them from the Plains Indians, until there was a complete ceremonial of confession, singing, drumming, and praying. The movement incorporated some Christian elements, reached many tribes of the Plains and the Southeast, and filled some of the void left by the passing of the Ghost Dance. Today, incorporated as the Native American Church, the peyote religion offers Indians the legal right to take peyote as their ritual sacrament.

Another postreservation trend has been **syncretism,** the blending of different religious traditions. This includes not just the sharing of rituals, symbols, and myths from one tribe to another, but also the blending of Christian and native traditions. A woman may be baptized as a member of a Christian denomination but still find some relevance in going through traditional puberty rites.

AFRICANS

The Africa most germane to our study in this chapter lies south of the Sahara. Whereas in the north Islam is now the major influence, in the south ancient religion competes with (or mingles with) Christianity or Islam. Africa is the world's second-largest continent in geographic area and its peoples vary greatly in terms of language, ethnic origins, and economic system. Some peoples are hunters in a rain forest, others are desert hunters, others herd cattle, and some have well-developed agricultural technology.

In analyzing traditional African religion, one first notes that most tribes have had a supreme being, sometimes fitting the concept of the high god. In East Africa, its most common name has been Mulungu, which connotes an impersonal spirit far away. Mulungu is creative, omnipotent, and omnipresent. It may be heard in thunder and seen in lightning. Originally Mulungu was intimate with the world, but in later days it withdrew.

Traditional West Africans build temples. They tend to pray every day, using simple, personal words, and frequently they pray at one of the many shrines that dot the countryside. Usually their prayers are quite practical—petitions for health, security, good farming, or safe travel. They commonly sacrifice something to a god, usually offering a liquid or cereal. The first-fruits offering at harvest time is especially important. Special occasions may prompt an animal sacrifice, and in ancient days humans apparently

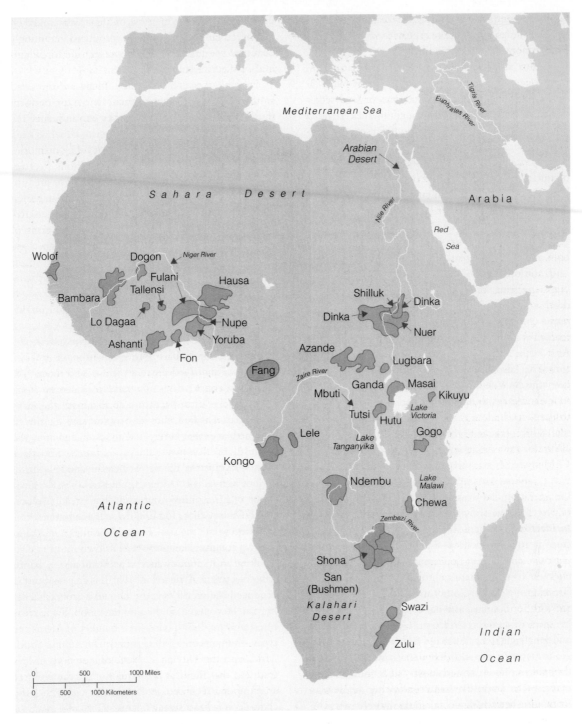

Indigenous tribal peoples of Africa

were sacrificed, largely to provide companions for deceased kings. (Kings were crucial mediators of cosmic harmony and so somewhat divine.)

The ox sacrifice of the Nuer shows African religious ceremony in high style. It only takes place on such important occasions as weddings or feud settlements. Once the ox has been brought in, the ceremony unfolds in four phases: presentation, consecration, invocation, and immolation (killing). The animal is tethered to a stake; officiants rub ashes on it to consecrate it; a priest raises his spear and invokes the spirit; then he spears the animal and all members of the community eat from it. (Africans in general show great regard for cattle, and the main idea in cattle sacrifice seems to be to revere and tap the powers of procreation that bulls and cows represent.)

Traditionally Africans also emphasize rites of passage, investing birth, adolescence, marriage, and death with religious significance and giving the self a sense of development. Usually these rites are performed at home under the guidance of a family elder. At a birth, the family makes offerings to the ancestors. They also use divination to determine to which deity the child should be dedicated. Adolescent ceremonies stress endurance. They are ordeals designed to toughen children into adults and to impart adult sacred lore. Frequently they take the form of circumcision for boys or **clitoridectomy** for girls.

Many tribes are polygynous (one man and several wives), and so African women often are co-wives. As the operation of a women's society such as the Sande of Sierra Leone shows, one of the purposes of *clitoridectomy* (euphemistically called female circumcision) is to develop deep sisterly ties, lest husbands play women off against one another. Thus, the painful excision of the initiate's clitoris is performed amid strong group support; other women console the initiate with food, songs, and dances, promising her that her present suffering will ensure her future fertility and be a sign to her husband of her moral and religious maturity. It is also likely that clitoridectomy is thought to remove any maleness (since the clitoris is perceived as a penislike organ), allowing the woman to fit into her female social status more easily. Understandably, feminist scholars have suspected a patriarchal desire to control women's sexuality.

For the BaMbuti, the forest pygmies of the northeastern Congo, female puberty rites have consisted of dancing and singing in praise of life, accompanied by a long tubal instrument that produced hauntingly beautiful sounds thought to represent the forest animals' collective voice.

Funeral rites are intended to separate the dead from the living without offense. One must perform these rites most carefully, for they can influence the dead person's peace in the spirit world. Funerals keep the living in view, too, stirring up consoling memories and reminding the bereaved that all life is fleeting. Africans have tended to place great stock in dreams, often because there they could meet their departed ancestors.

African religions are especially rich in terms of varied myths, so studying the tribes' tales has become a preferred way of understanding the African social outlook. In a Yoruba creation myth, the supreme God sends to a marsh an artisan who is carrying a bag that lay between the great God's thighs. From this bag the artisan shakes out soil and then a cock and pigeon, which scratch the soil until the marsh is covered. Thus, the land is holy, given from above. The Dogon say that God created the sun and moon like pots with copper rings. To make the stars he flung pellets of clay into space, and he also made the earth out of clay. The Fon think that a great snake gathered the earth together after God made it and that the earth still rests on this snake's coils. For the Kikuyu of Kenya, God is the divider of the universe. He made Mount Kenya, the "Mountain of Brightness," as evidence of his wonders and as a divine resting place. The Luyia say that God first made the moon brighter and bigger than the sun. The sun became jealous, and the two fought. The moon was thrown into the dirt, resulting in its muddy face. The Boshongo, a Bantu tribe of central Africa, said that the creator Bumba produced the world because he had a stomachache. In pain, he vomited up the sun, the moon, living creatures, and finally humans. In a number of myths, he creates humans out of the ground. The Zulu of South Africa and the Thonga of Mozambique both have a tradition that the first man and woman came out of an exploded reed bed. A Pygmy story says that the chameleon heard a strange, whispering noise in a tree. When it cut the tree open, out came a flood of water, which spread over the earth, and the first humans, who were light skinned. The Ashanti of Ghana revere Mondays and Tuesdays, because the leopard, who is sacred to some clans, emerged on those days. Also, the first human leader consoled his followers, who were frightened on coming out from under the earth. Because that leader was killed on Wednesday, Wednesday is a feared day.

The supreme deity fits a high-god pattern. There are numerous myths of the supreme being's withdrawal to the distant heaven. The Mende of Sierra Leone say that God moved away because humans were always bothering him. Ghanans and Nigerians say that humans became too familiar with God. Originally God's heaven was just above their heads, but children came to wipe their hands on it, women hit it when pounding grain, and finally a woman with a long pole hit heaven in the eye. God then moved away. The Burundi of central Africa say that God went off because a baby with a birth defect was born, and some humans wanted to kill God, whom they held responsible. In African mythology, God often leaves by climbing a spider's thread. If there were a great emergency, humans might be able to find the thread and obtain God's help again.

Though these stories stress God's distance and so reflect an African sense of a fall from heavenly grace, African prayers show that divinity is still thought to be present and operative, in ordinary times through intermediary gods and in times of crisis through the high god. Thus, a prayer to Imana, creator God of the Ruanda-Urundi, begs, "Give me offspring, give me as you give to others! Imana, what shall I do, where shall I go? I am in distress, where is there room for me? O merciful, O Imana of mercy, help this once." A hymn to Mwari, God of the Mashona of southern Zimbabwe, recites his attributes and accomplishments (he piled the rocks into mountains and sewed the heavens like cloth), then asks a hearing and mercy. A South African bushman asks his God Gauwa for help in hunting, complains that Gauwa is cheating him, but concludes on a note of hope: "Gauwa will bring something for us to kill next day, after he himself hunts and has eaten meat, when he is full and feeling well." The African God, then, is both far and near, both inscrutable and able to be petitioned. In general, he is considered kind and good, a father or friend. He creates and sustains all things, but no one has ever seen him.

Thus we have seen the African tendency to solve the problem of making God both transcendent of the world and immanent to the world by postulating a high god aloof from the world and lesser gods immersed in daily activity. Most other nonliterate religious cultures have worked out similar solutions, not agreeing with monotheisms that accept the otherness of full divinity, its lack of the limitations we find in all nondivine realities that makes it the realest, closest of beings.

Trickster figures were common in African myths. The Dogon viewed speech as a means of organization, and as such they thought it essentially good. Nonetheless, from the start of the world, speech had loosed disorder. This was because the jackal, God's deluded and deceitful son, desiring speech, had laid hands on the skirt (where speech was hidden) of his mother the earth and so had begun an incestuous relationship that set the world careening. As a result, there were many bad words whose utterance had manifestly physical effects. To Ogotemmeli they actually smelled, and their smell traveled from the nose to the throat and liver, and then to the sexual organs, where they affected potency and procreation. *self-denial*

Africans show little tendency toward asceticism. God's heavenly world is but a larger and happier version of their present good life. Many tribes hope that after death there will be a rebirth from the world of ghosts into another part of the sunlit earth. Because nature is bountiful, natural processes, including sex, are accepted without great question. The Ashanti of Ghana say that sexual knowledge came when the python sent man and woman to lie together. Consequently, many Ashanti thank the python for their children. If they find a dead python, they sprinkle it with white clay and give it a ritual burial. Africans tend to fear abnormal births, however, and disfigured people become outcasts. Twins are regarded differently by different tribes. Some tribes expose them to die, but others welcome and honor them. Like the Inuit, Africans think that souls are numerous, that the world is alive, and that a new child may inherit a soul from an ancestor in a form of reincarnation.

Several of the most poignant African myths deal with life's troubles, especially concerning ancestors and death and ghosts. A Zambian story tells of an old woman who wanted to follow her dead relatives because she had been left all alone. First she cut down tall trees and piled them on top of one another, trying to reach the sky. When this failed, she went looking for the road to heaven, which appears to touch the earth at the horizon. She could not find it, but in her travels she met many tribes. They assured her that suffering is normal. A myth of the Chaga of Kenya tells of a man determined to shoot God because his sons had died. When he found God, however, there were his sons, more glorious than they had been on earth.

From these and other sources, it follows that many Africans have attributed death to a mistake. The Kono of Sierra Leone, for instance, explain death as the failure of a messenger dog. God gave the dog new skins for human beings, but the dog put them down in order to join a feast and a snake stole them. Since then the snake has been immortal, changing skins, while human beings have died—and tried to destroy snakes.

The functions of the shaman are broken down into several different African roles. The religious functionary who merits most attention is probably the *diviner,* who is more of an intellectual, not an ecstatic or spirit-possessed functionary. His or her religious talent is to conceive a comprehensive view of how all events fit into a sacred scheme. However, possession and wisdom are not clearly differentiated; intermediate forms lie between. The Mwari cultists of the Matopo Hills of Zimbabwe, for instance, contend that God speaks through mediums whom he possesses deep in certain caves, and that these messages give a comprehensive view of his operations in the world.

Also, there are numerous African intuitive diviners, famed for their ability to find lost articles, identify thieves, recognize witches, and so on. Whether they are inspired by a spirit or instinctively sense particular events is unclear. These diviners can pick up oblique clues from their clients' stories and give evidence of extrasensory perception.

Another evidence that African worldviews reflect centuries of cultural exchange is the common divinatory systems that stretch from Zaire to South Africa. In one system, for example, a basket containing 205 pieces of bone or wood represents all reality. To answer a question, the diviner shakes the basket and analyzes the pattern into which the pieces fall. The possible combinations are enormous, so students travel long distances to study with famous teachers. In effect, the basket and its pieces are a microcosm of the African world's social institutions and forces. The diviner can feed into this system the problem at hand and then read out an answer. As with the shaman's report from the gods, the diviner's answer often becomes a means to healing or reconciliation.

Like the African witch doctor, who is a sort of physician, the diviner supports the forces of good, just as witches (to be distinguished from witch doctors) and sorcerers are agents of evil. Most tribes think that witches work at night, that they are usually women, and that they inherit or buy from demons a power to inflict harm. The sorcerer taps the power that witch doctors use but turns it to harm. He or she may make potions, cast spells, or put pins in an image of the victim.

SOUTHEAST ASIANS AND MELANESIANS

Just south and east of the Australian continent is a wide range of scattered Pacific islands known collectively as **Melanesia,** which includes Papua New Guinea. The indigenous peoples differ greatly in terms of language and culture but share many similarities with the Australian Aborigines—understandings of the sacred, animism, totemism, shamanism, and the Dreamtime. The Dyak of Borneo, for instance, thought of themselves as a sacred people. Their land was sacred, too, because it had been given to them by the deities, who made it from the remains of the sun and the moon.

One difference between the Melanesians and the Australians is that the former have agriculture and domestic animals such as pigs. One creation myth reflecting this is the story of **Hainuwele** from New Guinea. In some versions, a beautiful woman creates food in a disgusting way (e.g., she excretes it). Outraged, the people rise up and kill her, chopping up her body into many tiny pieces and burying them. These pieces become yams, the great dietary staple.

The various island cultures of Melanesia also have some notable male puberty rites. Some tribes were the original bungee cord jumpers: they built towers, fastened vines to their ankles, and jumped off as a test of daring. Other tribes would go on raids and try to capture the head of an enemy, and then shrink it.

FEATURES OF SPECIFIC TRIBAL TRADITIONS

PEOPLE	LOCATION	LEADER	DOCTRINES AND MYTHS	RITUALS
Aborigines	Australia	shaman	high god, animism, Dreamtime, totemism	puberty
Melanesians	western Pacific		Dreamtime, Hainuwele, ancestors	puberty, cargo
Polynesians	southeastern Pacific		taboo, animism, totemism, creation	puberty, cargo
Ainu	northern Japan	shaman	animism	bear sacrifice, divination
Eskimo	Arctic	shaman	afterlife, animism, creation	
Indians	North America	shaman	high god, tricksters, totemism, creation	puberty, peyotism, Ghost Dance
Africans	Africa	witch doctor, diviner, herbalist	high god, animism, tricksters, ancestors, ghosts	divination, puberty
Teutons	northern Europe		tricksters, apocalyptic hell and valhalla, pantheon, fairies	megaliths
Celts	western Europe	priests	tricksters, fairies	megaliths, sacrifice, calendars

The Ngaju Dayak of South Borneo saw marriage as a sacred stage in life's unfolding. Therefore, the two marital partners were made to die symbolically so that they could be reborn by sticking the stem of the Tree of Life, represented by a spear, in a human head taken in a raid or from a slave. Thus, the couple was made vividly aware that their new state dealt with awesome powers. (In recent decades the head has been replaced by a coconut.)

Ritual cannibalism was also practiced on these islands. The brains of ancestors were eaten as part of the funeral rites in order to assimilate the spirits of the departed. Unfortunately, after many generations this practice led to the transmission of a dementia based upon a slow-acting infection (not unlike bovine spongiform dementia, known as "mad cow disease").

In Indonesia and Melanesia, megaliths can be found: stone monuments that defended the soul during its journey to the beyond, ensured an eternal existence after death, linked the living and the dead, and fertilized the crops and animals through their sacred durability.

In the last century, contact with Europeans and North Americans led to the development of **cargo cults** among Melanesians in the western Pacific. Most of these cults arose during World War II, when these islands were occupied first by the Japanese, then by the allied forces of the United States, Britain, Australia, and

New Zealand. Docks and airfields were constructed and grew into oil depots, refueling stations, ammunition dumps and stockpiles of a variety of supplies produced in America. Local people developed myths that the cargo offloaded by the whites was really a gift from the ancestors and then expropriated by the white delivery men. The airplanes symbolized contact with the ancestors. The related ritual was to construct makeshift airfields and attempt to guide in planes loaded with cargo. More than one U.S. pilot landed on the wrong airstrip after being confused by these rituals.

POLYNESIANS

The Polynesians (e.g., the Samoans, Tahitians, Hawaiians, Tongans, Maori) settled the Pacific islands east of Melanesia, known collectively as **Polynesia**. They had complicated creation myths and totemic systems representing their arrival on the islands: a person's identity was determined by which canoes his or her ancestors were on when they arrived on the islands. The Polynesians had deities of the sun, seasons, and sea.

Puberty rites for men and women were popular. Many of the symbols and ceremonies that tourists associate with Hawaii, such as the flower lei and the hula dance, have their origin in these rites. Tattooing was used in puberty rites.

The term *taboo* is based upon a Polynesian word. Taboos were important in the explanation of natural disasters such as storms and volcanoes. Taboos were also useful in rationing the limited resources of the region. Fishing in certain areas might be forbidden for a while in order to allow for a replenishing of stocks. During certain times (such as the four-month winter period), war and heavy work might be forbidden. During that time they would also retell the myth of Lono, an agricultural god, symbolizing him with a pole and cloth banners. The explorer Captain James Cook arrived during this period, and his ship's masts and sails may have led some people to wonder if he was the god Lono returned to the islands.

Another concept related to the taboo was that of places of refuge. These were special locations that were generally uninhabited, but persons who had broken taboos could go there and seek sanctuary, escaping punishment and perhaps even obtaining some purification.

AINU

The **Ainu** were an indigenous people on the island of Hokkaido, the northern island of present-day Japan (and site of the 1964 Sapporo winter Olympics). The Ainu had many similarities to the Inuit, including the linguistic fact that their name for themselves means "the men." The Ainu had some millet-based agriculture, but most of their traditional diet was based upon salmon fishing and hunting. The Ainu were animistic and had diviners and shamans, but they are most notable for their bear festival. In this ritual a cub is captured, then kept and nourished for up to a year, and then ritually sacrificed as a messenger to the "Keeper of the Animals" so that more game will be sent. The festival is a three-day event with much music, dancing, and consumption of rice wine.

TEUTONS

The **Teutons**, the early inhabitants of Germany and Scandinavia, were also known as the Vikings or Norse. They were herding peoples with some agriculture.

flashcards and matching game
http://www.quia.com/jg/50585.html

jumbled words game
http://www.quia.com/jw/8253.html

millionaire game
http://www.quia.com/rr/41206.html

magic paragraphs
http://www.quia.com/cz/13541.html

Now take an online practice quiz at
http://www.quia.com/session.html

For session enter
relquiz4
download multiple-choice, true-false, and fill-in
drills from
http://www.ureach.com/tlbrink
click on the public filing cabinet and folder rel4
and download m4.exe, h4.htm, t4.exe, and f4.exe
and crossword puzzle CW4.html

The Teutons worshipped in groves and had some megalith ritual centers. Their mythology paralleled that of the Greeks, Romans, and Vedic Aryans: a similar polytheistic pantheon of anthropomorphic deities and creation myths. Odin was the father of the gods. Thor, his son, hurled the thunderbolt and represented the values of warriors and raiders. The gods lived in a palace known as Valhalla. There were also trickster figures, trolls, and fairies as well as Valkyries who flew over battlefields and swooped down to carry fallen heroes to join the gods at Valhalla. In addition to men who died in battle, the other humans who joined the gods were women who died in childbirth.

The Teutons thought that most people who died went to a place under the earth called "hell," which was not necessarily a bad place. There was also a doctrine of **eschatology** (a theory about the end of the world). The Teutons foretold of a final **apocalypse**, a battle between the gods and the forces of evil, in which the gods would be destroyed. The noblest act for a hero would be to fight on this losing side of the gods in the final battle.

CELTS

The **Celts** lived in western Europe—in present-day Brittany (France), Galicia (Spain), Ireland, Scotland, England, and Wales. The Celts had settled agriculture. (Indeed, it was usually the Celts who were the victims of the Teutons' raids.) The Celts had also developed megaliths as ritual centers. Some, such as Stonehenge in England, served as elaborate calendars.

A hereditary class of Celtic priests (the **Druids**) developed to officiate at these rituals (including some human sacrifice) and also engaged in astrological divination. Heroes, gods, and demons were often portrayed as clever tricksters. Some deities were similar to the Greeks, Romans, and Teutons. Celtic holidays have contributed some of their symbols to modern holidays such as Halloween, Christmas, and Easter.

CHAPTER 3

RELIGIONS OF ANCIENT CIVILIZATIONS

Date	Event
	RELIGIONS OF EARLY CIVILIZATIONS: 25 KEY DATES
7,500 B.C.E.	cereal grain agriculture; domestication of animals
8350–7350 B.C.E.	Jericho (first walled town, 10 acres)
6250–5400 B.C.E.	Catal Huyuk, Turkey (large city, 32 acres)
6000 B.C.E.	rice cultivation in Thailand; pottery and textiles in Catal Huyuk
5000 B.C.E.	irrigation of Mesopotamian alluvial plains; agricultural settlements in Egypt
4000 B.C.E.	bronze casting in Middle East
3500 B.C.E.	invention of the wheel
3100 B.C.E.	pictographic writing in Sumer; unification of Egypt
3000 B.C.E.	spread of copper working
2590 B.C.E.	great pyramids at Giza
1750 B.C.E.	Hammurabi has written code of laws
1370 B.C.E.	Akhenaton's "monotheistic" reform
600 B.C.E.	Zoroaster begins prophetic work
550 B.C.E.	Cyrus II founds Persian empire; Zoroastrianism the official religion
525 B.C.E.	Persian conquest of Egypt
521 B.C.E.	Persia extends from the Nile to the Indus
500 B.C.E.	first hieroglyphic writing in Mexico
332–329 B.C.E.	Alexander in Egypt, Persia, India
323 B.C.E.	start of Ptolemaic dynasty in Egypt
312 B.C.E.	start of Seleucid Era in Persia
247 B.C.E.	Arsaces I founds the Parthian Empire
224 C.E.	foundation of Sasanian dynasty
300 C.E.	rise of Mayan civilization
637 C.E.	Muslims invade Persia
1325–1530 C.E.	Aztec and Inca civilizations

Tribal peoples had technology, and the level of technology (if we can assume that technologies can be ranked) varied greatly from tribe to tribe. All eventually discovered the techniques for the making of fire, and its use in cooking. Most developed the bow and arrow, nets, hooks, and other tools for hunting and fishing as well as the making of houses, clothes, and containers. But in tribal cultures, these advances may take many generations to develop and diffuse from one tribe to another. With the earliest civilizations, the pace of technological innovation increased dramatically, as did the spread of ideas from one society to another.

A great shift in human diet and culture came when some tribes stopped following herds of game and domesticated some of those animals (cattle, sheep, goats, swine, llamas, camels, chickens) for meat, milk, and fiber. Other tribes noticed that the plant they had been gathering would give greater yields if they stayed around and nurtured its growth. Wheat, barley, rice, millet, corn were the cereal grains that permitted farmers to raise enough food to feed their families and have a surplus to trade with others who had dedicated their occupations to making plows or storage bins.

>The Mayas, like the Egyptians, used pyramids as sacred sites.

© Photodisc Blue

57

This change in the food supply led to a change in social organization. One of the earliest sociologists studying religion was Emile **Durkheim,** who referred to the tribal form of organization as *mechanical*. He chose this term not because hunter-gatherers used machinery but because members of a society mostly shared the same social function. Each man was a hunter. Each woman was assigned to gather vegetables, sew, cook, take care of the children. There was no real further specialization beyond gender roles (except for the one person who might be assigned the role of shaman). In such a society, it did not matter which man married which woman, much in the same way that in putting standard manufactured nuts and bolts together, you just reach in a bin, grab a nut, reach in another bin, grab a bolt, and you know that they will fit together. With settled agriculture, and especially large cities, came a different form of social organization that Durkheim referred to as *organic*. He chose this term not because city dwellers are closer to the processes of nature, but because their social organization seemed to parallel that of a large organism, with each individual assigned to some specialized function: soldier, miner, smith, potter, weaver, builder, miller.

With agriculture human beings made a great leap in mastery of their environment. Like the domestication of animals, agriculture meant people no longer were at the whim of natural cycles they did not understand. They could stabilize their food supply, lay in better stores for winter, and free some members of their group for artistic work, for developing religious lore, or for planning how to dominate neighboring peoples. The very successes of hunters and gatherers therefore moved these earliest people toward a significantly different way of life (and so toward significantly different religious interests and concepts).

Some of the inventions that spread in the early civilizations may have had roots in tribal cultures: pottery, metal smithing, weaving. But others, like the wheel, would have had little purpose in hunting or herding societies. The wheel is needed only when there are large concentrations of people and large quantities of goods to be moved (e.g., grain, construction materials, copper ore).

Metals deserve special attention. The principal metal was copper and its alloys bronze and brass (discovered about 3500 B.C.E. in the Middle East). They were useful for construction, numerous hand tools, and a simplified method of value exchange—money. More specialized work developed, such as mining, smelting, and casting metal. In turn, this work created more efficient farming implements, which led to the production of surplus food. Surplus food allowed a new class of religious specialists (who were agriculturally unproductive) to arise.

Perhaps the most important use of metals was as weapons of warfare against other humans. Tribal peoples such as the Melanesians and Teutons had been raiders, invading other tribes to carry off some wealth or trophies of conquest. But as the metal industry grew in importance, it stimulated the exploration and colonization of new territories for raw materials. The early civilizations became military empires designed to protect their flanks and sources of supply against other growing military empires.

From 1900 to 1400 B.C.E., following the Hittite invention of tempering, iron came into widespread use, and the production of bronze and iron further stimulated the human imagination and increased the symbolic content of mother earth. Whereas the earliest iron was a gift from the sky (coming in the form of meteorites), mined iron came from the womb of the earth. Indeed, miners developed regimes of fasting, meditation, and purification since they had to go into the sacred depths and extract a new form of life. Their mythology spoke of elves, fairies, genies, and spirits who inhabited the underground, assisting or witnessing the gestation of mother earth's strangest children, the ores. Metallurgists, like blacksmiths and potters, had to be "Masters of the Fire," which associated them with the shamans, who were masters of inner, magical heat. These metallurgists also took on some of the paradoxical nature of metal itself. Coming from mother earth and being a boon to humanity, metal was sacred. However, being invulnerable and easily made into an instrument of death, metal was also too close to evil for humans to handle comfortably. Thus, the smiths entered the mythology of the gods, fashioning weapons for their heavenly battles and tools for their heavenly enterprises. In India, Tvastr made Indra's weapons for the fight against Vrtra; in Greece, Hephaestus forged the thunderbolt that enabled Zeus to triumph over his enemies.

Perhaps the greatest innovations facilitating the development of civilization would be writing and mathematics. These are less important to a hunting-gathering

DIMENSION	TRIBAL PEOPLES	EARLY CIVILIZATIONS
Economy built on	gathering, hunting, herding	herding, agriculture, pottery, metals
Durkheimian solidarity	mechanical	organic
Contact with others	raiding	trade, conquest
Religious leader	shaman	priest
Group symbol	totem	patriarch
Ideas preserved by	oral tradition	writing
Control behavior with	taboos	law codes
Deities	primal monotheism, animism, polytheism	polytheism, pantheons, henotheism, monolatry, monotheism
Festivals	rites of passage	calendrical
Sacrifice	animal	animal, grain, human
Creation myths describe	specific origins	instability
Afterlife	contact with ancestors	reward for deeds
Sacred sites	natural hierophanies, taboo locations, megaliths	pyramids temples
Divination	yes	yes
Exorcism	yes	rare
Mythical figures	tricksters	conquering heros
Puberty rites	yes	rare
Syncretism	after contact with others	after contact with others
Secular society	no	no

society, which can rely upon oral traditions to convey information from one generation to another. (The Tasmanians only had three words for numbers: *one, two,* and *plenty;* but that was sufficient to understand how many hunters to bring.) Once there are agricultural surpluses of grain and trade of that grain for cloth and bricks and pots, some means of calculation and permanent records of transactions and contracts are needed. The rich symbolism of pictorial art does not suffice, for what is now required is the precise meaning of concepts that will be interpreted the same way by one person and another, today and tomorrow:

weights and measures and laws. To be steady producers of food, human beings also had to calculate the seasons much more precisely. This led to astronomical calculations, astrology, and the worship of planets and stars,

Writing makes the realities of the traditional world mediated, as they previously were not. Spoken language has a holistic quality, conveying its message immediately, in an imperative or at least solicitous way. Written language is more detached. To the benefit of science, and perhaps the detriment of religion, it tends toward scholarship. For example, once the biblical legends were written down, scholars could dissect them at leisure. In the development of the early civilizations, we glimpse sizable traditions at their very revealing transition from oral to written religion.

These technological changes proceeded alongside changes in the realm of the sacred. Hunters may have understood a sacred solidarity between themselves and the animals they hunted; now there was to be a sacred solidarity between cultivators and plants. Whereas in earliest times blood and bone were the symbolic, most sacred elements of life, in agricultural times the generative elements were seen as masculine sperm and feminine blood. Above all, women dominated agricultural life, and mother earth was the prime focus. Through the millennia before the biology of reproduction became clear, the earth was thought to give birth independently, without need of any male. Because women developed agriculture and controlled it, and because women issued all human life, Mesolithic culture connected women to mother earth. Thus, from this period came the best-known **Great Mothers,** goddesses of fertility. Sexuality became a sacred drive and process, because all nature—the whole cosmos—moved through a religious cycle of conception, gestation, birth, nurturance, growth, decline, and then death (which could be a new conception). Houses, villages, shrines, and burial vaults all reflected the womb architecturally. The earth itself seemed uterine: from it we come, to it we return. Accordingly, very old myths of human creation speak of first ancestors crawling forth from mines or caves, and funerary rituals consign the dead offspring back to the Great Mother. Even during this initial period of agriculture, there was an increased stress

on polarities—earth and sky, dirt and rain, yin and yang (the Chinese dual elements).

This focus on the earth in the Mesolithic era continued into Neolithic times, when village life developed into city life, agriculture became more extensive and secure, and arts and crafts such as pottery, weaving, and tool manufacturing were established. Also, in the Neolithic period, cults of fertility and death assumed even greater prominence. From sanctuaries excavated in Anatolia (modern Turkey), we know that around 7000 B.C.E. worship involved skulls and various gifts, such as jewels, weapons, and textiles. The principal divinity was a goddess who manifested in three forms: a young woman, a mother, and a crone (old woman). Figurines represent her giving birth, breasts adorn her cave sites, and drawings portray her among animals, especially bulls and leopards. In many caves the double ax, symbol of the storm god, underscores the fertility theme (stormy rain fecundates mother earth).

Representations of bees and butterflies relate this fertility theme to the burial skulls and gifts, since both bees and butterflies pass through distinct stages in their life cycles. Worshippers likely tried to fit death into such a scheme—to see it as another transformation of the life force, another stage. Subordinate to the goddess was a male god, a boy or youth, who seems to be her child and lover and who has some relationship with the bull.

Roughly ten thousand years ago, settled agriculture became widespread in the river valleys of the Nile, Tigris and Euphrates, Indus, and Huang Ho. The earliest civilizations arose around 4000 B.C.E. (i.e., *before* the *common era* marked in Western culture by the birth of Jesus). The term **civilization** refers to the cities that developed as commercial and ritual centers in the midst of settled agriculture. Unfortunately, the term has conveyed a false sense of superiority, as its opposite, *uncivilized,* is taken to stand for that which is crude, vulgar, unsanitary, or ignorant. Even the adjective *civil* conveys something socially acceptable and well mannered. In this book, all that we want to convey by the term *civilization* is a society based upon city life. When we speak of the "great" civilizations, we are not implying a judgment on their aesthetic accomplishments or moral virtues but refer to the technological, commercial, governmental, and military abilities that permitted and sustained a large-scale model of human organization.

RELIGIOUS THEMES

Syncretism is the process of blending elements from different religious traditions. One form of syncretism involves incorporating a symbol, myth, ritual, or ethical principle from one tradition into another. One example of this type, suggested in the previous chapter, is the presence of some elements of some Celtic and Teutonic traditions in the Christian holidays of Halloween, Christmas, and Easter. Another example is the spread of the peyote religion among various Native American tribes on the reservation.

Another type of syncretism consists of blending or assimilating different traditions, especially by combining their deities into a structured pantheon. The result usually has been an undigested mixture or rather infertile hybrid. This latter form of syncretism may have been minimal in tribal societies, probably because of the limited forms of contact with other peoples.

Yet another type of syncretism came about as a reaction to (or against) contact with other peoples. During the late nineteenth century, the forced relocation of Native Americans onto the reservations engendered something new: an apocalyptic movement known as the Ghost Dance. During the first half of the twentieth century, the South Pacific saw the growth of the cargo cults in response to airfields and docks constructed by white men.

The rise of civilizations foreordained the syncretism of religions. The heightened contact brought by ever-widening circles of trade was the first stimulus. Later, when civilizations became empires that conquered weaker, surrounding peoples, these contacts between cultures became clashes. As we will see in the remainder of this book, there are different ways that this clash can be resolved. The Hebrews who conquered Canaan and the Aryans who conquered India attempted to destroy the key elements of the religions of the vanquished. Those who later conquered China (e.g., Mongols, Manchurians) and Greece (e.g., Hellenes, Romans) assimilated much of what they found.

Myths also changed their structure, tone, and emphasis under the impact of the early civilizations. In tribal societies, creation myths might explain the origin of the world or the origins of specific things. Frequently these myths would contain totems (animal symbols of a tribe or clan) or tricksters (clever figures often credited with a certain innovation). In the early civilizations, the totem might be replaced by a patriarch (e.g., an ancestor such as Abraham for the Hebrews) and the trickster might be replaced by a culture hero who brought some cultural innovation or led some primal conquest. The creation myths of early civilizations became extremely important if the society was plagued by instability: these myths served to explain the origin of instability and suggested an approach for its solution.

Doctrines are statements about religious ideas, such as the nature of god (or gods). Both tribal religions and those of the cities could be called polytheistic in that several distinct deities were recognized and worshipped. The animism that characterized so many hunter-gatherers was absent in the early cities. Many of the agricultural societies of the Mediterranean and Middle East had Great Mother goddesses who governed the fertility cycle of plants and domesticated animals.

Conquering peoples (e.g., Aryans, Hellenes, Teutons) tended to have more masculine deities. As they assimilated conquered peoples, they may have kept some of these deities, renaming some to identify with what they had already or placing others in a subservient relation to the gods of the conquerors in a structured relationship known as a pantheon. In several (but not most) later civilizations, such polytheism may have led to henotheism (worship of some gods over others) or a monolatry (worship of one god among many), if not to a complete monotheism (only one god exists).

Another twist of doctrine was the elevation of living kings to a divine rank. Many ancient societies saw the monarch as mediating between the people and ultimate reality and concluded that the monarch should be considered a god. Thus the vitality of the king is extremely important, and the moment when the king dies and mediating functions pass to a new ruler is the most dramatic time in the people's existence. Some African tribes approach this doctrine, but its highest form can be found in stable empires such as the Egyptian and Incan, who claimed that their rulers were direct descendents of the sun god. Rituals changed greatly in the cities. Puberty rites became rare because the transition from boy to adult farmer, builder, weaver or potter is a slow process of apprenticeship. The festivals were now geared more to the seasons of the crops rather than the stages of life, and thus the calendar became even more important. Animal sacrifice was still prevalent in those societies with domesticated animals, but there was an increasing emphasis on other forms of wealth: grain, implements, and even human life.

The sites of rituals were located less and less in natural sites that may have been mentioned in myths as **hierophanies** (places where something sacred transpired). Now the emphasis was on sites that had been constructed by humans: pyramids and temples more elaborate than the older megaliths had ever been.

One possible impetus in the rise of the city would have been its importance as a ritual center. At first, people may have come to the city to trade and then were told to do some worship and sacrifice while they were there. Later, the temple may have become so important for the society that people traveled to the city to worship, whether or not they had trading to do. In some places, the ritual center may have emerged prior to trade, and the city may have grown around it.

There was also a shift in religious functionaries from the tribal shaman to the **priest.** The early civilizations had a decreased interest in exorcism. The main duties of priests were to perform sacrifices, rituals, and at least semiofficial interpretations of doctrine and morals. Priests tended to arise alongside writing and to become the custodians of the religious lore that multiplied after writing, but one can find ritualists in oral societies, such as the Druids of the Celts, who fit most of the rest of the priest's profile.

Divination (prediction of future events) was a major theme in many early civilizations, especially those subject to frequent foreign invasions, natural disasters, or problematic weather. The task of predicting the future was handled in certain societies by priests, or it could have had separate, specialized practitioners.

The ethical dimension of religion concerns rules of conduct. This dimension also underwent great changes in the city. Tribal society was composed of a maze of taboos: certain things were wrong because they would

Many of the religious traditions discussed in this course emphasized the importance of trying to predict the future: the Babylonians used astrology, the Chinese threw objects to the ground, the Africans and Greeks interpreted their dreams. Late-night television advertises many psychic hotlines claiming to predict what will happen.

Do you think that divination can be reconciled with Christian doctrine?

Contribute to this discussion at
http://forums.delphiforums.com/rel101

involve contact with the profane, disrespect of the sacred, or contact with a powerful sacred (or demonic) force. In the cities, these rules shifted toward the utilitarian dimension of ethics, resulting in the behaviors that kept the city functioning smoothly. There were rules for the builder, rules for the potter, rules for the soldier, so many rules that they could not all be remembered: they had to be written down in a code of law.

Neither tribal societies nor the early civilizations approximated anything like what we now regard as a secular society. The written laws and tribal taboos were enforced by the religious figures (whether priests or shamans) as well as the rulers (whether tribal chief or emperor). The priests enjoyed so much political power and the "divine" kings required so much priestly recognition that these city-states could be called **theocracies.** Indeed, the power of rulers to tax may have developed out of the power of priests to demand grain for sacrifice.

Afterlife doctrines also shifted in the cities. In tribal societies, the afterlife doctrines and funeral rituals surrounded issues of ancestral contact and veneration. In the cities, the doctrines of afterlife became more closely associated with a future reward for doing one's individual duties in that society.

MESOPOTAMIA

The name **Mesopotamia** means "between the rivers." The two rivers referred to were the Tigris and the Euphrates in the southern part of what is now Iraq. This was the site of several civilizations after 4000 B.C.E.: the Sumerians, the Akkadians, the Chaldeans, the

Assyrians, and the Babylonians. The one most important word to remember in the description of this region is *instability*. Agriculture in this area was dependent upon irrigation because the rainfall was uncertain and could lead to drought or flood. Other sources of instability were the constant conflicts between the cities to see who would be the ruling empire. The main features of Mesopotamian religion are a reaction to this chaotic instability: *creation myths* in which the gods forged an order out of a primal chaos, a written code of laws from King **Hammurabi** to provide order among human society, and a reliance upon astrology-based divination to find one's personal order in life.

The Sumerians arrived in Mesopotamia as colonizers in prehistoric times and were not related either racially or linguistically to their neighbors to the north, the Akkadians. Sumer was a flat, marshy region, and the first settlements consisted of huts built on mud. Flood was a constant, potentially devastating threat. Silt made the land fertile, however, and the Sumerians were able over the millennia to transform the swamp into a garden. They developed *cuneiform* (wedge-shaped) writing approximately two centuries before the Egyptians developed hieroglyphics. By that time they had already built great terraced, multistoried temple towers (ziggurats) with bricks, and they were using sailboats, wheeled vehicles, animal-drawn plows, and potter's wheels. The country included a dozen small cities, each belonging in principle to its local deity and centered on his temple. These cities included Eridu (traditionally considered the earliest, dating from about 4000 B.C.E.), Ur, Nippur, and Uruk or Erech. Sumerian kings served as representatives of the gods, enforcing their justice and promoting wealth to be used in their service. Cuneiform writing developed primarily as an instrument for recording contracts and accounts in the affairs of the temples, which controlled up to one-third of the land and owned great wealth.

It was also in Sumer, toward the middle of the twenty-fourth century B.C.E., that the idea of imperial rule was born, when a king named Lugalzaggesi (Zaggesi the Great) conquered a large part of the valley. An inscription that Lugalzaggesi placed on a monument in Nippur tells how Enlil, the supreme god and king of all countries, gave dominion to Lugalzaggesi, who then prayed that his rule might be peaceful and prosperous forever.

Sumerian political power never extended northward into Akkad, but Sumer had enormous cultural influence there. Over the centuries the Akkadians learned writing from the Sumerians and adopted much of their mythology and technology. Despite Lugalzaggesi's prayer for perpetual dominion, he was later defeated in battle and taken captive by an Akkadian, Sargon I, who founded an empire of his own, and also claimed the authority of Enlil. Sargon's rule was shortlived, however, and the Sumerians regained their independence for a while. But by the time of the lawgiver Hammurabi in the eighteenth century B.C.E., the Sumerians were completely absorbed into the civilization that is now known as Babylonian, after its principal city, Babylon (Babilani, or "the gateway of the gods"), which grew to prominence after the demise of Ur.

Although we have some Sumerian fragments, most of the writings now available come from the Babylonian period, so we see Sumerian myths through Babylonian eyes and with Babylonian adaptations. One reason that the evidence is so fragmentary, in addition to its enormous antiquity, is the fact that the cuneiform tablets were not used primarily for the recording of myths, but for business accounts. In many cases the tablets with myths seem to have been the exercise books of schoolboys learning to write by copying out stories. Still, we have enough evidence to provide a fairly clear picture of the religious conceptions not only of the Babylonians, but also of the Sumerians.

The great legacy of Mesopotamia is its creation myths. One of the earliest Sumerian creation myths was the story of Enki and Ninhursag. This takes place in a land pure, clean, and bright, free from death and disease, until the mother goddess, Ninhursag, was impregnated by Enki (variously interpreted as the god of earth or of water). These events took place in primordial time, the time of the ordering of the cosmos. In the myth, Ninhursag and Enki produce a daughter, with whom Enki also mates and who then gives birth to another daughter, with whom Enki also mates. This last birth brings Uttu, Enki's great-granddaughter. Ninhursag warns the girl that Enki lurks in the marsh and lusts for her and that she should not yield herself to him until he offers her the appropriate gifts for a bride. He does so, however, and she gives herself to him joyfully.

At this point it seems (the text is broken) that Ninhursag intervenes, takes Enki's semen, and uses it to bring forth eight plants. Enki, noticing the eight new plants, decides he must "know" them and decide their fate, and therefore he eats them. Ninhursag becomes furious at this usurpation. She curses him and says she will no longer look on him with the eye of life. Enki then languishes and the land becomes dry and dusty. Alarmed, the other gods, with Enlil as their spokesman, intercede through the help of a clever fox to get Ninhursag to restore Enki. She does so by placing her vulva next to the ailing parts of Enki's body and bringing forth eight goddesses, each of whom heals the part with which she is associated. The eight goddesses evidently replace the eight plants that Enki had misappropriated. The poem ends with the naming of the goddesses and the assignment of their destinies. It is not clear who speaks at that point, Enki or Ninhursag, but since the ending is one of reconciliation and restoration of life, it seems that the naming takes place with Ninhursag's approval. The last line of the surviving text praises Father Enki.

It is not easy to interpret a text that comes to us from a time so distant, in fragments, and possibly with many layers of revision along the way, but the main outline is not too difficult to discern. Clearly the myth depicts the beginning of the ordered world (or "cosmos") as we know it—a world in which nature brings forth living creatures. Before natural life with its cycles of birth, fertility, and death begins, there is no death or disease, but with life comes the problem of evil (theodicy) in its various forms. The form of evil that this story emphasizes is the evil of disorder.

Exactly why Enki's claim to preeminence (that is what his eating of the plants seems to imply) is a source of disorder is not altogether clear. Many ancient myths take the preeminence of the father god for granted, but this one does not. Possibly, therefore, there was an earlier version with a matriarchal emphasis, that is, with the idea that the female principle is preeminent in generation. At any rate, what we see is a struggle between the male and female sources of life to define their relative dignity. When Enki, the male principle, claims eminence that Ninhursag finds excessive, she demonstrates her own importance by withdrawing her life-giving power. The other gods subsequently realize her importance, as does Enki

himself, who must ask her to heal each part of his body that is afflicted. At the end an appropriate balance seems to emerge. The masculine principle's usurpation of knowledge and power is represented as a sort of fall that must be purged through suffering and the reestablishment of proper order.

Thus we see a fairly typical mythic pattern in which disorder in creation is repaired by dissolution, and right order is established through a new act of creation (the healing of Enki and the birth of the goddesses who replace the plants). Since this sequence of creation, death, and rebirth is also the pattern of the annual cycle of vegetation, the myth seems to do double duty as both a story of creation and commentary on the cycles of nature.

EGYPT

Modern **Egypt** is a major center of Arab and Muslim culture. Taxi drivers careen through Cairo with a *Qur'an* on the dashboard to protect them; common people lay rugs in the train station and kneel at the call to prayer. Yet the treasures of Tutankhamen, the Giza pyramids, and above all the Nile tie modern Cairo to the pre-Islamic Egypt of more than 5,000 years ago. Merely follow the Nile by train to Alexandria and you will see in its delta peasants drawing water with buffalo much as they did in the Old Kingdom.

Egypt described in this chapter is the pre-Arab, pre-Muslim civilization that developed along the Nile River in northeast Africa. The Nile's flow patterns are regular, predictable, and nonthreatening. Egypt had the Sahara desert to the west, mountains to the south, the Mediterranean to the north, and the Red Sea to the east. It was less susceptible to foreign invasion than was Mesopotamia. For the best part of 2,500 years, Egyptian life remained the same. At the Great Pyramids near the Sphinx, the desert seems to have mimicked the Nile's behavior. The endless sand, like the river water, changes with the wind. Actually, though, little changes. Sky, sun, sand, and water—they all endure. Like stable props, they are set on every stage. Egyptian civilization was remarkably *stable*, rigid, static, at least by comparison to its contemporary bronze age civilizations. Therefore, it had less need for divination or myths of primal chaos

Another widespread motif is that of a battle between creative and destructive forces. In the myth of Enki and Ninhursag, this motif takes the form of a personal conflict between mother and father deities. In the famous Enuma Elish myth, it becomes a regular military campaign. Both myths explain the seasonal renewal of nature and also the continuing need for the creative forces in the cosmos actively to counter threats of disorder and returning chaos. (*Cosmos* and *chaos* are Greek terms that have come to be used generally to refer on one hand to the ordered totality of things, including all the levels of being and even the gods, and on the other hand to a state of unformed, unordered being. The term *chaos* originally meant an abyss and comes from the verb "to yawn." *Cosmos* originally referred to the village as compared with its surrounding wilderness. Eventually it came to refer to whatever was harmonious, civilized, beautiful, and constituted an ordered whole.)

The *Enuma Elish* (the title means "When on high" and comes from the first words of the Akkadian text) has come down to us mainly in its Babylonian form, but some fragments of a Sumerian original have also survived. In the Sumerian version everything begins with the union of sky and earth, represented by the first "thing," a cosmic mountain whose base is earth (female) and whose summit is the sky (male). The Babylonian version begins with the precosmic chaos: "When on high the heaven had not been named. Firm ground below had not been called by name. . . . No reed but had been matted, no marsh land had appeared." Neither gods nor humans had yet been created. There was only the primordial pair, Apsu (male, associated with fresh water) and Tiamat (female, the sea), "their waters commingling as a single body." Time and the world begin when they give birth to the first gods (perhaps representing the accumulation of silt where the river water meets the sea). These beget other gods and goddesses who mate in turn to produce the gods of earth (Ea) and sky (Anu) and so on.

(Interestingly enough, earth and sky are here both represented by male gods, evidently because the Babylonians wanted to give honor to the earth god, Ea, progenitor of their own special god, Marduk. They seem to have been more emphatically patriarchal than the Sumerians.)

As the story proceeds, the younger gods annoy their original ancestors through their poor manners and overbearing character. Apsu complains that he can gain no rest by day or by night because of their incessant noise and he proposes to annihilate them. Tiamat, though she too is angry with them, urges restraint, but he ignores her. When the younger gods hear of his plans, they become virtually paralyzed with fear, except for Ea, who casts a spell of sleep on Apsu and then slays him. Afterward Ea builds his home on Apsu's body and begets Marduk. (The image suggests earth, perhaps mud from the river, building up above the level of the water so that habitations may be built and the Babylonians eventually generated.) The poem proceeds with lavish praise of Marduk (the sun), who is said to be the tallest and strongest of the gods. Marduk himself creates the four winds and produces streams, both of which annoy Tiamat. She decides to put an end to all of this nuisance and to avenge Apsu. She takes a new consort, Kingu, and raises an army with which to make war on the younger gods. When they hear of this they are at a loss until they think of asking Marduk to lead them. Ea bids Marduk come to the assembly of the gods. Marduk promises to be their champion but asks in return that he become supreme among them and receive all their authority to "determine the fates." They willingly proclaim him king and confer on him throne, scepter, and royal vestments.

When Tiamat sees Marduk ride into battle against her, she goes wild, taking leave of her senses and shaking to her lowest parts—an image not only of a stormy sea, but of chaos itself. Slaying her, Marduk splits her in two like a shellfish and thrusts one-half upward to make the sky and the other downward to make the sea, setting guards to ensure that her waters will not escape and threaten the world again. He makes the dome of heaven correspond to earth as its heavenly counterpart. Then he executes Kingu and creates human beings from his blood so that the gods will have servants to maintain the earth when they have withdrawn to the heavens. As their final work of creation the gods build Babylon and at its center, as a temple to Marduk, the great ziggurat of Esagila, described as reaching as high as Apsu, as high as the primordial waters were deep.

Notice in this myth that the gods need human beings that they may rest from labor. The gods are not unlimited in power, but constitute only a part of the larger system of things that is the cosmos as a whole. They themselves must struggle to establish creation and keep it in proper order. Also, they do not create the world from nothing but make it from a preexisting reality. The world as we know it comes from the body of the subdued Tiamat, and human beings come from the blood of Kingu. One might say that the gods do not "create" the world in the same sense that the God of the Judeo-Christian-Islamic tradition creates.

The plot of the *Enuma Elish* describes both the creation of the cosmos as a whole and the evolution of the political order of Mesopotamia, as seen from the perspective of Babylonians in the second millennium. The authors are looking back to the origins of an order in which they have preeminence over their neighbors but are themselves under the authority of the gods and divine justice. The movement from a democratic assembly of gods to a centralized monarchic system under the rule of Marduk, god of Babylon, parallels the historical movement from independent city-states in Sumer and Akkad to the Babylonian empire. That the Babylonian emperors interpreted their own authority as subordinate to and representative of an overarching divine order can be seen, for example, in the preamble to the Law Code of Hammurabi (approximately 1750 B.C.E.), which opens with a description of how Anu and Enlil, lords of heaven and earth, committed lordship ("the Enlil functions over all mankind") to Marduk and then called Hammurabi personally to enforce their justice in the land.

The underlying idea in this picture of historical development seems to have been that earthly kingship was conferred from a superhuman source and was an imitation of and participation in the ordering power of a divine original, the order established by the gods of the empire at the beginning of the world. This meant that royal rule was intended to be sacred rule in the service of divine justice. It also meant that human life and its order were connected with the cosmic order and the life of the gods. If human farmers did not cultivate their crops, if reverent worshipers did not offer sacrifices, if justice among human beings was allowed to deteriorate, then the life of the gods would also suffer injury.

This interpretation of the relationship among human beings, the world, and the gods is a good example of *cosmological symbolism:* symbolism in which human life and society are interpreted by analogy with the cosmic order. That was the predominant pattern of symbolism in ancient Mesopotamia, and we will see it again in Egypt. It is not the only possible pattern of symbolic interpretation, but all over the world it seems to have been the first to develop.

Anthropomorphic (human form) *symbolism,* such as that which flourished in classical Greece, likens society and the cosmos to a human existence. Specifically, it depicts reality in terms of the inner order of a wise and virtuous person. Anthropomorphic symbolism usually develops after cosmologically symbolized societies have broken down and disappointed their members so deeply that the members feel the need for an entirely new way of discovering relevance. This sort of disappointment never seems to have afflicted the ancient Mesopotamians, at least not enough to have caused a radically new development in their culture. Most of the myths the Mesopotamians have left us suggest that they found the evil of the universe intelligible in terms of the basic model we have seen: a precarious balance of interdependent forces.

Nonetheless, the Mesopotamians did finally wrestle with the problem of a suffering that is genuinely personal and calls the cosmological principle into question. The epic of *Gilgamesh* is their famous meditation on personal suffering. It concerns a famous early king of Uruk in Sumer and probably dates from the late third millennium B.C.E. The most complete surviving text is in Assyrian, but there are fragments of earlier versions in Sumerian and Akkadian.

Gilgamesh was of mingled parentage, divine and human, but he was a mortal all the same, and his mortality is the poem's main theme. At the opening Gilgamesh is a vigorous and effective ruler, in fact too vigorous: his constant demands for labor and military service lead the people of Uruk to appeal to the gods for relief. The goddess Aruru responds by creating another energetic creature, Enkidu, to attract the interest of Gilgamesh. Enkidu is humanity in its most primitive state. He is naked, covered with hair, enormously strong, and lives among animals in the wilderness. Befriending the animals, Enkidu protects them from hunters, who, unable to fight him themselves, appeal to Gilgamesh.

Gilgamesh sends a sacred prostitute, Shamhat, to civilize Enkidu. Shamhat goes to the wilderness to wait for Enkidu by a water hole. When he comes, she attracts his interest by uncovering her body. They enjoy a week of heroic lovemaking, at the end of which Enkidu tries to return to the company of his animals but finds them shying away from him. Shamhat tells him that he no longer belongs among animals but has become wise and godlike. She offers to take him to see the great walls of Uruk and mighty Gilgamesh. Enkidu decides to go with her and to challenge Gilgamesh. He arrives in Uruk at the moment of Gilgamesh's wedding procession and bars Gilgamesh's path to the bride. The two powerful figures hurl themselves at each other and fight like young bulls, shaking the walls of the bride's house. Gilgamesh turns out to be the stronger of the two, but his generous praise of Enkidu makes them fast friends.

Looking for adventure together (Gilgamesh seems to have forgotten all about his bride), they set out to kill a monster named Huwawa. When they return victorious, the goddess Ishtar falls in love with Gilgamesh and proposes to him. He turns her down. Furious, Ishtar appeals to her father, Anu, to unleash the bull of heaven. Anu warns her that this monster will be so destructive that there will be a famine for seven years, but she persuades him to unloose it anyway. However, Enkidu gets behind the bull and twists its tail while Gilgamesh plunges his sword into its neck. Enraged by Ishtar's curses, Enkidu tears off the bull's shank and throws it at the goddess.

This means trouble. The gods hold an assembly and sentence Enkidu to death. Enkidu is horrified and launches into a long lament in which he curses everything that has led to this end: his departure from the animals, his lovemaking with Shamhat, his migration to the city, and even his friendship with Gilgamesh. The sun god Shamash, however, intervenes and persuades him to withdraw his curses and bless his friend before dying. In a dream Enkidu has a vision of Irkalla, the land of the dead. It is a house of dust and darkness, devoid of real life, in which one is no more than a shadow. Far from representing a form of immortality, it is death depicted in the most graphic terms.

After his friend's death Gilgamesh falls into an extreme despondency, not simply because of the loss of his companion, but because death, which had always been a remote abstraction to him, has now become a vivid reality. He realizes that however long and glorious his life may be, death awaits. This thought becomes an obsession, undermining any joy in his own or his city's glory and any consolation from the balance of forces in the cosmos. The thought of his death haunts Gilgamesh day and night. Finally he decides to search for an escape from mortality. He has heard of an ancestor named Utnapishtim who once won eternal life as a gift from the gods and now dwells at the end of the earth. The sun god, Shamash, reproaches him for his lack of moderation, but

Gilgamesh is not interested in reasonableness; his heart is set on only one goal: not to die. Eventually he arrives at the shore of the great sea that encircles the earth, where he finds a tavern run by a woman named Siduri. She offers the conventional wisdom, urging him to accept his mortality, enjoy food, drink, and merriment, wear beautiful clothing, bathe in fresh water, rejoice in his children, and give satisfaction to his wife. This, she says, is the task of human beings. Gilgamesh refuses to listen and persuades her to tell him how to find Utnapishtim. She directs him to the boatman, Urshanabi, who takes him to Utnapishtim's island.

The result, however, is bitterly disappointing. Utnapishtim tells Gilgamesh that he did not win immortality through deeds of valor. It happened at a time when the gods had decided to destroy humankind in a great flood. Ea, more foresighted than the other gods, realized that without human beings to maintain the earth the gods would languish for lack of sacrifices. Ea told Utnapishtim to build an ark and save his family and pairs of all animals. (The story is similar in many details to the biblical story of Noah, which, as far as written records indicate, it may predate by perhaps a millennium.) After the flood, the gods realized the fault of their hastiness and were so grateful to Utnapishtim that they conferred eternal life on him. Unfortunately that was something that could happen only once.

Utnapishtim suggests, evidently mockingly, that if Gilgamesh wishes to conquer death, he might begin by trying to conquer sleep. No sooner does Gilgamesh take up the challenge than sleep overcomes him. Utnapishtim would happily let Gilgamesh sleep himself to death, but his wife takes pity on Gilgamesh and persuades Utnapishtim to wake him and let him go home. She also persuades him to tell Gilgamesh about a plant that will perpetually renew his youth. This thorny plant grows in the Apsu, the sweet waters deep under the earth. (In the Mesopotamian cosmology the earth is a great floating island.) Gilgamesh dives for it by tying stones to his feet and sinking to the bottom. When he gets the plant, he is overjoyed, thinking his basic goal achieved. On the way home, however, feeling the heat of the day, he decides to take a swim in a cool pond. He leaves the plant with his clothes and while he is swimming a serpent comes out of its hole and eats the plant. Immediately the snake sloughs off its old skin and is renewed, shiny and young. With that, Gilgamesh completely despairs. Following his despair, however, come resignation and composure. Essentially Gilgamesh accepts the wisdom of Shamash and Siduri that he had rejected earlier. At the end of the poem he takes the boatman around the great walls of Uruk, praising the grandeur of his royal domain.

Myths are told and retold to convey a society's values. Is this poem a lesson in moderation and the acceptance of human limitations, or is it a radical protest against those limitations? There is no easy answer. How far did the challenge to Mesopotamian cosmological assumptions proceed? Did anyone seriously doubt them to the point of considering another perspective? The ending of the poem seems designed to reassert the old doctrines and values. In the perspective of the conclusion, Gilgamesh's obsession becomes a temporary disorder that must be overcome if one is to live in proper harmony with the cosmos and the gods.

(so prominent in Mesopotamia). The greatest need was to keep the social order going, and so afterlife came to be emphasized. On the Egyptian stage, pharaohs and peasants enacted a mortality play. Beyond life under the sun, life in the flesh, lay deathlessness. The tomb then was an archway through which everybody passed.

The unification of Upper (southern) and Lower (northern) Egypt occurred about 3100 B.C.E., and with it began the central Egyptian religious dogma — divine kingship. In the prehistoric years before unification, Neolithic culture gradually developed small-town life, characterized by domestic animals, significant crafts (especially pottery), and probably the burial of the dead with hopes of an afterlife. From the beginnings of Egyptian history, local gods had great influence, and throughout the long dynasties

Sphinx and pyramids

they comprised a pantheon (in the form of an assembly of divinities).

Egyptian splendor began vigorously in the period 3100–2200 B.C.E., which historians divide into the Early Dynasties (3100–2700 B.C.E.) and the Old Kingdom (2700–2200 B.C.E.). A famous product of Old Kingdom religion is the Memphite theology, developed to justify the new, unified kingdom centered at Memphis. Central to the justification is that the god of Memphis, Ptah, is the foremost creator god. Ptah originated Atum, the supreme god of the older cosmogony, and the other gods by an idea in his heart and a command on his tongue.

The Middle Kingdom (2050–1800 B.C.E.) was centered at Thebes. It nurtured several trends that brought important changes, although they worked below the surface constancy of Egyptian life. The most important of these trends was a democratization of certain religious rights, as the distance between the pharaoh and the common people narrowed. Also,

there was an effort to elevate the more important gods and an increasing inclination to worship gods who were **theriomorphic** (in the form of animals). The most important religious rights that democratization brought the middle classes were privileges in the afterlife and a chance to participate in ceremonies that had been confined to the king and a few priests. By this time, most middle-class people could afford to have their bodies **mummified** after death.

An intermediate period (1800–1570 B.C.E.) dissolved the Middle Kingdom and included a century or so of rule by the Hyksos (Shepherd Kings), who were probably Syrians. The New Kingdom (1570–1165 B.C.E.) began with the famous eighteenth dynasty, which made Egypt a real empire that stretched to the Euphrates. For our limited review of the high points in later Egyptian religious history, the New Kingdom's speculation on the deities is important.

In the nineteenth dynasty under **Akhenaton** (1369–1353 B.C.E.), there was a move to make Aton, previously just the sun disk, the sole deity. Apparently Akhenaton himself bullied through this change (Egypt quickly reverted to polytheism after his death) because of his own spiritual perceptions (which many of his contemporaries considered fanatical and heretical). In a joyful climax, one of Akhenaton's hymns cries out: "The Aton is the creator-god: O sole god, like whom there is no other! Thou didst create the world according to thy desire, while thou wert alone." Moreover, Aton was not the god of Egypt alone. Akhenaton saw that a real creator god must have established all peoples, whatever their country, speech, culture, or skin. This was truly a remarkable leap toward universalism, especially coming from the leader of a resolutely ethnocentric people, and it was the centerpiece in the so-called Armarna Revolution that gave the New Kingdom a great charge of cultural energy. Whether Akhenaton should be considered an early monotheist (claiming the exclusive existence of just one god) or a mere monolatrist (advocating the worship of just one god, but not denying the existence of others) remains a point of scholarly debate, as does the relative role of political and psychological considerations in Akhenaton's actions.

Another high point of New Kingdom theology consisted of the Amon hymns, which probably date from the reign of Ramses II (1290–1224 B.C.E.). They illustrate a return to Amon and the demise of Aton as well as a deep sense that the first creator god must be mysterious. Amon is "far from heaven, he is absent from the underworld, so that no gods know his true form. His image is not displayed in writings. No one bears witness to him. . . He is too mysterious that his majesty might be disclosed, he is too great that men should ask about him, too powerful that he might be known." Along with the hymns of Akhenaton, these praises of Amon represent the greatest advance in Egyptian theology. Here we see traces of a "negative" theology—a rising of the mind to the true nature of divinity by denying that creatures can represent it adequately.

In the centuries after the New Kingdom, the capital moved to Manis, Bubastis, and Sais—a possible indication of some political turmoil of that era. Persians ruled Egypt from 525 to 405 B.C.E., and the last native dynasties in the fourth century B.C.E. ended with the conquest of Alexander. In the period from Alexander to about 30 B.C.E., the Hellenistic Ptolemies

ruled, and the city of Alexandria was the luminary of the eastern Mediterranean. Christian influence rose in the Roman and Byzantine periods (30 B.C.E.–641 C.E.), bequeathing Egypt the Coptic Church. Since 641 C.E., Egyptian culture has been predominantly Muslim.

Except for the brief episode of monotheism under Akhenaton, ancient Egypt was polytheistic. Indeed, the proliferation of Egyptian gods and symbols is overwhelming. The basic hieroglyph for God is a pole with a flag, the emblem flying in front of major temples, which designated purity and the creative life force. Since the Egyptians sensed purity and creativity in many places, they split divinity into many gods. The gods most important in the old cosmogony were four male-female pairs. The males bore the head of a frog, and the females the head of a snake—symbols, apparently, of self-renewal (the frog begins as a tadpole, while the snake sheds its skin). The idea (before the Memphite theology established Ptah as the creator) was that an invisible wind moved over primal waters and used these four pairs of gods to make life.

Throughout Egyptian history, the most important deities were associated with the sun and death (connoting a theme of resurrection). Their names and images varied from cultural center to cultural center, but the most common name for the sun god was Re, symbolized by either the sun's disk or the falcon. Another name was Khepri, represented by a scarab pushing the sun disk; a third name was Atum, whom people at Heliopolis worshipped and represented as the setting sun. In the mythology of Heliopolis, Atum generated himself on the primordial hill of creation (the Pyramids of the Old Kingdom represented this hill). He conquered chaos, took charge of the world, and established Maat, the eternal cosmic order. The *Book of the Dead* (17:3–5), from the New Kingdom, says that Re became king of the gods in the earliest times by defeating all his opponents. Maat is his daughter but also his mother, because in his course through the sky, the sun god follows her cosmic order. That course determined Egyptian reality. The west was the land of the dead, and the east was where the daily miracle of the sun's return from the dead occurred. On the walls of royal tombs near Luxor, twelve sections divide the night realm, or underworld, through which the sun god's boat travels. Although the sun god is dead during this time, he still possesses the power of resurrection. Middle night is the realm of Sokaris, who appears in human form with the head of a falcon. His area is a desert through which Re's boat has to be dragged before the sun can reemerge into the light.

It was the deity Osiris, however, around whom developed the funerary cult that made the underworld almost an Egyptian obsession. Nowhere is the myth of his descent to the underworld detailed, but it probably had the following plot. Osiris and Seth were brothers, and the deity Isis was Osiris' sister and wife. Osiris ruled the world as a good regent, but Seth hated him and killed him by guile. He got Osiris into a coffin and sent it down the Nile. Isis recovered Osiris' corpse and uttered a soulful dirge (which inspired litanies used in Osiris' worship). This dirge had a magic power that revived Osiris. Once again Seth moved against Osiris, this time hacking Osiris' body into fourteen pieces and then scattering them. Isis recovered them all and buried each piece properly wherever she found it (this explained the many Osirian sanctuaries). Furthermore, Isis conceived a son Horus by the dead Osiris and brought Horus up in the marshes to hide him from Seth. When Horus reached manhood, Isis arranged for a trial at which Seth was condemned for murdering Osiris and Horus was recognized as Osiris' heir. Osiris himself remained in the underworld, accepting the roles of lord of the nether realm and judge of the dead. Osiris seems to represent the growing power of vegetation, which roots in the earth, and he relates to all buildings that are set on the earth, to the moon, and to the dead. Isis represents the throne, the sacred seat of the king. As such, she "makes" the king and is his mother. For instance, on a relief in a temple at Abydos, the pharaoh sits on Isis' lap. Thus, Horus and the pharaoh are correlated. As Horus owed his throne to his mother Isis, so did the pharaoh.

Horus had many appearances, but most frequently he wore the head of a falcon. He was the model son but shows traces of an older sky god. In the Osiris myth, Horus fought Seth and lost an eye, while depriving Seth of his testicles. They reconciled, however, to suggest that life and death are paired. Thoth, originally a moon god, was the agent of their reconciliation. Usually Thoth was represented as a baboon or an ibis. He was also a god of the dead and is thought to have found Horus' lost eye and have

(c) Gianni Dagli Orti /CORBIS

Egypt had many theriomorphic deities, with part-animal bodies.

returned it to him. This eye became a token of life returned from the dead. All of these myths represent the Egyptian sense of a cosmic order. The term *Maat* described this order. Maat was something like the Law or Logos guiding creation. Personified as a goddess, it had the obligation of constraining or persuading creatures to follow the laws natural to them. The pharaoh mediated Maat to the common people, and the laws of the state sanctioned by the pharaoh spelled out what Maat was to mean in many concrete circumstances. The pharaoh had responsibilities to Maat, but he served as well as a metaphysical link between the order of heaven that Maat expressed and the order of earth that needed ordering. Maat had many competitors in the Egyptian pantheon, probably standing psychologically for the rights of reason in competition with will, desire, fertility, and the other urges of both the conscious and the unconscious mind.

This order was a major reason for the stability of the Egyptian culture. With divinity in their midst, what need the people fear? The greatest threat to social stability, understandably, was the king's death. The care taken for the transition from old pharaoh to new suggests how the office of pharaoh served Egypt as a fence against chaos. Consequently, the most influential mythic cycle was that of Osiris and Isis, which explained where the king (identified with Osiris) had gone at death. Relatedly, the most important ceremonies were the old king's burial and the new king's accession. For a hint of how effective this mythic-ritualistic approach was, consider the pyramids. The common people supplied the immense, brutal labor needed to build the pyramids, because they assured the king's happy afterlife and the state's continuance.

Ancient Egypt had a powerful caste of priests, and at times, despite the dogma of the king's divinity, this caste clashed with the crown. The conflict between Akhenaton and the priests of the old god Amon was a vivid instance of such friction, but conflict was almost always on the verge of breaking out. When Akhenaton moved the capital from Thebes to Amarna, he bruised theological, class, and local sensitivities all at once. The local priesthood, fighting for its own gods and people, consistently defended those sensitivities. As a result, the priesthood was a powerful sociological force.

Women were quite subordinate in Egyptian society but were not without influence and religious importance. The goddesses Hathor, Nut, Neith, Maat, and Isis represented the female aspects of divinity, while the queen had vital roles in the political theology. Hathor, Nut, and Neith were forms of the mother goddess—both sacred representations of fertility and figures of comfort. Maat ruled cosmic justice, while Isis was sister and wife of the god as king. On rare occasions a queen could rule (Hatshepsut, 1486–1468 B.C.E., is the most famous instance), and as the source of the divine king, the queen mother was much more than just another harem wife.

Egyptian proverbs encouraged husbands to treat their wives well so that their property would prosper, but they also pictured women as flirtatious, gossiping and spiteful. Women of the New Kingdom served in the temples and as popular entertainers, but in both cases they risked reputations as prostitutes. In both formal and popular religion, Isis was a focal point for women's own religion, especially in Hellenistic times, after 300 B.C.E. Related to Osiris, she was the ideal wife (and a potent exemplar of grief); related to Horus, she was the ideal mother. Through Isis, then, women in ordinary roles participated in divinity.

Perhaps because of this divinity, legal documents from about 500 B.C.E. suggest that Egyptian women had the right to own property, buy or sell goods, and testify in court. They were taxpayers and could sue; they could inherit from parents or husbands. On the other hand, husbands could dismiss wives at their pleasure (but not vice versa), and concubinage, adultery, and prostitution were widespread. Because many Egyptian women worked the fields or had other important economic roles, their lot was better than that of women in other ancient civilizations (Mesopotamia, for instance). Still, women were not regarded as equal to men.

The Egyptian religious conception of the self relates intimately to the Egyptian concern with death, burial, and the afterlife. The ancient Egyptians loved life, and they looked forward to another, better chapter after death. The remains of many burial sites, well preserved because of the desert sand and dry climate, show that the departed took with them favorite utensils and even favorite servants. The *ba* was that aspect of a person that continued after death, which contrasted with the *ka,* or vital force, the impersonal power animating the living. A third aspect, the *akh,* was the shining, glorious manifestation of the dead in heaven. With these three notions, the Egyptians had a sense of what moves the living and what continues on after death.

The key to a successful afterlife journey was good ethical behavior in this life. As indicated in our outline of his myth, Osiris judged the dead in the underworld. The Pyramid texts of the Old Kingdom, the Coffin texts of the Middle Kingdom, and the *Book of the Dead* from the New Kingdom show a constant concern with judgment, hence a certain awareness of personal responsibility. The *Book of the Dead* contains a famous "negative confession" that illustrates both the posthumous trial Egyptians imagined and some of their principal ethical concerns. The deceased claims before Osiris: "I have not committed evil against men. . . . I have not mistreated cattle. . . . I have not blasphemed a god. . . . I have not done violence to a poor man. . . . I have not made anyone weep. . . . I have not killed. . . . I have not defamed a slave to his superior. . . . I have not had sexual relations with a boy." In all, thirty-six declarations of innocence are made. Then, to complete his show of religious virtuosity, he gives each of the forty-two divine jurors, by name, a specific assurance. For example, "O Embracer-of-Fire, who comes forth from Babylon, I have not stolen. O Eater-of-Entrails, who comes forth from the thirty [judges in the world of the living], I have not practiced usury. O Eater-of-Blood, who comes forth from the execution block, I have not slain the cattle of the god."

We have less knowledge of the rituals in which the average Egyptian may have participated. In most agricultural ceremonies and many regal rituals, the common people could participate. There were probably festivals where grain and animals were sacrificed. Male circumcision and abstinence from pork were practiced, as in some other Middle Eastern traditions.

IRAN

Persia is the name for the ancient area north of Mesopotamia, east of Turkey, south of the Caspian Sea, and west of India and Pakistan. The most recent political regimes of the nation currently occupying that area have preferred the name Iran instead of Persia. That name comes from Aryans, nomadic peoples from the north who invaded and conquered this area during the second millennium B.C.E. We will use the terms *Iran* and *Persia* interchangeably.

Iran has had human habitation for well over 10,000 years. Those first inhabitants were great potters, and archeologists have found among their relics designs and figurines of a naked goddess, whose mate was likely a god who was her son. This doctrine would be the most direct explanation for the early Iranian customs of marriage between blood relations, descent through the female line, and, in certain tribes (for example, the Guti of Kurdistan), female army commanders. Later archeological remains, dating back to 2000 B.C.E., suggest a people both artistic and hopeful, for impressive pendants, earrings, bracelets, and the like found in gravesites imply a notion of an afterlife.

In the second millennium B.C.E., Indo-Europeans, pressured by population shifts in the neighboring geographic areas, left their homelands in the plains of southern Russia and migrated southeast across Iran. As we shall see in the next chapter, some of them eventually ended up as far south as India. In the west they established the Hittite empire, sacked Babylon, and confronted the Egyptians. From the east, Indo-European tribes called the Mittani conquered northern Mesopotamia and allied themselves with Egypt in about 1450 B.C.E. Linguistic, religious, and social parallels suggest that pre-Zoroastrian Iranian culture, as well as the culture of the peoples who conquered the Indus Valley in India and produced the Vedic culture, derived from the Mittani, Hittite, and other Indo-European **Aryans** (from an Indo-European word meaning "noble"). In particular, the Iranian and Indian Aryans had similar gods and similar social structures.

Recently Iran has been a nation in the throes of choosing its identity and direction. On first view, the principal choices Iran has faced in determining its identity have been Western secularism (almost unavoidable because of Iran's massive petroleum industry) and a form of traditional Islam. In a later chapter we will describe how Islam was brought to Iran and how it developed there.

This chapter will discuss an earlier religion developing in Iran, focusing on a man known as Zarathustra (called **Zoroaster** by the Europeans). He could be described as a priest, but even more so, a **prophet**. Most historical data indicate that he probably lived in the sixth or seventh century B.C.E., but many modern Zoroastrians claim that he (or his religion) was around several hundred years before then.

The native Iranian religion that Zoroaster challenged was probably controlled by the Magi, Median priests (the Medes were a later Aryan tribe from western Iran). Apparently that religion was an animistic polytheism (devotion to many divine spirits) similar to that of early Aryan India. After Zoroaster's death, the Magi fused their ideas onto some of his newer doctrines, making Zoroastrianism a syncretistic amalgam of conflicting gods and practices. Before Zoroaster, Iranian ultimate reality included a number of *ahuras*— good celestial spirits. The most prominent symbols were lucidity (the brightness that glances off the waters or that leaps from fire); the sacred liquor *haoma*, used in the old Aryan rituals; and plain water, symbol of purity and motherliness.

Ancient Iranian society established a pronounced caste system, but most of its ritual practices cut across class distinctions. Some common people were quite interested in magic, but the orthodox leaders feared the occult, treating sorcerers and witches as criminals. Folk remedies and totemic practices (for example, rubbing oneself with the wing of a falcon to ward off an evil spell) flourished, in part because of contact with Mesopotamia. Both divination and astrology were common, and other nations considered the Persian Magi to be specialists in dream interpretation. Occasionally there was trial by fire or molten lead (if the person survived, he or she was deemed innocent).

Zoroaster is estimated to have lived from 628 to 551 B.C.E., but the only direct source for his message is a fragment of the sacred Zoroastrian liturgical text, the *Avesta*. That portion, called the *Gathas*, along with later Greek and Persian traditions, suggests that Zoroaster's enemies (Magi and men's societies of the old religion) forced him to flee from his homeland into ancient Chorasmia (the area today of western Afghanistan, or Turkmenistan). There, when about forty years old, he found a patron in King Vishtapa and his message began to have social effect.

Zoroaster's doctrine was essentially **monotheistic.** The one supreme God had the name of Ahura Mazdah, although he was often called the "Wise Lord." This God is the creator of all, having thought it into existence. This God is holy, righteous, immortal, and generous. The great outward symbol of God's "Truth" and power is fire, and the center of the Zoroastrian ritual is the fire altar.

Zoroaster's doctrine was also **dualistic** in that he recognized the existence of two powerful and competing forces in the world. The world is divided between "the Truth and the Lie," by which Zoroaster meant God and Satan (the latter had several different names, including Angra Mainyu, the "destructive spirit").

Zoroaster advocated the doctrine of **free will**: that the creatures of the Wise Lord have the ability to freely choose whether to serve His cause or that of Satan. These creatures include human beings as well as spirit beings (angels). Sometimes the old deities are described as spirit beings who have chosen to serve the evil. Because human beings are free, they are responsible for their own fates. By good deeds they win the eternal reward of possessing Wholeness and Immortality; by evil deeds they merit pain in hell.

Historically, Zoroastrianism may be one of the earliest advocates of **eschatological** doctrine. The conflict between God and Satan was portrayed as **apocalyptic** (a final battle between these two sides) at which time the dead will be resurrected to fight on one side or the other. Unlike Teutonic eschatology (in which the gods are destined to lose) or Christian-Islamic eschatology (in which God is destined to win), the Zoroastrians say that the outcome hangs in the balance and will depend upon the choices freely made by men and angels.

Zoroaster generates his images of divinity and human destiny apart from nature and toward the inner light of human conscience. Two verses from perhaps the most autobiographical of Zoroaster's hymns suggest the religious experience at the core of his preaching:

> As the holy one I recognized thee, O Wise Lord, When I saw thee at the beginning, at the birth of existence, Appoint a recompense for deed and word: Evil reward to the evil, good to the good, Through thy wisdom, at the last turning-point of creation [43:5].
> As the holy one I recognized thee, O Wise Lord, When he came to me as Good Mind. To his question: "To whom wilt thou address thy worship?" I made reply: "To thy fire! While I offer up my veneration to it, I will think of the Right to the utmost of my power" [43:9].

In Iran in the early sixth century B.C.E., only an exceptional personality could have cut through the welter of Aryan gods, spells, and semimagical practices and discerned a clear religious call to identify God with justice. Similarly, only an exceptional personality could have lingered over abstractions such as Good Mind and the Right and made these terms God's best names. Zoroaster's revelations had a social background and significance. For instance, he championed the farmer over the nomad. Nonetheless, the deeper explanation of Zoroaster's religious power is the interior, spiritual experiences indicated by the *Gathas*. Like Jesus and Muhammad, Zoroaster met a holy, compelling divinity or ultimate reality. His mission was simply to spread this doctrine far and wide. The origins of Zoroastrian history, then, are the visions and insights of a founding genius. Through all its later changes, Zoroastrianism and the world religions that it influenced retained something of the dazzling vision of Zoroaster's Wise Lord.

Zoroaster's basic ethical imperative was to maintain goodness and life by fighting against evil and death. As a result, Zoroastrianism has frowned on fasting, asceticism, and celibacy. Rather, humans have been counseled to foster the powers of generation in nature and humanity alike. One basis for this view was Zoroaster's own stress on the holiness of agriculture, which to him was a cooperation with Ahura Mazdah. The farmer who sows grain, he said, "feeds the religion" of the Wise Lord. Zoroaster himself seems to have disapproved of blood sacrifices, going out of his way to try to protect cattle. Blood sacrifices survived in later Zoroastrianism, though, the most important being the bull sacrifice. Also important to later Zoroastrians was the preparation and offering of *haoma,* the sacred liquor, which until recently served as a sort of sacrament for the dying. The most important sacrifice and ritual focus, however, has been the fire sacrifice. The flame has to be "pure" (obtained by burning "pure" materials such as sandalwood), and it has to pass to another flame before its fuel becomes embers. The fire sacrifice has overtones of an ancient wonder at the source of light and heat, but its major emphasis has always been to symbolize the blazing purity and potential sensing of the Wise Lord.

Rituals for individuals, including rites of passage at maturity, marriage, and death are important, as are various purifications. Upon entering adulthood, both men and women receive a sacred thread and shirt. The thread is a compound symbol: cosmically it stands for the Milky Way, the thread of the stars through the heavens; mythologically, it recalls Ahura Mazdah's gift of *haoma;* personally, it symbolizes taking up adult responsibilities. The shirt is white, to symbolize purity and the garment that the soul dons after death. Death and bloodshed are prime occasions for purification, because they are prime pollutants. As noted, Zoroastrians have exposed the dead so as not to defile other persons, the earth, fire, or water. In some periods of Zoroastrianism, blood from a cut, an extracted tooth, or even menstrual flow could render a person ritually unclean.

In general, women have played only a small part in the Zoroastrian world. Their part in redemption has been to furnish males to fight against Angra Mainyu. Most of the tradition has held that in the beginning women defected to the Destructive Spirit. Theologically, then, Zoroastrianism has viewed the female nature as unholy.

After the death of Zoroaster, his religion invigorated the Persian empire. The great leaders of the Achaemenid empire who followed Zoroaster were the Persians Cyrus II (599–530 B.C.E.), Cambyses II (530–522 B.C.E.), and Darius I (522–486 B.C.E.). They conquered eastern Iran, the prophet's initial sphere of influence, and we can read in inscriptions that they left something of Zoroastrianism's function as the religious rationale for a new, energetic empire. Following Alexander's victory over Darius III in 331 B.C.E., the Achaemenid dynastic line begun with Cyrus II gave way to the Greek Seleucids. Under the Seleucids, for almost a century Hellenistic cultural ideals blended with Persian. Zoroastrian influence probably declined, overshadowed by a Greek-Iranian syncretism. While the practice of pure Zoroastrianism seems to have remained in Fars (the southern province called Persis), the old Iranian goddess Anahita, fused with the Mesopotamian goddess Nanai, complicated the religious picture in other provinces.

Also complicating the picture was the Greek hero Heracles (Hercules), who joined with local gods. Heracles was the patron of the gymnasium, the place of physical exercise, an important feature of Hellenistic culture. Also, he was one of several "savior" gods (gods who made life whole) whose influence grew apace with the disintegration of the previously secure city-state religions. The *Avesta* was probably still evolving at this time, incorporating hymns to the god **Mithra**, who had existed before Zoroaster and later became an important savior god for the Romans. In the *Avesta,* Mithra's main functions are to preserve cattle, sanctify contracts, and render judgment on human actions.

The Greek Seleucids yielded to the Parthians, who entered Iran from the area southwest of the Caspian Sea. The Parthians dominated Iran, bit by bit, from the first conquest by Arsaces in about 238 B.C.E. until about 226 C.E. While sources are scanty, Zoroastrianism apparently made some gains against syncretism under the Parthians, achieving a privileged status. Nonetheless, in Parthian times the cultures of the different geographic areas varied considerably. Coins, art, and other remains indicate different local preferences for a variety of gods. Ahura Mazdah and Mithra certainly were influential, but the worship of the goddess Anahita was probably the most important. The northern Magis had a custom of exposing the bodies of the dead on mountains or manmade "towers of silence" to be eaten by vultures. This was done because burial would pollute the earth and cremation would pollute the sky. This rite spread as far south as Susa, capital of the old Elamite kingdom. We also know that the Parthians were tolerant of religious minorities, so much so that Jews regarded them as great protectors.

The history of Zoroastrianism under the Parthians remains rather vague. Under the Sasanians (ca. 226–637 C.E.), it is more definite, as is the story of Persian culture generally. The early Sasanian king Papak probably was the director of the shrine to Anahita in Istakhr in Persis (south-central Iran), and his successor Shapur had quite liberal religious policies. That soon changed, however, largely because of the influence of Kartir, a zealous Zoroastrian priest. By the last third of the third century, he had made Zoroastrianism the established Persian denomination. Kartir favored proselytizing, establishing fire temples for worship and instruction, purging Zoroastrian heretics, and attacking all non-Zoroastrian religions. Consequently, he persecuted Jews, Buddhists, Hindus, Christians, and Manichaeans, destroying their centers and proscribing their rituals. From this time, marriage between blood relations became a common Zoroastrian practice, and the Zoroastrian clergy were a political power.

The **Manicheans**—followers of the native Iranian prophet Mani—came to be regarded as the chief heretics. Under Shapur I, Mani had been free to travel and preach, but soon after Shapur's death the Zoroastrians martyred him. Nonetheless, his ideas gained considerable acceptance, both in Iran and throughout the Roman empire. Manicheans stressed a **dualism** of good and evil, equating good with the spirit and evil with matter. Consequently, they denigrated the body, sex, marriage, women, and food—anything perceived as carnal. As we shall see, Manicheanism had significant effects on Christians, influencing St. Augustine and spawning several medieval

heresies. At the end of the fifth century C.E. Persian Manicheans led a socioeconomic movement called Mazdakism (after its leader Mazdak), which preached a sort of communism that included the division of wealth and the sharing of wives and concubines. Many poor people embraced this movement, but Prince Chosroes Anosharvan massacred the Mazdakite leaders about 528 C.E.

In the last decades of Sasanian rule, the Zoroastrian leadership sanctioned a rigid caste system based, somewhat like that of India, on an ideal division of society into priests, warriors, scribes, and commoners. Ritual tended toward a sterile formalism, and a number of speculative or *gnostic* (relating to secret knowledge) tendencies emerged. At the beginning of the Sasanian period, Zurvanism had become the dominant Zoroastrian theology, in good part because of an increasing interest in the problem of evil. Zurvan was Infinite Time. Slowly, he displaced Ahura Mazdah (now called Ohrmazd) as the first principle. Ohrmazd then became identical with Holy Spirit, and Zurvan became his father, as well as the father of Holy Spirit's twin, Destructive Spirit. Thus, Zurvanism begot a dualism: Holy Spirit and Destructive Spirit. However, unlike Mani's dualism, Zurvanism did not make matter evil. For Zurvanite Zoroastrians, nature remained God's good creation.

After the Muslims conquered Persia in the seventh century, the Zoroastrian communities that survived continued to have significant influence. Zoroastrian priests were instrumental in creating a renaissance of religious literature in Pahlavi, the native Persian language in its "middle" period. They kept alive the notion that the prior Sasanian empire had been a fortunate era for the "good religion" that had preceded the Muslims and also for such Zoroastrian doctrines as the coming of the future savior and the approach of an apocalyptic era when judgment would occur. Zoroastrians also fought against the Arabs, Romans, and Turks in their midst, assuring devoted followers that God would soon give them revenge against these interlopers.

However, the actual political revolts that the Zoroastrians attempted tended to be completely crushed. That was dramatically true of an uprising attempted in the city of Shiraz in 979 C.E., the result of which was a series of harsh repressions instituted by the Muslim rulers. As a consequence, around the end of the tenth century, Zoroastrians began to leave Iran and head toward India, where their small but successful community became known as the **Parsis.** They left a reduced community in Iran, centered in the regions of Yazd and Kerman. Both these Iranian Zoroastrians and the Indian Parsis have perpetuated the religion begun by Zoroaster, although what one finds practiced nowadays has been deeply transformed by a further millennium of historical changes.

Until the sixteenth century, the Zoroastrian communities in Iran and India had little contact with one another. In the sixteenth century, they began to exchange texts providing answers to questions that had arisen about ritual and doctrinal matters. The Iranian communities usually felt isolated in the midst of a hostile Muslim environment, but the Indian Parsis flourished and exerted considerable influence on their neighbors, all the more so when British rule gave them special privileges. Bombay (Mumbai) has been the center of India's Parsi community. The result of Parsi contact with the religions of India has been pressure to rethink traditional views about monotheism (Ahura Mazdah) and dualism (Truth and Lie). Indian Zoroastrians (Parsis) have also struggled with internal questions of reforming liturgical rites and doctrine to make them more attractive to modern members. Such matters as the exposure of the dead, questions related to the liturgical calendar for religious celebrations, and interpretations of the scriptures (the *Avesta,* rediscovered in the eighteenth century and thereafter studied with modern philological tools) have all been occasions for debate and division.

When British rule ended in India in 1947, a small group of Parsis (perhaps 5,000) were isolated in Pakistan. There was also a small community in Sri Lanka. There may be a quarter million Zoroastrians worldwide, perhaps half of them in India. The Iranian community has been persecuted under the Islamic Republic of the last two decades, and so many have fled to Europe and North America.

NEW WORLD CIVILIZATIONS

The civilizations of India, China, Greece, and Rome will be discussed in later units. Before we leave this chapter, we will also briefly discuss the civilizations that arose on the continents of North and South America. These civilizations differ in several dimensions from those which arose in the Old World (the continents of Africa, Asia, and Europe). One difference is the dates. Between 4000 and 2000 B.C.E. one could see the stirrings of civilization in Egypt, Mesopotamia, India, and China. In the New World, the civilizations arose in the common era (after the birth of Christ). While the Old World civilizations lasted for thousands of years, those of the Aztecs and Incas were cut short after a few hundred years by the Spanish conquistadores. Another difference is that Old World civilizations arose within river valleys: the Nile in Egypt, Tigris and Euphrates in Mesopotamia, Indus in India, Huang Ho in China. New World civilizations arose in less hospitable regions: the rain forest of the Yucatan (for the Mayas) and mountainous inland areas (for the Aztecs and Incas).

The Mayas and the Aztecs will be considered together, although they were separated by time and place. Mayan cities arose first, and were probably largely abandoned by the time the Aztecs began their empire. Although both cultures were centered in present day Mexico, they had little geographical overlap: the Mayans in the warm, flat, tropical rain forest of the eastern Yucatan and the Aztecs in the cool central highlands around present-day Mexico City. What unites these two traditions is a similar problem (*instability*) and a similar system of myths, symbols, rituals, and doctrines for coping with that instability.

If you have been to Cancún, Mexico, you know the Caribbean climate in which the **Mayan** civilization developed. If you arrived by air or cruise ship, you probably noticed how flat and green this area of Mexico is. You might be led to the assumption that the ground is very fertile. But take a handful of it: gravel. The locals have a saying: *La tierra chupa* (literally translated: "The earth sucks"). What they mean is that the frequent rainfall is not sufficient to keep the ground wet and fertile. If you flew in, you probably also noticed some smoke from local forest fires. The Indians learned centuries ago that the ground can only be prepared for corn by the ashes of the burnt rain forest. This fertility allows the harvesting of corn for a few generations, but then the ground becomes exhausted, and the farmers must move on, slashing and burning more rain forest. In a few decades, the rain forest may come back and reclaim the spent farmland.

If you venture out of the prefabricated resort of Cancún and travel a couple of hours south (Tulum) or west (Chichen-Itzá), you will come to some Mayan ruins and maybe see some of the descendents of the Mayas. (Some people in these southern Mexican states and the mountainous area of Guatemala still converse in their pre-Spanish languages.) Other Mayan ruins lie in remote parts of the Yucatan, overgrown by foliage.

Instability on the Yucatan peninsula was only partially the result of occasional hurricanes and warring tribes (the coastal city of Tulum was walled, but most were not). Instability was also geographical: the farmland, and the cities that grew around it, had to be relocated over and over again.

Much of what we know about the Mayas is pure speculation. Although the Mayas had a pictorial system of writing somewhat similar to Egyptian hieroglyphics, most of their books were destroyed by overzealous Spanish missionaries in the sixteenth century. What we think we know about the Mayas is based upon what has been pieced together from the writings that did survive plus the oral accounts of people several generations removed from the practice of these rituals.

Mayan deities were arranged in a great pantheon with specific functions being assigned to each. Many of the deities were **theriomorphic** (had animal form or parts). The need for multiple starts is reflected in Mayan creation myths: The theme is of multiple creation. Several worlds were created, and each was destroyed by a different disaster (e.g., a jaguar ate it). The Mayan priesthood was very powerful and developed a *calendar* based upon precise astronomical observation. The hope was that this calendar would be useful in divination, predicting when the present world would be destroyed (we have less than a decade to go!).

The great Mayan symbols for fertility were blood and semen. The Mayan kings would symbolically fertilize the ground to keep the corn crops coming by an annual ritual. A spine from a sea urchin was used to pierce the foreskin and a few drops of blood would fall to the ground. When the corn harvest eventually diminished, a new, more dramatic ritual was substituted. If a few drops of blood from the king was insufficient, perhaps the blood of dozens of commoners would do. The pyramids constructed by the Maya (the world's largest in land area) served as ritual centers for sacrifice).

At first, families regarded it a great honor to have their son or daughter selected for sacrifice. (There was a doctrine of an afterlife, with different levels of heaven and hell, but it is hard to tell how important this was.) Later, as the number of sacrifices increased, people may have fled the cities. After a few centuries, the Mayan cities were abandoned.

The **Aztecs** began as a tribe somewhere around Utah about a thousand years ago. A shaman had a vision commanding the tribe to migrate southward and to continue the journey until a powerful symbol could be seen: an eagle eating a snake. The journey lasted over two thousand miles until the band arrived at the shores of Texcoco, a stagnant lake in a mile-high valley in central Mexico. There they saw the eagle eating the snake. That site is now the Zócalo (central square of Mexico City), and the image of the eagle eating the snake is on every Mexican coin and flag.

The Aztecs did not create the civilization of central Mexico; they merely conquered what had been established by the Toltecs, Olmecs, and other peoples. Aztec ruins are largely confined to Mexico City (some were unearthed in the construction of the subway), but the great pyramids about 40 miles northwest of the city were built for ritual purposes at least a thousand years before the Aztecs arrived.

Central Mexico was also plagued by instability. Not only were there frequent and devastating earthquakes and incessant warfare between the tribes, but there was a climatic problem as well. Rainfall in central Mexico stretches from April through October (and then there is a dry spell from October to April). If the crops are sown early enough, just before it begins to rain, the first harvest should be due around July and a second crop can be sown at that time then harvested around October (if the rains last).

Aztec deities were comparable to those of the Maya: a complex pantheon in which many of the gods of the conquered tribes were renamed or included as subservient to the Aztec gods. Myths of multiple creation reflect the different empires established by previous tribes. The Aztec priesthood was

Aztecs and other early civilizations turned to human sacrifice in hopes of persuading the gods to show favor.

very powerful and used a calendar based upon precise astronomical observation. The hope was that this would be useful in divination: predicting when the rains would commence.

Aztec religion also showed an eschatological bent, coming from a myth of a culture hero named Quetzalcoatl. At times he is portrayed as a theriomorphic plumed serpent and at times as a white-faced anthropomorphic god with a beard. The myth foretold that Quetzalcoatl had quarreled with other gods but would return. The Aztec calendar calculated that return to be

around 1520 C.E. When Hernán Cortez and his band of a few hundred Spaniards landed on the Gulf Coast near Veracruz, the Aztecs failed to mount a decisive show of force against him, partly out of fear that he might be the returning god. (Cortez's cannon and horses seemed to be divine instruments.)

The core Aztec ritual was *human sacrifice*. Whereas the Mayas had been content to sacrifice dozens, the Aztecs required larger and larger numbers until thousands were being killed annually. The thinking went: If they sacrificed a hundred this year and the

79

SPECIFIC RELIGIOUS TRADITIONS OF EARLY CIVILIZATIONS					
DIMENSION	EGYPT	MESO-POTAMIA	PERSIA	MAYA AND AZTEC	INCA
Polytheist pantheon	yes	yes	yes	yes	yes
Deity form	therio-morphic	anthropo-morphic	anthropo-morphic	therio-morphic	anthropo-morphic
Mythic culture hero		Gilgamesh		Quetzalcoatl	Viracocha
Divine kingship	yes				yes
Person who changed religion	Akhenaton (pharaoh)	Hammurabi (king)	Zoroaster (prophet)		
What he brought	Monotheism (Aton)	written law code	Monotheism (Ahura Madzah)		
Pyramids	yes	no	no	yes	no
Mummies	yes	no	no	no	yes
Divination	no	yes	yes	yes	no
Environment	stable	unstable		unstable	stable
Creation myths	minor	major	minor	major	minor
Apocalyptic	no	no	yes	yes	no
Priests	yes	yes	yes	yes	yes
Sacrifice	minor grain	minor grain	minor grain animals	major human	minor human
Afterlife	major	minor	major	minor	major

rains came, better sacrifice at least a hundred next year. If the rains did not come on time, better sacrifice some more next year. The need for victims inspired more military campaigns (the goal was not just land or booty but people who could be captured and then killed as needed during sacrificial rituals). But military endeavors also required the favor of the gods, so victims had to be sacrificed before a battle to secure its success so that other victims could be captured (thus creating an endless cycle of sacrifice, war, and sacrifice). Part of Cortez's success was that he easily found allies among the other tribes who would take any opportunity to destroy or weaken the hated Aztecs.

The Incas were active about the same time as the Aztecs, but in the Andes region of South America.

Their empire stretched from southern Colombia to northern Chile, centering in what is now the nation of Peru. The key to understanding that empire is *stability:* major natural disasters and armed conflicts were occasional rather than frequent. Indeed, most of the Incan extensions had been accomplished by negotiations. Their empire was blessed with relative prosperity based upon potato agriculture and a vast public works system (especially roads). About a dozen years after Cortez had conquered the Aztecs in Mexico, another small band of conquistadores vanquished the Incas, with some of the soldiers boasting that the Indians had no weapons that could defeat an armored Spaniard on horseback.

Inca myths explained the origins of specific things. Potatoes were the result of a primordial murder (similar to the Hainuwele story from Melanesia). Many of the technological innovations of Inca culture were attributed to a mythic culture hero Viracocha, the first Inca emperor and direct descendent of the sun god. The pantheon of active deities was great, incorporating those of many neighboring peoples. There was a powerful caste of priests who performed various rituals at golden temples. Human sacrifice (usually of adolescents) existed, but it was performed on solitary victims.

There was a strict ethical code and the promise of an afterlife. The dead were **mummified**. The living were told to prepare for the afterlife by purifying themselves and confessing their sins to the priests. (Only the Inca emperor could avoid this ritual and confess directly to the gods without a priest

flashcards & matching game
http://www.quia.com/jg/50881.html

jumbled words
http://www.quia.com/jw/8323.html

millionaire game
http://www.quia.com/rr/41250.html

magic paragraph
http://www.quia.com/cz/13405.html

Now take an online practice quiz at
http://www.quia.com/session.html

For session enter
relquiz5
download multiple-choice, true-false, and fill-in drills from
http://www.ureach.com/tlbrink
click on the public filing cabinet and folder rel5 and download *m5.exe, h5.htm, t5.exe,* and *f5.exe and crossword puzzle CW5.html*

as intermediary.) The priests reacted to confessions by issuing penances, usually in the form of abstaining from sex, alcohol, chile, or coca leaves (the source of cocaine).

Note: We are indebted in this section to Professor Eugene Webb of the University of Washington, who furnished us his materials on Mesopotamian religion. Any errors, however, are entirely our responsibility.

CHAPTER 4

HINDUISM

HISTORY

Our sketch of the historical evolution of **Hinduism** unfolds in six chronological phases: the pre-Vedic phase; the Vedic phase; the phase of native challenges to Vedic orthodoxy; the phase in which Hindus responded to such challenges (by reforming, renovating, and elaborating the Vedic tradition); the phase in which outside, modern Western ideas challenged reformed Hinduism, and the present phase—what we might call recent or contemporary Hinduism. The tendency of Hindu culture not to discard previous ideas and practices so much as to place new ones alongside them means that one can seldom be precise about what was waxing when and what was waning. But one can suggest the "additive" logic of the Hindu religious story by noting the new ideas and movements that slowly enlarged Hinduism into the rich and varied entity one finds today.

PRE-VEDIC INDIA

Before the first Aryan invasions from the northwest around 2000 B.C.E., an impressive Indian culture already existed. Its beginnings stretch back to the second

> *Shiva, "the destroyer" deity.*

	HINDUISM: 25 KEY DATES	
Date	**Event**	
2750 B.C.E.	growth of civilization in Indus valley	
1500 B.C.E.	arrival of Aryans in Indus valley; composition of the Vedas	
800–400 B.C.E.	Upanishads	
600–500 B.C.E.	Mahavira and Buddha challenge orthodox Vedic doctrine	
500 B.C.E.	Aryans as far south as Sri Lanka	
500–200 B.C.E.	epic poetry: Ramayana, Mahabharata (Bhagavad Gita)	
322 B.C.E.	Chandragupta founds Mauryan Empire	
100 B.C.E.–100 C.E.	rise of Bhakti literature	
480 C.E.	fall of Gupta Empire	
680 C.E.	flourishing of Tamil Bhakti movement	
788–820 C.E.	Shankara, leading philosopher	
800–900 C.E.	rise of Hindu Orthodoxy	
1017–1137 C.E.	Ramanuja, leading philosopher	
1175 C.E.	first Muslim empire in India	
1469–539 C.E.	Nanak, founder of Sikhism	
1485–1533 C.E.	Chaitanya, leader of Krishna Bhakti	
1498 C.E.	Vasco de Gama visits India	
1526 C.E.	beginning of Mogul Dynasty	
1653 C.E.	completion of Taj Mahal	
1690 C.E.	British found Calcutta	
1818 C.E.	beginning of British Rule	
1869–1948 C.E.	Mahatma Gandhi	
1885 C.E.	founding of Indian National Congress	
1947 C.E.	independence from Britain; partition with Pakistan	
1971 C.E.	war with Pakistan, followed by founding of Bangladesh	

83

interglacial period (400,000–200,000 B.C.E.), and its earliest religion, if we conjecture on the basis of ancient peoples living in India today, was shamanist, focusing on the worship of nature—especially on the life force. The details of the religion of the pre-Vedic civilization are largely based upon inferences based upon archeology rather than surviving scripture or contemporary practitioners. In 1924, excavations at two sites along the Indus River, called Harrapa and Mohenjo-Daro, furnished the first extensive evidence of an advanced ancient Indian culture. This culture, called the Harrapan, stretched over about 500,000 square miles and was distributed in small towns between the two main cities of Harrapa and Mohenjo-Daro. Other excavations in what is now Pakistan have disclosed cultures predating the Harrapan, but this Indus Valley culture is the largest source of information about pre-Aryan Indian ways. Carbon dating suggests that the Harrapan culture flourished about 2150–1750 B.C.E., and some evidence suggests that the culture was remarkably stable throughout that period.

Harrapa and Mohenjo-Daro seem to have had populations of 30,000 to 40,000. Both were about 1 mile square. That few weapons have been found suggests that their people were not very warlike. Outside each city was a citadel, which was probably used for worship rather than for military defense. There were large granaries in the cities, two-room apartments nearby for the granary workers, and high city walls. Most building was done with kiln-dried bricks, which were standardized by size. Through the city ran an excellent sewage disposal system, with terracotta pipes and manholes through which workmen could enter to clean the pipes. The houses were multistoried dwellings with thick walls and flat roofs.

The entire city plan suggests orderliness: streets were wide and rectilinear, houses had chutes for sliding trash down into collection bins, and apartments had bathrooms and toilets. Larger buildings included a bathhouse 108 by 180 feet, with a tank 20 feet wide by 39 feet long by 8 feet deep. If this tank was used like similar ones outside Hindu temples today, probably its purpose was ritual bathing.

By about 1500 B.C.E., the Harrapan culture was destroyed, after perhaps a millennium and a half of existence. The destructive **Aryan** conquerors were a nomadic people who loved fighting, horseracing, drinking,

and other aspects of the warrior life. They came from the north, where they had wandered around the Eurasian steppe with their herds of cattle. (The later selection of the cow to be a specially revered animal in Hinduism is due to its connection with this ancient Aryan heritage.) Their name means "from the earth" or "noble." All European languages (except Finnish, Hungarian, and Basque) are related to the Aryans' language. The Aryans (or related tribes) pushed through Greece, Italy, Iran, and India during the second millennium B.C.

The Aryans moved by horse, ate meat, and hunted with bow and arrow. They knew about iron and fashioned good weapons. Like many other warrior, nomadic peoples (for example, the early Celts), they loved storytelling and singing. Indeed, their culture and religion were highly verbal. Their society was male dominated, with a primarily patriarchal family structure, priesthood, and pantheon of deities. Their main deity Indra was exuberant and warlike—a boaster, a thunderbolt thrower, a big drinker, a slayer of dragons. He ruled by seizure rather than inheritance. He had created this world by aggressively taking the waters of heaven, releasing them, and fashioning the earth. Perhaps Indra was originally a chieftain or culture hero and only later a leading god, but from their earliest time in India, the Aryans undoubtedly looked to him as the source and model of their prowess in war.

These two peoples, the conquerors and the conquered, thus contributed to the beginnings of Hindu culture. If the Harrapan culture was representative, the people who came before the Aryans in the Indus Valley were stable city dwellers who perhaps developed (or took from earlier peoples) important fertility rites. The Aryans were a rough, fighting people who had a much simpler technology than the Harrapans but whose poetry was imaginative. These Aryans became the dominant force militarily and politically, imposing their will and their deities on the subjugated Harrapans (also known as Dravidians or Sramanic people). Inasmuch as the Aryans produced the official scripture of Hinduism, the Vedas, Aryan culture always had more official status.

However, Indian culture never lost its native Dravidian features, especially in the less Aryanized south. At most these tendencies were dormant for a while. After the demise of Vedic culture, Dravidian interests

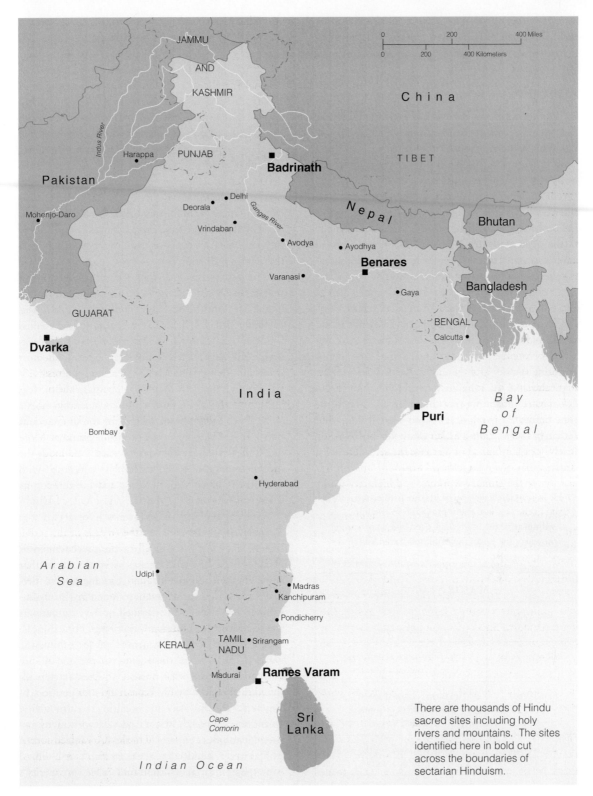

There are thousands of Hindu
sacred sites including holy
rivers and mountains. The sites
identified here in bold cut
across the boundaries of
sectarian Hinduism.

Sacred sites of Hinduism

in fertility reemerged. The complex devotionalism of later Hinduism may be best explained in terms of many non-Aryan factors.

VEDIC INDIA

By *Vedism* we mean the culture resulting from the mixture of Aryans, Harrapans, and other peoples of the Indus and Ganges valleys. This culture expressed itself in the earliest Indian writings, which are a collection of religious songs, hymns, spells, rituals, and speculations called the **Vedas**. It is convenient to consider these writings as representing the first stages of Hinduism, for although later India abandoned many of the Vedic gods and practices, the Vedas retained scriptural status throughout the later centuries, weaving themselves deeply into India's fabric.

The word *veda* means "wisdom" (cognates are the English *wit* and the German *wissen*). The Vedic pieces were originally oral. Some of the hymns found in the oldest Vedic literature may have been composed before the Aryans entered India. The hymns honoring the sky and the dawn, for instance, are remarkably like the religious literature of other Indo-Europeans, indicating that they may go back to the time before the Aryans split into their Iranian and Indian branches. Consider, for example, the following lovely verses in praise of Varuna, the deity of moral order:

He has put intelligence in hearts, fire in the waters, the
sun in the sky, and the soma plant on the hills. . . .
I will speak of the mysterious deed [*maya*] of Varuna
renowned, the Lord immortal, who, standing in the

MAJOR VEDAS	
Rig-Veda	hymns manifesting mythology and prayers
Atharva-Veda	materials concerning magic of special interest to Brahmins
Sama-Veda	mantras chanted at various sacrifices of soma (ritual liquor)
Yajur-Veda	priestly textbook on the Vedic ritual as a whole

firmament, has measured out the earth, as it were, with a yardstick. (*Rig-Veda* 5:85:2,5)

Although Hindu doctrine has evolved over the past three millennia, the Vedas are still regarded as *shruti* (divinely revealed scripture). *Shruti* does not connote that divinities outside the human realm broke through the veil separating heaven and earth in order to impart light from above; as we shall see, Hinduism does not have such a remote view of the divine. Rather, *shruti* implies that the eminent holy person has heard certain things in peak experiences (often induced by the ritual drink *soma*). Therefore, Vedic literature, representing what the rishis (holy men) had heard, was considered the best and holiest presentation of knowledge.

The Vedas consist of four separate collections of materials. Together, these four collections are known as the *Samhitas*. (Therefore, *Samhitas* can be a synonym for Vedas.) The individual collections are called the *Rig-Veda, Sama-Veda, Yajur-Veda,* and *Atharva-Veda*. The *Rig-Veda* is the oldest, largest, and most important. It contains more than a thousand individual units: hymns to the gods, poems, riddles, legends, and the like. They show considerable poetic skill, which argue against their being the spontaneous poetry of freewheeling warriors or rude peasants. More likely, they represent the work of priestly leaders—the careful creation of an educated class concerned with regulating contact with the gods and maintaining its own social status.

Most of the *Rig-Veda*'s hymns have a two-step formula. First, they praise the god being addressed; second, they ask the god for favors or benefits. For instance, the *Rig-Veda* praises Agni for deeds that show the splendor of his status as the god of fire. (These deeds appear to be not so much mythical allusions to feats the god performed in the beginning as similes drawn from human experience. For example, Agni's flame is like the warrior's battle rush: as the warrior blazes upon the enemy, so the god of fire blazes through the brush or woods.) Then, having admired the god, the hymn singer makes his petition. In *Rig-Veda* 6:6 he asks for wealth: "wealth giving splendor . . . wealth bright and vast with many heroes." The values expressed in the *Rig-Veda* are often utilitarian: a hundred years (longevity), a hundred sons (posterity), and a thousand cattle (prosperity).

Though this ritual exchange is the most usual focus, the *Rig-Veda* has other interests. For instance, it includes petitions for forgiveness of sins (such as having wronged a brother, cheated at games, or abused a stranger) indicating a developed ethical sense.

Some of the hymns of the *Rig-Veda* show a speculative wondering about the world, a theme developed in later sacred writings. A famous speculative text is 10:129, in which the poet muses about the creation of the world. At the beginning there was no air and no sky beyond. It was, in fact, a time before either death or immortal life had begun. Then only the One existed, drawn into being by heat that interacted with the primal waters and the void. However, from desire the One started to think and emit fertile power. Thus, impulse from above and energy from below began to make the beings of the world. But, the hymn asks in conclusion, who knows whether this speculation has intrinsic value? Even the gods were born after the world's beginning, so who can say what happened? Only one who surveys everything from the greatest high heaven knows, if indeed even that being knows.

THE VEDIC GODS. Hinduism is a great example of an evolving polytheism. A study of the Vedic gods suggests what the earliest Hindus thought about the deepest forces in their world. The gods are many and complex (tradition said there were 330 million), but of course a few stand out as the most important. Indeed, for many later sages, all the gods were manifestations of a single underlying divinity: "They call it Indra, Mithras, Varuna, Agni, or again the celestial bird Garutman; the one reality the sages call by various names . . ." (*Rig-Veda* 1, 164.46). They are all *devas* (good divinities), as distinguished from *asuras* (evil divinities). (In Iran the terminology is just the reverse, suggesting that the Iranian-Indian Aryans may have split along theological lines.)

The Vedas cast most deities in human (anthropomorphic) or animal (theriomorphic) form. Since the main feature of the *devas* was power, we may consider them functional forces: the warmth of the sun, the energy of the storm, and so on. To express these larger-than-life qualities, later Indian artists often gave the *devas* extra bodily parts. An extra pair of arms, for instance, would indicate prowess in battle; an extra eye would indicate ability to discern events at a distance.

Hermeneutical analysis of the Vedas suggests different generations of the Vedic gods. The oldest group consists of the gods of the sky and the earth that the Vedas share with other Indo-European religious texts. For instance, the Vedic Father Sky (Dyaus Pitar) is related to the Greek Zeus and the Roman Jupiter. Like them, he is the overarching power that fertilizes the receptive earth with rain and rays of sun. The Vedic earth is the Great Mother, the fertile female. These deities are not the most prominent Vedic gods, but they echo in the background as the oldest.

The second oldest group, whose age is confirmed by Iranian parallels, includes Indra, Mithra, Varuna, Agni, and Soma. As noted, Indra was the warrior god of the storm much beloved by the Aryan conquerors. Mithra was the god of the sun. Varuna was the god of cosmic and moral order, and Soma was the god of the exhilarating cultic drink. Known in Iran as *haoma, soma* gave visions so dazzling that it became integral to the sacramental rituals. Agni, finally, was the god of fire, whose importance increased as the sacrifice focused more and more on fire. It is worth noting that most of the deities in this second generation represent earthly and especially heavenly forces. Perhaps the storm, the sun, and the sky were all originally joined in Dyaus Pitar, but later they became separate objects of devotion.

The third generation of gods includes Brahma (the creator), Vishnu (the preserver), and Shiva (the destroyer). This Hindu "trinity" stands for the complete cycle of generation and regeneration. These deities arose after the Aryans arrived in India and so perhaps indicate Dravidian influences. We will consider them more fully below.

Finally, the fourth generation, which comes to the fore in the philosophical texts called the Upanishads, comprises abstract deities such as One God, That One, Who, and the Father of Creation (Eka Deva, Tad Ekam, Ka, and Prajapati). The Upanishadic writers had become dissatisfied with the concrete, world-affirming outlook at the core of the *Rig-Veda* and searched for more mystical approaches.

SACRIFICE. In the early Vedic period, the sacrifice was quite simple. The sacrifice intended to make human beings holy by giving them an operational way to please the gods. It required no elaborate rituals, no temples, no images—only a field of cut grass, some clarified butter for the fire, and soma (poured onto the ground for the gods and drunk by the participants). Later the sacrifice became more elaborate, involving chanting, reenacting the world's creation, and slaying a variety of animals. This elaboration went hand in hand with the increasing importance of the **Brahmin priests.**

One elaborate sacrifice conducted during that era involved a horse, a ceremony that lasted more than a year. In the first step of this complicated ritual, attendants bathed a young white horse, fed it wheat cakes for three days, consecrated it by fire, and then released it and let it wander for a year. Princes and soldiers followed the horse, conquering all territory through which it traveled. After one year, servants brought the horse back to the palace. During the next new moon, the king shaved his head and beard. After an all-night vigil at the sacred fire, the queens went to the horse at dawn, anointed it, and decorated it with pearls. A sacrifice of 609 selected animals, ranging from the elephant to the bee (and sometimes a human), followed.

The sacrifice reached its climax after attendants slaughtered the horse itself and placed a blanket over it. The most important queen then slipped under the blanket to have (simulated?) sexual intercourse with the horse, while the other queens and the priests shouted obscene encouragements. After this, participants ate the horse in a ritual meal. The entire ceremony fits the pattern of ancient celebrations of the new year, which often involved sacrifices and orgies designed to renew the world's fertility. Most of the symbolism centers on the virility of the king, in whose person the people hope to find strength like that of a lusty stallion.

CASTE. When one considers the distinctive organization of traditional Indian society that goes back to the Vedic roots, the word **caste** comes to mind. All human societies tend to stratify by developing social classes: differences in prestige, status, wealth, or privilege. In contemporary American culture, it is theoretically possible for an individual to rise or fall in the social order based upon educational or occupational attainments, or changes in income, though about three-quarters of Americans probably end up in the social class of their parents. In classical Indian society, these social classes were fixed at

birth, and one was not permitted to change one's caste assignment.

The Sanskrit word for caste was *varna*, the original meaning of which is uncertain but perhaps had connections with color (think of varnish, which emphasizes the exterior color of wood). *Varna* mainly has referred to the division of social ranks and tasks developed by the Aryans and established by them as regulative for the India that they came to dominate. Although this social structure became more pronounced and influential in India than in the other areas (Iran, northern Europe) where Aryan ancestral stock (the proto-Indo-Europeans) prevailed, one finds that ancient Persians, Celts, Greeks, and others shared its general delineation of the main social classes. This delineation was into the three groups of (1) priests, (2) nobles or warriors, and (3) commoners/farmers/merchants. The conquered Harrapan masses formed a fourth, lower caste of workers/servants/peasants. This way, the caste system was a racist attempt to keep Aryans and their descendents at the top of the social pyramid while keeping the conquered peoples out of positions of wealth and privilege.

The function of myth is to tell stories that vindicate the values by which we live. India thought of *varna* as part of the divinely ordered cosmos—part of the heavenly scheme of things. Thus, the *Rig-Veda* (10:90) speaks of a primal sacrifice of a proto-human being that gave society its four *varnas*. Later, the most influential law code, that attributed to Manu, repeated such Vedic justification, tying the ways Indians had come to think of their principal social classes to the divinely given order of things.

The second Indian word usually covered by the English caste is *jati*, which refers to the many particular, familial, clanlike groups that have made Indian society a complex quilt of different groups. Each has

THE FOUR CASTES		
Highest	Brahmin	priests
Second	Kshatriya	warriors, nobles
Third	Vaisya	merchants, artisans
Bottom	Sudra	unskilled workers, peasants

a different set of rules governing such issues as acceptable careers, diet, marriage. Most *jatis* require endogamy: that people marry within their own groups. *Jatis* can be considered as subdivisions of *varnas*. Thus, while there might be thousands of different brahmin *jatis* separating the priestly caste into various subgroups who could have only limited contact with one another, all such *jatis* held something in common and were more closely connected to one another than to such members of the third social echelon (the farmers/merchants) as barbers, potters, and leather workers.

In practice, the constraints of caste and *jati* have interacted to mean that most Indians have not grown up free to pursue what work and which spouses they might have preferred. The lowest of the lowest caste, the Dalits, are assigned to the most unappetizing tasks (e.g., working with animal hides, cleaning public toilets). Modern India has also tried to improve the lot of the Dalits (also called "untouchables") who lie at the very bottom of the caste system, but the social distinctions persist. Thus, even now, only certain groups of people carry garbage, clean homes, work in banks, and so on.

The doctrine of caste may have had an Aryan origin, but it soon came to be buttressed by doctrines of ethics (karma) and doctrines of afterlife (transmigration) that had not been part of the Aryan tradition. Ideas about reincarnation had been found in some tribal societies and involved the notion that the vital force survives after death and returns to animate a new body, usually in a nearly endless, cyclical way. Each body is merely a temporary housing for the soul. Transmigration of the soul might be human to human, or human to animal.

The notion of salvation in Hinduism and Jainism is that of release from a cycle of life, death, and transmigration. The solution is to meditate until we realize our spiritual identity and escape the hold of karma. This is a very different notion of salvation from that found in Christianity. However, can you find some passage in the Bible that (perhaps if removed from its context) might lend some support to the Hindu/Jain understanding of doctrine, ethics, or ritual?

Contribute to this discussion at
http://forums.delphiforums.com/rel101

Ganesha

Karma is an Indian term for the relations among past deeds, present character, and future fate. Karma is the law that governs advancement or regression in this physical world of deaths and rebirths. Karma is the reality that all acts have unavoidable consequences. Karma also explains one's status: A person's present life is shaped by that person's past lives. The only way to escape the round of rebirths, the pain of this *samsara* world, is to advance in one's next life, and this is done by meritorious deeds.

If we put all three together—caste, transmigration, and karma—we get a clever justification for the unjust assignment of social status at birth. The high-caste brahmin could say to the low-caste worker: "It is fair that I was born to the top of the social pyramid and you to the bottom. We are each merely reaping the rewards of our previous lives. If you want a better deal next time around, do the duties of your caste during this life. If you don't, you will be born in lowly animal form next time."

THE UPANISHADS. Even during the times of the *Rig-Veda,* people were unhappy with the priests' constant prating. A satire in 7:103, for instance, likens them to frogs croaking over the waters. Intellectuals desired something more satisfying than an understanding of sacrifice that tended to remain on the surface.

As the power of the Brahmin priests increased, the warrior-noble caste grew envious and frustrated. Some of them personally rejected the ritualistic sacrificial formula of spirituality and even their own place in the caste order. Leaving their assigned duties, they went off in the forest and attempted to attain spirituality by means of a more personal (as opposed to formal ritual) notion of sacrifice. The result of this was a series of books known as the *Aranyakas* ("forest books") that took the symbol of the fire's heat (used in the priestly sacrifice) and used it as a personal metaphor for self-discipline.

A related practice was that of **yoga.** It is an Indian term for discipline: to escape pain and gain enlightenment, one had to marshal one's energies and put oneself under discipline. Both Hinduism and Buddhism fostered several different yogas, most of which ideally were in the service of liberation from *samsara.* When we hear the term, we usually think of the physical yogas aimed at improving the body: posture, tone, relaxation, digestion, suppleness, and the like. Those were merely the means; the ends were liberation from the *samsara* world. A discipline focused on the breath might try to unify the matter-spirit composite. The most prestigious yoga was the *jnana* discipline, aimed at gaining an intuitive understanding of reality and so liberation. The yoga of trance and meditation sought to gain better mental concentration.

These practitioners of yoga and writers of the *Aranyakas* were not priests or prophets, but mystics who hoped that the concentration gained in meditation or yoga would lead to a state known as *samadhi.* This is an Indian term for the highest state of meditation or yoga. *Samadhi* usually is described as an imageless trance, an experience of pure human spirituality. Essentially, it means self-surrender, so that one's life more and more stands free of either worries about the past or troubling anticipations of the future. The yogi who realizes *samadhi* has such control over the body and spirit that the usual constraints of space and time seem broken.

Moksha is the Hindu term for release, liberation, salvation from the bondage of a *samsara* world of suffering in a cycle of death and rebirth. *Moksha* necessarily must be approached "negatively," by way of denying the limitations afflicting daily human experience. So it implies what is not limited, mortal, bound to the cycle of births and deaths, afflicted with desire, deluded, and the rest. Positively, Hindu thinkers have spoken of being, awareness, and bliss. *Moksha* is lasting, self-sufficient, truly real, in contrast to the fragility, passingness, and dubious reality of ordinary existence. It is full of the light of knowing and the joy of loving. As such, it can symbolize a good sufficient to justify the asceticism and toil necessary to escape *samsara.*

Insofar as yoga is trying to defeat *samsara* and lead the person (or the *atman*) to an unconditioned state (*moksha*), *samadhi* is a sort of down payment on *moksha,* much as mystical experience serves many theistic traditions as a down payment on heavenly communion with the deity.

The crowning achievement of this period was a series of books completed from 800 to 300 B.C.E. known as the **Upanishads,** a term that means "to sit apart" (in the forest, away from the workaday world). The Upanishads reveal the intellectuals' turn to interiority, which furthered this reinventing of the sacrifice (less a matter of slaughter, ritual, and words; and more a matter of soul cleansing and dedication to the divine powers).

The word *Upanishad* connotes the secret teaching that one receives at the feet of a guru (spiritual teacher). Out of hundreds of treatises (over the period from 800 to 300 B.C.E.), a few Upanishads came to the fore. They show that the intellectuals embraced a variety of styles and ideas and that their movement was poetic as much as philosophical. Whether poetic or philosophical, though, the movement's goal was quite religious: intuitive knowledge of ultimate truths, of the unity behind the many particulars of reality.

The Upanishads focus on two terms: **Brahman** and **Atman.** *Brahman is* the foundation of everything, a **pantheistic** conception that God is everything and everything is God. (Do not confuse this term with the Brahmin caste of priests or with the previously discussed Brahma creator deity of Hinduism.) *Atman* means the vital principle or deepest identity of the individual person—the soul or self. Probing this reality by thought and meditation, the Upanishadic seers moved away from Vedic materiality to spirituality. The internal world, the world of Atman and thought, was a world of spirit.

Combining these new concepts of Brahman and Atman, some of the Upanishadic seers found a coincidence—the basic reality within and without, of self and the world, was the same. Atman is Brahman. So in the *Chandogya Upanishad* 6:1:3, the father Uddalaka teaches his son Shvetaketu that Shvetaketu himself is, most fundamentally, Brahmanic ultimate reality: *Tat tvam asi* ("That thou art"). The soul and the stuff of the world are but two sides of the same single "be-ing" or "is-ness" that constitutes all existing things.

In the *Brihad-aranyaka Upanishad,* one of the most important, an interesting discussion occurs between the thoughtful woman Gargi and the sage Yajnavalkya about the ultimate "warp" of reality (the relevant definition of *warp* is "the basic foundation or material of a structure or entity"). Gargi has pressed the sage to tell her about the weave of reality: "That, O Yajnavalkya, which is above the sky, that which is beneath the earth, that which is between these two, sky and earth, that which people call the past and the present and the future—across what is that woven, warp and woof?" The sage answers that she is asking about space. Sensing that she still has not gained the final goal of her inquiry, Gargi presses one further question: "Across what then, pray, is space woven, warp and woof?" This is the capital question, eliciting from the sage the capital answer: the Imperishable.

To describe the Imperishable, Yajnavalkya launches into a long list of negatives: "It is not coarse, not fine, not short, not long, not glowing, not adhesive, without shadow and without darkness, without air and without space, without stickiness, odorless, tasteless, without eye, without ear, without voice, without wind, without energy, without breath, without mouth . . . without measure, without inside and without outside." Only by denying the limitations implied in each of these attributes can the sage suggest the unique, transcendent character of ultimate reality.

The Imperishable does not consume anything and no one consumes it. It is the commander of the sun and the moon, the earth and the sky, and all other things. Without the knowledge of the imperishable, other religious attainments are of little worth: "Verily, O Gargi, if one performs sacrifices and worship and undergoes austerity in this world for many thousands of years, but without knowing that Imperishable, limited indeed is that [work] of his." For the Imperishable is the unseen Seer, the unthought Thinker, the only One that understands. "Across this Imperishable, O Gargi, is space woven, warp and woof."

The Imperishable, then, is the Upanishadic sage's ultimate wisdom. When pressed for the material cause of things, the "that from which" everything is made, Yajnavalkya can only say "Something that is of itself, something that does not perish."

This is a characteristic answer, one that many sages, West as well as East, have fashioned. Pushing off from the perishable nature of the things of sensory experience, they have conceived of the ultimate foundation of reality as other than sensible things, other indeed than anything within the range of human experience. Reality does not perish, pass away, or suffer change. To uphold the world it must be different from the world. Either in the midst of worldly flux, or apart, it must surpass the "world," the mental construct of the material and spiritual whole that we limited humans fashion.

On the other hand, the ultimate material cause of things must be enough like us, discernible by us, to warrant our giving it negative names and seeking to know it. Were it absolutely other, completely apart from our human realm, we could not even discuss it negatively. It was by pondering this equally primordial fact that the Upanishadic seers came to focus on the human spirit or soul as the best analogue or presence of the Ultimate. This spirit or soul (Atman) seemed the best candidate for the presence of the Ultimate that makes human beings exist. While they live, human beings are imperishable: something keeps them from total change and decay. Thus, although they have a given identity, they draw upon the Imperishable, depend upon It, and express It. Between It and them must obtain a connection, maybe even an identity. Certainly the most real part of them is the presence of the Imperishable, without which they would actually perish. So perhaps the best way to regard them

The *Isa Upanishad,* one of the shortest, offers a good specimen of the Upanishadic style. Robert Hume, a respected translator of the Upanishads into English, divides the Isa into eighteen stanzas.

The strong emotions the stanzas of the *Isa* display remind us that the Upanishadic seers were religious philosophers—people pursuing a vision that would bring them *moksha.* The *Isa*'s passionate quest for a single principle to explain the diversity of the world's many phenomena also reinforces the impression that many of the Upanishadic seers had grown soul-sick from the complexity of the Hindu religion.

The first stanza of the *Isa* announces the monistic theme: Unless we see that the Lord (Isa) envelops all that exists, we misunderstand reality. There must be a stable principle giving rest to all the moving things. Religious people renounce all these moving things and so come to enjoy human life. Such renunciation takes them away from coveting the wealth or possessions of other people, which so frequently is a cause of sadness.

Stanza 2 develops this basis of freedom. It is possible to live in the world, performing the duties of one's station, without being attached to one's deeds. In that case, the deed does not adhere to the personality or weight it down. *Detachment* therefore is the antidote to karma. If one is free from concern about the effects of one's actions, one can work for *moksha.* But, as stanza 3 emphasizes, those who do not detach themselves receive a stern punishment after death. If they have slain the Self (the presence of Brahman within) by desirous, badly motivated deeds, they will go to dark worlds ruled by devils.

Stanza 4 shifts back to a positive viewpoint. The One that does not move, that stands free of the changing things of the world, is swifter than the human mind and senses. Wisdom is placing one's action in this One, reposing one's self in what is so swift it is stable.

Human life therefore faces a paradox, as stanza 5 shows. The principle underlying everything that exists seems both to move and not to move. Insofar as it is the inmost reality of whatever exists, it moves in all things' movement. Insofar as it gives all these things their basis, it is free of their movement, self-possessed rather than dependent on another. So, too, the One can be both far and near, both outside and within any being of the samsaric world.

Stanza 6 suggests a focus to bring this blur into clarity. By looking on all beings as though they reposed in the Self (the world's soul), and looking at the Self as though it were present in all things, the wise person stays close to the Brahman that is the world's ultimate significance.

According to stanza 7, the profit in this focus is the freedom from delusion and sorrow it brings. The person who perceives the unity of reality, seeing the single Self everywhere, achieves a knowledge and joy that the ignorant, mired in the world's multiplicity, never know.

This leads, in stanza 8, to an imaginative flourish. Picturing the world ruler, the human being who has realized full human potential, the Isa unfurls a flag of glowing attributes: wise, intelligent, comprehensive, self-sufficient. By dealing with what is bright, bodiless, pure, and unaffected by evil (by dealing with the Self), this person has reached the summit, come to stand close to eternity.

Stanzas 9 and 10 are quite mystical, probing the nature of religious enlightenment. If those who worship ignorance (who neglect the Self) go into a blind darkness, those who delight in true knowledge go into a greater darkness or mystery, a state beyond the dichotomy between knowledge and nonknowledge.

Stanza 11 adds another dimension: The wise person, holding knowledge and nonknowledge together, passes over death and gains immortality.

The "beyond" or transcendent character of true enlightenment appears even more clearly in stanzas twelve and thirteen. Both nonbecoming (changelessness) and becoming (change) can be illusory. The ultimate relevance of Brahman transcends such oppositions. The saving intuition that brings *moksha* takes the perceiver to another realm, where the dichotomies and antagonisms thrown up by ordinary human intelligence do not pertain. According to stanza 14, this saving intuition also conjoins becoming and destruction. If one understands their relation, he can ride destruction across the chasm of death, ride becoming to the far shore of immortality.

The *Isa* concludes prayerfully, in stanza 15 praising the sun as a cover of reality and asking divinity to uncover its face, that we might fulfill our primary human obligation, which is to grasp reality. (Note

that this prayer is answered in the Bhagavad Gita.) Stanza 16 calls divinity the nourisher, the sole seer, the controller of fortunes, the one who is yonder yet the inmost reality of the personality. Stanza 17 prays that while our body ends in ashes, our breath may take us to the immortal wind. This will happen if we remember our purpose, grasp the import of our deeds. The Isa's last prayers, in stanza 18, are addressed to Agni: Lead us to prosperity by a godly path, you who know all the ways. Keep us from the crooked ways of sin, for we want to offer you ample adoration.

ĪŚĀ UPANISHAD

Recognition of the unity underlying
the diversity of the world

1. By the Lord (*īśā*) enveloped must this all be—
   Whatever moving thing there is in the moving
      world.
   With this renounced, thou mayest enjoy.
   Covet not the wealth of anyone at all.

Non-attachment of deeds on the person
of a renouncer

2. Even while doing deeds here,
   One may desire to live a hundred years.
   Thus on thee—not otherwise than this is it—
   The deed (*karman*) adheres not on the man.

The forbidding future for slayers of the Self

3. Devilish (*asurya*) are those worlds called,
   With blind darkness (*tamas*) covered o'er!
   Unto them, on deceasing, go
   Whatever folk are slayers of the Self.

The all-surpassing, paradoxical world-being

4. Unmoving, the One (*ekam*) is swifter than the
      mind.
   The sense-powers (*deva*) reached not It, speeding
      on before.
   Past others running, This goes standing.
   In It Mātariśvan places action.

5. It moves. It moves not.
   It is far, and It is near.
   It is within all this,
   And It is outside of all this.

6. Now, he who on all beings
   Looks as just (*eva*) in the Self (*Ātman*),
   And on the Self as in all beings—
   He does not shrink away from Him.

7. In whom all beings
   Have become just (*eva*) the Self of the discerner—
   Then what delusion (*moha*), what sorrow (*śoka*)
      is there
   Of him who perceives the unity!

Characteristics of the world-ruler

8. He has environed. The bright, the bodiless, the
      scatheless,
   The sinewless, the pure (*śuddha*), unpierced by
      evil (*a-pāpa-viddha*)!
   Wise (*kavi*), intelligent (*manīsin*), encompassing
      (*paribhū*), self-existent (*svayambhū*),
   Appropriately he distributed objects (*artha*)
      through the eternal years.

Transcending, while involving,
the antithesis of knowing

9. Into blind darkness enter they
   That worship ignorance;

Into darkness greater than that, as it were, they
That delight in knowledge.

10. Other, indeed, they say, than knowledge!
Other, they say, than non-knowledge!
—Thus we have heard from the wise (*dhīra*)
—Who to us have explained It.

11. Knowledge and non-knowledge—
He who this pair conjointly (*saha*) knows,
With non-knowledge passing over death,
With knowledge wins the immortal.

The inadequacy of any antithesis of being

12. Into blind darkness enter they
Who worship non-being (*a-sambhūti*);
Into darkness greater than that, as it were, they
Who delight in becoming (*sambhūti*).

13. Other, indeed—they say—than origin
(*sambhava*)!
Other—they say—than non-origin
(*a-sambhava*)!
—Thus have we heard from the wise
Who to us have explained It.

Becoming and destruction a fundamental duality

14. Becoming (*sambhūti*) and destruction
(*vināśa*)—
He who this pair conjointly (*saha*) knows,

With destruction passing over death,
With becoming wins the immortal.

A dying person's prayer

15. With a golden vessel
The Real's face is covered o'er.
That do thou, O Pūshan, uncover
For one whose law is the Real to see.

16. O Nourisher (*pūsan*), the sole Seer (*ekarsi*), O
Controller (*yama*), O Sun (*sūrya*), offspring of
Prajāpati, spread forth thy rays! Gather thy
brilliance (*tejas*)! What is thy fairest form—
that of thee I see. He who is yonder, yonder
Person (*purusa*)—I myself am he!

17. [My] breath (*vāyu*) to the immortal wind
(*an ila*)! This body then ends in ashes! *Om!*
O Purpose (*kratu*), remember! The deed (*krta*)
remember!
O Purpose, remember! The deed remember!

General prayer of petition and adoration

18. O Agni, by a goodly path to prosperity (*rai*)
lead us,
Thou god who knowest all the ways!
Keep far from us crooked-going sin (*enas*)!
Most ample expression of adoration to thee
would we render!

(ourselves), or anything, is as a form of the Imperishable, one of its myriad extrusions or expressions. If so, one can say that, in the last analysis, only the Imperishable is real or actual or existent. Everything else at best receives a passing reality from the temporary presence to it, presence in it, of the Imperishable. For that reason, Yajnavalkya can rightly call it "that across which even space is woven, warp and woof."

For the Upanishadic thinkers, this realization was liberating because it avoided the multiplicity, externalism, and materialism that had often corroded the earlier stage of Hinduism. Though sacrifice and the gods continued to have a place in Upanishadic religion, they were quite subordinate to **monism** (the concept that every apparent different separate little thing was merely a manifestation of the same big thing: Brahman).

Upanishadic thinkers felt an urgent need for spiritual liberation (*moksha*), unlike the Vedists. Perhaps the writers of the Upanishads worked with experiences they found more dismal, depressing, and afflicting than the first Aryans had. Whereas those vigorous warriors had fought and drunk, living for the moment, these later meditative sages examined the human condition and found it sad. To express their views, they fashioned the doctrines of *samsara* and karma, which did not appear in the early Vedas.

Samsara (the doctrine of rebirths or reincarnation) implies that the given world, the world of "common sense" and ordinary experience, is only provisional. It is not ultimately relevant. To take it as ultimate is to delude oneself and thus to trap oneself in a cycle of rebirths. Only when one penetrates Brahman, the truly real, can one escape this cycle. Otherwise, one must constantly travel the scale of animal life (up or down, depending on one's advances or backslidings in wisdom).

THE PERIOD OF NATIVE CHALLENGE

From about 600 B.C.E. to 300 C.E., the Vedic religion, including its Upanishadic refinements, was seriously challenged by some Indians. The Upanishads themselves represent a critical reaction to the previous stage of sacrificial rituals, but they are considered to be a movement within Hinduism that charted its later course. The more serious challenges to Hinduism (e.g., materialistic, Jain, and Buddhist) first arose in northeastern India, where warrior tribes were more than ready to contest the priests' pretensions to cultural control. By this time (600 B.C.E.), the Aryans had settled in villages and India was a checkerboard of small kingdoms, each of which controlled a group of such villages.

The materialist approach denied the spiritual dimension of reality. These intellectuals, radically opposed to the Vedas, strongly attacked the doctrine that there is a reality other than the sensible or material. Ajita, a prominent materialist thinker, said that earth, air, fire, and water are the only elements—the sources of everything in the universe. According to Ajita, the differences among things just reflect different proportions of these elements. Human beings are no exception, and at death they simply dissolve back into these four elements. There is no afterlife, no reincarnation, no soul, and no *Brahman*. During the brief span of their lives, people should live "realistically," enduring pain and pursuing pleasure. Nothing beyond the testimony of the senses is to be taken as knowledge, and what the senses reveal is what is real.

A challenge from a different direction was posed by **Jainism.** This grew from the struggles for enlightenment of its main figure Nattaputta Vardhamana, called the Jina (conqueror) or *Mahavira* (great man). He is sometimes referred to by outsiders as the founder of Jainism, but Jains themselves have a different perspective. They see their movement as going back dozens of generations before Mahavira, mythically portraying him as the twenty-third in a long line of *Tirthankaras* (those who find a ford over the river of suffering). The story goes that Mahavira was born

to wealth (probably in the warrior caste). Elaborate myths have arisen about the pregnancy of his mother, Queen Trishala. She had over a dozen dreams foretelling the miraculous nature of her forthcoming son. The young prince found palace life unfulfilling, so he launched a life of **asceticism** (extreme self-privation). After gaining enlightenment by this self-denial, he successfully preached his method to others. He opposed both the ritualism and the intellectualism of the Vedic tradition. The only significant sacrifice, he said, is that which conquers the self.

Jains became critical of physical matter itself. They did not deny its existence but developed a **dualistic** view of reality: soul (good) and matter (bad). Their doctrine of the afterlife is that transmigration will continue as long as the soul is stained by karma. The Jains viewed karma as a semisolid entity that attached itself to the individual soul through acts involving material objects. Eventually, ascetic purification can lead to a soul entirely liberated from matter and not cursed to be reborn in a body. The purified soul, Siddha, then rests at the top of the universe, Siddh Shila, and stays there forever. Jain doctrine is sometimes labeled **atheist** insofar as it denies the existence of theistic deities who are paths to, or helpers in, our spiritual development. Mahavira challenged his followers to view reality as separate souls striving to cleanse themselves from the stain of karmic matter.

In order to purify themselves of karma, Jain followers became opponents of all forms of violence and pain inflicted on others. Consequently, they opposed the Vedic sacrifice of animals. In memory of the Jina, Jains rejected eating meat or harming anything thought to have a soul. Since total avoidance of harm was practically impossible, Jains tried to balance any injury that they inflicted or bad karma that they generated by acts of self-denial or benevolence. (Mahavira's death was the result of voluntary starvation.)

The Jain ethic of noninjury to all life forms is known as **ahimsa,** and has some parallels in the Upanishads. The liberated personality would feel no desire to hurt, abuse, manipulate, or otherwise disorder other finite beings and so would be a source of peace in nature as well as society. The preference for a vegetarian diet can be found among many Hindu holy men by this time, but the Jains carried *ahimsa* to a greater extreme: forbidding its followers to till the soil, lest a worm be severed by the spade. Jain monks walking through the forest carry a long-handled whisk broom (to sweep their path of insects) and are supposed to wear a cheesecloth mask to avoid inhaling insects.

The importance of *ahimsa* is apparent in this Jain teaching story. Once upon a time, there were six friends walking through the forest. They became very hungry and noticed a fruit tree. Each one responded differently, representing a different level of *ahimsa*. The first friend (representing the lowest level of *ahimsa*) wanted to chop down the entire tree in order to get some fruit. The second friend said it would be enough to chop off one big branch. The third friend said that they only needed to cut a small branch. The fourth one thought they should just get all the fruit they could carry, without chopping off any branches. The fifth friend only wanted to pick what they needed, leaving the rest. The sixth friend (representing the highest level of *ahimsa*) said that the tree should not be chopped, climbed, or disturbed in any way because there was enough fruit already on the ground.

The Jain ethic of asceticism also has its roots in Hindu self-discipline carried to an extreme. For the devout Jain, asceticism is more than the avoidance of self-indulgence, but a complete discipline of one's desires, sensual appetites, and spontaneous chatter. These *sadhus* (monks) have voluntarily left the worldly life and accepted five vows in order to purify their souls from karma. The *sadhus* remain in the forest or a monastery. They avoid preparing food for themselves and do not eat any food that has been cooked for them. They beg for food that has already been prepared for someone else. In contrast with Hindu filial obligations, the *sadhus* give up attachment for their relatives, even their parents. Their possessions are reduced to a few clothes, a food bowl, soft broom, and mouth cover, perhaps a water utensil to wash, but no shoes. They must not keep money, jewelry, or other possessions of great value (e.g., a house or car). *Sadhus* must not touch or sit with ladies or girls. They are not supposed to remain in one location for more than a few days (but this constraint is relaxed during the monsoon season). Further ethical commandments are to tell the truth, observe celibacy, and meditate.

The lay vows include commitments not to injure living beings, not to lie or steal, not to be unchaste, not to accumulate large sums of money, not to travel widely or possess more than what one needs, not to think evil of others, and not to pursue evil forms of livelihood. There were also positive vows to meditate and to support the community of ascetic monks.

Many rituals for Jain laity are similar to those performed by their Hindu neighbors. The fall festival of *Diwali* is one of the most important in India. For Hindus, *Diwali* celebrates the victory of the god Rama over an evil king. For Jains, *Diwali* marks the anniversary of the death of Mahavira in 527 B.C. Jains have temples in which instruments such as the gong-like Zalar are played with a wooden hammer before the statue of Mahavira. Jains also practice yoga and pray with rosary beads.

At the time of Mahavira's death, his followers were estimated to have numbered more than half a million. There were more women than men and many more laypeople than monks and nuns. Today there are a few million Jains in India. Prominent centers include Gujarat in the west and Karnatuku in the south. There is also a significant Jain population in Calcutta. In Jain temples one can see pictures of ascetics who represent an ideal of complete detachment, and the Jain doctrine of *ahimsa* (noninjury) has made a permanent impression on Indian culture.

Since we discuss Buddhism at length in a later chapter, we note here only that from a Hindu perspective, Buddhism arose, much like Jainism, as an anti-Vedic protest in the sixth century B.C.E. It was another stimulus to Hindu reform, another flowering of Vedic interest in improving people's ability to cope with an often painful world, another attack on the Vedic sacrifices and their rationale. If by "Hinduism" we mean the full-bodied tradition that evolved in response to the challenges of Jains and Buddhists, then those challenges were crucial to what Hindus later did.

BHAGAVATA. Especially in western India, movements arose that, unlike materialism, Jainism, and Buddhism, brought changes from less radical critics. A collective word for these movements is *Bhagavata* (devotionalism), which connotes an emotional attachment to personal gods such as Krishna and Shiva. Devotees (*bhaktas*) continue to claim that such devotion is a way of salvation or self-realization superior to sacrifice or meditation.

In the central Indian city of Mathura, devotion was focused on the god **Krishna**. Local people worshipped

Hindu Temple

him as a personal god and petitioned for gifts. A wealth of legends about Krishna's birth and adventures developed that ultimately made Krishna the most beloved of the Indian deities. In one, demons tried to kill the baby Krishna, but he was stronger than they. When the demoness Putana, who had taken the form of a nurse, tried to offer him a breast covered with poison, Krishna took it and sucked out all her milk and blood. When another demon approached him, Krishna kicked the demon so hard that the demon died. Another cluster of legends describes the child Krishna's pranks (he was always stealing his mother's butter, for which he had a great appetite) and the young man Krishna's affairs with young girls. In later Hindu theology, Krishna is seen as an **avatar,** or manifestation, of Vishnu, whom we discuss shortly.

The premier work of the Bhagavata tradition is a book known as the **Bhagavad Gita,** in which Krishna is the featured god. (The contrast between the warrior Krishna of the *Gita* and the pranksters of the Bhagavata tradition reminds us that we are dealing with a complex mythological character.) The *Gita* is set in the context of a great battle (the subject of the epic poem the *Mahabharata*), and it deals with the ethical problem of war. The conclusion that Krishna imparts to the reluctant warrior is that it is the caste duty of the warrior to fight. Drawing upon the insights of the Upanishads, Krishna argues that since individual souls do not die, but are recycled via transmigration, the killer does not really kill.

The *Gita* also concludes that there are many different but acceptable paths (*margas*) to salvation: meditation, caste duty, and *personal devotion* to a god. The *bhakti* (devotional love) appears to be the favored path given to Arjuna by his guru god (Krishna). In other words, if you cannot dedicate yourself to a life of meditation contemplating the nature of Brahman, just worship lovingly any of the 330,000,000 specific deities

MARGAS (PATHS)		
Dhyana	meditation	experience *samadhi*, unite with Brahman
Jnana	study	study scripture, understand the doctrine
Karma	work	do caste duties; detach action from its rewards
Bhakti	love	theistic devotion to a personal god or goddess

that Hinduism offers: it's all the same. The worshipper and the god will be in a reciprocal loving relationship, and through that individual god, the worshipper will reach God (Brahman). This theistic approach has made the *Gita* Hinduism's most influential text.

The devotional cult to Shiva was another reaction against Vedism, and one of its fascinating texts is the *Svetashvatara Upanishad*. For the devotees of Shiva, this text serves much as the Bhagavad Gita serves Krishnaites—as a gospel of the personal god's love. It is unique among the Upanishads for its theism (focus on a personal god), yet it shares with the monistic Upanishads an effort to think logically.

The author begins by asking momentous questions: What is Brahman? What causes us to be born? Then the author rejects impersonal wisdom, materialism, and pure devotion as inadequate answers. His own answer is to interpret Brahman (the ultimate reality) as a kind of god who may become manifest if one meditates upon him. In the *Svetashvatara Upanishad*, the preferred designation for Brahman is Rudra-Shiva. Rudra was probably the Dravidian form of Indra and Shiva, a god of fertility. In the post-Dravidian combination of these gods, the accent was on slaying and healing, destroying and creating—Shiva as the lord of the two rhythms of life.

According to this Upanishad, Shiva is in everything. He has five faces and three eyes, which show his control of all directions and all times (past, present, and future). The devotee of Shiva therefore deals with a divinity as ultimate and powerful as Krishna

but whose destructive capacities are more accentuated. Devotion to Krishna (Vishnu) or Shiva, then, satisfies the person who wants religious feeling and a personal god with whom to interact. Probably this sort of person predominated in Hindu history. From the legends about the gods and from the epics (especially the *Mahabharata* and the *Ramayana*), the *bhaktas* found models for religious love and for living as a good child, husband, wife, and so on.

SMRITI. During this period of challenge to Vedic authority, one other development merits attention because it was responsible for a great deal of Hindu religious literature. This movement was commentary on the Vedic literature that was intended to make it more comprehensible, practicable, and contemporary. The authority of this commentary movement is described by the word *smriti* (tradition). *Smriti* has less status than *shruti* and is considered less revelatory, more the product of human reasoning. Where the rishis intuited in mystical vision, the makers of tradition studied and reasoned. On the other hand, *smriti* had great influence in Hindu culture, because any elaboration of the social responsibilities (dharma) of the different castes involved such tradition.

Smriti provided such diverse literatures as the Dharma Shastras, or law codes (of which the Laws of Manu are the most famous); the writings of the six orthodox schools of philosophy; legendary works such as the *Mahabharata* and the *Ramayana*; the Puranas (more legendary materials, often from folk or aboriginal sources); commentaries appended to the Vedas (for example, the *Ayur-Veda*—the "Life Veda," devoted to systematic medicine—which tradition added to the *Athavara*); tantric writings on occult and erotic matters; writings (*Agamas*) peculiar to sects such as the Vaishnavites and the Shaivites; and writings on logical or ritualistic forms of thought.

The basic form of the *smriti* was the sutra, an aphorism or short sentence designed to expose the pith of a position. By the end of the third century C.E., the *smriti* tradition had developed some very important and common ways of understanding the Vedic heritage that greatly shaped Hindu social life.

PERSONAL LIFE. From the *smriti* elaboration of Vedic tradition came another influential doctrine, that of the four legitimate life goals. These were pleasure (*kama*), wealth (*artha*), duty (*dharma*), and liberation (*moksha*). *Kama* was the lowest goal, but it was quite legitimate. *Kama* meant sexual pleasure but also the pleasure of eating, poetry, sport, and so on. *Artha* was also a legitimate goal, and around it developed learned discussions of ethics, statecraft, manners, and so forth. Because the person of substance propped society, wealth had a social importance and was thus more significant than pleasure.

Dharma, or duty, was higher than pleasure or wealth. It meant principle, restraint, obligation, law—the responsible acceptance of one's social station and its implications. So in the Bhagavad Gita, Krishna appeals to Arjuna's dharma as a warrior: it is his duty to fight, and better one's own duty done poorly than another's done well. *Moksha* meant liberation, freedom, and escape. It was the highest goal of life, because it represented the term of one's existence: self-realization in freedom from karma (the influences of past actions) and ignorance. The concept of *moksha* meant that life is samsaric—precarious and illusory. It also meant that pleasure, wealth, and even duty all could be snares.

As a complement to its exposition of life goals, the *smriti* movement also analyzed the stages in the ideal unfolding of a life. For the upper classes (excluding the

IDEALIZED HINDU STAGES OF (MALE) LIFE		
First	student	young man studies scripture, meditation with a guru
Second	householder	marriage, caste defined career, children
Third	retired	retirement, disengagement from material concerns
Fourth	mendicant	renunciation of the material world, live as wandering beggar, life devoted to meditation

workers), the four stages, or *ashramas*, were student, householder, hermit, and wandering mendicant. In a hundred-year life, each would last about twenty-five years. In studenthood, the young male would apprentice himself to a guru to learn the Vedic tradition and develop his character. Depending on his caste, this would last eight to twelve years and dominate the first quarter of his life. Then he would marry, raise children, and carry out social responsibilities. Hindu society honored marriage, and the economic, political, and social responsibilities of the householder gave him considerable esteem. (Indeed, the competition posed by Jain asceticism and Buddhist calls for celibacy impelled some Hindu thinkers to reemphasize the dignity of this phase of the life cycle.)

When the householder saw his children's children, however, *smriti* urged him to retire from active life and start tending his soul. He could still give advice and be helpful in business affairs, but he should increasingly detach himself from the world. Finally, free of worldly concern, seeking only *moksha,* the ideal Hindu would end his life as a poor, wandering ascetic. Thereby, he would be an object lesson in the purpose of human life, a teacher of what mattered most.

In effect, this scheme meant an ideal development (not often realized but still influential) of learning one's tradition, gaining worldly experience, appropriating both tradition and experience by solitary reflection, and finally consummating one's time by uniting with ultimate reality. From conception to burial, numerous ceremonies have paced the Hindu through this cycle. The most important have been adornment with the sacred thread (signaling sufficient maturity to begin studying the Vedas), marriage, and funerary rites. Women have fallen outside this scheme. During most of Hindu history, their schooling, such as it was, took place at home, and they were not eligible for *moksha.*

THE PERIOD OF REFORM AND ELABORATION

From about 300 to 1200 C.E., the various movements that criticized or amplified the Vedic heritage resulted in a full reform and elaboration of Hinduism. We can see in the growth of the six orthodox philosophies (described here) and the rise of the major Hindu sects developments that effectively revamped Hinduism.

Two stories from the *Mahabharata* illustrate the ambivalent status to which the Brahmins had fallen by the time native Indian developments were challenging and expanding the religious outlook one finds in the Vedas.

The first story might be called "The Curse of a Brahmin." It shows the power attributed to Brahmins and also the colorful world of supernatural forces that has long delighted Hindus. Once the great King Parikshit went hunting. Wounding a deer, he chased it deep into an unfamiliar forest. There he came upon a hermitage with an old ascetic priest sitting near some cows. The king approached the Brahmin, told him who he was, and asked him whether he had seen the wounded deer. But the Brahmin gave the king no answer, for he had taken a vow of silence. The king repeated his question, and when he again received no reply, he got very angry. Gazing around, he spied a dead snake, lifted it with the end of his bow, and hung it around the priest's neck to shame him. The Brahmin still did not utter a sound, so the king gave up and returned home empty-handed.

The old Brahmin had a son, and when the son's friends heard of the incident, they teased the boy about his father's disgrace. The son asked his friends how his father had come to have a dead snake hung round his neck, and the friends told him the story of King Parikshit's visit. The son reacted angrily, cursing the king: "May Takshaka, the king of the serpents, kill this wretch who placed a dead snake upon the shoulders of my frail old father."

When he returned home, the son told his father how he had cursed the king. The old Brahmin was not pleased. Ascetics, he said, should not behave so impetuously. The son had forgotten that they lived under the protection of King Parikshit, who defended all the priests of his realm. The king had not known of the father's vow, so he should be forgiven much of his anger and bad behavior.

To try to repair the damage of his son's action, the Brahmin promised to send a messenger to warn the king. Both the father and the son knew, though, that the curse of a Brahmin could never be thwarted.

When the old Brahmin's messenger told the king of the curse, Parikshit was saddened by how he had abused the priest. He was also worried about his life, so he took counsel with his ministers about how to protect himself. They advised him to build a high platform, standing on tall posts, so that no one could approach him unobserved, and to remain there for seven days. The king followed this advice and moved his living quarters to the platform.

Toward the end of the seven-day period, the serpent king Takshaka sent several of his servants to King Parikshit disguised as ascetics. Not sensing any danger, King Parikshit allowed the ascetics to mount his platform and accepted their gifts of water, nuts, and fruit. When the ascetics had departed, King Parikshit invited his counselors to enjoy the gifts with him. But just as he was about to bite into a piece of fruit, an ugly black and copper-colored insect crawled out. The king looked at the setting sun, which was ending the seventh day, gathered his courage, and dared Takshaka to assume his real form and fulfill the Brahmin's curse. No sooner had he said this than the insect turned into a huge serpent and coiled itself around the king's neck. Bellowing a tremendous roar, Takshaka killed the king with a single mighty bite.

The story has several morals. First, it teaches the exalted status of priests. Dealing with holy things and marshaling great spiritual power by their ascetic practices, priests can perform marvels that ordinary humans can barely conceive. Therefore ordinary humans, including kings, ought to deal respectfully with priests.

Second, however, a Brahmin's very power imposes on him the responsibility to stay above petty emotions that might lead him to abuse this power. Thus the old father was deeply disturbed by his son's intemperate curse. A Brahmin's power ought to serve the people around him, improving their lives. The many Hindu stories in which priests do not act as ideally as they should suggest that the common people often found their priests wanting.

Third, the story piquantly illustrates the intimacy with nature that popular Hinduism has retained. Even though the Upanishads were pressing toward a purely spiritual conception of reality, in which a single Brahmin would relativize the reality of both human beings and snakes, the popular religion that came out of the period of native challenge stayed deeply immersed in the assumption that all things that exist live within physical nature. With this assumption, gods and human beings, serpents and kings, become more alike than unlike one another. This made for a very lively and imaginative "reality," in which curses such as the Brahmin's were plausible enough to teach both priests and commoners a religious lesson.

The second story from the *Mahabharata* might be called "The Well of Life." It offers a dramatic picture of the dangers of samsaric existence (life in this world).

Once there was a Brahmin who wandered into a dark forest filled with wild animals. Indeed, so ferocious were the lions, elephants, and other great beasts of this forest that even Yama, the god of death, would only enter it when absolutely necessary. The Brahmin only came to sense the wicked nature of the dark forest gradually, but then he grew more and more fearful. Panicking, he found himself running in circles, becoming more and more confused.

Finally the Brahmin looked about on every side and saw that the forest was caught in a huge net held by a giant woman with outstretched arms. There were five-headed serpents everywhere, so tall that their heads nearly reached the heavens. Then the Brahmin came to a clearing, with a deep well covered by vines and underbrush. Running frantically from a wild elephant that was pursuing him, he stumbled into the well, fell through the brush, and lodged halfway to the bottom, held upside down by a few vines.

At the bottom of the well was a huge snake. Above him waited the great elephant, which had six faces and twelve feet. To the side, in the vines that held him, were many bees that had built hives and filled them with honey. When the honey dripped toward him, the Brahmin reached out to catch it in his mouth. The more honey he ate, the more he could not satisfy his thirst for it. Meanwhile, black and white rats gnawed at the vines holding him. Though the elephant stood guard above, the serpent stood guard below, the bees buzzed on all sides, and the rats gnawed at his lifeline, the Brahmin continued to grope for more honey.

As many Hindu commentators have made clear, the story is an allegory for the human condition. The forest is the limited sphere of our life, dark and filled with dangers. The woman holding a net over the forest is the process of aging, which allows no human life to escape. The beasts of the forest are the diseases and other forces that can destroy us, while the serpent at the bottom of the well is time, which eventually receives all living things. The six-faced elephant with twelve feet is the year, with its twelve months, while the black and white rats are night and day, the devourers of our life spans. Finally, the honey is the pleasures of life, for which our thirst seems unslakable. The allegory, then, paints human life as tragic. Despite danger on all sides, we persist in pursuing transient pleasures. This is illusion with a vengeance. It is attachment making us oblivious to the great questions of what direction we should be taking and how we ought to be battling death. If we are ever to escape the painful circle of rebirths, which ensures that life after life we will suffer fear and pain, we must realize our self-imposed bondage. Plunging heedlessly into a dangerous life, we are soon fleeing in panic. We have gotten in over our heads, and before long we are upside down in an inescapable pit. Above and below, the many forms of time wait like jailers, ensuring that we stay in terrible danger. Meanwhile, day and night nibble our life span away.

Clearly, the story wants to impress upon its hearers the fearsome nature of unreflective living. If we simply pursue the pleasures of the senses and flee the pains, we will end up in the most trying of circumstances. Only by estimating correctly the lay of the land and refusing to get trapped in life's forests or fall into time's snares can we escape a tragic ending. Only by avoiding the whole battlefield of time can we enter into true freedom.

The Hindu keys to real freedom, therefore, are attention and detachment. We must watch where we are going, and we must stay free of worldly desires. The Brahmin of the story is pathetic because his calling or station especially should have educated him in these virtues. Were he noble in substance rather than just noble in name, he would not have wandered into the forest aimlessly. Similarly, he would not have abandoned himself to the sweet honey, forgetting his mortal peril. By meditation, sacrifice, austerities within and austerities without, he would have had hold of his time and been powerful in spirit. Then the beasts would have held no terrors, the well would have gaped to no avail. But, the story implies, few priests or few people of any station are true Brahmins, strong in spirit, so most people find aging a fearsome process.

A convenient distinction in the discussion that follows is that between those who reject the Vedas (for example, materialists, Jains, and Buddhists), called heterodox, and those who accepted the Vedas, called orthodox.

In other words, if you accept the Vedas (and caste) you are still part of the Hindu tradition, but rejecting those components means that you have gone outside of that tradition. Therefore, Jainism and Buddhism are considered different religions, but the Upanishads and the Bhagavad Gita are considered to be developments within Hinduism. The orthodox philosophies, or *darshanas,* were conceived as explanations of *shruti* (revelation). There are six such philosophies or schools: Mimamsa, Samkhya, Yoga, Nyaya, Vaisheshika, and Vedanta (the most celebrated darshana).

VEDANTA. Shankara, the greatest of the Vedanta thinkers, was a Brahmin who lived about 788–820 C.E. He taught a strict monist doctrine: reality is nondual and all variety and change should be attributed to illusion. Vedanta may be said to have systematized and deepened the teachings of the monistic Upanishads, taking their equation of Brahman and Atman to its logical consequence. Shankara urged celibacy and skipping the two middle stages of the life cycle so that one could pursue liberation wholeheartedly. He tried to systematize the Upanishads in terms of "unqualified nondualism" (*advaita*). In other words, he tried to explain the basic Upanishadic concepts of Brahman and Atman with consistency and rigor. To do this, Shankara first established that there are two kinds of knowledge, higher and lower. Lower knowledge is under the limitations of the intellect, while higher knowledge is free of such limitations.

The limitations of the intellect include its reasoning character, its dependence on the senses, and its dependence on the body to act. These limitations are all subjective, since they are limitations of the knower, or subject. The objective limitations to knowledge, due to aspects of the known thing, are space, time, change, and cause-effect relationships. Because of objective limitations, we tend not to see or grasp reality in itself.

Higher knowledge comes by a direct perception that is free of either subjective or objective limitations. In practice, it is the direct vision that the seers who produced the Vedas enjoyed. Quite likely, therefore, Shankara assumed that the Vedanta philosopher practices a yoga like that of the ancient sages. If so, he assumed that the Vedanta philosopher experiences a removal of the veil between the self and Brahman (with which the self is actually identified).

Shankara then applied this theory of higher and lower knowledge to hermeneutics, the study of textual interpretation. According to Shankara, all passages of the Upanishads that treat Brahman as one derive from higher knowledge; all references to Brahman as many or dual derive from lower knowledge. We can paraphrase this by saying that *Brahman in itself* is one and beyond all limitations, while *Brahman for us* (as we perceive it through sensation and reasoning) appears to be multiple—to be both in the world and beyond it, both material cause and prime mover.

With the subtlety of a great philosopher, Shankara wove the two edges of Brahman-in-itself and Brahman-for-us into a seamless whole. With the religious hunger of a mystic, he sought to correlate the within and the without. Shankara's core affirmation in his philosophical construction was that reality within is identical with reality without: Atman is Brahman. In other words, when one realizes through revelation, or higher knowledge, that there is no change, no space-time limitations, no cause-effect qualifications to the real, one then discovers that there is no self. Rather, there is only the Self, the Brahmanic reality that one directly perceives to be the ground of both internal and external being.

From the perspective of lower knowledge, there is, of course, a personal, separate, changing self. In absolute terms, though, there is one indivisible reality that is both subjectivity and objectivity, that is Atman-Brahman. Since we rarely perceive directly, we often live and move in *maya* (illusion). The world of maya is not unreal in the sense that there are no elephants in it to break your foot if you get in the way of a circus parade. The elephants in the world of maya are substantial, their dung is mighty, and their step will crush your foot. But this viewpoint has limited value. From a higher viewpoint, all that is going on is Brahman's illusion: Brahman imagining he is you and Brahman imagining that he is the elephant stepping on your foot.

VAISHNAVISM. In the period of reformation, then, keen speculative minds tried to rehabilitate the Vedic heritage by showing the reasonableness of *shruti*. It is doubtful that they directly converted more than a few intellectuals, but they did impressively demonstrate that orthodox Hinduism, through Vedic revelation, could enable one to make powerful interpretations of reality. The more popular reformations of Vedism were theistic movements that brought the energies of *Bhagavata* (devotionalism) back into the Vedic fold. Such movements centered on Vishnu and Shiva. Although both these movements were targeted at the common person's allegiance and presented quite different versions of divinity, they both advanced Vedic tradition and made a religion that combined some intellectual clout with much emotional enthusiasm. The main determinant of why one clung to one's particular god was a combination of social factors (the religion of one's family, *jati*, geographic area) and personal temperament.

The theistic religion centered on Vishnu (Vaishnavism) got its impetus from the patronage of the Gupta kings in the fourth century C.E. Perhaps the most winning aspect of Vaishnavite doctrine was its notion that the god is concerned about human beings, fights with them against demon enemies, and sends incarnations of himself (avatars) to assist humans in troubled times. In one traditional list there are ten avatars, the most important being Rama (the hero of the epic *Ramayana*), Krishna, Buddha, and Kalki (who is yet to come).

Vishnu himself is associated with water. According to tradition, the Ganges flows from under his feet while he rests on the coils of a great serpent. He is gracious to human beings, sending them many avatars of himself to help them when they are in need. Often he rides the great bird Garuda and is pictured as blue. Like an ancient monarch, he carries a conch shell, a battle discus, a club, and a lotus. Frequently he has four arms, to signify his great power to fight evil, and his consort is the much-beloved Lakshmi.

Vaishnavism promoted itself in several ways. Two of the most effective tied Vishnu to the *bhakti* cult. Between the sixth and sixteenth centuries, the *Puranas* (legendary accounts of the exploits of gods and heroes) pushed Vishnu to the fore. The *Bhagavata Purana*, perhaps the most influential, was especially successful in popularizing the avatar Krishna. In fact, the tenth book of the *Bhagavata Purana*, which celebrates Krishna's affairs with the girls who tended cows, mixes erotic entertainment with symbolism of the divine-human relationship. As the cow-girls were rapt before Krishna, so could the devotee's spirit swoon before god. When one adds the stories of Krishna's extramarital affairs with Radha, his favorite cow-girl, the religious eros becomes quite intense. The *Puranas* were thus the first vehicle to elevate Vishnu and his prime avatar to the status of *bhakti* (devotional) gods.

Vaishnavite *bhakti* was promoted in southern India during the seventh and eighth centuries. There Tamil-speaking troubadours spread devotion to Vishnu by composing religious songs. However, their wisdom was simply a deep love of Vishnu, a love that broke the bonds of caste and worldly station. The constant theme of the songs was Vishnu's own love and compassion for human beings, which moved him to send his avatars. They were so successful that they practically ousted Buddhism from India, and they were the main reason that Vishnu-Krishna became the most attractive and influential Hindu god.

Vaishnavism also had the good fortune of attracting the religious philosopher Ramanuja, who is now second only to Shankara in prestige. Ramanuja lived in the eleventh century, and his main accomplishment was elaborating the Upanishadic doctrine in a way that made divinity compatible with human love. This way goes by the name *vishishtadvaita*—"nondualism qualified by difference." It opposed the unqualified nondualism of Shankara, whom Ramanuja regarded as his philosophical opponent. For Ramanuja, the Upanishadic formula "This thou art" meant not absolute identity between atman and Brahman but a relationship: the psychological oneness that love produces. The highest way to liberation was therefore loving devotion to the highest lord who represented Brahman. Knowledge and pure action were good paths, but love was better. By substituting Vishnu or Krishna for Brahman or Ishvara, the Vaishnavites made Ramanuja a philosophical defender of their *bhakti*.

SHAIVISM. An alternative to Vaishnavism was Shaivism—devotion to Shiva. Shankara had been a Shaivite, but his intellectualism hardly satisfied the common person's desires for an emotional relationship with divinity. Shiva was the Lord of the Dance of Life and the Destroyer who terminated each era of cosmic time. From the earliest available evidence, Shaivism was a response to this wild god. It was frequently a source of emotional excesses, and its tone always mixed love with more fear and awe than Vaishnavism did.

For an extreme example, one of the earliest Shaivite sects, which the *Mahabharata* calls Pashupati, taught that to end human misery and transcend the material world, one had to engage in such rituals as smearing the body with cremation ashes; eating excrement, carrion, or human flesh; drinking from human skulls; simulating sexual intercourse; and frenzied dancing. Through such bizarre behavior, it wanted to symbolize the reversal of worldly, samsaric values that true religious devotion implied. Less defensibly, members of other sects, such as the eleventh-century Kalamukha (named for the black mark they wore on their foreheads), became notorious as drug addicts, drunkards, and even murderers. Even when Shaivites were thoroughly respectable, their religion was more fiery and zealous in its asceticism than that of the lovestruck but more refined Vaishnavites.

Shaivite priests came from all social classes, and Shaivite followers often regarded the lingam as Shiva's main emblem. The lingam symbolized the penis and sexual creativity in general as well as the dedication and intensification of this power through asceticism. There were Shaivite troubadours whose poetry and hymns were a principal factor in Shiva's rise to prominence, especially in southern India.

The Shaivite movement also received royal patronage in southern India from the fifth to the tenth centuries. During those centuries the Shaivites targeted both the Buddhists and the Jains. After winning that campaign, they turned on the Vaishnavites, singing of Shiva's superiority to Vishnu. In their theology they stressed not only the Lord of the Cosmic Dance and the god of fertility and destruction but also the hidden god. (Shiva also had such forms as the householder and the ascetic, representing several stages in the life cycle.) Even the worship of the phallus was enshrouded in mystery by placing it behind a veil. In addition, Shaivites often substituted representations of Nandi, Shiva's bull, or one of his *shaktis* (female consorts) for the god himself. Finally, to stress Shiva's ability to transcend all opposites, his followers often depicted him as androgynous. Since the Shaivite often became identified with the god, Shaivism was more like yoga than was Vaishnavism, in which the worshipper and deity remained two.

The follower of Shiva grew conscious that he or she was a sinner through mysterious rituals and Shiva's own symbols of fire and a skull. As a result, there was less equality, less of the lover-beloved relationship, between the devotee and Shiva than what one found in Vaishnavism. The Shaivite might deprecatingly refer to himself or herself as a dog. That the god would come to such a person was pure grace. Worship, then, was essentially gratitude that the tempestuous god chose to forgive rather than destroy.

SHAKTISM. Even in the Vedas, the male deity was accompanied by a female consort, who represented his energetic force (*shakti*). In developed Hindu speculation, the male principle was cerebral, passive, and detached. The female consorts were the bodily, active, involved, creative side of the divine dimorphism. The *shaktis* needed the control of their male counterparts if they were not to run amok. Many folktales depict the awesome power of a mother goddess or wife of a powerful god on the verge of annihilation.

Shaktism (and later **Tantrism**) focused on secret lore whose prime objective was to liberate the energies of imagination, sex, and the unconscious. Insofar as Shiva's *shaktis* represented the energy of female divinity, they exemplified tantrist powers. The general name of the ancient female divinity is Maha-Devi, whom we discuss later in her form of Kali.

It is hard to know exactly what *shakti* sects had in the way of doctrine or practice, because most of their rites were secret, but one of their main doctrines was that the union of coitus is the best analogy for the relationship between the cosmos and its energy flow. This symbolism seems to have spawned a theory of parallels or dualisms, in which male-female, right-left, and positive-negative pairings all had highly symbolic aspects. Like some of Shaivism, Tantrism downplayed class distinction and violated social conventions to symbolize the reversal of ordinary cultural values implied in religious conversion and realization (of union with divine reality).

One of the many Tantrist rituals for gaining *moksha* was called *chakrapuja* (circle worship). In it men and women (Tantrist groups tended to admit members without regard for gender or caste) used a series of elements (all having Sanskrit names beginning with

the letter *m*) that might facilitate union with Shakti: wine, meat, fish, parched rice, and copulation. In right-hand Tantrism, these elements were symbols. Left-hand Tantrism used the actual elements (not hedonistically but with ritual discipline, to participate in *maya*, reality's play). Other Tantrist practices involved meditation to arouse the *kundalini*—the snake of energy lying dormant at the base of the spine.

Overall, the reformation and elaboration of the Vedic tradition meant expanded roles for some Vedic gods and a shift of popular religion from sacrifice to devotional, theistic worship. The renovators tried to defend and extend their ancient heritage, allowing people to respond to any part of it that they found attractive. In this way they created an eclectic religion tolerant of diversity in religious doctrine and practice.

THE PERIOD OF FOREIGN CHALLENGE

From about 1200 C.E. on, Hinduism increasingly contended with foreign cultures, rulers, and religions. Islam and Christianity both made serious impacts on Indian life, and their presence is felt to this day. Islam, a factor in India from the eighth century on, first affected Indians of the Sind and Punjab regions in the northwestern part of ancient India, where Muslims

COMPARISON OF SECTS FROM INDIA				
DIMENSION	UPANISHADS	JAIN	BHAGAVAD GITA	TANTRICS
Date	800 B.C.E.–400 B.C.E.	500 B.C.E.	400 B.C.E.–200 C.E.	1000 C.E.?
Persons		Mahavira	Arjuna (fictional)	
Mysticism	yes	yes	tolerated	using sexual symbolism
Asceticism	yes	yes, extremely	tolerated	rejected
Caste	tolerated	rejected at first	advocated	ignored
Karma	accepted	accepted	accepted	ignored
Transmigration	accepted	accepted	accepted	ignored
Reality	monistic	dualistic	duty of caste	symbolic
Deity	Brahman	atheistic	theistic	paramour

traded and made military conquests. Invasions in the eleventh century put much of the Indus Valley region under Muslim control, and by 1206 Islam had conquered most of northern India. By 1335, Muslims controlled the south as well, and their final dynasty, the Mogul, did not end until 1858.

The policies of Muslim leaders toward Hinduism varied. Many were tolerant and allowed the Indians freedom to practice their traditional ways. Others, such as the Mogul zealot Aurangzeb (ruled 1658–1707), attempted to establish a thoroughly Muslim state and so tried to stop drinking, gambling, prostitution, the use of narcotics, and other practices that were prohibited by Islamic doctrine. Aurangzeb destroyed more than 200 Hindu temples in 1679 alone, and he discriminated against Hindus in the collection of taxes, custom duties, and various other ways. The permanent changes that Islam made in Hinduism and that Hinduism made in Indian Islam are hard to determine because the two traditions are intertwined. Islamic architecture and learning influenced Hinduism deeply. On the other hand, Muslim tendencies to regard many Hindu devotional practices idolatrous (for example, reverencing cows and praying to many deities) complicated relations between the religions. Indeed, in modern times tensions have led not only to the partition of India but to much bloodshed.

One definite result of Islam's presence in India was a new religion, **Sikhism,** a blend of Hindu and Muslim traditions. It began as a result of the revelations of the prophet Nanak, a Punjabi born in 1469. Nanak's visions prompted him to sing the praise of a divinity that blended elements of the Muslim Allah and the Hindu trinity of Brahma, Vishnu, and Shiva. This God he called the "True Name." The religious prescriptions for serving the True Name that he set for his followers were rather severe and anticeremonial, steering away from Hindu pilgrimages and devotions and favoring compassion and neighborly good deeds. The Sikhs developed into a small but hardy religious band, and on numerous occasions they proved to be excellent warriors. They number over 6 million in India today, and their golden temple remains in Amritsar in the northwest. Many of the other holy Sikh sites, however, are now in Pakistan because of the 1947 partition.

Christianity has been present in India since the first century C.E., according to stories about the apostle Thomas's adventures there. It is more certain that a bishop of Alexandria sent a delegation to India in 189 C.E. and that an Indian representative attended the Council of Nicaea (325). Only in the sixteenth century, however, did the Christian missionary presence become strong, in the wake of Portuguese (and later Dutch and English) traders. The British East India Company, founded in 1600, increasingly controlled the Indian economy and trade, and after the Sepoy Mutiny in 1857 the company, which had become a sort of government, gave way to direct colonial rule. When India became independent in 1947 after almost a century of British colonial rule, it had some experience with the political ideas and social institutions of the modern West. Christianity therefore usually has had a colonial character. Christianity has not been impressive statistically in terms of the numbers of converts, with less than 3 percent of the population. The impact of Christianity is felt in other ways: hundreds of charitable institutions, especially schools.

MODERN BHAKTI. For Ramananda, a follower of the philosopher Ramanuja, the important thing was to adore God, whom Ramananda called Rama, with fervent devotion. Rama considered all persons equal. In southern India, especially among the people who spoke Tamil, the Lord Vishnu increasingly appeared as a god of pure grace. Self-concern is useless and distracting, the Tamils told their northern Vaishnavite brethren. Not works but love is redeeming.

In west-central India, from the thirteenth to the seventeenth centuries, a poetic movement called the Maratha renaissance carried the message of *bhakti.* Tikaram (1607–1649), the greatest poet of this movement, stressed God's otherness and the sinfulness of human beings. His god was not the Brahman who was identical with one's innermost self, but a free agent and lover whose goodness in saving sinners was the more impressive because of their distance from him.

In these and other movements, modern Hinduism increasingly focused on *bhakti,* moving away from Vedic orthodoxy. The singers of *bhakti* cared little whether their doctrines squared with the Upanishads or the great commentators. The notions of *shruti* or *smriti,* in fact, meant little to them. They thought that the love they had found undercut traditional views of social classes, sex, and even religions. The god of love was no creator of castes, no despiser of women, no pawn of Hindus against Muslims. With little concern for intellectual or social implications, the singers and seers who dominated modern *bhakti* gave themselves over to ecstatic love.

Perhaps the greatest representative of *bhakti* was Chaitanya, a sixteenth-century Bengali whom his followers worship as an avatar of Krishna. Chaitanya, originally a Brahmin, converted to Vaishnavism and spent his days worshipping Lord Krishna in the great Bengali temple of Puri. Increasingly his devotions became emotional, involving singing, weeping, and dancing. Somewhat typically for modern *bhakti*, Chaitanya repudiated the Vedas and nondualistic Vedanta philosophy as opposing a gracious god. All were welcome in his sect, regardless of caste, and he even sanctioned worship of a black stone, thinking it might help some followers' devotion. He stressed the followers' assimilation with Radha, Krishna's lover, arguing that the soul's relation to God is always female to male.

Yet Chaitanya also stressed the necessity to toil at religious love and opposed those who argued that grace was attained without effort. His followers deified him, seeing his unbounded religious ecstasy as the ideal communion of divinity and humanity. He was the major figure in the devotional surge toward Lord Krishna that produced some remarkable Bengali love poetry during the sixteenth and seventh centuries. His movement has continued in the United States through the work of Swami Prabhupada, founder of the International Society for Krishna Consciousness. The monks in saffron robes on street corners, and his numerous publications, have made "*Hare Krishna*" part of our religious vocabulary.

Partly in opposition to the excesses of *bhakti* and partly because of the influence of Western culture, a group of Bengali intellectuals in the early nineteenth century began to "purify" Hinduism by bringing it up to the standards that they saw in Christianity. The first such effort was the founding of the group Brahmo Samaj by Rammohan Roy in 1828. Roy was a well-educated Brahmin whose contacts with Islam and Christianity led him to think that there should be only one God for all persons, who should inspire social concern and criticism of any abuses, Hindu or Christian. God should, for example, oppose such barbarism as suttee (*sati*), the relatively rare Hindu

practice in which a widow climbed on her husband's funeral pyre and burned with him. In 1811, Roy had witnessed the suttee of his sister-in-law, whom relatives kept on the pyre even though she was screaming and struggling to escape. He knew that in Calcutta alone there had been more than 1,500 such immolations between 1815 and 1818. Roy pressured the British to outlaw the practice, and in 1829 a declaration was issued that forbade it (though it did not completely stamp it out). Members of the Brahmo Samaj thought this sort of social concern was essential to pure religion.

Another movement to modernize Hinduism that originated in Bengal in the nineteenth century was the Ramakrishna Mission. Its founder, Ramakrishna, was an uneducated Brahmin who became a mystic devotee of the goddess Kali, whom he worshipped as a divine Mother. After visions of Kali and then of Rama, the epic hero, Ramakrishna progressed through the Tantrist, Vaishnavite, and Vedanta disciplines, having the ecstatic experiences associated with each tradition. He even lived as a Muslim and as a Christian, learning the mystic teachings of those traditions. From such eclectic experience he developed the joyous doctrine that we can find God everywhere: Divinity beats in each human heart. Ramakrishna's teachings achieved worldwide publicity through his disciple Vivekananda, who stressed the theme of worshipping God by serving human beings. The Ramakrishna Mission has sponsored hospitals, schools, and cultural centers, and it keeps an American presence through the Vedanta Society, which has chapters in many American cities.

TAGORE AND GANDHI. In the twentieth century, these currents of domestic and foreign stimuli to religious and social reform inevitably affected the controversies over Indian nationalism and independence. The controversies themselves largely turned on the assets and liabilities of the British and Indian cultures. Not all Indians opposed the British, largely because they did not have a single national tradition themselves. Rather, Indians tended to think of themselves as Bengalis or Gujaratis or Punjabis—natives of their own districts, with their own respective languages and traditions. What the Indian tradition meant, therefore, was far from clear. This fact emerges in the lives of two of the most intriguing modern-day personalities, Rabindranath Tagore and Mohandas Gandhi.

Gandhi memorial

J. T. Carmody

Rabindranath Tagore (1861–1941), modern India's most illustrious writer, won the Nobel Prize for Literature in 1913. His life's work was a search for artistic and educational forms that would instill Indians with a broad humanism. For this reason, he was leery of nationalism, fearing that it would crush individual creativity and blind Indians to values outside their own country. In the West, Tagore found a salutary energy, a concern for the material world, which seemed to him precisely the cure for India's deep cultural ills. However, he despised the Western industrial nations' stress on machinery, power politics, and democracy. In Tagore's renewed Hinduism, India would give and receive—give resources for individual creativity and receive Western energies for using that creativity to improve society.

Mohandas **Gandhi** (1869–1948) was a political genius who made some of Tagore's vision practical. He trained as a lawyer in England and found his calling as an advocate of the masses in South Africa, where he represented "colored" minorities. In India Gandhi drew in part on a Western idealism that he culled from such diverse sources as the New Testament, Tolstoy's writings on Christian socialism, Ruskin's writings on the dignity of work, and Thoreau's writings on civil disobedience. He joined this Western idealism with a shrewd political pragmatism of his own and Indian religious notions, including the Bhagavad Gita's doctrine of karma-yoga (work as a spiritual discipline) and the Jain-Hindu notion of *ahimsa* (noninjury). To oppose the might of Britain, he used the shaming power of nonviolent protests with the message: Indians, like all human beings, deserve the right to control their own destinies.

Gandhi provided an updated doctrine of *ahimsa*: We can strive to minimize our violence and destructiveness by not injuring any fellow creature needlessly. By a vegetarian diet, we can minimize our injury to fellow animals. By such traditions as the protection of the cow, India has long tried to focus nonviolence on a highly visible symbol of animal vitality. Such practices foster self-restraint and compassion, virtues especially needed in modern social affairs. The phenomenon of war, which for Gandhi probably reached its most tragic expression in the bloody conflicts between Indian Hindus and Muslims that followed upon independence from Britain, depends upon our lack of restraint and compassion. Surely a sagacious society, one that listened to the wisdom of its elders and traditions, would be able to muster the minimal spiritual power needed to keep itself from civil war. That India could not muster such minimal virtue sickened Gandhi's spirit. As a final irony, he ended his life as the victim of a Hindu assassin who blamed Gandhi for the civil strife.

CONTEMPORARY HINDUISM: POPULAR RELIGION

As we have already stressed, Hinduism is an umbrella for a great variety of different religious ideas and practices. Of necessity, we have concentrated on the ideas and practices that stand out when one attempts a historical overview. The outstanding ideas, however, tend to be the possession of intellectuals, at least in their reflective form. For the common people, it tends to be the many rituals of the Hindu religious year that mediate the sense of unity with the world that religion seeks to inculcate.

Most Hindus have chosen one or more specific deities (out of an estimated 300 million) to worship on a regular basis. Theologically, they all tie back to Brahman. Many are considered avatars of the Big Three: Brahma, Vishnu, and Shiva.

Most common rituals involve *puja*, a Hindu term for ceremonial prayer or worship, especially that which occurs in the home or local temple. The many small offerings, prayers of praise, prayers of petition, sacrifices, vows, and festival celebrations that punctuate the traditional Hindu year suggest that *puja* carried the Hindu spirit along from day to day. What the grand myths and ceremonies did on a great scale, the humble species of *puja* did in the home, for the small group, or for the individual concerned with personal problems. Women were prominent in *puja*, their many devotions to local goddesses, prayers for the health of their families, reverences to Lord Krishna, and the like being a prominent strand in the Hindu tapestry.

The rituals of folk Hinduism vary from geographic area to geographic area, depending on local gods and customs. Among Hindus of the Himalayas, a strong shamanistic influence remains. Many of these people's religious ceremonies involve a shaman's possession (much like the possession of central Indian mediums such as the weaver and carpenter). More often than not, a family calls upon a shaman because of some misfortune. When such things happen, people usually ask a shaman to hold a seance. The shaman may be from any caste, and he tends to make his living by acting as the medium of a particular god. Usually he opens a consultation by singing prayers in honor of his god, to the steady beat of a drum. As he enters into trance, often he becomes impervious to pain, as he demonstrates by touching red hot metal. When the god has taken full possession of the shaman, the god usually uses the shaman's voice to tell the client what is troubling him and what should be done to cure it. The god may also identify thieves or harmful articles that have brought the misfortune. If the clients do not like the god's diagnosis or advice, they simply go to a different shaman.

More often than not, the treatment the god suggests is performing a *puja* (short ceremony) in honor of the being that is causing the trouble. (In the case of a ghost, the *puja* amounts to an exorcism.) Other popular treatments are making pilgrimages or removing harmful objects causing disease. If the case is impossible to cure (for example, a person deranged beyond healing), the god may prescribe an impossible treatment (for example, the sacrifice of a cow; since the cow is sacred to Hindus, sacrificing a cow is unthinkable).

If the suggested cure is performing a *puja*, other religious specialists generally enter the scene. Their job is arranging and executing a ceremony in which the god can enter a human body, ideally that of the victim, dance in it, and make known any further demands. These *puja* specialists usually come from the lower castes, and their basic method of inducing the god's possession of the victim is playing percussion instruments. The ceremony tends to unfold in three parts: the dance, the *puja* or prayer proper, and the offering. Usually the ceremony takes place in the shrine of the god who is concerned. The shrine itself is very simple, generally consisting of one to four iron tridents about 8 inches high. The people place these in a niche in the wall, if the shrine is indoors, or at the base of a large stone, if it is outside, in effect marking off a sacred space. During the ceremonies the shrine is lighted by a small oil lamp, and often a container of rice and small coins hangs near it, as an offering to the god.

The dance, which begins the ceremony, is intended to attract the god (or any other spirit or ancestor who likes to dance in the bodies of humans). The gods are thought to like dancing because it gives them a chance to air their complaints and needs. Dancing most often occurs in the evening, but sometimes it is repeated the following day. As the drummers increase the intensity of the beat and the room fills with onlookers, smoke, and heat, the rhythms become more compelling, until someone, either the victim or an onlooker, starts to jerk, shout, and dance, first slowly but then more wildly. The possessed person is honored with incense and religious gestures and is fed boiled rice, because for the moment he or she is the god. After the god has danced his fill, he usually speaks through the possessed person, telling the cause of his anger (the source of the misfortune) and detailing what it will take to appease him. The victimized person and his or her family then make a short prayer to the god, expressing reverently their desire to comply with his requests, after which they make the offering the god has demanded.

The most frequent offering is a young male goat. The people place the goat before the shrine and throw rice on its back, while the ritual specialist chants mantras. When the goat shakes itself, the onlookers assume the god has accepted their offering. An attendant (usually from a low caste; higher-caste people tend to consider this act defiling) takes the goat outside and beheads it. The attendant then places a foot and the head of the animal before the shrine as an offering to the god, along with such delicacies as bread and sweet rice. The ritual specialist eventually gathers these up as part of his fee, and the family and guests share the rest of the goat.

A third sort of ritual common in contemporary Indian religion deals with rites of passage through the life cycle, helping a person cope with puberty, marriage, parenthood, or widowhood. Some of these rituals are based upon vows. The vows may last as short a time as a day or as long as the rest of one's life, but

whatever their time, they are serious business. As the stories of the *Puranas* emphasize, failure to fulfill a vow can lead to dire consequences.

Consequently, the person who makes a vow usually prepares assiduously to fulfill it by fasting, worshipping gods, taking frequent purificatory baths, abstaining from sexual relations, refraining from drinking water or chewing betel nuts, and not sleeping during daylight hours. From this asceticism, as well as the fulfillment of the vow itself, the vower gains spiritual power. For example, middle-aged women may go on a pilgrimage to a site sacred to Krishna in order to prevent the death of their husbands (trying therefore to protect themselves from the sad fate of the Hindu widow).

CRITIQUE. Modern India is not free of crime or warfare. Despite legal reforms, caste differences endure. To the ancient Aryans, the untouchables were "walking carrion." Gandhi—like other reformers before him—sought to make them part of the holy Hindu system. He called them *Harijans,* children of God. Still, it remains that Hindu caste has been a powerful ingredient in what to the outsider looks like the nearly unrelieved misery of millions of Indian poor. Simply by the accident of their birth, the majority of Indians have been assigned to the bottom levels of the social pyramid. Of course, to the traditional Hindu, birth was nothing accidental. One was born into a priestly caste, or into a caste of workers, in virtue of one's karma from previous lives. While this might provide some consolation—"my fate is what the gods have meted out to me, or what I have earned from previous existences"—it meant that Indian society as a whole could become static. If many people thought that their poverty, or their wealth, was fated, they were less likely to work hard. Certainly, talent and industry could make a difference in any individual life. On the whole, however, the tendency to think of themselves as fenced in by their caste or particular trade sapped the vitality of many Indians. In the worst cases, it also supported discrimination and outright cruelty.

Among all classes, but especially the poor, Indian women have suffered the worst burdens. The poverty, slavery, and general abuse into which untouchable women often have fallen, simply because they had been born into a certain social stratum, call into

Which theoretical approach would give you the most insight on the history, doctrine, rituals, ethics of Hinduism?

EXAMPLE: **Marx** reduced religion to a method of social control by which the segments of society which possessed power managed to oppress the disenfranchised and maintain power for themselves. In Hinduism power was possessed by the Aryan invaders of the second millennium B.C.E. The warrior-noble caste used military-political means to maintain power over the disenfranchised majority, and then the priestly Brahmin caste grew out of that and reinforced Aryan control over the social order by introducing karma and reincarnation. This served the Marxist function of "opiate," in that it distracted people from the plight of their powerlessness, focusing them on preparing for the next life by accepting the injustices of this life, and even justifying the inequities of this life by blaming it on an individual's conduct in previous lives. The result was a remarkably stable socio-economic order that resisted violent revolution for many centuries.

Contribute to this discussion at
http://forums.delphiforums.com/rel101

question all the religions' tendency to justify the status quo as a matter of divine ordinance.

WORLDVIEW

For Hinduism, as all other religious traditions, the relationship between history and worldview is dialectical—that is to say, each influences the other. What Hindus have assumed about the structures of reality (worldview) has developed in the course of their history. Conversely, their worldview has directed many of the choices that have determined the patterns of their existence over time (history).

Perhaps the most significant feature to emerge from Hindu history has been pluralism. Hindus have developed such a wealth of rituals, doctrines, devotions, artworks, social conventions, and other ways of dealing with ultimate reality, one another, and nature that they could not be uniform. More than such religious traditions as the Jewish, the Christian, the Muslim, and the Buddhist, whose basic doctrines have been relatively uncontested, Hindus have admitted variety and debate into the core of their religious culture. One sees this when examining the impact of such a Hindu notion as that of the four legitimate goals of life. To say that pleasure, wealth, duty, and liberation (salvation) are all legitimate ends for human beings to pursue, and then to allow numerous ways of interpreting each of these ends, has been to ensure that Hinduism would allow a vast range of options in prayer, family life, economic activity, and dealings with the natural environment.

NATURE

For the most part, Hinduism considers nature (the physical cosmos) to be real, knowable, and orderly. The cosmos is a continuum of lives; consequently, human life is seen as an ongoing interaction with the lives of creatures above and below it. Furthermore, most Hindus consider divinity to be more than physical nature and think human self-realization (*moksha*) entails release from the laws of karma. Let us develop these ideas.

The statement that the physical cosmos is real requires some qualification. Throughout history, the average Hindu, concerned with making a living and caring for a family, has had little doubt that the fields, flocks, and other physical phenomena are real. Also, the hymns of the Vedas that revere the sun and the storm express a vivid appreciation of nature. Even many of the philosophers spoke of the world as having being or reality. Only the idealistic thought of the Upanishads, as the Vedanta developed and somewhat organized it, called the reality of the physical world into question.

Furthermore, because of the Vedic notion of *rita* (order, duty, or ritual) and the later notion of karma, Hinduism found the natural world quite orderly. *Rita* presided over such phenomena as sunrise, sunset, and the seasons. Karma expressed the Hindu doctrine that all acts in the cosmos result from previous causes or choices and produce inevitable effects. To be sure, there are various religious paths (*margas*) for escaping karmic inevitability, and we discuss those paths here. Nonetheless, *rita* and karma suggest that the world is patterned, regular, and dependable. This does not mean that flood, famine, earthquake, sickness, or war cannot occur, but it does mean that none of these calamities makes the world absurd.

Karma is connected with the notion of transmigration and rebirth. *Rita* is involved with the vast space-time dimensions in which Hindu cosmology delights. Together these concepts give nature a gigantic expanse that is replete with connections. The connections that most interested the average Hindu linked the myriad living things. Shaivites expressed this interest by venerating the powers of fertility. Ancient rites honoring the Great Mother and other rites stressing Shaktism reveal other Hindu responses to the wonders of life. The symbolism surrounding Shiva and his consorts (such as Kali) explicitly links life with death. At a level above ancient concerns with the vegetative cycle of death and rebirth and the taking of life by life, Hinduism placed the connection between death and life in the context of the universal cycles of creation and destruction. The Jain notion of *ahimsa,* which many Hindus adopted to varying degrees, implied the connectedness of all lives through its practice of not harming animals. Many Indians refused to eat meat out of the desire not to harm animals. Nonviolence toward the cow, which one might not kill even to help the starving (but which might itself starve), epitomized for many Hindus a necessary reverence for life. Taking karma and transmigration (the passing of the life force from one entity to another) seriously, Hindus thought that life, including their own, was constantly recasting itself into new vegetative and animal forms. Such life was not an evolutionary accident or something that ended at the grave. The inmost life principle continued on, making nature a container of life forces.

Frequently, *maya* and *samsara* carry negative overtones. In fact, the whole thrust toward *moksha* suggests that the natural sphere is of limited value. For more than a few Indians, the natural sphere has been a prison or place of suffering. Yogis of different schools, for instance, have tried to withdraw from materiality to cultivate their mystical experience. Other Hindu mystics have sensed that there was something more ultimate than the ritual sacrifice, the play of natural processes, and even the emotions of the devout worshipper of the *bhakti* god. In this sense *samsara* opposed the freedom suggested by *moksha,* and *moksha* meant exit from what one had known as natural conditions.

However, it is misleading to label Hinduism as world denying or life denying, since India's culture has produced many warriors, merchants, artists, and scientists—a full citizenry who took secular life seriously. Nonetheless, Hindu culture was seldom secular or materialistic in our modern senses, usually stabilizing society by referring to a god or Brahman transcending human space and time. (We may say the same of traditional premodern societies generally.) In addition, Hinduism's reference to metaphysical concepts probably held back its concern with health care, education, and economic prosperity for the masses. When he argued for a secular state and a turn to science rather than religion, India's first prime minister, Nehru, spoke for many modern educated Indians.

Thus, Hinduism's Aryan beginnings, which were so bursting with love of physical life, and its Dravidian beginnings, which were tantamount to nature and fertility worship, were negated in some periods of history. The most serious blows came from intellectual Hinduism and *bhakti,* which found life good by spiritual exercises and thus were not concerned with social justice or transforming nature for human benefit.

SOCIETY

Hinduism structured society by caste and numerous occupational subclasses. In addition, families traced themselves back through their departed ancestors. Outside the four castes were instances of slavery. The basic structure of the four castes received religious sanction in the *Rig-Veda* 10:90, in which the priests, warriors, merchants, and workers are said to emerge from the Great Man's body after he was sacrificed.

The Laws of Manu, expanding the doctrine of casteism, specified the castes' social duties. The Brahmin, for instance, had six required acts to perform: teaching, studying, sacrificing for himself, sacrificing for others, making gifts, and receiving gifts. Brahmins also were to avoid working at agriculture and selling certain foods (such as flesh and salt). Were they to do these things, they would assume the character of people of other castes. In a similar way, Manu set duties and prohibitions for the warriors, merchants, farmers, and workers, giving the entire society a comprehensive dharma. As a result, Hindus considered their dharma to be something given rather than a matter of debate or free choice. Indeed, such caste obligations were the basic cement of the stability of Hindu society.

Nonetheless, various religious inspirations and movements introduced some flexibility. Many of the *bhakti* cults rejected caste distinctions, contending that all people were equal in the god's sight. The possibility of stepping outside the ordinary organization of things to become a full-time ascetic or seeker of liberation loosened the stranglehold of both dharma and caste.

WOMEN'S STATUS

We know little about the earliest Indian women's social status. There is evidence of fertility rites among the pre-Aryans, suggesting a cult of a mother goddess or a matriarchal social structure. In Vedic times women clearly were subordinate to men, but in earlier times they may have held important cultic offices, created canonical hymns, and been scholars, poets, and teachers. In the *Brihad-Aranyaka* Upanishad, the woman Gargi questions the sage Yajnavalkya, indicating that wisdom was not exclusively a male concern. It therefore seems likely that in early India at least, some girls of the upper castes received religious training like the boys'. However, between the first Vedas (1500 B.C.E.) and the first codes of law (100 C.E.), women's religious roles steadily declined. A major reason for this was the lowering of the marriage age from fifteen or sixteen years to ten or even five. This both removed the possibility of education (and consequently religious office) and fixed women's roles to wife and mother. In fact, in later Hinduism being a wife was so important that a widow supposedly was prohibited from mentioning any man's name but that of her deceased husband. Even if she had been a child bride or had never consummated her marriage, the widow was not to violate her duty to her deceased husband and remarry. If she did, it was thought she would bring disgrace on herself in the present life and enter the womb of a jackal for her next rebirth.

Thus, the widow was the most forlorn of Hindu women. Without a husband, she was a financial liability to those who supported her. If menstruating, she could be a source of ritual pollution. If barren, she was useless to a society that considered women essentially as child producers. In such a social position,

many widows must have concluded that they had little to lose by throwing themselves on their husband's funeral pyre. (Even suttee, though, was not simple. If the widow did not burn herself out of pure conjugal love, her act was without merit.)

Women were sometimes admitted as equals into the *bhakti* and Tantrist sects. However, two circumstances in Tantrism minimized the social liberation that the open admission might have effected. First, the Tantrist sects tended to be esoteric, or secret, which made their public impact minor. Second, the Tantrist interest in tapping *shakti* energies often led to the exploitation of women by men. Thus, the males sometimes tried to gain powers of liberation (*moksha*) by symbolic or actual sexual intercourse, with the result that the females became instruments rather than equal partners. Nevertheless, the Tantrist image of perfection as being androgynous tended to boost the value of femaleness. How much this ideal actually benefited Indian women is difficult to say, but it probably helped some. Nonetheless, women were not generally eligible for *moksha*; the best that a woman could hope for was to be reborn as a man. There is little evidence that Tantrism eliminated this doctrine, though the *Bhagavad Gita* 9:32 seems to contradict it.

The overall status of women in Hinduism was that of wards. They were subject, successively, to fathers, husbands, and elder sons. As soon as they approached puberty, their fathers hastened to marry them off, and during their wedded lives they were to honor their husbands without reservation. According to the *Padma-purana*, an influential text, this obligation held even if their husbands were deformed, aged, debauched, lived openly with other women, or showed them no affection. Worse than ward status, however, was the strain of misogyny (hatred of women) running through Hindu culture. The birth of a girl was not an occasion for joy. Hindus attributed it to bad karma in a previous life and frequently announced the event by saying, "Nothing was born." A girl was a financial burden, for unless her parents arranged a dowry there was small chance that she would marry, and the Vedic notion that women were necessary if men were to be complete (which the gods' consorts evidence) lost out to Manu's view that women were as impure as falsehood itself. In fact, Manu counseled "the wise" never to sit with a woman in a lonely place, even if that woman were one's mother, sister, or daughter.

Consequently, Hindu religious texts sometimes imagine a woman as a snake, hell's entrance, death, a prostitute, or an adulteress. In Manu's code, slaying a woman was one of the minor offenses. In the Hindu family, the basic unit of society, woman therefore carried a somewhat negative image; although, of course, some women entered happy households. The high status of the householder did not extend to his wife or female children. India mainly honored women for giving birth and serving their husbands.

MA JNANANANDA. To show the sort of exception that relativizes general statements such as those that we have been making about Hindu women, let us briefly consider a contemporary female guru, Ma Jnanananda of Madras. (*Ma* is a familiar form of "mother".) Jnanananda is a spiritual mother to numerous followers in present-day Madras. She is both a guru and a *sannyasi*. A guru is a religious teacher; a *sannyasi* is one who has taken a formal vow renouncing all worldly life, including family ties and possessions. Such a vow, in effect, means death to one's former life. This renunciation allows full-time pursuit of spiritual goals and fosters spiritual development.

Ma gained her lofty position as a guru because one of the leading Advaita Vedanta figures of contemporary India, Shankaracharya of Kanchipuram, recognized her mystical absorption with Brahman. Jnanananda had done this while living in the world, married and raising five children. That probably accounts for her great ability to relate the teachings of Vedanta to her disciples' daily problems at work or in family life. Photographs of Ma taken before she became a guru show a lovely woman, well dressed and well groomed. The beauty still lingers, but now it seems a reflection of her inner peace. She has traded her fine clothes for a simple sari of ochre cloth, cut her hair short, and painted on her forehead and arms horizontal stripes of a thick paste made from ashes, to symbolize her death to vanity and worldly desires.

In the regime Ma would have a disciple follow, the day begins with some prayer or meditation to the deity of the disciple's choice. After this, the disciple turns to the work of the day, trying to perform duties in such a way that they do not distract the mind from God. The ideal is always to surrender completely to God. When distracting thoughts enter the mind, one should return to God by substituting a prayer or *mantra* (sacred sound). The goal always is "realization" of God, experiential awareness of the divinity in everything. As this realization increases, worldly things lose their allure. Bit by bit, we are skirting the dark forest of fear and desire, moving away from the powers of samsara and time. We can never control all the events of our lives, but we can control our attitude toward them. If we regard what happens to us as intended for our detachment from samsaric things, intended for our attachment to God, all things will become profitable. Such is Ma's teaching.

The final state of realization brings a great love of God. As one's union with divinity increases, one's fulfillment overflows. In this conviction, Ma Jnanananda is a sister to the great mystics of other religious traditions. East and West, they agree that union with God or ultimate reality is the greatest success a human being can attain.

CONCLUSION. The social rewards of Hindu religion were in the hands of a relative few. By excluding most women, untouchables, and workers, intellectualist Hinduism told well more than half the population that their best hope was rebirth in a better station sometime in the future. (For the most part, only a member of a high caste could reach *moksha*.) However, in the family and the different trades, dharma gave all castes some legitimacy.

SELF

Obviously, the average Hindu did not think about the self in isolation from nature and society. The social caste system and the cosmic *samsara*-transmigration system were the framework of any self-examination. Within this framework, however, an individual might set about the task of trying to attain *atmasiddhi,* the perfecting of human nature. This was another way, more concrete perhaps, of posing what *moksha* or the *mahatma* (the "great soul") meant.

In the *Rig-Veda, atmasiddhi* was the pious man who recited the hymns and made sacrifices to the gods. Then the changes of Vedic tradition shifted the ideal to the priest who could faultlessly conduct the expanded ritual. The Upanishads shifted perfection toward the acquisition of secret knowledge about reality. The *smriti* literature such as the Laws of Manu valued more worldly achievement. There the most excellent man was he who could rule public affairs and lead in community matters. The Bhagavad Gita spoke of love as the highest attainment, but it described the realized human personality as being stable in wisdom and having overcome the desires of both the flesh and ambition. Recently Indian saints such as Ramakrishna and Gandhi have stressed, respectively, the mystic loss of self in God and the service of Truth. Clearly, therefore, Hindu tradition allows the self many ideals. Generally speaking, though, full success has implied emotional, intellectual, and spiritual maturity and has honored the social side of human beings, as well as the solitary.

The Upanishads jostled the classical life cycle for many. As we have seen, the Upanishadic self was the Atman identified with Brahman. For this revered part of the Hindu tradition, then, the most important aspect of the self was the spiritual core. More than the body, this spiritual core was the key to escaping rebirth. If one was serious about escaping rebirth, why wait for the final stages of the life cycle? Why not cultivate the Atman full time? Some such reasoning surely prompted those who became wanderers long before old age. Whether through study or meditation, they pursued a way that implied that the self's needs or aspirations could outweigh social responsibilities.

In the past thousand years or so, the individual Hindu has therefore had a variety of ways of viewing his or her life journey. The four stages of the life cycle, the Upanishadic or *bhakti* wandering, the household devotions—any of these concepts could give people's lives relevance. Hinduism explicitly recognized that people's needs differed by speaking of four *margas* (paths) that could lead to fulfillment and liberation. Among intellectuals, the way of knowledge was prestigious. In this *marga* one studied the classical texts, the Vedic revelation and commentators' tradition, pursuing an intuitive insight into reality. Shankara's higher knowledge is one version of this ideal. If one could gain the viewpoint where Brahman was the reality of everything, one had gained the wisdom that would release one from suffering.

But philosophy patently did not attract everyone, and many whom it did attract could not spare the time to study. Therefore, the way of karma (here understood as meaning works or action) better served many people. The Bhagavad Gita more than sanctioned this way, which amounted to a discipline of detachment. If one did one's daily affairs peacefully and with equanimity of spirit, then one would not be tied to the world of *samsara*. Doing just the work, without concern for its "fruits" (success or failure), one avoided bad karma (here meaning the law of cause and effect). Gandhi, who was much taken with this teaching of the Gita, used spinning as an example of karma-*marga* or karma-yoga (work discipline). One just let the wheel turn, trying to join one's spirit to its revolutions and paying the quantity of production little heed. When karma-yoga was joined to the notion that one's work was a matter of caste obligation, or dharma, it became another powerful message that the status quo was holy and relevant.

A third *marga* was meditation (*dhyana*). Contrasted with the way of knowledge, the way of meditation did not directly imply study and did not directly pursue intuitive vision. Rather, it was usually based on the conviction that one can reach the real self by quieting the senses and mental activity to descend without thinking to the personality's depths. In this progression, one approached a state of deep sleep and then went beyond it to nondualism. "Seedless *samadhi*" (pure consciousness) was the highest of the eight branches of yogic progress, but to enter *moksha* one had to leave even it behind. Along the way to *samadhi* one might acquire various paranormal powers (such as clairvoyance or telepathy), but these were of little account. For the many who meditated, the way of *dhyana* usually meant a great sensitivity to body-spirit relationships (through, for example, posture and breath control developed in yoga) and a deepening sense of the oneness of all reality.

Finally, *bhakti* had the status of a *marga*, and, according to the Bhagavad Gita, it could be a very effective pathway. Of course, *bhaktas* ran the gamut from emotional excess to lofty mysticism. The *Gita* qualified the self-assertiveness that could arise in *bhakti*, however, by making its final revelation not human love of divinity but Krishna's love for humans. On the basis of such revelation, the *bhakta* was responding to divinity as divinity had shown itself to be. In other words, the *bhakta* was realizing human fulfillment by imitating God.

We can get further glimpses into the Hindu sense of the self by considering how Hindus tended to regard their children.

The Hindu child was subjected to religious ceremonies well before birth. For devout Hindus, there were rituals to ensure conception, to procure a male child, and to safeguard the child's time in the womb. Birth itself involved an important ceremony, which ideally took place before the cutting of the umbilical cord, and that included whispering sacred spells in the baby's ear, placing a mixture of butter and honey in its mouth, and giving it a name that its parents were to keep secret until its initiation. Birth made both parents ritually impure for ten days, which meant they were not to take part in the community's ordinary religious rites. Ten days after birth, the child was given a public (as contrasted with the secret) name. Some households also solemnized both an early ear piercing and the first time the parents took the child out of the house and showed it the sun.

There was a pressing motive for parents to have sons, in that at least one son was thought necessary to perform the parents' funeral rites, without which they could not be sure of a safe transit to the other world. Adopted sons were better than nothing, but they were nowhere near so good as natural sons. Girls were of no use whatsoever, because girls could not help their parents in the next world, and at marriage girls passed into the families of their husbands. Although Indian history shows some evidence of female infanticide, this practice seems to have been relatively rare. Despite their lesser desirability, many girls were cared for and petted like sons.

Indian literature suggests that most Hindus had relatively happy, indulged childhoods. In Indian poetry, for example, children are often shown laughing, babbling, and being welcomed onto their parents' laps. On the other hand, poor children were set to work soon after they were able to walk, whereas wealthier children started their studies as young as four or five. Thus boys usually were set to studying the alphabet by their fifth year. Richer families engaged tutors for their children, and through the Indian Middle Ages (before the Muslim invasions) many village temples had schools attached. The education of girls was considered much less pressing than that of boys, but most upper-class women became literate. Before his initiation, when he was invested with the sacred thread and set to studying the Vedas, an upper-class boy usually concentrated on reading and arithmetic.

The initiation of Brahmin boys usually occurred when they were eight. For warriors the ideal age was eleven, and for merchants twelve. The key element in this initiation was hanging a cord of three threads over the boy's right shoulder. The cord was made of nine twisted strands (cotton for Brahmins, hemp for warriors, and wool for merchants). To remove this thread any time during his subsequent life, or to defile it, involved the initiate in great humiliation and ritual impurity. The initiation made the child an Aryan, a member of a noble people, opening the door to his first serious task, that of mastering the sacred Aryan lore. Accordingly, soon after initiation the child was apprenticed to a Brahmin in order to learn the Vedas. During this period he was to be celibate, to live a simple life, and to obey his teacher assiduously.

ULTIMATE REALITY

In the early Vedic literature, the gods are principally natural phenomena. It is the wondrous qualities of the storm or fire that elevate Indra and Agni to prominence. By the time that the emphasis on sacrificial ritual dominated, the gods had come under human control. The final stage of Brahmanism was the view that the ritual, if properly performed, inevitably attains its goals—it compels the gods to obey. When we couple this subordinating view of the gods with the notion of *samsara*, the gods become less venerable than human beings. Human beings have the potential to break with *samsara* and to transcend the transmigratory realm through *moksha*.

The gods, despite their heavenly estate, are still within the transmigratory realm and cannot escape into *moksha*.

The Upanishads moved away from the plurality of gods toward monism. Both the Upanishads and the Vedanta philosophers stated that the knowledge of Brahman or Atman is redemptive. Such knowledge is not simply factual or scientific but has the power to transform one's life—it is light freeing one from existential darkness. Therefore, from the side of the one who experiences Brahman's dominance, we can surely speak of "religious" (ultimately concerned) overtones. Brahman is the basis of everything, if not the creator. It is the supreme value, because nothing is worth more than the ultimate being, which, once seen, sets everything else in light and order.

Attending to Brahman, Hinduism's major concept for ultimate reality, we can note finally that the two aspects of Brahman approximate what monotheistic religions have made of their God. Being beyond the human realm (*nirguna*), Brahman recedes into mystery. This parallels the Christian God's quality of always being ineffable and inconceivable. But because it is within the human realm (*saguna*), Brahman is the basis of nature and culture. In this way it approximates the Christian conception of the Logos, in whom all creation holds together. Brahman is impersonal, whereas most monotheistic religions conceive their deities on the model of the human personality.

The *bhakti* cults have revered still another form of Hindu divinity. Vaishnavites do not strictly deny the reality of Shiva or Brahma, nor do followers of these other gods deny the reality of Vishnu or Krishna. The mere fact that *bhakti* sects devoted to different gods contend among themselves shows that they take the other gods seriously. But the emotional ardor of the devoted *bhaktas* suggests that they grant their gods the ultimate value of a monotheistic god. The same holds for devotees of goddesses, who may actually outnumber devotees of the male gods.

In Krishna's manifestation to Arjuna in the Bhagavad Gita, we can see how this monotheistic value took symbolic form. Krishna becomes the explosive energy of all reality. In the *Gita,* his theophany (manifestation of divinity) is the ultimate revelation of how divinity assumes many masks in space and time. Whatever reality is, Krishna is its dynamic source.

Much like the Upanishadic Brahman, he is the one source capable of manifesting itself in many forms. But whereas the atmosphere of Brahman is serene and cool, the *bhakti*-prone Krishna is turbulent and hot. When J. Robert Oppenheimer, one of the developers of the American atom bomb, saw the first nuclear explosion, Krishna's dazzling self-revelation came to his mind: "If the light of a thousand suns should effulge all at once, it would resemble the radiance of that god of overpowering reality" (*Bhagavad Gita* 11:12).

THE PROBLEM OF EVIL. The problem of evil (**theodicy**) is that so much in human experience seems to be dark and disordered. For many Western observers, Indian philosophy has seemed strangely silent about evil. (Their greater interest was the problem of ignorance—why human beings don't comprehend that only ultimate reality is fully real.) The Hindu doctrine of rebirth shifted the problem of evil away from the Western orientation, in which individuals (like Job in the Bible) can accuse God of having dealt with them unjustly, having caused them to suffer through no fault of their own. Rebirth, coupled with the notion of karma, meant that one existed through long cycles of time whose overall justice was beyond human calculation, and that one's fate in a given lifetime was the result of one's actions in a previous existence. Thus there was no unmerited punishment and consequently no "problem" of evil. The gods did not have to justify themselves before innocent sufferers.

One of the early reasons why Hinduism developed an articulate response to the problem of evil was the attacks of the Buddhists, who found evil a soft spot in Hinduism's armor. Thus Buddhist texts satirically ask why the Hindu gods do not set the world straight. If Brahman, for instance, is lord of all things born, why are things so confused and out of joint? Why is there such unhappiness and deception? If we are honest, it seems as though Brahman ordained not dharma (a good working order) but *adharma* (chaos).

Hindu thinkers struggled to meet this challenge. In trying to understand evil, they tended to regard natural disasters, such as earthquakes, and moral wrongs, such as murder, as but two aspects of a single comprehensive phenomenon. In the *Rig-Veda,* probably the moral sense prevails: People are evil-minded, committing adultery or theft. Still, the *Rig-Veda* does not necessarily see such evil as freely chosen. Moral evil or sin may occur without the sinner willing it. Therefore, one finds few prayers of personal repentance in the *Rig-Veda*, though numerous prayers for deliverance from the bad things other people can do.

The *Atharva-Veda* also tends to blend natural and moral evils, and to see moral evil as an intellectual mistake rather than a culpable flaw in character. There are exceptions to these tendencies, such as the Rig-Vedic hymn of repentance to Varuna (5:85), but the overall inclination of the Vedic texts is to regard evil not as something we humans do but as what we do not wish to have done to us.

KALI. One female deity whom scholars have studied thoroughly is Kali, the mistress of death, an important expression of Maha-devi, the ancient great goddess. In her, many of the popular ambivalences about ultimate reality come into focus. Part of the fascination Kali has evoked stems from her dreadful appearance. Usually she is portrayed in black, like a great storm cloud. Her tongue lolls, reminding the viewer that she has a great thirst for blood, and she shows fearsome teeth. Her eyes are sunken, but she smiles, as though enjoying a terrible secret. Round her neck is a garland of snakes, a half-moon rests on her forehead, her hair is matted, and often she licks a corpse. In her hand is apt to be a necklace of skulls. She has a swollen belly, girdled with snakes, and for earrings she has corpses. Her face projects a calm contentment, as if the savage realities of life, its evil and deathly aspects, suit her just fine. (It is interesting that the cult of Kali flourished in areas most profoundly influenced by British colonial rule, as though to express a sense that life had turned horribly oppressive.)

Moreover, certain historic associations have besmirched Kali's name, linking her with some of the most loathsome, degenerate streams in Hindu culture. For example, she has been linked with blood sacrifices, including those of human beings, and she has served as the patron goddess of the Thugs, a vicious band of criminals that flourished from ancient times until the late nineteenth century and devoted themselves to strangling carefully selected victims as a way of honoring the goddess of death. (It is from this group that our English word *thug* has come.)

Nonetheless, a careful study of Kali's full history as a major Hindu deity suggests that she has functioned as more than simply a lodestone for the soul's darker passions.

First, Kali does not appear in the earliest Hindu texts but comes on the scene fairly late. Second, throughout her history it is largely peripheral people, marginal groups, that populate her cults. In this respect her cult reminds one of Shavaism and Tantrism. Third, the geographic areas most devoted to Kali have been Bengal and the Vindhya mountain region of south-central India. Fourth, when Kali became associated with the **tantric** cults, her appearance changed, for a potential benevolence more clearly emerged. Tantrism's concern with tapping libidinal energies led to the rise of many female deities from the seventh century C.E. on, and by the sixteenth century Kali was intimately connected with the more adventurous "left-hand" tantric sects.

Kali is a personification of the most forbidden thing, death. Therefore, the tantric hero presses on to confront Kali, trying to transform her (death) into a vehicle of salvation. Consequently, the hero is apt to go to Kali's favorite dwelling place, the cremation grounds, meditate on each terrible aspect of her appearance, and try by penetrating her fearsomeness to pass beyond it.

The ordinary Hindu, man or woman, who was not a saint like Ramakrishna, tended to interact with a favorite god or goddess without understanding that this deity was merely the face of a universal divinity or ultimacy. Throughout history, most Hindus have not been literate, so their sense of the gods and goddesses has come from the oral tradition. It was the great cycle of stories about Krishna and Devi, about Rama and Sita, that filled the imagination of the ordinary person and so shaped what he or she said at prayer, thought during the religious festivals, or feared in the depths of night or at the bed of a sickly child. This is not to say that the average Hindu had no sense of the unity among the different deities. In all probability, even the humblest peasant accepted that the many different deities were reconciled in the realm of the gods. But for the present age, the trials of this round of the samsaric cycle, it was more helpful to focus on a particular deity than to speculate about a divine unity beyond or underneath all of the divine diversity.

A second feature of popular Hindu religion, the culture of the masses, has been a certain passivity. Ideally, karma moved people to live on the border between acceptance and resignation. Acceptance is something positive: thinking that one's life is in God's hands, thinking that Providence must in the final analysis be benevolent. Resignation is something negative: we can't do much about our situation, in the long run, so we had best detach ourselves from foolish hopes and let happen what will. In their prayers and rituals, Hindus tried to draw from their favorite deities a blend of acceptance and resignation fitting and powerful enough to keep them going. Popular religion certainly had its ecstatic moments, when love of a dazzling deity might move people to transports of delight, but on a daily basis Hindu piety or spirituality tended to be sober.

CONCLUSION. We suspect that Hindus have arranged nature, society, and the self in view of the Agni, Brahman, or Krishna who centered their lives in divine mystery. If Brahman is the ultimate reality, then nature, society, and the self are all versions of *maya,* are all illusion and play. If Agni, the god to whom one directs the fire sacrifice, is the ultimate reality, then nature stands by divine heat, society stands by priestly sacrificers, and the self strives after *tapas* (ascetic heat) or lives by ritual mantras (verbal formulas for controlling the divine forces). Finally, if Shiva is the ultimate reality, then ultimate reality destroys castes, is the arbiter of life and death, and reduces the self to a beggar for grace.

No system of interpretation can truly substitute for the system that the religion itself implicitly uses. In other words, we cannot reduce the religions to their cosmological, sociological, or psychological factors. They must remain essentially what they claim to be: ways emanating from and leading to the divine. For this reason, the concept of ultimate reality in a religion will always be the most crucial concept. God or ultimate reality is by definition the ultimate shaper of a worldview, because divinity determines the placement of the other dimensions and thus the worldview as a whole.

Having had many forms of divinity, Hinduism has had many worldviews. The membership requirements are quite simple: As long as one accepts the divine inspiration of the Vedas and the caste system, one can be called a Hindu.

SUMMARY: THE HINDU CENTER

How, overall, does Hinduism seem to configure reality for its adherents? What is the center, or summarizing pattern, that the Hindu "ways" appear to depict? It seems to us that the Hindu center is an alluring sense of unity. From the time of the Vedas, reflective personalities in India sought to put together the many disparate facets and forces of reality. Thus *Rig-Veda* hymns, the Upanishads, and the later theistic cults all proposed a mystery, or ultimate reality, or god that stood behind things, promising the devout adherent, or the self-disciplined yogi, a satisfying peace. The peace would come from the order that union with Brahman or Krishna would produce. Thus the individual was not to cling to the passing multiplicity of social, natural, or even personal life. *Samsara* was an enemy trying to keep the individual in a state of disunion, and so of suffering. Illusion was *samsara's* main ally. If one broke with illusion, appropriated the wisdom of the ancient seers who had fought through to, or been blessed by a vision of, the ultimate unity of all things, one could find being, bliss, and awareness.

Moksha is probably the watchword best symbolizing this typically Hindu cast of mind, yet *moksha* could have several different weightings. For the passionate, those either suffering with special pains or burning for being, bliss, and awareness with a special ardor, *moksha* could be an imperative. There being nothing more important than coming to right order, finding the ultimate relevance of life, the passionate Hindu could pursue *moksha* wholeheartedly, opting out of India's highly structured caste and family life. For personalities either less pressured by suffering or less drawn by the prospects of fulfillment, *moksha* could carry a somewhat comforting and palliative set of overtones. If not in this life, in some future life one could hope to attain *moksha*. With such a good future prospect, the turmoils and troubles of the present life could somewhat slacken.

Theistic Hindus, *bhaktas* devoted to Krishna, Shiva, or one of the goddesses, tended to picture the center in terms of their beloved God. Thus the **theophany,** or revelation, that Krishna gives Arjuna in the Gita shows Krishna to be the center of all reality, a sort of Brahman, but more personalized, dazzling, and energetic. As the force of life and death, Shiva could have a similarly universal power to organize reality, a similarly profound religious clout. Love for such a god could give the devotee's life ultimate relevance.

Be that as it may (and it may be more descriptive of the recent India than about the India of the pre-Muslim era), the impression remains that the Hindu center has been as ambivalent in its social effects as most other religious centers have been. By the standards of a radical contemplative wisdom that would penetrate to the core of reality's mystery and a radical social justice that would treat all human beings as equals who deserve fair dealing, the Hindu worldview emerges as more wise than just. So, of course, do most other worldviews, if only because it is usually easier to contemplate the grand source of order, the fair center of a mystery revealing itself as beautiful and healing, than it is to promote other human beings' equal access to the good life that such a mystery suggests.

JUDAISM

JUDAISM: 25 KEY DATES	
Date	Event
ca. 1200 B.C.E.	exodus: Moses leads Hebrews out of Egypt
1013–973 B.C.E.	David's rule
722 B.C.E.	fall of Northern Kingdom (Israel) to Assyria
586 B.C.E.	fall of Southern Kingdom (Judah) to Babylon; beginning of the Exile
331 B.C.E.	Alexander conquers Palestine
168 B.C.E.	Maccabean revolt against Hellenization
63 B.C.E.	Roman conquest of Jerusalem
70 C.E.	Romans destroy Temple; beginning of Diaspora
80–110 C.E.	assembly of Hebrew Scriptures
ca. 200 C.E.	promulgation of the Mishnah
ca. 500 C.E.	Babylonian Talmud complete in rough form
640 C.E.	Muslim conquest of Middle East
1041 C.E.	birth of Rashi, Bible and Talmud commentator
1135 C.E.	birth of Maimonides in Cordoba, Spain
1187 C.E.	Muslims reconquer Jerusalem from Christian Crusaders
1290–1309 C.E.	expulsion of Jews from England and France
1492–1496 C.E.	expulsion of Jews from Spain and Portugal
1516 C.E.	introduction of the Ghetto in Venice
1521 C.E.	beginning of Jewish migrations to Palestine
1648 C.E.	massacre of Polish and Ukrainian Jews
1654–1658 C.E.	Jewish communities in New Amsterdam and Rhode Island
1760 C.E.	death of Baal Shem-Tov
1897 C.E.	founding of Zionist movement
1938 C.E.	every synagogue in Germany burned
1948 C.E.	creation of modern state of Israel

The discussion of the tradition of **Judaism** must begin with a clarification of confusing and overlapping terms. Terms like *Jew* and *Judaism* came into being in the sixth century B.C.E. Judaism is the name of the religious tradition. The term **Jew** refers to a follower of Judaism. Non-Jews are described as *goyim* (**Gentiles**). One can be considered a Jew if one is a convert to Judaism (which is rare, since this denomination is non-proselytizing) or if one is the son or daughter of a Jewish mother (the father's status does not count). One of the most listened-to voices on the radio, Dr. Laura Schlessinger, proudly acknowledges the Jewish foundation of the advice she dispenses. Her father was an American Jew, but her mother was a war bride from Italy (a Catholic). As an adult, Dr. Laura decided to embrace her Jewish roots. She found that she did not qualify as a Jew solely on the basis of matrilineal parentage, so she had to make a formal conversion.

The term *Jew* has also come to serve as an ethnic description, such as Irish, Polish, Latino, or African-American. Many atheists, agnostics, or converts to other denominations still regard themselves as Jewish, at least in terms of ethnic identification. Indeed, some

> Menorah.

of the persecution (**anti-Semitism**) that the Jews have received throughout history was based more on ethnic rather than religious prejudice. Jews could not escape the Nazi death camps by converting to another religion. Indeed, one Auschwitz victim was a nun recently sainted by the Catholic Church, Sister Edith Stein. The Nazis tracked her down in a Dutch monastery and killed her because she was of Jewish parentage (although she converted to Catholicism and had become a nun as a young woman).

The figures of Abraham, Isaac, Jacob, and Joseph in the book of *Genesis* were known as the patriarchs of the tribe of **Hebrews.** Moses and the people who followed him out of Egypt used that name. The term may have come from a Mesopotamian term for "outside the city's walls" (implying "nomad" or even "outlaw"). We now use the term *Hebrew* to describe a language of the Semitic group (which also includes Arabic). The Old Testament was written in this language and Hebrew remains a language used in many Jewish rituals. (A different language was spoken in daily life by the Jews of eastern Europe: Yiddish, which has many similarities to German.)

The name **Israel** initially referred to a man, Jacob, another patriarch of the Jews. About five hundred years later, when Joshua led the Hebrews across the Jordan River into the promised land of Palestine, the name Israel was given to the land. About three thousand years ago, Israel became a kingdom ruled by such monarchs as Saul, David, and Solomon. The subjects of this biblical kingdom were known as *Israelites.* The terms *Jew* and *Judaism,* which emerged in the seventh century B.C.E., refer to the Kingdom of Judah (the "southern" kingdom) that had survived the Assyrian conquest of the northern kingdom of Israel.

In 1948, the United Nations created a modern homeland for the Jews and named this nation Israel. The citizens of this modern nation are known as *Israelis* (and the Arab peoples who lived in that land are now referred to as Palestinians).

HISTORY

THE BIBLICAL PERIOD

Even more than Hinduism, the development of Judaism is chronicled in its scripture. The **Torah** (also known as the **Pentateuch**) is found in the first five books of the Christian Bible. This Jewish scripture is sometimes simply referred to as "the Law" in order to distinguish it from the other, later parts of the Hebrew Scriptures. (Christians refer to these Hebrew Scriptures as the *Old Testament*).

Tradition says that the Torah was written by Moses after the **Exodus** (the movement of the Hebrews out from Egypt). Through the use of hermeneutical tools, secular and liberal scholars (such as Graf and Wellhausen) over the past hundred years have inferred that the books of the Torah might actually have been finally written down five hundred years later, a scissors-and-paste job from at least four different oral traditions. The more fundamentalist Jewish and Christian scholars have defended the plausibility of Moses' authorship. Rather than resolving the ongoing debate about the origin of the Old Testament, we point to a common agreement. Both sides agree that the Old Testament began as oral tradition (even those who take everything literally would say that Adam passed on what he knew to Seth, and then to his son, and so on until we get down to Moses). Both sides also agree that someone then put together oral tradition as a written document (if not Moses during the Exodus from Egypt, then the rabbis during the Babylonian Exile five hundred years later).

Materials such as these different strands of the Pentateuch were edited, probably several times, to form the biblical "books" that we find today. Each book of the Bible therefore is, to an extent, a composite work. Sometimes one finds different perspectives, if not apparent conflicts, within a given book or between one book and another.

Although the first five books of the Bible have been accorded the most dignity and authority, the second section of the Old Testament has also been revered. Traditionally called *Prophets,* this section contains reinterpretations of events (especially the establishment of the covenant between Israel and God) suited to later crises, such as the removal of many leaders of the Israelite community to Babylon in the sixth century B.C.E. Still a third section of the Hebrew Scriptures, traditionally called *The Writings,* collects later and disparate materials, and although as a group it has had less status than either the first five books (Torah) or *Prophets,* its works have still been considered authoritative interpretations of the relevance of

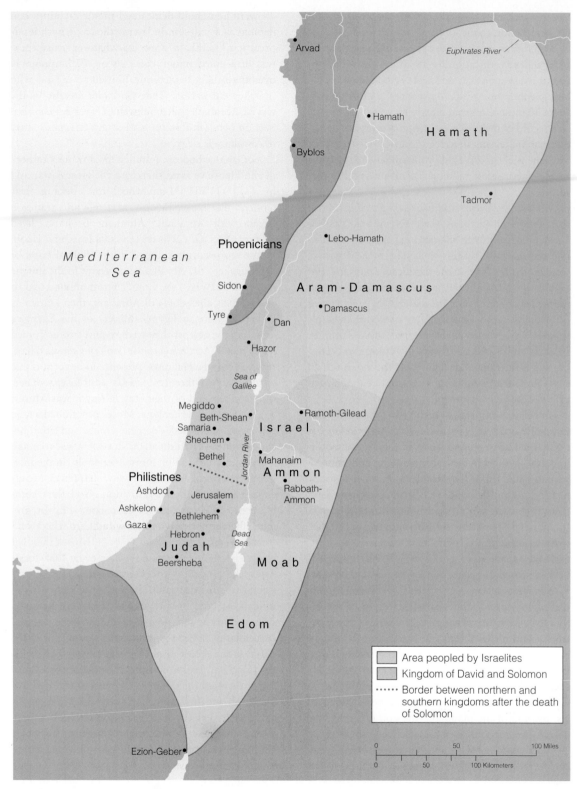

Kingdom of Ancient Israel about 1000 B.C.E.

Arvad

Euphrates River

Hamath

Hamath

Byblos

Tadmor

Phoenicians

Lebo-Hamath

Mediterranean
Sea

Aram-Damascus

Sidon

Damascus

Tyre

Dan

Hazor

Sea of
Galilee

Megiddo

Ramoth-Gilead

Beth-Shean

Samaria

Israel

Shechem

Bethel

Mahanaim

Ammon

Philistines

Ashdod

Jerusalem

Rabbath-
Ammon

Ashkelon

Bethlehem

Gaza

Hebron

Dead
Sea

Judah

Moab

Beersheba

Edom

Area peopled by Israelites

Kingdom of David and Solomon

Border between northern and
southern kingdoms after the death
of Solomon

0   50   100 Miles
0   50   100 Kilometers

Ezion-Geber

Kingdom of Ancient Israel about 1000 B.C.E.

125

Israelite existence. Together, these three sections of the Bible made up the *Tanak*.

Whether or not events of the Bible are capable of independent verification by historians and archeologists must be judged according to the standards of social science scholarship. Our concern in this book is less with these issues and more with viewing scripture as a record of myth. We use the term **myth** not to imply that the events described did not occur, but to view the Bible as a record of the values of the people who recited, wrote, compiled, and interpreted that record.

We see Bible events and figures as *paradigmatic* in that they can serve as three-dimensional lessons about the significance of Israel's experiences sojourning with its Lord though time. The biblical writers were more interested in the significance a given event had for the cultural challenges existing at the time of the writer or editor than in what may have happened (in a literal sense) originally (or how readers three thousand years later might interpret these writings). In other words, we are always involved in interpreting interpretations—dealing with the relevance of symbolism that people using the Bible paradigmatically found most absorbing.

To begin our historical survey, we take up an integrationist point of view, assuming a continuity between biblical Israel and later Judaism. In the beginning, the Jews were most likely a loose collection of seminomadic tribes that wandered in what is today Israel, Jordan, Lebanon, and Syria. They may have cultivated some crops, but their self-designation was "wandering Aramaeans" (*Deuteronomy*: 26:5). Thus, when scouts returned from Canaan (present-day western Israel) with grapes, pomegranates, and figs (products of settled cultivators), they caused quite a stir.

Members of an early Jewish extended family tended to worship their particular "god of the father," defining themselves largely in terms of their patriarch and his god. The cult therefore centered on clan remembrance of this god, who wandered with the tribe in its nomadic life. The common name for such a clan divinity was *el*. Before their settlement in Canaan, the people may have worshipped a variety of *el*s: the god of the mountain, the god of seeing, the god of eternity, and so on. Usually they worshipped at altars constructed of unhewn stones, which they considered to be the god's house. In addition to the *el*s were household deities and minor divinities and demons of the desert. In later orthodox Jewish interpretation, Abraham drew on whatever sense there was of a unity among these *el*s or of a supreme *el* over the others to dedicate himself to a God who was beyond nature. That God, the creator of the world, Abraham called **Yahweh** (YHWH). (The connection between *Exodus* 3:14 and the *Genesis* story of Abraham is clear.)

For later orthodoxy, **Abraham** became the "Father" of the Hebrews (and therefore the later Jews) and his God YHWH ("I am who I am") became their God. In that sense, Judaism as a religious tradition began with Abraham. Abraham probably lived around 1800 B.C.E. His descendants Isaac and Jacob, whose stories are recounted in the biblical book of *Genesis,* kept the Abrahamic covenant in the unique name of YHWH, "the Lord." From about 1650 to 1280 B.C.E., the people of Abraham, then known as Hebrews, were in Egypt, subjects of the Egyptian kingdom (or at least they were required to do forced labor there). According to the book of *Genesis* (chapters 39–50), the Hebrews' presence in Egypt was due to the success there of Jacob's son Joseph. Their leader at the end of their stay in Egypt was Moses.

In later Jewish theology, **Moses** functioned as the founder of the Jewish doctrine, ethics, and ritual because God revealed through Moses his will to make a covenant and fashion himself a people. In the incident at the burning bush (*Exodus,* chapter 3), Moses experienced God's self-revelation. God then commissioned Moses to lead the people out of Egypt, giving as his authoritative name only "I am who I am" (or "I am whatever I want to be"). Moses then led the Jewish people out of Egypt, an event that dominated the biblical authors' interpretation of everything that preceded and followed it. In the most significant episode in that exodus, Egyptian pursuers drowned in the sea. Free of them, the Israelites (the descendants of Jacob, Abraham's grandson) wandered in the desert until they entered the homeland that God had promised them. The deliverance from Egypt through the unexpected event at the Red Sea (probably not the present-day Red Sea) marked all subsequent Jewish doctrine. Looking back to this event, later generations clung to the hope that their God ruled history and would continue to liberate them from oppression.

In the desert, Moses and his people sought to understand the relevance of their Exodus experience. They developed the doctrine that they were bound to God by a **covenant**. In this contract, similar to the relation between a Near Eastern overlord and vassal, God pledged care and the people pledged fidelity. The commandments accompanying this covenant gave the binding relationship (which some later commentators saw as prefigured in the figures of Adam, Noah, and Abraham) an ethical code: the basis of the Law (Torah) and the revelation that bound the people together. From laws about how to keep the Sabbath to traditions about how to sway while praying, Torah has encompassed all the traditions cherished as the basis of the people's identity and way to live worthy of their Lord.

When the Israelites finally settled in Canaan (Palestine) in the latter half of the thirteenth century B.C.E. under Moses' successor Joshua, they changed from a nomadic to an agricultural people. They were still a group of confederated tribes, but in settlement their bonds tended to loosen, as each group kept to its own area and developed its own ways. Only in times of common danger would the groups weld together, but war was so constant a feature of the period from the Exodus to the sixth century Exile in Babylon that the people had to cooperate. Settlement also meant religious changes, as local sanctuaries replaced the wandering ark of the covenant as the house of God. A somewhat professional priesthood (the tribe of *Levites*) apparently developed around these sanctuaries. Canaanite religion itself was a great influence on the Israelites. Before long, it produced a conflict between Israelites who favored the older God YHWH—the God of Abraham, Moses, and the covenant—and those who favored the agricultural gods (baals) of the Canaanites.

KINGS AND PROPHETS. From about 1200 to 1000 B.C.E., the Israelites had a government by *judges*—charismatic leaders, usually men but occasionally women, who took command in times of common danger. However, they eventually adopted monarchical rule, organizing a sturdy little kingdom under David at a new capital: Jerusalem. This kingdom unified the tribes of both north and south, and under Solomon, David's son, it had a brief but golden age of culture and empire. Some of the most striking narratives of the Hebrew Scriptures (Old Testament) derive from this period, including the brilliant memoir we find in 2 *Samuel*, chapters 13–20. In these narratives, David is portrayed as the ideal king and yet a man undeniably human—lustful for Bathsheba (willing to murder to get her), tragically at odds with his son Absalom. Much later, David's achievements in war and his fashioning a kingdom for peace made him the focus of messianic hopes—hopes for a king anointed by God who would usher in a new age of prosperity and peace. David, then, was the Jewish prototype for sacred kingship. Similarly, David's son Solomon became the prototype for wisdom. Just as many pious Jews attributed the Psalms to David, so they attributed much of the Bible's wisdom literature (e.g., Proverbs) to Solomon.

Following Solomon's death, the northern and southern portions of the kingdom split apart. The north (Israel) lasted from 922 to 722 B.C.E., when it fell to Assyria. The south (Judah) lasted until 586 B.C.E., when it fell to Babylon. (Both Assyria and Babylon lay to the northeast.) These were centuries of great political strife and military conflict. They spawned a series of important religious **prophets**, who claimed to speak the will of God. These prophetic figures dominated the next phase of biblical history. Greatest of the prophets of this period was Elijah, who preached in the north against the corrupt kings Ahab and Ahaziah and the queen Jezebel. The legendary stories about Elijah portray him as a champion of YHWH and authentic prophecy against the false prophets of the Canaanite baals.

Around 750 B.C.E., the prophet Amos issued a clarion call for justice. Extending the notion that YHWH was simply Israel's protector, Amos made divine blessings dependent upon repentance from sin. His God was clearly in charge of nature, but the key access to divinity was social justice (human beings dealing with one another fairly). Hosea, another northern prophet, also spoke up for mercy and justice (and for a nonidolatrous cult), but he expressed God's role as symbolized by a spouse willing to suffer infidelity, unable to cast off his beloved (that is, the people covenanted to him).

In the south, the successors to these northern prophets were Isaiah, Jeremiah, and the prophet known as "Second Isaiah" (the source of *Isaiah*, chapters 40–55). They made the same demands, but with greater stress on punishment by foreign powers. Reading the signs of the times, they thought that God would subject his people to captivity because they had not relied on him in absolute commitment. However, both Jeremiah and Second Isaiah held out hope for a new beginning, assuring Judah that a remnant of the people would keep their commitment to the covenant. During the reign of the southern king Josiah (640–609 B.C.E.), there was a religious reform that many scripture scholars see as the source of the "Deuteronomic" recasting of the early Jewish tradition. It shaped not only the book of *Deuteronomy* but other historical writings as well. Among the influential ideas were that YHWH had elected Israel to be his people; that observing the covenant laws was necessary for religious prosperity; that Jews ought to repudiate contacts with foreigners and foreign gods; that sacrificial rituals should be consolidated in Jerusalem; and that Israel ought to rely only on YHWH, since he controlled history and oversaw nature.

COVENANTAL THEOLOGY. From their Exile to Babylon, Jews thought they had learned an important lesson: commitment to the covenant is essential, infidelity to Torah leads to national disaster. God had chosen them by covenanting with them in a special way, and unless they responded with fidelity, they would reap not blessing but judgment. Consequently, the returnees stressed their isolation and uniqueness. Some prophets and religious thinkers suggested that God himself was universal, Lord of all peoples. His dominion included the foreign nations, for they had obviously served as his instruments for chastening Israel. He had punished through the Assyrians and Babylonians and freed through the Persians.

The stress on covenant by the Deuteronomic and postexilic leaders exalted Moses as the religious figure par excellence. However much David stood for kingly success, indeed for the very establishment of Jerusalem, Moses stood for the Torah—revelation, teaching, law. The Torah was a much more solid foundation than either kingship or Jerusalem. By the words of God's mouth, the heavens were made. By the words God spoke through Moses' mouth, the Jews were made a people. If the people kept to those words, they would choose life. If they forgot them or put them aside, they would choose death. Thus, Moses had said: "I call heaven and earth to witness against you this day, that I have set before you life and death, blessing and curse; therefore, choose life, that you and your descendants may live, loving the Lord your God, obeying his voice, and clinging to him" (*Deuteronomy* 30:19–20). In the sober climate that followed the return from Exile, the wise way for Jews seemed to be to keep to themselves and their own special laws.

WISDOM AND APOCALYPSE. Two other movements marked the later Jewish biblical period. The first is found in the wisdom literature of the Hebrew Scriptures. As many commentators point out, *Ecclesiastes* and *Proverbs* bear the marks of the prudential, reflective thought, expressed in maxims, that was available from Egypt. Somewhat incongruously, it grafted itself onto Jewish speculation about God's action, which suggests that postexilic Judaism found its times rather trying. At least, the wisdom literature is dour and sober compared with the historical and prophetic sections of the Bible. It retains a trust that God still has his hand on the tiller, but it finds the seas gray and choppy. Suffering had tempered the fire in the Jewish soul for poetry and prophecy.

The book of Job, however, is an exception. Job probes theodicy (the problem of evil and suffering), which surely is a wisdom concern, but it reaches poetic depths. Job reveals that the innocent do suffer mysteriously—that we cannot understand our fate, because all human life unfolds by the plan of a God whose mind we cannot know. This God set the boundaries of the seas, made the different species of all living things. He is not someone we can take to court, not someone who has to account to us. Rather, we can only cling to him in darkness and in trust. Because Job does not profess the older theology, in which punishment was in response to sin, instead proposing a mystery beyond legalistic logic, it brings the postexilic centuries some religious distinction.

By the end of the third century B.C.E., however, the constraints on Jewish national life brought about another reaction to the problems of suffering and providence. Job refers to *Satan*, an "adversary," and, perhaps because of Iranian influences, in the last years before the common era, a dualistic concern with good and evil came to the fore. God and his

It will be useful to consider the personality, career, and message of Jeremiah, for Jeremiah is a striking example of both the prophetic vocation and biblical spirituality. Born in the middle of the seventh century B.C.E. (in 645, according to some scholars), and coming from a priestly family, Jeremiah preached during the reigns of kings Josiah, Jehoiakim, and Zedekiah, until he was deported around 582 to Egypt, where he died. We know more about Jeremiah's personal life than that of the other prophets, and this shows a man completely dominated by God's call. He did not marry, because he wanted to draw attention to the risk that most children would not survive the troubles coming because of Israel's infidelities (Jeremiah 16:1–4). He would not take part in mourning ceremonies or festivals because soon there would be none left to mourn and nothing good to celebrate (16:5–8). As one might expect, these dire forecasts made Jeremiah very unpopular. Enemies conspired against his life (11:18–23); he was confined in the stocks (19:14–20:6); and for announcing the coming destruction of the Jerusalem Temple he was tried for blasphemy. King Jehoiakim considered Jeremiah his deadly enemy and had him flogged. Jeremiah reciprocated Jehoiakim's enmity, attacking him verbally. Indeed, his indictment of King Jehoiakim reveals so much about Jeremiah's character that the verses are worth reproducing:

> Woe to him who builds his house by unrighteousness, and his upper rooms by injustice; who makes his neighbor serve him for nothing, and does not give him his wages; Who says, "I will build myself a great house with spacious upper rooms," and cuts out windows for it, paneling it with cedar, and painting it with vermillion. Do you think you are a king because you compete in cedar? Did not your father eat and drink and do justice and righteousness? Then it was well with him. He judged the cause of the poor and needy; then it was well. "Is this not to know me?" says the Lord. "But you have eyes and heart only for your dishonest gain, for shedding innocent blood, and for practicing oppression and violence." Therefore thus says the Lord concerning Jehoi'akim the son of Josi'ah, king of Judah: "They shall not lament for him, saying, 'Ah my brother!' or 'Ah sister!' They shall not lament for him, saying 'Ah lord!' or 'Ah his majesty!' With the burial of an ass he shall be buried, dragged and cast forth beyond the gates of Jerusalem." (22:13–19 RSV)

Whence came this lashing tongue, this need to accuse the mighty to their faces? Jeremiah concluded that his painful vocation had been laid upon him by God, who had chosen him to be a prophet from the moment of his conception (1:5–10). His mission would extend beyond Israel, bringing the Lord's message to all the nations. Jeremiah apparently came to this understanding of his vocation while still a teenager, and the responsibility it imposed overwhelmed him. But the Lord would hear none of Jeremiah's protests, assuring him that if he spoke divine words he would receive divine support: "Behold I have put my words in your mouth" (1:9). "Be not afraid of them, for I am with you to deliver you" (1:8). So a prophet was formed, a man dominated by "the word of the Lord," the message his God impelled him to deliver.

Along with Jeremiah's calling came two visions (1:11–19). The first vision was of an almond tree. Punning on the similarity of the Hebrew words for "almond tree" and "to watch," God told Jeremiah that his vision of the almond tree was symbolically relevant: the Lord would watch over his word to perform it. The second vision was of a boiling pot, facing away from the north. Just as boiling water spilled out of the pot and swept away twigs and pebbles, so foes would sweep out of the north and inflict evil on Jeremiah's countrymen. Jeremiah himself would face strong opposition for delivering these oracles, but his enemies would not prevail. The Lord would be with him, to deliver him.

From the outset, therefore, Jeremiah was a troubled man. He felt a charge to bring before his people the unpleasant news that hard times were coming, as the just deserts of their irreligion. From the outset Jeremiah was also a poetic man, brimming with powerful imagery. In a few lines he could sketch the whole career of a dishonest king, withering him by contrast with his righteous father. In a few phrases he could etch the king's coming demise, depicting the funeral that none would mourn. The word of the Lord pouring from the mouth of this troubled man riveted his people's imagination and lashed their soul. Jeremiah's passion for justice, his almost obsessive sense that the people had abandoned the very basis of their existence by falling away from God, gave him the courage to flay kings and leaders publicly. Thus he asked the people, in the name of God, "What wrong did your fathers find in me, that they went far from me, and went after worthlessness, and became worthless?" (2:5).

As Jeremiah read the political situation, God would punish this worthless people, using Babylon as his instrument. King Zedekiah consulted with Jeremiah about the political situation, but the king's advisers were bitterly opposed to the prophet, fearing that his predictions of woe were destroying the people's will to resist the Babylonians. Babylon did lay siege to Jerusalem, and when in 588 or 587 Jeremiah used a brief break in the siege to leave Jerusalem, his enemies arrested him for desertion. Zedekiah soon released him from the dungeon but had him kept in confinement. Undeterred, Jeremiah continued to proclaim that the Babylonians would defeat the Jews, and for this stubbornness his enemies threw him into a cistern, with the intention that he should starve there. When Jerusalem finally fell in 586, the victorious Babylonians treated Jeremiah well, offering him the choice of living either in Babylon or Judah. Jeremiah chose Judah, and he urged his countrymen left in Judah to try to live in peace. Peace was not to be, however, for some discontented Jewish fugitives from the army killed Gedaliah, the governor appointed by the Baby-

lonian ruler Nebuchadnezzar. Most of the Jewish community feared Babylonian vengeance for this murder, but when the community appealed to Jeremiah for a divine oracle on whether they should flee to Egypt or stay where they were, Jeremiah told them to stay in their own country. The people would not accept this oracle, however, so they took Jeremiah and his scribe Baruch with them to Egypt. In Egypt Jeremiah continued his unpopular ways, predicting that the Babylonians would defeat the Egyptians and castigating Jews who fell to worshipping a heavenly queen. The Jews in Egypt rejected this rebuke, and, according to later legend, stoned Jeremiah to death. Overall, most of Jeremiah's warnings, visions, symbolic actions, and oracles were gloomy. Thinking that his people had enmeshed themselves in secular politics to the neglect of their religion, the prophet saw Judah becoming crushed by the much larger foreign powers surrounding it and thought this fate a fitting punishment for Judah's defections. Still, not all Jeremiah's prophecies were gloomy. Like the other great prophets, his message balanced judgment with consolation. If God was judging the people harshly, because of their wanton irreligion, God was also assuring the people that the future would bring better times. Jeremiah's most consoling assurances occur in chapters 30–32, which are a high point of biblical poetry and theology.

Chapter 30 begins with the formulaic introductory phrase, "The word that came to Jeremiah from the Lord." This word was positive. The days were coming when God would restore his people's fortunes. He would bring them back to their land, lost when the northern kingdom fell in 722 to Assyria and was threatened by Babylon. No matter how great the present pains grew, God would save the people from them. He would break the yoke of their foreign rulers, leading them back to serve him, the Lord their God, and a king like David.

With great poetic skill, the prophet plays variations on this theme. Behind the people's present sufferings is the hand of the Lord, punishing them for their transgressions. But that same hand will punish Israel's enemies: "Therefore all who devour you shall be devoured, and all your foes, every one of them, shall go into captivity, those who despoil you shall become a spoil, and all who prey on you I will make a prey" (30:16).

Similar poetry sings of what the restored people will enjoy: good fortune for the tents of Jacob, compassion on all Jacob's offspring's dwellings, songs of thanksgiving throughout the city and the palace, many voices making merry. "And you shall be my people, and I will be your God" (30:22). Harkening back to the exodus from Egypt, the prophet has God say that the people who survived the sword and found grace in the wilderness would come to know God most intimately. Why? Because "I have loved you with an everlasting love; therefore I have continued my faithfulness to you" (31:3).

Both the prophets and the Deuteronomic historian-theologians testified to the dangers to survival that Jews of their time experienced. Political subjugation by the much larger neighboring powers was ever a possibility, but it was less ominous than cultural assimilation. To preserve their identity, Jews would have to keep clear of their neighbors' fertility religion. Only an adherence to a quite different god—YHWH, the God of Moses and Abraham—could keep the people unique. Thus, the stress on a nonidolatrous cult and detailed religious law that we find after the period of captivity to Babylon was most likely a reaction to the threat of adopting non-Hebrew influences. For instance, both adopt-

ing kingship and holding agricultural celebrations could be false steps, because they could take the Israelites away from YHWH. When the Israelites were exiled to Babylon, Jews of the southern kingdom tested the prophets' theology. A few realized what they had lost by playing power politics and relying on new gods.

This Babylonian Captivity (or Babylonian **Exile**), when Judah fell to Babylon in 586 B.C.E., was a major divide in biblical history, everything before it qualifying as pre-exilic and everything after (or everything after within the pre–common era) qualifying as postexilic. The Exile highlighted the paradoxes of trying to give theological interpretations of history (say what God's purposes were in the Babylonian captivity as well as the significance of autonomous rule in one's own land for the full flowering of biblical tradition). Some of the most profound prophetic poetry of the Bible came from the cauldron of the Exile—parts of the present books of *Isaiah, Jeremiah,* and *Ezekiel.*

When the Persians gained control of the region from the Babylonians, Cyrus allowed Jews to return to Jerusalem. The relatively small number who did return lived a reformed life under Nehemiah and Ezra, choosing to rebuild the Temple the Babylonians had wrecked and to reestablish themselves on the basis of a strict adherence to the covenant law. Marriage to foreigners was prohibited, and priests strictly controlled the new Temple.

supporting angels fought against Satan and his minions. The world, in fact, was conceived of as a cosmic battlefield, with God and the forces of light against the forces of darkness. For the first time, Jewish religion started to focus on an afterlife. Pressed by the problem that the good do not necessarily meet with reward nor the evil with punishment, Jewish religion raised the notion that a divine judgment would mete out proper justice. Correspondingly, it started to imagine heavenly places for the good who pass judgment and infernal places for the wicked who fail.

The book of *Daniel* expresses these concerns through what scholars call *apocalyptic* imagination of the end of the current unjust world order. This imagination purports to be a revelation (**apocalypse**) from God about how the future will unfold in a great battle between good and evil. Psychologically, it is an effort to comfort people who are under stress with promises that they will find vindication. Theologically, it puts a sharp edge on the question of whether God controls history. The historical context of Daniel was the pressure of Antiochus Epiphanes to profane Jewish worship. The revolt of

MAIN ELEMENTS OF JUDAISM	
Myths	Abraham was the patriarch of the Hebrews; Moses led the Exodus from Egypt and received the laws
Doctrines	*Monotheism:* There is only one God; *Covenant:* The Jews were a people chosen by God to receive special revelations, a promised land, and responsibilities
Ethics	Ten Commandments; pursue justice and mercy
Symbols	Star of David; Torah
Rituals	infant male circumcision; *bar mitzvah* coming of age; wedding; funerals; annual holidays; weekly Sabbath
Leaders	prophets in Old Testament times; priests conducting animal sacrifice (until 70 C.E.); rabbis (teachers) of scripture
Scripture	Torah (first five books of Bible); rest of Old Testament has lesser status
Commentary	Talmud (a later commentary)

the Jews led by the Maccabees stemmed from this pressure.

Daniel joins apocalyptic concern with the older prophetic concern with a messiah, casting the future vindication of the Jews in terms of a heavenly being (the "Son of man") who will come on the clouds. His coming is the dramatic climax in the **eschatological** (end times) scenario that Jews developed in postexilic times. Thus, the Son of man came to figure in many apocalyptic writings (most of them not included in the Bible's canon), and among those who were of a more apocalyptic orientation, he was the preferred version of the messianic king. (Christians seized on this figure as a principal explanation of Jesus.)

HELLENISM. From the end of the fourth century B.C.E., the political fate of the Jews lay in the hands first of the Greeks and then of the Romans. Thus,

Greek and Roman influences mixed with Israel's wisdom and apocalyptic concerns. The ideals that some Jews accepted from Alexander the Great are commonly labeled *Hellenism.* Contact with Hellenism divided the Jewish community. Some priests and intellectuals took to Greek science, philosophy, and drama, but the majority of the people, sensing a threat to their identity, reacted adversely. By the time that Antiochus Epiphanes tried to enforce worship of Greek gods and destroy traditional Judaism, most Jews supported the (successful) revolt that the Maccabees led in 168 B.C.E. Herod the Great was appointed king of the Jews by the Roman Senate in 40 B.C.E. and helped to promote Hellenistic influences in Judea after the Roman conquest.

Overall, Hellenism influenced the Jewish conception of law, and it sparked the first strictly philosophical efforts to make the Torah appear reasonable to any clear-thinking person. Philo, a contemporary of Jesus, was a great expositor of this sort of philosophy. In the final decades of the biblical period, however, political and religious differences divided the Jewish communities. Some people, called the **Zealots,** urged political action, in the spirit of the Maccabean rebellion. These small guerrilla bands or brigands hid out in rugged terrain and ambushed columns of Roman soldiers. They also ambushed merchant caravans, giving the Zealots the status of mere robbers in the eyes of many middle-class Jews. (Note how the figure of Barabbas appears in the Christian gospels: robber or revolutionary depending upon the author.)

A different approach was advocated by another small group, the **Essenes.** Their solution was physical withdrawal from the influence of Roman law and Greek culture. The Essenes moved from the cities and relocated to the Qumran community around the Dead Sea. (The Dead Sea scrolls, found just sixty years ago, were probably deposited by this sect.) The Essenes devalued this earthly world and advocated ascetic purification for the coming Messiah, perhaps celibacy (approaches that did not resonate with either Judaism's past tradition or future focus).

A larger first-century movement was the **Pharisees,** laypeople who defended the tradition of the oral Torah and tried to update its relevance. The Pharisees were somewhat distant from the Temple that was the center of priestly, ritualistic Judaism. (The portrait of the Pharisees in the New Testament is colored by

COMPARISON OF FIRST-CENTURY JEWISH SECTS

DIMENSION	PHARISEES	SADDUCEES	ESSENES	ZEALOTS
Greek culture	opposed	accepted	withdrew from	opposed
Roman rule	opposed	accepted	withdrew from	rebelled against
Laws of Torah	strictly followed	loosely followed	other new doctrines	ignored
Appealed to	poor	wealthy	alienated	robbers
Apocalypse	coming soon	ignored	ignored	start it!
Role of messiah	great	ignored	ignored	ignored
Angels	accepted	rejected	ignored	ignored
Resurrection	accepted	rejected	transmigration	irrelevant
Heaven and hell	accepted	ignored	ignored	ignored

Jewish-Christian polemics and cannot be considered objective in its charges of hypocrisy.) Indeed, most Pharisees were quite sincere in their efforts to follow strictly all of the more than six hundred rules of the Torah. Doctrinally, the Pharisees, like their contemporary Christian competitors, accepted the doctrines of angels, final judgment, a coming Messiah, and a resurrection of the dead. The Pharisees were probably most popular among the poor, who were attracted to the call to pride in Jewish traditions.

Another first-century movement was the **Sadducees.** They were composed of priests and upper-class members who were associated with the Jerusalem Temple and stressed the written Torah. They were willing to accommodate to Roman law and Greek culture. For example, their sons would participate in Greek-style athletics. The Sadducees disappeared after the fall of the Jerusalem Temple in 70 C.E. They are presented in the New Testament as denying the notion of a resurrection and agreeing with the Roman establishment that Jesus was a threat to security in Judea.

RABBINIC JUDAISM

The forces who urged revolt against the Romans suffered a crushing defeat in 70 C.E., when the Romans destroyed the Temple in Jerusalem and cast most of the Jews out into the **Diaspora** (the forced resettlement of Jews outside Palestine). Despite the heroic resistance of many Zealots at Masada, a fortress of King Herod near the Dead Sea Valley, foreign rule stamped down all the harder.

The Pharisees and their successors picked up the pieces. The Pharisaic movement owed much of its concern for the punctilious observance of Torah to the lay scribes (lawyers) who arose in the postexilic Hellenistic period, but the Pharisees did not organize themselves as a distinct party until the second century B.C.E. Maccabean revolt. The Pharisees stood for a close observance of the covenant law, applying it in all aspects of daily life, trying to adapt it as new times required. This approach had come to dominate the scribes who preceded the Pharisees, and it dominated the rabbis (teachers) who came after them. The Pharisees sponsored vigorous debate about the application of Torah, which became a feature of subsequent rabbinic Judaism.

In the Diaspora these rabbis became the center of communal life. The Temple had fallen and with it the cultic priesthood. So the alternative to cultic sacrifice—an alternative that had begun in the Babylonian exile, when Jerusalem and the Temple were far away—filled the religious void. This alternative was the **synagogue—** the gathering place where the community could pray and hear expositions of the Torah. The synagogue became the central institution of Judaism after the destruction of the Temple of Solomon and the deportation of many Jews to Babylon in the sixth century B.C.E. In the absence of a place to perform priestly rituals, the custom of gathering for common study and prayer gained momentum. The synagogue rather naturally gave rise to the rabbinic movement, in that it emphasized study of the tradition focused in the Torah more than ritualistic sacrifice. Following the Diaspora of 70 C.E., the synagogue became the major Jewish institution, although archaeological remains suggest that synagogues varied considerably in their architecture and their degree of involvement in the rabbinic hegemony over Judaism.

As the teachers wanted to base their expositions on the teachings of their eminent predecessors, so they gathered a great collection of commentaries. Eventually, this collection became the Talmud ("the Learning"), a vast collection of the oral law that was composed of the *Mishnah* (itself a collection of interpretations of biblical legal materials) and the *Gemara* (commentaries on the *Mishnah*).

The *Mishnah* arose at the end of the first century B.C.E. from the new practice of settling legal disputes by a systematized appeal to recognized authorities. This practice prompted a conflict between the Sadducees and the Pharisees. The *Mishnah* represented a Pharisaic effort to outflank the Sadducees, who denied the binding character of the oral law and relied on the literal biblical text alone. After the Temple fell in 70 C.E. and times became tumultuous, a written record of all the great teachers' legal opinions became highly desirable. The recording took place in Jabneh, a town on the coast west of Jerusalem. Many teachers moved to Jabneh, among them the great Rabbi Akiba (50–135 C.E.), who later set up his own influential academy at Bene-Berak to the north. They began the real systematization of the *Mishnah* (the word implies repetition). The *Mishnah* continued and even intensified the scrutiny of every scriptural jot and tittle, but it went hand in hand with more pastoral activities. The interest of the Mishnaic teachers was relatively practical, as they divided Jewish reality into different tractates and discoursed on how relationships ideally would be. For example, in the tractate on women they discussed especially the transitions that ought to occur when a woman passed from her

father to her husband at marriage or when she passed from marriage to widowhood.

The *Gemara* was comment on and discussion of the *Mishnah*. The *Gemara* represents a second stage in the evolution of rabbinic Judaism, as the rabbis who gained more and more control during the Diaspora of the early centuries of the common era elaborated their views of the oral Law (which they thought had long accompanied the *Tanak*) and moved from collecting the teachings of the revered early sages (accomplished in the *Mishnah*) to collecting reflections, additions, and commentaries upon this first stratum of collected oral tradition. The *Gemara*, which collected commentaries on the *Mishnah*, plus the Mishnah itself, yielded the Talmud.

As this grand collection of commentary, the **Talmud** became the primary source of Jewish law and focus of rabbinic learning, composed of the *Mishnah* and the *Gemara*. The Talmud was probably virtually complete around 500 C.E. and existed in at least two important versions, that from Babylon and that from Palestine. It collected teachings, opinions, and decisions of rabbis concerned with continuing the tradition of the oral law—the ongoing interpretation of the Mosaic Torah. As Talmudic scholarship grew throughout the Middle Ages, the Talmudic texts became an encyclopedia of Jewish learning—science, linguistics, and theology, in addition to halakic theory. A traditional Jewish education was based on the Talmud, and it inculcated a good memory, a concern for legal precedent, a willingness to weigh authorities against one another, and a realization that interpretation was intrinsic to the Jewish experiences of both scripture and God.

Under the Roman emperor Hadrian, the Jews were so oppressed, especially by his decision to build a temple to Jupiter on the site of the great Jewish Temple in Jerusalem, that they mounted the short-lived revolt led by Bar Kokhba. The Romans crushed it in 135 C.E., and thenceforth Jews could enter Jerusalem only on the anniversary of the destruction of the Temple, when they might weep at the Western Wall.

In Babylon (present-day Iraq), to which many of the teachers fled, the Talmudic work went on. When Hadrian died in 138 C.E., Palestinian Jews' fortunes rose, and a new intellectual center soon was established in Galilee in northern Israel. There, under Rabbi Judah, the *Mishnah* was elaborated to the point where, when written down (around 200 C.E.), it could be both a practical code and a digest of the oral law. It consisted of six parts, whose subject matter reveals a great deal about the rabbis' conception of religious life. The first Order (part) deals with the biblical precepts concerning the rights of the poor, the rights of priests, the fruits of the harvest, and other agricultural matters. The second Order deals with the Sabbath, festivals, fasts, and the calendar. The third Order (entitled "Women") contains laws of marriage and divorce and other laws governing the relations between the sexes. The fourth Order, entitled "Damages," addresses civil and criminal law. The fifth Order deals with cultic matters and the slaughtering of animals, and the final Order concerns ritual cleanliness.

LAW AND LORE. Perhaps the best-known portion of the *Mishnah* is the *Pirke Avot* ("Sayings of the Fathers"), the last tractate of the fourth Order. It contains opinions of some of the oldest and most influential rabbis, but it is especially venerated for the spirit, the animating love, with which it infuses both the study of the Torah and the ethical life that the Torah should inspire. The *Pirke Avot* suggests the thought of sober, disciplined, studious minds—minds not unlike that of Ecclesiastes and the other wisdom writers. However, further study shows that the Fathers' sobriety encourages a study that reaches the heart and brings joy. This is explicit in Johanan ben Zacchai (2:13), but surely it is implicit in Hillel (1:12), Simeon the Just (1:2), and many others.

The rabbis called the legal portion of the Torah *halakah*. Through reason, analogies, and deep thought, *halakah* made the most minute applications of the Torah. For instance, it concerned itself with the dietary laws intended to keep the Jews' eating practices clean or fitting (kosher). It also went deeply into the laws for the observance of the Sabbath. For centuries such laws, in their biblical forms (for example, *Leviticus* and *Numbers*), had kept the Jews separate from their neighbors. As the scribes, Pharisees, and then the Diaspora rabbis concentrated their legal expertise, however, *halakah* became very complex. Certainly in the Roman empire, non-Jews strongly associated the Jews with their laws. Thus, *halakah* partly contributed to anti-Semitism (prejudice and discrimination against the Jews), insofar as

it stressed the sense of "otherness" that often is used to justify bigotry.

Kosher meant habits that were considered consonant with the Torah. The dietary laws appear to have developed from a combination of ancient ideas about what was hygienic (apt to promote health and discourage disease) and what was fitting or normal in nature itself—for example, separating dairy and meat foods (that means no cheeseburgers, and for some strict homes, separate dishes for meat and dairy products). Some rules governed the preparation of meats (e.g., draining all the blood), while the flesh of other animals were entirely prohibited (e.g., swine, camels, snakes, vultures, shellfish).

Kosher observance became a badge of Jewishness in many periods, serving to demarcate Jews from Gentiles and helping to preserve the purity of the chosen people. Probably more Jews kept the laws for this reason than out of any strong sense that certain foods were intrinsically unclean or that God from all eternity had wanted housewives to need two sets of dishes.

THE KOSHER DIETARY RULES

1. Certain land animals are prohibited—
   Cannot eat: pigs, hares, camels, badgers
   Permitted animals must have cloven hooves and chew cud—
   Can eat: cows, goats, sheep, deer

2. Certain birds are prohibited, especially scavengers—
   Cannot eat: vultures, ravens
   Can eat: ducks, doves, turkeys, chickens, geese

3. Certain fish are prohibited—
   Cannot eat: crabs, shrimp, clams, oysters, lobsters
   Permitted fish have scales and fins—
   Can eat: trout, bass, red snapper

4. All rodents, amphibians, reptiles are prohibited—
   Cannot eat: frog legs

5. Butchering and preparation of meat must be done in a special fashion so as to be humane and to fully drain all blood—
   Cannot eat: blood sausage

6. Cannot mix dairy foods and meat—
   Cannot eat: cheeseburger, veal parmesan

Rabbis were most interested in **exegesis:** discerning the most relevant possible interpretation and elaboration of a given passage of scripture. Ancient techniques included the mystical and allegorical approaches. Modern approaches use *hermeneutics:* trying to determine the relevance intended by the original authors and latent in the text as a somewhat transhistorical entity. Exegetes usually stress knowing the original language in which the text was written, informing oneself about the original historical context, and studying the symbols through which the text seems to be trying to express its assumptions, messages, hopes, and the like.

Balancing the strictly legal teaching and lore, however, was the looser, more folkloric approach known as *aggadah,* a treasury of exegetical (interpretive) and homiletic (explanatory and preaching) stories that applied biblical passages to a congregation's present circumstances. Where *halakah* reasoned closely, *aggadah* was apt to employ symbols. *Aggadah* drew much of its authority from the fact that Jewish theology had always held (at least in the dominant Pharisaic opinion) that an oral Torah accompanied the written Law of Moses and the other books of the Hebrew Bible. *Aggadah* often presented pious reflection about traditional passages, especially those of scripture, that pictured God at work creating this world in which we live.

This approach probably began with Ezra in the postexilic period, and it flourished when the scribes came to dominate the reassembled community's spiritual life. *Aggadah* continued to develop side by side with *halakah* for at least a millennium, ministering to the needs that common folk had for a teaching that was vivid and exemplary.

In Babylon, under the rule of the Exilarch (as the head of the Diaspora community was known in the common era), scholars collected the fruits of discussions of Rabbi Judah's *Mishnah* conducted at various academies. In addition, they immersed themselves in the ideas and *responsa* (masters' answers to questions about the Law's application) that flowed back and forth between Babylon and Palestine. Both *halakah* and *aggadah* contributed to this broad collection of legal materials, and the final redaction of the Babylonian Talmud, probably accomplished early in the fifth century, amounted to an encyclopedia of scholarly opinion not only on the law but also on much of the other learning of the day, including biology, medicine, and astronomy, that formed the background for many of the discussions.

TALMUDIC RELIGION. In terms of theology proper, the Talmud (whether the Palestinian or the more influential Babylonian version) clung to scripture. Its central pillar was the Shema, the Jewish proclamation of God's unity based on *Deuteronomy* 6:4–9. The Shema has served to remind Jews that they are covenanted to the unique deity responsible for the creation of the world and the guidance of history. Their relation to this God ought to be one of wholehearted love, and they have the obligation to make this God the focus of the education they give their children, the culture they develop, and all the distinctive features of their community life. The call to "hear" implied listening, to the divine or prophetic or rabbinic word. It also implied obedience and loyalty, as well as a regular effort to remember the great things God had done for his chosen people, especially the victory of the Exodus and the gift of the promised land.

The Talmudic view of the Shema was practical rather than speculative. The oneness of God meant to them God's sole dominion over life. He was the Lord of all peoples. The most practical of God's attributes were his justice and his mercy, but how they correlated was not obvious. Clear enough, though, were the implications for ethics and piety: a person ought to reckon with God's justice by acting righteously and avoiding condemnation. A person also ought to rely on God's mercy, remembering that he is slow to anger and quick to forgive.

Through such righteous living, a person could look forward to God's kingdom, which would come through the Messiah. The **Messiah** would rejuvenate or transform this earthly realm, which was so often a source of suffering. The concept of God's kingdom eventually included a supernatural dimension (heaven), but Judaism rather distinctively has emphasized that personal fulfillment comes through daily life.

The thrust of the Talmud, therefore, is not so much theological as *ethical.* The rabbis were more interested in what one did than in how one spoke or thought. So they balanced considerable theological leeway with detailed expectations of behavior. One could hold any opinion about the subtleties of God's nature, but how one observed the Sabbath was clearly specified. A major effect of this ethical concern was the refinement of the already quite sensitive morality of the Hebrew Bible. For instance, the rabbis wanted to safeguard the body against even the threat of mortal injury, so they called wicked the mere raising of a hand against another person. Similarly, since the right to life entailed the right to a livelihood, the rabbis concerned themselves with economic justice, proscribing once-accepted business practices such as cornering a market, misrepresenting a product, and trading on a customer's ignorance. In the same spirit, they pondered a person's rights to honor and reputation. To slander another obviously was forbidden, but they reprehended even putting another to shame, likening the blush of the shamed to the red of bloodshed.

Despite the caricature that they were concerned only with legal niceties, their writings show that the rabbis were very sensitive to social interaction. Lying, hatred, infringement on others' liberty—all these were targets of their teachings. The rabbis held that the goods of the earth, which prompt so much human contentiousness, were to be for all people. Thus, after a harvest, the owner should leave his field open for the public to glean; the wealthy are obligated to help the poor; and no bread should ever go to waste. Moreover, the rabbis did not limit their lofty social ideals to the Jewish community. Glossing the injunction of *Leviticus* (19:34) to love the stranger "who sojourns with you . . . as yourself," the Talmudists made little political or social distinction between Jew and non-Jew. Human rights applied to all. The spirit of Talmudic ethics, thus, is both precise and broad.

The Talmud goes into extreme detail, but it applies to all humanity. According to the Talmud, the great vices are envy, greed, and pride, for they destroy the social fabric. Anger is also destructive, so the rabbis lay great stress on self-control. On the other hand, self-control should not become gloomy asceticism. Generally speaking, the Talmud views the goods of the earth as being for our enjoyment. We should fear neither the body nor the world. In fact, God, who gives us both the body and the world, obliges us to keep them healthy and fruitful. To spurn bodily or material goods without great reason, then, would be to show ingratitude to God—to withdraw from the order God has chosen to create. Wealth and marriage, for instance, should be viewed as great blessings that one should accept with simple thankfulness.

For the truest wealth, finally, is to be content with one's lot. The pious Jew tried to raise his sights beyond everyday worries to the Master of the universe, from whom so many good things flowed. The great purpose of religious life was to sanctify this Master's name—to live in such love of God that his praise was always on one's lips.

HALLOWING TIME. Through religious observances, the Talmudists designed the social program for inculcating their ethical ideals. In practice, every day was to be hallowed from its beginning. This worked itself out as intricate interactions between myths, symbols, and rituals. At rising, the devout Jew would thank God for the night's rest, affirm God's unity, and dedicate the coming hours to God's praise. He was supposed to pray at least three times each day: upon rising, in midafternoon, and in the evening (women were exempt, because of their family responsibilities). Ritual washings, as well as the kosher diet, reminded the devout of the cleanliness that dedication to God required. Prayer garments became powerful symbols, such as the fringed prayer shawl; the phylacteries, or *tefellin* (scriptural texts worn on the head and the arm); and the head covering reinforced this cleanliness. The *mezuzah* (container of scriptural texts urging wholehearted love of God) over the door was a reminder to the entire home to adopt this attitude. Home was to be a place of law-abiding love. When possible, Jews would say their daily prayers together in the synagogue. In addition to private rituals, congregational worship became a major feature of Judaism.

The synagogue, of course, was also the site of rituals on the Sabbath and on the great feasts that punctuated the year. Primary among such feasts have been Passover, a spring festival that celebrates the Exodus of the Israelites from Egypt; Shavuot, a wheat harvest festival occurring seven weeks after Passover; Booths (Sukkoth), a fall harvest festival whose special feature is the erection of branch or straw booths that commemorate God's care of the Israelites while they were in the wilderness; the New Year; and the Day of Atonement (Yom Kippur). The last is the most somber and solemn of the celebrations: the day on which one fasts and asks forgiveness of sins. It is a time when estranged members of the community should make efforts to reconcile their differences and when all people should rededicate themselves to the holiness that God's covenant demands. There are other holidays through the year, most of them joyous—like Hanukkah, a feast celebrating liberation by the Maccabees—and collectively they serve the several purposes of a theistic cult: recalling God's great favors (anamnesis), binding the community in common commitments, and expiating offenses and restoring hopes. In the home, celebration of the Sabbath did for the week what the annual feasts did for the year. It gave time a cycle with a peak that had special relevance. From midweek all looked forward to the Sabbath joy, preparing the house and the food for the day that came like God's bride. When the mother lit the candles and the Sabbath drew near, even the poorest Jew could view life as good. Special hospitality was the Sabbath rule; rest and spiritual regeneration were the Sabbath order. Regretful as all were to see the Sabbath end, a glow lingered that strengthened them so they could return to the workaday world.

The principal rites of passage through the life cycle were *bris,* infant circumcision, through which males entered the covenant community on their eighth day; *bar mitzvah,* to celebrate the coming of age; marriage under the symbolic *hoopa* tent; and *kaddish* (a funeral prayer requiring ten Jewish males). These rites reinforced the doctrine that life is good (or at least that we should be committed to finding goodness in every stage and challenge of life), that the Torah is life's guidebook, that marriage is a human being's natural estate, and that death is not the final word.

THE MEDIEVAL PERIOD

From the seventh century on, this Talmudic religious program structured the lives of Jews who were mainly under Muslim rule in the Middle East and Spain. As a subjugated people, the Jews tended to look inward for their fulfillment. Muhammad himself took rather kindly to Judaism, because he thought that his own revelation agreed with biblical thought: monotheistic doctrine, daily formal prayers, fasting and almsgiving, the prohibition of swine's flesh. However, things grew more complicated when the Jews refused to convert to Islam, and under both Muhammad and his successors the Jews had to endure some discrimination. Nonetheless, Muslims frequently found Jews useful as translators or businessmen, and Muslim countries were generally tolerant. As long as non-Muslim religious groups posed no threat to security or orthodoxy, they could have a decent, if secondrate, civil status.

During the first centuries of Muslim power, the Jewish community's prestigious center of learning was at the heart of its Diaspora in Baghdad (the former Babylonia). According to Talmudic tradition, the leaders of the Baghdad schools gave *responsa* to points of law and held sway over community religion. They also fixed the pattern of communal worship, which hitherto had been a source of confusion and controversy. During the ninth and tenth centuries, the scholars of the Babylonian schools also standardized the pronunciation for the Hebrew Bible. These scholars (called Masoretes) supplied the vowel points, accents, and other signs necessary to make readable a text that had consisted only of consonants. (Pronunciation, consequently, had been a matter of oral tradition.) The same work went on in Palestine, and eventually the version of a Palestinian author named Ben Asher won acceptance as the canonical Masoretic text. At the end of the first millennium of the common era, Talmudic scholars emigrated to Europe, North Africa, and Egypt, taking with them the scholarship of the Talmudic school to which they had the closest ties. The Babylonian traditions were more popular, but in countries such as Italy, which had close ties with Palestine, Palestinian influence was great.

The two main Jewish branches in Europe, the **Sephardim** (Spain) and the **Ashkenazim** (eastern European), can be characterized by their subjugation under either Muslim or Christian rule, respectively. The two traditions shared more than they held separately because of the Talmudists, and their different styles in intellectual matters and in piety largely derived from the different cultures in which they evolved.

The Sephardic branch of Jews trace their residence in Spain to the time when the Romans forcefully deported them from Israel in 70 C.E., and they looked for the furthest point in the Empire to which they might be conveniently sent, Spain. The Sephardim established a glorious civilization in the tenth and eleventh centuries, in which philosophy, exegesis, poetry, and scientific learning were at their peak. Medieval Jewish culture was favored in the southern cities under Muslim rule—Toledo, Cordoba, Sevilla, and Granada—but also did well in Christian areas such as Lisbon and even Avila before the Inquisition. The Sephardim suffered greatly from the Inquisition. When the Catholic monarchs Ferdinand and Isabela completed the reconquest of Spain from the Muslims in 1492, the Jews were given an ultimatum: convert or leave. This expulsion was a trauma so great it led many Jewish cabalists to expect the coming of the Messiah. Many left for the Netherlands (a colony of Spain at that time). Others emigrated to the Turkish empire, which they hoped would be more benign than the Christian. Even those who converted and remained in Spain were not free from discrimination or persecution. For centuries, the descendants of these *conversos* were accused of practicing Jewish rituals in secret.

PHILOSOPHY. The early medieval period saw a ferment in Talmudic learning. As well, a Jewish philosophical theology arose. Whereas Philo, in the first century of the common era, worked at what could be called philosophical theology, trying to reconcile Hellenistic thought with biblical thought, the medieval thinkers, especially Maimonides, brought philosophy into the Jewish mainstream. Philo's strong point had been reading of scripture on several levels so as to remove the problems that the philosophical mind might have with anthropomorphism. Though he never exerted a decisive influence on his contemporaries, Maimonides (1135–1204) did. This physician and scholar from Cordoba combined Aristotelian logic and science. His work was in the form of apologetics, making Judaism a strong contender in the debates that were being conducted by the Western religions on the supposedly common ground of rational analysis. However, Maimonides' work was also constructive, setting Talmudic and traditional learning in the context of a philosophical system. The philosophical services of thinkers such as Maimonides were very useful in internal fights with literalists such as the Karaites, who (despite their fundamentalism about points of biblical law) mocked both biblical anthropomorphism and much of *aggadah* (because it was poetic and symbolic).

The great questions of this period of philosophical debate were the criteria of biblical exegesis, the relation of doctrine to reason, the nature of the human personality and its relation to God, God's existence and attributes, the creation of the world, and providence and theodicy (God's justice). In debating these questions, the philosophers based their work on the Greek view that contemplation (*theoria*) is the most noble human work.

Whereas for the Talmudist study of the Torah was the highest activity, many of the medieval philosophers considered the contemplation of God's eternal forms (through which he had created the world) the highest human activity. Maimonides became the prince of Jewish philosophers largely because he was also learned in the Talmudic tradition and so could reconcile the old with the new. For him philosophical contemplation did not take one away from the Torah, because the proper object of philosophical contemplation was the one Law we find in both scripture and nature. A key teaching in Maimonides' system was divine incorporeality. God had to be one, which he could not be if he occupied a body, since matter is a principle of multiplicity. To rationalize the anthropomorphic biblical descriptions of God, where he has bodily emotions if not form, Maimonides allegorized as Philo had done. The dynamic to his system, however, was the conviction that philosophical reason can provide the key to scripture. Maimonides has probably been most influential through the thirteen articles in which he summarized Jewish doctrines and which even today are listed in the standard prayer book:

1. The existence of God
2. God's unity
3. God's incorporeality
4. God's eternity
5. The obligation to worship God alone
6. Prophecy
7. The superiority of the prophecy of Moses
8. The Torah as God's revelation to Moses
9. The Torah's immutability
10. God's omniscience
11. Reward and punishment
12. The coming of the Messiah
13. The resurrection of the dead

In this summary a philosopher gave the key headings under which reason and biblical revelation could be reconciled.

However, Jewish philosophy before Maimonides expressed a somewhat contrary position. The lyrical writer Judah Halevi (ca. 1086–1145), for instance, insisted that the God of Aristotle is not the God of Abraham and the biblical Fathers. (Halevi's position is reminiscent of the later Christian philosopher Blaise Pascal, and it draws on the same sort of religious experience that made Pascal visualize God as a consuming fire—no Aristotelian "prime mover" but a vortex of personal love.) Halevi did not despise reason, but he insisted that it is less than full religious experience, or love.

MYSTICISM. One of the earliest sources of Judaic mysticism was Ezekiel's vision of the chariot (*merkabah*). In medieval Germany a movement arose among Jews called the Hasidim who upheld a relatively new spiritual ideal. What characterized the truly pious person, this movement argued, was serenity of mind, altruism, and renunciation of worldly things. The renunciation, implying some degree of asceticism, especially ran counter to traditional Judaism, for it seemed to entail turning away from the world. Indeed, Hasidic speech relates to the experience that has always drawn mystics and caused them to neglect the world—the experience of glimpsing the divine being itself, of tasting the biblical "goodness of the Lord." Then the divine love exalts the soul and seems far more precious than anything the world can offer. Hasidism in its medieval Germanic form is not the direct ancestor of the modern eastern European Jewish pietism that goes by this name. Intervening between Hasidism's two phases was a most influential Jewish mysticism, that of the cabala.

Cabala (also known as *cabbala, kabala, kabbalah*) means "tradition," and the cabalists sought to legitimize their movement by tracing it back to secret teachings of the patriarchs and Moses. This Jewish mystical movement started in Spain and flourished during the Middle Ages. The cabalists usually considered themselves followers of the Torah who were developing an esoteric (secret) wisdom to complement the esoteric wisdom of the halakic law. In their mystical writings and exercises, the cabalists emphasized the emanations of the divinity into the created world and the symbolic marriage of God with the Torah, which gave religious living a nuptial or erotic symbolism. Such secret or esoteric overtones stamp cabalism as a sort of Jewish *Gnosticism* (secret knowledge). The fullness of knowledge the cabalists glimpsed in their ecstatic visions ordinary human beings can only conceive symbolically. Hence, cabalists engaged in their own brand of allegorical exegesis of scripture, trying to decode secret symbols about divinity that the Hebrew Bible couched in deceptively simple language.

In the cabalistic perspective, the divine and the human spheres are interdependent. The fallen state of the world (most acutely manifested in the suffering of the Jews, God's chosen people) signals a disruption within the divine essence itself. Human sinfulness, it follows, reflects this divine wounding. On the other hand, human holiness contributes to God's repair, and so every human act takes on cosmic significance. In fact, human life can become a sort of mystery play in which the significant aspect of people's actions is their wounding or repairing of the divine life. When the Spaniards expelled the Jews from the Iberian peninsula at the end of the fifteenth century, the cabalists had the perfect crisis on which to focus their somewhat fevered imaginations.

The paramount book of the cabalistic movement, and the most representative of its symbolism, was the *Zohar*, probably written by Moses de Leon in thirteenth-century Spain. Known as the "Book of Splendor," it consists of imaginative contemplations of the emanations of the divinity through the different layers of creation. From 1500 to 1800, the *Zohar* exerted an influence equal to that of the Bible and the Talmud. The *Zohar* is similar to aggadic materials in that it interprets scriptural texts symbolically and in pietistic fashion rather than in the legal manner of *halakah*. What distinguishes the *Zohar* from traditional *aggadah* is its suffusion with the Gnostic ideas mentioned earlier. For instance, its commentary on the first verse of the Hebrew Scriptures (*Genesis* 1:1) goes immediately to what the divine nature was really like "in the beginning." Within the most hidden recess of the infinite divine essence, a dark flame went forth, issuing the realm of divine attributes, but the mystics saw them as the emanations of God's own being. Such a view makes the world alive with divine essence. It gives human experience eternal implications, because the emanations move through our time, our flesh, our blood. The *Zohar* turns over each word of *Genesis*, searching for hidden clues to the divine plan. It concerns itself with the numerical value of the words' letters (for example, *a* = 1) and correlates clues in *Genesis* with clues from other visionary parts of the Hebrew Bible, such as *Ezekiel*, chapter 1, and *Isaiah*, chapter 6. To align its interpretation with respectable past commentary, it cites traditional rabbis, but the *Zohar's* immediate concern is not the rabbis' interest in ethics but an imaginative contemplation of divinity and the divine plan.

The *Zohar* stimulated many mystics, Hasidim, and even orthodox rabbis to view creation as shot through with sparks of the divine seeking to return to God in redemption. It supported the notion that God is metaphysically married to the Torah and that the splendor of God (Shekina) is a nuptial entity that sets sexual complementarity and love at the center of the heavenly realities. In the last few years, the study of cabalistic teachings has become popular again, and not just among orthodox Jews. Many Gentile celebrities (such as rock star Madonna) now wear red threads on their wrists, indicating study with cabalistic rabbis.

THE MODERN PERIOD

Thorough exposure to a secularized, technological culture did not come to most of the rural population of the eastern European Jewish *shtetls* (villages), where much of the Ashkenazic Jewish population lived, until the twentieth century. Until that time the eighteenth century Enlightenment and reform had made little impact, for Talmudic orthodoxy kept the tradition basically unchanged. But the center of eastern European Jewish culture was the restricted urban district known as the *ghetto*. It was in this environment that modern mystical **Hasidism** was developed by Israel Baal Shem-Tov (1700–1760). His movement sought to restore the traditional practices, which they saw as endangered by false messiahs, arid intellectualism, and Talmudic legalism. The key was the pursuit of divine wisdom and joy. The movement quickly caught fire in eastern Europe, and thousands rushed to the Hasidic "courts" where charismatic masters presided.

VILLAGE LIFE. Hasidism remained vigorous in the villages well into the twentieth century. Hasidism set the charismatic holy man rather than the learned rabbi at the center of the community: the *tzaddik* (righteous one). Hasidim revered this holy man for his intimacy with God, his ability to pray evocatively, and his gifts as a storyteller. (As a storyteller he was an updated version of the ancient aggadist.) But the simple ones among them held the *tzaddik* to be a wonder worker.

Hasidism in the *shtetl* commingled with Talmudic tradition, blending legal observance with emotional fervor. Jewish village life hinged on the Sabbath and on three blessings: the Torah, marriage, and good deeds. The Torah meant God's revelation and Law. In practice, it meant the exaltation of learning. *Shtetl* parents hoped that they would have learned sons, well versed in the Law, who would bring glory to the family. Thus, the ideal son was thin and pale, a martyr to his books. From age five or so, he marched off to a long day of study, beginning his education by memorizing a Hebrew that he did not understand and then progressing to subtle Talmudic commentaries. The Torah shaped the economic and family lives of *shtetl* Jews because men tried to free themselves for study, placing the financial burdens on women. The impoverished scholar, revered in the *shul* (synagogue school) but master of a threadbare family, exemplified the choices and value commitments that the Torah inspired. Many men did work in trades (the state usually prevented Jews from owning land and farming), but even they would try to gain dignity by devoting their spare time to learning.

Glory for women came from caring for the home, the children, and often a little shop. So much were those responsibilities part of religion for women that no commandments prescribed for them exact times for prayer, fasting, synagogue attendance, charitable works, or the like. Women's three principal *mitzvoth* (duties) out of the traditional 613 were to remove a portion of the Sabbath bread, to light the Sabbath candles, and to visit the ritual bath (*mikvah*) after menstruation.

In the *shtetl* (village) marriage was the natural human situation and children were its crown. Father and mother were obligated to create a home steeped in Torah and good deeds (fulfillment of the duties and acts of charity). In popular humor, nothing was worse than an old maid, while an unmarried man was pitied as being incomplete. Of course, kosher rules and keen legal observance marked the devout home, which was but a cell of the organic community. That community supported needy individual members with material goods, sympathy in times of trouble, and unanimity in religious ideals. One had to share one's wealth, whether wealth of money or of mind, and the seats of honor in the synagogue went to the learned and the community's financial benefactors.

TRIBULATIONS. The community exacted a steep toll through the pressure it exerted to conform to its ideals and through the gossip and judgment that ever circulated. Nevertheless, most Jews gladly accepted being bound by the common laws and custom, and few could avoid being bound by the equally overt and common suffering. The urban populations in the Russian and Polish ghettos shared an almost paranoid life, with *pogroms* (persecutions) a constant specter, while the rural populations of the rest of eastern Europe never knew when some new discrimination or purge would break out. In both situations, Jews' mainstay was their solidarity in commitment to their traditions. Consequently, we can understand how threatening were any movements to change those traditions, such as the Reform movement or the Enlightenment must have been. The old ways had been the foundation of Jewish sanity. New conditions, as in Germany and the United States, seemed much less solid than long familiar suffering and endurance.

The bulk of the Jewish population in the late 1700s was in eastern Europe: the Russian empire, Austria, and Prussia. Their life was rather precarious, and attacks by Russians and Ukrainians produced a stream of emigrants to the New World. Yet European Jews contributed to the formation of the notion of the modern secular state, probably because they hoped that it would offer them greater religious freedom. Thus, the Jewish philosopher Baruch **Spinoza** (1632–1672) suggested such a political arrangement, and Moses Mendelssohn (1729–1786), a German man of letters, plumped for a secular state before the French Revolution. Generally, Jews' civil status seemed to prosper in countries or under regimes that were open to the new, liberal ideas of equality. However, when nationalism prevailed, Jews tended to experience more anti-Semitism, since non-Jews then considered them to be outsiders.

DISSOLUTION OF TRADITIONAL JUDAISM. The eighteenth century European Enlightenment's emphasis on human reason rather than traditional institutional authorities in effect attacked the legal and philosophical underpinnings of traditional Judaism. By extending rights of citizenship to Jews ("Emancipation"), the Gentile thinkers of the Enlightenment in principle took away the basis of the Jewish community—it was no longer a ghetto or a world set apart from the national mainstream, because all citizens were to be equal. By its philosophical turn to individual reason, the Enlightenment attacked the Talmudic assumption that traditional law and its interpretation by the Fathers were the best guides for life. Thus, intellectual Jews who accepted the ideals of the enlightenment tended to abandon Talmudic scholarship (or at least deny that it was the most important learning) and devote themselves to secular learning. This movement spawned the distinguished line of modern Jewish scientists, social thinkers, and humanists, but it meant that the Jewish community lost some of its best talent to secular concerns. It also often meant intellectual warfare between the advocates of the new learning and the defenders of the old.

REFORM. Thus, the traditional legal authority at the heart of rabbinic Judaism crumbled because of both the new secular learning and the greater attractiveness of the charismatic *tzaddik*. In response to this crisis of the tradition came a "Reform" of orthodox conceptions. For the relatively educated, the **Reform** movement meant an effort to accept modern culture and still remain a Jew. In other words, it meant searching for new definitions of Jewishness that would not necessitate alienation from the intellectual and political life of Gentile fellow citizens.

Among some of the main personalities of the Reform movement, the emphasis was on rational Jewish ethics and theology (and so applicable to all people). In effect, emphasis shifted from what was distinctive in Judaism, what gave Jews their unique status as God's chosen ones, to what Judaism could offer to all humanity. The stress of Reform was ethical. Reform Jews saw their tradition as offering all peoples a moral sensitivity, a concern for the rights of conscience and social justice, that derived from the prophets and the great rabbis but could serve the dawning future age of equality, political freedom, and mutual respect.

The Hasidic masters made a deep impression on the Jewish imagination, and some of the tales about them are wonderfully entertaining as well as deeply instructive. For example, there is the story in which Satan was tormented by the good he saw the Baal Shem-Tov doing on earth, so he schemed to overcome the Master. Calling all his servants of darkness together, he disclosed to them a wicked plan. He would station devils on all the roads that led to heaven. Whenever a prayer rose upward, toward heaven's gates, the devils would be able to keep it from getting through. After some days without prayers getting through, Satan would be able to go to God and say, "Look, your people have deserted you. They no longer send you prayers. Even your favorite puppet, Rabbi Israel Baal Shem-Tov, has ceased to pray. Take back his wisdom, then. Take away his people's Torah."

The soldiers of the Evil One listened attentively, and then slunk out to execute the foul scheme. Leaving no bypath unguarded, they lurked silently in wait for any prayer. When a prayer came, they leaped upon it, pummeling and kicking it. They could not kill the prayers, but they flung them sideways into chaos. Thus all of space became filled with wounded prayers, whimpering and moaning, lost from their way. On Sabbaths, the flux of prayers was so great that many got through to heaven's gate, but there a great army of devils saw to it that the prayers were rebuffed. Three weeks passed in this fashion, and Satan thought it time to confront God.

Going before the divine throne, Satan said: "Take away the Torah from the Jews." But God said, "Give them until the Day of Atonement." Satan struck a hard bargain: "Give the command today, but hold back on its execution until the Day of Atonement." So God gave the terrible edict, and the Jews were to lose the Torah. On earth, the archbishop issued a proclamation. In ten days, the bishops were to have all the Hebrew books of learning confiscated. Men were to be sent into the synagogues to seize the Torah, and into all the Jews' homes. Then they were to heap all the Hebrew books into a great pile and set fire to them. The bishop of Kamenitz-Podolsky in Russia was the most zealous in obeying, sending his servants into all the Jews' homes. On the Day of Atonement, a great fire would destroy all the books of God's Law.

When the Baal Shem-Tov saw these things happening, he knew Satan was mounting a terrible attack. Yet he did not know how Satan was accomplishing this great evil, nor how to counteract it. Each day the horror mounted as Jews were stripped of the Torah. In home after home, cries of anguish rent the night. Fasting and sleepless, the Baal Shem-Tov struggled on behalf of his people, sending mighty prayers toward heaven day and night. They rose on colossal wings at incredible speed, but the Enemy himself caught them outside heaven's gate and cast them aside. So the heart of Baal Shem-Tov emptied, becoming a great cave of grief. At last the Day of Atonement dawned. Rabbi Israel went into the synagogue to hold the service, and the people saw the fever of his struggle on his face. Hope rose in their hearts. "He will save us today," they said. When the time came to sing the Kol Nidre ("All Vows"), Rabbi Israel's voice poured out the pain of his heart, freezing all who listened.

It was the custom for Rabbi Yacob to read each verse of the lamentations aloud and then for Rabbi Israel to repeat it. But when Rabbi Yacob read out the verse, "Open the Portals of Heaven!" Rabbi Israel did not utter a word. The people first were confused, then waited in growing fear. Once again Rabbi Yacob repeated, "Open the Portals of Heaven!" but still Rabbi Israel did not utter a word.

Then, like a trumpet blast into the monumental silence, Rabbi Israel threw himself upon the ground, beat his head, and roared like a dying lion. For two hours he remained doubled over, his body shaking with the force of his struggle. Those watching in the synagogue dared not approach him. They could only worry and wait. At last, the Baal Shem-Tov raised himself from the ground, his face shining with wonders. "The Portals of Heaven are open," he said, and then he ended the service.

Years afterward, it became known how Rabbi Israel had passed those terrible two hours. He had gone to the Palace of the Eternal, traveling by the road that goes directly to the throne. There he had found hundreds and hundreds of prayers huddled before the gate. Some were wounded, some lay gasping as though they had just ended a terrible struggle, some were emaciated and old, and some were blind from having wandered so long in darkness. "Why are you waiting here?" the Baal Shem-Tov asked them. "Why don't you go in and approach the throne?"

The prayers told Rabbi Israel that only his approach had scattered the dark angels. Before he came, no prayer could pass through the gate. "I will take you in," the Baal Shem-Tov told them.

But just as he started to pass the gate, the Baal Shem-Tov saw the army of evil spirits rush forth to close it. Then Satan himself came forward and hung a great lock, as big as a city, upon the heavenly gate. The Baal Shem-Tov walked all around the lock, looking for a crack through which to enter. It was made of solid iron, however, so there seemed no way he could pass through. Still, Rabbi Israel did not despair. Now, for each of us living on earth, there is an exact duplicate living in heaven. So Rabbi Israel called across the gate to his heavenly counterpart. "What shall I do," he asked, "to bring the prayers before the Name?" Rabbi Israel of heaven told him, "Let us go to the Palace of the Messiah."

They went to the palace, where the Messiah sat waiting for the day when he might go down to earth. As soon as they entered, the Messiah told them, "Be joyous! I will help you," and he gave the Baal Shem-Tov a token. The Baal Shem-Tov took the token back to the heavenly gate. When he brandished the token, the heavenly portals swung open, as wide as the earth is large. So all the prayers entered, going straight to the Throne of the Name. Heaven fell to ecstatic rejoicing, and all the angels sang hymns of praise. But the dark angels fled back to their hellish dungeons, routed and fearful again.

On earth, the bishop of Kamenitz-Podolsky was lighting a great fire. Beside him was a mountain of Hebrew books, which his minions had readied for the flames. He took a tractate of the Talmud and hurled it into the fire. He hurled another and another, until the flames leaped high as the clouds. But then his hand began shaking, and he fell down in a fit. The crowd was seized with terror, and ran out of the central square. The fire soon died down, and most of the books were saved. When the news of this happening spread to other towns, they abandoned their plans to burn the Torahs. Fearing they too would be struck by seizures, the other bishops gave back all the stolen books. That was how the Baal Shem-Tov saved the Torah for the Jews, on the Day of Atonement.

When we reflect on this little story, it reveals volumes about premodern Judaism. The Baal Shem-Tov is the central hero, but there are many other actors in the drama. The evil genius threatening Jewish life is Satan, the angel of power and light who had turned bad. Hating God and everything good, Satan is constantly plotting against God's people. If the Jews had not had saints like Rabbi Israel, there was no telling how their misfortunes might have grown. Bad as life was in the midst of unsympathetic Christians, it would have been much worse without the sainted rabbis.

Reform Jews tended to be talented people who were either formally or informally excluded from national and university life. As a result, their visions of a new day led them to stress what in their own religious past might abet equal opportunity. Today, most American Jews identify themselves as Reform.

A response to Reform within Judaism was the self-conscious **Orthodox** movement, which insisted that the Torah be the judge of modernity and not vice versa. Positively, however, the Orthodox conceded the possibility that living with Gentiles might be a good, God-intended arrangement. No doubt, the breakup of Christian control over culture that marked the Western shift from medieval to modern times played a strong role in this reevaluation. That is, the Orthodox saw the wisdom in the Reform argument that living among modern Gentiles might free Jews of the prejudice endemic in medieval Christianity by letting Christians see that Jews could be amiable fellow citizens (in its most virulent form, that prejudice branded all Jews as "Christ killers"). However, the most recent strains of Orthodoxy in the United States and Israel seem to favor a return to self-contained rural villages or urban neighborhoods in which Jewish culture may predominate. Although the Orthodox sect is the smallest branch of Judaism in the world, its high birth rates make it the fastest-growing sect of Judaism today.

Conservative Judaism represented an effort to find a centrist position between Reform and Orthodoxy. Its founder was Rabbi Zecharias Frankel (1801–1875), head of a theological seminary in Germany. Frankel's position was that Judaism should change slowly, remaining true to its traditional character and only allowing slight modifications of traditional practice. In the United States, Solomon Schechter of the Jewish Theological Seminary of America was the central promoter of Conservative Judaism. Its intellectual center is the Jewish Theological Seminary in New York, its rabbinical assembly numbers more than one thousand members, and its league of synagogues (the United Synagogue) numbers more than one thousand congregations. Building on Reform initiatives, the Conservative worship service has introduced family pews, developed a modernized liturgy in the vernacular, and allowed women a fuller role in the congregation's ritual life.

Reconstructionist Judaism, a U.S. Jewish movement founded by Mordecai Kaplan (1881–1983), has taught that past Jewish concern with otherworldly salvation is no longer credible and that consequently Jews should translate their traditional concern for salvation into this-worldly terms: human betterment in health, political rights, education, and the like. Other reconstructionists have kept the same this-worldly emphasis but focused more on Jewish culture than "salvation." Whether this is a specific denomination within Judaism, or more of a secular movement away from Jewish traditional ritual and doctrine, remains to be seen.

ZIONISM. The movement most responsible for the establishment of the modern state of Israel is **Zionism,** a nineteenth-century movement of European Jews to recreate a Jewish state in the land of Palestine. This return to the holy land has biblical roots, from the time that Israel gained a land of its own centered on Mount Zion in Jerusalem. During the Exile Jews longed to be back in their promised land, where they alone could sing their native songs joyously. The Diaspora that occurred in the first century C.E. made nostalgia for Zion and the Western Wall that symbolized the Temple ingredient in all Jewish culture. Most of the medieval piety movements anticipated Zionism insofar as their messianism regularly involved the notion of returning to the ancestral land (and to the holiest of cities, Jerusalem). In the eighteenth and nineteenth centuries, Hasidim in Poland sent many people to the holy land, with the result that there were circles of devout Jews in Jerusalem. During the nineteenth century, Jews led by Theodor Herzl (1860–1904) began practical movements to resettle Palestine. The upsurge of nationalism in modern Europe tended to make Jews consider their own national roots, while new movements of social thought, including those led by Marx and Tolstoy, caused many Jews to dream about a new society based on the *kibbutz* (collective).

The greatest impetus to Zionism, however, was the persecutions that convinced European Jews they were in peril on the European continent: pogroms in Russia from 1880 to 1905, Ukrainian massacres from 1917 to 1922, persecutions in Poland between 1922 and 1939, and, above all, the Nazi persecution that began in 1933 and climaxed in the **Holocaust** of perhaps 6 million Jews in Nazi death camps. The aftermath of World War II and the sufferings that Jews had endured in the Holocaust (as the climax of centuries of anti-Semitism in Europe) had made conditions ripe. By 1948, about 650,000 Jews lived within the British Mandate of Palestine, and at the birth of modern Israel many hundreds of thousands more emigrated from Europe and from Arab lands (where, after the 1948 war, conditions were difficult). The main ideologist for the modern Zionist movement was a Viennese named Theodor Herzl. His witness of anti-Semitism during the Dreyfus trial in France at the end of the nineteenth century had convinced him and many other Jews that only

JUDAISM IN THE LAST THOUSAND YEARS				
MOVEMENT	WHERE STARTED?	WHERE TODAY?	MAIN THEME	RITUAL
Kaballah	Spain	coming back	mysticism	study Torah code
Orthodox	Europe	New York and Israel	strict adherence	study Torah rules
Hasidism	Poland	New York and Israel	mysticism and strict adherence	singing
Reform	U.S.	U.S.	accommodation to secular world	minimal
Zionist	Europe	Israel	reestablishing nation of Israel	resettling Jews in Palestine

by having their own nation could Jews be free of constant persecution.

WORLDVIEW

NATURE

Generally speaking, nature has not been so important in Judaism as peoplehood. In the biblical period nature was quite important, because the earliest "Jews" were shepherds or farmers. The earliest theology appears to have been a veneration of different *els* (gods) related to natural powers, and the constant lament of the prophets and other biblical theologians that the gods of the neighboring peoples (the Canaanites especially) were seducing the people away from prophetic religion is testimony that the cosmological myth held considerable attraction.

Designated Jewish holidays, the liturgical feasts, though they began as nature festivals, ran through the agricultural year and were expressions of gratitude for harvests. In the Diaspora the sacrificial aspect of early Jewish worship was replaced by the sermonizing and Bible reading of the synagogue. Celebrations still involved food, drink, and dance, but they were probably due more to a social sense, from a desire to affirm a common identity, than from a close connection with mother earth or father sky.

(Interestingly, though, in their elaboration of the Torah, the rabbis were remarkably sensitive to animals' welfare. They glossed the biblical injunction not to muzzle the grinding ox, and they demanded that ritual slaughtering be as painless as possible.)

URBAN VALUES. Many of the countries in which Jews lived, as a distinct and often inhibited minority, forbade them ownership of land, while their tradition of study tended to lead them into intellectual occupations and business. The tensions between *shtetl* Jews and Gentiles in eastern Europe, for instance, were due as much to different occupations as to different theologies. The Gentile peasants worked the land and valued rather brutish strength. The *shtetl* Jews did not farm very much, tending rather to engage in small businesses and study. Jews were not to fight, engage in hard labor, drink, or carouse. They were to be disciplined, cultured, and family and community oriented. Because few Jews lived on farms, they had to concentrate on living in densely populated areas. The Gentile peasants needed customers for their goods, middlemen for their trades, craftsmen, and doctors, and Jews tended to fill these roles.

ZIONISM. With Zionism and the return to the holy land, Judaism has brought back to center stage a theme that was prominent in premodern times—the predilection for Israel and Jerusalem as the most religious places, favoring the prosperity of the Jewish denomination. In the centuries of Diaspora, the typical Jew felt something of what the first biblical exiles lamented—the inability to sing and rejoice in a foreign land. That did not afflict the descendants of the actual exiles as intensely, for few of them returned from Babylon when they had the opportunity, but it mixed a certain nature orientation with Jews' desire to have a place of their own. Consequently, Israel became not just a venerable place but also a beautiful, fruitful, arable, desirable land. Thus, the biblical theme of a promised land joined with messianic hopes to link the new age that the Messiah would usher in and the people's return to a place flowing with milk and honey. Zionism drew on these traditional themes, joining them to socialistic (if not utopian) theories of working the land and living together in close cooperation.

Though few American Jews farm, quite a few Israelis live on *kibbutzim* and work the land (and quite a few American Jewish youths join them for a summer or a year). The land, if not nature, is most important to kibbutzniks. Because of Israel's ancient history and Jews' present need to have their own place in the sun, the Israelis now are more agrarian than their recent predecessors were. How that affects their religious consciousness is hard to determine. Many do not consider themselves religious, and they often view their life on the land, even though it brings them close to nature, in sociological rather than naturalistic terms. Frequently, then, they resemble other idealistic groups who form communes and farm in order to augment their freedom (and often to "purify" their lives). On the other hand, those who do form *kibbutzim* out of religious motivations are often fundamentalists trying to regain their biblical heritage. Still, that heritage is not so much harvesting God's earth as living where God made the Jews his special people.

SOCIETY

Few religions are as community minded as Judaism. The Jews were the chosen people—chosen as a group or line rather than as individuals. From tribal beginnings, through kingdom, Diaspora, and ethnic diversification, Jewish religion has always been a group affair. Of course, the Torah is inseparable from this

Explain Judaism using one of the scholarly perspectives we have introduced: Freud, Marx, Otto, Tylor, Frazer, Malinowski, Muller, etc.

EXAMPLE: Emile Durkheim viewed religion as a system of rituals that served to celebrate and reinforce social cohesion. Each element of Jewish religion—doctrine, myth, ritual, and ethics—serves that function.

Jewish *doctrine* is that there is a sacred covenant between the one God and His people. It is easier to see your fellow man as your brother if you both acknowledge the same father: God.

Jewish *myth* involves many stories about their great patriarchs: Abraham, Isaac and Jacob. The relevance of these stories about the past is that they note common ancestors for the diversity of the twelve tribes.

Jewish *rituals* (e.g., sabbath, Purim, Hanukkah) keep alive those myths by reenacting them in an interpersonal, social context of family (sabbath, Passover) or synagogue (Yom Kippur).

Jewish *ethics* serve two functions. One is to preserve the sacredness of the symbols, rituals, and myths (do not worship idols) and another is to unify the community (helping the poor).

Contribute to this discussion at
http://forums.delphiforums.com/rel101

phenomenon, for it is a special law designed expressly for the chosen, covenanted people. It sprang from a group sense that life must flow to "our" God, who led us out of captivity to be his own people. The Torah also specified the theological direction of Jews by giving election and covenant the forms by which they shaped social life.

Thus, the synagogue has been a popular gathering place, uniting the action of the people. The Christian *ecclesia* ("church") has a similar etymological meaning ("gathering," "being called out"), but the building it names has been almost as much a place for private prayer as for public gathering. Perhaps the relative smallness of the Jewish population has helped it to gain a more worldwide sense of community than Christians have had. Perhaps, as well, the relative mildness of its sectarian divisions has helped to keep Judaism a family affair. In any event, Muslims,

This view of Jerusalem shows the Western Wall ruins of the old temple. The sacred Muslim Mosque, Dome of the Rock, lies directly behind.

despite their democratic worship and pilgrimage, have been less united than Jews have been, and Christians, despite their lofty theology of the Church, have been more individual oriented and divided.

WOMEN'S STATUS. Jews, then, have focused more on culture than on nature. Women have generally been associated with nature, because of menstruation, childbirth, nursing, and—to male eyes—more intuitive, less cerebral behavior. Men have been associated with culture: craft, art, literature, and politics. Though this is a stereotype that does not describe the specific abilities or interests of individuals, many societies have used it, more or less consciously, to characterize sex roles. Therefore, the construct is useful in analyzing how societies view the play of physical nature in human societies.

This gender stereotype is somewhat applicable among Jews. During many periods of Jewish history,

women worked or ran the home while the men studied. Women did not read the Torah in the synagogue (usually they could not read Hebrew), did not have many legal obligations (only three *mitzvoth* pertain solely to them), could not be priests or rabbis (until recently), were tabooed during menstruation, and were both indulged and criticized for their "flightiness." Under biblical law, Jewish women were partially considered as property—akin to animals and goods. For instance, the laws concerning adultery and rape were principally intended to protect the rights of the male—the injured husband or father. The principal value of women throughout Jewish history was motherhood. They seldom could have careers and usually had difficulty obtaining the education that would have enabled them to be their husbands' best friends. They were the source of the family line and of emotional support, not leaders. In good measure because he enjoyed being the cultural center, the male Jew traditionally prayed thanks to God for not having created him a woman.

JERUSALEM. It is hard for Gentiles to comprehend the dynamics of the current conflict in Palestine, especially the dispute over the holy sites of Jerusalem. From the Jewish perspective, David was the sacred king, the mediator between heaven and earth, the top of the human pyramid, and from his line would spring the Messiah. The city of Jerusalem was the city of David.

When the Jews gained a new homeland in 1948, fulfilling decades of Zionist longings, Jerusalem again became the real center of Jewish geography. All the biblical overtones of the city of David lie inside the old walls. Historically, Jerusalem summons images of kingship, prosperity, a golden age. Sociologically, Jerusalem gives the Jewish people a realized dream, a place of their own to which, next year, the Messiah just might come and all the blessed might journey. Psychologically, contemporary Jews are apt to overflow with feelings about Jerusalem, some of them quite conflicting. On one hand, there is a desire to support the powers in the new capital that are trying to promote Israel's survival and prosperity. On the other hand, there is the knowledge that the majority of Jews still live outside Israel, often more prosperously than if they lived inside Israel, and that not all the things done in the Knesset (parliament) merit full support. Some policies emanating from the Knesset have made barren land spring back to life. Yet on the West Bank the ecological policies have become so mixed with religious aims that they often seem to be a military weapon aimed against the troublesome Palestinians. It is hard for sensitive Jews to know where to direct their support.

The prophetic emphases on justice, commitment to God, and walking in the ways of the Torah continue to shape daily life in Jerusalem. Down the streets hurry bearded Hasidic Jews and visiting Americans, devout religionists and Jews nearly completely secularized. The land and the ethnic solidarity have become lodestones to chosen people all over the globe. The Jews of northeastern European origin (Ashkenazim) who have been the main reference point of our story increasingly find that they must accommodate the Jews of Spanish origin (Sephardim)

and Middle Eastern Jews. Within a small country, an amazing diversity exists. Fundamentalists (Orthodox) seeking to establish new settlements are committed to fulfill a biblical mandate. Twenty miles away in the Hebrew University, professors teach that such fundamentalism is foolish. Meanwhile, the specter of the Nazi death camps hovers outside Jerusalem at Yad Vashem, the memorial set in the nearby hills. This specter has led many to vow "Never again!"

PROPHECY AND THE CHOSEN PEOPLE. Of the three key biblical figures, Moses predominated, because the Law that came through him has been the backbone of Jewish religious life. As different cultures were assimilated by Judaism, Abraham's lineage became less important than his exemplary commitment to God. Similarly, as political sovereignty became a dim memory, David's kingship became rather metaphorical, propping future hopes more than guiding present living. Moses, however, stayed wholly relevant: he was thought to have authored the code that kept Jews united; he was the mediator of the covenant into which the community circumcised each male. When prophecy had become central to Jewish religion, Moses became the prophet par excellence.

Prophecy, which often distinguishes Western religion from Eastern wisdom religion, is not so much the predictions that appear in today's tabloids as a discernment of what the divine spirit is saying to the people of God. The establishment of Moses as the supreme prophet testifies to the social utility that Jews have expected communication with God to bear. They expected such communication to result in communal renovation, strengthening, and redirection. Prophecy was not a display of individual virtuosity or a matter involving crystal balls. The master of the universe, the Adonai ("My Lord," substituting for Yahweh, which was considered too holy to utter) that all prayers bless, has bound Jews together as his people.

THE LAW. Without abandoning their ideal of the perfect doctrine outlined in Maimonides' thirteen articles, the rabbis generally have focused more on performance than on motivation or thought. One's doctrines about the nature of God (within broad limits) has been less important than keeping the Sabbath and

Traditionally, Jewish social life has involved many rituals. To begin with, there was circumcision, the ritual through which males entered the covenant community. In the Jewish perspective, circumcision is not a matter of hygiene. It is a sign of the pledge made between Abraham and God, a sign in the very organ of life. For the rest of his life, the man signed this way stands out from the rest of unsigned humanity. Naked, the Jewish man is clearly a Jew. (At least this was the case before the twentieth century, when the operation became routinely performed on Gentile infants for supposed health reasons.) With or without such health benefits, Jews would continue to circumcise their males on the eighth day after birth, the time when Abraham circumcised Isaac.

The circumcision ritual is called a *bris,* the Hebrew word for covenant. When most children were born at home, the *bris* meant a family feast, with crowds of relatives and friends, learned speeches, and general merrymaking. Each step of the ceremony was something to be stored in the memory for later meditation.

Contemporary ceremonies retain what they can of this tradition, gathering relatives and friends to celebrate the new birth. The *bris* intensifies the ordinary joy parents feel at the gift of a child, by emphasizing that the covenant community is being extended another generation. So the father of the child pronounces a joyous blessing: "Blessed are you, Lord our God, Master of the Universe, who have made us holy with your commands, and have commanded us to bring this boy into the covenant of Abraham our father." Ideally the father would do the circumcision himself, as Abraham did, but the accepted practice has become to employ a *mohel,* or ritual circumciser, to perform it. The *mohel* may or may not be a medical doctor, but he has been well trained in medical safeguards and antisepsis.

The next rite of passage for the Jewish child is the **bar mitzvah,** or ceremonial accession to adulthood. Recently, American Jews have been quite sensitive about this ceremony. There may be elaborate preparations, incredible eating, and a swirl of family emotions. In the case of American Jews, the *bar mitzvah* seems to have become an occasion to celebrate a relative freedom from discrimination. The religious tradition behind the *bar mitzvah* assumes that a child does not develop the capacity to grasp the concepts of Judaism, nor to fulfill Judaism's disciplines, until the age of thirteen. Before that time, the father is responsible for the child. The *bar mitzvah* marks the child's transition to personal responsibility. Donning the phylacteries that an adult wears when he prays, the bar-mitzvahed boy can now receive a call to speak the blessing over a part of the weekly reading of the Torah. In many cases this leads to a renewal of Hebrew studies, so that the ceremony can express a genuine mastery of Judaism's foundations.

With the rise of a Jewish feminist consciousness have come rituals for bringing girls into the covenant and adulthood. Traditionally, women were exempted from most Jewish rituals, that they might be free for family tasks. But as the boys' *bar mitzvah* came to occasion a great party, there were good reasons for girls to want an equal celebration. Thus, there has arisen the *bas* (or *bat) mitzvah* ceremony for girls, an improvised way to ritualize girls' graduation from religious-school training and to recognize their new status as adults.

Judaism gives marriage a great deal of attention. Unlike Christian society, Jewish society had no monastic alternative (neither solitary nor communitarian) to marriage and family life. (The Essene community at Qumran, if it was an exception to this rule, was shortlived.) The command to be fruitful and multiply also influenced Jewish attitudes toward marriage. The emotional and social fulfillment of the spouses certainly was much valued, at least in Talmudic times, but a strong focus also remained on procreation. The relatively late development of the notion of personal immortality in Judaism resulted not only from the lack of a clear sense of a spiritual (immaterial) soul, but also to the tendency to think that one continued to exist through one's offspring. In other words, the family line was a sort of concrete immortality. To some extent, this limited the significance of the individual. Therefore, marriage was a treasure of Jewish tradition in part because it prevented the individual from being totally lost in the abyss of death. From this and other benefits attributed to marriage, sexual activity derived a certain dignity, even a certain obligation. Tradition encouraged couples to have relations except during the menstrual flow. One of the customs of the Sabbath was that in its leisure spouses should make love. As the cabalists stressed, the Sabbath was the bride of God.

Traditionally, marriages have taken place under a canopy (*huppah*) supported by four poles, the original purpose of which was to provide the ceremony a sacred space. The day itself usually entailed a fast, and other similarities to the Day of Atonement, in the doctrine that on their wedding day God forgives a couple all their past sins, so that they may begin their life together afresh. Another custom was for the bride and groom to wear white as a symbol of purity. Jewish betrothal occurred by writing a legal document binding on both parties. The rabbi asked the groom if he was prepared to fulfill his obligations as stated in the contract (*ketubbah*), and the groom answered affirmatively by taking hold of a handkerchief or some other object given him by the rabbi. After the groom signed the contract, the men present surrounded the groom and danced with him over to the bride, who sat regally on a throne. The groom lifted the veil from

the bride's face, while the rabbi recited the phrase, "O sister! May you become the mother of thousands of myriads" (*Genesis* 24:60). The bride and groom then processed to the *huppah*, the bride circled the groom seven times (entering all seven spheres of her beloved's soul), there were psalms, hymns, a blessing of wine, and then the essential act occurred.

The essential act was the groom putting a ring on the index finger of the bride's right hand and saying, "Behold you are consecrated to me with this ring according to the Law of Moses and Israel." After this the marriage contract was read, seven blessings were recited, and the groom smashed a glass by stamping on it, to conclude the ceremony.

Funeral rites, the last stage on life's way, have involved Jews in a final confession of doctrine. Ideally, the dying person said, "Understand, O Israel, the Lord our God is One. I acknowledge before Thee, my God, God of my fathers, that my recovery and death are in your hand. May it be your will to heal me completely, but if I should die, may my death be an atonement for all sins that I have committed." After death there was a ritual washing of the body, a funeral dominated by the recitation of psalms, a ritualized burial, a meal for the mourners, and then the *shivah*, a seven-day period of mourning, during which friends were expected to visit and a *minyan* (quorum of ten) was to gather each day. The mourning period concluded with visiting the synagogue the first Sabbath after the *shivah*.

fulfilling one's communal obligations. This attitude encouraged considerable intellectual freedom, including lively debate, tolerance, and theological ambiguity. Also, it prevented the establishment of a clear-cut religious authority and dogma, such as that encountered by Roman Catholics in the magisterium of their councils and popes. The Law, which seemed so specific, had dozens of interpreters. On and on the Talmud grew, because most interpreters had insights worth preserving. One's religious commitment was expressed in action, not in speculation or confession.

How one used one's body, money, and time was more important than how one used one's mind or tongue. Such a practical view meant that the community could bind itself through rituals, ethics, and laws without excessive concern about their accompanying doctrines.

THE HOLOCAUST. Last, contemporary Jewish identity has been annealed as a result of the Holocaust. While exodus and entry into the promised land characterized Jews in biblical times, suffering and persecution have characterized Jews since the expulsion

Infamous gate at Dachau

from Jerusalem in 70 C.E. Jewish commentators have no consensus on what the recent past and the Holocaust mean, but they do agree that we must not ignore, deny, or explain away the evil of the Holocaust. Thus, Jewish identity, the theme of so many American novels, has yet to be fully resolved.

SELF

After prophets such as Ezekiel and Jeremiah, individual responsibility separated from collective responsibility. Furthermore, both Hellenization and internal legal development set apart individual reason. Jewish thinkers in Alexandria, Egypt two thousand years ago, reflected Platonic, Aristotelian, Epicurean, and Stoic interests in mind and reason. Philo, the luminary of these thinkers, tried to correlate Mosaic teaching with a cosmic law. In the medieval period, Maimonides, Halevi, and others tried to square the Torah with rational demands for a less mythic, more

analytic explanation of doctrine. Since the individual soul is the site of reason, such concerns inevitably clarified the personality's partial independence of group thought. That is, it underscored that any particular person might grasp or miss the divine Law.

Moreover, the Torah and the Talmud themselves inculcated something of this sensitivity. As a scriptural religion, Judaism demanded literacy and encouraged learning. But literature and learning are obviously cultural developments deriving from a common human nature that tend to distinguish people according to their talent. Thus, the bright little boy may distinguish himself by the age of ten. Through his unique gifts he may stand out from the crowd and even increase regard for his family. If he develops into a sage, he will join the line of masters whose commentaries on the Law are the classics. So, by stressing personal insight, legal study encouraged individuation.

To a lesser degree, Jewish mysticism and Jewish attitudes toward wealth also encouraged individuation.

Mysticism, like study, is a personal inward phenomenon. Despite its debt to tradition and its occurrence within a community of commitment, mysticism is a solitary pursuit involving an "I-Thou" relation. When mysticism flowered in Judaism, it produced revered personalities, such as the Baal Shem-Tov and the Magid of Mezritch. To their disciples, these *tzaddikim* were stunning demonstrations of the ardor that divinity could inspire. Their personalities were special, set apart, distinguished. Despite the threats that mysticism posed for the traditional rabbinic authority, the mystics were precious for strengthening the common people's commitment. Thus, one could aspire to Hasidic distinction, as one could aspire to rabbinic distinction. Because mystical prowess edified the community, it was a worthy ambition. Analogously, one could aspire to the (lesser) distinction that came with wealth. Judaism is not, comparatively speaking, an ascetic religion. As much as Hinduism, it views wealth or prosperity as a legitimate life goal. For his good fortune and financial talent as well as for his philanthropy, a successful Jew could win recognition. True, with success he was sure to gain a host of petitioners, but their attestation to his generosity somewhat offset the burden they imposed.

This description of the self must be qualified in discussing women. Since their vocation was marriage and practicality, their distinction was basically reflected—that of being a rich man's wife or a scholar's mother. Nevertheless, women had rights to self-expression, at least regarding nonscriptural matters. The *shtetl* tradition that a woman had no soul did not mean that she had no say. In matters of the home or the shop, she probably had the dominant say. In matters of affection or emotion, she surely did.

MIND-BODY UNITY. Judaism has stressed the unity of mind and body, eschewing a body-soul or matter-spirit duality. Scholars usually contrast biblical Jewish notions of personhood and the then-contemporary Greek notions. This contrast can illumine the tendency of Judaism toward an existential concreteness that most of Western culture has been struggling for centuries to recapture. For instance, Descartes, the father of modern European philosophy, worked hard to reconcile the opposition within the human being between its *res cogitans* (thinking part)

and its *res extensa* (material part). In contrast, the "soul" (*nepesh*) of Hebrew biblical thought was a unity of mind and body that could not be divided into thinking and material parts. So the heart rather than the head stood for the center of thought and emotion. Out of the fullness of the heart the mouth would speak. This conviction fought against the Hellenization of Jewish theology, which would have made the mouth speak what reason dictated. It fought against the legalism possible in rabbinic theology, allowing space for aggadic tales whose appeal was more than mental.

THE HUMAN SPIRIT. In prophecy Jewish religion found understandings of God's relationship to the human spirit new to human history. That is, the ecstatic experience of the prophets, who seem to have begun as wandering bands of exultants (*nebi'im*), evolved into something other than ordinary shamanism (which we may take as the typical model of ancient ecstasy). For where shamanism usually kept the world divine and usually confused the relations between imagination and reason in the ecstatic experience (though some shamans were well aware of the divine incomprehensibility), the prophets had experiences that burned below imagination to the base of the spirit. The burning bush, for instance, occasioned the realization that we only know of God what the divine mystery shows in time. Elijah's small, still voice suggested that God comes more through spiritual recollection than through natural storms. Jeremiah, finally, went to the core of the matter: Divine creativity best expresses itself by writing its law upon the human heart. That did not mean that the prophetic, or later the mystical, Jews did not mix myth, symbol, and imagination. The *merkabah* (chariot) imagery dominated even the philosophers' ruminations about God, while the cabalists' bliss was to imagine the divine emanations. Still, the union of the entire *numinous* experience (the entire experience of divinity) with ethical demands refined what it meant to be religious by stressing communion with a transcendent God. Implicit in the prophetic and Talmudic program was the proposition that real religion is doing justice and worshipping purely. Implicit was the twofold commandment of loving God (who is one) and loving one's neighbor (who is another self). This outlook developed a powerful concept of individual conscience:

In the Jewish Prayer Book one finds praise for the One God who is King of the Universe: "Praised are you, O Lord our God, King of the Universe." This prayer then itemizes the great things the King of the Universe does. He fixes the cycles of light and darkness. He ordains the order of all creation. He is the source of the light that shines over all the earth. His mercy radiates over all the earth's inhabitants. Because he is so good, he recreates the world day by day. His manifold works reveal his great bounty. Their beauty and order reveal his great wisdom. And what does the devout Jew ask of the King of the Universe? That he continue to love his people. He, the only One exalted from of old, the One praised and glorified since the world began, has been all Jews' shield and protection: He has been the Lord of our strength, the rock of our defense. In his infinite mercy, may he continue to love us. His goodness is for all time, so we may hope for this mercy. Daily he renews the work of creation, so daily he may be our reliance. The Psalmist knew this and sang, "Give thanks to Him who made the great lights, for His loving-kindness is everlasting." O God, make a new light to shine on Zion. Make us worthy to behold its radiance. All praise to you, O Lord, maker of the stars. The One God is also the revealer of the Torah. The Prayer Book expresses this conviction in connection with God's compassion: Out of tender regard for his people's needs, the Lord has taught our Fathers the laws of life. For their sakes, may he continue to teach us. May we, too, learn the divine Laws, trust more and more in the divine guidance. May we observe all the precepts of the divine Law, fulfill all its teachings. If we are to do this, God must enlighten our eyes and open our hearts. He must gather together our scattered thoughts, uniting our whole beings in reverence and love. This reverence and love will keep us from shame, and help us to feel God's aid. If we trust in God's holiness, we will come safely from the corners of the earth to the dignity of our own holy land. It is you, God, who are our deliverance, you who have chosen us from all peoples and tongues. We praise and thank you for having

drawn us close to you: "We praise You and thank You in truth. With love do we thankfully proclaim Your unity, and praise You who chose Your people Israel in love."

When the Prayer Book reproduces the Shema, it includes much of the Shema's original biblical gloss. Thus after expressing the call to love God with whole mind, soul, and strength, the Prayer Book reminds the people that the words of the Shema should ever be in their hearts. They should teach these words diligently to their children. They should talk about the Shema at home and abroad, day and night. The words of the Shema ought to be a mark upon the hand, or as frontlets (browbands) between the eyes. They should be inscribed on the doorposts of the home and on every gate. If the people fulfill these injunctions, they will find God favoring. So all Jews should stay mindful of God's words of the Shema, keeping them in their hearts and souls. The words should guide all that the hand works. They should be stamped between the eyes, to guide all that the eye sees, all that the mind conceives. In speaking of God as redeemer, Jewish prayer spotlights his intervention on his people's behalf. God has been the king of each generation, the people's only sovereign guide. He has been the redeemer of each generation, the One to whom all Jews must go in time of need. Creator, he has been a victorious stronghold, a fort no enemy could overrun. Through his redemptive interventions, he has shown that there is no God but he. Though God dwells in the heights of heaven, his decrees reach all of creation. The very ends of the earth stand or fall by God's Laws. Happy is the person who takes these Laws to heart, obeying the commands of God's Torah. Such a person experiences what it really means to have a Lord, a defender and mighty king. The true God is the first and the last. The true people have no king or redeemer but him.

Addressing God directly, the weekly Prayer Book prays: "You, O Lord our God, rescued us from Egypt; You redeemed us from the house of bondage." As though retreating to a favorite haunt of memory, Jewish prayer again and again goes back to the Exodus. God slew the firstborn of the Egyptians, and saved his people's firstborn. He split the waters of the Red Sea, rescuing his followers and drowning the wicked. When the waters engulfed the enemies of Israel, not one of the arrogant remained.

God the redeemer is therefore God the powerful, God the One not to be trifled with. In the Exodus episode, Israel received its greatest lesson in redemption. Ever since, Jews have sung great hymns of thanksgiving to God. Ever since, they have extolled God with psalms of praise. Ever since they have known that the Lord their God is a mighty king, overseeing everything from his high heaven. Great and awesome, he is the source of all blessing, the ever-living divinity exalted in majesty. As the *Exodus* episode revealed, the God of Israel humbles the proud and raises the lowly. He frees the captive and redeems the meek. Helping the needy and answering the people's call, he shows himself no respecter of earthly persons, a respecter only of what is right. So let all voices ring out with praise for the supreme God: Ever praised be he! As Moses and the children of Israel sang, "Who is like You, O Lord, among the mighty?" Who is like God in holiness, wonderful deeds, worthiness of praise? There is none like God, because there is only One God. The people God saved in the Exodus sensed this stunning uniqueness. They sang a chorus of praises by the sea. The Lord will reign forever. Rock of Israel, may he ever rise to his people's defense. "Our Redeemer is the Holy One of Israel." Lord of Hosts is our God's name. May the Lord be praised, the Redeemer of Israel.

Such prayer combines a remembrance of God's past deeds with a meditation on God's constant nature. Its regular accent is thankful and praising. God has made everything that exists. He has revealed his will to Israel. And he has saved Israel from its enemies. For these and all his other splendors, he deserves his people's full worship and confidence. Though king, Lord, ruler of heaven, he has deigned to concern himself with his people's needs. Though holy and righteous, he has manifested mercy and steadfast love.

When a person or a group prays in this mood, its words and images fall into an easy rhythm. One image sparks another, one memory brings another memory to mind. Phrases tend to repeat themselves, for the point is not innovation. In their time, God was manifest in nature and was a fellow-warrior, with them against their foes. In their time, good harvests and military victories derived directly from God's hand, while bad harvests and military defeats suggested the people had faltered in their religion.

What has predominated in the Jewish liturgy, however, is the memory of God's saving deeds. In times past God has shown himself the people's redeemer. Reviving their commitment by journeying back to the biblical experiences, generations of Jews have been able to open their spirits to the God who lay ahead of them, in the mystery of the future. God has given his people a way to walk into the future with confidence. Not only has he promised he would reveal himself to Israel through time, he has given his Torah to detail what holy living with him requires.

God alone is the mystery that should dominate and constitute the human person in its being or its morality. When Jewish theologians clarified such a monotheism, they dealt a death blow to all idolatry.

ULTIMATE REALITY

The biblical beginnings were deep spiritual experiences: irruptions of divinity that seized and formed the soul (more than they clarified reason). The God who

was revealed was lively, personal, and free. Perhaps because the genius of Israelite religion was not reason but spirit, the biblical Jews expressed this God's character as the world's origin and destiny in myths. That is, they expressed the truth of order, of humanity's proper place in and with nature and God, symbolically, from the "dead spot," the bottom of the soul, which revelation seizes. Moreover, having expressed its order mythologically, the Israelite religious genius hardly criticized its symbols, making little effort to

COMPARISON OF HINDUISM WITH JUDAISM		
COMPARISON	HINDUISM	JUDAISM
Conquering tribe	Aryans	Hebrews
Original economy	herding	herding
Country conquered	India	Israel
Conquest took place	2nd millennium B.C.E.	2nd millennium B.C.E.
Conquered people	Mohenjo-Daro	Canaanites
Economy of those conquered	agriculture, cities	agriculture, cities
Religion of those conquered	mother-earth deities	mother-earth deities
Scripture recording conquest	Vedas	Torah
Individual's place in nation determined by	caste (heredity)	tribe (heredity)
Emerging doctrine about God	monism	monotheism
Dominant persons 1000 B.C.E.	priests	priests
Who were members of	Brahmin caste	Levite tribe
Dietary rules	vegetarian	kosher
Evil behavior	karma	sin
Axial Age figures	mystics	prophets
Axial writings	Upanishads	prophetic books of Old Testament
Doctrine of afterlife	transmigration	resurrection
Proselytizing?	no	no
Heterodox offshoots	Buddhism, Jainism	Christianity
Reaction and commentary	Bhagavad Gita	Talmud
Mystical sects	yes (e.g., Vedanta)	yes (e.g., Kaballah, Hadisim)
Tools used by mystics	meditation, yoga	Torah number code, singing
Had to live under the rule of	Mogul Muslims, British	Babylonians, Persians, Greeks, Romans, Muslims, Europeans
Gained independence	after World War II	after World War II
Victorious in wars with	Muslim neighbors	Muslim neighbors
Woman leader	Indira Gandhi	Golda Meier

interpret them in clearer, if less complete, conceptual terms.

So the God of Moses "is" only what time shows him to be; the God of *Genesis* makes the world "in the beginning" from primal chaos, the status of which is quite unclear; and the God of Isaiah is placed beyond the world by a dazzling cluster of symbols. The fight of the best Jewish theologians has been to preserve the insight, traceable to Moses and the prophets, that God is not one of the visual arts and that the nature of our race cannot be the measure of God. God has to be beyond our measures—visual, emotional, even intellectual. God has to be allowed to be as God presents the divine nature: sovereignly free, though deeply committed to the welfare of human beings. Human beings have to suffer the fact that God is always going to be strictly mysterious: a fullness that human beings can never comprehend, let alone control. The weight of Jewish theological tradition has been that Torah offers guidance on how to live with the God who cannot be visualized, who must always be allowed the divine mysteriousness—guidance that divinity itself had offered as a gracious gift and kindly command. The core of some of the most significant Jewish theology lies in the intimate connection between Torah and the divine mystery—in guidance to honor above all the unimaginable Guide of Jewish existence.

SUMMARY: THE JEWISH CENTER

The center of traditional Judaism is the Torah. That there is a law or guidance, coming from God and leading to God, has been Judaism's first conviction and main treasure. With such a guidance, life is relevant, reasonably clear. When such a guidance loses its persuasiveness, as it did for large numbers of Jews in modern times, almost all aspects of life demand rethinking. Then the zeal with which the rabbis studied Torah may shift focus to such new concerns as physical science, social justice, or simply making money. Kept under high pressure for centuries, Jewish intellectual abilities cannot just relax and take a leisurely stroll. In old tracks or new, it has pressed forward to set things clear, gain new knowledge, redress old wrongs. When a Jew marshaled intellectual or moral energy, the old summons suggested that things might subserve a higher plan, society ought to succor its widows and orphans.

CHINA AND

JAPAN

CHINA AND JAPAN: 25 KEY DATES	
Date	**Event**
3500 B.C.E.	earliest Chinese city
1600 B.C.E.	Shang bronze age sculpture
660 B.C.E.	Jimmu, first Japanese Emperor
551–479 B.C.E.	Confucius
530 B.C.E.	traditional date for death of Laozi
403–221 B.C.E.	warring States period
5 C.E.	Japanese build national shrine at Ise
206 B.C.E.	Han Dynasty reunites China
ca. 112 C.E.	"Silk Road" links China with west
ca. 150 C.E.	Buddhism in China
285 C.E.	Confucianism arrives in Japan
550 C.E.	Buddhism introduced in Japan
595 C.E.	Buddhism proclaimed state religion of Japan
712–720 C.E.	completion of Shinto chronicles
730 C.E.	invention of printing in China
845 C.E.	persecution of non-Chinese religions
1130–1200 C.E.	Ju Xi, leading neo-Confucian
1175–1253 C.E.	Pure Lane, Zen, and Nichiren sects arise in Japan
1234 C.E.	Mongols destroy Chinese dynasty
1275 C.E.	Marco Polo in China
1549 C.E.	Francis Xavier, Catholic missionary, in Japan
1585 C.E.	Matteo Ricci, Catholic missionary, in China
1854 C.E.	U.S. Commodore Perry forces Japan to trade with West
1945 C.E.	Japan surrenders in World War II; Shinto disestablished
1949 C.E.	Beginning of communist People's Republic of China

HISTORY OF CHINA

There was something special about the sixth century B.C.E. In India, monistic mystics were writing the *Upanishads*, while Buddha and Mahavira gained followers. In the Middle East, the Iranian and Hebrew prophets introduced apocalyptic ideas. In Greece, numerous philosophical and religious movements began. Nowhere did this **Axial Age** (600 B.C.E.—200 B.C.E.) have a more profound impact than in China, where it formed the basis for later East Asian thought.

PRE-AXIAL CHINESE RELIGION

Before the sixth century B.C.E., however, were centuries, perhaps even millennia, of nature- and ancestor-oriented responses to the sacred, during the long Chinese prehistory. China, like most ancient cultures, did not develop religion as a separate realm of human concern. The rites, sacred mythology, and ethics that bound the Chinese people were simply cultural phenomena not distinguishable from the daily routine. Keep in mind, then, that what we emphasize here for

> *Chinese shrine.*

Chinese herbalists selected a potion because of its presumed yin or yang properties. Of course, in modern medicine, which derives from organic chemistry, researchers formulate medicines based upon properties of specific molecules.

Geomancy is another blend of divination and magic based upon animist understandings of spirits and the symbolism of land, water, wind, and architecture. In China this practice is traditionally known as *feng-shui*. Its task is to intuit local auras, site a grave, or design a building so that the occupants will not be disturbed by the local spirits (or vice versa). In a convoluted symbolism employing dragons and tigers, it has tried to make the living forces of nature yield good fortune by figuring out the spiritual lay of the land. What nature disposed, according to *feng-shui*, architecture could oppose or exploit. For instance, straight lines were considered evil influences, but trees or a fresh pond could ward them off. Consequently, the basic design of Chinese villages has included trees and ponds for protection. Similarly, a winding approach to a house could divert evil forces. The *feng-shui* diviner would plot all the forces, good and evil, with a sort of compass that marked the different circles of power of these forces. *Feng-shui* has prevailed well into modern times, and some American interior decorators claim to employ its approach in their work.

CONFUCIANISM. When times are uncertain, some people remember the good old days and hope for a moral regeneration, a return to family values. Such a man was the philosopher known as **Confucius** (551 B.C.E.–479 B.C.E.), although his Chinese name was more like Kong Qiu, Kong Fuzu, or Kung Fuzi. He did not view himself as an innovator, coming up with some new approach to fix or transform a decaying society, but as someone calling for a return to ancient traditions and values. He succeeded in codifying them into a guide for present and future. Confucius never claimed divine inspiration in the style of a Middle Eastern prophet; he was merely a teacher. More than two centuries passed before his ethical principles became the state orthodoxy (during the Han dynasty, 206 B.C.E.–220 C.E.), but from the outset Confucianism had a healing effect on Chinese society.

For Master Kong (as his Chinese disciples knew him) the way out of social disorder and toward peace could be obtained from the ancients—the venerable ancestors who were closer to the beginning and wiser than the people of the present age. What the ancestors knew, what made them wise, were the decrees of heaven. As we have seen, heaven meant nature's overlord. Thus, Confucius accepted the ancient pre-Axial notion that nature has some order. In his view, the way to a peaceful and prosperous society was to adapt to that order rather than defy it.

The order begins internally. One had to know one's own mind, and the human mind had to be disciplined, set in *ren* (fellow-feeling or love). *Ren* (sometimes spelled *jen* in transliteration) is the primary Confucian virtue, human nature as it ought to be, full of fellow-feeling or even love. It is what makes social life attractive, what long study and practice ought to develop. Confucians have viewed ritual, filial piety, and the other important virtues (powers of the mature character) as expressions of *ren* or ways to build up *ren*. When you reach the point where what you are supposed to do is what your heart really wants to do, then you have *ren*.

People could adapt externally through sacrificial rites. *Li* (pronounced like Robert E. *Lee*) is the Confucian term for propriety, ritual, protocol, courtesy, manners, and etiquette. *Li* was the virtue that ideally presided over social interactions, the gentleman's participation in public life and external affairs. It required knowledge of the traditional ceremonies and mores, discipline, and grace. Probably the origins of *li* lay in ancient ideas about ritual, especially that surrounding the king. If such ritual were properly performed, it was bound to bring such good effects as bountiful harvests and social rest. *Li* tended to encourage politeness and social sensitivity, including a keen awareness of the different social ranks. It supported a somewhat formal persona, with considerable care given to preserving dignity, appearance, and face. At its best, when fully animated by *ren*, *li* suggested that all public living ought to be artful and sacramental. Confucius approved of the notion that ritual makes what we might call a liturgy or sacrament of the vital flow between heaven and earth.

A good general guide to external behavior was the concept of *yi* (duty, oughtness, responsibility). It is what eighteenth-century German philosopher Immanuel Kant would call the categorical imperative. For Confucians it meant that in every situation one ought to act not according to selfish motives of profit or pleasure, but according to one's greater duties, especially the duty to honor the heritage of the past.

Another general guide to social relationships was the "silver rule" (so called by Westerners because of its obvious parallel to the golden rule laid down by Jesus). Confucius stated the rule in its negative, prohibitory form: Do not do unto others what you would not have them do unto you.

External order also required formal, structured relationships. Confucians referred to this as the *rectification of names*, which we could interpret as the need to figure out one's proper role in each social encounter and perform the duties of that role. Confucius outlined five basic relationships. Notice that the key is never one of equality of rights, but of reciprocity of duties. The first such relationship (and the prototype for the others) is between father and son. The father had the duty to protect the son, to feed and clothe him, and provide him with an education. But the son had the greater duties: to obey as a youth, to support his father in later life, and to honor his father after death. The second relationship is between older brother and younger brother. Especially if the father died, the older brother had the duty to provide for the younger brother as a dependent child; however, the younger brother had an enduring responsibility to obey his elder sibling in family matters. The third relationship is between friends. The elder friend was accorded more respect but had a duty to advise the younger wisely, mostly by providing a good example. The fourth relationship, the marital, also reflected this inequality: the husband had to provide for the support of his wife and widow, but her duty was much greater, to selflessly obey and serve him and his sons. The final relationship is between ruler and subject.

The emperor was often seen as the earthly form of the Son of Heaven, conveying heaven's will to earth. With many other ancient societies China shared the notion that the king was the sacred intermediary between the realm of heaven and the realm of earth modeled upon it. What the king did for human society, then, was both priestly and exemplary. By officiating at the most important rites, through which his people tried to achieve harmony with heaven, the king represented society before the ultimate judge of society's fate. By the example that he set at court and by the way that he directed imperial policy, the king not only served as a good or bad model for his followers, he also led the state in following or defying heaven's intent. The king achieved his power simply through his close connection to heaven. Confucius approved of the model leadership of the legendary kings.

Confucius had little success in public affairs himself. He never attained high office, nor often found a ruler willing to hire his counsel. One story says that Confucius left one such position when the young prince had a greater interest in dancing girls than in his advice. The master then spent fourteen years on a sort of pilgrimage, wandering about China. He often met with ridicule and rejection from those who considered his ideas naive and old-fashioned. He then organized a school where he taught young men, free of charge, in hopes that some of them would then become leaders or advisers, or would teach others who would attain those positions of power.

Confucians came to revere four works as canonical expressions of the wisdom that the Master himself had inspired: the *Analects,* sayings and dialogues of Confucius; the *Great Learning,* a short study on how the cultivation of perfection can contribute to the ordering of society; the *Doctrine of the Mean,* a somewhat metaphysical treatment of how the moral person occupies the center of the universe; and the *Book of Mencius,* a collection of sayings and dialogues of the foremost exponent of Confucian thought. Both the *Great Learning* and the *Doctrine of the Mean* are excerpts from part of the *Canons on Ritual and Protocol.* Collectively, these nine works constituted the literary corpus that the Confucian literati strove to master.

> The Master said, At fifteen I set my heart upon learning. At thirty, I had planted my feet firm upon the ground. At forty, I no longer suffered from perplexities. At fifty, I knew what were the biddings of Heaven. At sixty, I could hear them with docile ear. At seventy, I could follow the dictates of my own heart, for what I desired no longer overstepped the boundaries of right. (*Analects,* 2:4)

We become what we study, meditate upon, and establish as the treasures on which our hearts are set. Perhaps that is why Confucius was so insistent on hard study—constant effort during one's youth and maturity to master the wisdom of the past. These classics were not just the sayings of Confucius, but

Do you think that Confucianism should be viewed as a religion? Present a definition of a religion and show why Confucianism does or does not qualify as a religion.

Contribute to this discussion at
http://forums.delphiforums.com/rel101

books that had already been accepted as expressions of the golden age. These sources included the *Book of History*, documents purporting to record the words and deeds of ancient leaders; the *Book of Songs*, an anthology of lyrics from the early feudal states and the court of Zhou; the *Yi Jing (I Ching*, the previously mentioned yin-yang manual for divination); the *Springs and Autumns*, the annals of the state of Lu; and the *Canons of Ritual and Protocol*, three works on *li* (protocol).

For Confucius, the Way manifests itself as a *golden mean*. This meant that moderation is a great virtue. It is wise for one to avoid all extremes: do not be a spendthrift or a miser, but show appropriate generosity; do not be recklessly bold, but neither be a coward; show the proper form and degree of courage. The golden mean opens a path between punctiliousness and irregularity, between submissiveness and independence. Most situations are governed by a protocol that will produce graceful interactions if it is followed wholeheartedly. The task of the *junzi* (true gentleman or superior person, "magnanimous man") is to know that protocol, intuit how it applies in particular cases, and have the discipline to carry it out.

The death of a parent, for instance, is a prime occasion for a *junzi* to express his love and respect for his parent. The funeral should not be showy, excessive according to the community standards, but neither should it fall too short of those standards. The external funeral and ancestral rituals are important, but the internal grief process is even more essential to the balanced life. According to the rites of mourning, a man should retire from public affairs, simplify his living arrangements, and devote himself to grieving (for as long as three years). Too brief a period would be an error, but so would be too long a time.

As that example suggests, *filial piety* (duty to family) was a cornerstone of Confucianism. If the relations at home were correct, other social relationships

would likely fall into line. The Confucian classic the *Great Learning* spells out this theory, linking the individual in the family to the order of both the state and the cosmos. Moreover, the family circle was the training ground for a *junzi*'s lifelong dedication to humanity (*ren*) and ritual propriety (*li*). When a man developed a sincere love for his parents and carried out his filial duties, he rooted himself firmly in both *ren* and *li*. (We consider the place of women below.) Confucius' own teaching, therefore, called for a balance between interior goodness and exterior grace. He thought that if people knew their inner minds and manifested their knowledge through social decorum, society would have both the substance and the appearance of humanity.

DAOISM. The term **Dao** had various implications and inspired various schools. *Dao* could mean "ultimate reality" or "the way of nature" (a kind of natural law), or the way of personal liberation (and also a formula for harmonious living). Later Confucians and adherents to other schools frequently used the term, but in this section we are going to discuss three movements that have been known as Daoist: the hedonist, the mystical, and the alchemical. The only things that they have in common is a commitment to discerning and following the way of nature and the rejection of social conventions.

The *hedonistic Daoists* were people who looked at the decaying society of the Axial Age, gave up on trying to save the social order, and sought to save themselves. Usually this was accomplished by becoming a hermit: leaving behind the chaos of the cities and the villages, the annoying and cumbersome obligations to government and family alike. Freed from these entanglements, the hermit would find joys among nature. These hedonists were pessimists, defeatists who sought only to preserve their own lives and avoid pain. Their **hedonism** was not one of seeking sensual pleasure or amassing wealth and power over others (which tends to characterize our society) but, at best, one of the quiet pleasures of a hermit's freedom. These recluses ridiculed Confucius and flaunted their own violation of duty and social convention.

The prototype of the hedonistic Daoist hermit was Yang Zhu (also transliterated Yang Chu). His own writings (if he wrote at all) did not survive the bonfires. We only know of him through the later Confucians

COMPARISON OF HINDUISM AND CONFUCIANISM		
DIMENSION	HINDUISM	CONFUCIANISM
Country	India	China
Time	400 B.C.E.–200 C.E.	500 B.C.E.
Book	Bhagavad Gita	analects
Person with ideas	Krishna	Confucius
Role	deity	teacher
Reaction to	Upanishads, Jainism, Buddhism	hedonism, warring states
View of Deity	pantheistic, polytheistic	monotheistic
Deist or theist	theistic	deistic
View of extremes	pragmatist, inclusive	moderation
Emphasis	duty	duty
Type of duty	caste	family
Inequality accepted	between castes	within family
Emphasis on ritual	yes	yes
Mystical pursuit	acknowledged, but discouraged	criticized

(e.g., Mencius) who used Yang Zhu as an example of what happens when you don't follow Confucius. Yang Zhu could have lived anywhere between 600 and 300 B.C.E. (and it is possible that he never was more than a fictional representation of the hermit). He dismissed the value of such things as long life, rank, reputation, and riches. We have two famous sayings attributed to Yang Zhu. One is "Each one for himself," reflecting his disdain of the Confucian concern with the broader social order. The other was the statement that if he were told that he could save all of China simply by plucking out a single hair from his head, he would not make the sacrifice. This shows his complete rejection of the Confucian concept of duty before the avoidance of personal pain.

The *mystical Daoists* were another branch of hermits who developed a pantheistic conception of nature. They responded to the troubled Warring States period quite differently from the Confucians. They agreed that the times were disordered and that the way to set them straight was by means of the ancients' Dao. But the great Daoist thinkers, such as Zhuangzi (also transliterated as Chuang Tzu, Chuang Tse) and Laozi (also transliterated as Lao Tzu, Lao Tse, Lao Tze), were more imaginative and mystical than the Confucians, less petty than the hedonistic hermits. In their broad speculation, the mystical Daoists probed not only the natural functions of the Way and the interior exercises that could align one with it, but also the revolt against conventional values that union with Dao seemed to imply.

Of the two great mystical Daoist writers, Zhuangzi is the more poetic and paradoxical. His stories stress the personal effects of living with Dao. Laozi's orientation is more political. For him, Dao gives a model for civil rule, lessons in what succeeds and what brings grief. Insofar as Zhuangzi is more theoretical and less concerned with political applications, he enjoys

Although the intelligentsia resisted efforts to deify Confucius, the Chinese people at large long reverenced the Master with rituals and cult. To communicate the flavor of this cult, let us briefly describe some of the ceremonies that regularly took place at Confucius' shrines in the southwestern part of Shandong Province. Before the communist revolution, such ceremonies were an important part of the Chinese ritual year.

The temple grounds covered about 35 acres well wooded with old cypress, yew, and fir trees. Tradition said that one of the trees was planted by Confucius himself and that others were planted later during the Song dynasties. The temple proper was divided into six courts, the innermost of which was venerated as the area where Confucius had lived. In front of this innermost precinct were various tablets with inscriptions of praise by various Chinese emperors.

Inside the central area stood an altar, commemorating the spot where Confucius had received people who came for his instruction. Behind this altar lay a great hall containing a statue of the Master. The statue was 16 feet high and portrayed the Master seated on a throne. Near it were screens, embroidered with dragons, that could be arranged as a shield. Magnificent pillars of white and black marble supported the great hall, its floor was lined with black marble, its roof was covered with yellow tiles, and its ceiling consisted of 486 square panels gilded at the edges and ornamented with dragons.

Two of the principal festival days for worshipping at the Confucian temple were the Ting days of spring and autumn, when the stems and branches of the foliage were supposed to be flourishing. The minister of music would open the ceremonies, which featured music used in Confucius' own day (but composed even earlier, supposedly about 2000 B.C.E.). The entire ritual employed symbols and artifacts considered to come from the ancient days, when the model heroes whom Confucius had revered had led Chinese society wisely by their commitment to following the dictates of heaven. The dominant cloth, for instance, was a pure white

silk, which ancient chiefs used to give people they wished to take into their employ. Other symbols of the Ting ceremony included the head of an ox (chief of the domestic animals, who leaves broad permanent footprints); a pig (an animal with a will of its own, as its bristles suggest); and a sheep (plump for food and useful for wool). The incense used suggested the fragrance of virtue, while the wine and food typified the abundance of a virtuous kingdom. The boys performing the ceremonial dance dressed in ancient costumes, bearing in one hand a flute and in the other a pheasant feather. The flute represented the refinement music produces, while the feather stood for the adornment of learning.

Obviously, this ceremony, like most of the others that took place in Confucius' temple throughout the year, was meant to convey elegantly the benefits of virtue and breeding. In tune with the cosmic rhythms, the dancers suggested how any diligent student of virtue might hope one day to live, how any well-ordered state might hope to flourish.

Some of the hymns sung during the sacrifices to Confucius suggest the respect, veneration, and religious need his cult expressed. In one hymn, the choir begins, "Great is Confucius!" He stands in the realm of heaven and earth, he can teach the ten thousand ages. His power brought lucky portents: the unicorn's horn gained a tuft of silk. He unveiled the sun and the moon, making heaven and earth fresh and joyful. During the offering of the gifts to Confucius, the choir members would sing: "I think of thy bright virtue." Never had there been a human being equal to the Master. His teaching was in all respects complete. The vessels people offer today are filled as vessels have been filled through thousands of years. From time immemorial, the Ting days have been sweet with the smell of sacrifice, adorned with clear wine.

Later in the ceremony, the choir referred to the traditional sounds of the drum and the bell. Echoing as the celebrant offered the ritual wine, the drum and bell expressed the reverence and harmony at the heart of the ceremony. The rites proceeded, the music cleansed the participants' hearts, and the liturgy reached a point of perfection—let all rejoice!

Then the choir would remember how people had performed these holy rites since antiquity. Even primitive people performed them, wearing rough skin hats. Though these ancient ancestors had only the fruit of the ground to offer, their music was orderly. Only heaven has ever guided any people well, and only a sage of Confucius' stature could have suited his instructions to the needs of any given hour. Following him, present-day people could carry out their moral duties properly, reverencing the emperor and their elders. Confucius taught his followers the link between sacrifice and happiness. Who would dare not be reverent in his hall? In their joy, all who prosper remember him as the source of their culture. Like the mountains of Fu and Yi, the rivers of Zhu and Si, Confucius' beautiful acts have spread his influence high above and all around. The sacrifice reminds all of his great virtue. He renovates thousands of the people. He inspires their schools and instruction halls. As elements of the cult of Confucius suggest, Confucianism built on Chinese customs that had long antedated the Master. Indeed, sacrifices such as the one we have described can be traced as far back as the Shang dynasty, which is the limit of current archeological research.

Most emperors after Confucius gravitated toward Confucianism rather than Buddhism or Daoism because Confucianism offered social thought more likely to produce docile subjects. Therefore, they found it useful to involve themselves in the Confucian sacrifices. Thus the emperor himself would officiate at the major ceremonies, as clan heads had since earliest times, while Confucian bureaucrats would officiate at lesser ceremonies in the capital and at state occasions in the provinces. This meant that there was no special caste of Confucian priests. In Confucianism, state official and religious priest merged, becoming but two faces of one public functionary. Thus Confucius was in effect the patron saint of the literati. As other clans had their divine protectors, so the literati had Confucius. The difference was that the literati headed the corps of civil servants. Their "clan" staffed the government offices, transmitted the imperial will. As teacher, cult figure, and model, Confucius gave civil servants the sanction of tradition and sober wisdom. Through him came the wisdom of the ancestors, the basis of good order in his or any time.

By the seventeenth century C.E., the diverse elements of the Confucian tradition had been merged into a rather unwieldy official cult. According to an official list of those to whom imperial worship was due in the seventeenth century, there were three classes of worthies. First came the Empress Earth, the imperial ancestors, and the guardian spirits of the land and the harvest. Second came the sun, the moon, the emperors of the preceding dynasties, the patrons of agriculture and sericulture (raising silkworms), the spirits of the earth, the planet Jupiter, whose revolution around the sun regulated the Chinese calendar, and Confucius. (In 1907 Confucius was moved up to the first class.) Third came the patron saints of medicine, war, and literature, the North Star, the god of Beijing, the god of fire, the dragons of several pools in Beijing, the god of artillery, the god of the soil, the patron saint of the mechanical arts, the god of the furnace, the god of the granary, the gods of the doors, and many official patriots.

This list illustrates the amalgamating tendency of the Confucian tradition. On the list's map of reality are the imprints of ancestor veneration, veneration of the deities of the earth, veneration of the patron gods or saints of particular clans, and veneration of Confucius, the mortal whose interpretation of the past was most congenial to the crown. Some of the deities in this list are very ancient, going back to the Shang and Zhou dynasties, at the very beginnings of Chinese history. During the Qing dynasty (1644–1911), the government instructed its officials in the particulars of worshiping the cult figures of the several ranks. The official was to bathe, fast, prostrate himself, and offer prayers. He was to make thanksgiving offerings of incense, lighted candles, gems, fruits, cooked foods, salted vegetables, wine, and other gifts. For special occasions sacrifices of whole oxen, sheep, pigs, deer, or other game were appropriate, as was a burnt sacrifice of a whole bullock. Music and dancing were to accompany these sacrifices. If the sacrifice was to a deity of the first rank, the official had to "fast" for three days before it. For sacrifices to deities of the second rank, two fast days sufficed. Fasting meant refraining from flesh, strong-smelling vegetables (such as leeks and onions), and wine.

Moreover, officials were to see to it that during important ceremonial seasons there were no criminal proceedings, no parties, no visits to the sick, and no mourning of the dead. They were especially to forbid entering the chamber of a dead woman, sacrificing to spirits, and sweeping a tomb. The government commissioned inspectors to check on the officials who had been delegated responsibility for the Confucian cult, to make sure that they followed these prescriptions scrupulously. Behind this concern that the officiants be properly prepared lay the Confucian conviction that a province follow the moral character of its officials. If the officials were scrupulous in performing the rites, the people would be orderly. As Confucius was reputed to have said (*Analects*, 2:3), people led by laws and restrained by punishments will avoid laws and punishments without qualm. People led by moral example and restrained by social ritual will develop a sense of shame and become good.

Present a verse from the Bible and explain how it is consistent with the teachings of Confucius.

Contribute to this discussion at
http://forums.delphiforums.com/rel101

a certain logical priority over Laozi. Thus, even though he probably came after Laozi historically, we discuss him first.

Zhuangzi. For **Zhuangzi** (369 B.C.E.–286 B.C.E.) the Dao, or Way, of nature was the way of happiness, while the artificial way of social convention was the way of sadness. The path to become one with nature is to change one's viewpoint or attitude. We must realize that identity is socially constructed: we are who we think we are. The famous butterfly story illustrates this precept. Zhuangzi dreamed he was a butterfly. Then he woke up and wondered if he were really awake, or just a butterfly dreaming that it was Zhuangzi.

The key is to cultivate "creative quietude" through meditative discipline. Anyone who advances in the "fasting of the spirit" that the ancients practiced can achieve this oneness. Apparently such "fasting of the spirit" was a meditative regime in which one laid aside distractions and let simple, deep powers of spiritual consciousness issue forth.

Zhuangzi pictured those powers rather dramatically: they can send the sage flying on the clouds or riding on the winds, for they free the soul so that it can be directed by Dao itself. Dao is the wind blowing on the ten thousand things, the music of the spheres. With little regard for petty humankind, it works nature's rhythms. The way to peace, spiritual ecstasy, and long life is to join nature's rhythms. But by joining nature's rhythms, one abandons social conventions. (Indeed, the creative quietude of meditation seeks to undo social conventions.) The Dao liberates our human judgments of good and bad, right and wrong. Indeed, the Daoist is totally committed to ultimate relevance, so he transcends all cognitive dichotomies of conceptual meaning. The sage realizes that the monistic, holistic Dao is not naturally divided. Things are only delineated by human description in the service of some social order. The sage even transcends the duality of self and non-self. He transcends his own ego (sense of individual self), liberating the true self, who is childlike, spontaneous, unpretentious.

Therefore, the mystical Daoist may be seen as eccentric from the conventional perspective of the rest of society, for he (or she, though women seldom predominated in Chinese society) prefers obscure peace to troubled power, leisurely contemplation to hectic productivity.

In rather technical terms, Zhuangzi attacked those who thought they could tie language directly to thought and so clarify all discourse. If Dao touches language and thought, he showed, they become highly symbolic.

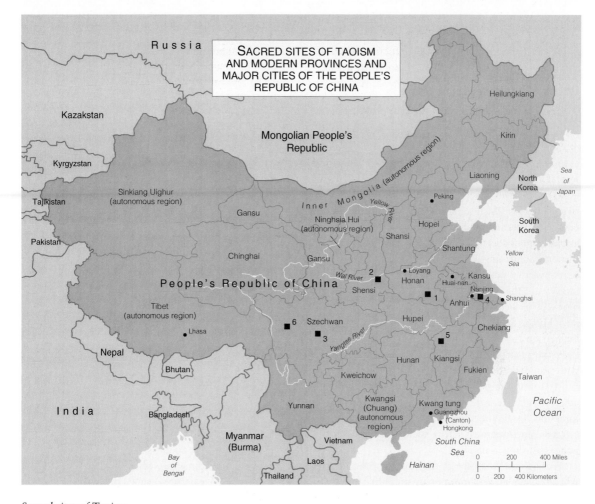

Sacred sites of Taoism

Moreover, Zhuangzi made his attack on conventional values and language into simple good sense. It is the worthless, cast-off, unpopular trees and people that survive. Those who would be prominent, who would shine in public, often end up without a limb (as punishment for crime or disfavor). When he was asked to join the government, Zhuangzi said he would rather drag his tail in the mud like a turtle than become as ornamental as a gold-inlaid tortoise shell in the Emperor's palace. When his wife died, he sang and drummed instead of mourning, for she was just following Dao, just taking another turn in the process by which matter keeps changing. For Zhuangzi there was no real death, for the individual self did not really exist to begin with. The Daoist sage achieves immortality in the sense that he or she is united with the Dao, and the Dao is immortal.

Puncturing cant, deflating pomposity, excoriating our tendency to trade interior freedom for exterior position, Zhuangzi ridiculed the sober Confucians. They, like other prosaic realists, seemed too dull for a life of spiritual adventure, for a Dao as magnificent as the heavens and as close as the dung.

Laozi. The mystical writing style of **Laozi** (ca. 600 B.C.E.) is more impersonal. The classic attributed to him is called the **Daodejing** (also transliterated as *Tao Te Ching*), and is often translated into English as, *The Way and the Power.* It is possible that Laozi the person never existed and is merely the fictional sage created by a committee of Daoist authors who compiled the book. (Laozi's existence is less certain than that of Confucius or Zhuangzi.) Confucius and Laozi could have been contemporaries, and there are legends about the two men meeting. In the Daoist versions of the legends, Laozi points out to Confucius that he has brought much confusion to humanity and separated people from the true source of order: nature.

Whether or not Laozi ever met with Confucius, or even existed, we do have an important text to analyze. The book itself has become a world classic, in good measure because of its mystic depth (and evocative vagueness). In it a very original mind meditates on Dao's paradoxical qualities, gleaning lessons about human society. The movement of the Dao is through something called *wuwei* (active not-doing or, conversely, passive action). Three of the principal images are the valley, the female, and the uncarved block. Together, they indicate Dao's distance from most human expectations. The valley symbolizes Dao's inclination toward the lowly, the underlying, rather than the prominent or impressive. (The valley fills with water because it does not resist it.) Laozi's female is a lesson in the power of passivity, of yielding and adaptability. She influences not by assault but by indirection, by nuance and suggestion. The uncarved block is human nature before society limits it. These images all show *wuwei*.

Wuwei is also shown in the power of the infant, whose helplessness can dominate an entire family. It is in the power of water, which patiently wears away rock. Wryly, Laozi reminds us of the obvious: a valley resists storms better than a mountain, a female tends to outlive a male, an infant is freer than a king, and a house is valuable for the space inside it, not the furniture or the wall hangings. The Dao moves nature by a subtle, elastic power. Were rulers to imitate Dao, moving others by *wuwei* rather than violent force, society might prosper. *Wuwei* follows, tries to short-circuit the cycle of aggression and reaction.

To gain *wuwei*, human nature must become like an uncarved block. It symbolizes the priority of natural simplicity over social adornment. A block of wood or jade, before it is carved, has infinite potential, but once we have made it into a table or a piece of jewelry, its use is fixed and limited. Impressed by the limitless creativity of nature, Laozi wanted to recover human nature's originality. In his eyes, the Confucians tended to overspecialize human nature. A society with fewer "modern" advances, less technology, and more spontaneous interaction with nature and fellow humans would be much richer than the Confucians'.

The Daoists, who took their lead from Laozi and Zhuangzi, tried to show how less could be more, how neglect could be cultivation. If people would shut the doors of their senses and thus cut off distractions, how less can be more would be obvious. The good life was not to be found in having but in being. By being simple, whole, alert, and sensitive to nature, one could find joy.

Throughout history, many commentators have criticized Laozi and his followers for both naivete and obscurantism. They have especially jumped on the Daoist precept that a good way to promote peace and simplicity is to keep the people ignorant. Daoists maintained that by not knowing about a wide range of possibilities and therefore not having many desires, a populace would be quite docile. Critics have maintained that it is but a short step from such docility to sheephood and being at the mercy of evil rulers. The commentators have a point: the ideas expressed in some of Laozi's sayings invite easy abuse.

However, a close reading of the *Daodejing* shows that *wuwei* is quite different from mindless docility or even complete pacifism. Rather, it includes the regretful use of force to cut short greater evil. As well, *wuwei* is not sentimental, which further distinguishes it from most Westerners' views of the "people." As easily as nature itself, *wuwei* discards what is outworn, alternating life with death. Because of this objectivity, Daoism can seem inhumane. For a people close to nature, though, humaneness is a less anthropocentric virtue than it is for ourselves.

> Dao is empty, but it never exhausts itself through use. Fathomless, it seems to be the genesis of all things. It dulls its sharpness, unties its tangles, dims its luster, and mixes with the dust. Hidden as it is [it] exists. (*Daodejing*, 4)

In this passage Laozi again and again makes the Dao the opposite of what human beings expect and honor. For example, Dao, the ultimate reality, is more like emptiness than fullness. The fertility that it lavishes upon the world comes from something unstructured, something rich in the mode of an infinite

COMPARISON OF UPANISHADS WITH DAODEJING		
DIMENSION	UPANISHADS	DAODEJING
How many books?	many	one
Authors	various	Laozi
Part of this denomination	Hinduism	Daoism
Time	800–300 B.C.E.	500 B.C.E.
Place	India	China
View of reality	monist	monist
View of Deity	pantheist	pantheist
Deity is	immanent	immanent
Name of deity	Brahman	Dao
exercise	meditation	meditation
orientation	detachment	detachment
virtues	vegetarianism noninjury	nonstriving passivity
opponent	corrupt priests	corrupt officials
view of government	ignored	antibureaucracy

treasure house, too vast or simple for us human beings to grasp. Where our minds crave clarity, sharpness, it is dull. Where we love complexity and sophistication, it unravels itself to appear completely plain. It has no polish or vanity. It is so real, so elementary, that it mixes with the dust of ordinary creation. Yet, though it is hidden in all of these ways, it is the most real thing we could know. If we doubt its reality, we miss the point of our human condition. We cannot know the lineage of the Dao, because it is at the very beginning of any world that we could grasp. So we have to make do with unknowing.

Like many mystics, Laozi finds that in his encounters with the ultimate he has to yield to the Dao. He cannot bend the Dao to his understanding or will. So the practical message of Daoism is both obvious and radical: Submit yourself to what is greater than you

are. Organize your reality in terms of what is objectively so: an Other has all of the priority.

Alchemical Daoism (also known as *magical Daoism*) was a popular movement in later times. It synthesized components from other schools such as alchemy and blended them with literal interpretations of the metaphors for the Dao used by Zhuangzi and Laozi. The alchemists became preoccupied about extraordinary powers and immortality, so much so that they actively pursued such gifts through chemical experiments and yogic techniques. Like medieval western alchemists who sought the patronage of kings by claiming to be able to change lead into gold, these Chinese alchemists sought the patronage of the noble and wealthy by promising to concoct an "Elixir of Immortality." This was not a potion to get one into a better neighborhood in heaven, but something that

Present a verse from the Bible and explain how it is consistent with the teachings of Daoism.

Contribute to this discussion at
http://forums.delphiforums.com/rel101

was supposed to extend longevity and decrease the physical deterioration of aging.

Other popular Daoist movements had sold variations on the theme of immortality. Some sponsored voyages to the magical islands in the East, where the immortals were thought to dwell. Another technique for immortality was physical exercises. The two favorite regimes were breathing air and practicing a quasi-tantric sexual yoga. Along with dietary oddities, some magical Daoists counseled trying to breathe like an infant in the womb so as to use up vital force as slowly as possible. Adepts would lie in bed all day, trying to hold their breath at first for a hundred and eventually a thousand counts. Perhaps some became euphoric through carbon dioxide intoxication. The "yogis" of sex practiced retention of the semen during intercourse, thinking that this vital substance could be rechanneled to the brain and thereby enhance one's powers and longevity. In these exercises, the proximate goal was prolonging physical life, and the ultimate goal was a full immortality.

Many of these later Daoist movements merged with the previous popular traditions (and performed seances with the dead and exorcisms) as well as with the Yin-Yang school performing divinations. In Taiwan, for example, these popular Daoist priests are known for their elaborate funeral rituals, lasting several days.

Over the centuries these magical Daoists formed a "church," generated a massive literature complete with ritualistic and alchemical lore, and earned the wrath of modern educated Chinese, who considered religious Daoism a bastion of superstition. Also, these magical Daoists sometimes became embroiled in politics and sponsored violent revolutionary groups. Their rituals and revolutionary politics went together, because from their rituals they derived utopian visions of what human society ought to become.

Magical Daoism and Aesthetics. Daoism had as strong an impact on Chinese aesthetics as it did on Chinese popular religion. As a guide to creativity, it stressed spontaneity and flow. Largely because of Daoist inspiration, calligraphy, painting, poetry, and music ideally issued from a meditative communion with the nature of things. Images for painters and poets might be a bird alighting on a tree, a rush of wind, the striking colors of persimmons at daybreak. Daoist artists owed a great deal to the "retirement" that Daoism advocated as a respite and counterpoint to Confucian "office." Mixed with Buddhist aesthetics, Daoism provided China most of its artistic depth. Nature, art, and the spirit so came together for the traditional Chinese that they considered their Way superior to the rest of the world.

LEGALISM. Another school, sometimes known as *Legalism,* advocated a strict "law and order" solution for China's problems. This movement began within a wing of Confucianism a couple of centuries later. Xunzi (also transliterated as Hsun Tzu, 335 B.C.E.–288 B.C.E.) proclaimed that human nature was basically evil, out for personal gain and pleasure. He doubted that the Confucian appeal to man's higher nature would be effective in checking those drives. Xunzi taught that only strong law could confine human nature to right action; for lack of strong law, a great many states founder. Furthermore, Xunzi connected this view with Confucius' own stress on ritual, arguing that law and etiquette have the pedagogical function of showing the inner spirit what goodness and justice really mean.

One student of Xunzi was Han Feizi (also transliterated as Han Fei-tzu), who severed all ties with the Confucian school. Han's approach was to use strict laws and brutal punishments for all classes of society. He also advocated enriching the state, strengthening the military, and a system of collective responsibility (e.g., punishing an entire town for the actions of one individual). Many forms of his ruthless statecraft sounded similar to those promulgated by Machiavelli in Italy almost two thousand years later. The legend of Han's life is that he finally found a position in the brutal Chin dynasty, who followed his teachings, executing anyone who might pose a threat to their continued rule—eventually including Han himself.

Although future brutal regimes were to recur throughout Chinese history, most rulers have preferred the more moderate Confucian approach of using the weight of tradition to secure compliance before resorting to brute force.

MOHISM. The opposite view of human nature was advocated by Mozi (also transliterated as Mo Tse, Mo Tzu, or Mo Ti), who probably lived sometime after 500 B.C.E. and may have begun as a Confucian. Mainline Confucians had a more deistic view of the deity (when Confucius speaks of "God" or the "Lord of Heaven," it is generally in the sense of an impersonal force for order and duty). For Mozi, God was theistic, a personal Creator who was both loving and righteous, and perhaps capable of answering individual prayer. Mozi criticized Confucianism (perhaps unfairly) for supporting elaborate funeral rituals and encouraging fatalism. Mozi argued that universal love was the solution to China's problems and that there was a need to transcend the Confucian tendency to limit the expression of love to the five formal relationships. The Confucians charged that Mozi would treat his own father as he would any old man. The Mohists responded that they would treat any old man as if he were their own father. Mohism had its major following among knights errant who opposed aggressive war, but the movement died out by the early common era.

SCHOOL OF NAMES. The smallest school of this period was known as the School of Names. It was composed of idle disputers, debaters, arguers, logicians, and lawyers. They valued knowledge, language and conceptual schemes for their own sake. Some of them, like Hui Shih, developed elaborate logical paradoxes. Others, like K'ung Sung-lung, pointed out that objects were different from the qualities ascribed to them. One of his favorite sayings was, "A white horse is not a horse," by which he meant that the property of whiteness was not the essence of being a horse. Although some of the later Daoist and Confucian thinkers incorporated such logical techniques, the School of Names died out as an independent movement. Lacking rituals, ethics, symbols, myths, or even a focus on deities in its rational deliberation, it never really developed into a religion.

LATER CONFUCIANISM.
Mencius. Different followers developed or elaborated upon different aspects of Confucius' teaching.

The most famous is known as **Mencius,** but his original Chinese name was Mengzi or Meng Ke (also transliterated as Meng Ko or Meng Tze, 371 B.C.E.– 287 B.C.E.). Mencius softened the Master's view of *ren*, drawing it down from the lofty status accorded it by Confucius and making it a possibility for every person. For Mencius, human nature was innately good. We are evil or disordered only because we forget our original nature. Like the deforested local hill (*Mencius* 6.A.8), the typical human mind is so despoiled by abuse that we cannot see its spontaneous tendency toward altruism and justice. If we would stop deforesting it with vice, we would realize that virtue is its natural state. Just as anyone who sees a child at the edge of a well rushes to save the child (*Mencius* 2.A.6), so anyone educated in gentlemanliness will rush to solve civic problems.

Living two centuries after the Master, Mencius tried to repeat Confucius' way of life. He searched for an ideal king who would take his counsel, but he had to be satisfied with having a circle of young students. Mencius, though, somewhat lacked Confucius' restraint in discussing heavenly things. Mencius proposed an ultimately religious theory that history moves in cycles, depending on how a given ruling family handles the *de* (the power to govern well) that heaven dispenses. The sharpest implication of this theory was that an unjust ruler might lose the mandate of heaven—that a revolutionary might be justified in establishing a new regime. Furthermore, Mencius advanced the view that the king brought prosperity only when he convinced the people that the things of the state were their own. This view was in part shrewd psychology of expectation and estimation: a people who have access to the royal park will think it small even if it is 100 miles square; a people denied access to a royal park 1 mile square will complain that it is far too vast. This view brought Confucius' stress on leadership by example and virtue up to date: only if the king demonstrated virtue could he expect the people to be virtuous.

The great importance of Mencius to the Confucian movement was that he was able to serve as its grand apologist, defending it from the other schools' attacks. Against Xunzi and the Legalists, Mencius argued that human beings were basically good, not evil. Against the Daoists, he chose their weakest spokesman (Yang Chu) and criticized the hermits for running away from their duties: a person can only perfect his

SIX SCHOOLS OF THE JHOU PERIOD			
SCHOOL	POPULAR AMONG	MAJOR FIGURES	MAJOR THEMES
Confucian	teachers	Confucius Mencius	duty to family, moderation, unequal relationships
Daoist	hermits	Laozi Zhuangzi Yang Zhu	nature, antisociety, mysticism, hedonism, alchemy
Legalism	officials	Han Fei-zi	people are evil, strict laws and punishments
Mohism	knights	Mozi	people are good, universal love, theism
Yin-Yang	diviners		unity of opposites, herbal medicine, divination, alchemy
Names	lawyers		idle disputation

basic goodness within the context of interpersonal relations and social hierarchy. Of his three opponents, Mencius was probably closest in doctrine to Mozi. Mencius co-opted the Mohists by agreeing that humans were essentially good but that the best way to develop goodness is through the structured relationships of the Confucian five relationships. He ended the old Mohist-Confucian debate ("you treat your father as if he were no one special") by saying that we should begin our practice of showing love to our fathers and then learn to apply it to everything old and venerable. Mencius rightfully won his title as founder of *orthodox* Confucianism, having defended this school from such heterodox internal schisms as Xunzi (whose group was then labled the *heterodox* wing of Confucianism) as well as the Legalists, Mohists, and Daoists.

Neoconfucianism. Much later, during the Song dynasty (960–1279 C.E.), the seminal Confucian thought that lay in the teachings of Confucius, Mencius, and Xunzi grew into a full-fledged philosophy that included metaphysical interpretations of nature and humanity. This movement was largely in response to the impressive systems that Buddhism, and to a lesser extent Daoism, had developed, and it produced a new synthesis known to scholars as *Neoconfucianism.* To Confucius' ethics the Neoconfucians added an explanation of all reality. They accepted the ancient worldview, granting an important place to sacrifices for the state and the family. Additionally, they accepted the moral supremacy of the sage, whose virtuous power might move society or even nature. But they went on to reason about the sort of reality that nature must be if the sacrifices or the sages were to be efficacious. This Neoconfucian development gave the Song rulers and their successors a doctrine that buttressed their practical preference for Confucian ethics.

The Neoconfucian philosophy of nature that gained the most adherents involved the interaction of two elements, principle and ether. *Ether,* or breath, was the basis of the material universe. All solid things were but condensed ether and eventually dissolved back into it. In the dynamic phases of this cycle, ether was an ultimate form of yang. In the still phases, it was the ultimate form of yin. The Neoconfucian view of material nature therefore preserved the tension of bipolarities—of, for example, hot and cold, male and female, light and dark—that had always fascinated the Chinese. One reason for the acceptance of Neoconfucianism, in fact, was that it appeared to be just an updated version of the ancient patrimony. The second element in nature's dualism, *principle*, etymologically related to the veins in jade or the grain in wood. It was the pattern running through all material things, their direction and purpose. If you opposed principle (went against the grain), all things became difficult. In terms of cognitive theory, the Neoconfucians invoked principle to explain the mind's ability to move from the known to the unknown. They also used it to ground the mind's appreciation of the connectedness of things. Principle was considered to be innate in human beings—it was nature's inborn guidance. The main task of human maturation and education was to remove the impediments that kept people from perceiving their principle. This task implied a sort of asceticism or moral diligence, sometimes involving meditation and self-denial.

Finally, the Neoconfucians tried to assimilate the folk aspect of Confucianism by finding a place for the spirits. They preferred not to venerate the ancestors' ghosts, but they allowed that *shen* and *kuei* (the two traditional kinds of spirits) could be the stretching and contracting of ether. In that way, they could agree that the "spirits" worked the planets, the stars, the mountains, the rivers, and so on. Once again, Neoconfucianism was less personal than the earlier traditions, but its new, rather rationalistic system stayed in touch with the old roots. Ju Xi (1130–1200 C.E.) was the master thinker who systematized these Neoconfucian ideas. His predilection was sober analysis, a sort of scientific philosophy, and he concentrated on physical nature. Another more idealistic wing of the Neoconfucians took up the Buddhist stress on mind and tended to place principle in the context of a meditative, as well as an analytic, cultivation of reason. Because Ju Xi's ideas became authoritative in such government-controlled areas as the civil service examinations, Neoconfucianism inculcated in the educated classes a realistic, affirmative view of material nature. It also stayed open to such artistic movements as the magnificent Song dynasty landscape painting. Despite these metaphysical developments, Neoconfucianism retained a commitment to the traditional Confucian virtues associated with character building. The paramount virtue continued to be *ren*. The ideogram for *ren* represented a human being in relationship: *ren* is humaneness—what makes us human. We are not fully human simply by receiving life in a human form. Rather, our humanity depends upon community, human reciprocity. *Ren* pointed in that direction. It connected with the Confucian silver rule of not doing to others what you would not want them to do to you. Against individualism, it implied that people have to live together helpfully, even lovingly. People have to cultivate their basic benevolence, their ability to put themselves in another's shoes. That cultivation was the primary educational task set by Confucius and Mencius.

The Neoconfucians also kept the four other traditional virtues: *yi, li, zhi,* and *xin. Yi* meant duty or justice, and it signified what is right, what law and custom prescribe. Its context, therefore, was the Chinese culture's detailed specification of rights and obligations. Where *ren* undercut such formalities, giving justice its heart, *yi* took care of contractual exactitudes.

Li, which meant manners or propriety, was less exact than *yi*. To some extent it depended on learning, so Confucius tried to teach by word and example what a gentleman would do in various circumstances, but it also required instinct, breeding, or intuition. Handling authority over household servants, men in the fields, or subordinates in the civil service involved *li*. So, too, did deference to superiors, avoidance of ostentation, and a generally graceful style. *Li* therefore was the unguent that soothed all social friction. In a society that prohibited the display of hostile emotion, that insisted on a good "face," *li* was very important.

Zhi (wisdom) was not a deep penetration of ultimate reality that depended on enlightenment or mystical union with the Dao. Rather, it was the prudent sense of right and wrong, decent and indecent, profitable and unprofitable that one could hope to gain by revering the ancients and living attentively. *Xin* meant trustworthiness or good intentions. It was related to *ren* insofar as what one trusts in another is his or her decency or humanity, but it pertained more to a person's reliability or dependability. A person of *xin* was not flighty or capricious.

THE TRADITIONAL SYNTHESIS. The key concept in understanding the interaction of these six schools, at least on the popular level, is not competition but **syncretism** (blending). We cannot look at the billion modern Chinese and classify each one into a specific category, a task that would result (hypothetically) in 460 million Confucians, 321 million Daoists, 274 million Buddhists, 17 million Christians, and so on. The nation and the individual people may turn to different parts of their tradition to answer different needs at different times. Confucianism probably remained the most influential religious tradition for the public functions of the Chinese family and the state. There were periods of exception, such as when the Daoist secret societies exerted influence. After the fall of the Han dynasty (third century C.E.), for instance, Confucian influence waned, and Buddhism gained great influence that lasted well into the ninth century. Nonetheless, in most periods the state bureaucracy hewed to the Confucian line.

For private worship, philosophy, and art, however, Buddhism and Daoism were quite influential. Daoism established monastic communities in the fourth century C.E. Along with the rituals of the Daoist priesthood and the Daoist political parties, these communities were strong sources of Daoist public influence. However, in their struggles against Confucian dominance, Buddhism and Daoism primarily depended on their greater appeal to individualist and artistic sentiments. In comparison, the sober Confucians offered relatively little to nourish a private, meditative, philosophical, or aesthetic life, although they were not completely lacking resources for meditation, self-improvement, and aesthetics. The Master's love of music, for instance, though he set it in a traditional and public context, could have inspired personal creativity in the arts. However, such inspiration tended to fall to Buddhists and Daoists.

In addition, the Buddhist and Daoist texts seemed richer and more mysterious to middle-aged people seeking meaning in their existence. Few Chinese could live fifty years and not suffer some surfeit from rules, laws, ceremonies, or traditions. At such point,

Chinese Lohan

the lean paradoxes of Zhuangzi, Laozi, and Buddhism could be very attractive.

Peasant Religion. Only the educated upper classes, of course, had the opportunity to immerse themselves in any of these three traditions. For the majority of the population, the influence of these traditions only vaguely affected a world dominated by family loyalties and naturalistic animism, largely because the Chinese population was always overwhelmingly composed of peasants. Close to nature, these people filtered Buddhist and Daoist ideas through a primal reverence and fear of nature's powers.

For instance, the Chinese peasants incorporated Buddhist demonology, Daoist demonology, and both traditions' concern with saints into their ancient world of ghosts and helpers, which was home to the ancestors.

The world of the spirits was alive. Daily the phenomena of the sky and the fields expressed that world's mysteries, and the wind and the sea carried great swans and dragons. What we might call basic Confucianism about family relations blended with a basic Daoism about nature to produce a curious mixture of formality and fear. Getting enough food, sheltering one's family, warding off sickness, continuing the family line—these were the concerns of the villagers. To meet them, different gods were honored at festivals for the New Year and for the changing seasons. As well, the Buddhist Goddess of Mercy drew those seeking easy births and strong children, and the Daoist cult of the immortals attracted a few who wanted longevity or knowledge of the rulers of their bodily organs. Tradition sanctioned these quests, but it was a tradition with many cracks. Daily life was shadowed by a greater need to avoid the wrath of the ancestors or the evil spirits.

Mercantile Religion. By the fourteenth century C.E., guilds of artisans and businessmen had developed, and folk religiosity in China had become more mercantile. The guild became a sort of family or clan with its patron gods and rituals. People now invoked the spirits who were the patrons of good selling, and a folk mentality affected the examinations that were part of the way to civil office. For instance, masters of the Confucian classics who did well in the examinations and secured good jobs took on an aura of religious power. Also, numerous stories were told of scholars who had received miraculous help from a patron deity, and these scholars gave the Confucians their own measure of magic and mystery. The common people could go to a great variety of shrines and temples to find out their futures. In addition, students prayed for success in their examinations, travelers prayed for safe journeys, and young people prayed for good marriages. Popular Chinese religion thus became almost economic in nature. Gods and powers were the foci of business—the business of getting along well with an unseen world of fate and fortune. Confucianism, Daoism, and Buddhism all were mixed into this economic popular religion, but its base was pre-Axial closeness to nature.

Few Chinese were so far from nature or so safe from adverse fortune that "secularism" was a live option. The state somewhat controlled religion by keeping the Buddhist and Daoist clergy in check, but the religious life of the family and the individual ran all the traditions together in a form that was largely outside the government's control.

COMMUNIST ERA

For more than two millennia, the ideas and rituals that we have described prevailed in China with amazing stability and consistency, eventually spreading to neighboring countries all over East Asia, including Korea, Japan, and Vietnam. Despite new dynasties, wars, changing artistic styles, and even dramatic new proselytizing religions such as Buddhism and Christianity, the general culture endured. In the family, the government bureaucracy, and the villages, the folk-Confucian tradition was especially solid.

However, that changed in the early twentieth century. From without, Western science and Western sociopolitical thought dealt ancient Chinese tradition heavy blows. From within, the decay of the imperial government led to the birth of the republic in 1912, and belatedly, China entered the modern world. By the early twentieth century its ancient culture showed cracks and strains everywhere. As a result, Chinese religious traditions, especially Confucianism, came under strong attack. Identified with the old culture, they seemed out of place in the modern world. Since the "cultural renaissance" of 1917, China has tried to cast off its Confucian shackles; since the communist takeover of 1949, it has espoused a program of ongoing socialism and modernization.

The paramount figure in this program, of course, was Mao Zedong (Mao Tse-tung). Mao was born in 1893 in Hunan (a south-central province) of a "middle" peasant family (that is, not one of abject poverty). His father had little culture or education, and his mother was a devout Buddhist. Mao himself received a traditional primary school education, whose core was memorizing the Confucian classics. (As a result, he developed a profound distaste for Confucius.) He had to leave school when he was thirteen to work the land, but prompted by his desire for more education, he ran away and enrolled in a modern high school. There he first encountered Western authors who challenged traditional Chinese culture. (At that time many educated Chinese felt humiliated by their defeat by the British in the Opium War of 1839–1842, their defeat by the Japanese in 1895, and the repression of their Boxer uprising in 1900 by a coalition of mainly Western powers). Mao got a job as an assistant librarian at the university library and came into contact with local communist intellectuals. He joined the Chinese Communist Party in 1921, took part in the communist collaboration with Jiang Kai-shek's Guomindang (Nationalist) party until 1926, and then led communist forces that opposed Jiang. By 1935, Mao was in charge of the Communist Party and engaged in what became his legendary "Long March." Through World War II, the communists and the Guomindang collaborated uneasily against the Japanese; after the war, the final conflict with Jiang led to the communist takeover in 1949. Throughout this period Mao pursued the twofold career of military general and political theoretician. While gaining power he collaborated with the Soviet Union, but he eventually decided that China had to go its own way. The result was a massive (but brutal) experiment in agrarian reform, trying to control economics by top-down Marxist-Leninist and Maoist dogma.

The reason for this brief biographical sketch of Mao is that he was the most important figure in China's break with tradition and plunge into modernity. Influenced by the Confucian classics and Buddhism, he nevertheless repudiated both. On the surface at least, Maoism took shape as a secular humanism (if humanism can be devoid of the concept of individual freedom). Some of its doctrines and programs dramatically changed the life of the people. The women's movement, for instance, and the related changes in the marriage law raised an entire segment of the population from subjection to near equality. By stressing agricultural production, local health care, and "cellular" local government, Chinese communism has become an even more grandiose socialist experiment than the Soviet one was.

As part of the program instituting these changes, Mao's party denounced religion. Instead of gods and sacrifices, it offered self-reliance, hard work, and the mystique that the people united are invincible. Temples became government property, religious professionals were persecuted, and religious literature was derided or proscribed. The party likewise attacked the Confucian classics, virtues, and traditions. Throughout, its goal was to destroy the old class society and produce a new people with one will and one future.

However, as one might expect, religion and tradition died harder than the communists had hoped. In the rural regions, peasant traditions continued to have great influence. Among the intellectuals, conforming to the party line resulted in rather wooden, if not second-class, philosophy, science, and art. As he aged, Mao pondered new ways of keeping his movement alive for the new generation that had been born after 1949. He launched the Great Proletarian Cultural Revolution in 1966 in an attempt to retrieve for a new generation the experiences of the Long March and the other peak events that had united the wills of the founding generation. This unleashed a flurry of anti-Western, anti-intellectual, and anti-traditional forces that disrupted much of the real progress that the country had made.

Since the death of Mao Zedong three decades ago, China has opened to the West. The "four modernizations" (in industry, science and technology, agriculture, and military affairs) urged by Mao's successors aimed at bringing China into the modern world. While the Chinese leaders who followed Mao are eager to copy Microsoft software or warhead technology, however, they are reluctant to let in Western religious proselytizing. Officially, people have a right to practice religion. The Constitution of 1975 stipulated in article 28 that citizens have the freedom to practice a religion as well as the freedom not to practice a religion and to propagate atheism. In practice, there is a Religious Affairs Bureau in Beijing that must license all religious activity. Official surveys conducted by the bureau claim the majority of Chinese are atheists and that less than 10 percent of the population is registered as Buddhist, Muslim, or Christian. But given the climate in China, it is doubtful that most people would want to admit their religious affiliation to the government. Some newer religious movements claim that they are meeting in secret "house churches" to avoid persecution from the government, while the government claims that the only reason it persecutes such churches is because they have not registered.

China's record during the last decade has not been encouraging. There has been a closure of almost 500 churches and temples: Catholic, Protestant, Buddhist, and Daoist. Individual Chinese Catholics have been detained and forced to deny the authority of the Pope. In the western provinces, theoretically ethnic Uighurs have an autonomous region but complain that their ability to practice Islam has been greatly constrained. Private homes in Tibet have been ransacked in order to search for pictures of the local spiritual leader, the Dalai Lama. Perhaps the most persecuted groups have been homegrown apocalyptic movements labeled as "cults" by the government. The Falun Gong and Zhong Gong movements have had thousands of members detained, with hundreds of members allegedly dying from police beatings and torture.

THE CHINESE WORLDVIEW

NATURE

All ancient societies lived deep in what we have called **cosmogony**, the cosmological myth, and China was no exception. However, Chinese thinkers did not have the tendency of their counterparts in India to call sensory experience into question. Throughout its Axial period, the Chinese attitude was that nature is utterly real—more primordial than human beings. The vast majority of Chinese doubted neither its reality nor its ultimacy. If there had been a question of subordinating one of the four dimensions of reality (nature, society, self, and divinity), nature would have been the last to go.

Physical reality took form through Dao. It was both Logos and mother. As Logos, it was the reasonable pattern, the intelligence running through nature. As mother, it was the womblike source of all things. Laozi, Zhuangzi, and the Buddhists consistently invested nature with an aura of ultimacy and preferred to bow before Dao.

FOLK VIEWS. Chinese folk religion is also distinctive in its concern for the compass directions. The geomancy of *feng-shui* is a clear expression of the Chinese emphasis on nature's four directions. Of course, other peoples were concerned with directions: Native Americans made a great deal of the four geographic directions, and early civilized peoples such as the Egyptians built their temples with great concern for their orientation toward the sun. However, China carried this concern to a high art. Even for the average person, the angle of the wind or the shape of the terrain was magically influential.

Chinese divination expressed another set of naturalistic assumptions. The *Yi Jing* (*I Ching*), for instance,

viewed yin-yang components as shaping human participation in nature's course of events. Like the African diviner who studied the patterns of chits in a magical basket, the Chinese fortuneteller saw nature's coherence in numbers and designs. In popular Chinese religion, then, there was a primal sense that nature coordinates with mind. That sense did not develop to the point of attempting to gain control over nature, as it would in modern Western science and technology, but for Chinese diviners, astrologers, and even fortunetellers, that sense had great relevance.

SOCIETY

Historically, China used Confucianism as its binding social force, and Confucianism thoroughly subordinated individuals to the community. Consequently, the Chinese individual felt inserted not only into a nature more impressive than the self but also into a society greater than its parts. Furthermore, the great Confucian thinkers based their theory of ideal social relationships on legendary rulers of the past. Rulers embodied a paradigm that ordered society by exemplary morality. Somewhat magically, the virtue (*de*) that went out from the legendary kings and dukes brought those it touched into harmony, at least according to Confucianism.

The Confucian mythic history evidences the common ancient notion of sacred kingship. Because the ruler stands at the peak of the human pyramid, he can conduct heaven's governing power to earth. The Chinese king manifested this holy mediating role by offering sacrifices to the gods of heaven and earth. In pre-Confucian times, he sacrificed human beings. The imperial cult, consequently, was the keystone in the Chinese social edifice, and the Confucian notion of *li* (propriety) applied especially to the punctilious execution of its ceremonies. To know the music and ritual appropriate to different occasions was the mark of a high gentleman. In fact, from this cultic center radiated something religious that touched all social relationships. Since human activities related to heaven, they partook of cultic propriety. By maintaining a harmonious family, for instance, individuals contributed to the most important order, that between natural divinity and humanity. The harmony that the Confucians encouraged, though it extended to all aspects of social life, expressed itself most importantly in its rating of key human relationships. It rated men over women (and so pictured marriage not as a partnership but as the wife's servitude to the husband). It rated children (among whom the eldest son was the plum) distinctly inferior to the parents—so much so that obedience and service toward the parents (most importantly toward the father) dominated the lives of children. Likewise, rulers were rated over subjects, masters over peasants, and, to a lesser extent, elder brothers over younger brothers.

In logical extension of their veneration of the past, the Chinese honored ancient ancestors more than more recent ones, and they rated children according to the order of their birth. Surely some parents loved a younger son more than an elder son or a gracious girl more than a mulish boy, but in determining the important matter of inheritance, age was the main standard. In these and many other ways, Chinese society looked backward. The past was the age of paradigms; the elderly were the fonts of wisdom. The Axial masters of Chinese political thought give little evidence of celebrating youth or brave new worlds.

Social space was similarly static. From the ruler's key connection to heaven, the social classes descended in clearly defined ranks with little egalitarian or democratic moderation. The Confucians especially focused on the importance of a person's rank. One said quite different things to a fellow noble riding in a hunting carriage and the carriage driver. A person of breeding knew and respected such differences. If Confucius and Mencius themselves are representative, such a person was almost prickly about his social rights. For example, a master would not visit just anyone, and for a pupil to come into town and not quickly pay a visit of homage was a serious slight. The Confucian master protected his dignity and honor.

WOMEN'S STATUS. The Disney animated movie *Mu Lan* is based upon an old story about Fa Mu Lan, the woman warrior. Although there were women warriors and shamans in China, theirs was not the life of most women. Among the Confucians, a peasant or a woman, however virtuous, had a hard time gaining respect. In fact, of the main Chinese traditions, Confucianism was the most misogynistic. The woman's role in Confucianism was to obey and serve her parents, husband, and husband's parents. She was useless until she produced a male heir, and her premarital chastity and marital fidelity were more important than a man's. No doubt some men genuinely loved their wives and treated them tenderly, but the Confucian view of marriage gave little place to romance or equality.

Since a Chinese woman's destiny was early marriage, childbearing, and household duties, her education was minimal. She was not necessarily her husband's friend, confidante, or lover—males and courtesans could fulfill these roles. A Chinese woman was primarily her husband's source of sons. They were the reason for her marriage—indeed, for her sex. As a result, the ideal Chinese woman was retiring, silent, and fertile. Custom severely curtailed her freedoms, but never more cruelly than through the practice of foot binding, which became the fashion in certain regions for at least a thousand years. This practice prevented girls' feet from growing; as adults, they could only take small, dainty steps. It may have been more than a misguided aesthetic preference (akin to our modern fascination with the slender figure, leading to an epidemic of anorexia). Foot binding may have been a conscious masculine attempt to reduce a woman's physical mobility. The only source of power for many Chinese women was to overcome their submissive role by cleverly manipulating gossip so that abusive husbands or mothers-in-law would lose face. Until the communist takeover, women had no place in the official political system and did very well if they merely outwitted it.

The Daoists were kinder to women and to the socially downtrodden generally. They were responsible for curtailing the murder of female infants by exposure, and their more positive regard for female symbols as examples of how the Dao worked upgraded femininity. By bestowing feminine or maternal attributes on the Dao itself, the Daoists made femininity intrinsic to ultimate reality.

SELF

The Chinese concepts of *ren* and *li* (goodness and propriety) indicate that the Chinese sensed that all people have something to share as a basis for mutual respect. In the structure of society, then, the self had some right to acknowledgment. Despite one's subordination to the whole (or, in many cases, one's near slavery), the common person found in such an author as Mencius a champion of the self's essential goodness. Mencius counseled princes to take their people's welfare to heart; his counsel was clearly more than a pragmatic bit of advice about how to avoid rebellions.

Furthermore, the Confucians exercised considerable care on the self's education, at least for the middle and upper classes. Their major motivation seems to have been societal needs (as opposed to the self's intrinsic dignity), but by stressing character formation the Confucians had to probe what the self's substance and dignity were. They decided, with considerable prodding from Confucius himself, that the paramount human faculty was the inner mind. If one could act from this inner mind with clarity and dispassion, one could act humanely and civilly. The core of the Confucian view of the self, therefore, was a certain rationalism. Confucianism did not stress speculative reason (that which gives rise to abstract theory), since Confucianism was not concerned with the human capacity to illumine or be illumined by the Logos of nature, but it did stress practical reason or prudence. Laying aside passion and prejudice (which required self-control), the good Confucian could hope with experience to discern the appropriate and harmonizing course of action.

Either through reflection on history or further rumination on the mind, the Confucians eventually linked practical reason with the ancients' Dao. It was clear from the myths handed down that the foremost ancestors were people of composed, effective good sense, which enhanced their subjects' common good and even prosperity. Because they were not venal or petty, the ancestors were able to lead by example— by radiating the power of *ren*.

On further reflection, the Confucians confirmed that the zenith of human achievement (which Confucius himself later came to epitomize) was such inner-directed action. In other words, the ideal human spirit feared no outer laws or sanctions. It was autonomous— it delighted in the good for its own sake. Though Confucius and Mencius both longed for public office, a major reason that neither ever achieved it was that neither would compromise his standards. This uncompromising integrity became a lesson to disciples for centuries. When a devout Confucian observed an inhumane ruler, he felt more pity than envy.

THE DAOIST SELF. The Daoists, who paid greater attention to the relationship between human consciousness and the cosmic Dao, produced a more paradoxical view of the self. They went against the Confucian standards of sagehood. Their masters were either cryptic eccentrics such as Zhuangzi or magical "immortals" possessing paranormal powers. The eccentrics' suspicion of human reason developed into a strong attack on logic and Confucian prudence. Daoists cast doubt on the entire realm of discursive reason, which plods along from premise to premise and often misses the whole. If one could argue either side of a proposition, as lawyers always have tended to do, one clearly was not in the realm of ultimate concern.

For the philosophical Daoists, the realm of ultimate concern pivoted on Dao. They attempted to reach that realm by meditation and *wuwei*. Consequently, they individualized the self more than the Confucians did. The Confucians, of course, realized that the talents of people differ, including the talent to reach the still inner reason from which humane action emanates. But the Daoists went beyond reason itself, encouraging each person to write his or her own script. What was important was that one write to the tune of the Dao. What the specific story was, how one chose to enact Dao's inspiration, was secondary.

The magical Daoists saw the self as a mortal physical body. Therefore, by the several physical regimes mentioned, they tried to prolong physical life. As a result, magical Daoists experimented with yogic practices, many of them in the vein of Indian kundalini or Tibetan Tantrism, both of which viewed the body as a repository of energy centers. Depending on the particular interest of a magical Daoist group, the self might focus on breath or semen or some other quintessence. Furthermore, the magical Daoists regarded the body as a warehouse of tiny gods, each in charge of a particular bodily part. In yogic exercise the adept was to visualize the god in charge of the spleen or the heart and so gain health or blessing there. By their quests for immortality (in the sense of continued physical existence), then, the magical Daoists simultaneously underscored mortality and suggested that humans can defeat death.

ULTIMATE REALITY

For most Chinese throughout history, nature has been the effective divinity. The physical world itself was something sacred and mysterious. This world intimated something beyond itself that was grasped by those who saw nature with mystic clarity, but the majority at best sensed this something beyond only vaguely. To sense clearly the Dao that cannot be named, one must reject the adequacy of all things nameable. Realizing that water, air, fire, wood, earth, yang, yin, and so on, do not explain the totality of heaven and earth, the mind senses that the ultimate is of a different order. It is without the limitations that characterize all the primal elements. As such, it must dwell in obscurity, too full or great or bright for mere human intelligence. A muted reference to ultimacy probably plays in Confucius' laconic references to heaven. For the most part, the Master refrained from speculating about heavenly things. But Confucius' reverence toward the sacrifice to heaven suggests that he would not have explained the sacrifice as a humanistic means of social bonding. Rather, he probably saw a link between the ancients' Dao and the way of sacred nature, and so viewed the sacrifice as humanity's chance to align itself with the power that most mattered, the power behind all life and all things.

Confucius made heaven the ultimate sanction for his ethical program. The judge of success and failure must be more stable than a human creation. Against the Daoist view that heaven treats all creatures as straw dogs, Confucius saw heaven as the great champion of *yi* (justice). Clearly, however, the Confucians justified their calls to virtue by appealing to suprahuman standards. Indeed, the depth of Confucius' analysis of what is necessary for a full humanity makes his overall program an invitation to explore the sacredness of the mystery of human potential.

For Zhuangzi and Laozi, natural harmony in the present was all important, and they paid little heed to future enjoyment of some otherworldly states. Consequently, the divinity of Dao was preeminently the undergirding and direction it gave cosmic nature.

Reaching back to prehistory, the magical Daoists conceived of a pantheon of divine forces, often giving them picturesque names and features. Furthermore, the goal of magical Daoist practices was to prolong life, and so they ventured into alchemy and yoga as well as voyages to the Lands of the Blessed (the Immortals). What they shared with their philosophical counterparts, however, was a characteristically Chinese concern with the body. The ideal of the magical Daoists was not a release in *moksha* but a consolidation of vital powers so as to resist death. Their divinities, consequently, were gods who could help this process, or "immortals" (who probably spanned the often narrow gap between saints and gods) who had successfully accomplished such a consolidation. In either case, they offered followers encouragement and models.

How did Chinese divinity appear in the popular amalgamation? Through ritualistic, emotional, and shamanic points of entry. The prevailing popular mind, which was primarily interested in warding off evil fortune and attracting good, and the great importance of ancestor veneration, gave ultimate reality a rainbow of colors. Ceremonies at the family hearth reaffirmed the clan by acknowledging the reality of its ancestors. Ceremonies in the fields, for building a new dwelling or for curing someone seriously ill, brought people face to face with spooky forces of life, luck, and disease. Shamans and mediums were the key figures, contacting spirits and ancestral souls. Diviners gave advice and told fortunes. The average person gathered talismans and totems, but also Buddhist and Daoist saints. The educated people patronized Confucius, but even they were open to other sacred figures who offered help. To say the least, then, the Chinese religious mind was syncretistic, and the study of folk religion, as recent studies suggest, has to be very comprehensive.

Which theoretical approach would give you the most insight on the history, doctrine, rituals, ethics of Chinese religion? Pick Durkheim, Freud, Malinowski, Tylor, or Frazer, and indicate how it explains the complex syncretism of Chinese religion.

Contribute to this discussion at
http://forums.delphiforums.com/rel101

In people's retirement, Daoist and Buddhist insights yielded poetry and metaphysics. If one backed away from the bureaucratic mind, accepted the lure of Zhuangzi and Laozi, the Way took on sharper angles, more vivid hues. So Zhuangzi carries across the thousands of years, speaking playfully to any generation that values wit. So Laozi remains a highly relevant political study, challenging all our established views of power and virtue. How, in fact, does the successful natural organism survive and prosper? What, in reality, are the evolutionary and ecological virtues? As a matter of experience, how lasting or thorough is the victory that does not conquer the enemy's heart? In the best of personal times, when does one hear the Way in the morning, and what is the contentment for which one would willingly die?

These are the sorts of questions that make a culture profound, concerned with ultimate realities or religion. China was fortunate in having Buddhists and Daoists who kept these questions throbbing. Through their influence on art, philosophy, and social ethics, they made the Way properly empty. Emptying the Chinese mind of the excesses to which its Confucian practicality tended, Daoists and Buddhists gave this great people inner space. Thus Chinese landscape paintings can haunt the beholder as few other artworks do. Thus a lonesome, allusive poetry let thousands of gentlemen give voice to their inmost feelings.

There is much irony in this world, much well-tested humor. The Way that collects us, giving us our vision and our depth, turns out to be sportive and unpredictable. To the sober-sided it is quite regular, but the sober-sided are more mummified than enlightened. To the sage, each day is fresh, each particular fights generalization. The sage does not master life by formulas and bureaus. The sage does not master life at all. Mastery is really discipleship, docility, and constant attention. When a docile, empty mind meets a fluid, allusive way, things fall apart. There is no center fixed or certain. There is only a center moving, always being recreated, ever arranging itself in new yet ancient patterns, like a kaleidoscope. The way that can be told is not the real way. The real way is compressed in a glance, hinted in a gesture, sounded in the pure tones of an emptied life.

THE HISTORY OF JAPAN

THE ANCIENT-FORMATIVE PERIOD

Shinto, the indigenous religion of Japan, cannot be traced to any particular historical founder. The prehistoric period in Japan lasted until the early centuries of the common era. Clay figurines that archeologists have excavated from this earliest Jomon period indicate a special concern with fertility. As the hunting and gathering culture of the earliest period gave way to agriculture and village settlement, religious practices came to focus on agricultural festivals, revering the dead, and honoring the leaders of the ruling clans. According to the primitive mythology, which existed long before the written versions that date from the eighth century, such leaders were descendants of the deities—once again a version of sacred kingship.

In the villages outside the leading families' influence, people probably conceived of a world with three layers. The middle is the realm of humans, where we have a measure of control, but the realms above and below, which spirit beings control, are far larger. The *kami* (nature and clan spirit deities) dwell in the high plain of heaven and are the objects of worship; the spirits of the dead live below, condemned to a filthy region called *Yomi*. (In some versions, the dead go to a land beyond the sea.) Apparently *Yomi* was especially important for the aristocrats' cult, which suggests not only a connection between folk and imperial religion but also indicates why later religion came to stress ritual purification, especially from polluting contacts with the dead.

THE KAMI. The *kami* represented the sacred power involved in the principal concerns of prehistoric Japanese religion (kingship, burial of the dead, and ritual purification). They were rather shadowy figures or spiritual forces who were wiser and more powerful than humans. Traditionally they numbered at 800,000. Although most of the *kami* apparently originally were natural forces (wind, storm, sun; spirits of various striking local phenomena—tall trees, distinctive rocks), heads of the clan and other heroes also could be *kami*. From time to time, *kami* would descend to earth, especially if a human called them down and helped them assume a shape (in their own world the *kami* were shapeless). They were called down by means of *yorishiro*—tall, thin objects that attracted the *kami*. Pine trees and elongated rocks were typical *yorishiro*, and they suggest that the *kami* had phallic connotations. To a lesser extent, rocks of female shape also attracted the *kami*, and relics from the great tombs of the third and fourth centuries—a profusion of mirrors, swords, and curved jewels—suggest that these artifacts also drew the *kami*. (Such objects became part of the imperial regalia as well as the special objects of veneration in shrines.) There were also *kami* on earth and revered ancestors who assumed a status like that of *kami*, so not all *kami* came from heaven.

Because the *kami* held key information about human destiny, it was important to call them down into human consciousness. That occurred through the *kami*'s possession of shamans, or mediums. Most of the early shamans (*miko*) were women, and they functioned in both the aristocratic and the popular cults. The *miko* shamans tended to band together and travel a circuit of villages, primarily to act as mediums for contact with the dead but also to serve as diviners and oracles. They also ministered to spiritual and physical ills, which popular culture largely attributed to maligned spirits. As a result, the *miko* developed both a poetic and an herbal lore. In composing songs and dances to accompany their ministrations, they contributed a great deal to the formation of traditional Japanese dance, theater, balladry, and puppetry.

Essentially, the *kami* were the sacral forces of nature and impressive aspects of social life. They impressed the Japanese ancient mind, as they impressed the ancient mind elsewhere, by their striking power. Sensitive individuals could contact them, but the *kami* remained rather wild and unpredictable. Later Shinto shrines stressed natural groves of tall trees, and founders of religious cults were often possessed by spirits. As the early mythology shows, however, the *kami* remained in charge.

As the eighth-century chronicles, the *Kojiki* and the *Nihon-shoki*, have preserved it, Japanese mythology adapted to Chinese influences early on. For example, redactors regularly changed the Japanese sacred number 8 to the Chinese sacred number 9, and they were influenced by the Chinese cosmogonic myths. The result was a creation account in which the world began as a fusion of heaven and earth in an unformed, egg-shaped mass that contained all the forces of life. Gradually the purer parts separated and ascended to heaven, while the grosser portions descended and became the earth.

SHINTO MYTHOLOGY. Chinese influence disappears when the chronicles come to the myths of the *kami*'s origin and to the related question of how the Japanese islands came to be. The first *kami* god was a lump that formed between heaven and earth; he established the first land. Six generations later, the divine creator couple, Izanagi and Izanami, arose by spontaneous generation. They married and by sexual union produced the many *kami*, including the Japanese islands. For instance, heaven commanded Izanagi and Izanami to solidify the earth, which hitherto had been only a mass of brine. Standing on a bridge between heaven and the briny mass, they lowered a jeweled spear and churned the brine. When they lifted the spear, drops fell, solidified, and became the first island. The couple descended to this island, erected a heavenly pillar (the typical shamanistic connector to heaven), and proceeded to procreate. The account of their interaction is both amusing and revealing:

> Now the male deity turning by the left, and the female deity by the right, they went around the pillar of the land separately. When they met together on one side, the female deity spoke first and said: "How delightful! I have met with a lovely youth." The male deity was displeased, and said: "I am a man, and by right should have spoken first. How is it that on the contrary thou, a woman, should have been the first to speak? This was unlucky. Let us go round again." Upon this the two deities went back, and having met anew, this time the male deity spoke first, and said: "How delightful! I have met a lovely maiden."

This account influences the Shinto wedding ceremony to this day, tabooing the bride from speaking first (under pain of perhaps having a deformed child).

In tortuous logic, the myth describes the fate of the first two. Izanami died giving birth to fire, and

Shinto Torii

Izanagi followed her to the underworld. Izanagi then produced many deities in an effort to purify himself of the pollution of the underworld. By washing his left eye he produced the sun goddess **Amaterasu,** and by washing his right eye he produced the moon god. When he washed his nose, he produced the storm god Susanoo. In this story of descent to the underworld and divine creation, scholars see an expression of the aboriginal Japanese rites of purification and fears of death. The sun goddess, who became the supreme being of the Yamato clan, a powerful Japanese family, and the focus of the clan's cultic center at Ise, presided over the land of fertility and life. Opposing her was the domain of darkness and death. Rituals were performed to keep darkness and death from afflicting sunny fertility—harvests, human procreation, and so on. As Izanagi purified himself of death by plunging into the sea, the Japanese throughout their history have used salt as a prophylactic. People still scatter it around the house after a funeral, place it at the edge of a well, set a little cake of it by a door jamb, and even scatter it before the bulging sumo wrestler as he advances toward his opponent.

In subsequent myths, Amaterasu and Susanoo have numerous adventures arising from the antagonism between the life-giving sun and the withering wind. These figures also demonstrate both the trickster and noble dimensions of the divinity found in nature. Susanoo, the Trickster, committed "heavenly offenses" that later became a focus of ritual purification: He broke the irrigation channels for the imperial rice field that Amaterasu had set up; he flayed a piebald colt and flung it into the imperial hall; and, worst of all, he excreted on the goddess's imperial throne. These offenses reflect practical problems of an agricultural society (respecting others' fields), cultic problems (a sacrificial colt was probably supposed to be of a single color and not be flayed), and speculation on the tension between divine forces of nature.

From these and other materials in the earliest chronicles, it is clear that the ancient-formative period of Japanese history centered on natural forces, some of which were anthropomorphized. In the background were the *kami,* whom we may consider as foci of divine power. Anything striking or powerful could be a *kami.* To relate themselves to the natural world, the early Japanese told stories of their love for their beautiful islands (worthy of being the center of creation) and of the divine descent of their rulers. The fact that Amaterasu is a sun goddess suggests an early matriarchy, as does the fact that kingship on the Chinese model of a rule possessing the mandate of heaven (rather than by heredity) only came with the bika reforms of 645 C.E. Shinto maintained the divinity of the emperor until the mid-twentieth century, when the victorious Western Allies forced the Japanese emperor to formally renounce these claims at the close of World War II.

ARRIVAL OF BUDDHISM. During the Kamakura period, Buddhism sometimes eclipsed Shinto, but the native tradition always lay ready to reassert itself. Whenever there was a stimulus to depreciate foreign influences and exalt native ones, Shinto quickly bounced back. Also, Shinto only defined itself in the seventh century, when Buddhism, Confucianism, and Daoism started to predominate. In defining itself, Shinto picked up something from Buddhist philosophy, Confucian ethics, and Daoist naturalism. The result was a nature-oriented worship with special emphasis on averting pollution. Furthermore, Shinto modified Confucian social thought to include the emperor's divine right. Buddhist deities were enshrined by Shintoists (and *kami* by Buddhists), another example of East Asian syncretism.

Later in the medieval period, a number of Shinto scholars took issue with this syncretism. The most important of these medieval Shinto reformers were Kitabatake and Yoshida, who worked in the fourteenth and fifteenth centuries. They drew from writings of Ise priests, who wanted to give Shinto a scripture comparable to that of the Buddhists. Another step in the consolidation of Shinto's position was the organizing of its shrines, which began in the tenth century and continued through the fifteenth century. The resulting network provided every clan and village with a shrine to represent its ties with the *kami.*

ARRIVAL OF CHRISTIANITY. In the mid-sixteenth century, Christianity came to Japan in the person of the charismatic Jesuit missionary Francis Xavier. It flourished for about a century, until the Tokugawa rulers first proscribed it and then bitterly persecuted it. By impressing the shoguns, or local warrior rulers (often by holding out prospects of trade with the West), the Christians gained the right to missionize much of Japan and made some lasting converts. Western artifacts fascinated the Japanese as well, and for a while things Western were the vogue.

However, before the missionaries could completely adapt Christianity to Japanese ways, the shoguns became suspicious that the missionaries had political and economic designs. The shogun Ieyasu (1542–1616) killed many who had converted to Christianity, and after his death Christianity's brief chapter in Japanese history came to a bloody close.

SUMMARY. At the end of the medieval period of elaboration (around 1600), then, five traditions were interacting. Buddhism brought Japan a profound philosophy and system of meditation that stressed the flux of human experience. In return, it was revamped to suit Japanese tastes and the interests of the diverse social classes: rulers for rituals, warriors for discipline, common people for devotional love and hope. Confucianism furnished a rationale for the state bureaucracy and for social relationships. It stressed formality and inner control, which especially suited merchants and government officials, and one can see its imprint in the Bushido Code, which prevailed during the Tokugawa period. Daoism most influenced folk religion, whereas Shinto developed a rationale for the *kami* and a strong shrine system. Christianity came to represent foreign intrusion, but since it converted perhaps 500,000 Japanese, it also satisfied a hunger for other ways to salvation. Probably the average person mixed elements from these traditions with folk traditions to fashion a family-centered religion that would harmonize human beings with the forces—*kami,* evil spirits— that presided over good fortune and bad.

JAPAN'S MODERN-REFORMATIVE PERIOD

During the Tokugawa shogunate (military dictatorship), which lasted from 1600 to 1867, Japan experienced peace and stability. The Tokugawa rulers expelled the Christian missionaries and severely limited contacts with the West. The biggest shift in the social structure was the rise of the merchant class, which went hand in hand with the growth of cities. Regarding religion, the Tokugawa shoguns made sure that all traditions served the state's goals of stability. In the beginning of the seventeenth century, those goals had popular support because the preceding dynasties had allowed great civil strife. Neoconfucianism eclipsed Buddhism in state influence, perhaps because it was less likely to stir thoughts of independence or individualism. Shinto suffered some decline in popular influence but retained a base in folk religion. As well, Shinto generated a clearer rationale for separating from Buddhism. Early during the Tokugawa period there arose a movement called Kokugaku ("National Learning"), designed to furnish Japan a more impressive native religious/cultural tradition. In terms of positive goals, the leaders of this movement wanted to improve historical learning about Japanese culture, thinking that scholarship about Shinto and other aspects of the native ways were in a deplorable state. Negatively, many of the leaders attacked the way that Japan had adopted Confucian and Buddhist ways. The tendency of the leaders of the Kokugaku movement was to schematize Japanese history into three phases. In the early period, a pristine native culture and spirit had flourished. During the middle period, foreign imports had contaminated Japanese culture. The Kokugaku leaders hoped to make the modern period a time when the ancient native ways would be restored and their country would be purged of foreign contaminations. In fact, the beginnings of this reform movement owed something to the Buddhist priest Keichu (1640–1701), who proposed aesthetic reforms that would return poetry to ancient forms and who noted the differences between Shinto and both Buddhism and Confucianism. He showed special respect for the *kami,* claiming they were beyond human understanding and generally provided some of the initial impetus to restore ancient Japanese traditions. A Shinto priest from Kyoto, Kada Azumamaro (1669–1736), contributed one of the first influential critiques of the synthesis between Confucianism and Shinto that had arisen, arguing that Shinto ideas were not well interpreted through such Confucian notions as yin and yang or the five basic elements constituting reality.

A second generation of Shinto reformists came with Kamo no Mabuchi (1697–1769) and Motoori Norinaga (1730–1801), who sharpened the focus of Kokugaku to precisely religious matters. Mabuchi founded a school of "ancient learning" dedicated to reviving the Japanese spirit that had prevailed before the introduction of Buddhism and Confucianism. Norinaga edited the *Kojiki,* the chronicles that became regarded as the Shinto scriptures. His commentaries on the *Kojiki,* along with his other writings on such topics as the *kami* and his poetry, gave the Shinto revival much more intellectual clout than it had had previously. Hirata Atsutane (1776–1843) represents a third generation of the Kokugaku movement. He was the most passionate advocate of Shinto religiosity, arguing that the way of the *kami* was superior to all other religious ways.

Despite their claim to be purifying Japanese religious traditions of the foreign accretions that had denatured them, the later reformers in fact drew on the Daoist philosophers Laozi and Zhuangzi. Atsutane even borrowed from Christianity, which the Tokugawa leaders had proscribed. In their attacks on Buddhism and Confucianism, the Shinto reformers argued that those traditions had arisen through human contrivance, while the way of the *kami* was natural—completely in accord with the dictates of heaven and earth. The Daoist notions of spontaneity and nonstriving (*wu-wei*) seemed to support the superiority of such naturalism and so were adapted to the argument on behalf of the superiority of Shinto. Norinaga used the further Daoist concept that things are self-explanatory (do not require a full chain of causes) to rebut Neoconfucian ideas about the workings of nature that he thought had invaded the Shinto view of the world. He also explored medicine, his profession, with an eye to reviving ancient theories, which were quite empirical (concentrated on simple facts and cures), and to ousting the complex, more rarefied theories of the Neoconfucians. The religious payoff Norinaga found in this contrast was a support for his view that one ought to give the *kami* complete obedience, respecting the mysteriousness of their ways and not poking into how they had arranged nature. Thus what he considered Shinto naturalism, bolstered by Daoist views (Chinese naturalism), seemed more properly religious (worshipful) than what had infiltrated Shintoism through neo-Confucianism.

Some later Shinto scholars have argued that Norinaga also was shaped by Christian views of the Creator, but the clearer Christian influence appears in the works of Atsutane, who apparently incorporated materials from translations of books on Christian doctrine brought by Western missionaries to China such as Matteo Ricci (1552–1610). The missionaries had been searching for ways to show the superiority of Christianity to Confucianism, and some of their arguments seemed relevant to Shinto attacks on Confucianism. As well, Atsutane adapted Christian notions of the Trinity and the Last Judgment to a theology of the nature and works of the *kami*. A third feature of his theology was its special emphasis on Japanese ancestor veneration, which he found superior to Chinese ancestor veneration because it was broader in its range of devotion (Japanese ancestor worship was dedicated not only to members of one's own clan but also to the great *kami* associated with the imperial family). This latter point was extremely important in the nineteenth-century Meiji restoration of the power of the imperial family, for it provided a basis for discrediting the Tokugawa leaders (who were shoguns, not members of the imperial line) and bolstering the sacredness of the restored royal line. The subsequent "divinization" of the Japanese emperor, which went hand in hand with the extreme nationalism of late nineteenth century and early twentieth century Japan, owed much to the last phases of the Kokugaku movement, when the *kami* had come to reoccupy the royal ancestral line.

THE NEW RELIGIONS. The first "new religions" arose during the Tokugawa period. They were eclectic packagings of the previous medieval elements, and they gained their success by contrasting favorably with the highly formal, even static, culture that had prevailed in the early nineteenth century. The new religions usually sprang from a charismatic leader who furnished a connection with the *kami*—indeed, whom his or her followers took to be a *kami*.

Since the government was pushing Shinto, the new religions tended to join the nationalistic trend. Tenrikyo, a modern faith-healing denomination, is a good example. It sprang from a revelation that its founder, Nakayama Miki, had in 1838. She had been a devout Buddhist, but while serving as a medium in a healing ceremony for her son, she felt a *kami* possess her—the

"true, original *kami* Tenri O no Mikoto" ("God the Parent"). Thereafter, her religion had a distinctively shamanic character. Miki embarked on a mission to spread her good news, healing sick people and promulgating the recitation of "I put my faith in Tenri O no Mikoto." The Tokugawa authorities harassed her somewhat, but in time a large number of followers accepted Miki as a living *kami*. Her writings became the Tenrikyo scripture, her songs became its hymns, and her dances shaped its liturgy. Recalling the creation myth of Izanagi and Izanami, she built a shrine "at the center of the world," where she thought the first parents had brought forth the land. The shrine had a square opening in its roof and a tall wooden column—ancient symbolism for the connection to heaven.

Miki's teachings stress joyous living. In the beginning God the Parent made human beings for happiness, but we became self-willed and gloomy. By returning to God the Parent and dropping self-concern, we can restore our original joy. The way to return is commitment to God the Parent and participation in Tenrikyo worship. By stressing gratitude for (sacred) creation, social rather than individual good, hard manual work, and the like, this sect has generated great popular enthusiasm. By the end of the nineteenth century, Tenrikyo claimed more than two million members, testifying to the power of combining old shamanistic elements with new organizational forms and liturgies. Tenrikyo even revived the ancient Shinto concern for purification by focusing on an interior cleansing of doubts and untoward desires.

THE BUSHIDO CODE. Bushido was the ethical and disciplinary code of Japanese samurai, warriors of the feudal period who swore fealty to their lord under pain of death. The samurai became renowned for their courage, sense of honor, and discipline as well as for their outbursts of cruelty and their share in the infighting of Japanese politics. The samurai developed swordsmanship, archery, and hand-to-hand combat as holistic disciplines. Bushido was more cultural than expressly religious, but it drew on Confucian notions of responsibility to one's superiors and Buddhist (especially Zen) notions of the disciplined spirit. Those formed by the Bushido Code considered dishonor worse than death and offered their superiors (the lords for whom they fought and served) complete loyalty.

Bushido was especially significant for gathering together the sense of honor most samurai warriors and their consorts held to be more precious than life itself.

For women, the Bushido virtues of chastity and honor offered a parallel field for spiritual discipline. Manuals instructed young girls who had been compromised how to commit suicide (with the dagger each girl received when she came of age), including details of how, after plunging in the blade, she should tie her lower limbs together so as to secure modesty even in death.

RECENT HISTORY. At the close of the Tokugawa period in 1867, Japan abolished the military dictatorship and restored the emperor. It also changed from a largely decentralized feudal society into a modern nation organized from Tokyo. Japan made astonishing strides in education and culture, assimilating Western science and again opening itself to the outside world (at first under duress, supplied by Commodore Perry and the U.S. gunboats during 1853 and 1854, then voluntarily). Success in two major wars with China and Russia between 1895 and 1905 gave the Japanese great confidence, and the first third of the twentieth century was a time of increasingly strident nationalism. One of the main foci of this nationalism was what became state Shinto. Because of its chauvinist potential, some Japanese thinkers and politicians stressed the divinity of the emperor and the unique dignity of the Japanese people.

During this period Buddhism lost its official status as a branch of the government, Shinto was established as the state religion, and Christianity was reintroduced. In addition, more new religions appeared, which, like Buddhism and Shinto, took on nationalistic overtones.

For our interests the modern period, beginning with the Meiji Restoration (of the emperor) in 1868, is most significant because of the revival of Shinto. This was largely a political operation, designed to glorify the imperial family and to unify the country around its oldest traditions. To bring their tradition up to date and do what their revered ancestors had done, the modern Japanese had only to be utterly loyal to the emperor.

Japan's defeat in World War II produced great national trauma, prompting the emergence of hundreds of new religions. Culturally, defeat meant a shattering

of national pride; religiously, it meant a body blow to state Shinto. The Western conquerors, led by allied commander General Douglas MacArthur, force-fed the Japanese democracy and the concept of individual liberties. On its own, Japan rebuilt with incredible speed, soon becoming the economic giant of Asia. The new constitution disestablished Shinto and allowed complete individual religious freedom. The older traditions, which people identified with the national self-consciousness of prewar times, were shattered, and the new religions rushed in to fill the void. In the past two decades or so, the older traditions have regrouped, especially Buddhism, but secularism has been a strong trend. Caught up in its technological spurt, Japan has seemingly put aside nationalistic and religious issues. The contemporary culture is secularistic, at least outwardly, but in the byways Buddhism and Christianity struggle to revive themselves. Confucian and Daoist elements remain part of the Japanese psyche, but in rather muted voice. Strangely, perhaps, it is Shinto—the ancient version rather than the state— that is the strongest religious presence. Divinity in nature, which Japanese religion has always stressed, continues in the shrines that connect present times to the original *kami*. The place of the emperor remains a touchy issue.

JAPANESE WORLDVIEW

As Confucian, Daoist, and Buddhist influences penetrated Japan, the Japanese people worked steadily to make them their own. Shinto arose as the articulation of the native traditions and the strong social cohesiveness of the Japanese gradually shaped how the new ways would color the old. As in China, the different religious traditions seldom competed on the Western, individualistic model. By and large, people did not feel forced to choose between a wholehearted allegiance to Shinto or a wholehearted allegiance to Buddhism. Confucianism proved useful in expressing Japanese convictions about social relations. Daoism provided help in articulating native feelings about nature, in aesthetics, and also in expressing aspects of Buddhist philosophy. But the typical Japanese person felt free to pick and choose from the wealth of ideas and rituals that the several traditions offered. Any showdown that occurred tended to be between Shinto and Buddhist loyalties, and Shinto always had the great advantage of being intimately bound up with the symbolism of the royal family and the birth of the Japanese islands. The Confucian influence was more indirect or internal than imposed from without. Many more people thought about family life and social relations in Confucian terms than studied the Confucian classics or considered themselves disciples of Master Kong.

From the relative homogeneity of its people, Japanese religion could rely on many tacit assumptions. People long schooled to living closely together and taking pride in their beautiful land did not need to be lectured on consensus or veneration of natural beauty. Certainly, modern technology has shown that Japanese respect for nature is vulnerable; ecological problems are serious. But Japan's genius for taking foreign ideas, technology, and other accomplishments into itself and refashioning them to fit its own sense of peoplehood and social values has continued strong into the contemporary era. What seldom cracks is the ability of the people to work cooperatively for a common good. In the case of religion, that has meant creating a digest of foreign influences that mixed well with Shinto convictions about the significance of beauty and the primacy of the Japanese people. It should prove useful to focus on the ways that Japanese religion has not only offered the usual ministrations (ways of coping with death and other deep questions, ways of hallowing everyday life) but has also helped to energize the Japanese people. The Shinto sense of being the people privileged to live on a beautiful string of islands has moved the Japanese to draw from other traditions what might enhance such a life—give it more vitality, increase its pleasures and decrease its pains.

NATURE

From its earliest beginnings, Japanese religion has been enraptured by nature. Ancient mythology featured the sun goddess Amaterasu and the wind god Susanoo. Furthermore, we best describe the *kami* as nature forces (though they could also possess human beings). Japanese folk religion, which exerted a hardy influence, viewed nature with a peasant's eye. Nature was fertile and fickle, nourishing and devastating. The early myths reflect this paradoxical quality. The

sun goddess was benevolent—a source of warmth, light, and the power to make things grow. The wind god was unpredictable, often destructive. Susanoo's punishment for his misdeeds belies a peasant hope that nature's order and benevolence will prevail. However, Susanoo and his like might have destructive outbreaks at any time; Japan has been a land of earthquakes, volcanoes, floods, and typhoons. Japan is a very beautiful land, but rugged and not easily tamed, and controlling the effects of nature has been a herculean task. Perhaps that accounts for the Japanese delight in gardens and groves—places where they have brought peace to nature.

As we noted in describing the Japanese innovations in Buddhism, this sort of delight showed in the Japanese embellishment of religious ceremonies. Not only do most temples have some sort of grounds, often quite lovely, but their liturgies employ flowers, incense, candles, and other adornments. Along with the Japanese stress on order and cleanliness, which goes back to ancient concerns for purification, a desire has grown to make living graceful. In Shinto shrines, such as Ise, Heian, and Meiji, gardens, pools, fields of flowers, and lofty trees also reflect this desire. The mode in which the Japanese have received these nature lessons, we suggest, has been *religio-aesthetic*. Its religion appears to move by a sense of harmony. If the folk interest is nature's agricultural energies (and the powers responsible for sickness), the higher-class interest is nature's ability to soothe. Sensing that the groves and gardens represent something primal, the warrior, merchant, and bureaucrat have returned to it to escape the human concerns that threatened to swamp them. By communion with nature, the samurai warrior could collect his spirit for a single-minded attack. By slipping away from his accounting, the merchant could anticipate a "retirement," which, in Japan as well as China, allowed more poetic, Daoist preoccupations. The same applies to the bureaucrat. Even Emperor Hirohito, who after World War II was merely a figurehead, specialized in marine biology. Somewhat inept in social situations, he came alive in his pools and gardens.

This interest in nature is religious in the sense that nature has regularly represented to the Japanese something ultimate. Thus, concern for nature has often been an ultimate concern. Japanese religion tries to gain access to the core of the personality, where the personality touches nature's flow. It tries, probably semiconsciously, to let the moss and rocks work their influence. The religious veneration of nature, or even the religio-aesthetic use of nature for soothing the soul, implies an impersonal ultimacy. Furthermore, it implies that humanity, as well as divinity, is more at one with nature than over or against it. Religion based on nature, in fact, tends to collapse humans and gods into nature's forces or nature's flows. As a result, Japan has not seen the world as created by a transcendent force. Rather, Japan has let nature somewhat suppress knowledge and love of divinity, subordinating them to energy and flow. Human beings have been encouraged not to exploit nature (though recent technological changes qualify this statement). Through most of Japanese history, individuals would prune or rake nature rather than lay waste to it, at least in part because human beings did not have a biblical writ to fill the earth and subdue it. Rather, they had a call to live with nature. Today we might hear that as a call to be ecological, grateful, and thus graceful.

This emphasis on nature relegated intellectual concerns to second place. The reasoning of theoreticians tends to be sharp, attacking, and dialectical. The reasoning of contemplative monks tends to be poetic, symbolic, and expressive. Those who ponder the "feminine" intelligence of Eastern cultures must seek to understand this contemplative mind. Generally, Japan has sought the whole rather than the part, the movement rather than the arrest, the beauty as well as the utility. These are feminine characteristics only if masculine refers to only one sort of logic (the shortest distance between two points). If a culture moves more circuitously, Western men will likely call it feminine. We are fortunate to live in a time that challenges such stereotypes.

SOCIETY

Women's Status. It is ironic that a culture that has displayed many stereotypically feminine refinements has been male dominated, almost oppressively so. Although there are traces of an early matriarchy and strong influences from female shamans and their successors in the new religions, women have regularly occupied a low position in Japanese society. Expert in the very refined Japanese tact, wives and mothers have found ways of influence despite their institutionalized powerlessness. In addition, they have run the home and controlled the purse strings. Officially, however, Japan accepted Confucian notions of social relationships (no doubt because they fit traditional predilections), so the female was almost always designated as the underling. The important religious roles played by females in Japanese history require further research. Perhaps their phallic overtones made it fitting that the *kami* should possess females. Or perhaps shamanism offered the powerless a chance to gain attention and influence. Whatever the reasons, women were the prime contact with divinity in folk Shinto, despite strong menstrual taboos. They were the prime contact with the spirits of the dead as well, and so were central in maintaining the sense of the clan. The figurines from the prehistoric Jomon period suggest that women were originally considered awesome because of their power to give birth. The difficulty of the women's liberation movement in contemporary Japan suggests that the powers of women represented by these former roles have long been suppressed.

No doubt for a variety of reasons, the men dominating Japanese society have found it advantageous to place religion and femininity in opposition to warfare and business. As the recourse to nature has been in contrast to things official, so the recourse to monasteries, female shamans, and even geishas has been in contrast to workaday life.

CLAN EMPHASIS. The modern stress on a man's work, identifying him with his corporation, is the result of the group structure of Japanese business. Consequently, the typical businessman takes much of his recreation with his fellow workers apart from his family. A characteristic of the traditional family was concern with the dead. As in China, ancestor veneration was a significant portion of the average person's religious contacts with ultimate powers. Originally, the Japanese probably worried that the departed continued to hover around the places where they had lived. The Japanese tended to associate their ancestors with *kami.* Therefore, in its petitions and venerations, the clan reminded itself of its own identity (the function that some sociologists, such as Durkheim, have considered the main rationale for religion) and kept attuned to the natural forces of life and death.

Thus, the family tended to be the locus of daily worship, and the family shrine tended to predominate over the village or national shrine. Still, there was not a sharp division between the family clan and the national clan. The emperor was often considered the head not only of his own line but also of the entire Japanese people; the gods of Shinto mythology were the gods of the collective Japanese group; and national shrines such as Ise were the site of ceremonies performed on behalf of the entire nation.

The Confucian cast of much traditional Japanese social thought is evident from the first article of a constitution developed by Prince Shotoku in 604 C.E. The implication is that throughout the land, harmony ought to be the watchword.

ETHICS. This historical sense of clan was accompanied by certain ethical assumptions that were immensely influential in shaping the Japanese conscience. The medieval samurai conceived of their own lives as belonging to their feudal lords. If a samurai failed his lord, by being defeated or less than fully successful, he was expected to offer to commit ritual suicide—to petition his lord for this "favor," so that he might mend the honor he had violated. In contemporary Japan, the individual worker is supposed to promote the honor of his bosses above all. He is to assume any failures by his group and to attribute any successes to the group's leader. Thus, the boss (or at most the group as a whole) always gets credit for a bright idea or increased productivity. If the worker does not rock the boat, the corporation will take care of all his needs until he dies.

SELF

Shinto defined the self less clearly than it defined nature or the group. Thus, when Confucianism brought an elaborate social protocol, the sense of self in Japanese religious consciousness was bound to be de-emphasized. In fact, Japanese religion does not emerge as a champion of freethinking. Compared with religion elsewhere, Japanese religion does not support individual initiative or responsibility to a significant degree. Japan has told the individual that fulfillment is a matter of harmonizing with nature and society.

Perhaps as a consequence of selflessness, the individual Japanese may appear ethically underdeveloped to the Westerner. Such a description can provide confusion as well as misperception and offense. Still, a Western student has to begin with existing Western categories, even if they prove inappropriate. In Western ethics, the individual person judges right and wrong, largely because Greek philosophy and Israelite religion, the bases for Western culture, made the individual an intellectual and moral subject of revelation—in the Greek case, revelation from a nature or personal experience structured by reason (Logos); in the Israelite case, revelation from a willful God. By the time of the Enlightenment (eighteenth century), the West had developed this patrimony to the point that the individual could be autonomous and ethics a matter of individual reasoning. Even though recent thought has found this view to be inadequate, it remains influential and at least partially true.

In some ways Shinto was more concerned with ritual pollution than with individual morality. Pollution did not pertain to the intentions of the actor, and no distinctions were made between accidental and deliberate violations. Merely to shed blood or encounter death was polluting. Consequently, the polluted person did not have to assume responsibility, to repent, or to renew the self morally. Essentially, both the pollution and the purification were external to the violator and amoral. Polluting acts occurred in the context of rather physical forces, akin to electricity or the shark's response to blood.

In the medieval period, the warrior or serf let his master be his will. The master held the power of life and death over the servant; morality was more a matter of loyalty to conscience. This de-emphasis on conscience in personal life has persisted even in the modern period. As the honor accorded ritual suicide suggests, the individual has been subject to the social code in nearly all matters. From medieval times, as we suggested earlier, an individual's proper bearing toward the group was loosely codified in Bushido, the warrior's way. Bushido discipline may be a factor for the vitality of the modern Japanese economy. The watchwords for the individual in Japanese religious history, then, were discipline and self-effacement. Fulfillment would come from submission to nature and service to the group, not from self-development or personal contact with God. The religious traditions, consequently, tended to help satisfy society's need for good workers and compliant citizens. Although this is true of religious traditions in most places, it stands out in Japan. The happy life that a new religion such as Tenrikyo holds out to its adherents is the result of reviving ancient concepts, including the submersion of the individual in the group.

ULTIMATE REALITY

Japanese divinity, though complex, is essentially an impersonal collectivity of natural and clan forces. The sharply defined personage of Western religion hardly appears in Japan. The gods of Shinto mythology, for instance, have a distinctly finite knowledge, love, and power; they have not separated from the cosmos to make particular demands. In the course of Japanese history, there have been numerous personal claims to divinity, such as Miki's.

To the present, the times and spaces that are most wonderful, though, are the folk festivals and the popular pilgrim shrines. At special festivals or shrines, one passed a threshold (limen) and went from the ordinary to the sacred world. To set off places where people might venerate the *kami*, the Japanese have long fashioned wooden shrines with encompassing groves. They have not designed the shrines for communal worship but rather as simple sites where people might recite ritual prayers and make offerings to the *kami*. Unlike the Buddhist temples, the Shinto shrines originally did not contain statues. The official focal point of veneration usually was an old sword or mirror, which was considered to be the *kami*'s resting place or "body." However, these ritual objects were seldom seen, even by the Shinto priests, so the general impression most visitors received was of a simple wooden pavilion where one might make a personal petition or venerate the *kami* in the course of a village celebration.

Usually the encompassing grove was almost as important as the wooden pavilion. The grove typically was of rectangular shape, and one entered it through a sacred archway, or *torii*. At the entrance stood a well, where visitors were to take some water in a wooden dipper and purify their hands. At the entrance to many Shinto shrines two stone lions stood guard. Even today the tall trees create an atmosphere of quiet, which the trees' association with the *kami* turns in the direction of religious respect. The general appearance of both the grove and the shrine buildings

is unadorned. Thus the grove's vegetation burgeons almost wildly and the shrine buildings usually are of rough wood. Exceptions occur, as in the red-painted Heian shrine of Kyoto, but even there the total effect is subdued, in flight from anything fancy or garish. The roofs of the large Heian buildings are shingled with natural materials, and the gardens behind the buildings are understated. As with the great shrine at Ise, the grove keeps a fairly dense appearance, probably so that the natural influences of the *kami* can seem to outweigh the cultural influences of human beings.

When visitors approach a main shrine, they usually clap their hands and ring a suspended bell to attract the gods' attention. Then they bow, in reverence or prayer, and deposit their offerings in a money chest. Another building, at the innermost part of the shrine, is a sort of holy-of-holies, where the deities actually dwell. Laity have no access to this building, and the popular attitude has been that to peek into it and observe the ritual objects that attract the *kami* would be to court blindness or death. Because of Buddhist influences, some Shinto shrines erected pictures of human beings or images of gods, but generally the "bodies" of the *kami* have been impersonal objects. In addition to the old swords and mirrors, stones, sacred texts, ancient scrolls, jewels, and balls of crystal have predominated. All these objects have associations with natural forces (or, on occasion, heroic human figures) thought to embody the *kami*. When the influence of Buddhist *bodhisattvas* came to color the Shinto notion of the *kami* and so led to deifying especially loyal subjects of the emperors, the headgear, batons, weapons, clothing, writing implements, and other possessions of such deified subjects also became "bodies" of the *kami*.

Before the disestablishment of Shinto after World War II, the government classified shrines on twelve levels. At the head of the list was the Great Imperial

Which theoretical approach would give you the most insight on the history, doctrine, rituals, ethics of Japanese religion? Pick Durkheim, Freud, Malinowski, Tylor, or Frazer, and indicate how his theory explains the complex syncretism of Japanese religion.

Contribute to this discussion at
http://forums.delphiforums.com/rel101

Shrine at Ise. Below Ise came the various large government or national shrines, such as the Heian Shrine in Kyoto and the Meiji Shrine in Tokyo, and then the smaller local shrines. Not even on the list were the tens of thousands of little-village or domestic shrines, at which a great deal of Shinto worship actually occurred. Before World War II there were about 111,000 official shrines and about 15,500 Shinto priests.

SUMMARY: THE JAPANESE CENTER

Characteristically, the Japanese have shown a remarkable talent for taking other peoples' works and giving them a distinctive polish or perfection. This has happened recently with Western technology, and historically it has happened with non-Japanese religion. Most of the religious influences that Japan appropriated and perfected came from China. To its native Shinto orientations, Japan welded Confucian, Daoist, and Buddhist components. The result was an energetic, disciplined, elegant religious ideal. Aesthetic as well as philosophic, solitary yet bounded by clan allegiances, the Japanese way could take nationalistic and militaristic turns without completely losing sight of a beautiful center.

The Japanese center that provokes such responses is not personal. The nature that gives serenity and proportion is not warm. No divine face waits to break the stillness of the Rock Garden.

At the Japanese center, reality is polite. Cleanliness and formality, mediated through Shinto concerns with purity and the vital forces of nature, obtain. The rituals of the traditional religious year express different aspects of this vitality. For harvests, marrying, the New Year, and burials, different measures of Shinto and Buddhist traditions color life's mystery fertile, familial, regenerative, or transmigratory. It is a beautiful land that the Japanese people celebrate. It is a cohesive national identity.

The polite center judges all brutality harshly, but brutality has had many inglorious seasons in Japan. For peasants, women, and ordinary people, it has been easy to be in the wrong place at the wrong time. Then the ruling powers have crushed people thoughtlessly, like a cart rolling over a bug. The consolations of nature never shroud the fact that nature itself can be very cruel. In a land of volcanoes and fierce storms, beauty and violence have often commingled. In a land of warriors and artists, discipline has had several faces. The Japanese center lets these disparities be, instead of reconciling them in some thicker mystery. Atonement and redemption are not the Japanese way.

CHAPTER 7

GREEK AND

HELLENISTIC

RELIGION

GREEK AND HELLENISTIC RELIGION: 25 KEY DATES	
Date	**Event**
ca. 6500 B.C.E.	First farming in Aegean areas
2000 B.C.E.	Minoan civilization begins on Crete
1200 B.C.E.	collapse of Mycenaean civilization in Greece
776 B.C.E.	first Olympic Games
750 B.C.E.	writings of Homer and Hesiod
ca. 600 B.C.E.	Eleusinian mysteries spread around Greece
570–500 B.C.E.	Pythagorus
ca. 550 B.C.E.	Thales says everything is water
540–480 B.C.E.	Heraclitus says that everything is in flux
525–406 B.C.E.	playwrights: Aeschylus, Sophocles, Euripides
ca. 500 B.C.E.	Orphics become popular
ca. 470 B.C.E.	Parmenides says everything is one
ca. 450 B.C.E.	Zeno's paradoxes
500–430 B.C.E.	Empodocles recognizes earth, water, air, and fire
470–399 B.C.E.	Socrates
ca. 390 B.C.E.	rise of Cyrenaics (pleasure) and Cynics (asceticism)
429–347 B.C.E.	Plato
384–322 B.C.E.	Aristotle
342–270 B.C.E.	Epicurus says that pleasure is the greatest good
342–260 B.C.E.	Zeno of Citrium, founder of Stoics
332–329 B.C.E.	Alexander conquers Egypt, Persia, India; beginning of Hellenistic era
200 B.C.E.	Goddess Cybele is brought to Rome from Phrygia
1st century C.E.	Isis and Osirus brought to Rome from Egypt
1st century C.E.	Christianity brought to Greek and Roman cities
2nd century C.E.	Mithra brought to Rome from Persia

The key word to the understanding of Greek and Hellenistic religion is **syncretism,** the tendency to run together several gods, ceremonies, doctrines or other aspects of two or more religious traditions. The cases of China and Japan show that syncretism could produce more than an undigested mixture or infertile hybrid. Greece stood at the crossroads of the ancient Mediterranean world, and its culture tended to mix and match rather than resist and reject that which was foreign (the strategy employed by the Jews).

HISTORY

Greece is a mountainous peninsula and archipelago in the eastern Mediterranean (also called the Aegean Sea). Much trade activity with the Sumerians and Egyptians stimulated development in this area in the middle of the third millennium B.C.E. This first Bronze Age culture became known as Minoan because it was centered on the island of Crete (named after Minos, the legendary king of Crete). By about 1700 B.C.E., the Minoans had a linear script, and in the period 1580–1450 B.C.E. a splendid civilization flourished.

> *Mycenaean tomb figurines*

The first peninsular Greeks, called Minyans, were Aryan-speaking Indo-Europeans. They established relations with Minoan Crete, and around 1400 B.C.E. (at which time they were known as Mycenaeans) these Greeks had settled at the Cretan capital city of Knossos. The Mycenaean period (1400–1150 B.C.E.) constituted Crete's last glory; a people known as the Dorians invaded from northern Greece and instituted a "dark age" in the Aegean region from 1100 to 650 B.C.E. During that period, literacy largely passed from the Greek scene. Consequently, much of our knowledge of Minoan religious culture comes from archeological excavations. These reveal that caves were great cultural centers from Neolithic times, serving as dwellings, cemeteries, and religious sites all in one.

THE EARLIEST RELIGION

As the archeological excavations show quite clearly, the foremost deity of Cretan cave religion was a goddess whose primary features were fertility and mastery of animals. This finding corresponds with remains found on Cretan mountains, where Minoans also celebrated fertility. However, the goddess cult probably did more than simply venerate natural life. The many burial remains, symbols of butterflies and bees (change-of-state beings), and other artifacts suggest a complex religious interest in life, death, and rebirth. Probably participants underwent initiation into these mysteries, much as tribal Africans or Australians have long done. The remains or artistic representations of bull horns, double axes, trees, animals, cosmic pillars, and blood sacrifices testify to a particularly rich Neolithic agricultural goddess religion, perhaps one involving **theriomorphic** (animal-form) spirit beings. A related ritual may have been human sacrifice (or at least a ritual trial of human wits against animal brawn, such as in the legend of Theseus), but this practice seems to have been over by the dawn of the sixth century B.C.E.

In light of later Greek initiations—for example, those into the Eleusinian and Orphic mysteries—it is likely that the Minoan goddess cult aimed at ensuring a happy afterlife. If so, it probably had conceptions of immortality that continued through the dark age.

It is possible that the worship of this single discovered goddess was merely one example of a broader pattern of worship of gods of the earth. Several investigators have suggested that a broad animism (viewing spirits in everything) probably ranged in this area in the first agricultural settlements, at least until specific deities could be identified (probably at the time of the settlement of the first cities).

These earth spirits were known as the *chthonioi*. Such *chthonic*, or earth, deities probably remained, at least at the popular level, throughout the course of Greek culture, perhaps to the coming of Christianity. Similar to what we saw in China, these agricultural deities were local: the god one village worshipped may not have been the one worshipped by the next village. These earth spirits had two main functions (as we inferred from the archeology of the goddess on Crete): fertility and rule of the dead. For the most part, the *chthonioi* were local spirits, concerned with a particular town's crops or deceased members. These two themes are connected: Greece is further north than Egypt, Mesopotamia, the Indus Valley, or Israel, and although winters are not cold, there is a definite growing cycle. Grapevines wither and appear dead in the winter, and it seems like a miracle when young vines shoot forth in the spring (hence, the prevalence of dying and rising gods in this region).

Additional focus must be given to the importance of the dead. (Indeed, this is something every later movement in Greek religion seems to address, and no two of them seem to have the same answer.) The only thing that we can say for sure about this earliest stage is that **funerals** were considered an important ritual, a right of the deceased, and a sacred obligation of the surviving relatives. One of Sophocles' plays, *Antigone*, represents this duty: The heroine, Antigone, has two brothers fighting for the throne of Thebes. When both were killed in the battle, uncle Creon takes charge. He declares that one brother had the legitimate claim to the throne, so the other is the usurper. Creon then decrees that the rightful heir to the throne will be buried with the full honors befitting a king, but the other will not receive any burial (and anyone who attempts to give him this will suffer pain of death). Antigone's sacred duty to provide burial for both of her brothers transcends the issue of who was right or wrong on the battlefield. It also transcends any duty she may have to preserve the stability of the state by obeying her uncle, and even any interest she has in preserving her own life.

When one village of Greeks heard about the spirits or deities of another village, their first response

The Olympic games began in Greece, and their name comes from Mt. Olympus. The athletes competed in the nude. The Greeks had no sense of shame about the human body.

was not always to think: "Our gods are better than your gods." Rather, they tended to ponder how the different gods might be related. Could your goddess be ours with just another name? Could they be long-lost sisters with an interesting tale to tell about how they became separated? The Greeks loved to spin a yarn, embellish upon a legend. (Playwrights such as Euripides and Sophocles might take a standard myth as the basis for a play and then have full license to change the ending without fear of upsetting the audience.)

Sometimes the local earth spirits blended with the cult of a local hero. At other times sacrifices to the *chthonioi* had overtones of devotion to Gaea, Demeter, Pluto, or Trophonious—divinities of fertility or Hades. Whether the *chthonioi* were gods or shady figures imagined to populate the afterlife is not clear. Regardless, they elicited considerable fear, and the common people tried not to offend them.

A key difference between these ancient Greeks and modern (especially Protestant) Christians is that there was no canon of myths that was considered sacred.

There were some myth collections, like those attributed to Homer, but even these were not universally considered a canon for clarifying doctrines about deities. A layperson could dispute a myth or counter one myth with another competing explanation, and no great offense would be perceived. The only way to really deny the deities their due was in the realm of ritual: the layperson who refused to perform a ritual duty (such as burial) ran the risk of offending the spirits (and incurring the wrath of his or her fellow citizens).

THE OLYMPIAN PANTHEON

The **Olympian pantheon** is so named because these gods were said to reside atop Mount Olympus. The name is associated with the Olympic games: the games were named after the gods, not the gods after the games. The gods were not called Olympian because they were athletic; the athletic contests were seen as a ritual honoring these gods.

COMPARISON OF ANCIENT GREEK AND ROMAN RELIGIONS

GREEK	ROMAN	FAMILY	CHARACTERISTICS
Achilles		son of Peleus and Thetis	hero of Trojan war, killed by arrow in heel
Adonis		son of Myrrha	lover of Aphrodite, killed by wild boar
Antigone		daughter of Oedipus and Jocasta	risked execution by burying dead brother
Aphrodite	Venus	daughter of Zeus, wife of Hephaestos	goddess of love
Apollo		son of Zeus and Leto	god of reason, father of medicine, Delphi was his oracle
Ares	Mars	son of Zeus and Hera	god of war
Artemis	Diana	daughter of Zeus and Leto	goddess of the hunt, virgin
Athena	Minerva		goddess of war, wisdom, Athens
Atlas		brother of Prometheus	Titan condemned to carry earth on his shoulders
Cronus	Saturn	son of Uranus and Gaea	Titan defeated by his son, Zeus
Demeter	Ceres	daughter of Cronus and Rhea	goddess of grain, mother of Persephone
Dionysus	Bacchus	son of Zeus and Semele	god of vegetation and wine, inspired a cult
Gaea		mother and wife of Uranus	first being to come out of chaos, mother of the Titans
Hades	Pluto	son of Cronus, brother of Zeus	god of underworld, ruler over the dead

The Olympian deities came with the Minyan peoples and represented a patriarchal order similar to that of the Aryans who invaded Iran or India. There was a warrior god who hurled a thunderbolt (**Zeus**), similar in name to the Indo-Aryan Dyeus, and similar in role to the Teutonic Thor.

The more systematized myth of the Olympian pantheon of deities is usually attributed to a blind poet named Homer. This polytheistic hierarchy of deities was one of the most **anthropomorphic** (humanlike) in history. Indeed, these myths were more like soap opera tales of lust, revenge, jealousy, pettiness, and poor decision making (but remember, Greek gods were not insulted by the content of the myths about

them). Did Homer, however, create these figures out of whole cloth? Probably, he merely took figures that his audience (relatively enlightened nobility who could pay) was already familiar with and gave clever and entertaining explanations of how one god got his assigned celestial role, or how another got a certain personality quirk. These deities are in the form of a **pantheon** (a systematic structure). Arranging the deities in a kind of family tree, and explaining their origin from a previous generation of Titans and back to original chaos, was probably the work of Hesiod (ca. 750 B.C.E.), if not someone before him.

Archeologists discovered a written script called Linear B, traceable to the Greeks on Crete from

GREEK	ROMAN	FAMILY	CHARACTERISTICS
Hecate		daughter of Uranus and Gaea	only Titan to retain power under Zeus, goddess of sorcery
Hephaestos	Vulcan	husband of Aphrodite	god of the forge
Heracles	Hercules	son of Zeus	cursed by Hera, brave and strong
Hera	Juno	sister and wife of Zeus	jealous
Hermes	Mercury	son of Zeus	god of commerce
Hestia	Vesta		goddess of western star, Roman temple tended by virgins
Orpheus		son of Apollo	musician, inspired a cult
Pandora		first woman created by Zeus	let human problems out of the box
Persephone or Kore		daughter of Zeus and Demeter	abducted by Hades, inspired Eleusinian cult
Perseus		son of Zeus	killed Medusa
Poseidon	Neptune	son of Cronus	god of sea
Rhea		wife and sister of Cronus	earth goddess, mother of Zeus
Theseus		son of Aegus	slew the minotaur, escaped from labyrinth
Titans			giants who preceded Olympian gods, then were defeated by them
Uranus	Caelus	son and husband of Gaea	defeated by his son, Cronus
Zeus	Jupiter	son of Cronus	king of gods, creator of men

1400 B.C.E. The existence of this script shows that by that time, Minoan and Mycenaean cultural forces were interacting and Olympian myths were being developed. The important effect was that later Greek religious culture appropriated Minoan Crete as its golden age. For instance, according to Olympian legend, Zeus was born on Crete, and Apollo, Heracles, and Demeter (and even the non-Olympian Dionysus) performed prodigies or had high adventures on Crete. Crete thus became the *omphalos,* the navel or birth center, of the classical Hellenic world. At the end of his life and literary career, when he composed his masterpiece the *Laws,* Plato placed his characters on Crete, walking from Knossos into the hills to the temple cave of Zeus.

But wait just a minute! If Zeus was born on Crete, how could he have come from the northern Minyan invaders? If that apparent inconsistency bothers you, you are employing biblical standards of canonical consistency where they should not be applied. The stories about the Greek gods kept changing to reflect the ongoing changes of peoples and places. Having an obviously northern, mainland deity like Zeus born in Crete is just a myth that attempts a little syncretism: making him relevant to a new geographic area.

One of the outstanding characteristics of Indo-European religion was its interest in sky phenomena — storms, wind, lightning, the sun, and stars. Zeus, the prime Greek Olympian god, is comparable to Vedic and Iranian sky gods. (In proto-Indo-European religion, mother earth was polar to father sky but less powerful.) Furthermore, the Indo-Europeans were much concerned with the human word—in sacrifices, chanting, spells, and sagas. Their traditions were largely oral, and they opposed writing when they first encountered it among Near Eastern peoples. It is worth underscoring that they had a powerful, double sense of the sacred—the sacred was both charged with divine presence and forbidden to human touch. Throughout its later development, Greek religion never lost this sense of awe-filled unapproachability. Finally, as we noted in connection with Iran, Indo-Europeans divided their society and gods into three groups. As a result, Vedic India, Aryan Iran, and preclassical Greece all had priests, warriors, and commoners (though in Greece the priestly class was underdeveloped). If both Crete and mainland Greece maintained earlier traditions during the dark age, we can assume that the emergence of Homeric Olympian religion was quite slow.

By the time of the great poet Homer, however, the Indo-European religion had a distinctively Greek flavor. For instance, Zeus had acquired a mythological lineage. According to a later work, Hesiod's *Theogony,* he was born in the third generation of gods, after the original period of Earth and Heaven and the second period of the Titans. When Zeus overthrew his father Cronus or Kronos (Saturn), the present world resulted. (This is one of the world's few myths where the son rebelled against the father, and triumphed.)

In terms of his success in being recognized by the common people as the main deity, Zeus came to preeminence slowly. Most likely, his many liaisons with local goddesses symbolize a religious and political takeover, as a unified Greek culture emerged out of local traditions. These local traditions did not disappear but instead were incorporated into the large complex of Greek religious notions, enriching both Greek mythology and religious practices. For instance, the local Cretan dances of armed youths during their initiation ceremonies became part of the colorful story of the infant Zeus' birth in Crete. The noise of the youths' clashing shields drowned out the infant's cries, and so saved him from Cronus, who wanted to devour him. Furthermore, the Cretan Zeus merged with the child and lover of the Cretan goddess, linking him to the island's Neolithic past. In classical Greece, Zeus was first among the gods dwelling on Mount Olympus, as Homer portrayed him. He was the father of humans, the ruler of their destinies, and, despite his own moral waywardness, the ultimate upholder of justice.

In addition to Zeus, the roster of the foremost Olympian gods included Hera, Zeus' wife; Poseidon, god of the sea; Hephaestus, the divine blacksmith; Apollo, god of law and order; Hermes, the divine messenger; Artemis, mistress of wild beasts; Athena, patroness of feminine and practical arts; and Aphrodite, goddess of love. Of these gods and goddesses, Apollo deserves special mention, because he came to symbolize many virtues that seemed typically Greek, such as serenity, harmony, balance, and order. Through his oracle at Delphi, Apollo gave counsel on matters of liturgical propriety and ritual purification. For example, Apollo had charge of purifying homicides, who had to be cleansed of their "pollution." One would take serious matters needing counsel to Apollo's *pythia* (priestess) at Delphi. In trance, she would exclaim the wisdom with which Apollo filled her. The origins of the *pythia*'s exclamation may lie in shamanism, but by classical times Apollonian wisdom had distanced itself from the emotional and irrational, becoming primarily intellectual *theoria*—relatively serene religious contemplation. As epitomized in the Delphic oracle's command "Know thyself," Apollonian religion deified thought and spirit. For that reason, it encouraged science, art, philosophy, and music.

ORACLES AND DIVINATION

The main function of these **oracles,** however, was not worship of a deity but **divination** (foretelling the individual fortunes of persons and city-states). Ancient Greece was similar to ancient Mexico, China, Mesopotamia, and Africa: there were periods of extreme instability (due largely to the shifting power centers within the Greek city-states). The solution for instability is knowledge about one's personal future. These oracles, like other types of shrines, were out of the main cities and required a pilgrimage. Each one had a different gimmick for foretelling the future. At Dodona, there would be the rustling of the leaves within a cave like a wind tunnel. At Delphi, there was a priestess who went into a trance and made utterances that may have required someone else's interpretation. (One theory was that the cave in which the

Parthenon

ritual took place had fumes that could have physically induced the trance and hallucinations.) Other oracles (e.g., Epidarus) specialized in the interpretation of dreams. Many Greeks also turned to wandering seers and soothsayers, who might use any of the aforementioned techniques along with traditional approaches of watching a flight of birds, lightning, animal entrails, or the casting of lots. The oracles became an important part of Greek culture, and pilgrimage may have had some semblance of rites of passage: expectant parents would try to get a glimpse of the destiny of their future child; at age eighteen, young men would get what amounted to career advice, while young women might have had an insight into their future husbands. Part of the awe-inspiring aspect of visiting the oracle was the fear that one would learn the inevitable details of one's own death.

The story of Oedipus began as a Greek myth and was retold in the play by Sophocles, *Oedipus Rex*. This is a great example of the power of oracles in Greek culture. Anticipating the birth of his first child, the king of Thebes is goes to an oracle for a divination

concerning the child. The king is told that his wife, Queen Jocasta, will give birth to a son who will kill his father and marry his mother. When a son is born, the king resolves that this must not come to pass. He tells a servant to take the child up to the mountaintop and slay him. The servant merely abandons the child, but tells the king that the deed was done. A passerby finds the abandoned child and carries him over the hill to the next little kingdom. There the king and queen have been childless, and when they hear of the abandoned child, they adopt him, call him Oedipus, and resolve never to tell him of his origin. Upon turning 18, young man Oedipus goes to an oracle to get a divination about his adult life. He is told that he will kill his father and marry his mother but resolves to leave the land of his (adoptive) parents so that he will not fulfill this future. Going back over the hill, and entering the kingdom of Thebes, he meets an old man on the road. The two quarrel, and Oedipus kills the old man, who happens to be none other than his biological father. Eventually, Oedipus solves a riddle posed by a theriomorphic sphinx and is rewarded by being declared the new king of Thebes. Part of the deal is that he will marry the widow of the last king, Queen Jocasta (his biological mother). Freud's interpretation of the power of the Oedipus myth was that humanity is so driven by the forces of sex and aggression that young boys have the desire to sexually possess their mothers and kill their fathers. The ancient Greeks understood the story of Oedipus to reflect the power of fate. Both Oedipus and his father before him strove to prevent the catastrophe foretold from coming about, yet their actions set in motion events that resulted in the final outcomes predicted by the diviners.

THE OLDER MYSTERY CULTS

The sky-oriented, rational aspect of Olympian religion never was the whole story. From the Minoans came an earthly religion to balance the sky. There were many mother goddesses. Hera, Artemis, and Aphrodite, for example, all relate to fertility and mother earth. In Hesiod's *Theogony,* Gaia (earth) actually precedes and produces heaven. The result of this earth-oriented counterweight to the somewhat overbearing Olympian gods who resided in heaven was a view that humans should aim to become, in Plato's phrase, "as much like God as possible." Through contact with the forces of life and fertility (in the Eleusinians' case) and with the forces of intellectual light (in the philosophers' case), the limits of mortality were challenged. "No," many Greeks said, "we are made for more than a few days in the sun. If we truly know ourselves, we can find undying life."

The form of religion known as the **mystery cult** was a recurring phenomenon in Greek and Hellenistic times, from about 600 B.C.E. to 300 C.E. Although these religions were proselytizing, and tended to gain new followers and spread geographically, they had an element of secrecy, either of doctrine and/or ritual. The complete story would only be revealed after initiation (or in the next world) and the initiated members of the cult were sworn not to reveal the secrets to outsiders. Membership in these cults might also be a secret. In a great example of syncretism, members of mystery cults might be indistinguishable from other citizens of the Greek city-states (or later Roman empire) in that they would participate in local rituals to the Olympian pantheon, seek counsel from the oracles, and study philosophy, but then on some occasions they

would sneak out and participate in the rituals of the mystery cult.

DIONYSIANS. Somewhat the antithesis of Apollo was **Dionysus,** an eccentric among the gods of the Olympian period. A son of Zeus by a mortal woman, Dionysus apparently always remained an outsider. His cult was not native to central Greece but may have come from Asia Minor, where a similar deity named Bacchus was the god of the vine. Dionysus was a god of vegetation who would disappear to the underworld and then spring back to life. His concern with the irrational and emotional made many fear his cult. Unlike the ecstasy of the Apollonian *pythia,* that of the followers of Dionysus (for example, of the women called *maenads*) was wild, frenzied, and orgiastic. Such ecstasy represented the enthusiasm (being filled with divine force) that could come from dancing and wine drinking. The most influential literary source on the Dionysian cult, Euripides' play *The Bacchae,* portrays the god's followers as wildly joyous. If the play depicts the actual rituals of this cult, their mountain revels culminated in tearing apart live animals and eating the flesh raw (so as to commune with the god of animal life).

Strangely enough, the Greeks recognized something essential in the non-Olympian Dionysus. Call it the need to reverence the life force, or the value of temporarily escaping one's moral bonds—they blessed it and called it good. As a result, Apollo vacated Delphi during the three winter months and allowed Dionysus to reign. This cult seems to have been most popular among urban married women, perhaps out of frustrations with their limited roles.

ELEUSINIANS. This mystery cult is named for its place of origin, Eleusis, where it was no doubt an ancient system of myth and ritual. After about 600 B.C.E., it seems to have been exported to other Greek city-states but probably remained strongest in Athens (which was not far from Eleusis). The **Eleusinian cult** involved a mother-daughter pair of deities. Demeter was an earth deity ("goddess of the grain"). The growing season was explained by the myth that Hades (god of the underworld) had decided to make off with Demeter's adolescent daughter Persephone (also known as Kore) and take her to the underworld to be his wife. In the ensuing dispute between Demeter and

Hades, Zeus intervened with a compromise: Persephone would spend part of the year above with her mother and part of the year below with her husband. So, when Persephone is above, Demeter is happy and yields the harvest, but when winter comes, the ground lies fallow. The myth also had a subplot about Demeter's unsuccessful (because of human folly) attempt to make Demophoon, the infant prince of Eleusis, an immortal. Thus, the mysteries consisted of rites and revelations that gave initiates precious knowledge in this life and bliss in the world to come.

We do not know the particulars of the mysteries, which were strictly secret, but the mystery religions probably grafted Neolithic agricultural ideas onto the Olympian theme that the gods are immortal. If so, the mysteries moved beyond the myths of the Melanesian Hainuwele type, in which agriculture entailed ritual murder and gods that died. The result was a new and powerful synthesis of sexuality and death (as reflected in Persephone's being carried to the underworld by Pluto) and of agriculture and a happy existence beyond the grave (as in Demeter's representing mother earth). This religious synthesis made Eleusis an important cultic center for almost 2,000 years. Adherents to the Eleusinian mysteries lived in all parts of the Greek world and came from all social classes. Anyone who spoke Greek and had "clean hands" (including women, children, and slaves) could take part. Poets of the stature of Pindar and Sophocles praised the mysteries.

ORPHICS. The **Orphic** mystery cult also had a focus on entering the underworld to defeat death. Orpheus was a prominent Thracian hero, the son of Calliope by Apollo. His great gift was for music—when he played the lyre wild beasts grew calm, trees danced, and rivers stood still. Orpheus married the nymph Eurydice, who died from snakebite while fleeing Aristaeus, another son of Apollo. Orpheus could have regained Eurydice from the underworld if he had been able to resist looking at her. But he could not, so he had to wander inconsolably until followers of Dionysus tore him apart (because of his devotion to Apollo).

Unlike most Greeks, the Orphics had an unfavorable view of life: while the soul is immortal, the earthly body is its tomb. Death is only apparent, for there will be reincarnation. We will not remember our past lives in our future ones, we will just continue to suffer. For eternal blessedness, Orphics preached, one had

to follow a strict moral code, abstain from the flesh of living creatures and avoid wearing wool. In some accounts, the prohibitions also included sex. When fully pure, the soul would be reincarnated no more. No more would it drink of the spring of Lethe (forgetfulness), but, light as air, it would live in union with the divine mind. The Orphics, which can be traced back to about 500 B.C.E., appealed to persons of refinement; they were one of the few Greek religions that had a sacred book. Orphism certainly influenced Plato, the natural philosopher Empedocles, and the Roman epic poet Virgil.

Both the Eleusinian mysteries and the Orphic rites sought immortality, the one by a profound ritualization of the life force, the other by purification of the divine soul. Together, they were a strong counterforce to the pessimism fostered by the heaven-oriented Olympianism, which taught that once one passed from the sun everything became a shadowy darkness.

PYTHAGOREANS. The founder of this cult was The same Pythagorus who brought an interest in mathematics, especially geometry. He lived in the sixth century B.C.E. in Sicily, which was then one of the western-most colonies of Greece. Imagine a monastic brotherhood of mathematicians who were convinced that there was a secret knowledge as precise as geometry that could be used to save the soul. The soul was seen as immortal, but it became imprisoned in earthly bodies, human and animal. It retains some memory of previous lives. In order to escape the cycle of reincarnation, it is necessary to live an ascetic life, avoid meat and beans, and study math as a key to cosmic law. The Pythagoreans also contributed to the study of music with their mathematical relationships of harmonics. The Pythagoreans may have also influenced Plato's ideas about forms. Despite the striking similarities between the Orphics and the Pythagoreans, there is no evidence of direct contact between the two schools.

PHILOSOPHY

Most textbooks in world religions do not touch Greek philosophy, claiming that it is a separate discipline. However, we think of it as an attempt to address two of the key elements of religion, doctrine and ethics, and in some instances (e.g., Plato's writings) there is a powerful use of symbol and a suggestion of myth.

The only thing that made some philosophical systems fall short of the complete definition of religion would have been ritual.

The common people did not build Athenian culture or develop the breakthrough called *philosophy* (the "love of wisdom"). Rather, an aristocratic elite, working for several centuries, slowly distinguished the realms of myth and reason and in so doing wrote a pivotal chapter in the history of human consciousness.

Before philosophy, the concept of reason was vague. Only the culture of the Greek city-state identified reason and controlled it. Only the line of pre-Socratic thinkers—most prominently, Pythagoras, Xenophanes, Parmenides, and Heraclitus—so disciplined their dissatisfaction with Olympian culture that they saw the human mind (*nous*) itself as being divine and real. India approached this position but never came away with Greece's counterbalancing view of the reality of the material world.

The earliest recorded Greek philosophers speculated about the nature of reality and considered the same elements as those considered by the ancient Chinese. In the mid-sixth century B.C.E., **Thales** was considered one of the seven wise men of Athens. He was renowned for his skill in international diplomacy as well as for his business acumen. He had a great interest in the natural world, predicting eclipses and changes in weather patterns, but he was also interested in abstract things. He is credited with five geometric theorems. Thales' main claim to fame is that he was regarded by Aristotle to be the founder of philosophy. He had noticed that ice, steam, and liquid water are just different forms of the same element and concluded that water was the basic element in all of reality, especially life. He is alleged to have said, "All things are full of gods," which means that Thales viewed water more as a spiritual force than a molecular foundation for reality.

Other Athenians arose to identify other primary substances. Anaximander called the prime element the "boundless," whereas Anaximines regarded it to be air. The most interesting philosopher of this group was **Heraclitus** (540–480 B.C.E.). Writing in short, vivid fragments, he identified the primary substance as fire. The flickering character of the flame symbolized change. "All things *change*, except change" was his motto. To symbolize this, he said "You cannot step into the same river twice," because its continued flow makes it a different river second by second. Heraclitus spoke of a divine *Logos*, a universal divine formula. God stands above the flux of the world and understands its internal logic. The soul is like a flame and is extinguished upon death (except for some extremely fiery types who might linger a while as demons). Nevertheless, Heraclitus ridiculed the rituals of traditional religion.

Heraclitus's vision of flux was challenged by the **Eleatics**. This school was founded by Xenophanes (569–480 B.C.E., who was originally from Asia Minor (modern-day Turkey). Xenophanes argued against Heraclitus, maintaining that things were constant, and change was but an illusion. He also argued against the anthropomorphic Olympian pantheon. He countered with a monistic pantheism but then reflected that we cannot really know anything about God except that He is everything. Parmenides (ca. 470 B.C.E.) explained this extreme monist position that only one thing exists and that one thing does not change: "How can being nonexist, and nonexistence exist?" That which exists exists and will never cease to exist. That which exists fills all space and remains constant in time, having no beginning and no end. There was no creation of the world because something cannot arise from nothing. When we think we see multiplicity, change, or even time or space, these are mere illusions. Parmenides' most famous student was Zeno of Elea, who wrote in the mid-fifth century B.C.E. that it was only possible to divide reality into measurable units of distance or time in our minds. His famous paradoxes (e.g., "Achilles and the Tortoise") challenge the empirical frame of mind on the observation of motion.

The different speculations about the primal element finally reached synthesis with Empedocles (500–430 B.C.E.), who put together the four Greek elements: earth, water, fire and air. (If we drop air and add wood and metal, we will have the ancient Chinese formula.) Empedocles wrote about biology and medicine and was convinced that a multiplicity of views of reality was necessary for the advancement of empirical science. Later in life he seems to have fallen under the spell of the Orphics.

The prestige accorded to the rational philosophers was diminished with the emergence of the **Sophists**. These were roving teachers who used specious arguments for self-advantage (e.g., "This doesn't matter because the rivers all flow into the sea, but the sea never fills.") The Sophists were *relativists*, denying the possibility of objectivity, finality, or ultimacy when it came to "truth" or religion or morals. The Sophists worked out the logical extreme of agnosticism: since nothing can be proven, we should try to get as much pleasure as possible out of life.

One story shows their dog-eat-dog mentality. A Sophist ran a school for sophistic reasoning and charged a hefty fee, but he offered a money-back guarantee: "If you do not win your first legal case, I will refund your tuition." He usually charged his fee up front, but one young man was so convincing that the Sophist teacher let him start his studies with just the promise of payment. Time passed, but still he had not paid. Finally, the persuasive student graduated from the Sophist's course and refused to pay what he owed. The Sophist took him to court and pleaded his case. The judge was thoroughly convinced but allowed the student to plead his case. To the judge's surprise, the student had to agree with everything his teacher had said. When the judge found for the teacher, the student said, "I have lost my first case, so I invoke my money-back guarantee."

SOCRATES. The Sophist excesses poisoned the environment for wandering philosophers, especially those who appeared to skirt the issues without taking a firm stand. One unfortunate fellow to fall into this milieu was **Socrates** (469–399 B.C.E.) Later revered by his students for his high moral character, he did not deny either the existence of the Olympian deities nor the appropriateness of traditional rituals. Plato described Socrates as a man of private prayer for divine guidance. Nevertheless, he was accused of corrupting the morals of Athenian youth. This verdict probably resulted from the fact that Socrates may have been seen as a Sophist because of his method of teaching. He appeared to be taking no particular stand, but merely asking a series of questions. In this way he would draw out his opponent in a dialogue and then reveal the weakness of the opponent's position. This technique had been used very effectively against some overly assured Athenians, much to their embarrassment. Socrates had simply alienated too many powerful figures, and so he was tried and sentenced to die (by drinking hemlock).

The execution of Socrates left his students convinced that Athenian society and democracy were evil.

One disciple, Aristippus of Cyrene (435–356 B.C.E.), simply gave up on Socrates' goal of teaching as a way of transforming society. The **Cyrenaics** urged a withdrawal from social roles (similar to the approach of Yang Chu) and advocated *hedonism* (the maximization of pleasure over pain). Although the Cyrenaics favored physical pleasures, they did acknowledge the need for prudence (e.g., not going beyond the limits of law and custom), because the unwise pursuit of physical pleasures can lead to pain.

Another of Socrates' students was Antisthenes, whose reaction to his master's death was to found the school known as the **Cynics.** The name came from the hall where Antisthenes lectured, but it has come to mean those who are pessimistic about human nature. Taking the exact opposite approach from that of Aristippus, the Cynics argued that all pleasure was evil (yes, even the pleasure of studying philosophy). The good life was being freed from all nonessential constraints such as wealth and family. One must reduce one's possessions to the bare essentials and reject social conventions such as the city, marriage, religion, and other traditions. The key is **asceticism,** self-denial, privation, and keeping our desires in check. The most famous Cynic was Diogenes (400–325 B.C.E.), who lived in a barrel so that he could roll his house from town to town. His symbol was a lighted lamp, which he would carry during midday, saying that he was searching for something extremely hard to find: an honest man.

PLATO. Perhaps the most famous of Socrates' students was **Plato** (427–347 B.C.E.). Much of what we know about Socrates is through Plato. Like Laozi, Plato developed a view of the ideal sociopolitical order (an antidote to the Athenian democracy that had executed Socrates). Where Plato differs from Laozi is that the Greek philosopher envisioned a benevolent totalitarian order in which wise rules would enforce a common property scheme, arrange marriages, and raise all children. Only in this way could the limitations of present society be overcome.

Metaphysically, Plato was a **dualist** who divided reality into a lower realm of matter and a higher level of forms (e.g., geometric shapes, aesthetic concepts). The material world is in flux, but the forms are unchangeable, constant. The material world is known by the senses, but the forms are known by reason.

The forms had independent existence in a heavenly realm, and whatever could be seen in the material world was at best an imperfect copy. Plato contended that the soul was immortal and would be reincarnated. Although we do not remember the details of our previous lives, we do come into this life with a foreknowledge of the forms (presumably learned in the heavenly realm prior to our incarnation).

Although Plato's philosophical method was pre-eminently rational, there is a mystical core to his doctrine. "The good, the true, and the beautiful" are the core of wisdom and must be directly experienced. To understand the journey that one must make to have this experience, Plato consciously employed an allegory that had the symbolic structure of a myth. Imagine a cave used as a prison. Each prisoner in the cave is tied to a pole and faces the wall of the cave. By the opposite wall of the cave is a raging fire. Between the fire and the prisoners is a walkway where the guards walk back and forth talking. But the prisoners cannot see the guards, only the shadows cast on the wall by the raging fire. For the prisoners, those shadows are the only "reality" they know. In order to understand higher reality, we would have to untie a prisoner from his pole and turn him around to see the actual form that casts the shadow. Slowly the prisoner would revise his understanding of his reality. If we brought him outside the cave so that he could see the sun, that would be an even more terrifying view of higher reality. Decoding the symbols Plato uses: the prisoner is man in his regular state, the shadows on the wall are the material objects of the everyday world, the guards walking back and forth are the forms, and the sun is "the good, the true and the beautiful" that we can comprehend only at the end of the journey.

Later developments of Platonism were even more obviously mystical, such as the Neoplatonism of **Plotinus** (203–279 C.E.). He spoke of the Platonic "good, true and beautiful" as the One. The One devolves into the spirit, which devolves into soul, which devolves into objects. The great sin is individuality, forgetting the One that is our foundation. The task of the mystic is to undo the process and rediscover the One. In the early Christian era, Platonism would be the basic inspiration for the theology of Augustine.

ARISTOTLE. Aristotle (384–322 B.C.E.) was not born until fifteen years after the death of Socrates, so he escaped the event that had seared the conscience of Plato and the other students of Socrates. Aristotle studied under Plato but developed a broader range of interests (e.g., drama, biology, physics) and held less extreme positions than his mentor about metaphysics, ethics, and politics. He did not insist on Plato's radical dualism but recognized that all matter has some form to it and questioned the idea of the independent existence of forms (apart from God).

Paralleling Confucius, Aristotle advocated a course of moderation between extremes. He also acknowledged that people were at their best when they interacted with others in society, performing their roles dutifully rather than seeking private self-interest.

Aristotle influenced great theologians for the next two thousand years, such as **Averroes** (1126–1198), an Arab physician in Cordova, Spain, who looked to Aristotle for insights in Islamic theology; **Maimonides** (1135–1204), another Cordovan physician, who harmonized Aristotle with rabbinic Judaism; and St. Thomas **Aquinas** (1224–1274), a Dominican monk who blended Aristotle's thought with systematic Christian doctrine.

EPICUREANS. Epicurus (342–270 B.C.E.), founder of **Epicureanism,** agreed with the Cyrenaics that happiness was the greatest good (hedonism). Epicurus only disputed the hedonistic emphasis on the physical pleasures. Epicurus stressed the higher pleasures of the mind, but he agreed that prudence and self-control were the best guides to happiness, which is best accomplished by a quiet, simple life. We must avoid whatever causes fear and pain. (Unfortunately, the term *Epicurean* is often used today to mean gross physical hedonism, such as gluttony for food.)

Metaphysically, Epicurus accepted the atomistic theory of Democritus: everything is composed of these tiniest of particles. He even acknowledged the existence of the traditional gods: they too were composed of these atoms. But Epicurus doubted that the gods had any interest in human affairs. He denied the immortality of the soul, viewing death as the end of personal consciousness and pain: "Death is nothing to us because when death comes, we are no longer there."

STOICS. The Stoics were a less ascetic outgrowth of the earlier Cynics. The founder of **Stoicism** was Zeno of Citrium (342–260 B.C.E.), a student of Crates the Cynic. Zeno had a view of the afterlife similar to that of Epicurus. Fearing nothing from death, Zeno eventually took his own life. The school he founded continued throughout the Roman empire. Later Stoics assimilated and expanded Heraclitus's doctrine of the Logos, which they understood as God's great plan for all of us. (This doctrine found its way into early Christian theology as "natural law".) The Stoics urged a life guided by both self-control and service to others. A good example of a later Stoic would be Epictetus (50–120 C.E.), a one-time Roman slave. Epictetus taught that happiness was a matter of the will, and as long as we can control our will, we can be happy. He accepted the existence of one theistic God and the brotherhood of all men.

THE HELLENISTIC MYSTERY CULTS

Following the cultural flowering of Greek religion in science, the arts, and philosophy, the Hellenistic religions dominated. This postclassical period resulted from Alexander the Great's conquests (**Hellenism** is the term for his vision of an ecumenical, transnational culture). The Hellenistic era extended from the rule of **Alexander the Great** (who died in 323 B.C.E.) well into the Roman and Christian periods. From our standpoint, perhaps the most significant feature of Hellenistic religion was its syncretism. In an imperial area populated by numerous ethnic groups, many different gods, doctrines, and rituals swam together. We conclude our historical survey of the main movements of Greek religion by describing the most important aspects of this syncretism.

Alexander himself was something of a visionary, for what lured him to empire building was the idea of a realm in which conquered peoples "were to be treated not as uncivilized and barbarous members of subject races but as equals with whom one must live in concord." Before Alexander, the Greeks had some knowledge of foreign religions through travel and trade, but, in general Middle Eastern deities had made little impact on Greek piety. However, from the time of the Diadochi, the rulers who succeeded Alexander, Middle Eastern cults began to spread. By the beginning of the second century B.C.E., they were predominant. The most popular of the early common era were mother goddesses. They may have paved the way for the worship of Mary in the early Christian Church.

CYBELE. Originally from Phrygia (central Turkey), Cybele was a mother goddess often identified with Rhea, the mother of Zeus. This mother goddess (and Mistress of the Animals) was often accompanied by her young lover, Attis. (We may assume that to the Greeks Cybele and Attis echoed the Minoan cave goddess and her consort.) Cybele was severe and vengeful, and accompanied by lions. When Attis was unfaithful, she drove him mad. Eventually Cybele became a maternal deity like Demeter, Hera, and Aphrodite—a patroness of life, protectress of particular cities, and defender of women.

In Cybele's ceremonies, devotees reenacted Attis's insanity and consequent self-castration. They would take the pine tree (Attis's symbol), bury it, mourn for the dead god, and then observe his resurrection. Resurrected, Attis would rejoin Cybele, which was cause for great feasting. The cult seems to have promoted fertility, and its rituals have overtones of the vegetative cycle and sexuality. Celebrants went to emotional extremes, dancing, scourging themselves, and even on occasion imitating Attis's castration. We could say that the worship of Cybele attracted Dionysian energies.

The cult of Cybele was officially imported to Rome about 200 B.C.E. when the Romans were desperate with the advance of Hannibal. So a stone from a sacred meteorite in Phrygia was installed in a Roman temple. Rome survived, and Cybele's cult grew. In the first and second centuries of the common era, it may have been the most popular religion in Rome and many parts of the empire.

ISIS. In ancient Egypt, as we saw, Isis was the wife of Osiris and the mother of Horus. In the Hellenistic period she achieved a wider influence, often in the company of Serapis. Serapis was an artificial creation, the result of the Greeks' aversion to the Egyptian tendency to worship gods in animal form. Fusing Osiris with his symbol (Apis, the bull), the Greeks made a new god: Serapis. He was bearded and seated on a throne, like Zeus, Hades, and Asclepius, some of whose functions he shared (such as rule of the sky, rule of the underworld, and healing). Joined with Isis, Serapis was primarily a fertility god, bedecked with branches and fruit.

Isis rather overshadowed Serapis, for she became a full-fledged, several-sided deity. As the consort of Osiris-Serapis, she was the heavenly queen of the elements, the

MAJOR GREEK AND HELLENISTIC SCHOOLS

SCHOOL	PRE- OR POST-HELLENISTIC	MAIN THEMES
Chthonics	pre	earth deities, fertility rites, funeral rites
Olympians	pre	myths about deities, temple rites
Oracles	pre	divination
Dionysians	pre	drunkenness, orgy of devouring live animals
Heraclitians	pre	all is change
Eleatics	pre	Parmenides and Zeno: monism and no change
Pythagoreans	pre	ascetic, vegetarian, mathematics, transmigration
Orphics	pre	ascetic, vegetarian, music, transmigration
Sophists	pre	moral relativism, dispute for private gain
Socratics	pre	moral absolutism, question to find truth
Cynics	pre	people are evil; asceticism, hermits
Stoics	post	self-control, use reason to understand harmony of natural law, brotherly love, allegorical interpretation of myth
Cyrenaics	pre	hedonism: pursue pleasure with prudence
Epicureans	post	hedonism: pursue pleasure with prudence; atomism; no afterlife
Platonists	pre	dualism of matter and forms; transmigration; ideal, structured society
Neo-platonists	post	mysticism, transmigration
Aristotelians	pre	empiricism, moderation, stay in society
Eleusinians	pre	mother-daughter deities, rituals of purification for afterlife
Followers of Isis	post	mother deity, answered prayer, rituals of purification for afterlife
Followers of Cybele	post	mother deity, resurrected son, castrated priests
Mithraists	post	sun deity, rituals of purification for afterlife, bull sacrifice, for men only, popular among soldiers
Gnosticism	post	dualism of matter and spirit, ascetic, only a few will be saved, inspired early Christian heresies
Christianity	post	son deity who submitted to Father, crucified and resurrected, apocalyptic, highly persecuted

ruler of stars and planets. Because of such power, she could enter the underworld to help her devotees or to stimulate the crops. Indeed, as a vegetative goddess Isis blended with Demeter and also the moon goddess Selene. Perhaps her most important role, though, was to represent feminine virtues. In distress, she had sought the slain Osiris and brought him back to life. Sensitive and compassionate, Isis would do the same for her followers. As the mother of Horus (she was often represented suckling him), she would help women in childbirth and with child raising. Unlike Cybele, the Hellenistic Isis was soft and tender. This cult was theistic: Isis answered prayer. Her devotees assumed a code of high ethics and her cult was strikingly free of orgiastic tendencies.

Like those for Cybele and Attis, the ceremonies for Isis and Osiris-Serapis amounted to a cycle of mourning and rejoicing. Mourning, followers reenacted Isis' search for Osiris and her discovery of his dismembered parts. Rejoicing, they celebrated Osiris' resurrection and the return of Isis' joy. The rituals may have included preparation by bathing and ten days of abstinence from sex. The actual ceremonies were elaborate, much as the Eleusinian mysteries must have been. Through the cycle of Osiris' death and resurrection, followers would gain confidence that their own lives were in good hands. Through the dramatic symbolization of the afterlife, they could anticipate security and bliss.

MITHRAISM. The deity Mithra, whom we know from Iran, never took strong hold among the Hellenistic Greeks, but he did become important among the Romans influenced by Hellenism, especially the Roman soldiers. Indeed, his transformation illustrates almost perfectly the religious amalgam that cross-cultural contact produced at this time. In Mithra's romanization, Jupiter (Zeus) took on attributes of Ahura Mazdah and became a great champion of "Truth." Mithra, in turn, became Jupiter's committed helper in the battle against the Lie. In this later mythology, Mithra was born of a rock (symbol of the celestial vault) and from birth carried a bow, arrows, and dagger (much like a Persian noble). He shot the arrows into the heavens from time to time to produce a heavenly spring of pure rain water. Very important was his sacrifice of the bull, from whose blood sprouted the corn (symbol of vegetation).

Thus, Mithra was both a celestial deity (later associated particularly with the sun) and a fertility god. His followers would trace his circuit through the sky, reenact the mythology of his birth, and celebrate a bull sacrifice in his name. After the sacrifice they would feast together, convinced that the bull's meat and blood contained the substance of eternity. Another important ritual was the celebration of his birthday on December 25. As the Mithraic doctrine developed, it generated a complicated astrology, by which the progress of initiates' souls through the heavens was shown. This involved secret rituals for purification for different levels of heaven. At its peak, Mithraism ran underground "churches" and schools. Today excavations under Christian churches, including St. Clement's in Rome, reveal statuary, classrooms, and altars used by Mithraists. This denomination was open to males only and was popular among Roman soldiers. Its popularity eclipsed that of Christianity in the early common era. In 304 C.E., Mithra was named protector of Rome.

In summary, the Hellenistic period was a time of profuse religious activity. Onto Greek and then Roman religious culture, a cosmopolitan era grafted elements from the Egyptians, Persians, Phrygians, and others. Thrown into close contact with foreigners, all people in the new empire had to face new divinities, doctrines, and rituals. Partly as a result, many people sought salvation or assurances of a happy afterlife. The upshot was a frenzy of mysteries through which devotees could feel stirring emotions or see marvelous sights. With a rush of sorrow, sexual excitement, or hope for rebirth, an initiate would feel passionately alive. In a time of disarray and ceaseless warfare, when the city-state or clan no longer offered security or guidance, such a sense of vitality was more than welcome.

WORLDVIEW

NATURE AND ULTIMATE REALITY

Nature and divinity run together in pre-Christian Greek religion. Throughout its history, the Greek religious mind associated all major natural phenomena with particular gods. As noted, the sky, sea, and earth were powerful deities. The major stress was on fertility (which was the focus of most local festivals), perhaps due to the poor quality of the rocky Greek soil.

The Homeric hymns, for instance, sing praise to mother earth, who feeds all creatures and blesses humans with good crops. Relatedly, they make the man with good crops a symbol of prosperity. The earth, mother of the gods and wife of the starry heavens, has blessed him—his children can play merrily. As a result of its prehistoric roots, then, Greece saw much divinity in natural growth.

SOCIETY

In social terms, Greek religious culture reflects the ethical ideas that bound first the early clanspeople and then the citizens of the city-state. The ethics of the early historical period evolved from the extended family. There was no money and banditry was rife, so a man's great virtue was to provide food, shelter, and defense—whether by just means or otherwise. Consequently, most men (it was a patriarchal culture) petitioned the gods for material prosperity and success in arms. They called one of their number good and praised him for excellence if he was a survivor. The more elevated notions of justice later developed by philosophers clashed with the less moral early tradition. Since early Greek religion did not associate godliness with justice, the philosophers called for its overthrow.

Another primitive concept that died hard was that of "pollution." This was the dangerous state of being unclean or at odds with the natural powers because of some dread deed. Homicide was especially polluting, but incest, contact with a dead person, or even a bad dream or childbirth could also be polluting, each in varying degrees. Washing in a spring would cleanse away a bad dream; purification by fire and the offering of pig's blood cleansed a homicide. The concept of pollution seems to have been a way for the Greeks to deal with dreadful, amoral happenings that might bring destructive contact with the sacred, even though they were unintentional. Since polluted persons could contaminate others, they were often banished. Greek cults used magical formulas, prayers, sacrifices, dances, and dramatic scenes—a wealth of creative expressions. Magical formulas probably were most prominent in agricultural festivals, in which peasants mixed models of snakes and phalluses with decomposing organic materials, such as pine branches and remains

of pigs, to excite powers of fertility. Greek prayers would recall a god's favors and the sacrifices that the praying person had offered previously. This implied a sort of barter: We will honor you and offer a sacrifice if you give us success in crops (or war, or family life, or whatever).

Occasionally texts indicate pure admiration for divine power or beauty, but the ordinary attitude was quite practical. Since the gods were not necessarily rational or holy, they had to be cajoled. Indeed, a Greek tended to pray and sacrifice rather parochially, addressing the family god Apollo or Athena, who might remember fat sacrifices offered in the past. Each family or city-state had its own traditions, customs, myths, and gods, which served both to bind the members together and to keep the different tribes from uniting.

Sacrifice was a primary way to keep local religion in good health. By giving the local god good things, one could expect prosperity in return. (Significantly, this implied that the gods blessed those who were wealthy and had good things to sacrifice and that those who sacrificed and met bad luck had secret sins or wicked ancestors. Either way, human success and goodness were rather arbitrary.) In a sacrifice, usually parts of an animal were offered and the rest was consumed. According to a Homeric account, for instance, a pig was cut up, pieces of each limb were wrapped in fat and thrown on the fire, and barley grains were sprinkled on the fire. The meal that followed was a mode of communion with the deities.

Greek cults produced many priests, but their status and functions were limited. In principle, any person could pray and sacrifice to any god, so priests had no monopoly. They tended to be limited to particular temples and were seldom organized into bands or hierarchies. A large clan might have its own officiating priest, and the priest of a prosperous

> Explain Greek religion from one of the theoretical perspectives introduced in this course: that of Müller, Durkheim, Freud, Malinowski, or some other.
>
> Contribute to this discussion at
> http://formums.delphiforms.com/rel101

temple might make a good living from sacrifice fees. Otherwise, priesthood was not a road to status or wealth. Priests seldom gave instruction or performed divination, though some priests in the mystery rites did both.

WOMEN

Women did have legal rights in Athenian society, but their lives were largely circumscribed by male control. Their basic function was to bear children. Many Greek religious authors were rather harsh on women. Hesiod, for instance, reported the myth of Pandora and the box of evils, which made woman the source of human woes. Socrates, when asked about the advisability of marriage, balanced the boon of heirs against the woes of a wife: "One quarrel after another, her dower cast in your face, the haughty disdain of her family, the garrulous tongue of your mother-in-law, the lurking paramour." In Plato's *Republic,* women were to be equal to men socially and sexually, having rights to education and rule. Nonetheless, Plato tended to consider women less independent than men, in good part because of their physique: "The womb is an animal that longs to generate children." Aristotle, however, was the most unequivocal misogynist. To him women were simply inferior, both intellectually and morally. In his matter-and-form theory, women supplied only the matter for human reproduction, men supplying everything effective and active.

Nonetheless, we have seen that Greek divinity frequently was powerfully feminine. In the Minoan-Mycenaean period, a great goddess was the prime deity. In the Olympian period, Demeter, Hera, Athena, Artemis, and Aphrodite all exerted great influence. In the Hellenistic religions, Cybele and Isis more than equaled Mithra. Psychologically, then, Greek culture never doubted the divinity of the feminine. More than Israelite, Christian, or Muslim culture, Greek divinity was androgynous. Furthermore, certain religious groups offered women escape from social oppression, for example, the Eleusinian and Dionysian sects. There, in a sort of utopian free zone, women could experience equality and dignity. Although these cults never compensated for women's lack of dignity or status in ordinary life, their egalitarianism was an implicit admission that ordinary life was quite imperfect.

SELF

The personal side of Greek religion is perhaps most manifest in myths dealing with human creation. In the most famous collection of myths, Hesiod's *Works and Days,* ancient Greeks read that they were the last and lowest in a series of human generations. During the first ages, races of gold, silver, and bronze had flourished, but they came to various bad ends. A flood intervened, followed by the age of the heroes. Finally the present iron people arose. In other words, Hesiod's myth put into Greek form the widespread idea of a golden age or a previous paradise, with the accompanying message that the present age was a low point, a period of decline.

Partly on account of this religious heritage, the prevailing mood of many Greek writers was pessimistic. Delphic wisdom was more positive: gain self-knowledge and practice moderation. Self-knowledge, above all, was accepting one's mortality. By moderation, one could avoid hubris (overweening pride) and tragedy. There were overtones of jealousy in this advice from Apollo, however, as though the god feared humans yearning for immortality or resented their craving a life of passion. Indeed, passion was ever a danger, for the Greeks were competitive and lusty. In the end, they would not give up their dreams of immortality, so becoming godlike became a central theme of philosophy and mystery religion. The philosopher Empedocles, for instance, thought that his wisdom made him a god among mortals. Plato taught that the soul is divine and deathless. The common person would more likely find divinity in one of the

The doctrine of the transmigration of souls was the afterlife accepted by Hinduism, Buddhism, Jainism, the Orphics, the Pythagoreans and Plato. What is your view on reincarnation?

Do you think that reincarnation can be *verified* (e.g., proven logically or empirically)?

Do you think that reincarnation can be *vindicated* (e.g., proven as a valuable or helpful world view)?

Contribute to this discussion at
http://formums.delphiforms.com/rel101

mystery rites, through a union with Demeter or knowledge from Isis, either of which could bring victory over death.

The personal implications of Greek religion were greatest in the philosophers' clarification of reason, universal humanity, and the participation of divinity in human thought. As we have noted, the poets, dramatists, and early philosophers slowly clarified the nature of human reason, separating it from myth. By focusing on mind (*nous*) and its relations with being (*ousia*), the pre-Socratics prepared the way for Plato and Aristotle, who realized how mind and being coincide. Moreover, this work did not take the Greek intellectuals away from either religion or politics. Rather, it introduced them to an order that set all the fundamentals—nature, society, self, and divinity—in harmony. In other words, it took them to the heart of what it means to be human.

Finally, the philosophers' order meant a new perspective on death. In early times, death was shadowy. For Homer, the dead had only a vague existence around their graves or in the underworld. There was no judgment or punishment for injustice toward one's fellows. Only those who had directly affronted the gods had to suffer. The mystery cults said one could conquer death by union with an immortal divinity, and their great popularity indicates the hold that death had on Greece starting in the sixth century B.C.E. The philosophers spoke of judgment and punishment because they were acutely aware that justice rules few human situations. In quite deliberate myths, Plato symbolized the inherent need we have for a final accounting. Without it, he suggested, reason would lose balance.

In the eyes of many scholars, the Greeks were among the most religious of ancient peoples. From heaven to under the earth, from crude emotion to the most refined spirituality, their great culture put a religious shine on everything. Today, if we find the world "sacred" (deeply relevant) through science or art, if we find the human being "sacred" (deeply valuable) through medicine or philosophy, if we find the political order alive with counsels to flee disorder and pursue justice—if we ever think in these ways, it is largely because of the Greeks. They made the transcendental qualities—unity, truth, goodness, and beauty—part of all subsequent Western religion.

COMPARISON OF CHINA WITH GREECE		
DIMENSION	CHINA	GREECE
Earliest deities	fertility rites, ancestor worship	fertility rites, ancestor worship
Key ritual	funerals	funerals
Elements	earth, fire, water, wood, metal	earth, fire, water, air
Divination	yin/yang	oracles, seers
Strict rules	legalists	Spartans, Draco
Focus on pleasure	Yang Chu	Cyrenaics, Epicureans
Idle disputation	school of names	Sophists
Ethics	Confucius, Mencius	Socrates, Aristotle
Moderation	Confucius	Aristotle
Stay in society	Confucius	Aristotle
Universal love	Mo	Stoics
Mystic with vision of ideal society	Lao	Plato
Foreign religion(s) that arrive	Buddhists	Cybele, Mithra, Isis, Gnostics, Christians
Militaristic neighbor that copies culture	Japan	Rome

Compare Greek or Hellenistic religion with Judaism, Hinduism, Aztecs, or Zoroastrians.

Contribute to this discussion at
http://formums.delphiforms.com/rel101

It would be tempting to say of the Greek center, like Gertrude Stein's description of Oakland, that "There is no there there." It is useful to see the Greek center as the center of a circle, a theoretical point from which the circle can be seen, but not a point on the circle itself. If we think the Greek religious mind is defined by reason (represented by Apollo), we just follow the diameter of the circle from one side to the other, where we find the polar opposite (frenzied followers of Dionysus). If we think of the Greek religious mind to be embodied by the masculine Zeus or Mithra or Hercules, we find Gaia, Athena, Artemis, Demeter and Persephone, Isis, Astarte, Cybele 180 degrees later. Likewise devotion to Aristotle's vision of life in the community of the city-state is counterbalanced by the Cynics and Cyrenaics, who wanted to avoid social obligations and conventions. For every advocate of asceticism, we can find a hedonist. For those who speculated about dualism (Plato), there were monists (Parmenides). For those who said that there was nothing but change (Heraclitus), there were those who said that change was pure illusion (Eleatics). For those obsessed with afterlife and reincarnation, there were those who assured us, "When you are dead, you are dead."

The human is the measure of all things, and in the Greek and Hellenistic world, this was the case with the gods. They were constantly reinvented by humans with changing spiritual horizons. The gods were mere actors, with the humans serving as producers, directors, scriptwriters, and audience. The gods may not have received much respect, but they may also have been regarded much like today's celebrities. The myths told about them have the flavor of the scandalous and fantastic reports that fill our tabloids.

flashcards and matching game
http://www.quia.com/jg/51744.html

jumbled words game
http://www.quia.com/jw/8536.html

millionaire game
http://www.quia.com/rr/41391.html

magic paragraph
http://www.quia.com/cz/13519.html

Now take an online practice quiz at
http://www.quia.com/session.html

For session enter
relquiz9

download multiple-choice, true-false, and fill-in drills from
http://www.ureach.com/tlbrink
click on the public filing cabinet and folder rel9
and download *m9.exe*, *h9.htm*, *t9.exe*, and *f9.exe*
and the crossword puzzle *cw8.htm*

CHAPTER 8

BUDDHISM

> *Buddha.*

BUDDHISM: 25 KEY DATES	
Date	**Event**
563–476 B.C.E.	life of Siddhartha Gautama Sakya, the Buddha
519 B.C.E.	Gautama's enlightenment
473 B.C.E.	first Buddhist Congress
363 B.C.E.	second Buddhist Congress
273–236 B.C.E.	reign of Buddhist Emperor Asoka
236 B.C.E.	rise of Mahayana tradition
160 B.C.E.	*Prajna-paramita* literature
80 B.C.E.	*Lotus Sutra*
ca. 200 C.E.	Nagarjuna, leading philosopher
220–552 C.E.	Vietnam, China, Korea, Java, Sumatra, Japan missions
430 C.E.	Buddhaghosa, leading philosopher
594 C.E.	Buddhism proclaimed Japanese state religion
749 C.E.	first Buddhist monastery in Tibet
805–806 C.E.	foundation of Tendai and Shingon sects in Japan
845 C.E.	persecution of Chinese Buddhists
1065 C.E.	Hindu invasions of Sri Lanka
1175 C.E.	Honen; Japanese Pure Land Buddhism
1193–1227 C.E.	rise of Japanese Zen sects
1260–1368 C.E.	Tibetan Buddhism influential in China
1360 C.E.	Buddhism becomes state religion in Thailand
1543–1588 C.E.	final conversion of Mongols
1603 C.E.	Tokugawa government dominates Japanese Buddhism
1646–1694 C.E.	Basho, Great Japanese Buddhist poet
1868–1871 C.E.	Meiji persecution of Buddhism in Japan
1954–1956 C.E.	Sixth Buddhist council in Rangoon, Burma

HISTORY

OVERVIEW

The term **Buddhism** derives from Western scholarly efforts to organize the movements, ideas, and practices that appear to have been spawned by a mystic who founded this religion, a man who bears the title of the Buddha (ca. 563–476 B.C.E.). It also covers the diverse acts and thinking of followers of the Buddha, who spread this religion from India throughout Asia and recently have established roots on other continents. Buddhism is the world's first great **proselytizing** religion seeking transnational converts: starting in India and spreading east to the other nations of Asia. Originating in Axial Age India, Buddhism simply shared the assumptions of Jainism and the Upanishads: that earthly existence was a sorrowful cycle perpetuated by rebirths (transmigration) and influenced by the deeds and thoughts of this life (karma) and the need to employ meditation to seek a release. Wherever Buddhism went, it blended with local traditions, modifying the doctrines of karma, transmigration, and the practice of meditation, creating a diversity of syncretism.

THE BUDDHA

The man who would later become known as the Buddha was born about 536 B.C.E. outside the town of Kapilavastu in what is now a part of Nepal just below the Himalayan foothills. His people were a warrior tribe called **Sakya** (sometimes spelled *Shakya*), and his family or clan name was **Gautama**. His given name was **Siddhartha**, so his complete name was Siddhartha Gautama Sakya, and he might be referred to by any one of those names (or **Sakyamuni**, as the Japanese termed him) or as just the *Buddha*, a term meaning the Enlightened One. Unlike Christianity, which has only one figure who bears the title of Christ (Jesus), Buddhist sects may recognize other Buddhas. Some were mythological figures of the past; others were real people who dedicated their lives to good works and meditation (and therefore earned the title of Buddha) or future Messiahs who would come and end the evil age of a deteriorating society.

The religious climate of the Axial Age in which Gautama grew up was quite heated. Some objectors were challenging the dominance of the priestly Brahmin class. As we saw in the chapter on India, there was dissatisfaction with sacrifice burning among intellectuals, while the accounts of the *Mahavira* are evidence of the ascetic movement that also challenged the priestly religion of sacrifice. In secular culture, the sixth century B.C.E. saw a movement from tribal rule toward small-scale monarchy, a growth in urban populations, the beginnings of money-based economies, the beginnings of government bureaucracies, and the rise of a wealthy merchant class. Thus, the Buddha came of age in a time of rapid change, when people were in turmoil over religion and open to new teachings.

Myth heavily embellishes the accounts of Gautama's birth and early life, so it is difficult to describe this period with historical validity. One legend describes his birth as follows: he came out of his mother's side without causing her any pain, stood up, strode seven paces, and announced, "No more births for me!" In other words, the child would conquer transmigration's cycle of death and rebirth and would be an Enlightened One.

As Gautama grew, his father surrounded him with pleasures and distractions to keep him in the palace and away from the sights of ordinary life. When Gautama came of age, the father married him to a lovely woman. So Sakyamuni ("sage of the Sakyas") lived in relative contentment until his late twenties. By the time of his own son's birth, however, Gautama (the future Buddha) was restless; he named the child Rahula (fetter). What really precipitated Sakyamuni's religious crisis, though, were experiences he had outside the palace. On several outings he witnessed examples of old age, disease, and death. They shocked him severely, and he became anxiety ridden. How could anyone take life lightly if these were its constant dangers? Meditating on age, disease, and death, the young prince decided to cast away his daily round of pleasures and solve the riddle of life's ultimate relevance by becoming a wandering beggar concerned only to gain enlightenment.

Renouncing his wife, child, father, and goods, he set off to answer his soul's yearning. (Indian tradition allowed renouncing the world after one had begotten a son.) The teachers to whom Gautama first apprenticed himself when he started wandering in pursuit of enlightenment specialized in meditation and asceticism. Their meditation, it appears, was a yogic pursuit of enlightenment through *samadhi* (trance). From them Gautama learned much about the levels of consciousness but was not fully satisfied. The teachers could not bring him to dispassion, tranquility, enlightenment, or **nirvana** (a state of liberation beyond *samsara*). In other words, he wanted a mystical experience, a direct perception of how things are, necessitating a complete break with the realm of space, time, and rebirth. He sensed that to defeat age, disease, and death he had to go beyond ordinary humanity and tap the power of something greater.

Gautama spent about seven years on this spiritual quest before he found enlightenment. First, Sakyamuni turned to asceticism—so much so that he almost starved himself. The texts claim that when he touched his navel, he could feel his backbone. In any event, asceticism did not bring what Sakyamuni sought either.

Because of this, he and his followers have always urged moderation in fasting and bodily disciplines. Theirs, they like to say, is a **Middle Way** between indulgence and severity that strives to keep the body healthy, as a valuable ally should be, and to keep the personality from excessive self-concern. From our perspective of material luxury and comfort, the life of a Buddhist monk would seem ascetic, but the Buddhists were comparing themselves with much stricter zealous

Hindus, who would sleep on a bed of nails, or dedicated Jains, who would sit in meditative postures until their limbs atrophied.

According to the traditional accounts, Gautama's enlightenment (mystical experience) came after he sat under a tree and meditated for forty days. At that point, he became the Buddha (Enlightened One). One symbol used in the mythical account of this experience is that of Mara, the personification of evil or death, who tried to tempt Buddha away from his pursuit. First, he sent a host of demons, but the Buddha's merit and love protected him. Then, with increased fear that this man sitting so determinedly might escape his realm, the evil one invoked his own power. However, when Mara called on his retinue of demons to witness to his power, the Buddha, who was alone, called on mother earth, which quaked in acknowledgment. As a last ploy, Mara commissioned his three daughters (Discontent, Delight, and Desire) to seduce the sage. But they, too, failed, and so Mara withdrew.

ENLIGHTENMENT. The experience of enlightenment can be conceived as the realization of pure ultimate relevance. According to tradition, Buddha had his experience on a night of the full moon. Buddha ascended the four stages of trance (a progressive clarification of consciousness): (1) detachment from sense objects and calming the passions; (2) nonreasoning and "simple" concentration; (3) dispassionate mindfulness and consciousness with bodily bliss; and (4) pure awareness and peace without pain, elation, or depression.

Another traditional way of describing the Buddha's enlightenment is to trace his progress through the night. During the first watch (evening), he acquired knowledge of his previous lives. This is a power that some shamans claim, so it is not Buddha's distinguishing achievement. During the second watch (midnight), he acquired the "divine eye" with which he surveyed the karmic state of all beings—the cycle of dying and rebirth that is their destiny. With this vision he realized that good deeds beget good karma and move one toward freedom from *samsara*, while bad deeds beget bad karma and a deeper entrenchment in *samsara*. This second achievement made Buddha a moralistic philosopher, one who saw the condition of all beings as a function of their ethical or unethical behavior.

During the third watch (late night), the Buddha reached the peak of perception, attaining "the extinction of the outflows" (the cessation of desire in favor of samsaric existence) and grasping the essence of what what was to become the **Four Noble Truths:** (1) All life is suffering; (2) The cause of suffering is desire; (3) Stopping desire will stop suffering; and (4) the Eightfold Path (explained below) is the best way to stop desire.

The **Eightfold Path** outlines the lifestyle that Buddha developed for people who accepted his teaching and wanted to pursue nirvana. As such, it is more detailed than a description of what he had directly experienced in enlightenment—something that he or his disciples elaborated later on. The explanation of reality that Buddha developed out of his experience of enlightenment, which became known as the doctrine of *Dependent Co-arising,* also came later. It explains the connections that link all beings. Beings not only depend on one another in what might be called a field of relations, they also arise (come into being) together, thus the "co" in co-arising.

Enlightenment seems to have been the dramatic experience of vividly perceiving that life, which Sakyamuni had found to consist of suffering, had a solution. One could escape the terror of aging, sickness, and death by withdrawing one's concerns for or anxieties about them—by no longer desiring youth, health, or even life itself. By withdrawing in this manner, one could lessen the bad effects of karma, since desire was the means by which karma kept the personality on the wheel of dying and rebirth. Removing desire therefore took away karma's poison. To destroy desire for karmic existence, though, one had to penetrate and remove the illusion of its goodness. That is, one had to remove the ignorance that makes sensual pleasures—financial success, prestige, and so on—seem good. Buddha designed the Eightfold Path and the doctrine of Dependent Co-arising to remove such ignorance and rout desire.

The picture of the Buddha sitting in repose after having gained enlightenment has always been a great consolation to his followers. With the pictures and stories about his kindness as a teacher, his affection for his disciples, his wisdom in instructing kings, and the like, it has given the Buddha the human qualities most followers of a religious leader seem to need if they are to follow the path with enthusiasm. The general rule

COMPARISON OF SECTS FROM INDIA					
DIMENSION	UPANISHADS	JAINISM	BHAGAVAD GITA	TANTRISM	BUDDHISTS
Date	800 B.C.E.–400 B.C.E.	500 B.C.E.	400 B.C.E.–200 C.E.	1000 C.E.	500 B.C.E.
Persons		Mahavira	Arjuna (fictional)		Gautama
Mysticism	yes	yes	tolerated	using sexual symbolism	yes
Asceticism	yes	yes, extremely	tolerated	rejected	yes, but limited
Caste	tolerated	rejected at first	advocated	ignored	rejected
Karma	accepted	accepted	accepted	ignored	accepted
Trans-migration	accepted	accepted	accepted	ignored	accepted
Reality	monistic	dualistic	duty of caste	symbolic	
Deity	Brahman	atheistic	theistic	paramour	ignored

seems to be that followers must love the leader if they are to love the path. Admiring the clarity of the leader's teaching and experiencing the benefits of the path are not enough. The leader inevitably becomes the model, the prime evidence, the vindication that the teaching indeed is wholly wise, that the path in fact is fully efficacious. Students did not find his **detachment** something cold and forbidding. They found it just the far side of the **compassion**, the kindness, the charm that made him seem to reach into their very beings and loosen the bonds in which ignorance and fear had kept them tied. These became the central yet polar virtues of Buddha, and the challenge to his followers was to balance the two: to have detachment from the sufferings of the world, yet have enough compassion to stay in the world and minister to those who yet suffer.

THE DHARMA (BUDDHIST DOCTRINE)

Buddhists have seen in Sakyamuni's enlightenment the great act centering their religion. The Buddha is worthy of following because in enlightenment he became shining with knowledge (*bodhi*). What he saw under the *bodhi* tree in the third watch was nothing less than the formula for measuring life and curing its mortal illness. The Four Noble Truths and Dependent Co-arising are two favorite ways of presenting the essential truths of Buddha's knowledge.

DEPENDENT CO-ARISING AND THE EIGHTFOLD PATH

Often Buddhists picture the doctrine of Dependent Co-arising, which provides their basic picture of reality, as a **wheel** with twelve sections or a chain with twelve links (the first and the last are joined to make a circuit). These twelve links explain the round of samsaric existence. They are not an abstract teaching for the edification of the philosophical mind, but an extension of the essentially therapeutic analysis that the Buddha thought could cure people of their basic illness.

The wheel of Dependent Co-arising turns in this way: (1) Aging and dying depend on rebirth; (2) rebirth depends on becoming; (3) becoming depends on the appropriation of certain necessary materials; (4) appropriation depends on desire for such materials; (5) desire depends on feeling; (6) feeling depends on contact with material reality; (7) contact depends on the senses; (8) the senses depend on "name" (the mind) and "form" (the body); (9) name and form depend on consciousness (the spark of sentient life); (10) consciousness shapes itself by *samsara*; (11) the *samsara* causing rebirth depends on ignorance of the Four Noble Truths; and (12) therefore, the basic cause of *samsara* is ignorance.

One can run this series forward and back, but the important concept is that ignorance (of the Four Noble Truths) is the cause of painful human existence, and aging and dying are both its final overwhelming effects and the most vivid aspects of *samsara*. Thus, the chain of Dependent Co-arising is a sort of practical analysis of human existence. It is coordinated influences—of how the basic factors shaping reality impact on one another. This chain straddles what we might call the physical and the moral realms, linking desire with death and rebirth but also specifying how desire works through the senses and intellect.

In the Buddha's enlightenment, as he and his followers elaborated it, there is no single cause of the way things are. Rather, all things are continually rotating in this twelve-stage wheel of existence. Each stage of the wheel passes the power of movement along to the next. The only way to step off the wheel, to break the chain, is to gain enlightenment and so detach the stage of ignorance. If we do detach ignorance, we stand free of karma, karmic consciousness, and so on, all the way to aging and rebirth.

The result of enlightenment, then, is no rebirth. **Nirvana** is the state in which the chain of existence does not obtain—in which desire ceases and one escapes karma and *samsara*. A good metaphor for the Buddhist conception of transmigration and nirvana is that a flame (one's life) can be passed from one candle (existence in a body) to another. Nirvana occurs when the flame is blown out. Thus, nirvana begins with enlightenment and becomes definitive with death. By his enlightenment, for instance, the Buddha had broken the chain of Dependent Co-arising; at his death his nirvana freed him from rebirths.

The Eightfold Path (which is the Fourth Noble Truth) details how we may dispel ignorance and gain nirvana by describing a middle way between sensuality and extreme asceticism that consists of (1) right views, (2) right intention, (3) right speech, (4) right action, (5) right livelihood, (6) right effort, (7) right mindfulness,

and (8) right concentration. *Right views* means knowledge of the Four Noble Truths. *Right intention* means dispassion, benevolence, and refusal to injure others. *Right speech* means no lying, slander, abuse, or idle talk. *Right action* means not taking life, stealing, or being sexually disordered. *Right livelihood* is an occupation that does not harm living things; thus, butchers, hunters, fishers, and sellers of weapons or liquor are proscribed. *Right effort* avoids the arising of evil thoughts. In *right mindfulness,* awareness is disciplined so that it focuses on an object or idea to know its essential reality. *Right concentration* focuses on a worthy object of meditation.

The first two aspects of the Eightfold Path, right views and right intention, comprise the wisdom portion of the Buddhist program. If we know the Four Noble Truths and orient ourselves toward them with the right spiritual disposition, we are wise and come to religious peace. Tradition groups aspects three, four, and five under morality. To speak, to act, and to make one's living in wise ways amount to an ethics for nirvana, a morality that will liberate one from suffering. Finally, aspects six, seven, and eight entail meditation. By setting consciousness correctly through right effort, mindfulness, and concentration, one can perceive the structures of reality and thus personally vindicate the Buddha's enlightened understanding.

The three divisions of the Eightfold Path compose a single entity, a program in which each of the three parts reinforces the other two. Wisdom sets up the game plan, the basic theory of what the human condition is and how one is to cope with it. Morality applies wisdom to daily life by specifying how one should speak, act, and support oneself. Regular meditation focuses one on the primary points and the reality to which they apply. In meditation the Buddhist personally appropriates the official wisdom, personally examining the ethical life. As a result, meditation builds up the Buddhist's spiritual force, encouraging the peaceful disposition necessary for a person to be nonviolent and kindly.

THE BUDDHA'S PREACHING. Buddha himself apparently debated what to do after achieving enlightenment. On one hand, he had a potent medicine to dispense as a cure for humanity's greatest suffering. On the other hand, there was dreary evidence that humanity, mired in its attachments, would find his teaching hard to comprehend and accept. Out of compassion (which became the premier Buddhist virtue), the Enlightened One finally agreed to teach. According to tradition, his first sermon occurred in Deer Park near Benares, about five days' walk from where his enlightenment took place. He preached first to some former ascetic companions who had rejected him when he turned away from their harsh mortification, and his calm bearing won them over. What Buddha first preached was the Four Noble Truths, but he apparently prefaced his preaching with a solemn declaration of his authority as an immortal enlightened one. From this preface Buddhists have concluded that one must offer the authority behind the **dharma** (the teaching) if the dharma is to have its intended effect.

Let us imagine that we are listening to his famous Fire Sermon, preached after the sermon in Deer Park.

> O priests, [monks], all things are on fire. The eye is on fire, as are the forms the eye receives, the consciousness the eye raises, the impressions the eye transmits, the sensations—pleasant, unpleasant, or indifferent—that the eye's impressions produce. All that has to do with our seeing is on fire. And in what does this fire consist? It consists in the flame of passion, the burning of hate, the heat of infatuation. Birth, old age, death, sorrow, lamentation, misery, grief, and despair are all expressions of the fire that comes into us through our eyes.

> In the same way, the ear is on fire with burning sounds. The nose is on fire with burning odors. The tongue is on fire with flaming tastes. The whole body is on fire with flaming touches. Even worse, the mind is on fire; hot ideas, burning awareness, searing impressions, smoldering sensations. Again I say, the fire of passion, birth, old age, death, sorrow, lamentation, misery, grief, and despair is burning you up.

> What, then, should you do? If you are wise, O priests, you will conceive an aversion for the eye and the eye's forms, the eye's consciousness, the eye's impressions, and the eye's sensations, be they pleasant, unpleasant, or indifferent. If you are wise, you will conceive an aversion for the ear and its sounds, the nose and its odors, the tongue and its tastes, the body and the things it touches, the mind and all that passes through it.

> If you conceive this aversion, you will divest yourselves of passion. Divesting yourselves of passion,

you will become free. Being free, you will become aware of your liberation and know that you have exhausted rebirth. This will prove that you have lived the holy life, fulfilled what it behooved you to do, and made yourselves subject to this world no longer.

When the Buddha finished his sermon, many of the monks' minds became free from attachment and they were delivered of their depravities. This set them on a path toward the heights of meditation where they might defeat the problem of suffering by understanding the illusions on which it feeds.

Can we appreciate the relevance of the Fire Sermon across 2,500 years? We are still possessed of eyes, ears, nose, tongue, and hands eager to touch. We are still the strange animals possessed of minds flowing with ideas, reflex awareness, sensations to drive our days and bedevil our nights. As with the Buddha's contemporaries, unless we have these faculties under control, we are burning with useless passions. Look around you. See how many of your contemporaries rush after money. Others rush after pleasure. A third group hustles to gain power. From dawn to midnight, their brains teem with schemes, images of success, numbers adding up to bigger and bigger bank accounts. Do they not seem feverish? Is there not within them a fire wisdom would have to douse?

The Buddha's preaching won him innumerable converts, men and women alike, many of whom decided to dedicate their lives to following him and his way. A great number entered the sangha (a monastic order) as monks and nuns, assuming a life of celibacy, poverty, and submission to rules of discipline. Other followers decided to practice the dharma while remaining in their lay state, and they frequently gave the Buddha and the Buddhist community land and money. In both cases people became Buddhists by taking "refuge" in the three jewels of the Enlightened One's religion: the Buddha himself, the teaching (dharma), and the community (*sangha* can mean either the monastic community or the entire community of Buddhists, lay and monastic, past and present). By uttering three times the vow of taking refuge, one became a follower in a strict, official sense.

BUDDHIST CATECHETICS. In time a catechism developed to explain the Buddha's teaching. One of the catechism's most important notions was the "three

BUDDHISM BY THE NUMBERS	
Three jewels	• the Buddha • the Dharma • the Sangha (monastery)
Three pillars (main concerns)	• wisdom • morality • meditation
Three marks of all reality	• painful • fleeting • selfless
Four noble truths	• All life is suffering. • The cause of suffering is desire. • We must remove desire to end suffering. • Desire can be removed by the Eightfold Path.
Five ethical principles	• Do not kill. • Do not lie. • Do not steal. • Do not have sex outside of marriage. • Do not take intoxicants.
Eightfold path	• right views • right intention • right speech • right action • right livelihood • right effort • right mindfulness • right concentration

marks" of reality. The first mark is that all life or reality is painful: the reality of suffering. By this Buddhists do not mean that one never experiences pleasant things or that one has no joy. Rather, they mean that no matter how pleasant or joyous one's life, it is bound to include disappointment, sickness, misunderstanding, and finally death. Since the joyous things do not last, even they have an aspect of painfulness.

Second, all life is fleeting, or passing. Everything changes—nothing stays the same. Therefore, realistically there is nothing to which we can cling, nothing that we can rely on absolutely. In fact, even our own realities (our "selves") change. On one level, we move through the life cycle from youth to old age. On a more subtle level, our thoughts, our convictions, and our emotions change.

Third, there is no self. For Buddhists, the fleetingness of our own consciousness proves that there is no Atman—no solid soul or self. In this the Buddhists directly opposed Hinduism. All people, it seems, naturally think that they have personal identities. Buddhists claim that personalities consist of nothing solid or permanent. We are but packages of physical and mental stuff that is temporarily bound together in our present proportions.

The tradition identifies the component parts of all things, which number five: body, feeling, conception, karmic disposition, and consciousness. Together these *skandhas* make the world and the person of appearances, and they also constitute the basis for clinging to existence and rebirth. To cut through the illusion of a (solid) self—Buddhists do not deny that we have (changing) identities—is therefore the most important blow that one can strike against ignorance. This is done by being open to the flowing character of all life and decisively pursuing nirvana.

The early teachers described the realms of rebirth to which humans were subject and in so doing developed a Buddhist version of the Indian cosmic powers and zones of the afterlife. Essentially, the Buddhist wheel of rebirth focuses on six realms or destinies. Three are lower realms, which are karmic punishment for bad deeds. The other three are higher realms in which good deeds are rewarded. The lowest realm is for punishing the wicked by means befitting their particular crimes. However, these punishments are not eternal; after individuals have paid their karmic debt, they can reenter the human realm by rebirth. Above the lowest realm is the station of the "hungry ghosts," who wander the earth's surface begging for food. The third and least severe realm of the wicked is that of animals. If one is reborn in that realm, one suffers the abuses endured by dumb beasts.

The fortunate destinies reward good karma. The human realm is the first, and in it one can perform meritorious deeds. Only in the human realm can one become a buddha. The two final realms are those of the demigods (Titans) and the gods proper. Both include a variety of beings, all of whom are subject to rebirth. Since even the Buddhist gods are subject to rebirth, their happiness is not at all comparable to the final nirvana. Better to be a human being advancing toward enlightenment than a divinity liable to the pains of another transmigratory cycle. Perhaps for that reason, the Buddhist spirits and divinities, as well as the Buddhist ghosts and demons, seem inferior to the human being. Apparently Buddhism adopted wicked and good spirits from Indian culture without much thought. In subjecting these spirits to the powers of an *arhat* (another term for a buddha, one who achieves nirvana), however, Buddhists minimized their fearsomeness.

Despite its sometimes lurid description of the six realms, the dharma basically stated that each individual is responsible for his or her own destiny. The future is neither accidental, fated, nor determined by the gods. If one has a strong will to achieve salvation, a day of final triumph will surely come. As a result, karma is less an enslavement than an encouragement. If one strives to do good deeds (to live by the dharma in wisdom-morality-meditation), one cannot fail to progress toward freedom. At the least, one will come to life again in more favorable circumstances. Thus, Buddhism ousts the gods and the fates from control over human destiny. This is interesting sociologically, because Buddhism has been most appealing to people who have wanted control over their own lives, such as warriors and merchants. The simpler folk, who might have had to spur themselves to such a sober and confident state of mind, drew encouragement from Buddhist art, which illustrates the delights of heaven and the torments of hell. Many renditions of the wheel of life, for instance, show Mara (Death) devouring the material world and those who cling to it. In the center of the wheel are such symbolic animals as the cock (desire), the snake (hatred), and the pig (delusion), who work to keep the wheel turning.

The dharma, therefore, began as a proclamation of diagnosis and cure. Likening himself to a doctor, the Buddha told his followers not to lose themselves in extraneous questions about where karma or ignorance comes from. Furthermore, he told them not to concentrate on whether the world is eternal or how to conceive of nirvana. To ponder such issues, said the Buddha, would be like a man severely wounded with an arrow who refuses treatment until he knows the caste and character of the man who shot him. The point is to get the arrow out. Similarly, the point to

Original Buddhism was a simple religion:

DOCTRINE: Life is suffering, suffering is caused by desire, desire can only be controlled by a life structured around meditation.

MYTH: The life of the Buddha: a man who meditated, found Enlightenment, shared it with others

RITUAL: Meditation

ETHICS: Do not kill, do not steal, do not lie, do not take intoxicants, do not commit sex outside of marriage

Which aspects of Buddhism could you accept?

Which would you have to reject?

Contribute to this discussion at
http://forums.delphiforums.com/rel101

human existence is to break the wheel of rebirth, to slay the monstrous round of suffering, fleetingness, and emptiness.

For about forty-five years after his enlightenment, the Buddha preached variants on his basic themes: the Four Noble Truths, Dependent Co-arising, and the three marks. His sangha grew, as monks, nuns, and laypeople responded to his simple, clear message. He had to suffer painful threats to the unity of his group, but on the whole he did his work in peace. At his death he had laid the essential foundation of Buddhism— its basic doctrine and way of life. Thus, his death came in the peace of trance. When he asked his followers for the last time whether they had any questions, all stood silent. So he passed into trance and out of this painful realm. According to legend, the earth quaked and the sky thundered in final tribute.

EARLY BUDDHISM

After the Buddha's death his followers gathered to organize the dharma (which for some centuries remained largely oral) in part because he had said it should be their guide after his death. According to tradition, they held a council of monks to settle both the dharma and the monastic rules. Supposedly the canon of Buddhist scriptures we now possess is the fruit of this council: This is the three baskets of law, the *Tipitaka* (the authoritative collection of materials also known as the *Pali canon* because it was written in the Indian vernacular derived from Sanskrit). The scriptures consist of five collections of discourses (*sutras*) that the Buddha supposedly preached. Just one of these collections runs to 1,100 pages in modern printing.

In addition to these sutras and the monastic rules, early Buddhists added to the canon the *Abhidhamma* treatises of the early philosophers, who tried to analyze reality by correlating the Buddha's teaching with the experiences of meditation. Therefore, the Buddhist goal in forming a canon of scripture was to establish an authoritative standard by which to measure doctrine and ethics.

However, within a hundred years of the Buddha's death, dissensions split the movement. These were the precursors of the major division of Buddhism into the Theravada and Mahayana schools, which we consider

Which theoretical approach would give you the most insight on the history, doctrine, rituals, ethics of *Hinayana Buddhism*?

EXAMPLE:

I shall use the example of the perspective of Freud.

Freud's psychoanalytic approach reduced religion to a social attempt to control unconscious drives of sex and aggression. He also postulated that the human mind could be divided into three components:

ID, which contains those unconscious drives

SUPEREGO, the conscience which attempts to repress those drives

EGO, which is the sense of self, charged with the responsibility of balancing the demands of external reality as well as balancing the id and superego.

From this perspective, Buddhism can be seen as a strategy. The communal life of the *sangha* (monastic order) serves to strengthen the superego. The first target is the id: both sex and aggression are limited by the rules of the Sangha. After these id-based forces are controlled, the Buddhist strategy then targets the ego, using meditative exercises that help the monk transcend any remaining sense of individuality, and tie to external reality. Then, only the superego exists, but it has no more opponents, so it may fade away, yielding a tension-free state known as Nirvana.

Contribute to this discussion at
http://forums.delphiforums.com/rel101

below. The apparent forerunners of the Mahayana schools were the Mahasanghikas, who seem to have considered the monastic rules adaptable, while the Sthaviras (Elders), the precursors of the Theravadins, stressed the importance of the letter of the monastic code. About two hundred years after the Buddha's death, the Pudgalavadins branched off from the Sthaviras. They taught that there is a person or self (neither identical with the *skandhas* nor separate from them) that is the basis of knowledge, transmigration, and entrance into nirvana. These first schisms prefigured later Buddhist history. New schools have constantly arisen as new insights or problems made old views unacceptable. As a result, the sangha has not been a centralized authority and Buddhism has not kept a full unity. Nonetheless, the sangha has given all Buddhists certain essential teachings (almost all sects would agree to what we have expounded of dharma so far). Also, it has fostered a very influential monastic life. The monastic order, which has always been the heart of Buddhism (monks have tended to take precedence over laity as an almost unquestioned law of nature), has been a source of stability in Buddhism.

MONASTICISM. A major influence on the Buddhist monastic routine has been Buddha's own life. This routine became a model for the monks: rise at daybreak, wash, and then sit in meditation until it was time to go begging for food. Usually devout laity would invite him in, and after eating lightly he would teach them the dharma. Then he would return to his residence, wash, and rest. After this he would preach to the monks and respond to their requests for individual guidance. After another rest he would preach to the laity and then take a cool bath. Originally the monks always wandered except during the rainy season, but later they assumed a more stable setting with quiet lands and a few simple buildings.

The four misdeeds that merited expulsion from the order were fornication, theft, killing, and "falsely claiming spiritual attainments." (This last rule implied that one was not to go around trying to impress people by working miracles or performing divination.) Committing any of thirteen lesser misdeeds led to a group meeting of the sangha and probation. They included sexual offenses (touching a woman, speaking suggestively to a woman, urging a woman to gain merit by submitting to a "man of religion,"

Head of Buddha from third century C.E., *found in Afghanistan. Some of the largest stone statues of the Buddha in Afghanistan were destroyed in March of 2001 by the Taliban, a group of Muslims who declared that the statues were idols to be smashed.*

and serving as a procurer), violating the rules that limited the size and specified the site of a monk's dwelling, falsely accusing other monks of grievous violations of the rule, fomenting discord among the monks, or causing a schism. With appropriate changes, similar rules have governed the nuns' lives. There are hundreds of other things that monks and nuns cannot do, and all of them suggest something about the ideals of the sangha. Prohibitions against lying, slander, stealing another's sleeping space, and "sporting in the water" testify to an ideal of honest and direct speech, mutual consideration, and grave decorum. Similarly, prohibitions against digging in the ground and practicing agriculture reflect the ideals of not taking other creatures' lives and of begging one's food.

Rules for good posture and table manners indicate that an ideal monk stood erect, kept his eyes downcast, refrained from loud laughter, and did not smack his lips, talk with his mouth full, or throw food into his mouth. The refined monk also cannot excrete while standing up or excrete onto growing grass or into the water. Finally, he is not supposed to preach the dharma to monks or laypeople who carry parasols, staffs, swords, or other weapons, or wear slippers, sandals, turbans, or other head coverings.

The sangha accepted recruits from all social classes, and many of them were youths. From this circumstance one can understand the concern for the rights of the growing grass and the water. Monks often carried their two principal fears (of taking life or being sexually incontinent) to extremes. Especially regarding matters of sex, the monastic legislation was quite strict.

THE LAITY. From earliest times, Buddhism encouraged its laity to pursue an arduous religious life. Though his or her white robe never merited the honor that a monk's saffron-colored robe received, a layperson who had taken refuge in the Three Jewels and contributed to the sangha's support was an honorable follower. From early times Buddhism has specified morality for the laity in five precepts. The first of these is to refrain from killing living beings. A vegetarian diet was preferred but not always followed. Unintentional killing is not an offense, and agriculturalists have only to minimize their damage to life. The second is to refrain from stealing. The third precept deals with sexual matters. It forbids intercourse with another person's wife, a nun, or a woman betrothed to another man. It also urges restraint with a

> The monastic lifestyle of monks and nuns involves vows of poverty, chastity (celibacy), and obedience. That lifestyle has attracted thousands of Buddhist and Christian men and women over the centuries. Do you think that such a lifestyle has any place in the modern world? If not, do you think that any modifications (e.g., a limited commitment of time in a monastery) would be appropriate for today's world?
>
> Contribute to this discussion at
> http://forums.delphiforums.com/rel101

wife who is pregnant, nursing, or under a religious vow of sexual abstinence. Apparently relations with courtesans were licit. The commentators' explanation of this precept assumes that it is the male's duty to provide control in sexual matters (because females are by nature wanton). The fourth precept imposes restraint from lying, and the fifth precept forbids drinking alcoholic beverages.

This ethical code has been the layperson's chief focus. Occasionally he or she received instruction in meditation or the doctrine of wisdom, and later Mahayana sects considered the laity fully capable of reaching nirvana. (In the beginning only monks were so considered; nuns never had the status of monks, in part because of legends that the Buddha established nunneries only reluctantly.) The principal lay virtues were to be generous in supporting monks and to witness to Buddhist values in the world. The financial support, obviously enough, was a two-edged sword. Monks who put on spiritual airs would annoy the laity sweating to support them. On the other hand, monks constantly faced a temptation to tailor their doctrine to please the laity and so boost financial contributions. The best defenses against such abuses were monasteries in which the monks lived very simple, poor lives.

Beyond meditation and the routine of monastic life, early Buddhism did not develop many new ceremonies or rites of passage. The closest was the initiation rite of shaving one's head. Buddhism got its rituals by integrating some of the local celebrations and customs. To this day, most localities do not involve Buddhist priests in birth and wedding ceremonies, but funeral services do. Indian Buddhists commemorated the Buddha's birthday and the day of his enlightenment. However, the *bodhi* tree under which the Buddha came to enlightenment prompted many Buddhists to revere trees. Such trees, along with *stupas* (burial mounds) of holy persons, were popular places of devotion.

Originally, a stupa was simply a mound of earth or stone that served as a shrine to a Buddha or bodhisattva and so became a focus of Buddhist piety. Stupas became more ornate temples as time went on, points of pilgrimage, giving Buddhists access to some of the religious effects pilgrimage regularly produces (entrance into a zone free of ordinary profane concerns, divisions, and sulliedness).

The worship of statues of the Buddha grew popular only under the influence of the Mahayana sect after 100 C.E., but earlier veneration of certain symbols of the Buddha (an empty throne, a pair of footprints, a wheel or lotus, or a *bodhi* tree) had paved the way. These symbols signified such things as the Buddha's presence in the world, his royal renunciation, and the dharma he preached. The lotus became an especially popular symbol, since it stood for the growth of pure enlightenment from the mud of worldly life.

MEDITATION. A central aspect of early Buddhist life was meditation, which has remained a primary way to realize the wisdom and inspire the practice that lead to nirvana. Meditation designated mental discipline. For instance, one could meditate by practicing certain devotional exercises that focused attention on one of the three jewels—the Buddha, the dharma, or the sangha. These would be recalled as the three refuges under which one had taken shelter, and the meditator's sense of wonder and gratitude for protection would increase his or her emotional attachment. Thus, such meditative exercises were a sort of *bhakti,* though without sexual overtones.

Indeed, both the saints (bodhisattvas) and the Buddha could become objects of loving concentration. However, such devotion was not meditation proper, for this was a discipline of consciousness similar to yoga. As is clear from the story of his own life, Buddha's enlightenment came after he had experienced various methods of "mindfulness" and trance. It is proper, then, to consider Buddhist meditation a species of yoga. From early times the mindfulness of Buddhists has usually been a control of the senses and imagination geared to bringing "one-pointed mental consciousness" to bear on the truths of the dharma. For instance, one fixed on mental processes to become aware of their stream and the *skandhas,* and to focus on the idea that all is fleeting, painful, and selfless. In addition, meditation masters sometimes encouraged monks to bolster their flight from the world by contemplating the contemptibleness of the body and its pleasures.

However, wisdom was more than just attacks on hindrances to freedom and nirvana. In careful meditations, Buddhist adepts tried to replicate the Enlightened One's experience during the night of vision, cultivating first his one-pointedness of mind and then his dispassionate heightening of awareness. Adepts also composed meditations focusing on doctrinal points such as the Four Noble Truths or the three marks in order to see their reality directly. This was similar to the insight practices or the way of knowledge (*jnana-marga*) that Hinduism offered, though of course Buddhist doctrines often differed from Hindu.

MAHAYANA. *Maha* means "large" (*maharaja* is a great king; *mahavira* is a great sage), *yana* means "boat," so *Mahayana* is the "large raft" (big ferryboat) approach to Buddhism. This theistic approach eventually viewed Buddha as captain of the ferryboat: he is a personal savior and all we have to do is get on his boat. This approach developed about five hundred years after Buddha's death, though there may have been some earlier trends in this area. The role of the laity differed greatly between Theravadins and Mahayanists. Even more, the notion of the Buddha and the range of metaphysics varied considerably. Before its emergence, early Buddhism was fairly uniform in its understanding of Buddha-dharma-sangha and wisdom-morality-meditation. (Theravada has essentially adhered to early Buddhist doctrine, so the description of Buddhism thus far characterizes Theravada.)

The hallmark of Mahayana was its literature, which placed in the mouth of the Buddha sutras describing a new ideal and a new version of wisdom. Why did Mahayana conceive the need for a greater vehicle? The answer seems to be twofold: the sense that the career of the Buddha showed him to be so full of compassion that one could not limit Buddhist doctrine or practice in any way that confined the outreach of the Enlightened One's mercy, and the sense that people everywhere, indeed all living creatures, needed such compassion—were burning with desire and could only be saved by the wisdom of Gautama. Thus the Mahayanists came to think that the ideal follower of the Buddha, the saint they call a **bodhisattva** (one who had the knowledge and being of a Buddha, who essentially was an Enlightened One, but who decided to remain on this earth a little longer in order to teach others), would so extend compassion that any notion of self-concern would fall away. Somewhat in contrast to the *arhat*, the holy person whose concentration on self-perfection had brought deep wisdom, goodness, and peace, the bodhisattva would

vow to postpone entrance into nirvana (postpone gaining the fruits of his or her perfection) and stay in the samsaric world to labor for the salvation of all living human beings. In Mahayana, therefore, the self-giving symbolized by Gautama's decision to return to the world and preach the dharma empowered a considerable outreach. Emotionally, horizons expanded to include all beings in need. In terms of missionary impulse, the Mahayanists felt impelled to preach to people everywhere. Culturally, Mahayanists sensed that all aspects of life ideally would be colored and enriched by the Buddha's compassion. As well, they realized that laypeople had to be better appreciated and shown how any state of life, married life and work in the world as much as monastic living, could be a means to enlightenment and a place where one could do good. Finally, the Mahayanists put great effort into developing Buddhist wisdom so that it could accommodate the large-heartedness they found in the Buddha's career. Thus their metaphysics came to look for traces of *bodhi,* liberating wisdom, everywhere, and they soon came to question any facile distinction between nirvana and *samsara.*

Historically, Theravada spread to southern India and Southeast Asia, while Mahayana became the "northern" tradition, spreading to Central Asia, China, Korea, and Japan. Today Theravada Buddhism dominates Sri Lanka (Ceylon), Thailand (Siam), Myanmar (Burma), Vietnam and Kampuchea (Cambodia), and Laos. Other Asian countries are dominated by Mahayana Buddhism. Tibet has been dominated by an offshoot of Tantric Buddhism, as we shall see. In focusing on Mahayana doctrine, let us deal first with two innovative teachings of the Mahayana schools, emptiness and mind-only, and then consider the Mahayana views of the Buddha himself.

EMPTINESS. The doctrine of emptiness (*sunyata*) is a hallmark of Mahayana teaching. In fact, the Mahayana sutras known as the *Prajna-paramita* ("wisdom-that-has-gone-beyond") center on this notion. By the end of the Mahayana development, emptiness had in effect become a fourth mark of all reality. Besides being painful, fleeting, and selfless, all reality was empty. Thus, further rumination on the three marks led Mahayana philosophers to consider a fourth mark, emptiness, as the most significant feature of all beings. No reality was a substance, having an "own-being."

The **Theravada** tradition is called "the way of the elders" because it claims ties with pristine early Buddhism. It is sometimes called *Hinayana* (small raft) because it assumes that each individual has to cross the river of suffering by his own efforts: Buddha only provides an example of how to do it. (The followers of this approach prefer to call themselves Theravada, regarding the term *Hinayana* to be one of derision concocted by their opponents.) This approach prevails in Southeast Asia and stresses the importance of meditation for gaining freedom from the illusions of the self. This teaching has experienced a vigorous renaissance in contemporary Myanmar (Burma). By and large, most of the recent Burmese meditation masters have emphasized attaining insight into the true nature of reality, in contrast to meditation masters in other eras or lands who have emphasized attaining a formless yogic trance. Since they claim that insight was the original Buddhist emphasis while trance was the Hindu emphasis, the recent Burmese masters have rather self-consciously striven to give preference to the Buddhist, rather than the Hindu Brahmanistic, influences that Indian history bequeathed them.

The preferred Burmese focus for observing the human unity is the breath or the body's *tonus* (feeling). By cultivating a regular breathing that integrates the body-mind components and stressing feeling, the Burmese masters have shifted away from the visual emphasis of the yogic tradition. They urge that one try to grow more sensitive to the touch of the breath at the nostrils or the rise and fall of the abdomen. Then, with practice, one can expand this tactile awareness to other dimensions of experience, for example the pleasures or pains one is experiencing. The result should be a heightened attention to what seems most really stimulating, pleasing, or irritating to the body-mind unity at a given moment. Behind the efforts to gain this heightened attention lies the conviction that the three marks, if vividly experienced, will bring one great spiritual progress.

Obviously, therefore, none could be an *Atman,* be constant, or be fully satisfying.

DIALECTICS. The *Heart Sutra* is an example of this tradition. It employs dialectics (the act of playing both sides of an issue) in analyzing the five *skandhas*: Form is emptiness, and this very emptiness is form. Feeling, perception, impulse, and consciousness are all emptiness, and emptiness is feeling, perception, impulse, and consciousness. This identification, the sutra emphasizes, can be seen by anyone "here"— from the viewpoint of the wisdom that has gone beyond. Therefore, reminiscent of Shankara's two levels of knowing Brahman, the *Prajna-paramita* says that there are several ways of looking at ordinary reality. From the lower point of view, feeling, perception, impulse, consciousness, and form are all "something." From the higher viewpoint of enlightenment or perfect wisdom, however, these terms all designate something that is empty, that has no solid core or own-being.

To deal with any dharma as though it were full, therefore, would be to deal with it at least erroneously and possibly desirously—thus, karmically. If, however, we see that nothing is pleasant, stable, or full, then we will deal with all things in detachment, moving through them toward nirvana. So, according to the sutra, a bodhisattva sees things without "thought coverings," does not tremble at the emptiness that this attitude reveals, and thereby attains nirvana.

MIND-ONLY. The second major Mahayana school, the Yogacara, which became influential from about 300 C.E. on, proposed another influential teaching on ultimate reality, mind-only. Like the teaching on emptiness, it went beyond early Buddhist teaching, and the Theravadins rejected the sutras that attributed this teaching to the Buddha. The teaching of mind-only held that all realities finally are mental. The Yogacarins wanted a fuller explanation of mental reality, probably because their intuitions grew out of meditational or yogic practices (whence their name).

One of the principal Yogacarin sutras, the Lanka-vatara, described a tier of consciousness in the individual culminating in a "storehouse" consciousness (*alayavijnana*) that is the base of the individual's deepest awareness, the individual's tie to the cosmic. The storehouse consciousness is itself unconscious and inactive, but it is the repository of the "seeds" that ripen into human deeds and awareness. Furthermore, Yogacarins sometimes called the storehouse consciousness the Buddha's womb. Thereby, they made the Buddha, or Tathagata (Enlightened One), a metaphysical principle—a foundation of all reality. From the womb of the Buddha issued the purified thoughts and beings of enlightenment. The symbolism is complex (and interestingly feminine, suggesting a Buddhist version of androgyny or primal wholeness). Its main point, though, is clear: The womb of the Buddha (Tathagata-garbha) is present in all living beings, irradiating them with enlightenment. Like the feminine *Prajna-paramita*, then, the ultimate reality of the Yogacarins "mothers" the many individual things (that are themselves empty). It is the great mental storehouse from which they issue, the matrix that holds them all in being. It stimulates their dancing flux.

MAHAYANA DEVOTION. Most major Mahayana schools developed sophisticated theories to correlate the many beings of experience with the simple finality of nirvana. It was not philosophy that brought Mahayana popular influence, though, but its openness to the laity's spiritual needs, its devotional thought. Early Buddhism held monks in great regard, considering them the only true followers of Buddha. They were the teachers, the determiners of doctrine, and the guardians of morality. They were the stewards of tradition who made the sangha a jewel alongside the Buddha and the dharma. Consequently, the laity considered themselves to be working out a better karma, so that in their next lives they might be monks (or, if they were women, so that they might be men). The central lay virtue, as we have seen, was giving financial support to the monasteries, and the sangha seldom admitted laity to the higher occupations of philosophy or meditation.

Mahayana changed this view of the laity. As we have seen, by stressing the Buddha's compassion and his resourcefulness in saving all living creatures, it gradually qualified the Theravadin ideal of the *arhat*

(individual saintly monk who worked on his own spiritual perfection) and fashioned a new, more socially oriented ideal, the bodhisattva. Mahayana thereby prepared the way for later schools that were in effect Buddhist devotional sects, such as the Pure Land sect. Such sects preached that through graceful compassion, a buddha or bodhisattva only required that one devoutly repeat his name and place full trust in him for salvation. In this "degenerate age," the difficult paths of wisdom and meditation were open only to the few. Therefore, the Enlightened One (Buddha) had opened a broader path of devotion, so that laity as well as monks might reach paradise and nirvana. (Or to use the raft analogy: Buddha is the captain of the ferryboat; to get your ticket you just have to accept him as your personal savior.)

Mahayana did not destroy monastic dignity. Rather, it stressed the social side of the ideal. The Mahayanists saw the Theravadin monks as too individualistic. To pursue one's own enlightenment and salvation apart from those of other living beings seemed selfish. Out of great compassion (*mahakaruna*), the full saint would remain in the samsaric world, for eons if need be, content to put off final bliss if that would help save other living beings.

Mahayanists stress six great "perfections" in becoming a bodhisattva, and these effectively summarize Mahayana religious living. First is the perfection of giving: giving material things to those in need, but also giving spiritual instructions, one's own body and life, or even one's own karmic merit. In a life of compassionate generosity, everything could be given over to others. Mahayanists understand the five other perfections of morality, patience, vigor, meditation, and wisdom in a similarly broad fashion. Thus, they have applied the traditional triad of wisdom-morality-meditation in more social ways. Giving, patience, and vigor have meant that one became selfless in more than a metaphysical way. For the love of others, for the grand vision of a totally perfected world, the saint may cheerfully donate his goods and talents, suffer abuses, and labor ceaselessly.

Finally, Mahayanists began to contemplate the Buddha's preexistence and the status he had gained as a knowledge being. In this contemplation, his earthly life receded in importance, so much that some Mahayanists began to say that he had only apparently assumed a human body. Then, linking this stress on the Buddha's metaphysical essence with the Indian doctrine of endless *kalpas* of cosmic time and endless stretches of cosmic space, Mahayanists emphasized the many buddhas who had existed before Sakyamuni and the buddhas who presided in other cosmic realms. All became potential objects of adoration and petitionary prayer.

In this way the notion of buddhahood greatly expanded. First it was the quality shared by many cosmic beings of wisdom and realization. Later, in East Asian Mahayana, buddhahood became the metaphysical notion that all beings are in essence enlightenment beings. As we have seen in the *Prajna-paramita* sutra, enlightenment implies grasping how all beings are empty of individual solidity. Enlightenment, therefore, is just realizing one's buddha nature, the knowledge and light that dawn when the grasp of emptiness allows true human nature to show itself. It is the beginning of nirvana, the break with samsara, and the achievement of perfect wisdom all in one.

Buddhahood thus became complex and many-sided. The Buddha came to have three bodies: The dharma body, in which he was the unmanifest aspect of Buddhahood or Enlightenment-being; the human body, in which he appeared on earth; and the glorification body, in which he was manifest to the heavenly beings, with all his marks and signs. Moreover, the distinction between buddhas and great bodhisattvas blurred and largely dissolved in the popular mind, giving Buddhist "divinity" a full spectrum of holy beings. Citing the Mahayana understanding of divinity, therefore, is a sure way to refute claims that Buddhism is not a religion. By the fifth or sixth century after the Buddha's death, Mahayana Buddhists were venerating a variety of divine figures. This was especially true in East Asia, where Mahayana devotionalism built on pre-Buddhist traditions (for example, many Japanese *kami* became bodhisattvas).

TANTRISM

Tantrism's sexual symbols (if not rituals) affected (or infected) orthodox Buddhism as well as orthodox Hinduism in the early common era. Buddhist Tantrism in India seems to have originated around the sixth century C.E., flourishing first in the northwest. From the eighth century on it prospered around Bengal, combining with *Prajnaparamita* philosophy and native

symbolic practices. It later reached Sri Lanka, Myanmar (Burma), and Indonesia. Often it merged with Shaivism, but in Tibet it combined with native *Bonism,* or shamanist practices, and became the dominant Buddhist sect.

Tantrism had antecedents in both Buddha's teaching and in the surrounding Hindu Brahmanism. Buddha appears to have allowed spells, and the canon contains reputed cures for snakebite and other dangers. *Prajna-paramita* sutras such as the *Heart Sutra* often ended with spells, transferring certain key ideas and words from strictly intellectual notions to mantras. In Brahmanic sacrifices, as we noted, the prayers were understood so literally that they became mantras; if a priest recited a prayer properly, it was sure to accomplish its end.

Buddhist Tantrists took over such sacred sounds as *om,* as well as esoteric yogic systems, such as kundalini, which associated sacred syllables with force centers (*chakras*) in the body. They also used mandalas (magic figures, such as circles and squares) and even stupas (shrines). The Buddhist Tantrists were thus hardly bizarre or innovative, mainly developing ancient Hindu esoteric practices in a new setting.

What novelty the Tantrists did introduce into Buddhism came from their creative use of rites that acted out mandalas and esoteric doctrines about bodily forces. Perhaps under the influence of Yogacara meditation, which induced states of trance, the Tantrists developed rituals in which participants identified with particular deities. If it is true that many meditation schools, such as the Yogacara, employed mandalas for the early states of trance in order to focus consciousness, then the Tantrists probably built on well-established practices. In their theoretical elaboration, however, they retrieved certain ancient cosmological notions.

For instance, they came to see the stupa burial sites as replicas of the cosmos. The railings that separated the stupa precinct from secular ground divided the sacred from the profane. The edge of the moving mandala that the Tantrist troupe would dance or act out had a function similar to that of the railings. Often Tantrism strove to symbolize the entire cosmic plan. Indeed, the Tantrists tried to draw heavenly worlds (bodhisattva realms) and gods into their meditations and rituals. A principal metaphysical support of Tantrism was the Madhyamika doctrine of emptiness, which the Tantrists interpreted to mean that all beings are intrinsically pure. Consequently, they used odd elements in their rituals to drive home the doctrines of emptiness, purity, and freedom. For the most part, these ways did not become public, since the Tantrists went to considerable pains to keep their rites and teachings secret. In fact, they developed a cryptic language that they called "twilight speech," in which sexual references were abundant. For instance, they called the male and female organs "thunderbolt" and "lotus," respectively. As with Hindu Tantrism, it is not always possible to tell whether such speech is symbolic or literal. Some defenders of Tantrism claim that it tamed sexual energy in the Indian tradition by subjecting it to symbolization, meditative discipline, and moral restraints. Other critics, however, view Buddhist Tantrism as a corruption of a tradition originally quite intolerant of libidinal practices. For them the Tantrist explanation that, since everything is mind-only, the practice of erotic rites means little is simply a rationalization.

In a typical Tantrist meditation, the meditators would begin with traditional preliminaries such as seeking refuge in the three jewels, cleansing themselves of sins (by confession or bathing), praying to past masters, or drawing a mandala to define the sacred space of the extraordinary reality that their rite was going to involve. Then the meditators would take on the identity of a deity and disperse all appearances of the world into emptiness. Next, using their imaginations, they would picture themselves as the divinities whose identities they were projecting.

So pictured, a man and his consort would sit on the central throne of the mandala space and engage in sexual union. Then they would imagine various buddhas parading into the sacred space of the mandala and assimilate them into their bodies and senses. In that assimilation, their speech would become divine, they could receive offerings as gods, and they could perform any of the deities' functions. So charged with divinity, they would then return to the ordinary world, bringing back to it the great power of a buddha's divine understanding.

The relation of the master (**guru**) and the disciple was central in Tantrism, because the master represented the tradition. (Zen has maintained this stress on the master. The Tantric guru was the authority needed to help the striver receive the original enlightenment disclosed by the Buddha. Texts were too pale and ambiguous.) The Tantric gurus occasionally forced their pupils to engage in quite bizarre and painful practices, to teach them to examine the mirror of their minds, to learn the illusory character of all phenomena, and to stop the cravings and jealousies that clouded their mirror. Pronouncing the death of old judgments and the birth of new ones of enlightenment, the guru might confuse pupils, punish them and push them to break with convention and ordinary vision. When Buddhism had become vegetarian, some Tantric masters urged eating flesh. When Buddhism advocated teetotalism, some urged imbibing intoxicating spirits.

TIBET. Perhaps the best place to examine the Mantric and Tantric tradition full blown is Tibet. Tantrism was welcomed in Tibet and came to dominate in this land between India and China. Our first historical records date from only the seventh century C.E., when Chinese historians started mentioning it. Under King Srongsten Gampo in 632, Tibet borrowed both writing and Buddhism from Kashmir. Toward the end of the eighth century, two notable Indian Buddhist monks came to Tibet and founded a lasting Tibetan sangha. Since that triumph, Tibet has owed more to Indian scholarship and philosophy than to Chinese.

The mandalas, mantras, and chakras (ritual circles within which the gods could be encountered or impersonated) furthered the Indian academic structures that greatly influenced Tibetan Buddhism. During the Indian Gupta dynasty (320–540 C.E.), great monastic universities became the pillars of Buddhism. The "curricular Buddhism" of these schools encompassed all the arts and sciences. Furthermore, meditation integrated with scholasticism, assuring that the academic efforts to correlate Buddhist doctrine with existing knowledge never divorced themselves from practical religion. The Tibetan adoption of an Indian rather than a Chinese religious style correlated with this union of study and meditation, for the Indian schools favored a gradual penetration of enlightenment in which study could play an important role.

One characteristic of Tibetan Buddhism has therefore been its line of scholars based in monastic universities. They have produced voluminous translations and commentaries for the canonical scriptures, as well as a tradition that learning should inform ritualist life. Learning and ritual, in fact, became the primary foci of the Tibetan monastic life. The king and the common people looked to the monastery for protection through ritual against evil powers, while individual monks utilized both meditation and ritual in their pursuit of enlightenment.

The typical day of a traditional Tibetan monk began with a private ritual contemplation (Tantrist) before dawn for an hour and a half. During the morning, the monk regularly participated in the community's prayers for two hours and then worked in the monastic library. He devoted the afternoon to more work and public ceremony and again meditated in the evening.

Before the Chinese communists occupied and incorporated Tibet into China (and transplanted many ethnic Chinese into Tibet), about a fifth of the adult male population was living in the monasteries. Many monks spent a lifetime in this regime, coming to the monastery at the age of nine or ten and receiving a thorough training in the scriptures, meditation techniques, and ceremonial details. As suggested, the king supported this lifestyle, because ritual could prop his authority. (Pre-Buddhist Tibetan culture thought of the king in ancient sacred terms, as the tie between heaven and earth. Something of this ancient view continued when monks prayed and conducted rituals for the king's good health.) The common people, whose shamanist heritage emphasized many malevolent spirits of sickness and death, saw in the ritual spells and ceremonies a powerful defense. As a result, the monasteries were quite practical institutions for them, too.

One ritual engaged in by both monks and laity in Tibet is the prayer wheel. This is a twelve-sided wheel of stone or bronze. The worshipper spins it rapidly by hand so that the different faces whiz by. Each face has a different prayer stamped upon it. Each time the wheel turns, all dozen prayers are credited to the worshipper. But this can be viewed as more than a relatively high tech approach to send more prayers in less time. The process of spinning focuses the attention and induces a meditative state.

By emphasizing ritual in both public ceremonies and private meditations, Tibetan Buddhism created its own version of the Tantrist doctrine that the imagination, senses, and psychological and bodily powers are all potential sources of energy for enlightenment and wisdom. The Yellow Hat sect of Tantrism is the largest, and the one with the Dalai Lama. They have symbolized the tantric acts. (The Red Hat sect is considered more extreme, with some debased tantrics and some extreme ascetics.) The Tibetan Tantrist cult acted out symbolic situations representing the cosmos, so that the common people could find something comfortingly universal. The worship of the local goddess, for instance, which monasteries and popular festivals promoted, gave the world a motherly and protecting aspect. Monks and laity both prayed personally to Tara for help, while many of Tibet's musical and dancing arts developed through festivals devoted to her.

The success that Buddhism enjoyed in Tibet may also be linked to its ability to capitalize on native shamanist themes and political institutions. The ancient Tibetan *bon* ("he who invokes the gods") was a shaman very like the archetypal Siberian shaman. Beating his drum, whirling in dance, weaving his spells, he fought against the demons of sickness and death. In addition to developing its own Tantrist rituals to cover these interests of the older religion, Tibetan Buddhism also produced a type of wandering "crazy" saint who drew much of the awe and respect that the older shamans had.

The prototype of this ascetic, visionary holy man in Tibet was the much-beloved Milarepa (1040–1123). After a harsh initiation by a cruel guru, he took to the mountain slopes and gained a reputation for working wonders. In his songs he poetically expressed profound insights into both the nature of dharmic reality and the psychology of the ascetic life.

Buddhism capitalized on the demise of kingship in Tibet in the ninth century to establish a theocratic regime with the monastery at its heart. Despite early persecutions during a period of kings' intrigues and assassinations, by the eleventh century the monasteries were strong. Until the communist takeover, in fact, the monasteries and the Dalai Lamas (religious leaders) dominated Tibetan politics (often with much intrigue and sectarian strife). The Mongol emperor Kublai Khan granted Buddhist abbots temporal power over all Tibet, firmly establishing a theocratic rule. By the fourteenth century, however, Tibet was a cauldron of various Buddhist sects vying for power.

Of the sects that developed after the demise of the Chinese Tang dynasty in the ninth century, the most important was the Ge-lug, which shrewdly employed

Japan

Kamakura

BUDDHISM ARRIVES
6TH CENTURY

BUDDHISM ARRIVES
4TH CENTURY

Korea

Kyoto
Nara

Kyongju

Pacific
Ocean

INTRODUCED IN 1ST CENTURY C.E.,
FLOURISHED UNTIL 9TH CENTURY

Mongolia

▲ Mt. Wu'tai

Loyang

Ch'ang-an

Yellow R.

China

▲ Mt. Omei

West R.
(Xun)

Kuang Chou
(Canton)

Taiwan

Yangtze R.

Hanoi

Mekong R.

Vietnam

SOUTH
CHINA
SEA

Brunei

BUDDHISM TAKES
HOLD IN 7TH CENTURY

Laos

Angkor

Thailand

Cambodia

Phnom Penh

Malaysia

Indonesia

Bali

Java

Turfuang

TIBET

Lhasa

Bhutan

Brahmaputra R.

Mandalay

Myanmar
(Burma)

Pagan

Salween R.

Sukhothai

Irrawaddy R.

Rangoon

Sumatra

BUDDHISM INFLUENTIAL
FROM 1ST TO 8TH
CENTURIES

Kucha

Khotan

Kathmandu

Nepal

Sravasti

Vaisali

Bodhgaya

Ganges R.

Calcutta

Bangladesh

SHAKYAMUNI LIVES IN THE
REGION OF MAGADHA
DURING 5–6TH CENTURIES C.E.

Bay
Of
Bengal

Kyrghyzstan

Tajikistan

Gilgit

KASHMIR

India

Jumna R.

BUDDHISM ARRIVES
2ND CENTURY B.C.E.

Uzbekistan

GANDHARA

Afghanistan

Pakistan

Indus R.

Bombay

Sri
Lanka

IN DECLINE FROM 7TH CENTURY,
DISAPPEARS FROM 8TH–10TH
CENTURIES

Arabian
Sea

Indian Ocean

1500 Miles

1500 Kilometers

1000

500

1000

500

0

0

Sakyamuni's birthplace and dispersion of Buddhism to East Asia

the idea of reincarnation. Consequently, the Mongols both recognized the Dalai Lama as a spiritual leader and considered him a grandson of the Mongol chief. From the sixteenth century onward, the Ge-lug wielded great political clout. The Dalai Lamas, for the most part, have been men of considerable spiritual and political acumen, and their rule has meant a vigorous sangha. The fourteenth, and current, Dalai Lama (b. 1935) was exiled by the Chinese communists, but he is still the spiritual leader of tens of thousands of Tibetan Buddhists, working for the day when Tibetans will again govern their own lives and be free to practice their religion.

One of the implications of the political role of the Tibetan Buddhist leaders and this emphasis on reincarnation is the practice of identifying small boys as the reincarnation of the Buddha, and therefore the next Dalai Lama. Such a boy would be taken away from his parents and specially trained for his future role. There was a major dispute between Tibetans and the Chinese leadership in the mid-1990s when they had identified different small boys as future leaders of Tibet.

Tibetan Buddhism thus stands out for two things: its Tantrist bent and its especially knotted political history. Few cultures have so absorbed one version of Buddhism as Tibet has absorbed the "thunderbolt vehicle" (Tantrism). Perhaps the most famous Tibetan religious text to reach the West is the *Tibetan Book of the Dead,* which purportedly describes the experiences of the deceased during the forty-nine days between physical death and entry into a new karmic state. By employing vivid imagery and specifying rituals designed to help the deceased to achieve nirvana, the *Book of the Dead* exemplifies the Tantrist mentality well. It is a journey through the imagination and unconscious that severely challenges most notions of reality, since it maintains that the period right after death is the most opportune time for liberation.

THE DEMISE OF INDIAN BUDDHISM

Buddhism declined in India after the seventh century, only in part because of Tantrist emphases. Invaders such as the White Huns and the Muslims wrecked many Buddhist strongholds, while the revival of Hinduism, especially of Hindu *bhakti* sects of Vishnu and Shiva, undermined Buddhism. Mahayana fought theistic

Hinduism quite fiercely, not at all seeing it as equivalent to the Buddhist theology of bodhisattvas and buddhas, but Hinduism finally prevailed because of its great ability to incorporate other movements. Indeed, Buddha became one of the Vaishnavite avatars.

By the seventh century the Indian sangha had grown wealthy and held much land—facts that contributed to a decline in religious fervor and to antipathy among the laity. From the time of its first patronage under Asoka (around 260 B.C.E.), Buddhism had enjoyed occasional support from princes and kings, and its ability to preach the dharma, to enjoy favor at court, and to influence culture depended on this support. The Kusana dynasty (ca. 78–320 C.E.), for instance, was a good time for Buddhists, while the Gupta age (320–540 C.E.) revived Hinduism. When the Muslims finally established control in India, Buddhism suffered accordingly. Early missionary activity had exported it to the south and east, however, and Buddhism proved to be hardy on foreign soil. So Hinduism, which has largely been confined to India, became the native tradition that opposed the Muslims.

BUDDHISM IN CHINA

Buddhism may have entered China by the beginning of the first century B.C.E., and possibly earlier. Buddhist missionaries traveled along the trade routes that linked northeastern India and China. Probably the first incursions of Buddhism were not well received by the Chinese. Buddhist monks showed their denial of the body by calling it a "stinking bag of bones" and by shaving their heads. The Chinese revered the body as a gift from the ancestors and wore their hair long to reverence the body. The idea of personal transmigration of souls (which underlay the Buddhist understanding of life's problem and its solution) must have sounded quite foreign to the Chinese.

But the Chinese missionaries were persistent, and by the end of the first century of the common era, a foothold had been established. By 148 C.E., monks such as Anshigao had settled at Luoyang, considerably to the east, and begun translating Buddhist texts. The first interests of these translators and their audiences appear to have been meditation and philosophy, which suggests that the Chinese first considered Buddhism similar to Daoism. However, as the translating progressed through the Han dynasty (ended 220 C.E.), sutras on morality became popular, too.

From this beginning, Buddhism slowly adapted to Chinese ways. Most of the preachers and translators who worked from the third to the fifth centuries C.E. favored Daoist terminology. This was especially true in the south, where the intelligentsia had created a market for philosophy. By the middle of the fifth century, China had its own sectarian schools, comparable to those that had developed in India. Thus, by that time most of the major Buddhist philosophies and devotional practices had assumed a Chinese style, including the *Abhidhamma* (a system that employed erudite philosophy and psychology in interpreting the scriptures) and the Indian Madhyamika and Yogacara schools. In general, Mahayana attracted the Chinese more than Theraveda, so the native schools that prospered tended to develop Mahayana positions.

The Chinese brought to Buddhism an interest in bridging the gap between the present age and the age of the Buddha by constructing a line of masters along which the dharma had passed intact. The Master was more historical than timeless scriptural texts were, and the authority-minded Chinese were more concerned about history than the Indians had been.

Indeed, conflicts over the sutras were a sore problem for the Chinese, and in trying to reconcile seemingly contradictory positions, they frequently decided to make one scripture totally authoritative. A principal basis for the differences among the burgeoning Chinese Buddhist sects, therefore, lay in which scripture the sect's founder had chosen as most authoritative.

CHAN. The most popular sects were the Chan (later known as **Zen** in Japan), the Jingtu (which was devoted to meditation), and Pure Land (which was more theistic). The Chinese took to meditation from the beginning of their encounter with Buddhism, probably because it was the one aspect of Buddhism with which they could most easily identify (from the Daoist heritage). There are evidences of yogic practices in the Daoist works attributed to Laozi and Zhuangzi, and certainly Daoist imagery of what the sage who knows the "inside" can accomplish had made many Chinese eager to tap interior powers. Chan capitalized on this interest, working out a simple regime and theory that focused on meditation. (*Chan*

is the transliteration of the Indian dhyana; the Japanese transliteration is *Zen*.) Its principal text was the *Lankavatara Sutra*, which the Yogacarins also much revered.

Chan (Zen) Buddhism is the most mystical school in all of Mahayana. It urges meditation and other spiritual exercises in order to achieve a Satori experience (similar to the *samadhi* or *moksha* of the Upanishads). The Chan school understands this state to be a pure experience of no-mind action (and Chan found an easy way to conceptualize this in China using Daoist concepts such as *wu-wei*). According to legend, Bodhidharma, an Indian meditation master devoted to the *Lankavatara*, founded Chan in the fifth century C.E. Paintings portray Bodhidharma as a fierce champion of single-mindedness, and he valued neither pious works nor recitations of the sutras. Only insight into one's own nature, which was identical with the dharma-nature of all reality, was of significance; only enlightenment justified the Buddhist life. Tradition credits Bodhidharma with developing the technique of "wall gazing," which was a kind of peaceful meditation—what the Japanese later called "just sitting" (*shikan-taza*).

Probably the most eminent of the Chan patriarchs who succeeded Bodhidharma was the sixth patriarch, Hui-neng. According to the Platform Sutra, which purports to present his teachings, Hui-neng gained his predecessor's mantle of authority by surpassing his rival, Shenxiu, in a demonstration of dharma insight. To express his understanding, Shenxiu had written:

The body is the Bodhi Tree
The mind is like a bright mirror and stand.
At all times wipe it diligently,
Don't let there be any dust.

Hui-neng responded:

Bodhi really has no tree;
The bright mirror also has no stand.
Buddha-nature is forever pure;
Where is there room for dust?

This juxtaposition and evaluation of the two rivals' verse reflects the doctrines of the southern Chan school, which looked to Hui-neng as the authoritative spokesman for its position that enlightenment

Chinese Buddha

fingers, the purpose of *koan* is to get the monk to give up trying to find cognitive solutions to life's problems. One rather gross example occurred when one monk asked the master Ummon, "What is the Buddha?" Ummon replied, "A dried shit-stick." (This is a stick used in China instead of toilet paper.) Ummon, asked about the wonderful Buddha-nature that is the true self, makes this shocking and iconoclastic answer. What does he mean? He means that however noble our aspirations, we must remember that we are (in the words of one commentator) "a bag of manure." Nor is it sufficient to give an intellectual assent to this proposition. One who would solve the *koan* must live it, realize it, act it out with his or her body, demonstrate to the master that one has identified with this ugly shit-stick.

PURE LAND. The most popular sect in China was usually Pure Land Buddhism derived from Tanluan (476–542). He sought religious solace from a grave illness, and after trying several systems, he came to the doctrine of Amitabha Buddha and the Pure Land. Amitabha is the Buddha of Light, devotion to whom supposedly assures one a place in the Pure Land (Heaven or Western Paradise). Tanluan stressed commitment to Amitabha and the recitation of Amitabha's name as ways to achieve such salvation. This, he and his successors reasoned, was a doctrine both possible and appropriate in the difficult present age. The Pure Land sect greatly appealed to the laity, and it developed hymns and graphic representations of paradise to focus its imagination. In stressing love or emotional attachment to Amitabha (called *A-mi-to fo* in China), it amounted to a Chinese Buddhist devotionalism. By chanting "*na-mo a-mi-to fo*" ("greetings to A-mi-to fo Buddha"), millions of Chinese found a simple way to fulfill their religious needs and made A-mi-to fo the most popular religious figure of Chinese history.

POPULAR BUDDHISM. Medieval Buddhism also permeated the life of the common people, including the village peasantry, for the government developed a network of official temples that linked the provinces to the capital. On official feast days, ceremonies held throughout the land reminded the people that they shared the same religion. The provinces also used the Buddhist temple grounds for their fairs, thereby making them the centers of the local social, economic, and

comes suddenly. Because all Buddha-nature is intrinsically pure, one need only let it manifest itself. The northern school held that enlightenment comes gradually and thus counseled regular meditation. (Huineng himself probably would have fought any sharp distinction between meditation and the rest of life: in wisdom all things are one and pure.) The southern school finally took precedence.

One development of Chan was the use of **koan**, mind puzzles, to break the hold of cognitive meaning, thus liberating the individual to perceive ultimate relevance. Perhaps the most famous is "What is the sound of one hand clapping?" Rather than come up with Bart Simpson's quick response of snapping his

artistic life. The great feast days were the Buddha's birthday and the Feast of All Souls, when large crowds would gather to honor the Buddhist deities, listen to the sutras, or hear an accomplished preacher expound the dharma.

When local organizations met for vegetarian dinners, clergy and laity had a fine chance to socialize. Fashioning close bonds of mutual interest, these dinners became a great source of fund raising for the monasteries and blessings for the mercantile and personal interests of the laity. The village clergy usually were not well educated, but they tended to know the laity intimately and to provide them considerable solace at such important times as weddings and funerals. Many of the village Buddhist clergy also functioned as healers and mediums, as well as storytellers and magicians.

CHINESE PHILOSOPHY. It was also during its medieval flourishing that Buddhist philosophy became fully Chinese. A hallmark of this domestication was the rendering of the abstractions in which Indians delighted into the concrete images the Chinese preferred. Chan, the school that most stressed meditation, carried the Chinese spirit to the heart of Buddhist spirituality, distrusting abstract words and stressing metaphors, paradoxes, gestures, or direct, person-to-person intuitions. Chan and the other native schools also stressed living close to nature, in the conviction that nature held many of the secrets of enlightenment. This had great appeal for medieval Chinese artists, poets, and philosophers, many of whom would refresh themselves in retreats at Buddhist monasteries.

The concept of nirvana only won acceptance in China after the Buddhists had adapted it to Chinese thought. At the outset, ultimate Buddhist reality seemed wholly contradictory to Chinese concreteness. Thus, Chinese Buddhists accomplished a rather thorough cross-cultural translation. They had predecessors in the Indian Mahayanists, who identified *samsara* with nirvana, but the Mahayanists were far more abstract than the Chinese. Indeed, Chan probably became the most successful of the sects rooted in Mahayana metaphysics because it most thoroughly domesticated nirvana. Little interested in words or speculations, Chan focused on meditation, by which one might experience nirvana. It also stressed physical work, art,

and ritual. Since meditation expresses this commitment to experience via bodily postures that one assumes, one has only to sit squarely in the midst of natural reality and focus on its is-ness. (Not incidentally, one does not close one's eyes. The proper focus is neither a direction within nor a withdrawal to fix on the passing mental stream. In Chan it is a gaze with eyes open toward the end of one's nose.) The objective is to see without reasoning the reality that is right here. Such seeing should not focus on particulars, nor concern itself with colors and forms. Rather, it should appreciate reality's wholeness by not making distinctions.

Through Buddhism, China received a heavy dose of the doctrine of karma. That was most effective in the popular Buddhist sects, among which Pure Land headed the list, but it entered the general religious stream, influencing even those who rarely participated in Buddhist rites. Karma, of course, meant that the self was immersed in a system of rewards and punishments. All its actions, good or bad, had their inevitable effects. Past lives pressed upon the present, and the present was but a prelude to a future life. In popular Buddhism, this doctrine encouraged a sort of bookkeeping. Sometimes quite formally, with ledgers and numbers, Buddhists tried to calculate their karmic situation and plan out a better destiny. More generally, the concept of karma prompted the idea that the self's present existence was a trial that would be evaluated at death. How heavily this sense of trial pressed on the average person is hard to say. Combined with the rather lurid popular pictures of the several hells awaiting the wicked, karma probably sparked its share of nightmares.

The philosophical and meditative Chinese Buddhist sects accepted the traditional doctrine of no-self. So the Chinese thinkers who followed Madhyamika or Yogacara speculation agreed that emptiness or mind-only implied an effort to rout the illusion of a permanent personal identity. To grasp Buddha-nature and join the dance of reality, the individual had to annihilate samsaric misconceptions about the substantiality of the self. The Chinese appear to have been more concrete than the Indians in such efforts. That is, where the Indians often reasoned over the self very closely, trying by dialectics to understand the illusion of selfhood, the Chinese tried to get the self to see reality's totality. Such seems to be the intent of pictures that Tiantai and Hua-yen masters drew, as well as the intent of the more radical techniques of Chan. Bodhidharma's "just sitting" and "wall gazing," for example, were exercises designed to make clear that only Buddha-nature is real.

GOVERNMENT RELATIONS. The Tang dynasty (618–907) was the golden age of Buddhism in China. A major reason for this growth was the perception of the rulers that Buddhism could help them knit together the northern and southern cultures. Thus the founder of the Sui dynasty presented himself as a universal monarch who was both a pious Buddhist and a generous patron of the sangha. He likened his wars to campaigns to spread the ideals of Buddha, calling his weapons of war incense and flowers offered to the Enlightened One. It is hard to see how this squared with Buddhist nonviolence, but the popularity of Buddhism among the emperor's subjects led him to associate himself with the dharma as much as he could.

On the other hand, both the Sui and the Tang rulers feared the power of the sangha and took steps to limit its influence. Thus they insisted on regulating the admission, education, and ordination of the Buddhist clergy and on licensing the Buddhist temples. As well, the emperors put pressure on the sangha to enforce the monastic rule strictly, for its rules governing monastic life tended to restrict the clergy's economic enterprises. Such imperial efforts to control Buddhism were only partly successful, for many medieval empresses and wealthy merchants saw to it that temple wealth grew. The merchants' support of Buddhism is an interesting example of fitting a religious rationale to economic goals. For the merchants, the Mahayana notion that money gifts should be put to productive use became a justification for widespread commercial enterprise. Since the prevailing economy was, by imperial design, focused on agriculture, the Mahayana notion in effect buttressed the merchants in their conflict with the state comptrollers.

The government did its best to limit the ways that Buddhist doctrines might become politically subversive, guarding against the revolutionary implications of Mahayana dharma. For example, potential rebels had available to them the Mahayana doctrine that Buddhism would pass through three ages. In the third age, religion would come close to extinction and no government would merit the full allegiance of the Buddhists. A wealthy and powerful sect called the Sanchieh chiao seized on this notion and tried to use it to undermine the imperial authority, but the Tang rulers reacted vigorously and had the sect suppressed. The Mahayana teaching about Maitreya, the future buddha (a sort of messiah), was similarly dangerous. Enough Buddhists expected that the advent of Maitreya was close at hand to present the government a sizable problem. The popular understanding was that when Maitreya came, a new heaven and a new earth would begin. Thus both the Sui and the Tang emperors had to battle rebels moving against them under banners of white (the color associated with Maitreya). Still, the golden age that Buddhism enjoyed in these dynasties flowed from the positive support the emperors gave it. For all their care that Buddhist fervor not become subversive of their own rule, the Sui and Tang leaders made Buddhist ritual an important part of the state ceremony. Thus the accession of a new emperor, the birth of a prince, and the ceremonies in honor of the imperial ancestors all incorporated Buddhist sutras, spells, and prayers. When the emperor ritualized important occasions, the monasteries and temples received handsome donations, which of course increased their patriotic loyalty and pliability.

At the great capital of Changan, Buddhist art dominated a vibrant cultural life. The architecture of the pagodas and temples gracefully blended Indian and native Chinese elements, producing a distinctively Chinese Buddhist appearance. The images and paintings that adorned the temples drew on the full range of sources with which the great Chinese Empire came in contact. With sufficient freedom married to sufficient imperial support, Chinese Buddhist artists enjoyed a period of great prosperity and created a distinctive new style. This sort of syncretism—a core of Chinese Buddhist inspiration in touch with many other sources of inspiration—extended to literary art. The Tang dynasty was a high point in the history of Chinese poetry, and the moving forces behind this poetry were the two congenial streams of Buddhist and Daoist philosophy.

The state and the sangha therefore had a symbiotic relationship throughout the Sui and the Tang dynasties. Whether pulling in the same direction or wanting to go opposite ways, they were mutually influential. One place where Buddhist views considerably modified traditional Chinese customs was the penal codes.

The traditional customs were quite cruel, so the Buddhist ideals of compassion and respect for life served as a mitigating influence. Both the Sui and the Tang rulers granted imperial amnesties from time to time, and when the rulers remitted death sentences they often justified their actions in terms of Buddhist compassion or reverence for life. Specifically, both dynasties took up the custom of forbidding executions (indeed, the killing of any living thing) during the first, fifth, and ninth months of the year, which were times of Buddhist penance and abstinence. The emperors also converted Buddhist notions of the soul to their own ends, using them for the psychological conditioning of the imperial armies. Whereas the traditional Chinese cult of filial piety had weakened martial fervor, teaching that a good son should return his body to the earth intact, out of gratitude to his parents, the Buddhist stress on the soul (or spiritual aspect of the "person") downplayed the importance of the body. The traditional cult had also taught that immortality depended on being buried in the family graveyard, where one's descendants could come to pay tribute. Thus a soldier buried far from home would have no continuing significance. The Sui and Tang dynasties made it a practice to build temples at the scene of foreign battles and endow these temples with perpetual services for the souls of those slain in military service. In this way, they lessened the conflict between a generous service in the army and a generous filial piety.

CHINESE SOCIETY. Medieval Buddhism also increased the charitable helps available in Chinese society. Monks were the first to open dispensaries, free hospitals (supported by the Tang government), and hostels for travelers. They built bridges, planted shade trees, and generally broadened China's ethical sensitivity. Whereas the native ethic seldom took much charitable interest in affairs outside the clan, Buddhism encouraged an interest in the welfare of all living things. For example, it said that giving alms to poor people outside one's clan was a fine way to improve one's karma. This Buddhist universalism never displaced the formative influence of the Chinese clans, but it did move many Chinese to great magnanimity.

Buddhism downplayed social differences in another way. By teaching that the Buddha-nature is present in all reality, it said that equality is more basic than social differentiation. The monastic sangha institutionalized this equality. It would be naive to think that background or wealth played no part in monks' evaluations of one another, but the sangha was governed by a monastic code that underplayed wealth and severely limited monks' possessions.

Furthermore, during many periods in Chinese history, the sangha was genuinely spiritual. That is, its actual raison d'etre was religious growth. In such times, the only "aristocracy" was determined by spiritual insight. For instance, though Hui-neng, who became the sixth Chan patriarch, was born poor (and, according to legend, brought up illiterate), his spiritual gifts mattered far more. Because he was religiously apt, a reading of the *Diamond Sutra* opened his mind to the Buddha's light. After enlightenment, his peasant origins became insignificant.

The Buddhist sangha also improved the lot of Chinese women. It offered an alternative to early marriage and the strict confinement of the woman's family role. In the sangha a woman did not have full control of her life, but she did often have more peer support and female friendship than she could have in the outside world. In fact, Confucian traditionalists hated Buddhist nuns for their influence on other women, because they demonstrated alternatives to wifely subjection.

One of Daoism's greatest influences on Buddhism shows in Chan's acceptance of individualism. Placing little stock in doctrines or formulas, the Chan master determined enlightenment by the pupil's whole bearing. The flash of an eye, the slash of a sword—a single gesture could indicate an enlightened being. One could even "slay the Buddha"—throw off all traditional guidance—if one had drawn near to the goal. To the unenlightened majority, one's actions and life would be strange. Quite literally, one would be eccentric. But if the Dao or Buddha-nature really became the self's treasure, such eccentricity was but the near side of freedom.

BUDDHISM IN JAPAN

Buddhism infiltrated Japan by way of Korea during the second half of the sixth century C.E. It first appealed to members of the royal court with overtones of the prestige of Chinese culture. The Japanese rulers, in the midst of trying to solidify their country,

SCHOOLS OF BUDDHISM		
SCHOOL	LOCATION	MAJOR THEMES
Theravada (Hinayana)	Myanmar (Burma), Thailand (Siam), Sri Lanka (Ceylon), Kampuchea (Cambodia), Laos, Vietnam	monasticism, meditation, Buddha as guide
Mahayana	China, Korea, Japan	heaven, Buddha as savior
Lamaism	Tibet	Dalai Lama, monasticism, reincarnation, prayer wheels
Tantrism	Tibet	symbolized sex
Zen	China, Japan	monasticism, meditation, mind puzzles
Nichiren	Japan	national shrine, chanting for prosperity

thought of the new religion as a possible means, along with Confucian ethics, for unifying social life. So, during the seventh century, emperors built shrines and monasteries as part of the state apparatus. In the eighth century, when the capital was at Nara, the Hua-yen school (called Kegon in Japan) established itself and began to exert great influence. The government ideologues expediently equated the emperor with the Hua-yen Buddha Vairocana. Kegon has survived in Japan to the present day and now has about 500 clergy and 125 temples. In general, Buddhism coexisted with Shinto, sometimes in a mutually beneficial syncretism. From Buddhism, Shintoists developed the notion that the *kami* were traces of the original substances of particular buddhas and bodhisattvas. As a

result, Buddhist deities were enshrined by Shintoists (and *kami* by Buddhists).

TENDAI. The first decades of the Heian era saw the rise of two new schools of Japanese Buddhism, Tendai and Shingon. Dengyo Daishi (767–822), the founder of Tendai, went to China to learn about the latest forms of Buddhist doctrine and practice. Upon returning to Japan, he established a new monastic foundation on Mount Hiei. The school that Dengyo Daishi founded derived from the Chinese Dien-dai sect. Dien-dai taught a quite syncretistic outlook, laying special importance on the *Lotus Sutra*. It was especially interested in joining philosophical speculation to meditation. Dengyo Daishi broadened the syncretistic outlook by adding moral discipline and ritual to the program he wanted his monks to follow. He also gave Tendai a nationalistic aspect, hoping that Buddhist practice would help protect the Japanese nation. The result was a well-rounded school in which just about any traditional Buddhist interest could be pursued. Dengyo Daishi struggled with the government to gain recognition for his group, but after his death his followers got a full go-ahead and could ordain monks. It is difficult to overemphasize the importance of the establishment of Tendai on Mount Hiei, because from its ranks in the Kamakura era (1185–1333) came the leaders of the Pure Land, Zen, and Nichiren sects.

SHINGON. The Shingon sect was founded by the monk Kobo Daishi (774–835), who, like Dengyo Daishi, went to China to find fresh inspiration. The term *Shingon* derived from the Chinese term for mantra, and the school that Kobo Daishi established in Japan amounted to a branch of Buddhist tantra. Through elaborate rituals, Shingon expressed deep metaphysical notions thought capable of achieving magical power. Kobo Daishi was a talented writer, so he was able to furnish Japan a full manual on esoteric Buddhism. Through his influence, mantras, mandalas, and *mudras* (ritual gestures) became influential religious vehicles. As well, they made a great impact on Japanese iconography and fine arts.

Both Tendai and Shingon were open to outside influences, so during the Heian period Shinto and Buddhism came into closer contact than previously had been the rule. For instance, there arose numerous

Another good example of the *Prajna-paramita* literature that Mahayana Buddhism developed is the *Diamond Sutra,* which probably originated in India in the fourth century C.E. This sutra begins by setting the stage for a dramatic discourse. Once when the Buddha was dwelling in the garden of a person named Anathapindika, with a group of 1,250 monks, he rose, went on his round of begging, returned, washed his feet, and sat down to meditate. Many monks approached him, bowed at his feet, and seated themselves to await his teaching. One of them, a monk named Subhuti, ventured to ask the Enlightened One how a son or daughter of good family, having set out on the path toward enlightenment, should stand, progress, and control his or her thoughts. The Buddha graciously replied that such a person ought to entertain the thought that although the Enlightened One has led many beings to nirvana, in reality he has led no being to nirvana. How can this be? Because, as any true bodhisattva or enlightened person understands,

the notion of "being" or "self" or "soul" or "person" is actually an illusion. With various subtleties, examples, and further inferences, this is the sutra's main teaching. Thus somewhat later the Buddha repeats the message: bodhisattvas are those who do not perceive a self, a being, a soul, or a person. They do not perceive a dharma (individual item of reality), or even a no-dharma. They neither perceive nor nonperceive. Why? Because they have reached a realm beyond the dichotomies that perception usually entails, beyond our ordinary tendency to organize things in terms of beings, persons, or selves.

Such a tendency seizes on individuals and turns aside from the whole. By concentrating on beings, it neglects nirvana. Nirvana is not a thing, nor an entity. Those who think in terms of things or entities cannot enter nirvana. Only those who have gone beyond, to the higher knowledge that is unified, intuitive, and comprehensive, can enter nirvana.

---

jinguji (shrine-temples), where Buddhist rituals took place within the precincts of a Shinto shrine. Belatedly, the idea arose that the *kami* were manifestations of the Buddhist bodhisattvas. Until the beginning of the Meiji era (1868), when there was an official reform aimed at cleansing Shinto, Tendai and Shingon fostered such a syncretism between Shinto and Buddhism.

AMIDA. Last, we should note that during the Heian era there arose the conviction that Buddhism was bound to devolve through several ages (on the order of the Indian kalpas), and that the present age was the lowest—a time when religious practice was especially difficult. This eventually laid the foundation for the rise of various savior figures during the Kamakura period—for example, Amida Buddha, the merciful figure who presided in the Western Paradise so eagerly pursued by the Pure Land sects. The Amida, bodhisattva of light, became the most influential form of devotional Buddhism. It was popularized by evangelists such as Ippen (1239–1289), who encouraged songs and dances in honor of Amida. By practicing

the recitation of "homage to Amida Buddha," followers could gain great merit or even full salvation (entry to the Pure Land). This prescription was simple, practical, and available to all. It did not require deep philosophy or meditation, simply theistic commitment. The laity found Ippen's message very appealing.

Honen (1133–1212) personally suffered persecution for his position and for his success in winning converts. In a letter written to the wife of the ex-regent Tsukinowa, Honen described the essentials that a convert to Pure Land would have to embrace. Sakyamuni came into the world only to reveal Amida's vow to help human beings discover Amida's grace. By prayer even the worst of sinners will come to Amida's mercy, as surely as all mountain water finally comes to the ocean.

NICHIREN. This son of a fisherman named Nichiren (1222–1282) came the closest of any Buddhist figure to fulfilling the role of prophet. He agreed with the Pure Land Buddhists that simple devotional forms like the nembutsu were desirable, but

Japanese Amida Buddha

he found their stress on Amida unwarranted. For Nichiren the be-all and end-all of Buddhism was the *Lotus Sutra*. He considered this scripture the final teaching of Sakyamuni. Nichiren urged the practice of chanting homage to the *Lotus Sutra*. He also articulated an apocalyptic message: We are in the last days, an evil time. Nichiren demanded the building of a national shrine. Like a stern Israelite prophet of the Old Testament, he warned of disasters to come if the shrine was not built. Legend has it that he predicted the 1257 earthquake, the 1258 typhoon, and the 1259 famine; the Mongol invasion was forestalled only when the government agreed to the building of the shrine, and the divine wind (*kami kazi*) blew the Mongol ships away from Japan.

The strongest contemporary Japanese sect that traces its roots to Nichiren is **Nichiren Shoshu** with its *Soka Gakkai* ("Value-Creating Society") layman's organization and *Komeito* (clean government) political party. This movement derives from Makiguchi Tsunesaburo (1871–1944). During World War II, the

leader of Soka Gakkai refused the government's request that all religionists support the military effort, arguing that compliance would compromise the truth of the *Lotus Sutra* (by associating Soka Gakkai with other Buddhist sects and with Shintoists). For this he went to prison. Makiguchi died in prison, but his movement revived after the war through the efforts of Toda Josei, and currently by the leader Daisaku Ikeda. In a time of national confusion, Soka Gakkai's absolutism carried great appeal. According to Soka Gakkai, commitment to the *Lotus Sutra* (and to itself) would dissolve all ambiguities. Many observers have criticized the Soka Gakkai of the 1950s and 1960s as cultlike: Nichiren and contemporary leaders were charismatic and intolerant, and the movement has a rigorous proselytizing with a "cellular" structure like that of communism, a strict program for daily devotion, pilgrimages to the National Central Temple near Mount Fuji, and an extensive educational program. This was the new religious movement that won over millions of displaced rice farmers and fishermen who were in transition to becoming factory workers in post war Japan. Under the name Nichiren Shoshu, a somewhat more restrained movement, it has exported itself to the West, now boasting a new private university in California's Orange County.

JAPANESE ZEN. Two of the great pioneers who launched Chan on its illustrious career in Kamakura Japan were Eisai (1141–1215) and Dogen (1200–1253). Eisai studied Chan in China and then established himself in Kamakura, the new center of Japanese political power. His teaching won special favor among the hardy warlords who were coming to dominate Japan, and from his time Zen and the samurai (warrior) code had close bonds. For Eisai, mind was greater even than heaven. Buddhism, which concentrated on the mind, had known great success in India and China. Among the different Buddhist schools, the one founded by Bodhidharma especially stressed mastering the mind. From Bodhidharma's missionary ventures in China, Zen had made its way to Korea and Japan. Now it was time for Japan to capitalize on Zen's great potential. By studying Zen, one could find the key to all forms of Buddhism. By practicing Zen, one could bring one's life to fulfillment in enlightenment. To outer appearances, Zen favored discipline over doctrine. Inwardly, however, it brought the highest wisdom, that of enlightenment itself. Eisai was able to convince some of the Hojo regents and Kamakura shoguns of this message and make them patrons of Zen, so he planted Zen solidly in Japan.

If Eisai proved to be a good politician, able to adapt to the new Kamakura times and to benefit from them, Dogen proved to be the sort of rugged, uncompromising character Zen needed to deepen its Japanese roots and gain spiritual independence. After studying at various Japanese Buddhist centers without satisfaction, he met Eisai and resolved to follow in his footsteps and visit China. After some frustration in China, Dogen finally gained enlightenment when he heard a Zen master speak of "dropping both mind and spirit" (in other words, dropping dualism). Returning to Japan, he resisted the official pressures to mingle various forms of Buddhism and would only teach Zen. Nonetheless, within Zen circles Dogen was quite flexible, teaching, for example, that study of the Buddhist scriptures (scholarship) was not incompatible with a person-to-person transmission of the truth (the guru tradition).

Within Zen circles, Dogen also distinguished himself for his worries about the use of *koans*. The Rinzai school of Chan that Eisai had introduced to Japan stressed the use of these enigmatic sayings as a great help to sudden enlightenment. In Dogen's opinion, the Chinese Soto school was more balanced and less self-assertive. He therefore strove to establish Soto in Japan, teaching a Zen that did not concentrate wholly on the mind but rather on the total personality. This led him to a practice of simple meditation (*zazen*) that ideally proceeded without any thought of attaining enlightenment and without any specific problem in mind. Disciplining the body as well as the

mind, Dogen aimed at a gradual, lifelong process of realization. The other Japanese Zen approach, Rinzai, has tended to seek sudden enlightenment, urging disciples to strive hard and keep up a firm discipline of work, silence, and obedience.

JAPANESE SOCIETY. Buddhism offered an alternative to the Japanese group orientation. Though the Buddha's own thought was quite social, as manifested by the sangha, his original message stressed the uniqueness of each individual's situation. It is true that each being possessed the Buddha-nature (at least according to Mahayana Buddhism, which introduced the Buddha to Japan). This doctrine, coupled with that no-self, led to a conception of the relatedness of reality. Practically, however, the Buddha made the existential personality the religious battleground. Only the individual could remove the poison of karma and rebirth; only the individual could pronounce the Buddhist vows for himself or herself, let alone live them out. However, early Japanese attempts to appropriate Buddhism were sponsored by the state because the state leaders thought they might enlist its magical or ritual power.

CONTEMPORARY BUDDHIST RITUALS

Devout Burmese (Myanmar) Buddhists begin and end the day with devotions performed in front of a small household shrine. This shrine usually consists of a shelf for a vase of fresh flowers and a picture of the Buddha. It is always located on the eastern side of the house (the most auspicious side) and placed above head level (to place the Buddha below head level would be insulting). During the time of devotions, householders light candles and place food offerings before the Buddha. Coming before this shrine, the householders begin by saying: "I beg leave! I beg leave! I beg leave! By act, by word, and by thought, I raise my hands in reverence to the forehead and worship, honor, look at, and humbly pay homage to the three gems—the Buddha, the Law, and the Order—one time, two times, three times, O Lord." Then they would petition to be freed from the four woes (rebirth in hell, as an animal, as a demon, or as a ghost), from the three scourges (war, epidemic, and famine), from the eight kinds of unfortunate birth, from the five kinds of enemy, from the four deficiencies (tyrannical

J.T. Carmody

Thai temple

kings, wrong views of life after death, physical deformity, and dull-wittedness), and from the five misfortunes, that they might quickly gain release from their pains. They end the morning prayer by reciting the five precepts, renewing their commitment to abstain from taking life, from stealing, from drinking intoxicants, from lying, and from sexual immorality. Clearly, therefore, the Burmese Buddhists seek to orient each day by honoring the Buddha, begging his protection against misfortune, and rededicating themselves to the Buddhist ethical code. In the evening many Burmese, especially the elderly, conclude a similar session of homage, petition, and rededication by praying a rosary. The Buddhist rosary consists of 108 beads, one for each of the 108 marks on the feet of the Buddha (which, in turn, represented his 108 reincarnations). While fingering a bead, the devotee usually says either "Painful, selfless, fleeting," or "Buddha, dharma, sangha" three times.

Public ceremonies sometimes have a syncretistic mixture with some of the animistic themes that predate the arrival of Buddhism. Villagers may have a public ceremony every evening after sunset in the village chapel. This is located in the center of the village and consisted of a shed open on three sides. The fourth side encloses an ark containing a statue of the Buddha. Attendance usually is sparse, except in special periods such as the Buddhist Lent, and more sophisticated laity, who think meditation was the central expression of a mature Buddhism, speak disparagingly of the chapel services as magical or superstitious.

Nonetheless, the village service is interesting because it is led by laypeople, rather than monks, and because it uses the Burmese vernacular, rather than Pali, the formal liturgical language. Thus, it is a place where common folk and Burmese youth can experience their religion in a form easy to understand.

The ceremony usually begins with an invocation of the gods and then an invocation of the Buddha, before whose image fresh cut flowers have been placed. The worshipers ask permission to reverence the Buddha and pray that their worship might bring them to nirvana or the higher abodes (the states near to nirvana). Other prayers follow, asking the Buddha to grant the petitioners strength to fulfill the five precepts and understand the three marks.

The central portion of the village ceremony begins with an offering of flowers, candles, and water—symbols of beauty, reverence, and purification. Following this, the committed laity express their veneration of the Buddha, the teaching, the order, their parents, and their teachers. Next come recitations of parts of the scriptures, a profession of love for all creatures, a recitation of the doctrine of Dependent Co-arising, a recitation of the Buddha's last words, a recitation of the five "heaps" (*skandhas*) of which human individuality is composed, a prayer to the eight planets, and a confession of doctrine.

The ceremony concludes with a water libation that calls the merit of the worshipers to the attention of an ancient earth goddess, the release of the gods who had been called into attendance, and an enthusiastic "sharing of merit" (of the benefit the participants had gained from the service) with the participants' parents and all other beings. Overall, the ceremony reinforces the main points of Buddhist teaching, reminding the participants how to orient their lives and encouraging them to express both their reverence for the Buddha and the main concerns for which they wanted the Buddha's aid.

Since 1970, there has been a successful Buddhist monastery near Mount Shasta in northern California. It has seventeen buildings (a Zendo or meditation hall, a founder's shrine, a shrine to the bodhisattva Kannon, a sewing room, a laundry, a tool shed, a store room, a library, eight residences, and a common room). The monastery was founded by an English-woman named Peggy Kennett (Jiyu Kennett-Roshi), who is a guru in the Soto Zen tradition. (Soto and Rinzai are schools that began in China but underwent a further development in Japan.) While maintaining traditional Soto teachings, the Shasta monastery has tried to adapt to American cultural forms. Thus members eat their meals American style at a table rather than Japanese style sitting on the floor, they chant in Gregorian tones rather than Japanese tones, they usually wear Western clerical garb rather than Japanese robes, and they serve English rather than Japanese tea. The central occupation of the monastery is *zazen*, or sitting in meditation. Most members of the monastery spend two to three hours in meditation each day.

During the morning service, the trainees make three bows and offer incense to the celebrant, Kennett-Roshi. The community then intones and recites portions of the Buddhist scriptures. There are three more bows, and then the community processes to the founder's shrine, where they recite more scriptures. During the evening ceremony, in addition to the scripture recitations, there is a reading of the rules for *zazen*. At meals someone recites portions of the scriptures while the food is passed, to help community members increase their sense of gratitude for what they are about to receive. Since the meditation hall is closed on any day of the month having a 4 or a 9 (for reasons not disclosed), six times in most months there is a "closing ceremony." Vespers finish the evening service, and through the day monks say prayers before such activities as shaving their heads and putting on their robes.

The recitation of the Buddhist scriptures potentially has the effect of creating mantras, for when sounds enter consciousnesses that have been purified by discipline and made alert by meditation, they can develop almost mesmerizing cadences. The ritual bows, use of incense, use of flowers, and the like help to engage all the senses and focus all the spiritual faculties, so that the prayer or meditation to be performed can be wholehearted. A major difference between the monastic ritualism of Mount Shasta and the lay ritualism of the Burmese Buddhism we described is the stress the lay ritualism places on petitioning the Buddha for protection against misfortune and help with worldly needs. Part of this difference stems from the greater stress that Theravada lay doctrine places on gaining merit. Whereas the monastic doctrine of Soto Zen stresses the enlightenment, Buddhists live in a thought-world filled with ghosts and gods that constantly make them aware of a need to improve their karmic state. Consequently, Burmese ritual seems more anxious. While the Burmese stress the merit one must attain for a better future, the Soto ritual stresses the grace, harmony, and peace that enlightenment brings. (Of course, Soto ritual is also an effort to inculcate the dispositions that conduce to enlightenment, such as inner silence, gratitude, and a sense of harmony with all of creation.)

WORLDVIEW

Naturally enough, Buddhism has made accommodations for the laity, since they were bound to be the majority of the members of the community. The worldview that we now study has usually come to ordinary laypeople through ceremonies, festivals, traditional stories, and Buddhist culture at large. Music, poetry, views of sickness, views of good fortune—all aspects of a popular religious culture—carry parts of the core religious message. If the core religious message has always been the Four Noble Truths, young people have heard it differently from old people, women have heard it differently from men, the wealthy are bound to stress one side of the message, and the poor bound to stress another. That is how popular culture works. It is never straightforward, completely clear, univocal. It is always complex, many layered, and many voiced. Thus, you have to imagine the intellectualism that we have stressed working its way out in terms of images and feelings—thoughts and hopes that the average Buddhist seldom brought to clarity or full articulation. The Japanese holy man Shinran (1173–1262) made explicit what many other Buddhist leaders have done implicitly, adapting the dharma to the needs of married people, unlettered people, people who have to work in the world. Shinran went farther than most others, stressing a theistic commitment to the Buddha more than a grasp of the dharma, but whenever it allowed rituals and devotions to multiply, the sangha accommodated the Buddha's Way to the needs of ordinary people.

For example, you have to imagine the typical devout Buddhist family centering its religious life on the little altar in its home. When family members decorate the altar with flowers and fruit and incense, they express concretely their love of the Buddha, their trust that Buddhist tradition would make their lives relevant, their inclination to go to the Buddha and tradition in time of trial. We should not despise religious traditions for being most powerful in time of trial. We ought to accept the fact that, the world over, most human beings only think completely seriously when suffering, death, injustice, evil, and other trials or hardships force them to. Paradoxically, and mercifully, that is how the bad things that happen to good people sometimes turn out to have brought a blessing. The blessing does not remove the badness, but it can become a solid consolation.

In the same way, we have to accept the fact that the majority of Easterners, like the majority of Westerners, have gone beyond what a restrained orthodoxy might have preferred and sought human faces in which they might concretize the ultimate reality that they needed to worship. For example, a great many Buddhists have worshipped Gautama, even though some schools of Buddhism have taught that he was only a man who embodied a universal wisdom. The distinction between venerating a holy man and worshipping a truly ultimate, divine reality escapes many laypeople in many different traditions. The popular treatment of the Virgin Mary in Christianity and of Muhammad in Islam are cases in point. Rather than debating about the propriety of the cult that grew up around Gautama, as around central figures in other religious traditions, we do better to appreciate the human needs that the cult expresses. In the case of the Buddha, the people who have bowed, offered gifts, chanted verses from the scriptures, and in various other ways given flesh to their vow to place their trust in the Buddha (as in the dharma and the sangha), have expressed their need for a center—a holy place of refuge. The Buddha has functioned for most Buddhists as such a place, just as Christ has functioned that way for Christians. The Buddha has meant that reality is not chaotic, suffering is not the final word. More positively, the Buddha has meant that, in the ultimate analysis, human existence is blessedly good and carries a wonderful potential. That is what human beings most need to hear. That is the sort of "place" the human heart most needs to be able to go, if it is not to feel like a motherless child—an orphan in an uncaring, hostile world.

NATURE

Stepping back from the historical view of Buddhism, we find that Buddhist attitudes toward nature do not fit together neatly. From its Indian origins, Buddhism assumed much of Hinduism's cosmological complexity. That meant taking up not only a world that stretched for vast distances and existed for immense eons (kalpas) but also the Aryan materialism and yogic spiritualism that lay behind such a cosmology. However, Buddhism came to contribute its own worldviews. Its numerous "buddha-fields," for instance, are realms with which our earthly space-time system shares the boundless universe. Buddhism has had few equivalents to Vedic materialism, but Buddhism used the doctrine of *samsara* early in its history to justify acceptance of one's worldly situation and working only to improve it (rather than to escape it for nirvana). On the other hand, the ancient Indian yogic practices impressed the Buddha and his followers deeply. Since Gautama had in fact become enlightened through meditation, and since this enlightenment expressed itself in terms of the antimaterial Four Noble Truths, Buddhism could never settle comfortably in the given world of the senses and pleasure.

Initially, therefore, Buddhism looked on nature or physical reality as much less than the most real or valuable portion of existence. Only consciousness could claim that title. Certainly the doctrine that all life is suffering reflects a rather negative attitude toward nature, and it indicates that what the eyes see and the ears hear is not the realm of true reality or true fulfillment. Also, to analyze physical reality in terms of three negative marks (pain, fleetingness, and selflessness) further devalues nature. At the least, one is not to desire sensory contacts with the world, because such desire binds one to illusory reality and produces only pain. Thus, Indian Buddhists separated themselves from nature (and society and self).

PHILOSOPHY AND POPULAR BUDDHISM.
Because the great interest of early Buddhist philosophy was an analysis of dharmas (elements of reality) based on probings of consciousness sharpened by intense meditation, the material aspects of the natural realm fell by the way. At best, they were background realities and values. The scholastic Abhidharmists did not deny nature, for they were acutely aware of the senses, but they did deflect religious consciousness away from it. Far more impressive than natural phenomena were the states of consciousness that seemed to go below the gross phenomena to more subtle phenomena. They were the places where the Indian Buddhists preferred to linger. In considering the Buddhist view of nature, we must distinguish between the inclinations of the meditators and scholars, who were interested in nonphysical states of consciousness, and the inclinations of the laity, who saw the world more concretely and less analytically. As we might expect, the laity were more worldly than the monks. When they heard that all life was suffering, they probably thought of their family burdens, their vulnerability to sickness, and the many ways in which nature seemed out of their control. The

comforts they received from Buddhist preaching, therefore, lay in the promise that right living would take them a step closer to the kind of existence where their pain would be less and their enjoyment greater.

Thus, it is no surprise that the most popular Buddhist movements were built on the Indian traditions of devotion. Just as popular Hinduism fixed on Vishnu, Krishna, and Shiva, popular Buddhism fixed on Amitabha, Avalokitesvara, and Vairocana. These celestial buddhas, or bodhisattvas, drew the popular religious imagination away from the historical Buddha and the commonplace world of the here and now to the realm of future fulfillment. In that way, popular Buddhism lay in between the deemphasis of the physical realm that the monks and scholars practiced and the simple acceptance of physical life that a worldly or naturalist outlook (such as that of the early Vedas) produced.

SAMSARA AND NIRVANA. We have seen that as
the intellectuals and contemplatives worked further with immaterial consciousness and its philosophical consequences, they changed the relationships between samsara and nirvana. In the beginning, Buddhists thought of *samsara* as the imperfect, illusory realm of given, sense-bound existence. Nature, therefore, was part of the realm of bondage. The Buddha himself exemplified this view when he urged his followers to escape the world that was "burning" to achieve nirvana. His original message regularly said that spontaneous experience makes one ill and that health lies in rejecting attachments to spontaneous experience. With time, however, the philosophers, especially the Mahayanists, came to consider the relations between nirvana and samsara more complex. From analyzing the implications of these concepts, the philosophers determined that nirvana is not a thing or a place. The Buddha realized this, for he consistently refused to describe nirvana in detail. But while the Buddha's refusal was practical (such a description would not help solve the existential problems of being in pain), the refusal of the later philosophers, such as Nagarjuna, was largely epistemological and metaphysical. That is, they thought that we cannot think of such a concept as nirvana without reifying it (making it a thing), and that the reality of nirvana must completely transcend the realm of things.

Therefore, nirvana could be the deepest reality of nature. To follow this line of thought is no easy task, so only the elite grasped the philosophy of the *Prajna-paramita,* with its concepts of emptiness and transcendence. That philosophy influenced the devotional life of Mahayana and the ritual life of tantrism, however, because even the simple people could grasp its positive implications as presented by the preachers. These positive implications, which blossomed most fully in the East Asian cultures, amounted to seeing that all reality is related. The other side of saying all dharmas are empty is to say that the Buddha-nature (or nirvana, or the other ways of expressing the ultimate totality) is present everywhere. Even if one had not entered into nirvana fully, so that no mark of karma remained, one could sense the presence of nirvanic ultimacy as the foundation of nature. For instance, if all things contain the buddha-nature, then the natural and social worlds can become glowingly fresh and beautiful, as one realizes their potential.

Tantric Buddhism, finally, shared the doctrine of the nonduality of *samsara* and nirvana that Indian Mahayana developed but differed in its expression of this doctrine through ritualistic imagination. Tibetan practices, for example, played with the world, both loving nature and kicking it away, through sights (mandalas), sounds (mantras), and ceremonies (symbolic intercourse) that engaged the participant both psychologically and physically. All of this, of course, implied using nature as a somewhat sacramental way to gain liberation.

SOCIETY

The Indian society of the Buddha was divided into castes, which were religiously sanctioned as a way of maintaining social order. Moreover, casteism was part of Vedic India's cosmological myth, since according to legend human society's order resulted from the sacrifice of Purusha, the primal human being. In Brahmanism, the priests merited their primary status because they derived from Purusha's mouth.

Buddha, himself a member of the warrior class, brought a message that clashed with this hierarchy. He rejected both Vedas and caste (and therefore his sect would not become just another Axial-era sect within Hinduism). His dharma taught that beings are to free themselves from painful worldly life. His sangha accepted all persons: both men and women, whether Indians on Nepalese, and from every caste.

The Buddhist doctrine and practice refuted the cosmological myth that legitimated casteism. Many warriors and merchants no doubt also found Buddhism a convenient weapon in their struggles with the brahmins for power. So they and others who wanted to change the status quo gave Buddhism a close hearing.

WOMEN'S STATUS. Buddhism offered Indian females considerably more than had been available to them previously. Women were capable of enlightenment and could join the monastic community as nuns. This practice was in stark contrast to the classical Hindu view, which held that women had to be reborn as men to be eligible for *moksha.* By opening religious life to Indian women, Buddhists gave them an option besides marriage and motherhood—a sort of career and chance for independence. No longer did a girl and her family have to concentrate single-mindedly on gathering a dowry and arranging a wedding. Indeed, Buddhists viewed Hindu child marriage darkly, and they thought it more than fitting that women should travel to hear the Buddha preach. In later times, women could preach themselves, but from the beginning they could give time and money to the new cause.

Moreover, by offering an alternative to marriage, Buddhism inevitably gave women more voice in their marriage decisions and then in their conjugal lives. In fact, Buddhism viewed spouses as near equals. The husband was to give the wife respect, courtesy, and authority, while the wife was to give the husband duties well done, hospitality to their parents, watchfulness over his earnings, skill, and industry. One concrete way in which a Buddhist wife shared authority was in choosing their children's careers. For instance, to enter a monastery, a child needed both parents' consent. Married women could inherit and manage property without interference. Buddhism did not require or even expect that widows be recluses, and suttee was abhorrent to a religion that condemned animal sacrifice, murder, and suicide. Finally, Buddhist widows could enter the sangha, where they might find religious companionship, or they could stay in the world, remarry, inherit, and manage their own affairs.

Still, Buddhism never treated women as full equals of men. Though the logic of equal existential pain and equal possession of the Buddha-nature could have run to equal political and educational opportunities, it seldom did. Nuns had varying degrees of freedom

Nagarjuna gained such a lofty reputation in later Buddhism, especially that of Tibet, that he deserves special consideration as an example of the the ideal Buddhist. He probably lived between 150 and 250 C.E., most likely in south India, and his style of argumentation, as well as his analyses of his opponents' positions, suggests that he was trained as a Hindu Brahmin before he converted to the budding movement of Mahayana Buddhism. Although Nagarjuna is known as the most acute of the Mahayana dialecticians, Tibetan tradition also reveres him as a guru who offered his disciples sound ethical advice.

First, Nagarjuna insists that the only way to gain the real relevance of the dharma, the Buddhist sciences, and the holy mantras is directly to experience them. Those who merely analyze the cognitive meaning of words never come to the core. This insistence expresses the conviction of all Buddhist gurus that words can be deceptive. If we allow words a life of their own, detached from the experiences they are trying to describe, words can distract us from reality. To grasp the dharma or the treatises of wisdom, we must both meditate on the realities to which they point and practice the virtues they extol. The same with the holy mantras that the tradition urges us to pray. Unless we experience the states from which they flow, the realities to which the saints have spontaneously directed them, the mantras will be but nonsense sounds.

Nagarjuna then reflects on the sort of knowledge that is intrinsically valuable. We only know what this knowledge is in time of need, when we are hard pressed. Then it is clear that the knowledge contained in books is of little use. Unless we have made an insight our own, it will give us little light or peace. In this, knowledge is parallel to wealth. Time of need shows us that wealth we have borrowed

from others is no real wealth. It is nothing on which we can depend, for it can be taken from us at a stroke. Whether it be a matter of knowledge or of wealth, need, pressure, or suffering shows us the stark contrast between what we truly own and what we have merely borrowed. Thus hard times can have a silver lining. If they strengthen our resolve to gain our own wisdom, possess our own (incorruptible) wealth, they can advance us toward fulfillment.

Some people teach with words; others instruct silently. This is reminiscent of the reed-flower, which has no fruit, in contrast to the walnut, which has both fruit and flower. It is also reminiscent of the kataka tree, the fruit of which clears mud from the water. If you only mention the name of the kataka tree, you will not remove the mud. You must make your teaching bear fruit, make it deal with more than words. You must extend it to the realm of action, instructing by silent deeds as well as wordy lectures. Indeed, if you do not apply your knowledge, you are like a blind man with a lamp. Though you have in hand a source of great illumination, you do not shed it on the road, do not light the way for others to travel. Stanza after stanza, Nagarjuna tosses out aphorisms like these. Line after line, his advice is poetic, symbolic, image laden. From deep meditation and reflection, he finds emptiness a font of great illumination. For one who sees, the spiritual life is paradoxical and parabolic. As we come close to enlightenment, the main structures of the holy life stand clear, but these structures (meditation, wisdom, and morality) are capable of endless application. The key is having the experience, grasping the center, knowing emptiness directly. When we realize that reality is a seamless cloth, we can enjoy all its various designs. At that point, Buddhist selfhood will be properly achieved (and empty).

to run their own affairs in the monasteries, but they were regularly subject to monks. Women never gained regular access to power over males, either in Buddhism's conception of the religious community or in its conception of marriage.

POLITICS. In its relations with secular political powers, Buddhism had varying fortunes. The Buddha seems to have concerned himself little with pleasing public authorities or worrying how his spiritual realm related to the temporal. No doubt his assumption was that if people became enlightened they would relativize social problems and solve them fairly easily. At the time of Asoka, however, the importance of royal patronage became clear. Much of Buddhism's influence outside India began when Asoka dispatched missionaries to foreign lands, and his efforts to instill Buddhist norms of ethics and nonviolence in his government became a model for later ages. As Christians rethought Jesus' dictum about rendering unto Caesar the things that are Caesar's when it found a potentially Christian Caesar in Constantine, so after Asoka Buddhists longed for a union of dharma and kingly authority, thinking that such a union would beget a religious society.

Historically Buddhists tried to gain favor at courts. In Sri Lanka, Burma, Thailand, and the rest of Southeast Asia, this effort often succeeded, and temporal rulers played a large role in Theravada's victory over Mahayana and Hinduism. In China, Buddhism's fortunes depended on whether it fared better or worse than Confucianism in getting the emperor's ear. During the worst periods, it became the object of imperial persecution. The same was true in Japan, where such persecution had much the same rationale: Buddhism was not the native tradition. Overall, however, Buddhism fared well in East Asia. It had to coexist with Confucian and Daoist cultural forces, but it regularly dominated philosophy, funeral rites, and art. Tibet realized the theocratic ideals that Asoka had sparked: throughout most of its history religious leaders doubled as temporal powers. However, the intrigue, murder, and moral laxity that this binding of the two powers produced during certain periods of Tibetan history suggested rethinking the relation between the religious and the secular powers.

As with Christianity, there is a built-in tension between the Buddhist religious community and any temporal state. The sangha and the church both make claims upon their followers that can bring them into conflict with secular powers. Since these claims are made in the name of dharma or God, they carry an aura of sacredness or of coming from a higher authority. Things that rightly are Caesar's are limited. So long as there is a Christ or a Buddha, a God or a nirvana, Caesar cannot claim everything. One ploy that Caesar can develop, however, is to claim that he, rather than the priests or monks, is the representative of God or dharma. In other words, employing the aspect of the cosmological myth by which the human ruler is the link between heaven and earth, the king can claim a sacredness of his own. Many Christian successors to Constantine claimed this, and in effect many Buddhist rulers after Asoka did also.

Despite its focus on otherworldly matters, then, Buddhism remained knotted in secular-religious controversies. Since it did not clearly establish an authority outside the cosmos (for instance, by coming to a doctrine of creation from nothingness), it was always liable to attack from kingly Buddhists who wanted to make doctrinal dharma serve the state.

THE SANGHA. The sangha alternately raised and dashed hopes that most human beings might live together in harmony and peace. Energetic monasteries, run by learned and holy monks or nuns, were models of what human society could be. Living simply, obeying a common rule and a common authority, such Buddhist professionals acted out a vision of equality and cooperation. When a monastery was in good spiritual fettle, one survived there only if one's motivation was religious. Meditation, hard work, austerity in diet and clothing, long periods of silence, celibacy— these staples of Buddhist monastic life offered little to the worldling. However, monasteries of the devotional sects could be quite different. Often people entered them rather grudgingly and briefly, to learn the minimal ritual and doctrine necessary to function at the inherited family temple. Meditation-centered monasteries also differed from the pampered, court-favored centers of learning, art, and intrigue frequently spawned by East Asian Buddhism. Still, as long as the genuine articles existed, Buddhism was alive and well.

The life of Buddhist laity has always reflected the state of the monastic sangha. When the monasteries were spiritually active, the laity tended to support them generously. In return, the monks usually served the laity spiritually. During these periods, the notion that the layperson's vocational obligation was primarily to support the monks evoked no cynicism. The monastery was embodying the social ideal and so encouraging the whole sangha to think that dharma could be an effective social philosophy. On the other hand, when the monks were lax, the reaction of the laity was ambivalent. The laity enjoyed seeing clay feet under yellow robes, but they missed the examples and teachings that might have dissolved some of their own clay.

Ideally, then, the monks and nuns and the laity have provided mutual supports. A lively interaction between monks and laity could grow from the notion that by giving generously to the monks lay people could draw on the "field of merit" created by monastic holiness. Mahayana and Tantra have acted on this ideal by relating nirvana and samsara in such a way that vocational differences between the laity and the clergy are lessened. Even for these schools, however, the monasteries have symbolized idealistic places of retreat, meditation, study, and ritual devotion.

BUDDHIST AHIMSA. Traditionally, Buddhism laid great stress on the precept of nonkilling, not only because this precept inculcates a respect for all living things but also because carefully observing it leads to great self-control and promotes peace. For example, if one is to stay away from killing or injuring other creatures, one must control anger, greed, hatred, and the other vices that usually spur our injurious actions and inhibit social justice. Nonetheless, in contemporary countries such as Myanmar (Burma), where many political figures profess to be devout Buddhists, the question of how to apply the precept of nonkilling in public policy has grown quite vexing. Nonviolence probably has been closer to the core of Buddhist tradition than to the core of Christian tradition. Leading Buddhist politicians, such as U Thant, who became head of the United Nations, therefore have had to make some distinctions. Generally they have tried to moderate public policies in the direction of nonkilling but have conceded that a thorough application of *ahimsa* (for example, prohibiting all military action) is not always practical.

Capital punishment is another problem that the precept of nonkilling heightens. Ideally, most Buddhists probably would oppose a law of capital punishment, urging sentences of life imprisonment for capital crimes. Not only would this honor *ahimsa,* it would also offer the criminal an opportunity to repent and be converted to Buddhist convictions. Still, through history to modern times most Buddhist countries have practiced capital punishment. This has caused some analysts to speak of a conflict between the mundane morality of the state and the ideal morality of the Buddhist religion. In their view, the state needs capital punishment to maintain order, so one must reluctantly kill the worst social offenders. This view

might seem to relegate Buddhist ideals to complete impracticality, but further reflection has led some ethicists to a more dialectical notion of nonkilling. For these dialecticians, there are circumstances in which not slaying heinous offenders would be a great violence. Those charged with protecting the common good would seriously fail their charge were they to allow murderers to continue operating without fear of capital punishment. So the dialecticians come to the conclusion that committing the lesser evil is doing a species of good. In other words, they justify capital punishment as a necessary evil, a means public officials must employ if they are to honor the precept of noninjury in more general, far-reaching terms. To prevent great injury to the public at large, one must injure some criminal offenders. Once again, it would not be hard to draw parallels to Western debates over capital punishment.

SELF

The practical accent of Buddha's original preaching made the issues related to self paramount. Buddhism has directly addressed individuals, insisting that only the individual can change his or her life. On the other hand, Buddhism has counseled that to escape *samsara* and achieve nirvana, we have to rid ourselves of the notion that we have or are an *Atman,* a soul, or self. This doctrine has prompted some of Buddhism's central meditational practices and philosophical speculation.

Historically, the teaching of "no self" most distinguished the Buddha's way from that of his Hindu predecessors. As we have seen, a staple of Upanishadic wisdom was that the self is part of the great Atman (the interior aspect of Brahman). In yogic meditation, the Hindu tried to realize this ultimate identity, to experience the oneness of everything in Atman. When Buddha turned away from this teaching, calling human identity just a bundle of elements (*skandhas*) temporarily fused, he laid down a philosophical challenge that Hindu and Buddhist philosophers seldom neglected in later centuries. What motivated this new conception of the human being?

The principal motive, it appears, was Buddha's conviction that the key to human problems is desire. If pain expresses the problem ("All life is painful"), then desire expresses its cause ("The cause of suffering is desire"). These, we have seen, are the first two Noble Truths. The Third Noble Truth ("The removal of desire leads to the removal of suffering") extends the first two, and when Buddhists pondered its implications, they came to the doctrine of no-self (*anatman*).

The Third Noble truth itself is psychological. For instance, we may analyze the suffering in human relations in terms of desire. Parents desire their children's success and love. When the children choose paths other than what the parents have dreamed, or when the children demand distance in order to grow into their own separate identities, the parents suffer pain. They feel disappointed or rejected, or they feel that their toil and anxiety have gone for naught. Buddhists would tell such parents that their relations with their children have been unwise or impure. Because they have desired success and love, instead of remaining calm and free, they have set karmic bonds that were sure to cause pain. But to cut the karmic bonds, the Third Noble Truth implies, one must get to the root of the desire. At this point one must turn psychology into metaphysics—one must realize that the self from which desires emanate is neither stable, fixed, permanent, nor, ultimately, real. In our distraction and illusion, we gladly accept the fiction that we have stable selves.

In simple terms, the prime reality in our interior lives is flux. At each moment we are different "selves." True, some continuity exists in that we remember past events and project future ones. But this continuity hardly justifies clinging to or relying upon a permanent self. What Buddhists stressed, therefore, was the change and coordination of the components, just as they stressed the interconnectedness and flux of the entire world (through Dependent Co-arising). They developed a view of both the interior realm of consciousness and the exterior realm of nature that became quite relational. Their metaphysics focused on nature's coordinated interdependencies, its continual movement. The self could not be the exception to such a worldview. Humans were too clearly a part of the total natural process to violate the process's fundamental laws. And just as analysis showed all the natural elements to be empty, so, too, analysis showed the self to be empty.

Therefore, Buddhists directly denied what Western philosophers such as Aristotle called a "substance." To live religiously, in accordance with the facts of consciousness, one had to cast off the naive assumption that the human person is a solid something—

one had to slide into the flux. In so doing, one could both remove the basis for desire and open up the possibility for union with the rest of coordinated reality.

This movement toward coordination with the rest of reality became the positive counterweight to the Buddhist negative view of the self. That is, as people advanced in their meditation and understanding, they started to glimpse what Mahayana saw in enlightenment: the realization that all Buddha-nature is non-dual. According to the *Prajna-paramita*, ultimately only Buddha-nature existed. All multiplicity or discreteness resulted from a less than ultimate viewpoint. Such a realization, of course, meant the death of the illusion that one was an independent *Atman*.

We have belabored this teaching of no-self because it seems most important to the Buddhist attitude toward the individual. It is also the key to the Buddhist view that nature flows together and that society should strive for ultimate reality by means of enlightenment. Because of no-self, the individual could move toward greater intimacy with nature. There were no barriers of separate identity, no walls making him or her isolated. For those who attained enlightenment through the dharma, this nonseparation of self, nature, and society was a personal experience.

Buddhism regularly counseled the individual to regard the body, the family, society, and even a spouse or a child with detachment. One was to revere and discipline the body according to the Middle Way. Clearly, though, the body was only a temporary station on the way to nirvana or one's next incarnation. Wealth and pleasure were not, as they were for Hinduism, worthy life goals. The family was a necessary unit, biologically and socially, but frequently it was also an impediment to spiritual advancement, as the Buddha's own life showed. Society would ideally be a context for mutual support in realizing enlightenment. Personal bonds, therefore, could not be passionate and karmic, and even a spouse or a child came under this law.

Tantrism seems to qualify the Buddhist view of the self, since it allowed a more intense connection with food, alcohol, sex, and material ritual items. However, according to its own masters, the watchword in Tantrist rituals was still discipline and detachment. To use alcohol or sex licentiously was just a quick way to attachment and bad karma. The point to Tantrist ritual was to master these items and retain the energies that would have flowed out to them.

Buddhist religion was vigorous, the doctrine of no-self was influential. In fact, we often can sense its effects in the peace and humor of Buddhist texts. Many texts, of course, are complicated and complex. However, some raise serenity, irony, paradox, and wit to a high religious art. For instance, in one story two monks meet a fetching damsel by a rushing river. One charitably hoists her and carries her across. Later the second monk chastises the first for such sensual contact. The first monk replies, "I let the woman down when we crossed the river. Why are you still carrying her?" The Buddhist ideal was to carry nothing, to have a self utterly free.

ULTIMATE REALITY

Debate has raged over the question of whether Buddhism is a theistic religion. The simple answer is that Theravada has said that it is not, that Buddha has just shown the way; Mahayana has said that it is and encourages us to accept Buddha as savior. Devotional Buddhism certainly has venerated a variety of buddhas and bodhisattvas, treating them as other religions treat gods and saints. To be sure, the Buddha himself does not appear to have claimed divinity. Gautama seems to have been a human being who thought that he had found the key to living well. The key was enlightenment, whose expression was the Four Noble Truths. In the enlightenment experience, Gautama encountered ultimate reality. The overtones to this encounter gleaned from the texts are not those of meeting a personal God. Whether that differentiates Gautama's ultimate reality from the God of Western religion is another question, the answer to which depends on careful analysis of peak experiences and conceptions of ultimate reality. The personal character of the Western God is not so simple as many Westerners assume, and the impersonal quality of Gautama's encounter with nirvana is less absolute than many assume.

SUMMARY: THE BUDDHIST CENTER

The Buddhist center seems to us to lie in enlightenment. This is the experience that gives the religion its name; this is the experience from which the Middle Way proceeds, to which it conduces. All the philosophical speculation about whether mind exists and about whether there is a big raft or a small one are merely attempts to figure out how to explain or achieve enlightenment.

Nevertheless, as history's first great transcultural religion, it is safe to say that there is more difference in interpreting what all this means within Buddhism than between an Indian Buddhist and an Indian Hindu devoted to the Upanishads.

BUDDHISM

flashcards and matching games
http://www.quia.com/jg/51966.html

jumbled word game
http://www.quia.com/jw/8563.html

millionaire game
http://www.quia.com/rr/41399.html

magic paragraph
http://www.quia.com/cz/13520.html

Now take an online practice quiz at
http://www.quia.com/session.html

For session enter
relquiz10

download multiple-choice, true-false, and fill-in drills from
http://www.ureach.com/tlbrink
click on the public filing cabinet and folder rel10
and download *m10.exe, h10.htm, t10.exe,*
and *f10.exe*
and crossword puzzle CW10.html

CHRISTIANITY

© Photodisc Green

If we gather all its parts, *Christianity* is the largest religion in the world, with about a third of the earth's
population expressing at least nominal adherence to
a specific Christian denomination. What began as a
proselytizing sect within Judaism was carried around
the world and mixed with other heritages.

HISTORY

JESUS

Christianity was spread by first-century **apostles**
who dedicated their lives to one very singular man,
Jesus of Nazareth. It is likely that the word *Jehsus,*
a Greek form, derives from the Hebrew *Yeshua,*
which means "savior." There is no doubt that Jesus
existed, preached, gathered followers, and was executed by the Romans. The historical validity of these
facts is attested by such non-Christian authors as
Josephus, Tacitus, Suetonius, and Pliny the Younger.
Jesus was born about 4 B.C.E. (by current calendars)
in Palestine.

	CHRISTIANITY: KEY DATES	
Date	**Event**	
ca. 30 C.E.	death of Jesus of Nazareth	
ca. 65 C.E.	death of Apostle Paul	
ca. 100–165 C.E.	Justin Martyr, leading apologist	
ca. 185–254 C.E.	Origen, leading theologian	
313 C.E.	Christians freed of legal persecution	
325 C.E.	First Council of Nicea	
354–430 C.E.	Augustine, leading theologian	
451 C.E.	Council of Chalcedon	
ca. 480–500 C.E.	Benedict, founder of Western Monasticism	
ca. 540–604 C.E.	Pope Gregory I, founder of Medieval Papacy	
787 C.E.	Second Council of Nicea	
869–870 C.E.	intensified disputes between Rome and Eastern bishops	
1054 C.E.	Great Schism between Rome and Constantinople	
1096–1099 C.E.	First Crusade to conquer Palestine	
1225–1274 C.E.	Thomas Aquinas, leading theologian	
1369–1415 C.E.	John Hus, Bohemian Reformer	
1517 C.E.	Luther's *Ninety-five Theses*	
1509–1564 C.E.	John Calvin, leading theologian	
1545–1563 C.E.	Council of Trent	
1620 C.E.	Pilgrims sign Mayflower compact	
1703–1791 C.E.	John Wesley, founder of Methodism	
1869–1870 C.E.	First Vatican Council in Rome	
1910 C.E.	beginning of Protestant ecumenical movement	
1962–1965 C.E.	Second Vatican Council in Rome	

> *St. Thomas the Apostle.*

BOOKS OF THE NEW TESTAMENT

BOOK	WHEN	AUTHOR	THEME(S)
James	45	James	social justice; need for good works
Galatians	48	Paul	need for salvation by grace; against Judaizers
I Thessalonians	52	Paul	second coming
II Thessalonians	53	Paul	rebuke idleness while waiting
I Corinthians	54	Paul	order within Church; resurrection; spiritual gifts (tongues); morality
II Corinthians	55	Paul	sex, gossip
Romans	55	Paul	need for salvation by Grace, not works
Philemon	60	Paul	forgiveness and restoration
Colossians	60	Paul	against Gnosticism
Ephesians	60	Paul	stand against Satan
Philippians	61	Paul	rejoice in the Exaltation of Christ
I Timothy	62	Paul	roles of women, bishops in Church
Titus	62	Paul	against Judaizers and Antinomians
I Peter	63	Peter	persistence and patience
II Peter	63	Peter	against false teachers
II Timothy	63	Paul	nature of the Church
Hebrews	60s	?	Jesus fulfills Jewish tradition
Jude	66	Jude	against apostates
Mark	60s–70s	Mark?	Jesus as miracle worker; Son of Man, servant of God; second coming is near
Matthew	60s–70s	Matthew?	Jesus as King of Jews, Messiah; fulfills Jewish tradition
Luke	60s–80s	Luke	most comprehensive story of Jesus
Acts	60s–80s	Luke	chronology of major apostles in the 50s
I John	80s	John?	against Docetism; sin and Christians
II John	80s	John?	against false teachers
III John	80s	John?	encouragement to friends
Revelation	90s	John?	second coming of Christ
John	90s	John?	theological view of Christ as God, the Son

NEW TESTAMENT. Beyond that, little can be verified to the satisfaction of objective secular historians. Most of what we know about the life of Jesus is reported in the New Testament. This is a compilation of books including the **Epistles** (letters to early Christians written by the apostles Paul, John, Peter, James, and Jude), the *Acts of the Apostles* (a history written by Luke), and the **Gospels** (the first four books of the New Testament, describing the life of Jesus). While the Gospels undoubtedly contain historical facts (such as names of persons and places and descriptions of events) that have not been disputed by any other sources, they also contain other claims that will probably never be verified by sources outside the New Testament. Clearly, the Gospels contain some mixture of factual description, myth (in the sense of stories being told because of the values they demonstrate), and interpretation of both myth and fact in order to argue a point of doctrine or explain some ritual developed by the early Christians.

There is a general split of opinion in how the Gospels are viewed. In general, more fundamentalist Christian biblical scholars argue that each gospel was written by the man whose name appears at the front (e.g., *Mark* was written by Mark, rather than a committee). Also, fundamentalists assume that the authors were (except in the case of Luke) eyewitnesses to most of the events they described, especially the crucifixion and the resurrection. The fundamentalists also assume that the Gospels were written within a generation of the life of Jesus. Biblical scholars with a more secular orientation assume that the oral recounts of Jesus' life lasted for over a generation before being put in writing (but agree that at least the three synoptic gospels were pretty much in their present form by the end of the first century C.E.). The secular scholars also question if *Mark, Matthew,* and *John* were really written by the individual eyewitnesses of the same name, but could represent composite documents from different sources. The least amount of debate is about Luke, who was a first-century physician turned historian who traveled and may have interviewed eyewitnesses to give a thorough account of the life of Jesus (the gospel of *Luke*) and the movements of the early apostles (*Acts of the Apostles*). One group of secular scholars, the so-called Jesus Seminar, doubts that most of the statements attributed to Jesus (highlighted in some red-letter Bibles) were actually spoken by him at the time (instead, they were added by the authors to make theological points). Both the more fundamentalist and the more secular scholars tend to dismiss most of the noncanonical writings as written in the next century or written by someone other than the purported author. (The exception seems to be the gospel of *Thomas,* which secular scholars date to about 50 C.E., and which offers some confirmations of many of Jesus' sayings.)

ROLE OF JESUS. We know little about the youth of Jesus except through gospel stories, such as those of his circumcision and his dialogues with religious teachers, and these seem consistent with the assumption that he grew up as a typical Jewish youth of his times. About the year 27 C.E., he started from his native Galilee on a career as an itinerant preacher and healer. (This was not unusual for the time and place, and reflected the frustration of many Jews with Roman rule). When we read the **synoptic gospels** (*Mark, Matthew, Luke*), what is so impressive about Jesus is not the accounts of the healings, but the power of his words: they have the lofty symbolism of a mystic, the tie-in to the past of a teacher, but the new revelatory authority of a prophet, yet are uttered by someone who exorcises and heals like a shaman. Buddha could simply be classified as a mystic, Muhammad a prophet, and Confucius a teacher, but Jesus seems to fill all of these roles. His followers concluded that he had to be more than a man, he must be the Son of God, and the Jewish Messiah.

Apparently Jesus linked his work with that of **John the Baptist,** who called for a spiritual renewal and the expectation of a Messiah. Jesus championed the poor and the socially outcast. He criticized the hypocrisy of the Jewish temple priests, the Sadducees and the Pharisees. The fact that he came from the district of Galilee also seemed to reduce his credentials

> Would you describe first-century Christianity as an *ascetic* denomination? Compare the nature and degree of ascetic tendencies in early Christianity to those of Orthodox Jews, Jains, Orphics, or Pythagoreans.
>
> Contribute to this discussion at
> http://forums.delphiforums.com/rel101

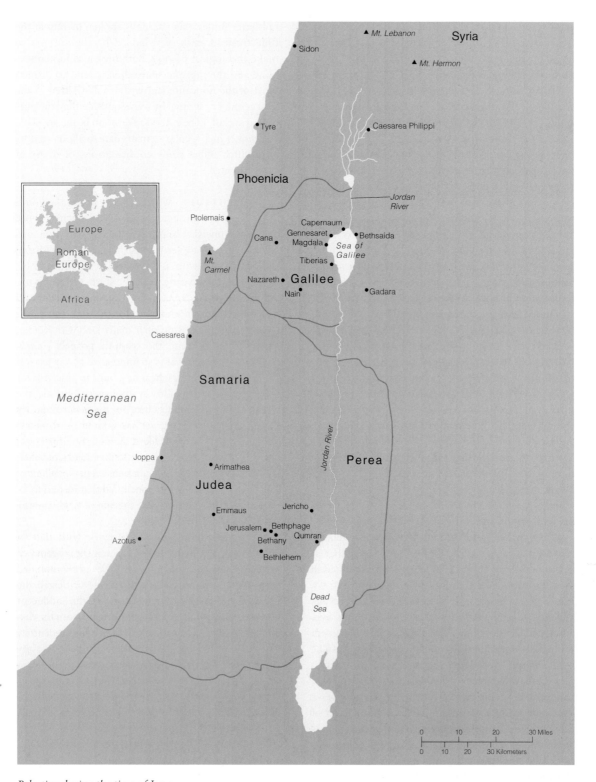

Palestine during the time of Jesus

COMPARISON OF FIRST-CENTURY JEWISH SECTS					
DIMENSION	PHARISEES	SADDUCEES	ESSENES	ZEALOTS	CHRISTIANS
Greek culture	opposed	accepted	withdrew from	opposed	at first ignored, later assimilated
Roman rule	opposed	accepted	withdrew from	rebelled against	persecuted by
Laws of Torah	strictly followed	loosely followed	other new doctrines	ignored	other new doctrines
Appealed to	poor	wealthy	alienated	robbers	poor
Apocalypse	coming soon	ignored	ignored	Start it!	coming soon
Role of messiah	great	ignored	ignored	ignored	great
Angels	accepted	rejected	ignored	ignored	accepted
Resurrection	accepted	rejected	transmigration	irrelevant	accepted
Heaven and hell	accepted	ignored	ignored	ignored	accepted

among the Jerusalem–based Jewish priesthood. To both the Jews and the Romans at the time, that sounded like a call to rebellion against the establishment. His death came by order of the Roman procurator Pontius Pilate on the dubious grounds that he threatened the peace.

Beyond this bare outline, historical and theological interpretations diverge. Indeed, all of the Gospels are theological interpretations of Jesus, developed in the light of at least a generation's worth of the Christian community's experience, of controversies with Jews who did not accept Jesus as the Messiah, and of efforts to explain the relevance of Jesus to Gentiles. According to the New Testament and the mainstream doctrine of later centuries, after death Jesus was raised (resurrected) and was disclosed to be "Lord," or the divine Son whose dying and rising brought the world salvation. Another interpretation of Jesus found in the New Testament is that he was the **Messiah**— the anointed king of the age of grace which Judaism had long been anticipating, where grace came to mean not just peace and material plenty but intimacy with God and sharing in divine life. From the titles that the New Testament gives to Jesus, his own reported claims, and the miracles (healings, raisings from the dead, and so on) that the New Testament attributes to Jesus, we can conclude that the New Testament writers found him most remarkable—so remarkable that he had to be more than human. For them he was the bringer of salvation, God's Word incarnate, the **Christ** (Greek term for God incarnate), the Messiah, and the divine Son.

In the earliest portions of the New Testament, the Pauline **Epistles** (letters), Jesus is a living spiritual reality. The assumption behind Paul's directions for church life, for instance, is that the "Lord" lives in Christians' midst. After Jesus' death, his followers apparently thought that his movement was finished, but the events of the resurrection convinced them that he had assumed a new form of existence. They stayed together in Jerusalem; at Pentecost (fifty days after Passover, when Jesus had died), they experienced what they called the Holy Spirit, whom they thought Jesus and the Father had sent. The Spirit charged them to go out and preach about Jesus. Thus, the early Christians proclaimed that Jesus' life and death were the definitive act of salvation. The disciples also preached that Jesus was the Messiah.

As such, he was in accordance with Jewish tradition and yet responsible for its transformation. From a historical perspective, then, the first Christians appear as sectarian Jews with a new interpretation of messianism. The early Christians thought of themselves as the new Israel because they thought that Jesus had brought, and the old Israel had rejected, the kingdom of God sought by Jewish messianic expectation. This was an apocalyptic position that envisioned a second coming of Jesus, a resurrection of the dead, a final battle with Satan, and a day of judgment.

It took some time for the first interpretations of Jesus to sift out and clarify, and a principal catalyst in that process was **Paul.** From the accounts in *Acts* and his own writings, Paul was a Pharisaic Jew whose conversion on the road to Damascus (*Acts* 9:3–9) was quite dramatic. After his conversion, he tried to show his fellow Jews that Jesus was their Messiah, but their opposition to his preaching, plus his own further reflection on Jesus' life and death, led Paul to think that in Jesus God had opened the covenant to all people—Gentiles as well as Jews. Consequently, Paul made the *gospel* (good news) about Jesus a transformation of the Torah. Because God had fulfilled in Jesus the intent of the Law, the Law's many detailed prescriptions were passe. Adherence to an external code could not make one righteous (acceptable to God). Only by opening to God's love and healing could one stand before him acceptably. Paul called that opening "faith" by which he understood an absolute and complete personal commitment to Jesus. For him, Jesus was the agent of a shift from the Torah to the gospel, from the old covenant of works to the new covenant of commitment. Jesus the Christ was a new Adam, a new beginning for the human race. Paul began to use the term "body of Christ" to stand for the growing Christian community. All who clung to Jesus became members of his "body." Christ and the Church formed a living entity.

Paul's interpretation of Jesus was the key to early Christianity's developing into a universal religion. Although Paul and the original disciples of Jesus had been Jews, Paul's decision to drop the requirements of the Jewish Law (e.g., circumcision, kosher diet) and extend membership to all (Jew and Gentile alike) who would base their lives on Jesus, the early church

broke with Judaism irreparably. In the beginning, some followers of Jesus ("Judaizers") had urged keeping the precepts of the Jewish Torah, but they lost out to Paul's vision. The Torah had been the cornerstone of covenantal life. Most Jews, understandably, were not willing to throw the Torah over or enter a new covenant. Unfortunately, Paul and the later gospel writers seem increasingly frustrated with traditional Judaism for not accepting the Christians as the legitimate leaders of Judaism.

The **Gentiles** (non-Jews) who warmed to the gospel lived in a Hellenistic milieu that was ripe for foreign religions offering new concepts of salvation. Just as Judaism was in turmoil, with Zealots, Pharisees, Sadducees, and Essenes all urging different reactions to Roman rule, so, too, were the denominations of the Gentiles. But lacking the Jewish foundation, many of the Gentiles found it difficult to interpret Christian doctrine. Some, such as those in Corinth, fell into an **antinomian** view that since Jesus had died for their sins, they could do whatever they wanted without fear of God's retribution.

A NEW WORLDVIEW. As a result of the gospel and Paul's theology, within a generation of Jesus' death Jewish and Greek thought had combined into a powerful new worldview. From Judaism came the concepts of prophet and messiah. From Hellenism came the notions of savior and god. Jesus was the successor to Moses, the giver of a new Law, Daniel's concept of the Son of Man come to inaugurate the messianic age, the conqueror of death and disorder, and the Logos (Word) of eternal divinity come into time. All past history, from the first parent Adam, had been but a preparation for his coming. All of the future would unfold his implications, climaxing in a final judgment and a fulfillment in heaven.

The new denomination was apocalyptic. The early Christians expected the future to be short: Jesus would soon return in power and glory to consummate his work. As the years went by, the expectation shifted. Jesus had accomplished the essentials of salvation through his death and resurrection. However long it took in God's dispensation for Jesus' salvation to work itself out, there was no doubt of the final success. In the meantime, Christians were to spread the gospel (good news of Jesus).

One of the main reasons Jesus has remained fresh for each generation of his followers is that the New Testament authors set down some of Jesus' lively teaching stories, his parables. Puzzling, enigmatic, and vivid, these parables have drawn the attention of preachers and audiences through all the Christian centuries. Today the parables have become a favorite topic of scholarly discussion. We can only hint at the main lines of this discussion, but studying one of Jesus' parables, that of the Great Supper (*Matt.* 22:1–10; *Luke* 14:10–24), will take us a few steps into what New Testament scholars are currently conjecturing about Jesus' own outlook.

As a background to our consideration of the parable of the Wedding Banquet, let us first note the tendency of current New Testament scholars to emphasize the parables' underlying conviction of God's oneness, an absolute mystery. The authors of the parables (Jesus and the writers who set them in their New Testament form) used a paradoxical speech, through which they might hint at God's transcendence—God's overspilling of all human conceptual containers. The parables imply that God cannot be captured in any single set of images. The best way to indicate the divine nature is to juxtapose stories that flash forth now one, now another aspect of what God seems to be like.

Moreover, some of Jesus' parables opposed the assumption of some of his contemporaries that the only way righteous people could experience the rule of God would be through a dramatic, even cosmic, overturning of the prevailing political patterns, so that the sinners presently in charge would be thrown out. Not so, Jesus' preaching suggested. God does not need earthquakes or revolutions. The reign of God is subtler, and more powerful, than any prevailing political or religious conditions. No matter how bad the times, one could always find something of God in them. For Jesus, God was always active, always reaching out to people in need. His gentle speech had a powerful edge; the forgiveness and reconciliation imaged is

demanded for everyone's life. The holiness appropriate to the rule of God belongs to all.

Applied to Jesus' liking for parables, this attitude meant a calm "take it or leave it." A parable was an invitation to enter the world of Jesus' Father, to open oneself to Jesus' view of what God was doing. It was not an oppressive command. The parable of the Banquet suggests that one could meet Jesus and not even realize that this was the most important encounter of one's life. Jesus would not beat his hearers over the head. God would not flash forth lightning or bellow thunder. The Kingdom of God was in people's midst. To find it, they had only to turn around and open themselves to Jesus' good news.

The parable itself tells of a man (or a king) who once gave a great banquet. Deciding to throw this feast, he sent his servants to announce it to those he wanted to invite. The servants told the invitees, "Come, for all is now ready." But the invitees began to make excuses. Not sensing the significance of the invitation, they told the servants such lame tales as "I have bought a field and I must go take a look at it," or "I have bought five yoke of oxen, and I must go examine them," or "I have just gotten married, so I cannot come." (However, *Deuteronomy* 20:5–7 and 24:5 suggest that these may traditionally have been considered legitimate excuses.) In each case, they asked to be excused. The man hosting the banquet got very angry. In Matthew's version, the invitees had treated the man's servants shamefully, even killing them, so the man (who was a king) sent his troops to destroy the murderers and burn their city. In Luke's milder account, the host simply told his servants to go out into the streets and lanes of the city and bring in the most wretched people they could find: the poor, the maimed, the blind, and the lame. When the servants came back to report that they had done this and that there still was room in the banquet hall, the host told them to go out again, this time into the highways and hedges, and make people come in, until the banquet hall was completely full.

Those whom he had first invited had shown themselves unworthy of the banquet, but one way or another he would have his house filled.

For Matthew, the story is an occasion to indulge in a bit of allegory. By playing up the theme of the king's punishment of the invitees' bad treatment of the servants, he can allude to the Roman destruction of Jerusalem in 70 C.E., which perhaps he saw as a retribution for the slaying of Jesus. Luke, on the other hand, presents a simpler plot line, and he is more interested in the redoubling of the host's invitation than in any rejection and punishment. Where Matthew makes an irreparable break between the king and the original guests, Luke passes over this relation, allowing the possibility that it might mend. Accenting the good fortune of the new invitees, he stresses that they are an unlikely group, outcasts and strangers. For Luke, the drama lies in the host's seizing the occasion of the original invitees' (the Jews') refusal or inability to come and making it a chance to be generous to another class of people. Thus, when most Jews rejected Jesus' message, God offered the gospel to the Gentiles. In the background of the New Testament's use of the parable is the bitterness between Jews who had accepted Jesus (become Christians) and those who had rejected him. Although they tend to stress the literary structure of the evangelists' different accounts, today's scholars do not neglect the historical or theological dimensions of the parables. For example, they point out that Jewish lore contemporary with Jesus had a story that praised a tax collector for doing one good deed during his (otherwise hateful) life: inviting some poor people to a banquet when the original guests did not come. Similarly, research into the social customs of Jesus' day has revealed a tendency in sophisticated Jewish circles to invite people twice. Important people, at least, did not take seriously a single invitation but had to have their egos stroked a second time. One of the rabbis used a person dressed and ready to go by the time of a second invitation as an example of wisdom, while a person not ready to go by the time of a second invitation, and so excluded from the good time, became an example of foolishness.

Moreover, by choosing the figure of a banquet, both Jesus and the gospel writers inevitably conjured up the messianic time. In the messianic time, when Israel's deliverer had come, Jewish tradition said the people would eat and drink joyously, banqueting together. It may be stretching the original intent of the parable to make it a full symbol of the messianic or heavenly time, as later Christian preachers often have, but the figure itself was bound to suggest inclusion in the occasion of celebrating God's victory or exclusion from it. If one stresses the confrontational side of the invitation and rejection, as Matthew does, one develops a rather harsh, judgmental view of Jesus' messiahship and the invitation to join the Christian community. The understated version of Luke simply hints at what a human situation—a generous host's disappointment that the people he first invited could not come—can reveal about God's ingenuity and goodness. Undaunted, the host finds new outlets for his largess.

Behind Matthew's harsher version probably lie the bitter experiences of the early Christian missionaries, who were confused and hurt that their proclamation of Jesus' good news brought them persecution rather than gratitude. However, this harsh attitude seems to contradict Jesus' own tendencies, which were to keep contact with people, avoid unnecessary ruptures, and find creative alternatives to strategies that had run into dead ends. Behind Jesus' own mission there seems to have lain a rather constant goodwill. If the members of the establishment were not interested in his message, there were always the crowds on society's margins. If the Jews were intractable, there were always the Samaritans and the Gentiles. Jesus may not have worked all this out into an explicit theology of his mission, but it seems latent in his regular style. For all that he seems to have been disappointed by the stupidity and hardness of heart he encountered, he kept speaking provocatively of the Kingdom of God, always hoping he would come upon a few people whom God's Spirit had prepared to accept his words.

In Luke's version of the parable, the social implications of the gospel also are important. It is no accident that the outcasts come into the banquet hall.

Luke sees the good news of the Kingdom as especially intended for those people who have little other good news in their lives: the poor, the sick, the despised. At the least, his parable implies, those who have received much from God should share it generously with people less fortunate. The host who insists that his banquet not go to waste should be a role model for Christians.

In recent years, excavations at Nag-Hammadi in Egypt have made available to New Testament scholars Gnostic versions of the gospel (see later) that they can compare with the canonical four **Gospels.** The gospel of *Thomas,* for example, has a version of the parable of the Banquet that is quite spare, more like Luke's than Matthew's account. Interestingly, however, the gospel of *Thomas* makes several of the original invitees excuse themselves for monetary reasons. Thus, one man has some merchants coming the evening of the banquet to pay him money they owe, while another man has bought some property and must go to collect the rent. When the host hears these excuses, he tells his servants to go into the streets and bring back whomever they find. The conclusion of the story is ominous: "The buyers and the merchants shall not come into the places of my Father." Not only does this conclusion make Jesus pass stern judgment on those who reject the invitation, it also castigates business (and by implication all this-worldly affairs) as incompatible with the Kingdom of Heaven.

Overall, the parables remain an absorbing topic for study. Because they stand so close to Jesus' own way of thinking and preaching, they offer some of the best keys to Jesus' intriguing personality. But the parables seldom admit of a clear-cut interpretation, any more than Jesus' other teachings or actions do. They contain so many different levels, possible allusions, and strata of metaphors that one is finally forced to leave off analyzing them and let them make a more synthetic, holistic impact. When one does this, it seems clear that Jesus, like many Eastern gurus, was a man filled with lively speech, because he was a man filled with God's presence, pregnant with God's love.

COMPARISON OF MOHISM AND CHRISTIANITY		
DIMENSION	MOHISM	CHRISTIANITY
Who founded?	Mozi	Jesus
Where?	China	Palestine
When?	4th century B.C.E.	1st century C.E.
Who appealed to?	knights	poor
Which commandment?	love	love
Rigid opponents	Confucians	Pharisees
Mystical competition	Daoists	Essenes
Brutal opponents	Legalists	Zealots, Romans
Scripture	fragments in Mencius	New Testament
Fate of founder	unknown	crucified
Fate of movement	died out	grew with proselytizing around Roman Empire

Three apostles

THE EARLY CENTURIES

The gospel writers (Mark, Matthew, Luke, and John) all interpreted the life of Jesus. Even in the most journalistic portions of the New Testament, they have cast Jesus' sayings and doings in terms of their own theologies. Matthew, for instance, works largely with Jewish notions, trying to show that Jesus is the successor to Moses, the gospel is the successor to the Torah, and so

on. The other gospels, as well as the *Epistle to the Hebrews* and the *Book of Revelation,* are similarly theological. John arranges Jesus' public life, giving him a sacramental glow. The second half of John's gospel concentrates on Jesus' "glory": his intimacy with the heavenly Father and his victorious death and resurrection. *Hebrews* tries to show that Jesus fulfilled Jewish types of sacrifice, while *Revelation* is a Christian apocalypse (final disclosure) designed to shore up the Christians' commitment against Roman persecution.

By the end of the first century, then, the Church had a variety of theologies. The majority were extensions of Jewish religion in the light of Jesus as the Messiah. The *Apostolic Age* is the period that elaborated what Jesus meant and how the Church was to organize itself. It embraces roughly the period from the death of Jesus (ca. 30 C.E.) to the last decades of the first century. A central concern in both those years and the next centuries was authority. For the early church, an *apostolos* was a person to whom God had delegated church authority.

During Jesus' ministry, his twelve intimate disciples were the apostles par excellence, since they had received their commission from Jesus himself. Clearly the Twelve formed a collegial group with Peter as their head, and the Church accepted their authority. However, balancing this apostolic "official" authority was a looser, charismatic leadership expressed through prophecy, teaching, speaking in tongues, and so on. The earliest Church preaching was intended to show that Jesus fulfilled the promises of Jewish scripture. In their teaching, the first apostles relied on oral tradition about Jesus' person and words. The first great problem in the Apostolic Age, as we saw, was the Pauline (pertaining to Paul) problem of opening the Church to the Gentiles.

During the second century, the leadership of the Church passed from those who had seen Jesus themselves to those who had received the gospel from eyewitnesses but had not themselves known the Lord. The "Fathers" who led the second-century Church are therefore apostolic in the sense that they had direct contact with the Twelve.

Externally, from the time of Nero (54–68 C.E.) the Church was ever liable to persecution by the Roman authorities, who worried about secret societies that might sow seeds of revolution. Since the Romans looked on religion as the bond of their realm, they were especially sensitive to groups who did not worship the traditional Roman deities. But Christians continued to expand throughout the Roman empire during the second and third centuries. By 300, they probably constituted the majority population in Asia Minor and Carthage, and they were at least a noticeable fraction of the population along the northern shore of the Mediterranean. Their major political problem, gaining sufferance from the Roman authorities, was not solved until Constantine came to power early in the fourth century.

GNOSTICISM. More potentially destructive than Rome were the heresies known under the general label of **Gnosticism**. This is sometimes covered as another Hellenistic mystery cult, but most of Gnosticism's growth was within Christianity as a competing (later deemed heretical) set of doctrines. Most Gnosticism involved a *dualistic* mythology: spirit was good, but matter, the negative principle, came from a Demiurge (something like Satan, a subordinate being whom the spirit Father God begot as Wisdom but who fell from grace). Gnosticism offered a revelation to certain "elect" persons: if they would hate this lower world of material creation (which was under the fallen Demiurge) and commit to the higher spiritual and divine realm, they might return to glory with God. To explain their revelation, the Gnostics taught the myth that each of the elect had a hidden spark from God's eternal world. The sparks fell into matter because of a heavenly war between darkness and light (or, in other versions, because of an accident during the production of the divine emanations). Higher beings would one day dissolve this fallen world, but in the meantime they called to people's hidden sparks by means of saviors, revelations, and rites of baptism.

Gnosticism blended the Hellenistic notion of divine emanation, mystery religion notions about salvation through sacramental rites, and Jewish notions of sin and redemption. It stressed the division between this world and heaven, the evil of matter and the flesh, and the need for asceticism (celibacy and bodily discipline) to gain freedom from matter.

Some Gnostic thinkers, such as Mani, offered a separate denomination that directly competed with Christianity for gentiles open to Middle Eastern religions offering salvation. Mani (216–276 C.E.) lived in Mesopotamia. At age twenty four, he claimed to be the final revelation, completing the messages started by Zoroaster, Buddha, and Jesus. His system supposed a primeval conflict between light and darkness, and it, too, stressed asceticism. The goal of **Manicheanism** was to release the particles of light that Satan had stolen and placed in the human mind. His movement spread to Egypt, north Africa, and even Rome. (During the early years of his adult life, the great Christian

COMPARISON OF JAINISM WITH GNOSTICISM		
DIMENSION	JAINISM	GNOSTICISM
Time	500 B.C.E.	1st and 2nd centuries C.E.
Started in	India	North Africa and Middle East
Spread to	nowhere	Roman Empire
Major figures	Mahavira	Mani, Marcion
View of reality	dualism: spirit and matter	dualism: spirit and matter
View of creator deity	nonexistent	evil
Metaphor	wheel	light
Metaphor adopted by	Buddhism	Christianity
Ethics	asceticism and noninjury	asceticism or antinomianism
Monasticism	encouraged	encouraged
Opposed	Hinduism	Judaism
Rejected scripture	Vedas	Old Testament
Rejected doctrine of	caste	incarnation (Docetism)
Verdict of other denominations	declared heretical by Hinduism	declared heretical by Christianity
Core constituency	merchants	
Current status	a few million followers in India	doctrines and symbols recur in new movements

thinker Augustine was, for a time, a Manichean.) Mani wound up in Persia, where his Gnostic doctrine had converted the king, who spread it throughout his empire. Unfortunately for Mani, the next king returned to traditional Zoroastrianism and threw Mani into jail, where he died.

The greatest threat from Gnosticism was that it moved within Christianity and tried to shape its doctrine. The ascetic Marcion (85–160 C.E.), who ended up being excommunicated for his preachings, maintained that the Christian gospel is wholly a matter of love rather than a matter of law. On that account, **Marcionism** completely rejected the Old Testament (Jewish scripture), declaring that the God of the Old Testament (who had created the material world) was not the Spirit God, but the Demiurge, Satan.

About the same time, there arose another Gnostic doctrine within Christianity, **Docetism**. It proclaimed that Jesus was the pure Man of Light who brought salvation from the material darkness. It further denied that Jesus could have a material body of flesh. Therefore, his death upon the cross (and his physical resurrection) were merely apparent. Although this doctrine was clearly condemned in the second century, it had great staying power and motivated the Church to issue creedal statements affirming that Jesus did come in the flesh, was crucified, died, and was resurrected.

OTHER CHALLENGES. Other threats to Christianity during the early period included Ebionism (an effort to restrict the understanding of Jesus to Jewish categories) and people who claimed revelations setting dates for

Forces within Early Christianity

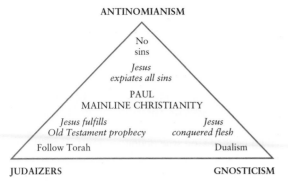

ANTINOMIANISM

No
sins

*Jesus
expiates all sins*

PAUL
MAINLINE CHRISTIANITY

*Jesus fulfills
Old Testament prophecy*   *Jesus
conquered flesh*

Follow Torah   Dualism

JUDAIZERS   GNOSTICISM

---

the second coming of Jesus. This no doubt started in the first century, for Paul and even the later gospels had to caution against setting dates. Perhaps the greatest challenge in this area was that of Montanus in Asia Minor. About the year 160, the ascetic Montanus led a heretical apocalyptic movement based on the primacy of the Holy Spirit. His followers expected the outpouring of the Holy Spirit on the Church. In its own prophecies, **Montanism** saw the beginnings of the bestowal of the Spirit. Montanus set dates for the return of Christ, and many of his followers sold their possessions or decided to stop tilling their fields. When the Church declared Montanism a heresy, it was an important point in its self-definition: Christians were to be an enduring church and not trust a self-appointed prophet who set dates for the imminent return of Christ.

Donatism was an internal challenge dealing with the question of the purity of membership in the Church and clergy that arose in the fourth and fifth centuries, primarily in the north African churches. To understand how this came about, we must understand the gravity of the ongoing persecutions against the Christians. The Roman emperors Decius (249–251 C.E.) and Diocletian (284–305 C.E.) made enough *martyrs* to make professing Christian doctrine a serious risk to personal safety. Christians had to meet secretly in catacombs (caves) or private homes, and their organization had to be informal. Their leaders (bishops and elders) were indistinguishable from ordinary people, and their teaching had a *disciplina arcani*—a strict code of secrecy. Those who died as martyrs were great heroes, whom heaven would greet with open arms. But many Christians did not have that degree

of courage and fell into *apostasy* (they recanted their commitment to Christ) in order to avoid torture or death. When the threat of persecution was over, many of these apostates (also known as *lapsi*) felt guilt and asked readmission to the Christian community. Donatus was a local bishop who led a party of rigorists who insisted that such traitors had no place in the Church. He went one step further, declaring that if these lapsed Christians had been readmitted to the priesthood and had administered the sacraments,

Which theoretical approach would give you the most insight on the history, doctrine, rituals, ethics of early Christianity? Consider that of Freud, Marx, Tylor, Malinowski, Otto, Muller, and others.

EXAMPLE: Durkheim viewed religion as a social phenomenon which served to celebrate and reinforce the cohesion of the social group.

Christians in the first century were a small and persecuted band drawn from the ranks of the slaves, workers, and displaced immigrants of the Roman Empire. They could not trust the greater Roman society or Jewish authority, only themselves and their savior Jesus.

Luke's history of the apostles (*Acts* 4:32–35) records how they shared material possessions. Although they had come from different lands, they were seen as being of "one blood" (*Acts* 17:26).

Paul's first epistle to the Corinthians sets out both the ethical rules and the symbolism for the new community. The guiding rule is to avoid offending a brother Christian (8:13). We are not to be concerned with private gain, but with what is best for the community (10:24). Wealth is to be shared (II *Corinthians* 8:13–15).

The powerful symbol Paul uses of the unity of this community comes from the central ritual of the early church, the Lord's Supper. The bread eaten by all is the Body of Christ. As all partake, they become the Body of Christ, and each individual is merely a part (e.g., a toe, an ear) and must serve the whole.

Each one must appreciate (rather than covet) the diversity of gifts bestowed on other Christians (I *Corinthians* 12).

Contribute to this discussion at
http://forums.delphiforums.com/rel101

the holy rites would not be acceptable in God's eyes. Donatism was opposed by many Church thinkers, most conclusively by his fellow north African *Augustine* (354–430 C.E.) who argued for greater clemency and for Christ's decisive role in the inner effect of the sacraments: the Church is holy even if the people in it are not.

THE CONCILIAR AGE

The Christian church had little power in the secular world until the conversion of the emperor **Constantine** (312 C.E.), so even when it was not suffering active persecution, it was not very influential. From the time of the Edict of Milan (313 C.E.), however, Christianity was free to proselytize within the Roman empire.

During the fourth and fifth centuries, a number of meetings (**councils**) of church leaders were held that formally established the rituals and official doctrine (dogma) that any group in union with the Apostolic Church had to adopt. From those meetings came the name for the next period of Christian history. Above all, the meetings, many of which were called by emperors concerned about the unity of the empire, dealt with the central issues of the Christian creed, hammering out the dogmas about God, Jesus, salvation, and the like that became the backbone of Christian theology. Various controversies made church leaders realize that it was imperative to determine which apostolic sources were genuine expressions of doctrine and which were not. That imperative resulted in the establishment of a Christian scriptural **canon** (list of official books in the Bible).

Three main factors determined the final canon: whether the writing in question came from an apostle or a close associate of an apostle, whether it was accepted by the Church at large, and whether its contents were consistent with doctrine. As early as 170, leaders in Rome had determined a canon of authoritative books in response to the canon drawn up by the heretic Marcion. Yet for many decades no list was agreed upon by the entire Church because local traditions varied. For instance, the East long hesitated to accept *Revelation,* while the West was uncertain about *Hebrews.*

The first great dogmatic (official doctrinal) council occurred at Nicaea by the Black Sea in 325. It produced a consensus that was especially important for

clarifying Jesus' divine status as Logos or Son. The Council of Nicaea was called by the emperor Constantine, and without imperial support the Nicene party would not have triumphed. Before Nicaea, most churches had been content to repeat what scripture (Jewish and Christian) had said about God and Jesus. However, Church theologians did not know how to respond to questions that scripture did not address. One such question came from Arius, a priest of Alexandria, in Egypt, who proposed that Jesus, as the Logos of God (the divine Son), was subordinate to the Father. **Arianism** (which was the doctrine of Arius and had nothing to do with the Aryans) assumed that if one drew a line between created beings and the uncreated divine substance, the Logos (Christ) would fall on the side of created beings.

Arius's principal opponent was **Athanasius,** who represented the theologians of Alexandria in Egypt, who descended from Clement of Alexandria (ca. 150–215 C.E.), one of the first Christian theologians to cast Christian doctrine as a philosophy that might persuade educated Hellenists, and Origen (ca. 185–254 C.E.), the first great Christian speculator. (Working with Platonic philosophy, Origen had written immensely influential commentaries on scripture and expositions of Christian doctrine.) Athanasius, drawing on this Alexandrian tradition, assaulted Arius' argument. Speaking for what he held to be orthodoxy, he said that the Logos was of the same substance as the Father, possessing the single divine nature. Nicaea agreed with Athanasius, making his position dogma. There were many political machinations, as different political factions chose different theological sides, and Arianism thrived among Germanic tribes well into the sixth century. However, the *Nicene Creed,* which codified the position against Arius, was official doctrine.

TRINITARIAN DOCTRINE. The doctrine of the Trinity cannot be found clearly stated in the Bible, but most mainline Christian denominations accept it. While most theologians regard the Trinity as a doctrine consistent with scripture, it was not until the fourth century that Church councils finalized it. Athanasius perceived that the canonical literature gave the Holy Spirit divinity equal to that of the Father and the Son. Therefore, he suggested the term *homoousios* ("of one substance") to include the Holy Spirit and so set the lines of what would become, at the Council of Constantinople in 381, the doctrine of the Holy Spirit's divinity. That completed the doctrine of the **Trinity:** one God who was three co-equal "persons," each of whom fully possessed the single divine nature, co-eternal and present at creation.

Augustine, bishop of Hippo, in North Africa, was greatly influenced by Plato. It was Augustine who expressed Trinitarian doctrine in terms of a psychological analogy that shaped Western Christian speculation. He proposed that as memory, understanding, and love are all mind, so (but without human imperfections) are Father, Son, and Holy Spirit all divinity. The Father is like an inexhaustible memory (from which all creation comes), the Logos is like the Father's self-awareness, and the Spirit is like their boundless love.

MONASTICISM. Not all early Christian ascetics were Gnostics. The increasing tie between the Church and civil authorities stimulated new religious movements within the Church that opposed the laxness or "accommodation" that worldly success easily begot. The most important reforms generated interest in monasticism and virginity (which overlapped, insofar as monks took vows of celibacy). Communities of celibate, frequently very ascetic monks and nuns grew in this period. Both males and females found a monastic life of dedication to prayer and charitable works a way of maintaining their martyrlike intensity of commitment. Many found that it led them to the north African desert for solitude and asceticism.

The great hero of the day, in fact, was the desert father Anthony, who made a great impression on Athanasius. Partly because of the dangers of desert solitude, many monks soon formed communities, and before long these communities admitted women (nuns). In the East, communal (cenobitic) monasticism took form under the guidance of Basil, bishop of Caesarea. In the West, the rule of Benedict predominated. So the dedication that had previously been an informal option (largely in terms of virginity or widowhood) took institutional form. That, too, was an innovation added to New Testament religion, which had no monastic life. The Church's decision that monastic life was truly in keeping with New Testament religion was analogous to the decision to coin new doctrinal concepts. It should not be surprising that the Protestant reformers of the sixteenth century opposed the development of monasticism (as being unbiblical), just as they opposed the development of the Catholic notion of the central authority of the Roman Pope.

CHRISTOLOGY. The councils not only set the pattern of Trinitarian doctrine that dominated the following centuries but also dealt with a host of problems that arose when people started to think about Jesus as the divine Word. Nestorius from Antioch and Cyril from Alexandria squared off in Christological controversy, and Alexandria won. **Nestorianism,** after the teachings of Nestorius, stressed the unity of the Christian God, though he affirmed Christ's two natures (human and divine). Cyril thought that Nestorius's affirmation was not strong enough to safeguard the single personhood of Jesus Christ the God-man, so he pressed for a *hypostatic* (personal) union of the two natures. The Councils of Ephesus (431 C.E.) and Chalcedon (451 C.E.) affirmed Cyril's doctrine of one "person" and two "natures." Later Christological development clarified that Jesus had a rational soul, two wills, and two sets of operations, human and divine. This orthodox Christology resulted from trying to systematize the scriptural teaching about God and Jesus. It stressed that only the union of the divine with the human in Jesus could save human beings from sin and give them divine life. Orthodoxy cast many groups in the shade, branding their positions as heretical, but it also developed the mainline conception of Christ considerably.

CATHOLIC SACRAMENTALISM. The Gospels only record two rituals instituted by Jesus. One was a ritual of initiation, baptism, and the other was to be done regularly, the Holy Eucharist (Lord's Supper). Eventually, the Church (which was becoming known as the Holy **Roman Catholic** Apostolic Church) had developed seven **sacraments** (liturgies or rituals), which it understood as being efficacious for channeling God's grace through the Church to its members. The development of these sacraments involved an interesting interplay with the development of doctrines about heaven and purgatory.

The first sacrament was **baptism**. In the Gospels, baptism was a rite of initiation into the Christian fold. It was performed in a natural body of water, such as a river, and it was by complete immersion. There is no direct evidence of infants being baptized, although some passages suggest that "whole households were baptized" and we can infer that they might have included children or infants. A doctrine associated with baptism was that it washed away not only original sin but also any individual sins that the person had committed prior to baptism. Some people petitioned to be rebaptized,

because they had fallen into sin again after their conversion and wished to cleanse themselves of that new stain upon their souls. The Church finally agreed that baptism would be a once-in-a-lifetime, nonrepeatable ritual of initiation. Many people then decided that they would hold off on getting baptized so that it would cover a broader spectrum of life's sins. Deathbed conversions were common into the fourth century.

The Church accordingly made a decision to emphasize baptism as a birth rite, urging that Christian parents get their infants baptized. This entailed a change in the ritual: sprinkling instead of dunking. It also meant that its relevance would not be the initiate's decision to convert to become a Christian; rather, the rite would be more for the parents (and godparents, and the entire local community attending the ceremony), for it would symbolize their commitment to raise the child as a Christian.

This shift opened up several theological issues about the impact of baptism (or its lack) upon an individual in the afterlife. What is the downside if parents do not get the infant baptized? **Pelagianism,** after Pelagius (d. 430 C.E.), took the humanistic perspective that Adam's sin was an individual fall, not a fall for the entire human race, and therefore, we had no reason to presume that unbaptized infants would go to hell. Augustine challenged Pelagius and reaffirmed Paul's conception of original sin: the entire human race had been stained by the disobedience of Adam, and without the grace of Christ, channeled through the Church, there was no salvation. Medieval theologians, hoping to soften the harshness of this condemnation of the unbaptized, suggested the existence of **limbo,** a place not as bad as hell (for the infant had not been guilty of any personal sins, especially the conscious rejection of Christ) but not as good as the Beatific Vision that was reserved for those in Heaven.

Purgatory, a related concept, tries to answer the question of what happens to adults who, after baptism, commit individual sins. Assuming that these sins are venial (not so serious as to keep one out of heaven), then the soul might have to do a sort of penance in purgatory prior to entering heaven. This is not a place where souls who had rejected Christ while they were on earth will get a second chance to convert, but a place where those Christians who are bound for heaven must serve a little more time in preparation for their eventual destination. Nevertheless, purgatory was not considered that great of a place, and so the motivation was to sin less on earth (or do penance on earth in order to avoid having to spend so much time in purgatory).

While the doctrines of purgatory and limbo were never accepted by any future Christian denomination other than the Catholic, the ritual practice of infant baptism became the norm and has remained so in the Catholic, Eastern Orthodox, Lutheran, Episcopalian, Presbyterian, and Methodist churches. (The return to adult baptism exclusively was later advocated by the Baptists, Pentecostals, Mormons, Seventh Day Adventists, Church of Christ, and Jehovah's Witnesses.)

This move toward infant baptism in the third and fourth centuries occasioned the need for additional sacraments to take the place of adult baptism. If baptism is not going to be a ritual of personal decision, initiation, for Christians who have come to the age of discretion, then a new sacrament must be developed to fill that void: **confirmation.** This was usually performed by making the sign of the cross with oil on the forehead of the initiate, transforming him or her into a "soldier of Christ." The age at which a Catholic undergoes this ritual has come to vary, culture by culture, from elementary school age up through adolescence.

The main attraction of the deathbed conversion and baptism was that it erased a lifetime of sins. If baptism was to be a birth rite and nonrepeatable, some new sacrament would have to be developed to handle those sins committed after baptism. The earliest form, **confession**, was a public statement of sins to the rest of the Christian community. By the sixth century, a Celtic practice of private confessions of sin directly to a priest became popular, usually associated with the granting of absolution and the assigning of certain penances. (Even serious sins would be forgiven, but the more severe the sin, the greater the time in purgatory to compensate for it.) After Vatican II, the sacrament has been reformulated as the Sacrament of Reconciliation and more public, symbolic options are now available for penitents.

Another attraction of the deathbed baptism was that it helped bring closure to a person's life with a special pre-death ritual. After the shift to infant baptism, that was replaced with **last rites** (also known as *extreme unction*). This is a rite of penance (like confession) and anointing with oil (like confirmation). In recent years it has been expanded to the Sacrament

for the Sick and can be given to anyone who is ailing or has the risk of death.

The Holy **Eucharist** (Holy Communion, Lord's Supper) has been the principal sacrament in the majority of the Christian traditions. It is practiced weekly (even daily) by the most devout and is based upon the description of the Last Supper that Jesus had with his disciples. The key words recited in the ritual are:

For in the night in which he was betrayed, he took bread; and when he had given thanks, he brake it, and gave it to his disciples, saying, "Take, eat, this is my Body, which is given for you. Do this in remembrance of me." Likewise, after supper, he took the cup; and when he had given thanks, he gave it to them, saying "Drink ye all of this; for this is my Blood of the New Testament, which is shed for you, and for many, for the remission of sins. Do this, as oft as you shall drink it, in remembrance of me."

Paul's *Epistles* point out that this ritual not only reaffirms the vertical bonds between the Christian and Christ, but the horizontal bonds with his/her community who share the ritual bread and wine.

Marriage also became recognized as a sacramental occasion. The Christian theology of marriage has likened the conjunction of man and woman in matrimony to the union between Christ and the Church, and it has found in the *Genesis* creation account, in which God gave Eve to Adam, a prototype of the nuptial union. A Christian marriage was meant for both the mutual comfort of the spouses and the procreation of children. It had to be entered into freely by both parties, and usually the minister called upon the assembled community not only to witness the parties' vows but also to support them in their marital venture.

Marriage inside the Catholic Church is considered an important sacrament that the individual will not be allowed to repeat again with another spouse (unless the first spouse has died). The current Catholic stand against divorce is seen as the most rigid among Christian churches, but it is quite a bit more complicated than first meets the eye. The Catholics take literally the part about no man being able to put asunder the sacrament of marriage. Although the Church recognizes the right of abused spouses to seek legal redress in the form of a divorce granting separation and property settlement, it does not consider such a civil action as freeing the parties to engage in the sacrament of remarriage in the Church. (Indeed, if a divorced Catholic remarried in a secular or non-Catholic marriage ceremony, the spouses would then be seen as committing adultery). The Catholic Church does have a loophole, nullification or annulment, which says that there must have been something wrong with the first marriage to begin with; therefore, we can say that it never really existed, and so the remarriage is really only the first real marriage. Unfortunately, this process of a canon law annulment is not well understood, even among Catholics, and tends to be thought of as a favor granted more often to the rich and powerful than to others.

An additional sacrament (and one not undertaken by the laity) is the **ordination** of the Church's ministers. In churches with several ranks of ministers, the bishop has usually presided at the ordination. After satisfying himself that the candidates were qualified, he solicited the approval and support of the community, prayed over the ordinand and then laid hands on the ordinand's head and prayed, "Therefore, Father, through Jesus Christ your Son, give your Holy Spirit to ———; fill him [or her, in churches that ordained women] with grace and power, and make him [or her] a priest in your Church."

Although not an official sacrament, another important ritual was burial rites. These usually focused on the Holy Eucharist for the occasion of death and burial. The Liturgy of the Word featured psalms and scriptural passages concerned with death and the Christian hopes for resurrection, and the person would be buried in consecrated ground with prayers for forgiveness and the life of the blessed in heaven.

RELICS AND SAINTS

Even in the first century, as Christianity moved north and west, the proselytizers often carried with them physical symbols of the religion: perhaps a palm leaf from the Holy Land, or a splinter of wood from the true cross, or a tooth from one of the apostles. These relics were intended to serve as credentials for the missionary, but many times the new Christians venerated these relics as if they possessed magical powers. Later, as the churches became more elaborate, there would be paintings, stained glass windows, and statues representing Jesus or the saints. While these

were supposed to be powerful symbols to put the worshipper in a spiritual frame of mind for the worship of Jesus, no doubt some people thought that they were praying to the statue (and thereby committing idolatry).

A related issue is the practice of identifying deceased people as **saints.** Paul used this term broadly to refer to all members of the Christian community. After a generation or two, this title became reserved for exceptional Christians: perhaps the apostles, martyrs, hermits, or exemplary leaders. The Church came to recognize saints as having two functions: their lives could serve as models of piety for the living, and after death they had a role to play in mediating the interaction of heaven and earth. A Christian sometimes prays to a saint in hopes of the saint's serving as an intermediary, someone who will plead the case before God in heaven. The process of selecting saints is a two-step procedure known as beatification (sort of a nomination process) and canonization (the maintenance of an official list of saints) and requires action by the Pope.

The greatest of all the saints was **Mary**, mother of Jesus. There is evidence that Christians were praying to her in the earliest Church. The Catholics have introduced some additional doctrines about her: that she was forever a virgin, that when she herself was conceived in her own mother's womb, it was a special immaculate conception so that she would be a vessel free of the taint of original sin, and that after her death she was directly assumed into heaven without having to go through purgatory.

Many Christians from non-Catholic denominations have come to criticize the Catholic leadership for changing the rituals or doctrine from what was reported in the New Testament. Some contemporary Protestant fundamentalists might consider the Catholics to be a cult unworthy of the title "Christian." The Catholics respond that all of these extensions of ritual and doctrine were attempts to make the core of Christianity (the worship of Jesus) more relevant to new times and peoples and that it is inappropriate to try to freeze doctrine or ritual to the first century. Furthermore, although the Catholics do respect scripture, they do not consider themselves limited to it (as some fundamentalist Protestants might perceive). The Church sees itself as canonizing the books of the

Madonna and child

Critique a specific Catholic doctrine, ritual, or ethical stance by citing scripture. You might consider:

- Veneration of Mary
- Use of statues
- Purgatory
- Confession
- No remarriage in Church
- Papal authority
- Prohibition of birth control

Contribute to this discussion at
http://forums.delphiforums.com/rel101

EASTERN ORTHODOX CHURCHES

Orthodoxy has two principal meanings. It may refer to the **Eastern Orthodox Church** that separated from Rome in the **Great Schism** of 1054 or to the "correct doctrine" established by scripture, tradition, and the councils. In this section we address the first concept, describing the growth of Eastern Christianity after the Conciliar Age (most of the great councils took place in the East). The term *Orthodox* was adopted for both of the aforementioned reasons: the Orthodox Church thought of itself as keeping the traditional doctrine and rituals alike.

LITURGY. Liturgy means "the work of the people" and refers to public ritual. During the Apostolic Age, the Church had developed a sacramental system in which baptism and the Eucharist ("the Lord's Supper") were especially important. In the early medieval period, when Orthodoxy took form, the liturgy flowered. The result was a full calendar of holy days and a full ritual that involved music, art, incense, iconography, and more. Thus, communal worship became the dramatic center of church life, especially in the Eastern Church.

From the ninth to the fifteenth century, a complicated process of alienation between Byzantine (Eastern) Christianity and Roman Christianity resulted in their separation. Some of the factors in the separation were the fall of the Eastern Roman empire, the failure of the Crusades, the growing antagonism of Islam, the growth of the papacy, the stirrings of what developed into the sixteenth century Protestant reactions against

New Testament (and later changing that canon over a thousand years later). As one Catholic layman put it, "Jesus did not come to write a book, but to establish a Church." But Catholics can also find scripture to back up the Church's authority to modify doctrine and ritual (e.g., *Matthew* 16:18, which gives Peter as first Pope the keys to the kingdom).

Byzantine Book Cover

the papacy, and the rivalry between Russia and western Europe. These factors take us to the beginning of modernity in Eastern Christendom, explaining why East and West have remained divided to the present.

RELIGIOUS ISSUES. Thus, the break between Eastern and Western Christianity owed a great deal to political and cultural conflicts. For instance, the patriarch Photius, who presided at the Eastern capital of Constantinople from 858 to 886, drew up a list of what Byzantines considered to be Latin (Western) errors in doctrine. This list reveals how the two portions of Christendom had developed different understandings of orthodoxy. In this list Photius cited irregularities in the observance of Lent (the period of penance before the great feast of Easter when the resurrection of Christ was celebrated), false teaching about the Holy Spirit, and most importantly compulsory celibacy for the clergy (most Eastern priests were married, and now the Pope was trying to make celibacy a requirement).

The most acute point of theological difference between the East and the West was a doctrine about the

Holy Spirit, which came to be known as the *filioque.* According to the Nicene Creed, within the life of the Trinity the Holy Spirit proceeds from the Father. The Western Council of Toledo (589) made an addition to the Nicene Creed: the Holy Spirit proceeds not just from the Father but also from the Son (*filioque* means "and from the Son"). East and West each became attached to its Trinitarian formula, so the *filioque* became a sharp bone of contention. The East claimed that it was heretical; the West claimed it merely articulated a tacit understanding of traditional doctrine that Nicaea had assumed. The practical significance of the difference is not clear, but it probably shows the East's tendency to appreciate the Father's primal mystery—the Father's status as a fathomless source from which everything issues.

In response to Photius, Western theologians composed their own list of complaints about Eastern usage. In their view the Eastern discipline that allowed clerics to marry, that baptized by immersion, that celebrated the Eucharist with leavened bread, and that had different rules for fasting deviated from tradition. The debate even descended to such details as whether bishops should wear rings, whether clergy should wear beards, and whether instrumental music was appropriate at the liturgy. However, the main theological issue continued to be the *filioque*, while the main political issue emerged as the difference in the churches' understanding of authority. The Eastern Church's tradition was a loose federation of bishops, all of whom were considered successors of the apostles. The Eastern Church also stressed the rights of individual churches and ethnic groups. The Western tradition was a "monarchical" leadership by the bishop of Rome. As successor to Peter, he claimed primacy over the other churches.

When the Byzantine empire was about to fall to the Turks, the Eastern and Western factions met for the last time at the Council of Florence (1439). That was long after the mutual anathemas of 1054 (described later), but the East hoped to secure both church unification and Western help against Islam. On the agenda were only four points (the other disagreements having fallen away as trivial). They were the prerogatives of the bishop of Rome, the *filioque* clause, the doctrine of purgatory (the Roman Catholic teaching that there is an intermediate state between heaven and hell, which the Orthodox condemned as unbiblical), and whether to use leavened or unleavened bread in the Eucharist. In retrospect, theologians have judged the last two items as relatively inconsequential. The first two were interrelated, because the Council of Florence came to focus on the question of whether the Pope had the right to alter an ecumenical creed (that is, add *filioque* to the Nicene Creed). Because of their political problems (the menace of the Turks), the majority of the Greeks (Easterners) accepted the *filioque* and agreed to certain papal prerogatives. The union was confined to paper, though, because back at home Orthodox **synods** (councils of bishops) refused to ratify the agreements signed by their delegates.

Separation. The pivotal moment in the East-West division was the mutual excommunications of 1054, which were due more to politics (or to snappish personalities) than to irreconcilable differences in the core elements of religion. Pope Leo IX had sent a Western delegation to Constantinople headed by one Cardinal Humbert. The Normans were menacing Leo and also the emperor Constantine Monomachus, so a major goal was to unite the churches to oppose a common foe. Humbert seems to have been a narrow, contentious type, as was his Eastern counterpart, the patriarch Michael Cerularius. When Pope Leo died in 1054, Cerularius held that Humbert's credentials were void. Humbert responded by laying on the altar of Saint Sophia in Constantinople a letter that excommunicated the patriarch and all his associates. The patriarch then assembled his own council, which excommunicated Humbert in return. The emperor dispatched the cardinal back to Rome with presents, hoping that the next Pope would appoint a new legate who could heal the breach. But the Normans prevented the popes from resuming negotiations, so the mutual excommunications stood until after the Second Vatican Council in the early 1960s.

In the opinion of many contemporary theologians and historians, the division between the Eastern and Western branches of the Church was a tragic accident. (Historians now say much the same of the sixteenth-century Reformation split in Europe.) Political circumstances, differences in traditional ways of celebrating liturgy, and, above all, differences in temperament and cultural backgrounds were more decisive than hard theological differences. What Orthodox and Catholics (and Protestants and Catholics) held in common was far more significant than what they held apart.

It may be more appropriate to speak of Eastern Orthodox Churches (e.g., Greek, Russian) rather than just one Church, because the East has always respected ethnic differences in tradition and local control of church matters (probably because many bishops were under the control of local political leaders, such as the Byzantine emperor, whereas the Pope in Rome often enjoyed much greater power than Western European kings). All the Eastern churches together probably have about 200 million adherents. Most of the priests are married, but most of the bishops are not. The archbishops are sometimes called metropolitans.

In an Orthodox Church, a Catholic will notice fewer statues but more paintings (icons) on the wall. The sign of the cross is made right to left. At the Orthodox liturgy, one feels a Christian *pneumaticism*: The Holy Spirit is dramatically present to effect the sacraments. In the invocation made over the Eucharistic gifts (the *epiclesis*), Orthodoxy stresses the Holy Spirit's role in transforming the bread and wine into Christ's substance. In its baptism and confession of sins, Orthodoxy's accent is sharing God's life—beginning divine life in baptism or repairing it in penance. Overall, Orthodoxy places the mystery of the Christian God to the fore. For the East, God is less a lawgiver or a judge than a spiritual power operating through creation. Creation ought to respond to God's power and beauty, so the Divine Liturgy becomes a song of praise, a hymn to the goodness and love that pour forth from the Father of Lights. Orthodoxy especially venerates Mary, the Mother of God, for her share in the design of grace that raises human beings to participate in the divine immortality.

Both major branches of Eastern Orthodoxy, the Greek and the Russian, have fostered a strong monastic life, and from this strong monastic life has come a steady stream of holy people wise in the ways of the religious spirit, prayer, asceticism, and mysticism. The Orthodox mystical tradition continues, alive and well, in places like Mount Athos in Greece, where monks meditate in the old ways and read the old classics. Like Hasidim lost in the world of Torah, the Orthodox holy men and women are lost in the world of the gospel. For them the gospel words are shining jewels, the gospel scenes are blazing icons. Contemplating those icons, the Orthodox saints have enjoyed wonderful visions of the life of God that fills the holy soul, the mercy of God that courses through the world.

Their meditations have made the scriptural scenes contemporary, much the way Jewish prayer has made the Exodus contemporary.

It is shocking to enter the thought-world of the Orthodox monks and nuns, and perhaps equally shocking to realize that a similar thought-world predominated in the Christian West less than 500 years ago. Less than 500 years ago, even theologians studied the Bible more for its religious feeling than for its literary structure. Even theologians were more interested in feeling compunction than in knowing its definition. Similarly, the terms of reference are not the historical or literary aspects of the Bible, but the spiritual experiences and verities of his tradition tells the monastic what the Bible can promote. What the Holy Spirit did for the apostles, and for all who came after them, the Holy Spirit is poised to do today. After all, Jesus, the eternal Son of God, came from God precisely to give us human beings God's life, which the Holy Spirit wants to nurture in us. God's life, the East always has emphasized, is the perfect community of the Father, Son, and Holy Spirit. It is the Trinity not as the subject of conciliar controversies, or the subject of theologians' dry reflections, but as the spiritual atmosphere in which human beings can live, move, and have their being, if they would open their souls to its power. What the Eastern liturgy has always sung, the Eastern holy people have always stressed: the substantial love of God poured out for the salvation of human beings; humanity's potential elevation to a new, heavenly mode of life.

THE MEDIEVAL PERIOD

In the West, during the third and fourth centuries, most of the Celts converted. During the fifth and sixth centuries, Christian missionaries made considerable inroads among the Germanic tribes. Frequently they would convert tribal leaders from Teutonic religion or Arianist versions of Christianity, and then the entire tribe would convert. From 800 one could speak of the Holy Roman Empire—a tense mixture of political and religious drives for unity. Local bishops found that they could increase their freedom from local secular rulers by increasing their allegiance to the bishop of Rome. The friction between church and state therefore shifted to the interaction between the Pope and the Germanic emperor. A key issue was who should appoint local bishops. The investiture controversy, as it is called, was solved by a compromise in the Concordat of Worms (1122). Secular rulers had to recognize the independence of the local bishop by virtue of his loyalty to the Pope, and the Pope had to consult the emperor and appoint bishops acceptable to him.

During the twelfth century, the **Crusades** to the holy sites in Palestine riveted the Christian imagination, but they tended to increase the alienation between Eastern and Western Christendom. When the Fourth Crusade (1204) conquered Constantinople, set up a Western prince, and tried to Latinize the Eastern church, relations deteriorated to their lowest point. By 1453, after the Councils of Lyon and Florence had done little to heal the wounds of division, and after Easterners had suffered centuries of Western domination, a popular slogan circulated to the effect that Turks would be better rulers than Western Christians.

During the twelfth century, considerable resistance to the established Church power and doctrine arose among some groups, such as the Waldenses, who urged a return to apostolic simplicity and poverty. Groups that owed a debt to the old Gnostic views, such as the French **Cathari** or Albigensians, pushed dualistic views in their war on the flesh and their contempt for the material world.

To meet the challenge of such reformers, the Roman church developed new orders of priests and monks, the most important of which were the **Dominicans** and the Franciscans. Dominic (1170–1221) organized his group to preach against the heretics, and one of the devotions it added was the rosary—a string of beads for counting prayers to the Virgin Mary. The **Franciscans** stemmed from the charismatic Francis of Assisi (1181–1226), who dedicated himself to simple living. His angelic love of nature and of the infant Jesus made a deep impression on subsequent generations of Christians. Both Dominicans and Franciscans were innovations on the established (largely Benedictine) model of Western monasticism. Principally, they had more freedom than Benedictines to move out of the cloister. They were mobile and therefore quite effective in responding to different religious trouble spots.

SCHOLASTICISM. The thirteenth century was the high point of medieval intellectual life, and the movement known as **Scholasticism** reached its peak then. The Scholastics systematized the conciliar and patristic (the Fathers') theological doctrines. Augustine (354–430 C.E.) was their great inspiration, but where Augustine worked with Neoplatonic thought categories (worked out by thinkers such as Plotinus, who developed Plato's ideas), Thomas **Aquinas** (1225–1274), the greatest of the medievals, worked with Aristotelian categories. Between Augustine and Aquinas lived **Anselm** (1033–1109), who said that, on the basis of a firm Christian commitment (rooted in scriptural, conciliar, and patristic doctrines), the theologian ought to learn as much as the divine mysteries allowed. Anselm's definition was a writ of intellectual emancipation. Though they accepted the disciplines of tradition and the Church's teaching office, the medieval theologians seized the right to develop reason and use it to illumine doctrine.

It was Aquinas who gained the greatest following. For Aquinas, philosophy was a universal basis for discussion, regardless of religious allegiance. Jews, Muslims, Christians, and pagans all had reason, and so all could philosophize. Theology, which rested on divine revelation, perfected philosophy, taking it into realms that it could not penetrate on its own (for instance, without revelation philosophy would not know of the Trinity or the Incarnation, the divine Word made flesh). Aquinas developed a powerful system of philosophical theology, but he was by no means the only impressive medieval thinker. His school, Thomism, trusted in reason, had a hopeful view of the world, thoroughly analyzed the Trinity, Christology, grace, and human virtues and vices.

HIERARCHY. The clergy had separated themselves from the laity, and within the clerical order there were numerous ranks: monks, priests, canons, bishops, abbots, archbishops, cardinals, and more. The papacy had a considerable bureaucracy and wielded great secular power. Because the general culture held a Christian worldview, heaven and hell had a vivid reality. Thus, the papal power to bar people from Church membership and so from heaven made people fear the pope greatly. Considerable worldliness entered into the papal use of excommunication, interdict, and the like, because by medieval times the Church had largely laid aside the *parousia* (second coming of Christ) and was concentrating on shaping daily life.

The medieval cathedrals also exhibited hierarchy through their stretching from earth toward heaven.

Exterior view of elaborate cathedral

They instruct us about medieval mentality, for towns built them to be a means of indoctrination. One can see this today in the gothic masterpieces of Notre Dame de Chartres and Notre Dame de Paris. The basic architectural thrust is toward heaven, as all commentators point out, yet within the cathedrals are windows and statues that bring God down into daily life. Most cathedrals were built over centuries, and sometimes the townspeople contributed free labor, as if they wanted the cathedral to praise God doubly. Significantly, Chartres and Notre Dame de Paris both bear Mary's name. As the Virgin Mother of God, Queen of Heaven and recourse of weak human beings, Mary was a mainstay of medieval Catholicism.

Around the cathedral walls, in wonderful stained glass, were biblical scenes, pictures of saints, and the like, that told even the illiterate what the doctrine meant.

With the statues of the Virgin and Jesus, they gave comfort to the person who slipped into the cathedral's darkness to pray. In its majestic space, one gained a proper perspective on one's problems. At a time when hard work, early death, and many sufferings were the rule, the cathedrals were for many a great support.

Monastic life progressed during the Middle Ages, though new orders such as the Franciscans and Dominicans neither completely replaced the more stable Benedictines nor completely abandoned their regimes. The great work of the monastic community was to celebrate the divine "office": liturgical prayers throughout the day and a communal Mass. By the thirteenth century, the Eucharist involved a rather complex ceremony, with choral music, gorgeous vestments, and precious vessels for the bread and wine. Gregorian chants best represent the music, which was lively and alert, giving many psalms a joyous lilt. For solemn moments, such as the celebration of Christ's Passion, chant could express deep sorrow, prefiguring, for instance, the music of Johann Sebastian Bach.

As it developed, the mass increasingly tended to represent Christ's sacrificial death. That did not deny the motif of a common meal, but it shifted emphasis to the consecration of the elements (bread and wine), because in the theologians' interpretation, the separation of the bread and wine stood for the sundering of Jesus' body on the cross. As a prayer (the "sequence") for the feast of Corpus Christi (attributed to Thomas Aquinas) shows, the consecrated host (bread transformed into Jesus' body) came to epitomize God's presence and redemptive action. The consecration was a miracle that the liturgy enacted each day. Paradoxically, the host defied the senses and nourished the soul. Because Jesus' body remained in church, the church was indeed God's house. Indeed, in the host, Jesus made himself available for reverence and prayer. Along with the cult of the Virgin and the cults of the many medieval saints, the cult of the Eucharist gave people at the bottom of the church pyramid another source of comfort.

Thus, the average person went through a harsh medieval life in fear and trembling but with many sources of hope that such a life would lead to heaven. The worldliness of much church life was balanced by the sacramental ceremonies that stressed the primacy of heaven. Rather clearly, the laity knew that they stood between heaven and earth. They were citizens of two worlds, and the best medieval theology and religious art counseled them to live their dual citizenship gracefully. For instance, the cathedral and monastic schools joined piety to learning. The mystery plays and even the *danse macabre* (dance of death) brought home to the common people that death leveled Pope and pauper to strict equality.

THE PERIOD OF REFORM

During the late fourteenth and fifteenth centuries, the papacy was in great disarray. At one point there were two claimants to the chair of Peter, one in Rome and one in Avignon. In the East the Muslims held Asia Minor and Greece, their most dramatic victory being at Constantinople in 1453. Well into the fifteenth century, southern Spain was under Muslim control, while in Italy the spirit of the Renaissance seemed stronger than conciliar attempts to reform the papacy. In addition, there were frictions among local rulers within the Italian, French, and German realms; the middle classes emerged as a result of city life and economic changes; and the pre-Lutheran attacks on Church corruption by the Lollards (followers of John Wycliffe, [1329–1384] in England) and the Hussites (followers of John Hus [1369–1415] in Bohemia) took place.

The spark that set the Protestant **Reformation** blazing was the German, Martin Luther (1483–1546), an Augustinian monk whose study and spiritual searches had convinced him that the heart of the gospel was the Pauline justification by "faith" (the doctrine that it is only one's personal commitment to Christ that makes one right with God). Only by reviving this Pauline theme could Christianity regain its pure beginnings. This view claimed that the entire Catholic sacramental system was to be dismissed as a covenant of "works": the mass, the rosary, and so on. Luther was precipitated into action by the prevailing practice of **indulgences** (papal remissions of purgatorial punishment due for sins), which one could obtain for various good deeds, including almsgiving. Behind this practice lay some simple economics. The popes had spent lavishly in their Renaissance enthusiasm for art and culture. Leo X, for instance, was perhaps 125,000 ducats in debt at the time that he endorsed the preaching mission of Johann Tetzel (Luther's great adversary in the debate over indulgences in Germany), the mission included granting an indulgence for a contribution to the building of St. Peter's in Rome. To Luther the whole system—the Pope's extravagance, his pretension to control a treasury of merits generated by the saints, out of which he might draw "credits" to cover sinners' debts, and his focusing his economics on the mass—was blasphemous. On October 31, 1517, tradition says, Luther nailed his *Ninety-five Theses* to the door of the castle church at Wittenberg, which amounted to a formal challenge to the system.

Many Germans who for political or religious reasons had grievances against Rome supported Luther. As his thought expanded, he made scripture the sole arbiter of Christian doctrine and ritual, declared the primacy of individual conscience, upgraded the status of the layperson, and urged the use of the vernacular rather than Latin. Luther also stressed the uniqueness of Christ's death on the cross and so taught that the Eucharist principally commemorates the Last Supper, rather than representing Christ's sacrificial death. On the basis of scripture, he judged the doctrine of purgatory unfounded and the practice of monastic life an aberration. Because Luther was a fine preacher, he made these ideas matters for discussion in the marketplace. By translating the Bible into marvelous German, he put the central basis for his reform within reach of all literate people (and just about standardized High German in the process). Finally, Luther's departure from monastic life and subsequent marriage led thousands more to leave their monasteries and convents.

THE SPREAD OF REFORMATION. Luther's reform in Germany quickly generated uprisings elsewhere. Not only were many people eager for religious reform, but separating themselves from Rome furthered their nationalistic sentiments. In Switzerland, Ulrich Zwingli (among the German speaking) and John Calvin (among the French speaking) led movements with similar themes. In England, Henry VIII and Thomas Cranmer separated their church from Rome. As the Reformation worked out, Lutheranism took root in countries with a primarily agrarian economy, such as Germany and Scandinavia, while Calvinism took root in countries with a commercial economy, such as French Switzerland, France, Flanders, and the Netherlands.

John **Calvin** (1509–1564) was a French lawyer who traveled to Geneva in order to establish a religious community based upon his doctrines. These

Martin Luther, sixteenth-century German Protestant Reformer

became known as double *predestination*, and can be summarized in five points, sometimes symbolized by the acronym TULIP. Point one is the *T*, and that stands for the *total depravity* of human nature, and therefore all of humanity is deserving of an afterlife in hell. The second point is the *U*, that God's grace is completely *unmerited* by its human recipients. There is nothing that people can do to earn their own salvation, and, going beyond Luther, Calvin said that humans even lacked the free will to muster their own powers of commitment to turn toward God. Therefore, the salvation accorded any human is completely due to the mercy and sovereignty of God (who has therefore elected, predestined, some for salvation). The third point is the *L*, the *limited* atonement of Christ on the cross: he died for the sins of the elect, not for the sins of all. In response to the criticism that this makes God an unfair or capricious dispenser of salvation, Calvin responded that if God were really

ROMPTE   ET SINCERE

(c) Archivo Iconografico, S.A. / CORBIS

John Calvin, advocate of predestination

were advanced by a Flemish bishop, Cornelius Jansen, 1585–1638.) To his credit, Calvin's doctrine opened up a new vista among the Protestants in his Reformed Churches: now, one did not have to wonder about salvation and could concentrate on the more arduous task of sanctification, the never-ending task of spiritual perfection via the action of the Holy Spirit.

Critics of Calvinism came from many sectors: Protestants, Catholics, and secular humanists rallied to defend the doctrine of free will. Jacobus Arminius, a Dutch Protestant, argued that although humans were depraved, they had free will, and could always call on God to accept His unlimited atonement. The one downside to **Arminianism** (as his doctrine was called) is that one can lose one's salvation by backsliding.

just, He would consign all humans to hell, but the fact that He decides to save some is entirely within his right and reflects His great mercy. The fourth point is the *I*, which stands for *irresistible* grace: if one is the recipient of God's grace, one will manifest "faith" (and good works) because one has no free will and cannot resist the call of God. The *P* stands for the last point, the *perseverance* of the saints. This is also known as the doctrine of secure salvation: if you are saved, you cannot lose your salvation. If someone commits major sins after baptism, that person was obviously not one of the elect to begin with. (Within the Catholic Church, similar ideas about predestination

---

CALVIN'S TULIP

- Total depravity of all mankind
- Unmerited grace from God
- Limited atonement: only for the chosen
- Irresistible grace draws the chosen to God
- Perseverance of saints: salvation is secure forever

Calvin maintained that humans were so evil that they could not, on their own, muster the "faith" necessary to commit themselves to God's Grace. So, it is God who elects certain persons to receive His Grace, and all others will get their just desserts (hell). Therefore, the redemptive act of Christ on the cross was not for all, but only a limited atonement for the elect. If someone has this elect status, then God will not allow that person to fall away. One cannot lose one's salvation. The elect will manifest their status by good deeds: if they don't, then they were not elect in the first place. Calvinist doctrine was accepted by churches such as the Reformed and the Presbyterians.

Arminius opposed Calvin, maintaining that the redemption of the cross was for everyone who freely chooses to accept it. Those who then turn away from God lose their salvation, unless they confess and return to His saving Grace. Arminian doctrine was accepted by the Methodists.

Which side of this debate do you accept?

If you accept the Calvinist position, attempt to address a passage of scripture that *appears* to support your side (God has already chosen who will be saved).

If you accept an Arminian position, perform an exegesis of a passage of scripture that *appears* to support the idea that anyone can be saved via an act of free-will acceptance of Jesus.

Contribute to this discussion at
http://forums.delphiforums.com/rel101

CHAPTER 9

THEOLOGIANS CIRCA 1600				
APPROACH	CALVIN	ARMINIUS	JANSEN	JESUITS
Where?	Geneva	Holland	Belgium	Spain
Catholic?	no	no	yes	yes
Denominational impact	Presbyterians, Puritans, Pilgrims, Reformed	Methodists, Salvation Army	declared heretical	Catholic
Free will	no	yes	no	yes
Predestination	yes	no	yes	God knows what each one will decide
Human nature	depraved	fallen	depraved	fallen
Salvation open to	a few	all	a few	all
Salvation secured?	forever	can be lost by sin		can be lost by sin
Sinners	never were saved	must return to God		must return to sacraments

(Arminius greatly influenced one Anglican priest, John Wesley, 1703–1791, whose movement became known as **Methodism.**) Within the Catholic Church, the major opponents of Jansenism were the Jesuits who defended the doctrine of free will, arguing that God had created man with free will (and that's why Adam fell). Therefore, in order for God's grace to be efficacious, the individual must use his free will to work with Grace (through the sacraments of the Church). The Jesuit position was affirmed by Church councils, and Jansenism was declared heretical.

English **Puritanism** began when the Puritans were inspired by Calvin's desire to honor God by consecrating all of life to his kingship. Consequently, they tried to develop a theocratic state. Calvin's notions of God's sovereignty guided Jonathan Edwards, the first major American theologian, and through Edwards much of the Great Awakening (the revivalist movement that Edwards sparked in New England from 1740 to 1743) and subsequent American religious life bore a Calvinist imprint. Through the preaching of John Knox, Scotland also became a home to Calvinism, and when they came to America, Scottish immigrants brought their Calvinist tradition (called **Presbyterianism**) to

bear on business as well as Church life. Calvin's main work, *Institutes of the Christian Religion*, became the leading text of Reformed (i.e., Calvinist) doctrine, while his efforts to establish a Reformed commonwealth in Geneva provided a model for other communities seeking to live by the gospel.

One recurring theme among all of these aforementioned reformers has been the desire to get back to original Christianity. That usually involves stripping away some of the accretions that have characterized the Roman Catholic Church over the centuries. For the Eastern Orthodox, it was diminishing the authority of Rome. For Luther, it was rejecting indulgences and monasteries and celibacy. **Baptists** strip away all of these and infant baptism. The different forms of Baptists (or *Anabaptists*) that have arisen over the past five hundred years have very little in common doctrinally (there are those who affirm free will and those who affirm predestination), but they agree on the importance of baptism by immersion as a ritual of adult initiation.

From the mid-sixteenth to the mid-seventeenth century, religious wars ravaged much of Europe. The Edict of Nantes (1598) preserved the status quo:

Ignatius Loyola, Basque founder of the Jesuit Order of Catholic priests

Protestant areas would remain Protestant, Catholic areas (the majority) would remain Catholic. In the Netherlands, the wars had the character of a rebellion against Spain. The northern Netherlands became largely Protestant, while the southern Netherlands remained under Spanish power and so Catholic. Germany was the most furious battlefield. Until the Peace of Munster (1648), there was constant carnage. The upshot in Germany was the famous dictum: each area would follow the religion of its prince.

In England, **Henry VIII** found the Reformation currents useful in his struggle with the papacy to have his marriage to Catherine of Aragon annulled. Henry declared the king supreme in all matters that touched the Church in England, and he eagerly took monastic lands and income to finance his war against France. (This church became known as the **Anglican** "Church of England," or the Episcopalian denomination in the U.S.) From 1553 to 1558, Mary Tudor made England Catholic again, but in 1571, under Henry's daughter Elizabeth I, the English bishops published their

Thirty-Nine Articles of Faith, which formalized their special blend of Protestant doctrine and Catholic ritual.

CATHOLIC REFORM. The Catholic response to the Protestant Reformation took place at the Council of Trent (1545–1563). Trent affirmed the reliance of the Church on both scripture and tradition, the effective power of the sacraments, and the possibility of sin after justification (denied by some reformers). It also provided for reforms in clerical education and a general housecleaning to remove the laxness and venality that had made the reformers' charges more than credible. Probably the most powerful single agent of the Catholic Reformation was the Society of Jesus (the **Jesuits**), which Pope Paul III approved in 1540. Its founder was **Ignatius of Loyola** (1491–1556), a Basque. Ignatius' companions quickly demonstrated themselves to be the best combination of learning and zealous commitment around. Therefore, they were assigned many of the tasks of teaching and missionizing that were central to Catholic renewal. Peter Canisius in Germany, Robert Bellarmine in Italy, and Francisco Suarez in Spain were intellectuals and educators (the first two also became prelates) who had a great deal to do with revitalizing Catholicism in their countries. Jesuit missionaries to Asia such as Francis Xavier, Matteo Ricci, and Roberto di Nobili also had great success. Xavier was a charismatic figure able to stir crowds without even knowing their language. Ricci and di Nobili took on the customs of the people with whom they worked (Chinese and Indians) and confronted the vast task of forming indigenous versions of Christianity. Jesuits also ministered underground to Catholics in England (several lost their lives in the effort), and they went to the New World to missionize Canada, the American Southwest, and Latin America.

WORLDVIEW

NATURE

Christianity's Greek and Israelite sources both gave Christianity a realistic orientation toward the natural world. Moreover, the body of Jesus, insofar as Christian doctrine made him the Logos incarnate, was an anchor to realism. Against the Gnostics, who were their foremost adversaries, the early Christian writers insisted on the reality and goodness of matter. If God himself had made the world, and God's own Son had assumed flesh, both the world and human flesh had to be good. Nonetheless, because of the early controversies about the being of God and Christ, the word *physis* (nature) connoted divine and human "whatness" more than it connoted external reality. During the early controversies about free will and sin, Christian speculation finally concluded that the redemption and salvation that Christ had worked were beyond that to which human beings had any right. Thus, they were supernatural gifts that came only by grace. Grace, it followed, was a generosity that God does not owe us. Furthermore, redemption and salvation so transformed human nature that it could share in God's own divine nature (2 *Peter* 1:4). By itself, apart from grace, nature was unredeemed, unsaved, something far from the glory of divinity. These doctrines dominated classical Christian theology (Catholic, Orthodox, and Protestant alike).

As for creation, God stands to the world as its independent, uncaused source, who made it from nothing by his simple free choice. The first mark of the natural world for the traditional Christian, then, has been its subordination to divine creativity. Considerable time passed before the full conceptualization of creation as a Divine making of the world from nothingness developed (from a combination of biblical and philosophical sources), but from the beginning the God of the burning bush was sovereignly free.

In most periods of Christian history, nature was considered mysterious and overpowering, but the *Genesis* story that God gave human beings dominion over nature shaped a doctrine that the physical world existed for humanity's sake. Thus Christianity has taught its followers to husband the physical world and use it. Little in the Christian message proposed that human beings should ravage the world, but equally little proposed integrating human life with nature's ecology or preserving nature's gifts through frugality and reverence. In most periods Christians found nature abundant and generous, so conservation was not a major concern.

Furthermore, the biblical fear of nature gods contributed to a semiconscious Christian effort to make nature undivine. In rural places (among European peasants, for instance), this effort succeeded only partially. Overall, though, it was quite central to the Christian theology of creation. Coming from God,

the world was good. But since it came from God by his free choice, springing from nothingness, the world was definitely not divine. Thus, the Christian interest in transforming human nature combined with a continuance of the biblical prophets' objection to the nature gods; thus, the physical world was made a subordinate, even a somewhat ambivalent, concept. Inasmuch as nature and the human body could seem antagonistic to the spiritual destiny of human beings, nature could seem something that human beings had to restrain and control.

SCIENCE. The relative profanity (nonsacredness) that Christians attributed to nature played a rather complex role in the rise of Western science. When the Greek protoscientists, or early natural philosophers, developed a primitive demythologizing of nature, they established the principle that the physical world is open to rational investigation. Thus, it was not blasphemous to pry into nature's secrets, and it could be profitable: Nature yields valuable information to those who pry well.

In Christian hands this demythologizing went several steps further. Pre-Renaissance scholars (many of them monks) worked at what we would call physics or biology, although such work was subordinated to theology. In other words, the basically religious culture preceding the Renaissance determined that theology would be the queen of the sciences. Thus, before the Renaissance, the Catholic Church kept physical science on a rather short leash. The controversy that the new theories of Galileo Galilei (1564–1642) raised shows the Church attitude that still prevailed in the seventeenth century: the doctrine of **geocentric order** had to predominate over the **heliocentric order** supported by the evidence of the senses. Shoring up theological notions (that the earth was the center of the universe was a theological axiom) was more important than allowing intelligence the freedom to investigate nature as it would.

SACRAMENTALISM AND MYSTICISM. Christian sacramentalism has somewhat closed the gap between the place of nature in Christian religion in contrast to pagan religion that was opened by the Western separation of reason from myth. As well, Christian mystics played a large role in the Middle Ages. An example would be figures such as St. Francis who have sensed a divine presence in woods and birds have been rather naturalist in their style. In its worship and sacramental theology, Christian religion often has pressed the scriptural reference that God called creation good. Often, it has applied a mythic and poetic intelligence that made the world mysterious, awesome, and alive. Baptismal water, eucharistic bread and wine, wax, incense, flowers, salt, oil—they have all enriched the liturgy. On the most solemn feast of Easter, the liturgy spoke as though all of creation got into the act, joining in the Exultet—the song of great rejoicing. In the liturgy of Good Friday, which commemorates Christ's death, the tree of the cross (the holy rood) became a new *axis mundi*—a new cosmic pillar linking heaven and earth. Taking over Psalm 150, Christians praised God in his firmament. Taking over other psalms, they made the mountains and the beasts coconspirators to God's praise. All creation, then, was to resound to the music of the spheres. All creation ought to sing as it labored for redemption. Nature was part of a divine drama, part of a cosmic play of sin and grace. Partly from such liturgical encouragement, Christian mystics have often shown a delight in nature like that of their East Asian counterparts. The accents have been different, since the Christian God is not the impersonal Buddha-nature, but they have not been contradictory. For instance, Francis of Assisi felt free to praise God as manifested in nature, and he composed famous canticles to "brother sun" and "sister moon." For the early desert fathers, the wilderness was a place to become sanctified. For many Puritans and early Americans, the wilderness brought to mind Israel's wanderings in the desert—the place where its religion was pure. Thus, a romantic strain of Christian thought has kept nature close to God. Sometimes it has made the city less desirable for religious life than the country. Often it has made solitude close to the elements a privileged place for prayer. As a result, the Christian God has been strong as the seas, everlasting as the hills, lovely as the lilies of the field.

SOCIETY

Central to the Christian notion of how people ought to join together has been the Church. It could oppose the state, standing as the religious collectivity against the secular. It has also been the place where Christian life was supposed to show itself as something mysteriously organic—as the "body" of Christ. In the

earliest periods of church history, before Christianity became the official church of the Roman empire, church leaders led quite unpretentious lives. Meetings of the community tended to be small gatherings in members' homes, and the bishop who led the liturgy might earn his bread as a cobbler or a craftsman. New Testament models suggested that carpentry (the occupation of Jesus) and tentmaking (the occupation of Paul) were more than honorable occupations. The decision to have deacons care for temporal affairs (*Acts* 6:1–6) suggests that Christians quickly established a hierarchy of tasks parallel to the hierarchy of Christian authorities.

POLITY. Christian society has centered on worship through Word and Sacrament. Still, its structural organization was rather fluid at first and varied from place to place. In those early arrangements we can discern elements of all three of the later Church polities: the episcopal, presbyterial (of the elders), and congregational forms of Church government. With time, though, came the monarchical structure of Roman Catholicism, the collegial model of Orthodoxy, and the government by elders that has characterized much of Protestantism. In the West before the Reformation, the structure of the Catholic Church was pyramidal. At the top was the Pope, along the bottom were the laity. In between, in descending order, were cardinals, bishops, and priests. The "religious" (those who had taken vows of poverty, chastity, and obedience, usually in the context of a communal life) were in the middle, though technically most religious groups had both clerical and lay members. Status, naturally and unbiblically enough, was accorded those at the top. Thus, the Council of Trent, reacting against Reformation notions that all Christians are "saints," denounced any diminution of virginity in favor of marriage. As a result, for many Roman Catholics the Church long meant the clergy. That was less true for the Protestants and Orthodox, because their theologies stressed, respectively, the "priesthood" of all Christians (lay and cleric) and the mystical union of all Christians with Christ their head.

WOMEN'S STATUS. In principle, the Christian Church was democratic in that all people, regardless of sex, race, or background, were welcome. Each church member had her or his own gift from God, and each was a unique reflection of God. Thus, there was the Pauline dictum (*Gal.* 3:28) that in Christ there is neither Jew nor Greek, male nor female, slave nor free. In practice, however, women have been second-rate citizens in all branches of Christianity. Neither the Catholic nor the Orthodox churches would ordain women (that remains the case), nor would many Protestant churches. By associating women with Eve, the cause of Adam's fall (1 *Tim.* 2:14), the Church often suggested that they were responsible for human misery and sin. Thus, the fulminations of ascetics (usually celibate males) against women's wiles were a staple of the literature on how to avoid sin.

From the New Testament, men could buttress their supremacy by citing Pauline texts (*Eph.* 5:22–23; 1 *Tim.* 2:11–12) stating that wives were subordinate to their husbands and ought to keep silent in church. From the patristic age they could draw on what we can only call the misogyny of Jerome, Chrysostom, Tertullian, and others, who portrayed woman as the gateway to hell. Augustine, perhaps from his personal experience of concubinage, made sexual congress the channel of original sin. Medieval theologians, such as the Dominican authors of the *Malleus Maleficarum* (Hammer of Witches) cited witches as the cause of much psychological imbalance. In the name of preserving the Church, its authorities tortured and killed thousands of witches. Moreover, the Reformation did not relieve women's plight. Luther thought that woman's vocation was to "bear herself out" with children, while John Knox trumpeted against "petticoat" power in the Church. Reformation biblicism, then, meant merely a return to the patriarchy of the scriptures.

With a patriarchal God and an ambivalent role model in Mary the Virgin Mother, Christian women for the most part heard and obeyed, keeping any dissent to themselves. They had some measure of religious self-expression in their convents, and some of them gained leadership roles in the Protestant sects, but from the standpoint of today's egalitarian sentiments, their fate through most periods of Christian history was quite dismal.

CHURCH AND STATE. The Christian view of society outside the Church varied over time. According to the New Testament book of *Revelation*, Roman society was a beast that the coming Messiah had to slay if the earth were to become worthy of God. During the Roman persecutions, which some recent scholarship

has downplayed, this view was influential. As a result, earthly life was held cheap compared to heavenly life. When the Church gained security with Constantine, it changed its tune. Eusebius, for instance, virtually ranked Constantine with the twelve apostles. In reaction against this secularization, as we noted, the monastic movement restored the tension between time and eternity. The Western father Tertullian cast doubt on the worth of secular culture, asking what Athens had to do with Jerusalem. However, other patristic figures, such as Clement of Alexandria and Augustine, recognized that Christianity needed an intellectual respectability if it were to prosper, so they started to give their theology an infrastructure of Greek philosophy. By the medieval period, a certain harmony was achieved, as most of the culture was formed in accordance with Christian ideals (if not practice). There was a balance between reason and revelation, between emperor and pope. In practice, however, the competition between the emperor and the pope was fierce, for each tended to claim ascendancy over the other. Consequently, church leaders such as Ambrose and Hildebrand, who stood up to kings or even brought them to heel, were accounted great heroes. In the Christian East, however, the emperor had more clearly God given rights.

The Reformation depended in good measure on the political power plays of its day. Through application of the principle that a region would follow the religion of its ruler, a great deal of religious power returned to the local prince. Theologically, Luther tended toward a dualism of powers, religious and secular, whereas Calvin promoted a theocratic state in which citizens would live under Christian law. Thus, the Reformation did not initially encourage the modern pluralistic state.

SELF

The conceptions of nature and society that we have sketched here suggest the Christian view of the self. The biblical teaching that God placed human beings over nature has meant to Christians that the human person is of much greater value than the plants and animals. Furthermore, as Christian social theory interacted with the secular elaboration of human nature through Western history, the individual acquired greater stature than in Asia. In Asia, as in ancient societies generally, the group predominated over the individual.

One was most importantly a member of a tribe and only secondarily a unique person. As an image of God, the individual was more significant under Christianity. Of course, at times both secular and religious authorities crushed individuals ruthlessly. Nonetheless, because they bore the life of Christ, individuals commanded respect. In matters of ethics, for instance, the notion of individual conscience counterbalanced the finespun codes of the canon lawyers and the moral theologians. The sacrament of **penance** epitomized this, for penance was essentially a self-accusation in which the individual, helped by the Church's representative, passed judgment on his or her standing before God.

By standing out from nature and having personal rights, the Christian individual was conscious of being a unique self. Historically, the Church did not lay great emphasis on fulfilling one's unique self by communing with nature, but it did lay great emphasis on fitting into the social body of Christ. In fact, the charity of the community united was to be the primary sign of God's presence. Beyond social fulfillment, however, Christian theology encouraged the self to commune with divinity itself—with the Father, Son, and Holy Spirit. During the biblical period that meant putting on the "mind of Christ." During the Patristic Age it meant that grace was considered a share in divine nature and that religion was a process of divinization. Since the Hellenistic divinity was above all immortal, religion was also a process of immortalization. In medieval speculation, the self's fulfillment was the "beatific vision." By directly perceiving God's essence, our human drives to know and love (Augustine's famous "restless heart") would find a restful bliss. For the Thomists, participation in the divine nature through grace meant sharing in the "missions" of the Son and Holy Spirit. Thus, one's contemplation, knowing, and loving flowed into and out from the dynamic relations that characterized God's own inner life. The Reformation returned to biblical emphases, sending people to study the Word and to work in the world. For Orthodoxy the Divine Liturgy, with special accents on the Holy Spirit and the Mother of God, nourished one throughout life. In many periods, Christians never quite found the balance between life in the world and life that looked to heaven as its true home. Before the Reformation, Christians probably gave greater emphasis to the latter. Since the Reformation and the Enlightenment,

they have emphasized social and political commitments in the world.

RELIGIOUS DEVELOPMENT. Stressing communion with God, traditional Christian spiritual masters developed certain models of what happens in the life of the serious religious person. One of the most influential traditions involved the "three ways" that the self would travel. First, one had to walk the purgative way, which meant purging oneself of sin and developing virtuous habits. Then one would enter the long way of illumination, by which the Christian Word and Sacrament would slowly become one's own. No longer would they be external concepts—in time they would become inner principles of judgment and action. Finally, consummating the spiritual life was the unitive way, by which the self would unite with God as in a deep friendship or even a marriage. Occasionally such union would produce experiences of rapture, and then one could speak of mysticism strictly so called ("infused contemplation"). Clearly, then, the paradigm of the three ways depended on the notion that final fulfillment was communion with God. The saints who modeled Christian selfhood tended to be wholeheartedly given to communion with God. They also had to manifest charity for their fellows, but the spotlight was on their love of God. Because solitude or monastic withdrawal seemed to foster love of God, by allowing the freedom of deep, leisurely prayer, most saints went outside of family or civic life to lose themselves in devotion. That was the pattern up to the Reformation, and it took Christian selfhood some distance from the New Testament's view that prayer is important but not dominant. Still, as the world became more important, the concept of saintliness expanded to include the service of other human beings. The Church had always honored certain holy married people, certain holy civic leaders, but by late medieval times it had to contend with a more dynamic society.

SIN. Related to the capital question of what the self should most value is the complicated Christian teaching about **original sin** (most developed in Western Christianity—Eastern Christianity has not stressed original sin to the same degree). At its crudest, the teaching said that all people not baptized were in thrall to Satan and on the road to hell. Hell was essentially the deprivation of God (the loss of the beatific vision), but because of a gruesome imagery of fire and brimstone, it was popularly conceived of as a place of physical suffering. The ceremony for infant baptism, then, contained an exorcism of Satan—to save the little one from evil and make it pure for God. (Unbaptized babies who died before reaching the age of responsibility, and so before the possibility of personal sin, went to limbo, a state of "natural" happiness without beatific vision. Although limbo was never a matter of fully official Church teaching, it exerted considerable influence.)

A key moment in the development of the doctrine of original sin was Augustine's reading of the Fall as a social act. Adam's sin had alienated all human beings from God, for Adam was the head of the entire race. Augustine took the seeds of this view from Paul (for instance, *Rom.* 5:12–14). It suggested that Christ is the head of a new holy race, but that those not baptized into Christ belong to an old human nature destined for punishment.

The classical Protestant thinkers owed a great deal to Augustine; thus, their reform of theology emphasized original sin. Like Augustine, they interpreted *Genesis* and Paul rather literally, thinking in terms of corporate sinners and saints. The famous double predestination of Calvinism was an attempt to explain human beings' different fates (going to hell or heaven), as members of Adam or members of Christ, without removing the mystery of God's creative vision and providence. Those whom God has destined for heaven will surely end up there. Likewise, whom God has set for hell will fall into the flame.

In a fateful development of Calvinistic predestination, the signs of election to heaven became outward decorum and even material prosperity. That meant the double burden of being both poor and damned and the double blessing of being both rich and saved. Eventually more careful Bible readers recognized that this correspondence contradicted the Sermon on the Mount, but a lot of Calvinists thoroughly enjoyed storing up plenty in their barns and letting their souls wax fat. How inherently wicked or good the self is was an important question in the Reformation debates between Protestants and Catholics. Protestants, following Luther's stress on justification by "faith" and Calvin's stress on God's sovereignty, tended to emphasize the corruption of human nature through sin. Catholics, partly in reaction to that Protestant position and partly from their own emphasis on the sacraments and the Incarnation, saw an essential goodness in human nature (though they spoke of sin as darkening the mind and weakening the will). Clearly, though, Christianity made the West suspicious of human intuition. Many Christians were indoctrinated that they were virtually bound to be wicked sinners. Often that led them to oscillate between self-punishment and, in compensation, self-indulgence. However, most were taught that through penance one could experience God's mercy—the almost delicious sense of being loved gratuitously. Then the Johannine promise (1 *John* 3:20)—that even when our hearts condemn us God is greater than our hearts—could break out into joyous effect.

The Pauline discussion of sin and grace in terms of "flesh" and "spirit" focused Christian understanding of the self as embodied. That Paul's original language did not intend a matter-spirit dualism was almost forgotten after Christianity took up Greek thought. As a result, extremists tended to deprecate the body, marriage, and the world of human affairs as fleshly pursuits. In response to the Manichean and Albigensian heresies, the Church affirmed the goodness of the body, but the Church's general orientation toward heaven, its introduction of celibacy for holders of high Church offices, and its preference for ascetic saints tended to make the average person regret his or her flesh. For women, this caused considerable suffering, because the male Church teachers often projected their sexual problems onto women. In that case, women became by nature wanton, seductive, and dangerous.

On the other hand, a certain realism about worldly life, in which imperfection if not sin was inevitable, tended to soften this rigorism. Christian moral theologians have usually taught that sins of the flesh are less grievous than sins of the spirit (such as pride, anger, or hatred). And, although at one point Roman Catholic moralists classified all sexual offenses as serious ("mortal" as opposed to "venial" sins), there were usually effective if unauthorized counterforces in the bawdiness of Chaucer and Boccaccio and the frequent concubinage of members of the clergy.

ULTIMATE REALITY

The first Christian conception of God was Jewish. Jesus himself accepted the God of the Fathers—Abraham, Isaac, and Jacob. This God, as we have seen, interacted with human beings and was personal.

His guidance of humanity peaked in his liberation of Israel from Egypt and his covenanting with Israel on Mount Sinai. As numerous theologians have pointed out, it was difficult for Jesus to designate himself as divine, because to do so would have confused his identity with that of his "Father." In other words, the God of the Jews was Jesus' Father, his source.

In dealing with the revealed God's inner nature, the concept of the Trinity became paramount. Orthodox catholic (universal) doctrine held that Father-Son-Holy Spirit was attested by the scriptures and defined by the councils. Thus, the God of Christian speculation was perfection, in need of nothing outside himself. He was the Creator and Redeemer, moved only by his own goodness. The Incarnation was the main instance of his outpouring, but glimpses of God abounded everywhere. Subhuman creatures were his "vestiges" (footprints); human beings were his images. Christians were images of his great Image, for they reflected the eternal icon, the Logos-Son. Regarding the Trinity, Christians stood in the Son's position, receiving their likeness to God from the Father and expressing it through Spirit-carried love. The similitude broke down, however, because the divine persons were only relationally distinct (that is, Son and Father differed only as begotten and begetter), while humans remained creatures distinct from God.

BIBLICAL RENEWAL. When Reformation thought returned to biblical conceptions as it found the medieval synthesis too abstract and unhistorical, it revived the notion that "faith" is a living interpersonal relation to God, an ongoing commitment. Between the time of Luther and the nineteenth century Danish theologian Søren Kierkegaard, such "faith" became paradoxical—a leap. Kierkegaard jumped into the intellectual abyss, proposing that what reason could not fathom divinity could yet do, because it moved by reasons the mind knew not, by reasons of the heart. The Hebrew notion of *hesed* (steadfast, merciful love), which kept God to his freely chosen covenant, encouraged Christians to trust that no situation in their lives was hopeless. If Ezekiel's God could raise dry bones back to fleshly life, Jesus' God could use even suffering and evil to his own inscrutable ends. Was not God's chosen way of salvation, the death of his only begotten Son, the surest sign that no one had

ever understood him? As the heavens are above the earth, so were God's ways above the ways of human beings. For that reason, the Reformers wanted only a Pauline formula: God's power and wisdom are Christ crucified.

In contrast to other religions' versions of divinity, Christian theology has stressed the personal, loving character of God that Jesus' flesh disclosed. Jesus was God in human terms. (He was also humanity fulfilled by union with divinity.) As a result, Christianity did not appreciate the impersonal divinity of nature so dear to East Asian and Indian thought. This divinity was implicit in Christian theology, but the personalistic emphasis placed it in the shade.

At its better moments, Christianity was grateful to Judaism, since it had adopted most of Judaism's doctrine of God. As well, it was mindful of the continuing election of Israel that Paul had proclaimed (*Rom.* 9–11). At its worst, Christianity condemned Jews as Christ killers and spoke of their responsibility for Christ's blood. Islam confronted Christianity with claims of a later, perfected revelation and prophecy, and with an adamant insistence on God's unity. For Islam, and for Judaism, the Christian doctrine of the Trinity violated monotheism. Christian claims that God is both one and three seemed to Muslims and Jews incoherent, while Christian allegiance to Jesus clashed with Muslim allegiance to the Qur'an and Jewish allegiance to the Torah. Those clashes remain with us yet.

As the center of the Christian worldview, God in Christ dominated Christian conceptions of nature, society, and self. Nature was but God's cloak. It was a lovely gift, but it sprang from nothingness and was wholly under God's control. With each extension of space and time by science, the awe of the sophisticated increased: a more complex nature only magnified their God all the more.

Similarly, God was the norm and goal of Christian society, because his law was the source of all natural law and because eternal life with God in heaven was the goal of all people. God wanted human beings to form a community. Christ showed them the love that could bring that about. Thus, the vocation of the self was to obey the great twofold command: to love God with whole mind, heart, soul, and strength and to love one's neighbor as oneself.

COMPARISON OF BUDDHISM WITH CHRISTIANITY

DIMENSION	BUDDHISM	CHRISTIANITY
Country of origin	India	Israel
Century of origin	6th century B.C.E.	1st century C.E.
Founder	Gautama	Jesus
His title	the Buddha	the Christ
Social origin of founder	warrior caste	Galilean
Age at beginning of spiritual quest	29	30
Tempted by	Mara	Satan
Duration	40 days	40 days
Reaction to previous scripture	rejected Vedas	accepted Old Testament
Accepted local doctrines	karma and transmigration	sin, resurrection, and apocalypticism
Rejected	priestly rituals	priestly rituals, rigid interpretation
Proselytizing?	yes	yes
Followers from all social strata accepted?	yes	yes
Religion went to	East Asia	Roman Empire
Canon set	500 years later	300 years later
Decisions about canon and doctrine	Councils of monks	Councils of bishops
Doctrine infected by	Tantrism	Gnosticism
Mysticism preserved by	monastic orders	monastic orders
Mystical doctrine brought in from	Daoism	Platonism
Large vehicle of salvation	Mahayana	Catholicism
Small vehicle of individual salvation	Hinayana (Theravada)	Protestantism
Prophet 1800 years later who demanded a temple	Nichiren	Joseph Smith, Jr.

SUMMARY: THE CHRISTIAN CENTER

The Christian center is Jesus, for the God worshipped in the Christian liturgy, served in the Christian ministries, and crucial for the Christian Church is the Father known through the revelations of Jesus. In the New Testament (*John* 14:6) Jesus is the way. For the Christian monk, martyr, or layperson, Jesus has been the strong soldier in combat with Satan, the sacrificial victim dying for human beings' sins, or the good shepherd ever seeking his lost sheep.

The centrality of Jesus the Christ has meant that Christianity is supremely **incarnational**. Its theology, if not always its Church practice, has pivoted around the enfleshment of divinity. Orthodox and Roman Catholic Christians have developed this theology into rich sacramental rites. Protestant Christians have developed it into a profound reverence for the holy scripture.

SEPARATION OF THE CHURCH

flashcards and matching game
http://www.quia.com/jg/52666.html

jumbled words game
http://www.quia.com/jw/8669.html

millionaire game
http://www.quia.com/rr/41405.html

magic paragraph
http://www.quia.com/cz/13525.html

Now take an online practice quiz at
http://www.quia.com/session.html

For session enter
relquiz12

download multiple-choice, true-false, and fill-in drills from
http://www.ureach.com/tlbrink
click on the public filing cabinet and folder rel12
and download *m12.exe, h12.htm, t12.exe,*
and f12.exe
and crossword puzzle CW12.htm

ISLAM

ISLAM: 25 KEY DATES	
Date	Event
570 C.E.	birth of Muhammad
609–610 C.E.	first Qur'anic revelations
622 C.E.	Hejira: flight to Medina
630 C.E.	Muhammad returns to Mecca in conquest
632 C.E.	death of Muhammad
636–640 C.E.	conquest of Damascus, Jerusalem, Egypt, Persia
ca. 650 C.E.	establishment of the canon of the Qur'an
661–750 C.E.	Umayyad Caliphate
680 C.E.	murder of Husain, Shi'ite saint
711 C.E.	Muslims enter Spain
713 C.E.	Muslims enter Indus Valley
750–1258 C.E.	Abbasid Caliphate
762 C.E.	foundation of Baghdad
909 C.E.	rise of Fatimids in North Africa
956 C.E.	conversion of Seljuk Turks
966 C.E.	foundation of Cairo
1099 C.E.	Christian Crusaders capture Jerusalem
1111 C.E.	death of Al-Ghazzali, leading theologian
1258 C.E.	Mongols sack Baghdad
1453 C.E.	Ottoman Turks capture Constantinople
1492 C.E.	end of Muslim presence in Spain
1707 C.E.	decline of Mogul India
1803–1804 C.E.	Wahabism victorious in Mecca and Medina
1924 C.E.	secularization in Turkey
1947–1948 C.E.	creation of Pakistan and Israel

HISTORY

Islam is an Arabic word that means "submission, surrender" (to the will of *Allah*, God). **Muslim** is another Arabic word, this one meaning "one who submits," in other words, a follower of Islam. Muslims understand this God to whom they are submitting to be the same God described in *Genesis* and to whom Jesus prayed.

Islam is one of the best examples of a religion influenced by the place, time, and person who developed it. We will begin our discussion of Islam with the Arabs. Most, but not all, Arabs are Muslims. Outside Saudi Arabia, there are Arabs who still adhere to various Eastern Orthodox churches (such as the Maronite in Lebanon). Furthermore, most of the world's Muslims are not Arabs but Indonesians, Bangladeshis, Pakistanis, Afghanis, Turks, Uzbeks, Azerbajanis, Chechens, Bosnians, Albanians, Kosovars, Persians, and Africans. It is estimated that there will soon be more Muslims than Jews in the United States.

The place and time that influenced Islam were the western coast of the Arabian peninsula at the beginning of the seventh century of the common era. At that time, it was not the oil-rich region that we find in modern Saudi Arabia. The main economic activity of this area was trade: shipping across the Red Sea and camel caravans inland. This tribal society was rough and lawless. Some tribes functioned like modern street gangs trying to control the trade. If one

> *A mosque in Alexandria, Egypt.*

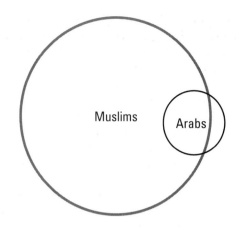

Most Muslims are not Arabs, but most Arabs are Muslims

group of bandits attacked a caravan and killed one of the drivers, the clan of the victim would resolve to take vengeance against some member of the clan of the (alleged) perpetrators. Clan deities were an important aspect of religious worship.

Arab religion at this time was animistic and polytheistic. Another term sometimes used to describe it was *polydemonistic*, since many of the deities or spirits worshipped did not claim divine status. Some of these were good, some evil. The evil spirits or demons had to be warded off with prayers, sacrifices, amulets, and spells. One aspect of polydemonism was a geographic worship of stones, stars, caves, and trees. As the drivers went through various places along the routes, they would have to stop, worship, and pay tribute (such routes were not unlike modern toll roads).

The city of Mecca had special status in this regard. It had very many and very important deities honored at a special shrine, a large black stone (possibly a meteorite) set in a shrine known as the Kaaba. This powerful symbol was explained by a myth: that this stone was first consecrated by the father of all Arabs, Ishmael and/or by his father, Abraham. (Recall that Abraham had a son before Sarah gave birth to Isaac. Abraham sired Ishmael through Hagar, the Egyptian handmaiden of Sarah.) A ritual of pilgrimage developed: Arabs who were passing through Mecca should stop at the Kaaba and worship. This ritual became so important that people were convinced they were obligated to come to Mecca to worship, even if they did not have a caravan journey that was passing through Mecca anyway. Some

of the local people may have longed for a purer approach to religion, but the Meccan city leaders knew that they had a great attraction to keep business going, and they jealously guarded against any threat to this shrine or the business it generated.

MUHAMMAD

It was into this milieu that **Muhammad** was born in 570 C.E. (His name is sometimes spelled Muhammed, Mohammed, or Mohamet). Little is known of his early life, except that he was born to a widow (his father died during his mother's pregnancy). He was brought up by uncles and he may have lacked much tribal protection. He had to work as a driver on the caravans. Competent and scrupulously honest, he came to the attention of one of the caravan owners, a wealthy widow named Khadijah. She gave him more responsibilities and when he was about the age of 25 she proposed marriage (she was 40). They had six children, of whom four daughters survived. This marriage was an important factor in his future career, not just economically, for it was his wife's support and encouragement that enabled him to pursue his religious motives.

Around the year 610, Muhammad began to receive revelations. He often slept in a cave and had visions (perhaps dreams). The revelations are explained by Islamic doctrine as the text of a divine book written by God in heaven, brought by the angel Gabriel, and recited by Muhammad. That book is known as the **Qur'an** (Koran). His first visions, according to the Qur'an (53:1–18, 81:15–25) were of someone "terrible in power, very strong." That person hovered near him on the horizon and imparted a revelation. It and subsequent revelations finally convinced Muhammad that God was choosing him to be a messenger, a prophet of God. Muhammad continued to receive revelations for the rest of his life (over twenty years), and those messages, which either he or early disciples wrote down on stones, palm leaves, and leather, form the basis of the Qur'an.

From earliest revelations given to Muhammad, five major themes emerge: God's goodness and power; the need to return to God for judgment; gratitude and worship in response to God's goodness and pending judgment; generosity toward one's fellow human beings; and Muhammad's own vocation to proclaim the message of goodness and judgment.

At first, Muhammad's proclamation met with considerable resistance, principally because it threatened some powerful vested interests. For example, the absolute monotheism of the Islamic vision of God threatened the traditional polytheism. However, his message was much more than just a challenge to custom and traditional religion—it was a mortal challenge to the commerce that had grown up around the Kaaba. The livelihoods of the merchants who sold amulets, the soothsayers who sold fortunes, and the semi-ecstatic poets who lyricized the old gods were all imperiled. Second, Muhammad's call for social justice implied a revolution—if not in contemporary financial arrangements, at least in contemporary attitudes. Third, the message of God's pending judgment was hardly welcome, for no age likes to find itself set before divine justice, hell fire, or the sword of retribution. Last, many Meccans ridiculed Muhammad's notion of the resurrection of the body and apocalyptic images of judgment day.

RISE TO POWER. Initially rejected, Muhammad drew consolation from the fate of prophets who had preceded him. Increasingly, it appears, he learned about Judaism and Christianity from followers of those traditions who either lived in the area or traveled it for trade. The first converts to Muhammad's revelations came from within his own family. When he started to preach publicly, around 613, the leaders of the most powerful clans opposed him vigorously. He thus tended to be most successful among the low-ranking clans and those with young leaders ripe for a new order. Also, those who were considered "weak" (without strong clan protection) found the new prophecy attractive. Muhammad was proposing a religious association based on commitment to Allah that transcended clan allegiances and so might make the weak stronger.

In 619, Muhammad suffered a personal crisis. His wife and uncle, who had been his foremost supporters, both died. Local pressures against him mounted in Mecca. He left, taking a small but loyal band of Meccan followers with him. In 622, he went to Yathrib, to the north, to arbitrate a longstanding dispute between two leading tribes. He settled the dispute with a revelation, and both parties were so impressed that they invited him to remain. The town became Medina, the town of the Prophet.

Muslims call Muhammad's departure or flight from Mecca the **Hejira,** and they view it as the turning point in the history of early Islam. Muhammad became the religious and political leader of Medina. He organized the Meccans who had followed him and the Medina clans into a single group. In Medina he developed a blueprint for a Muslim state.

One problem for Muhammad in Medina was the local Jewish community. Initially, he expected them to recognize him as a modern prophet of the one true God, the God of Abraham, Isaac, and Jacob, the God of the Jews. However, they refused to accept him as a genuine prophet and ridiculed his interpretation of the Hebrew scripture. In the falling out that followed, the Medinans have been accused of driving out the local Jews, or killing them, or selling them into slavery.

After consolidating his power base and building support among the neighboring Bedouin tribes, Muhammad started to challenge his old foes at Mecca. He disrupted their trade in an effort to overturn the city's commercial base, and in 624 his vastly outnumbered troops won a surprising victory at Badr. Finally, after several further skirmishes, Muhammad won a decisive victory at the Battle of the Ditch. Muhammad's greatest triumphs came through diplomacy among the tribes, however. Mecca finally fell in 630 without the stroke of a single sword. In control, Muhammad cleansed the Kaaba of pagan idols. He then consolidated his victory by a final military triumph over resistant Meccans at Hunayn. This settled the matter for most onlookers, and thenceforth the surrounding tribes were in Muhammad's hands.

In the two remaining years of his life, Muhammad further developed the educational program that he had set up in Medina. Muhammad soon became the focus of Arab solidarity throughout the peninsula, and just before his death, he apparently contemplated action against the Byzantine powers in the north, perhaps because Muslim nationalism meant a growing hostility toward the Greeks and their Christian Arab allies. The quick military victories of his successors make most sense on the assumption that they simply executed plans that Muhammad himself had formulated.

PERSONALITY AND RELIGIOUS IMPACT. Although critics have decried Muhammad's violence toward his enemies, he certainly demonstrated an abundant humanity. In addition to his religious sensitivity and his political and military skills, the Prophet apparently manifested a notable sympathy for the weak, a gentleness, a slowness to anger, some shyness in social relations, and a sense of humor. According to the *hadith* (a plural term for written traditions about Muhammad) one day the Prophet's second in command, Abu Bakr, started to beat a pilgrim for letting a camel stray. Muhammad began to smile and then indicated to Abu Bakr the irony that a pilgrim like Abu Bakr (a pilgrim through life) should beat a pilgrim to Mecca.

In glimpses obtained from the Qur'an and the earliest levels of the tradition, Muhammad seems to have been an ordinary man whom God singled out to receive revelations. Muhammad's virtue was to accept his calling and keep his commitment until death. The emphasis in the Prophet's own preaching on the sovereignty of God and the divine authority for the Qur'anic message led him to stress his own ordinariness, his liability to error, and the like. For example, at one point he thought that Muslims could compromise with Satan (the "Satanic Verses"), but then he realized that only God could receive Muslim devotion. He made no claim to miraculous power. The central miracle was the Qur'an itself—a message of such eloquence that it testified beyond doubt to a divine source.

In keeping with Muhammad's own humility, orthodox Islam has condemned any move to exalt Muhammad above ordinary humanity or to worship him as divine. (There are no statues of Muhammad for Muslims to bow down or pray to.) Nonetheless, popular Muslim religion sometimes seized on hints in the Qur'an and made Muhammad superhuman. The most famous of its images is Muhammad's "night journey" (miraculous flight) to Jerusalem, after which he ascended to Paradise, talked with the prophets who had preceded him, and experienced an ineffable vision of God. This story became so popular that it finally entered orthodox doctrine. Later traditions also elaborated on Muhammad's preaching of the coming Last Judgment and tended to think of the Prophet as its shield and intercessor on the Last Day.

QUR'ANIC RELIGION

After Muhammad's death, his followers collected the texts of his revelations and established the orthodox version of the Qur'an during the rule of Othman (644–656). However, since this version contained no indication of vowels or diacritical points, variant readings exist and are recognized by most Muslims as of equal authority. Most Muslims insist that the Qur'an be recited in Arabic. Muslims consider the Qur'an to be written in the purest Arabic, and therefore, the style of the Qur'an, as well as its message, shows that it must have come directly from God.

The present version of the collection of revelations follows the editorial principle that the chapters (*suras*) should be ordered in decreasing length. The result is that the present text tells the reader nothing about the chronology (or theme) of the revelations. While scholars have attempted to distinguish the Meccan utterances from the ones given at Medina, their work is often so refined (distinguishing separate verses within a *sura*) that no one theory of the chronology of the revelations has won universal acceptance. A probable early Meccan passage (96:1–5) emphasizes that Muhammad experienced his call as a command to recite, although what he was to recite only became clear as time passed. *Sura* 53, lines 1–18, richly symbolizes how Muhammad experienced his call. Because of Muhammad's vision of the angel Gabriel, the Muslim theology of revelation granted Gabriel an important role as the mediator in transmitting the Qur'an. In *Sura* 81, lines 15–29, are suggestions that Muhammad's early preaching met with rejection and even contempt. Indeed, the Prophet seems to have had to defend himself against the charge of *jinn* (demon) possession. *Suras* 73 and 74 buttress the tradition that Muhammad regularly used to go off to a cave to pray. Wrapped in a mantle against the night cold, he would seek God's comfort. This image has been a model for countless later Sufis and ascetics as they have sought an experiential knowledge of God. Other Qur'anic passages that are considered reflections of Muhammad's early experiences boom forth a praise of God, a sense of God's overwhelming majesty, that suggests Rudolf Otto's classic definition of the holy: the mystery that is both alluring and threatening.

The later passages of the Qur'an, those that likely were written in Medina, concern more practical matters. As the head of an established political and religious community, Muhammad had to deal with questions of law and order. Thus, we can find the seeds of later Islamic law on inheritance, women, divorce, and warfare. Generally, Muhammad's law and social teaching are advances on the mores of his day. They improved the lot of the downtrodden and humanized both business and war. For instance, Muhammad made widows and orphans the prime beneficiaries of the *zakat* (almsgiving) required of all Muslims. Two points on which outsiders frequently have faulted Muhammad and the Qur'an are the doctrines of holy war (*jihad*) and polygamy. Nevertheless, in both cases Muhammad's views were improvements on the pre-Muslim practices and benefited both women and prisoners of war.

THE FIVE PILLARS. On the basis of the Qur'an's prescriptions for Islam, a religion of submission to the will of God, Muslims have elaborated five cardinal duties known as the Five Pillars of Islam: (1) witnessing (proclaiming the creed), (2) ritual prayer, (3) fasting during the lunar month of Ramadan, (4) almsgiving, and (5) pilgrimage to Mecca. The witness of Islam epitomizes the Muslim's orientation in the universe: There is no God but God, and Muhammad is his Prophet. God is the only fit object of worship, and Muhammad is the last of the prophets—the "seal."

The rigorous monotheism of Islam has both negative and positive aspects. Negatively, in what amounts to an attack on false religion, Islam makes idolatry (associating anything with God) the capital sin. At the onset, then, Muhammad's revelation implied an attack on the prevailing Arab polytheistic idolatry. Later it led to a polemic against Christian Trinitarianism and a check on any worldly pride or Mammon that might diminish God's sovereignty.

Positively, Islamic monotheism generated great praise for the "Lord of the Worlds"—the Creator who guided all things, who was the beauty and power by which the world moved. For the later Muslim mystics, the words of the creed swelled with hidden relevance. Like the Jewish cabalists, some Muslim mystics assigned each letter a numerical value and then composed numerological accounts of how the world hung together. Some Muslim mystics pushed the concept of divine sovereignty so far that they denied the existence of anything apart from God. Not only was there no God beside him, there was no being apart from his Being. While the orthodox Muslims found such pantheism blasphemous, the mystics tended to stress the oneness of the Lord's domain. Last, rigorous monotheism implied that Muhammad himself was not divine. His high status was to be the prophetic mouthpiece. (In later devotion, as we have seen, there was a tendency to exalt Muhammad, while later theology often

viewed the Qur'an as co-eternal with God, much as rabbinic theology saw the Torah as co-eternal with God.)

In this clear statement of monotheism, Muhammad tried to cleanse the Arab psyche of its polytheistic impulses, but he himself accepted the existence of angelic spirits and *jinn*. The *jinn* and angels certainly were not on the same level as God, but they had influence in human life and had to be dealt with. Popular Islamic religion frequently remained quite involved with fighting the *jinn*, retaining longstanding notions about the influence of the evil eye and the need to protect oneself against bad spirits by prayers and regular submission of one's fate to the will of God.

The second pillar of Islam is prayer, which has worked out as an obligation to pray five times daily. Authoritative authors such as Al-Ghazzali went to great lengths to specify the postures, words, number of bows, and proper places and times for prayer, but the primary effect of the second pillar on the common people was to pace them through the day in the great Muslim practice of remembrance (*dhikr*). This linked with the Muslim conviction that forgetfulness (rather than intentional sin) was the main reason people disregarded God, fell into idolatry, violated the laws, and so on. Thus the Qur'an called for constantly remembering the goodness of God, the promises and favors God had vouchsafed, the teachings of the Prophet, and the like. The call to pray five times a day externalized the importance of *dhikr,* and in general much Islamic spirituality sought to keep the disciple in the presence of the Qur'anic word or attentive to the presence of God to both human beings and the signs of physical nature.

At each call from the minaret (prayer tower), they were to remember the one God whom they served—remember his compassion, his mercy, and his justice. Ideally, by praying fervently at the appointed hours, one might forge a chain that linked together more and more moments of remembrance, so that God progressively came to dominate all one's thought, action, and emotion. Witnessing Muslim prayer is a moving experience. The slow chant of the Qur'anic words becomes haunting, stirring even the non-Arabist. The voice (usually recorded today) is passionate—a lover's near sob, a tremulous witness to God's grandeur.

Fasting is the third pillar. What the prayer times are to the day, the holy month of Ramadan is to the year.

Ramadan is the month of fasting and (interestingly enough) of celebration that helps give the year its rhythmic turning around God. This lunar based celebration moves around (akin to Easter), but it is not limited to just April. Ramadan may occur when the days are either short and cold or when they are long and hot, which means the severity of the exercise can vary considerably. Through all the daylight hours of Ramadan (from the time that one can distinguish a black thread from a white), no food or drink is to pass the lips. There is as much joy as penitence in this ritual, for there is feasting before dawn and after dusk.

The fast is supposed to discipline both body and mind, reminding all Muslims that their first obligation is to the will of God and that to fulfill the will of God they need to be masters of their own personal beings. Thereby, the Muslim learns discipline, sacrifice, and the price that divine treasures cost. In contrast to a secular succession of months, in which no time is finally more significant than any other, the Muslim acknowledges the special time of Ramadan, fencing off a portion of time as sacred.

The fourth pillar is pilgrimage. Islam has developed a similar paradigm of the sacred for space by praying toward **Mecca** and by the obligation to make a pilgrimage to Mecca (the Hajj) at least once in one's lifetime. For Muslims, Mecca is the center, the *omphalos* (navel) where the world was born. It is the holy city where Qur'anic revelation was disclosed to the world. Thus, the psychodynamics of the pilgrimage run deep. Without doubt, devout pilgrims understand that they are going to the holiest spot in creation.

On pilgrimage, Muslims dress alike, go through the same traditional actions tying their religion to that of Abraham, their spiritual father, and often experience an exhilarating sense of community. By going through ritual actions associated with Abraham, they dramatize their position that Islam is not an innovation but the religion that preceded Judaism.

The fifth pillar, almsgiving, focuses this sense of community in a practical, economic way. The *zakat* is not a charitable gift but a matter of obligation. How much it should be has varied with local custom (it might be one-fortieth part of one's wealth in some societies, while in others it might be 15 percent of a grain crop, but only 10 percent if irrigation is used). Everywhere it has symbolized the community all Muslims share and the obligations they carry to care for one

another. In Muhammad's day clan society had broken down, with considerable suffering for widows, orphans, and others who had no immediate family. The alms in the first place were aimed at helping such unfortunates, but it can also take the form of endowing hospitals, schools, and mosques. The Muslim alms, then, is more than a tiny dole or act of charity—it is an act of social, corporate responsibility. Furthermore, it reminds the advantaged that they are one family with the disadvantaged and that the stern Judge will demand a strict account of what they have done with his gifts.

THE AGE OF CONQUEST

At Muhammad's death in 632, most of Arabia had accepted Islam, though often the allegiance was superficial, as some tribes had been won over more by the political, economic, or military strength of Islam than by a pure attraction to the religious elements. Some tribes took the occasion of the Prophet Muhammad's death to attempt a revolt. General Khalid al-Walid, who served the first caliph (leader), Abu Bakr, crushed them within a year. Thus, when Abu Bakr died in 634, Arabia was united and poised for adventure. The obvious foes were Byzantium and Persia, which threatened Arabian prosperity and were ripe for religious and military conquest. The Muslim armies were amazingly effective. By the end of 636, they controlled both Damascus and Jerusalem. As important in this lightning conquest as their military skill, though, was the unrest of the peoples they conquered, who may have seen the Muslims as liberators from Byzantine exploitation. On the eastern frontier, Muslim armies spread into Persian territory, and by 649 all of Persia was in Arab hands.

The quick conquest of Syria released men for further expeditions in the west; by 640 there were conquests in Egypt. Alexandria soon fell, and despite resistance from the Roman emperor Constans, the Arabs established themselves as a marine power operating from the southeastern Mediterranean. By 648, they had conquered Cyprus; by 655, they were in charge of the waters around Greece and Sicily. On land in North Africa, the Muslims conquered the Berber region of Tripoli in 643 and then proceeded to Carthage and to the Nubian regions along the Nile, conquering the Nubian capital city of Dongola. When the Umayyad

Sura 19, entitled "Mary," shows some of the connections between the Qur'an and both Judaism and Christianity. The *sura* begins with an interpretation of the story of the birth of John the Baptist (Luke 1:5–80). Zacharias, the father of John the Baptist, approached God and prayed for an heir. He received the answer that he would have a son, to be called John, despite the fact that he and his wife were advanced in years. God instructed John to observe the scriptures with a firm resolve, bestowing on him wisdom, grace, and purity. John grew up to be a righteous man who honored his father and mother and was neither arrogant nor rebellious. So the Qur'an blesses the day John was born and blesses the day of his death.

Then Muhammad receives a command to recount the story of Mary, who left her people and betook herself to a solitary place to the east. God tells Muhammad that he sent to Mary the divine spirit in the semblance of a grown man. Mary saw the spirit and was seized with fear. But the spirit explained that he was a messenger of Mary's Lord, come to give her a holy son. When she asked how this could be, since she was a virgin, the spirit said that nothing was difficult to God and that this miracle was God's will. Thereupon Mary conceived. When her time of delivery came, she lay down by a palm tree, wishing that she had died and passed into oblivion. But a voice from below her cried out that she should not despair. God had provided her a brook to run at her feet, and if she would shake the trunk of the palm tree it would drop ripe dates in her lap.

Mary took her child to her people, who abused her as a harlot. So she pointed to the baby in the cradle, who spoke up and said: "I am the servant of Allah. He has given me the gospel and ordained me a prophet." The child explained that God had commanded him to be steadfast in prayer, to give alms to the poor, to honor his mother, and to be free of vanity and wickedness. God had blessed the day of his birth and would bless the day of his death.

The *sura* then makes a polemical point: This is the "whole truth" about Jesus, the son of Mary, which "they" (probably the Christians) are unwilling to accept. In other words, though Jesus had a marvelous birth, he was in no way the divine Son of God. Only God is Muhammad's Lord, and the Lord of Muslims. Therefore only God is to be served. That is the right path. Any other path is erroneous. Those who cling to the view of Jesus as a member of a divine Trinity (instead of being a mere human prophet, no higher than Muhammad) will experience woe on the day they appear before God, since they are in the grossest error (idolatry).

Next the *sura* takes up the story of Abraham. Abraham was a prophet and a saintly man. He asked his father, "How can you serve a worthless idol, a thing that can neither see nor hear?" Furthermore, he told his father to follow Abraham away from the worship of Satan, who had rebelled against the Lord of Mercy. But Abraham's father only became angry, banishing him from the house and threatening him with stoning. Abraham prayed that the Lord would forgive his father, but he departed, since he could not worship idols. God rewarded Abraham with sons called Isaac and Jacob, prophets of high renown.

The next story in the *sura* on Mary concerns Moses, who was a prophet, an apostle, and a chosen man. God called out to Moses from the right side of a mountain. When Moses came, Allah communed with him in secret and gave him his brother Aaron, also a prophet. Then there was Ishmael, also an apostle, a seer, and a man of his word. Ishmael enjoined prayer and almsgiving on his people, and thereby he pleased the Lord. Last there was Idris (Enoch), another saint and prophet, whom the Lord honored and exalted.

To all these men, God has been gracious. They are the line of prophets, from the descendants of Adam and the people God carried in the ark with Noah. They include Abraham and Israel (Jacob), Moses, David, and Jesus, and they stand out as the line God has guided and chosen. When they received divine revelations, these prophets humbled themselves, falling down on their knees in tears and adoration. In contrast, the generations that succeeded the prophets neglected prayer and succumbed to temptation. Assuredly they shall be lost.

However, those that repent, embrace what Muhammad is preaching, and do what is right will be admitted to Paradise. They shall not be wronged, but shall enter the Garden of Eden, which the Merciful has promised to his servants as their reward. What God has promised, God shall fulfill. In Paradise the just will hear no idle talk, only the voice of peace. Morning and evening they shall receive their sustenance. That is the bliss that the righteous shall inherit. The *sura* then interposes a strange transition: "We do not descend from Heaven save at the bidding of your Lord." Muslim commentators tend to interpret this as the voice of the angel Gabriel, answering Muhammad's complaint that the revelations he was receiving sometimes stopped, making for long intervals of silence. Gabriel reminds Muhammad that revelation like this is solely God's affair. To God alone belongs what is before us and what is behind us, and all that lies between.

Gabriel goes on to comfort Muhammad. His Lord does not forget his servants. God is the ruler of the heavens and the earth and all that is between them. Muhammad's task is simple: Worship him and be loyal in his service. After all, what god compares with God? To whom else can a sane or devout person go?

But all human flesh is weak, so human beings regularly ask, "When I am once dead, shall I be raised to life again" (resurrection)? God's answer is a call to remembrance and patience. Why do human beings forget that God once had to create them from the void?

Unless people put their lives in order, God will call them to account, placing them in the company of the devils, setting them on their knees around the fire of hell. Each sect of dissidents will have its stoutest rebels cast down into hellfire. God alone knows who most deserves to burn. God will deliver those who fear him, but wrongdoers will endure the torments of the fire. God will record every word of vain boasts and determine punishments long and terrible.

Again the *sura* lashes out at Christian doctrine, that God has begotten a son. That is such a monstrous falsehood that the heavens should crack, the earth should break asunder, the mountains should crumble to dust. Those who ascribe to God a son know nothing of the nature of the Merciful. It does not become him to beget a son. His sovereignty is beyond any such thing. For there is none in the heavens or the earth who shall not return to the Lord in utter submission. God keeps strict count of all his creatures. One by one, they shall all approach him on the Resurrection Day. Those he shall cherish are they who have accepted the doctrine Muhammad is preaching and shown charity to their fellows. Concluding, the *sura* has God remind Muhammad that he has revealed the Qur'an in Muhammad's own tongue so that Muhammad can proclaim good tidings to the upright and warnings to a contentious nation.

From reading this remarkable bit of the Qur'an, one senses the overwhelming sovereignty of Muhammad's God. Not to accept him exclusively is tantamount to blindness or utter corruption of heart. Muhammad finds this way prefigured in the prior prophets of Judaism and Christianity, who deserve high esteem. Jesus, the miraculous child of Mary, the great heroine of commitment to God's plan, was a worthy precursor. But the Christian notion that Jesus was God's son is sheer blasphemy, an effort to diminish the absolute uniqueness and sovereignty of God. The Creator is solely responsible for all that happens in the world. Those who confess this will merit good things in the Garden of Eden. Those who reject it will go to hell, the place of punishing fire and devils.

caliphate established itself in 661, the ventures became even more far-reaching. Soon Muslims were as far away as China, India, and western Europe. By 699, Islam occupied Afghanistan, while various campaigns south of the Caspian and Aral Seas brought Armenia, Iraq, Iran, and eastern India into the Muslim fold by 800.

At the beginning of the ninth century, Arab rule along the southern Mediterranean stretched from Palestine to the Atlantic. Muslims controlled three-quarters

Courtyard of Cairo mosque

J.T. Carmody

of the Iberian Peninsula, and most Mediterranean traffic had to reckon with Muslim sallies. European campaigns had brought Arab soldiers as far north as Orleans, and they strongly influenced the southern portions of the Frankish kingdom. In 732 Muslims had taken Toulouse and then the whole of Aquitaine, moving into Bordeaux and Tours. Charles Martel stopped them at Poitiers, but in 734 they crossed the Rhone and captured Arles, Saint-Remy, and Avignon. Then they fortified Languedoc and recaptured Lyons and Burgundy. In the ninth century, from their positions in southeastern France, they pushed northeast as far as Switzerland. By daring naval raids, they harassed such ports as Marseilles and even Oye on the coast of Brittany.

Toward the end of the ninth century, Islam controlled most of western Switzerland and ruled many of the Alpine passes. In the mid-tenth century Muslims were at Lake Geneva, taking Neuchatel and Saint Gall. Only the attacks of the Huns and the Hungarians

from the north and northeast and the deterioration of the Spain-based Umayyad caliphate kept them from ruling all of southern Europe. However, Muslim expansion ended after 1050, when the Normans pushed Islam out of southern France, southern Italy, Corsica, Sardinia, and Sicily.

By 1250, Islam's European presence had weakened considerably. Only southernmost Spain and eastern Anatolia (Turkey) held secure. However, Islam had spread through all of Persia, crossed northern India, and reached the western Chinese border. In East Asia, it had a discernible presence in Sumatra, Borneo, and Java. All of North Africa was securely Muslim, while down the East African coast as far as Madagascar it exerted a strong influence. In many of these regions, of course, substantial portions of the populations remained non-Muslim. For instance, in Egypt many Christians of the Monophysite and Coptic churches remained loyal to their own traditions, as did many Christians in Anatolia and Syria. Nestorian Christians in Iraq north of Baghdad held out, while portions of southern Persia remained Zoroastrian strongholds. In India the majority remained Hindu, especially in the central and southern regions.

MOTIVATIONS. Through this age of conquest and expansion, the basic Muslim strategy revolved around the use of the desert. Just as modern empires, such as the British, made great use of naval power, so the Arabs exploited their experience with the desert, using it for communication, transferring supplies, and retreating safely in time of emergency. In their spread through North Africa, they established main towns at the edge of the desert. In Syria they employed such conquered cities as Damascus to the extent that they lay close to the desert. Through the Umayyad period (to 750), these garrison towns at the edge of the desert were the centers of Arab government. By dominating them and by introducing Arabic as the language of government, the conquerors exerted a disproportionate influence (they usually remained a minority of the total population). The towns served as the chief markets for the agricultural produce of the neighboring areas, and around their markets clusters of artisan quarters developed. By imposing discriminatory taxes on the outlying populations, the Arabs encouraged the citizenry to congregate in the cities, making their control easier.

Religion served as a rallying point for the Arab cause. It stressed the common bond to a single Lord, and it dignified the Arab movement with a sort of manifest destiny. Certainly the generals who dominated the era of conquest were as accomplished in worldly affairs as they were in religion. For Khalid and Amr, two of the most outstanding, the utilitarian values of the Islamic expansion seemed to have been clear.

The Islamic administration of the conquered territories was also quite pragmatic. Rather understandably, the interests served were not those of the conquered subjects but those of the aristocracy that conquest created—the interests of the Arab rulers. Thus, the temper of the Arab military commanders and then of the quasi-military Arab governors most determined how Islam treated its new peoples. At the beginning of the conquest in Byzantium and Persia, Muslims kept the old administrative structures. In the 640s, though, they shifted to a new format, through which the caliphs could impress their will more directly.

However, at first there was no unified imperial law. The conquerors struck different bargains with different peoples, and some stipulated that local customs or laws remain in force. The Arabs tended to take only the property of the state (and that of the new regime's enemies); other landowners who were willing to recognize the new regime could keep their holdings provided they paid a sizable tax. Nevertheless, there were opportunities for Muslim "speculators," as we might call them, to gain lands outside the garrison center on which they would have to pay only light levies.

At first, the conquered peoples were allowed to retain most of their traditional civil and religious rights. The Muslims grouped most of the conquered non-Muslims together as *Dhimmis*—members of religions that Arab law tolerated. As "peoples of the book," Jews and Christians were *Dhimmis,* with title to special respect. There were nevertheless frictions, especially if Jews or Christians were blatantly derogatory of the Prophet Muhammad and his Book, but usually people were not compelled to convert to Islam. Because Arab rule regularly promised to be more just than Byzantine rule, many Jews and Christians are on record as having welcomed the change. For example, in Palestine the Samaritans actively assisted the invaders. The Arabs were not always sure how to handle such complicity, especially when it developed into a desire to convert to Islam. Islam and Arabism were so synonymous that the first converts had to become Mamali—clients of one of the Arab tribes. In fact, converts seldom gained status equal to born Muslims, especially regarding such material benefits as the booty that warriors received after a conquest.

INTERNAL STRIFE. Despite its enormous outward success in the age of conquest, the Islamic community suffered notable internal divisions. With the exception of Abu Bakr, the first caliphs, known as the rightly guided, all left office by murder. (Despite these assassinations, modern Islam has considered their time the golden age.) Ali, the fourth caliph, was the center of a fierce struggle for control. His main opponent was Muawiya, the head of a unified stronghold in Syria. Muawiya maneuvered to have the legitimacy of Ali's caliphate called into question. As a result, Ali lost support in his own group, and dissidents called Kharijites appeared who had a hand in many later conflicts.

A Kharijite killed Ali in 661, and the caliphate passed to the Umayyad dynasty—the followers of Muawiya.

However, Ali's influence did not end with his assassination. In fact, his assassination became part of Islam's deepest division, the one between the **Shia** (party), who were loyal to Ali, and the **Sunni** (traditionalists). The "party" supporting Ali maintained that the successors to Muhammad ought to come from Muhammad's family—in other words, that Islamic leadership should be hereditary. (As the cousin and son-in-law of Muhammad, Ali was his closest male relative and so his heir.) This conviction was supported by certain verses of the Qur'an, in which the Prophet supposedly indicated that Ali would be his successor. The Shia therefore consider the first three caliphs, who preceded Ali, as having been usurpers. After Ali's death, they took up the cause of his sons, Hasan and Husain.

The word that the Shia gave to the power that descended through Muhammad's family line was *imamah* (leadership). Through its history, the Shia has made it a cardinal doctrine that Muhammad's bloodline has an exclusive right to *imamah*. The slaughter of Husain in Iraq in 680 was an especially tragic event, and the Shiites (who have been strongest in Iran) have come to commemorate it as the greatest of their annual festivals. This has developed a religious consciousness dominated by suffering, persecution, and martyrdom. Another distinctively Shiite doctrine has been the expectation for a future prophet (**imam**) to consummate history. Although they are dominant in Iran and southern Iraq, Shiites have usually been the Islamic minority.

The majority did not follow Ali, but stayed within the **Sunni** (well-trod) path of traditionalism. The Sunnis have considered themselves both more traditional and more moderate than the Shia (or the later Sufis). They have tended to take the generally accepted principles of law and doctrine as the backbone of Muslim culture and to favor religious life that balanced between profession of the uniqueness of God and conviction that God had made the material world good for human beings to develop. Sunnis have predominated in most cultural areas other than Iran. Historically, they supported the view that the successors to Muhammad in leadership of the Muslim community need not be members of the Prophet's bloodline—a

position with some foundations in pre-Islamic Arab political custom. During the past quarter century, with strife in Lebanon, Iran, and Iraq, the relations between Shiites and Sunnis have been tense, even combative. Shiites and Sunnis share more doctrines and practices than they hold separately, although the Shiites do have certain distinctive doctrines, such as the expectation of the return of the hidden imam, and certain distinctive festivals, such as the commemoration of the martyrdom of the sons of Ali.

THE GOLDEN CIVILIZATION

The Umayyads had been auxiliaries of the Romans in Syria, so when they established the caliphate in Damascus in 661, they brought an enthusiasm for Hellenistic culture. In particular, they became patrons of the sciences. For example, in 700 they founded an astronomical observatory at Damascus. However, the Umayyads fell to the Abbasids in 749, Umayyad rule continuing only in Spain. The Abbasids set their caliphate in Baghdad and turned to Persian rather than Hellenistic culture, supporting the Persian specialties of medicine and astronomy. Al-Mansur, the second Abbasid caliph, was also devoted to learning, bringing Indian astronomers and doctors to Baghdad and having many Indian scientific treatises translated. Under his successors, translation continued to be a major project, any nation's heritage being fair game. As a result, many Greek treatises (for example, those of Galen and Ptolemy) became available to Muslims. Partly because of Babylonian and Zoroastrian influences, the Baghdad caliphs deemed astronomy especially important. They imported Indian mathematicians to help in astronomical calculations and made Baghdad a center of astronomical learning.

Al-Razi (865–925) collected voluminous lore on medicine from Greek, Indian, and Middle Eastern sources. Indeed, he may even have drawn on Chinese sources, for there is a story that he entertained a Chinese scholar who learned to speak Arabic, and his successors' works include what seems to be the Chinese doctrine of what one could learn from the body's pulses. A Muslim alchemy arose in the ninth century with Jabir ibn-Hayyan, but in Islam alchemy remained somewhat suspect because the authorities linked it with non-Muslim religion. Some radical Sufis became

Mosque in New Delhi

deeply involved in alchemy, but orthodox Sunni had the works of at least one such group, the "Brethren of Purity," declared heretical and burned. The orthodox Muslims had less of a problem with the rational geometry and science of the Greeks.

From 970, the Spanish branch of the Muslim Empire had a distinguished scientific center in Cordoba. Similarly, the religious authorities patronized science, especially medicine and astronomy, at Toledo from the early eleventh century. The Spanish Muslims tended to be critical of Ptolemy and to favor Aristotelian doctrines. **Averroes** (1126–1198), who lived in Cordoba at the same time as the Jewish theologian Maimonides, was a great Aristotelian synthesizer who composed a full philosophical corpus. By conquering the territory between the Muslim East and the kingdom of Sung China, the Mongols expedited trade and the flow of learned information between East and West. Marco Polo (1254–1324) was able to travel to the East because of Mongol rule, which also enabled

the Chinese Mar Jaballaha (1244–1317) to come West and become the Nestorian Christian patriarch. When the Mongols conquered China, they left its bureaucratic structure intact. They set up an observatory in Peking and staffed it with Muslims. In the West they conquered the Abbasid capital of Baghdad in 1258, where they continued to support astronomical studies.

Muslim art concentrated on architecture and ornamentation of the mosque rather than painting or sculpture. The preponderance of Muslim art during the golden age was nonpictorial, including rugs, vases, lamps, and mosques. It reached its peak in the sixteenth and seventeenth centuries, leaving impressive monuments in Ottoman Turkey, Safavid Persia, and Mogul India.

A distinctively Islamic calligraphy developed from the trend to decorate pages from the Qur'an. The Qur'an itself praises the art of writing (96:4) and speaks of being written on a heavenly tablet (84:2122).

The Taj Majal, a Muslim building from Mogul India. Muslim art, restrained from making images of God or Muhammad, focused on architecture.

The favorite script was Kufic, which originated in the new Islamic town of Kufa near Babylon, and it was the standard scriptural model from about the seventh to eleventh centuries. It is vertical, massive, and angular, while its prime alternate, the Naskhi script, is horizontal, flowing, and rounded. A favorite subject of embellishment has been the *Bismallah,* the prefix to the Qur'anic *suras* ("In the name of God"). Through an extension of calligraphic swirls and loops, Muslims developed an ingenious ability to suggest flowers, birds, lions, and so on. The Sufi interest in numerology also encouraged artistic work.

POETRY. Poetry had always held a place of honor among Arabs, for eloquence had always been considered a trait of a great man, even before the advent of Islam. The ancient poetry was born in the desert, so it was replete with desert images and themes. With expansion and conquest, however, Islam became largely an urban culture, so there was need to reshape its poetry. Meter, rhyme, and new imagery became the chief tools. The result was a very complex style. The thirteenth-century poet Ibn al-Khabbaza fashioned an elegy that epitomized Arab eloquence. The themes that dominate some poetic selections are not especially religious: the beauty of a beloved, trees, battle, and, for humor, the flanks and shanks of an ant.

Still, some of the religious mystics, such as Junaid, Rumi, and the woman Rabia, gained fame for their poetic skills. Most were Sufis—devotees of religious emotion and feeling. Among the religious poets of Islam, the Persians were most eminent. Their themes and images centered on the Sufi goal of self-effacement in the divine immensity. For instance, Rumi often portrayed the soul's sense of abandonment in moments of trial when it could not feel the divine embrace: "Hearken to this Reed forlorn, Breathing ever since 'twas torn from its rushy bed, a strain of impassioned

As we suggested, Islam also influenced architecture. The mosque was a sort of theology in the concrete. Muslim architects tried to embody the conviction that all of life stands subject to God and so that no great distinction should be made between sacred dwellings and profane. The guiding idea in the construction of a mosque was simply to house a space for prayer and prostration. The *hadith* reported that the Prophet led his first companions outside the city, so that they could pray together in an open space. At Medina, the usual place for prayer was the open courtyard of Muhammad's own house. For convenience, the architects tried to construct a churchlike building that had the character of an open space where many Muslims might go through the same rhythmic motions of bowing, kneeling, prostrating, and praying together.

Mosque architecture tended not to differ radically from that of Muslim palaces. Most of the renowned Muslim palaces have crumbled, but the Alhambra, in Granada, Spain, still stands, a glorious tribute to the Muslim golden age. The Alhambra was built between 1230 and 1354 and served as a great citadel for the Moorish kings. It was mutilated after the expulsion of the Muslims in 1492 but extensively restored from 1828 on. Its beauty suggests the Muslim notion of how religion and secular life ought to interpenetrate.

Physically, the Alhambra is located on a hill overlooking the city of Granada. Although it is surrounded by walls and has the look of a fort, only the lowest parts of the enclosure were actually used for military purposes. According to early Islamic tradition, palaces were supposed to be placed as the Alhambra is: close to the city, yet a little bit apart. Thus the Alhambra strikes us as a country villa, yet also like an urban citadel. One gets the same impression from similar palaces in Aleppo (northwest Syria) and Cairo. There, too, the effort was to retain the amenities of a royal palace while fortifying the ruler's residence against possible incursions. Such military considerations led to architectural innovations in the vaulting, gateways, and towers of the urban citadel.

The Alhambra goes beyond a simple fusion of the villa and citadel traditions, however, by breaking its sizable area into a series of separate units. Some of these units are lovely gardens, in the Muslim paradisiac tradition. For example, both Iranian and Indian Muslim palaces frequently sought to prefigure Paradise by developing lovely royal gardens. Of the other units of the Alhambra, the most celebrated is the Court of the Lions. The Court of the Lions has an impressive portico running along several sides, with slim, delicate pillars supporting strong arches. The open space in the center is handsomely tiled, and a small fountain with flowers at the base adds splashes of color. Off the court run complexes of square and rectangular rooms, as though the architect wanted to suggest sumptuousness. This is what one commentator calls the "additive" principle: adding room after room, to imply that the royal resources were limitless. The delicate, filigreed work on some of the wall panelings gives an impression of exquisite lace.

A third feature of the Alhambra, beyond its fortified and multipurpose aspects, is its extraordinary attention to decoration. When one is inside the Alhambra, the most gripping feature is the careful ornamentation of the pillars, walls, ceilings, and floors. If one asks why Muslims lavished such care on the internal aesthetics of their palaces, the Alhambra provides an important clue to the answer. The impressive stalactite domes, and the thin pillars of the Fountain of the Lions, apparently derived from the medieval Muslim understanding of Solomon, the famed biblical king. In the medieval mythology surrounding Solomon, the *jinns* (spirits) made wonderful scenes of beauty for him and his queens. Thus medieval Muslim rulers had a certain stimulus to create scenes of an otherworldly, separate Paradise. Wanting to produce by natural means beauty such as that which Solomon achieved by supernatural power, they came to stress gardens, delicate decorations, and almost tours de force of engineering (thin pillars holding stupendous domes, for instance).

Less spectacularly, the motivations behind architecture like that of the Alhambra led to the "monumentalization" of many ordinary Muslim buildings. Thus in many urban areas, schools, shops, hostels, hospitals, baths, and even warehouses were built with great facades and intricate decorations. The caravanserais (motels, we might say) of thirteenth-century Anatolia, for example, employed the latest and most sophisticated techniques of construction. A religion that had a large place for "works"—business, pragmatic affairs, military matters—placed great stress on housing its social activities and secular affairs well. Also, in the medieval period Muslims tended to invest in land or buildings rather than trade or industry. The result was an architecture that little distinguished between the mosque and the secular building. Facades, for instance, seldom gave external viewers a basis for determining what sort of building they were entering. It was the internal decorations of the buildings, or the activity that occurred within them, that gave them their distinction.

From the time of the building of the famous Jerusalem Dome of the Rock in 691, the decoration we stressed in the case of the Alhambra preoccupied Muslim builders. Indeed, increasing the decorative beauty of their buildings seems to have been a prime motivation in the Muslims' development of stucco, in their laying bricks to make bold designs, and in their creation of colored tiles. This concern with ornamentation leads to the question of how Muslim construction and decoration relate, a question historians of Islamic architecture debate with some vigor.

A good case to study is the mosque of Cordoba. In the *mihrab* (niche to designate the direction of Mecca) of the Cordoba mosque the domes contain such unusual features as ribs that appear to support the cupola yet form a static mass with the cupola. The squinches (a characteristic support of domes) that accompany the ribs do not really support anything. In other words, the ribs and squinches are present for decorative, rather than constructive, reasons. The north dome of the great mosque in Isfahan, Persia, built a century after the *mihrab* of the mosque in Cordoba, has an unusual articulation of supports that also seem more decorative than constructive. The supports correspond to every part of the superstructure and give the impression of being a grid or net filled with decorative masonry. Third, the Muslim use of *muqarnas*, three-dimensional shapes used in many different combinations, seems clearly intended for decorative, rather than constructive, purposes. The *muqarnas* draw attention to some principal parts of a building, but they usually have little significance in terms of engineering.

The basic ornamental motif in much other Islamic art is repetition, seemingly endless patterns, whether representational (roses and leaves), semiabstract (vine tendrils and rosettes), or completely abstract (geometric patterns). This motif is known as the *infinite pattern*, and some suggest that it has theological significance. It does not want to rival God by creating anything fixed or permanent. Popular art often violated this pattern, suggesting that it most applied to mosques and official constructions. For instance, a Persian manuscript painting of the sixteenth century portrays Muhammad's ascent to Paradise, complete with winged angels, dishes of fruit, showers of pearls, and rubies.

love and pain." In this way, the talented Sufi writers won considerable respect from cultured people. To be able to express a religious vision with eloquence made the Sufis seem less eccentric, more representative of traditional Arab cultural ideals.

LAW AND THEOLOGY. Within the inner precincts of Islam, neither science nor art constituted the main cultural development. Rather, the most important flowering of Qur'anic doctrine was the law *Sharia* (the path, teaching). This concept is similar to the Catholic canon law, or Jewish Torah, or Buddhist dharma. It rose from reflections on the Qur'an and the *hadith* that passed on the example and teachings of the Prophet. Generally it tends to connote the orthodox law codes Islam developed, which codified the consensus of the community and the conclusions the Muslim teachers had reached by reasoning from precedents.

Built in the seventh century C.E., *the Dome of the Rock, Jerusalem, is one of Islam's most splendid shrines. Jerusalem is a city holy to Christians and Muslims as well as Jews.*

Traditional Muslims have looked to Sharia for guidance on the path to salvation, although they have admitted notable debate among their teachers over fine points of interpretation. Sharia has been the backbone of traditional Muslim culture. As the opening verses of the Qur'an suggest, a fundamental concern in Islam is guidance, and Islam went to lawyers, not to scientists, poets, or even mystics, for its most trustworthy guidance.

Traditional Islamic law has thought of itself as derived from God's plan for the proper ordering of human life. Its province has extended to whatever impinged on human beings' passage to Paradise. A term equivalent to *Sharia, fiqh* ("understanding" or "knowledge"), implied that the laws developed by the lawyers expressed what was understood to be behavior that would keep Muslims on the straight path.

The main thrust of the *fiqh* rules is on the "vertical" obligations of the Muslim to God: prayers, pilgrimage,

fasting, and the like. Another interest of these treatises bears on what we might call "horizontal" relationships: marriage, divorce, freeing slaves, oaths, criminal penalties, relations with non-Muslims, partnerships, contracts, the slaughter of animals, use of the land, fines, wills, sports, prohibited drinks, and much more. Some of these topics traditionally got more attention and development than others, in part because the religious courts were more able to detail and enforce laws concerning them: inheritance law, family law, and law concerning pious endowments for good works (schools, hospitals, etc.), for example.

On the whole, Islamic law has most concentrated on what sometimes is called "personal law": marriage, divorce, and inheritance. These areas continued to receive great attention and stay under the influence of religious lawyers even into the twenty-first century, somewhat in contrast to the secularization of such other areas as taxation, criminal law, and

Meeting of the theologians

analogous situations. These were the four main sources of religious authority.

The *hadith* were sayings attributed to Muhammad or stories about Muhammad apart from the Qur'an. The *hadith* function in Islam as one of the principal sources of authoritative teaching, standing with the Qur'an, community consensus, and analogical reasoning. They affirm the paradigmatic role of the Prophet, whose life Muslims have taken as the model or template for Muslim existence. Complicated rules govern how sayings became authenticated and entered the collections of *hadith*. Muslims tend to be confident that what is housed in the several authoritative collections reports what the Prophet said and did, but scholars using the detached techniques of textual criticism find much that seems folkloric and incapable of independent historical verification.

To be sure, Muslims did not view religious law or theology as a human creation. Rather, it was divine guidance, the expression of God's own will. The goal of the teachers was to offer comprehensive guidance for all of life—much as the Jewish rabbis' goal was to apply the Torah to all of life. As they refined their craft, Muslim teachers also distinguished all human actions according to five headings: obligatory, recommended, permitted, disapproved, and forbidden. Thus, one had to confess the unity of God and the Prophethood of Muhammad, one was counseled to avoid divorce, and one was forbidden to eat pork. Since Muslim society was a theocracy, Sharia was the code of the land. (While that made for a certain unity and order, it also prepared the way for the Sufi mystic's emphasis on personal devotion as a counterweight to legalism.)

THE PERIOD OF DIVISION

A minor source of division within the Muslim community was the differences in law developed by the various schools. The Hanafite school came to dominate Muslim countries north and east of the Arabian Peninsula. Within Arabia itself, the dominant school was founded by ibn-Hanbal. Northeast Africa was under Shafite and Hanafite lawyers, while Malikite opinions were the most prestigious in northwestern Africa. In Persia the Shia sect had its own law. On the whole, that distribution still holds today.

Given the four recognized legal codes of Sunni, the large Shia minority, and the division of the Islamic

constitutional law. Interestingly, however, with the rise of fundamentalist influences in many Muslim countries during the last quarter century has come a trend to rethink even these latter, secularized legal areas in terms of older traditions that assumed there was no unreligious, secular dimension in a good Muslim's life.

The early theological discussions dealt with doctrine and types of sins (e.g., idolatry). Later debates focused on the unity of God (in the context of discussing the divine attributes) and on the relation of the divine sovereignty to human freedom. While there was a full spectrum of opinions, in Sunni quarters the more moderate positions tended to win favor. Before long, however, Islam effectively curtailed speculation, favoring instead careful efforts to ascertain what legal precedents any practical problem had in the Qur'an, the *hadith* of the Prophet, community consensus, or

empire into eastern and western parts centered at Baghdad and Cordoba, respectively, one can see that religious and political unity was less than perfect. Still, Muslims holding to the Five Pillars and the Qur'an had much more in common with one another than they had with any non-Muslim peoples. Thus, legal or creedal differences did not divide Muslim religion severely. In contrast, different devotional styles, such as Sufism, caused considerable conflict.

SUFISM. The **Sufis** were the best known sect of Islamic mystics. The term *Sufi* comes from the Arabic word for wool, which Sufis wore as a gesture of simplicity. In the beginning, the Sufi movement stood for reform and personal piety. In a time when political and military success tempted Islam to worldliness, and the rise of the law brought the dangers of legalism, the Sufis looked to the model of Muhammad at prayer, communing with God. For them the heart of Islam was personal submission to God, personal guidance along the straight path. In later centuries, through its brotherhoods and saints, Sufism set a great deal of the emotional, anti-intellectual, and anti-progressive tone of an Islam that had lost its status as a world power.

Several cultural streams ran together to form the Sufi movement. First was the ascetic current from traditional desert life, which was basic and simple—a daily call for endurance. Out of a keen sense of the religious values in such a harsh life, Abu Dharr al-Ghifari, a companion of the Prophet, chastised the early leaders who wanted to lead a sumptuous court life after their conquests. Second, many of the Sufi ecstatics drew on the Arab love of poetry. Their lyric depictions of the love of God, coupled with the Qur'an's eloquence, drew sensitive people to the side of a living, personal commitment to realize the beauties of Islam. Third, the more speculative Sufis drew on Gnostic ideas that floated in from Egypt and the Fertile Crescent. By the ninth century, Sufi contemplatives (especially the Persian Illuminationists) were utilizing those ideas to analyze the relations between divinity and the world. (The Sufis seem to have found most attractive the emanational ideas—the theories of how the world flowed out of the divine essence—rather than the dualistic theories of good and evil.) This kind of understanding, along with the alchemical interests noted previously, was the beginning of the esoteric

and sometimes magical lore for which the orthodox theologians and lawyers held the Sufis suspect. Last, Indian (especially Buddhist) thought apparently influenced the eastern portions of the Muslim realm, and it perhaps was a source of the tendencies toward self-annihilation (loss of personal identity in God) that became important in Sufi mystical doctrine.

Taken at their own word, the Sufis desired to be committed followers of Muhammad and the Qur'an. The more honored among them never intended any schismatic or heretical movements. The most famous theologian among them was **Al-Ghazzali** (1058–1111), who withdrew from his prestigious teaching post in Baghdad to pursue the mystic's life. Like the Jewish Hasidim, the Sufis fashioned stories to carry their messages about the paradoxes of the spiritual life, the need for being focused and wholehearted, the way that God comes in the midst of everyday life. In these stories, the poor man turns out to be rich; the fool turns out to be truly wise. Like their counterparts in other traditions, the Sufis left no doubt that riches and prestige tend to be obstacles to spirituality. Predictably, this challenge to the expectations of society, of the religious authorities, and of the literally minded won the Sufis no love. Perhaps to intensify their opposition, some Sufis became even more provocative, challenging the establishment and suggesting that its religion was little more than dead convention. Along similar lines is a story of a Sufi who meets the devil. The devil is just sitting patiently, so the Sufi asks him why he is not out making mischief. The devil replies, "Since the theoreticians and would-be teachers of the Path have appeared in such numbers, there is nothing left for me to do."

Sufi followers had a *sheikh* (master, similar to a guru in Hinduism) who would help the novice learn meditation. Typically, at the order's local lodge, a small number of professionals resided to teach and lead worship. Most members have been lay adherents who came for instruction when they could and who supported the lodge by contributing money, manual labor, and so on. Each order tended to have its own distinctive ritual, whose purpose was usually to attain ecstatic experience. The ritual was the group's interpretation of the general virtue of *dhikr* (remembrance) that all Muslims seek. For instance, whirling dances characterized many of the Mevlevi *dervish* meetings, while Saadeeyeh Sufis developed a ceremony in which the head of the order rode on horseback over prone devotees.

LATE EMPIRE AND MODERNITY

During the period of empire, at least three general changes occurred in Arabic-speaking society. The first was the transformation of the Islamic Near East from a commercial economy based on money to a feudal economy based on subsistence farming. The second was the replacement in positions of authority of Arabic-speaking peoples by Turks. The Arab tribes retained their independence in the desert regions, where they held out quite well against Turkish rule. In the cities and cultivated valleys (the plains of Iraq, Syria, and Egypt), however, the Arabs became completely subjected, and the glorious language that had been the pride of Islam became the argot of an enslaved population. Psychologically, the Turks grew accustomed to taking the initiative and commanding, and the Arabs grew accustomed to passivity and subjection. The third change was the transfer of the seat of Islam from Iraq to Egypt. Iraq was too remote from Turkey and the Mediterranean to be the base for the eastern wing of Islam, so Egypt—which was on the other principal trade route and which was the most unified area geographically—became the new center.

The Ottoman Turks finally defeated the crumbling Byzantine empire, taking Constantinople in 1453 and renaming it Istanbul. They moved into southeastern Europe, gaining many converts to Islam among the Albanians and Bosnians. At first many of the subject peoples welcomed the Ottoman takeover from the Mamluks or Byzantines as a return to political order. By the eighteenth century, however, the Ottoman empire was in decay—corrupt, anarchic, and stagnant. The principal religious form of revolt during this period was Sufism. At first Sufism was mainly an escape for oppressed individuals, but with the organization of more brotherhoods, it became a social movement that was especially powerful among the artisan class. The long centuries of stagnation finally ended, however, with increased contact with the West. From the beginning of the sixteenth century, European expansion brought some of the new learning of the Renaissance and the Reformation. The French in particular had considerable influence in the Middle East, and Napoleon's easy conquest of the Ottoman Turks at

the end of the eighteenth century was the final blow to Islamic military glory.

THE WAHABIS. Also during the time of Napoleon arose an Islamic reform that was designed to check what it considered to be the infection of Sufism. One of the first leaders in this reform was a stern traditionalist named Muhammad ibn Abd al-Wahab, whose followers came to be known as Wahabis. They called for a return to the doctrines and practices of the early generations, of the ancestors whom they venerated. In law, the Wahabis favored the rigorous interpretations of the Hanbalite school, and they abhorred the veneration of Sufi masters as saints. Thus, they inveighed against supposed holy personages, living or dead, and went out of their way to destroy the shrines that had become places of popular piety or pilgrimage. They further objected that the worship of saints presumed that they were "partners" of God and so was idolatrous. The punishment due such idolatry was death. Some of the more rabid Wahabis went so far as to classify the more lenient lawyers and schools as being guilty of idolatry (and so punishable by death). The Wahabis were based in Arabia, whence they waged war on their dissenting neighbors. They went down to military defeat in their 1818 campaign, but their puritanical reform had much ideological success and spread to other parts of the Islamic world.

An immediate effect of the Wahabi movement was great hostility toward the Sufi brotherhoods. In fact, Muslims interested in renovating orthodoxy singled out the Sufis as their great enemies, although they also attacked the Scholasticism of such theological centers as Al-Azhar in Cairo. One of the leaders of the nineteenth-century reform was the apostle of Pan-Islam, Jamal al-Din al-Afghani, who proposed the political unification of all Muslim countries under the caliphate of the Ottoman sultans. While Pan-Islam has never been realized, it stimulated the widespread search for an effective Muslim response to modernity. In India and Egypt, conservative groups arose that gravitated toward the Wahabi position. Many of the Sufi organizations lost their strength, and those that survived tended to back away from gnosis and return to a more traditional theology.

Even before this conservative threat, however, the Sufis had reformed on their own, sponsoring a number of missions in Africa, India, and Indonesia. For the most

The rest of the Islamic world followed the Iranian upheavals of 1979 with great interest, to say the least, and many interesting commentaries on the relevance of Islam for today have arisen because of the Iranian events. One such commentary appeared in Cairo, at the instigation of the Islamic Student Association of Cairo University. Studying the reflections of this commentary may open a window on the likely future of Islam's blend of religion and politics.

The commentary begins with a quotation from the Qur'an (3:26) to the effect that God, the possessor of all sovereignty, gives earthly sovereignty to whomever he wishes. Just as freely, God takes earthly sovereignty away. Only God is powerful over all things. If God wishes to raise someone up, he does. If God wishes to debase someone, he does.

From this theological foundation the commentary moves to the Khomeini revolution in Iran, which was then riveting the whole world. This revolution, says the article, the violence and restraint of which surpassed the calculations and wildest imaginings of most observers, deserves deep study. Muslims must ponder such marvelous happenings, if they are ever to fulfill their Qur'anic destiny (see 3:110) and "assume the reins of world leadership of mankind once again and place the world under the protection of the esteemed Islamic civilization."

Beginning such study, the first lesson the commentary would underscore is the influence of the creed on the Islamic people. The Iranian people, who had appeared completely submissive to death and tyranny, exploded like a volcano, tossing their fears aside. Their spiritual conquest of the steely forces that opposed them recalls the heroes of earliest Muslim times, and it should remind everyone that religious commitment might muster similar power in many situations. Islam is the religion with the power to redress the injustices of all peoples everywhere.

Second, the Iranian revolution reminds us that Islam is a comprehensive religion, legislating for both this world and the next. It provides alike for religion and state affairs, education and morals, worship and holy war. In fact, the Iranian revolution

clarifies the errors in modern secularism, which would separate religion from state affairs. Clearly, it shows that secularism is the recourse of idolaters, who want to keep religion out of politics, so that they can plunder the wealth of the common people. The only adequate laws and constitutions are those that derive from the Sharia of Islam. When laws and constitutions are manmade, their status is no greater than the idols of the pre-Muslim Arabs. If the pre-Muslim Arabs got hungry, they would eat the Goddess of Pastry. In contrast, the Sharia of Islam, which comes from God, is permanent, just, wise, and perfect.

Third, Iranian affairs show that the real leaders of the Muslim people are the sincere, learned men of religion. These men (the *ulama*) have been the guiding lights of all the best modern Muslim liberation movements. The touchstone is justice. For forty years the tyrant shah betrayed his community and brought down on it the most repulsive forms of injustice. God takes his time with the wrongdoer, but when he takes him there is no escaping.

Fourth, shrewd observers will note how the false Iranian leaders had the courage of lions when dealing with their own people but were puppets in the hands of the rulers of the East and the West. Yet the West quickly disowned the shah, abandoning him like a worn-out shoe. To the lesson implied in this, one should add the patent effort of Islam's enemies to exploit the sectarian differences between Shiites and Sunnis and tear the Muslim community apart. As well, the enemies of Islam tried to use the Iranian revolution to instigate local governments to strike out at Islamic movements.

Therefore, rulers in other Islamic locales must realize that their real strength lies in the strength of their people, and that the real strength of their people lies in Islam. Wise leaders are those that place their allegiance in God, his apostle Muhammad. As the Qur'an (5:49) teaches, only those who rule by what God has revealed can expect to be strengthened. Thus, to those who would instigate strife against Islamic movements, one should reply: God suffices for us. The Qur'an has said the last word in these matters: "God promised those of you who believe and perform good works that he would make you viceroys on earth as he did with those before and will make it possible for you to follow the religion which pleases you and will change your fear into safety. You will worship me, associating nothing else with me" (24:55).

Several concerns of the Cairo Students' Association merit special comment, because they have been present in the recent resurgence of a passionate Islam in other countries, such as Iran, Afghanistan, and Pakistan. First, some students obviously long for a return to traditional Muslim law. Chafing under what they think is their recent rulers' secularism, the students hope that returning to the principles of the Qur'an and traditional Muslim law will speedily redress all current wrongs. In its early stages, the revolution in Iran seemed a great vindication of this viewpoint. Even fervent Muslims were amazed that they were able to bring down so powerful an enemy as the shah. Today, at a greater distance from the events of 1979, and with more experience of what the Ayatollah Khomeini understood the revolution to imply, even zealous students might take pause. The bloody chaos that afflicted the Muslim ranks in Iran after the revolution argues that the Sharia is open to markedly diverse and violent interpretations. The long war between Iran and Iraq was a festering sore in the Muslim community.

Second, a great deal of the world does not want to be placed under the protection of Islamic civilization, even when one grants Islamic civilization its great due. Pluralism is a more powerful force than the students seem to realize, and any peaceful assumption of the reins of world leadership will have to handle pluralism quite sympathetically. Any forceful assumption of the reins of world leadership is almost unthinkable, both because Islam is hardly in the position to challenge the West militarily and because military means to power inevitably raise the specter of nuclear war. No nations would profit from a contemporary translation of Islamic "holy war" that led to nuclear confrontations.

Third, students of religion might most profitably focus on the somewhat tacit pleas that run through the Egyptian students' commentary. For example, there is the tacit plea that the rest of the world take seriously and duly honor a proud religious tradition. Islam came on hard times when the West took charge of modernity. Its pride was wounded, and one can trace much of its strong rhetoric, even its hyperbole, to this wounded pride. Now that Islam is on the march again, more than competitive with the Western religions in Africa and other parts of the Third World, it is trying to recoup some of its emotional losses.

Still another plea running through the students' manifesto is for simple justice. Iranians had been suffering injustice. Enough of them had been tortured and abused by the shah to make his regime hated. The popular support for the Khomeini revolution was only explainable on the basis of this hatred. Had the shah's innovations, his programs for modernization and economic development, not been perceived as brutally unjust, as well as destructive of the people's cherished religious heritage, the shah probably would not have become the Iranian Satan. Even when one allows for a considerable emotional excess in the rhetoric of the shah's opponents, and their considerable manipulation by religious leaders quite ambitious for power, the political facts seem clear. The clarion call of the religious revolutionaries was for a restoration of justice. A major attraction in the prospect of restoring a Qur'anic government was the possibility of achieving a much greater justice.

For many secular observers, Khomeini's authoritarianism soon became precisely a demand for idolatrous obedience, precisely the arbitrary rule of a false god.

part these were peaceful, but occasionally they involved military ventures. In fact, some groups quite consciously took up the Qur'anic tradition of holy war, including the "Indian Wahabis" and the Mahdists in the Sudan. However, even in decline the Sufi brotherhoods kept dear to Islam the notion of bonding together for mutual support.

The organizations that have grown up in recent times, such as the Association for Muslim Youth and the Muslim Brotherhood, seem in good measure an effort to fill the void created by the demise of the Sufi brotherhoods. The new groups differ by operating primarily in pluralistic cultures, where Muslims live in the midst of non-Muslims.

WESTERN INFLUENCE. A characteristic of Islamic modernity was the invasion of Western secular ideas. These ideas came on the heels of modern Western takeovers in the Middle East, at first through the administrations of the Europeans who governed the newly acquired territories and then through the educational systems, which were westernized. The new classes of native professionals—doctors, lawyers, and journalists—frequently trained abroad or in native schools run by Westerners. One political effect of such training was to raise Muslim feelings of nationalism and to provoke cries for westernized systems of government. The new ideas challenged the madrasas, or religious schools, too, for it was not immediately apparent that these new ideas could be taught along with traditional theories of revelation and Qur'anic inspiration.

From the nineteenth century on, the economics, politics, education, social habits, and even religion of Muslims were increasingly affected by the upheaval that resulted from the European Renaissance and Enlightenment. Some countries remained largely insulated from Western notions, but they tended to be backward portions of the old empire with little political impact. As we might expect, the cities bore the brunt of the challenge. In theology the outward Muslim reaction was to close ranks. Still, even in the most fiercely traditionalist schools, modern notions—such as the freedom of human beings to shape their own destinies—softened the old propositions about providence and predestination.

Indeed, when it was convenient, theologians incorporated modern science into their argumentation. For instance, some Muslim theologians justified the doctrine that God creates the world continuously by citing atomic theory. The less theologically inclined among the modern educated classes contented themselves by asserting that Islam, as submission to the God as "the Master of Truth," in principle cannot conflict with modern science or with any empirically verified truths.

Controversy over societal matters has been more heated than that over theology because the guidance provided by the traditional legal schools diverged more sharply from Western mores than Muslim theology diverged from Western theology. Slowly Islamic countries have developed civil codes and separated civil courts from religious courts. In the mid-nineteenth century, the Turkish Republic breached the wall of tradition when it abolished the authority of the Sharia in civil matters. In other countries the Sharia has remained the outer form, but new legislative codes direct the interpretations. The tactic has been to invoke the Qur'an, the *hadith*, and the traditions of the schools but to leave the legislators and judges free to choose the authority that is most appropriate. Specifically, the legal reforms have applied primarily to marriage contracts (protecting girls against child marriage), divorce proceedings, and polygamy—central factors in the traditional family structure.

In considering recent Muslim fundamentalism, one must realize that Islamic secularism never got so advanced as Western secularism. True, fundamentalism attracts a noteworthy number of Christians and Jews, but Christianity and Judaism more clearly differentiate the civic realm, the realm shared with citizens of other religious convictions (or of none), than Islamic culture has done. Conversely, Islam has kept the sacred and the secular more tightly conjoined than Christianity or Judaism has, professing that there is no secular realm—that everything lives by the will and touch of Allah, who is as near as the pulse at one's throat.

WORLDVIEW

NATURE

The key to the Muslim notion of nature is Islam's concept of creation. As much as the biblical religion on which it is built, Islam sees God as the maker of all that is. Several Qur'anic passages establish this doctrine. For instance, *Sura* 10 describes the Lord as "God, who created the heavens and the earth in six days, then sat Himself upon the Throne directing the affair." This is the biblical imagery of creation: Genesis spreading God's work over six days. Moreover, the Qur'an finds significance in this creation in that through creation God has given God-fearing people signs of his dominion. By making the sun a radiance and the moon a light, by giving them "stations" so that astronomers can calculate time, and by alternating night and day, God has set over humankind a heaven full of signs. *Sura* 13 repeats this theme, adding earthly phenomena: It is he who stretched out the earth, set firm mountains and rivers, and placed two kinds of every fruit. The abundance of nature testifies to the abundance of nature's source and ought to remind human beings of God's power and provision. Thus, the Creator is not only strong but also admirable in his design of the world and praiseworthy in his concern for human welfare as evidenced by his bounty. In this way the best features of nature become analogies for God in the Qur'an. The "Light-Verse" of *Sura* 24 gives one of the most famous of these analogies: God is the light of the heavens and the earth. His light is as a niche where there is a lamp. The lamp is in a glass, the glass is like a glittering star. The lamp is kindled from a Blessed Tree, an olive neither of the East nor of the West, whose oil would shine even if no fire touched it. Light upon light, God guides to the light whom he will.

Religiously, then, nature is replete with evidence from which wise people discern God's creative presence. However, nature is not itself a divinity or a form of God's presence. Unlike East Asian thought, Islamic thought does not mix divinity with the cosmos. Islam separated from the ancient cosmological myth, in that God transcends the world. One may say that the biblical prophets' critique of nature gods combined with Muhammad's negative reaction to the polytheism of his times to correlate transcendence and anti-idolatry. So the signs that nature gives to the God-fearing are not themselves sacraments. They point beyond themselves; the divinity does not come in them. Water, oil, bread, wine—they are not miniature incarnations of divinity. The God of Islam has no incarnation, no personal or material forms by which he becomes present. Creator is Creator, creature is creature, and never the twain shall meet.

Nature never dominated Arab or Muslim culture. The earliest poetry deals more with war and nomadic life than with father sky and mother earth. Pre-Muslim Arabia worshipped natural and agricultural forces, but Qur'anic monotheism attacked them harshly. In religious art, the prohibition on images was not absolute, although religious art tended to avoid representations of natural scenes, let alone representations of God. Still, the prime material for worship, the Qur'an itself, contained natural figures and not merely in the context of creation. Thus, it embellished its theme of judgment and recompense with naturalistic imagery. Thus, the Qur'an considered nature a factor in the mysteries of judgment, punishment, and reward, as the images of Fire and Garden clearly show. Moreover, mythological elaboration of these themes in popular religion was quite unrestrained. In the popular conception, angels presided over hell, meting out punishments, while heaven became a place for enjoying fruit, wine, and the charming black-eyed virgins.

Islam maintained that justice would be served in the afterlife through reward for the pious and punishment for the non-Muslims. Sex was high on the list of pleasures, so Paradise was rich with sex. Islam depicted sex from the male point of view, with details of "maidens restraining their glances, untouched before them by any man or *jinn*" (55:55). As we shall see below, Islam did not declare the goodness of sex so loudly and clearly for women. In fact, there has often been a double standard concerning sex in Muslim society. Still, the basic fact that Islam does not paint heaven as an ethereal, wholly spiritual realm shows that it blesses human nature.

Muslim spirituality manifests something of the emphasis of keeping human nature under control. By fasting, a Muslim tames the nature closest to the self. By confessing that there is no God but God, a Muslim clears the world of competitors to the Creator and Judge. That means that many devout Muslims' ideal is a bare vista. The Sufis manifested this ideal most fully, for many of them saw life as a pilgrimage to union with a God much more valuable than anything worldly. In less deliberate but still consoling ways, the poor merchant or soldier learned from misfortune how precarious a worldly vista was. Although the physical world was definitely real and on occasion quite good, the human being's role was to observe it closely enough so that it served as a guidepost to heaven. A Muslim can be comfortable in the natural world, then, but only as a visitor. Life in the natural world soon passes, and Judgment depends on higher things, such as one's commitment, one's prayer, and one's generosity in giving alms. The tradition does not teach people that the Judge will ask them how they treated the environment or whether they tore the bosom of mother earth. Those issues are far less important than whether they remembered God and his Prophet.

SOCIETY

The Muslim social unit has been the *Ummah*, the brotherhood and sisterhood of all Muslims. The Prophet was the head of the entire community in his day, but after his death the question of headship of the community became entangled in political and cultural battles. The differences between Shiites and Sunnis have complicated estimates of how the *Ummah* actually subsists in time. But such occasions as the annual pilgrimage to Mecca have allowed Muslims to affirm their solidarity.

The Muslim social ideal has never distinguished between secular and sacred aspects of community life. The Prophet and his successors bore a theocratic power. That is, they had authority in both the religious and the secular spheres, because Islam does not much distinguish between the two. Muslims were to bring their disputes to the Prophet or his successors, and they all had a common duty to worship God, to obey God's commands, and to do good and avoid evil. Members were to be to one another as brothers and mutual guardians (*Qur'an* 9:71), respecting life and enjoying its good things.

The Islamic state made a threefold division of humanity: Muslims, covenanters, and enemies. The Muslim peoples who constituted the Dar al-Islam (House of Islam) could not legitimately resort to war against one another. Covenanters were non-Muslims who had made "compacts of peace." Examples would be those Jews and Christians living in Spain and the Zoroastrians of Iran. Muslims had the right to preach to them but not to force them to convert. As long as the covenanters accepted Muslim law in the society, their civil rights and duties were the same as those of Muslims.

Presumably, holy war only resulted when enemies rejected both conversion and covenant. If an enemy responded with hostility, Muslim security necessitated war. Muslims had to fight for brethren in other places who suffered tyranny (*Qur'an* 4:75). For Muslim leaders, the consensus of the community was an important goal, for they wanted a single divine rope to bind the *Ummah* together.

ETHICS. Despite the doctrines of God's sovereignty, Islam considered people to have free will and be morally responsible for their actions. As we noted, the law distinguishes five kinds of action, from the commanded to the forbidden. The Qur'an deals with adultery, murder, and theft, prescribing stern punishments for them. Homosexuality is likewise forbidden (though its practice was not absent in Muslim societies which so thoroughly excluded women largely from the daily life of single men).

Muslim dietary rules are comparable to the Jewish kosher restrictions, but they are not as elaborate. Pork is not to be eaten. Meat must be obtained from a butcher skilled in the proper techniques of slaughter. (Today Islamic *halal* butchers can be found in many European and North American cities with large Muslim populations.)

Two other prohibitions are on alcohol and gambling. These may have had their origin from the need of controlling male behavior on a long caravan (or military campaign). In some Muslim countries (e.g., Saudi Arabia, Afghanistan), alcohol may not be manufactured or consumed. In other Muslim countries, alcohol may be produced and sold to non-Muslims (e.g., Pakistan has a very successful gin distillery started by the British colonialists). Just as not all Catholics are committed enough to avoid committing the sins specified by that denomination, so some Muslims sometimes lapse and go into a bar or casino (especially in non-Muslim countries). But, God is most merciful and does forgive.

Racism was an evil targeted by the prophet Muhammad. In the beginning, there was to be no discrimination between Muslims based upon the Arab tribe to which a Muslim belonged. There was never any idea that God was just the God of the Arabs, so this proselytizing religion accepted as converts Turks, Persians, Indians, Slavs, Indonesians and Africans. One story about Muhammad was that one of his later wives was an African woman. Another story is that one of his own daughters was given to an African husband.

The Qur'an takes slavery for granted, but it commends humane treatment and the freeing of slaves. Only non-Muslim prisoners of war could legally become slaves. Discrimination because of color and race was unlawful, though some racial prejudice mars Islamic history. When the law reached its final stage of development around 1000, its detailed specifications tended to become mechanical. The mystics therefore tried to make ethics spring from a deeper relationship with God. The first virtue they taught was abstention from everything unlawful or dubious. In other words, one was not to nitpick but to act from the heart and turn away from anything that might displease God. Masters such as Al-Ghazzali advocated living every moment in the presence of God. Finally, the general effect of Muslim ethics was to heighten awareness of one's distance from the divine purity and so lead one to beg Allah's mercy and forgiveness.

WOMEN'S STATUS. In the Qur'an there is some basis for sexual equality in theory: reward and punishment in the afterlife depend on deeds, not gender. However, Islam has had a gnawing sense that in practice women had too many limitations, such as monthly menstruation, which were bound to interfere with prayer and fasting.

In practice, Muslim law improved the lot of women over what it had been in Arab lands prior to 600 C.E. Before Islam, women had status little better than that of slaves or livestock. If there was a time of famine, female infanticide would be widely practiced so that the clan did not have to make an investment in a future member who could not drive camels or exact vengeance in the desert. Before Islam, she could be given in marriage or sold as a sex slave before she reached her teens. Islam encouraged formal marriage (but did not ban slavery or concubinage), and (at least in theory) even gave her the right to refuse a marriage proposal. Islamic rules on polygamy limited the number of wives a man could have to four (and having more than one was granted on the condition that he treat them equally, which many theologians have suggested was a back door approach to monogamy). Before Islam, women would not have legal rights to inheritance, but they did under the Qur'an. Before Islam, there were few practical hindrances to a man divorcing his wife on a whim. Islamic law still permitted this, but it deterred such a practice by requiring the man to return a portion of the dowry he had received at marriage. Islam also granted women the right to remarry after being widowed, and most importantly, Muslim males the duty to protect pregnant and nursing women.

However, women's rights are not equal to those that the Qur'an gives males in either divorce or inheritance. Her value as a witness in court was only half of that of the man. Moreover, the Qur'an does not even consider the possibility that women might assume leadership roles in the community, receive an education equal to that of males, teach law or theology, or obtain multiple spouses (as males could). The prime role of a woman in this life was to serve and obey her husband, bearing and caring for his children, and it was in her fulfillment of these duties that her value to Muslim society was judged. At its stereotypical worst, women were portrayed as empty headed and best left illiterate, veiled, and secluded in a harem.

Although on the issues of slavery and women's rights, Muhammad must be viewed as a sincere reformer, making significant improvements by broadening the rights of these classes, the fact that his specific seventh century reforms have been frozen has created a basis for discrimination in modern times. As Afghani women under the Taliban hoped for the right to work outside the home, and Iranian women struggle for greater opportunities for advancements in education and career, their challenge will be to use the rock of Muhammad's reforms as a steppingstone under their feet rather than a millstone around their necks.

WAR. Muhammad sought to greatly limit the fratricidal strife among Arab tribes. He proclaimed that all Muslims were brothers and abolished the cycle of vengeance for past wrongs. He promulgated the doctrine of **jihad** in order to limit the situations that could justify war. Jihad is frequently misunderstood by non-Muslims (and it does not help matters that there is a terrorist group named "Islamic Jihad" planting bombs against civilian targets). *Jihad* is a Muslim term for holy struggle, warfare in defense, or pursuit, of a good cause. It can connote the whole range of effort necessary to promote Islam in both personal and social life. Moreover, even when it refers to military matters, it need not primarily be offensive. The more ordinary reason for going to war, in the Muslim view of past history, was opposition that would have denied Muslims the chance to practice or spread Islam. Seeing such a denial as opposition to God, the Qur'an, and the Prophet, Muslims have felt obliged to fight, as they could feel obliged to fight on behalf of brother and sister Muslims who came under attack. The unity of the Muslim community justified such a sense of social solidarity, Muslims having ties among themselves that relegated their relations with non-Muslims or outsiders to a lower level.

However, most experts on the Sharia are clear that the ethics of Islamic warfare protect noncombatants, women and children, the aged, and prisoners of war. Islamic terrorists are condemned by most Islamic theologians, just as terrorist splinter groups of the Irish Republican Army (fighting for the Catholic side in Northern Ireland) have their violence condemned by the Pope.

OFFSHOOTS. The different Islamic cultures have all been bonded by the Qur'an despite their geographic, linguistic, ethnic, and even theological differences. While each of these owes a debt to Islamic doctrine and myth, each can be viewed as a new and distinct revelation that subsequently blended elements of Islam. In India, as noted in a previous chapter, Islamic elements fused with Hindu elements to create **Sikhism** under the inspiration of Guru **Nanak** (1469–1539). *Sikh* is a Punjabi word meaning "disciple." They had a sequence of later gurus who blended Muslim monotheism with the Hindu doctrine of reincarnation. They celebrate some traditional Indian holidays (e.g., *Diwali*) along with special days commemorating their founders and martyrs. Life cycle rituals include the naming of a child, baptism, marriage, and funerals. After baptism, Sikhs commit themselves to keep their hair uncut, but neatly held in a comb and turban. Other items to be on one's person would be a steel bracelet, small sword, and special underwear. Sikhs came to reject many rituals associated with Islam and Hinduism: circumcision, pilgrimages, fasting, idol worship, celibacy, and the caste system or established priesthood. Most Sikhs have the last name Singh (but not everyone with that Indian name is necessarily a Sikh). Sikhs now number almost 20 million in India (and perhaps 5 million outside). They are prominent in the Punjab district and in India's military. (Most of India remained either Muslim or Hindu, and one of the results of the independence after World War II was a division of the country into a predominantly Hindu republic of India to the south, and the Muslim republics of Pakistan and Bangladesh in the northwest and northeast, respectively.) So, Sikhs are a minority, but

prominent, in India. Although there was some tension between the Sikhs and the Indian federal government in the 1980s, that has largely been resolved. In 2003 India elected its first non-Hindu prime minister, a Sikh.

A thousand years ago, the **Druses** sect was formed by an imam, al-Hakim in Egypt, who had a revelation that only his small group of followers would be saved and that they were not to accept any additional converts beyond their own descendants. They now number about a quarter million, largely concentrated in an area of southeastern Lebanon.

Islam was also the inspiration behind **Baha'i,** a tolerant, universalist religion that stresses the unity of all traditions and the basic oneness of the human race. It arose in nineteenth-century Persia when a Shiite Muslim, Sayyid Ali Muhammad, declared that he was the twelfth imam—the last messianic leader whom the Shia awaits. Sayyid took the designation Bab ("gate"), and his follower Baha Ullah produced writings that became classic works of Baha'i. Today Baha'i has about 5 million adherents. Its world center is on Mount Carmel in Haifa, Israel, where a lovely garden and shrine are dedicated to the Bab, and there is a beautiful temple just north of Chicago in Wilmette, Illinois. These Baha'i temples are characterized by many entrances, symbolizing the world's different denominations (e.g., Buddhist, Christian, Muslim) all of which are considered acceptable pathways to God.

In Detroit in the 1930s, African Americans formed a movement called the **Nation of Islam** (also known as the Black Muslims). Although it accepts the Qu'ran and traditional Islamic prohibitions against pork and alcohol, it included doctrines quite different from those of traditional Islam. For example, the movement's mysterious founder, Fard, disappeared and was then heralded as an incarnation of God. The Nation of Islam did not preach racial equality and integration. They had a myth that Satan had created the white man. They advocated a separate homeland in order to secure self-determination. Malcolm X had converted to the movement in prison and became a major spokesman. But after a pilgrimage to Mecca, where he experienced a profound fellowship with blond, blue-eyed Slavic Muslims from Bosnia, he came to see the racist doctrines of the Nation of Islam as heresy. Malcolm was assassinated in 1965, allegedly by gunmen directed by the Nation of Islam leadership.

SCHOOLS OF ISLAM		
SCHOOL	LOCATION	APPROACH
Sunni	Saudi Arabia, Turkey, Bosnia, Albania, Africa, Pakistan, Syria, Palestine, Afghanistan, Indonesia, Bangladesh	consensus interpretation of Qur'an
Shia	Iran	living prophet (Ayatollah, imam)
Druses	Lebanon	no more converts
Sikh	India	Hinduism and Islam
Sufi	Iran	mysticism
Bahai	Iran	ecumenism
Nation of Islam	African Americans	evil whites and Jews

Although the current head of the movement, Louis Farrakhan, has won widespread praise for his Million Man March, his occasional anti-Semitic remarks have left him a controversial figure. Some of the more famous members of this sect (e.g., boxer Muhammad Ali and basketball star Kareem Abdul-Jabbar) have left it and made full conversions to orthodox Islam.

SELF

The orthodox conception of the self began with the notion of creation. In *Sura 96* the self is described essentially as a small thing that God made from a blood clot or a drop of sperm. The essence of Islam and of being a Muslim was to recognize the creator-creature relation: a sovereign God who is completely the Lord of a very insignificant vassal. The basic scriptural message of Islam is complete submission.

This attitude was no false humility. Rather, it was seen as the acceptance of the human condition. Human beings came from God, and their destiny depended on living out the pattern that God had in making them. Thus, they had no basis for self-glorification. Thus, the exclamations of an Al-Hallaj, who claimed identification with God (through mystical union), could only sound blasphemous to the majority, who were immersed in the literal text. Between the divine Lord and the human vassal stretched an impassable gulf. However much genuine love might have drawn the spirit up to God, however much God's intimate mercy might have descended toward human flesh, the essential difference in their states remained.

From other Qur'anic accounts of creation one can gather the impression that, despite their lowliness, human beings have a special status among all creatures. In the stories of Adam's creation (for instance, 2:28, 15:29, 32:8), the angels object to God's making human beings, but God forms this first man from clay and water, gives him a most beautiful form, and breathes his spirit into him. Then he makes the angels bow before Adam, for Adam is the first prophet and vice-regent on earth, having in this capacity the right and duty to carry out God's orders. Echoing *Genesis*, *Sura* 2:31 speaks of God's teaching Adam the names of all things, which means giving him power over all things, since to control a being's name was to have power over it. The end God had in mind for such a creature, the recompense that He expected, was adoration: "We have created men and *jinn* only for adoration" (51:51). God made the earth subject to human control. Along with the doctrine of God's transcendence, this anthropocentricity in creation helped to de-emphasize nature.

The traditional view of human nature conceives of the spiritual faculties having several names. The *nafs* was essentially the animal soul, the source of concupiscence (desire). It had the connotation of belonging to the lower part of the personality—to the flesh that incites evil. (Sometimes, though, it just means "self.") The *ruh* was the spirit, come from God, that animates the human body. Muslims often pictured it as a subtle matter that permeates the human body. Reason (*aql*) was the spiritual faculty by which human beings discern right and wrong. Finally, the mystics spoke of the *qalb*—the heart that is the faculty by which one obtains direct knowledge of God.

Yoruba Muslims of West Africa have ritualized their religion for the life cycle, the religious year, and the ordinary week. By studying these rituals, we may glimpse how Islam has adapted itself to such new geographic areas as West Africa and created a syncretism with tribal aspects of religion.

The life cycle of Yoruba Muslims begins on the day they become members of the worshipping community. This may be the day when, as adults, they formally convert to Islam, or the eighth day after their birth, when they receive their name. The major action in the adult conversion ceremony is an ablution, to symbolize the pure life the convert is entering upon. The candidates take off their clothes and don loincloths. The presiding cleric washes each candidate's right hand three times, the left hand three times, the right leg three times, and the left leg three times. Then three times he washes the elbows, blows each one's nose, and washes the ears. Concluding, he pours water on the head and chest of each candidate, who, having been washed and become clean, is a Muslim.

For the naming ceremony of a newborn child, the presiding cleric receives money in a covered dish. The cleric prays for the child, preaches a solemn sermon (often in Arabic), and then gives the child its name. Some West African Muslims also sacrifice a sheep or cut the infant's hair. (The Yoruba Muslims practice male adolescent circumcision, as well as the drawing of tribal marks on the face or body. Apparently Islam did not introduce these customs to Africa but rather gave them a new interpretation.)

The second major stage on the Yoruba Muslim's way is marriage. The presiding cleric must divine that the proposed match is a good one and pray for the marital partners. Before the wedding, the groom has to pay the bride's family several monies and gifts. In modernized West African Muslim rituals, the presiding cleric asks the groom: "Do you take Miss as your wedded wife? Will you love her, honor her, feed her, clothe her, and lodge her in proper lodging?" Then he quotes the Qur'an (4:34), to the effect that one of the signs God has given

human beings is creating mates for them, that they may find quiet of mind. Putting love and compassion between these mates, God gives reflective people a sign of his goodness and care. The presiding cleric also asks the bride similar questions, including whether she will love, honor, and obey her husband. He repeats most of the quotation from the Qur'an and reminds the bride that "the good women are therefore obedient, guarding the unseen as Allah has guarded." The ceremony concludes with prayers to Allah that he bless this wedding. (Most of the West African Muslim community supports the traditional polygyny.)

Funeral rites complete Islam's ritual impact on the Yoruba life cycle. When a person has died, the neighbors come together and dig a grave. They then wash the corpse, repeating the ablutions of the conversion ceremony. They dress the corpse in a white cap, loincloth, and sewn sheet, and then put it into the grave and cover it with earth. The presiding cleric prays for the deceased person, that God may forgive its sins. The dead person's family is expected to pay the cleric handsomely, with food as well as money. Some modernized sects hold a second ceremony, on the eighth day after the burial, with readings from the Qur'an, a sermon, and a eulogy of the deceased.

In addition to these three major ceremonies for the life cycle, Yoruba Islam has an annual cycle of feasting and fasting. The cycle begins with the Muslim New Year, which is a day for hearty eating in most sects and for orgiastic nude bathing and mock battles in a few. The New Year festival recalls Noah, who disembarked from the ark very hungry.

The next festivals in the annual cycle are two celebrations of Muhammad, his birthday and the night of his heavenly journey to Jerusalem and Paradise. The more conservative Yoruba Muslims have made much of the Prophet's birthday, using it as an occasion to display their learning. In their circles children act out scenes from the Prophet's life, and those who teach the Qur'an receive special stipends.

The month of Ramadan is the great time of fasting, but many of the Yoruba elderly fast during the month of Rajab as well. The last Friday of Ramadan is especially important, because then one may ask forgiveness for one's laxities in worship during the past year. Among the modernizing Yoruba Muslims the Ramadan ceremonies include the prayer, "O Allah! whom our obedience does not benefit and our disobedience does not harm, please accept from us what does not benefit you, and forgive us what does not harm you."

The two greatest feasts in the Yoruba Muslim calendar are the Feast of the Breaking of the Fast and the Feast of the Immolation. Each entails two days of public holidays in Nigeria. For the Feast of the Breaking of the Fast, worshippers dress elaborately and bring expensive prayer rugs. The ceremony includes an almsgiving, to solemnize gratitude for a successful conclusion to Ramadan, a visit to the ruler of the Yoruba, and a visit to the graves of the first two imams (religious leaders) of the community. The Feast of the Immolation reminds the Yoruba that their fellow Muslims in Arabia are performing this sacrifice in Mecca, as part of their pilgrimage. The immolation itself usually is the sacrifice of a small goat. After the communal ceremony many individuals also sacrifice goats or rams at the entrances to their own houses.

The last feast of the annual cycle is the Hajj, the pilgrimage to Mecca. Since Nigerian independence, the government has supported the pilgrimage, making the Hajj available to the prosperous farmer, shopkeeper, or local leader. If the individual can make an initial outlay of money, he or she usually will receive supplementary gifts from friends. Once the pilgrims return to their local communities, they enjoy great status, since they have been to the center of the Muslim world. Usually the experience of Islam as a worldwide fellowship greatly broadens the Yoruba pilgrim's horizons. Not all Yoruba Muslims have the opportunity to travel to Mecca, but each year at the time of the Hajj all turn their imaginations to the holy city and picture what is taking place there.

In the weekly religious cycle of Yoruba Muslims, Friday is the crowning day, but Wednesday and Thursday also have special significance. The last Wednesday of each lunar month is esteemed as a day of special blessings. All are encouraged to increase their prayers, that they may protect themselves from the evil every month contains. The darkness of the moon at the end of the month is probably the spark for this attitude.

In folk Islam, Wednesday is considered replete with blessings, as is Thursday. Most Yoruba groups have adopted this folk attitude. Thus, most marriages, celebrations of a student's completion of the Qur'an, and groundbreakings occur on Wednesdays or Thursdays. One of the many functions of the Yoruba cleric is to divine an auspicious date for these celebrations. Conservative Muslims, who tend to be better educated, downplay such divinations, and do not attribute any special significance to particular days of the week.

However, Thursday evening has a special significance, because it is the threshold to Friday, the Muslim Sabbath. Indeed, most Yoruba Muslims offer prayers for the dead on Thursday night. A popular tradition says that on Thursday evening God allows the dead to come back to the world and see what is going on. This ties into a Yoruba tradition of leaving gifts for the deceased. If a dead person does not have gifts left for him, he loses prestige among his peers.

A certain conflict between traditional, pre-Muslim notions about the dead and Muslim ideas confuses many Yoruba Muslims. The traditional pictures show the dead existing in a shadowy heaven, where they need the care of those they have left behind. The Muslim doctrines of judgment and resurrection do not square with these pictures, so the status of the dead is rather murky. Some Yoruba Muslims translate resurrection so that it becomes a state much like the old view, but others accept the more orthodox Muslim notion that resurrection is a wondrous event that will occur in the future.

Friday is the center of the weekly cycle, when all good Muslims are supposed to gather at noon in the main mosque for communal worship. In the large towns the mosques are crowded with male worshippers. (A smaller number of women is allowed to worship, segregated from the males, at the back of the mosque.) The service begins with the call to prayer and then has a sermon in the vernacular. Often this "sermon" turns out to be more like a group session of petitionary prayer. People come up to the prayer leaders and whisper their intentions, which "megaphonists" then repeat in a loud voice, so that God and the community at large can hear them. The sermon sometimes amounts to no more than a few moral exhortations tossed in as editorial comments on the prayers people have offered. The people also contribute money. After the sermon comes the heart of the Friday service, the communal ritual prayer. Together the group goes

through the actions of the fivefold daily prayer—bowing, kneeling, and touching their foreheads to the ground. Muslim prayer is essentially this doing, this performative act.

Through the life cycle, the annual cycle, and the weekly cycle, the great lesson the Yoruba or any other Muslims are learning is the lesson of prostration. Bowing before God, the Almighty, the Muslim deepens her or his sense that only one power is in charge of the world. To be at peace with God is life's greatest accomplishment; to be at war with God is life's greatest tragedy.

For some of the Sufis, the doctrine of creation in God's image was crucial. On occasion, Neo-Platonic or gnostic notions colored this doctrine to mean that the soul wanders in exile. It can return to its home, though, if it appropriates secret teaching or learns certain meditative techniques. From the notion of creation in God's image, the Sufis also developed their concept of the perfect man. Usually they applied it to Muhammad, who contained all the divine attributes and served as a microcosm of divinity.

Islam did not consider man and woman to be laboring under a "fallen" human nature, for Muslims did not regard the sin of Adam and Eve as being contagious or passed on to their offspring. Thus, Islam did not speak of redemption. The Prophet was a revealer or a medium of revelation; he was not a ransom, a victim, or a suffering servant (as Christians had portrayed Jesus). Instead of sin (in the deep sense of alienation from God by irrational actions), Islam tended to stress human forgetfulness (of God's goodness). Human nature was weak—prone to a kind of religious amnesia.

In the Prophet's own conception of human destiny, men and women have a common responsibility to remember God's goodness and to respond by fulfilling his will. Originally, both men and women were to offer prayer and alms; in later times, however, women's status deteriorated, and they did not have this obligation.

Historically, the major theoretical question concerning the self was the relation of human freedom to divine will. At least in the Meccan sections, the Qur'an takes human freedom for granted. Muhammad's call and his preaching make no sense without a capacity

to respond. Similarly, the scenes of Judgment Day assume that human beings have been responsible for their actions—that they could have done otherwise than they did. However, later Qur'anic passages emphasize God's omnipotence. As a result, the question arises: Does God lead some people astray—or at least leave them in error? In the Umayyad period a group of strict predestinarians (the Jabriya) stressed God's complete control. Opposing them were the Qasriya, who defended human responsibility. A third group, the Mutazilites, defended both human freedom and God's perfect justice. Still another position, that of Al-Ashari, satisfied many people with the following formula: "God creates in man the will to act and the act, and man acquires the act by performing it." The common people frequently behaved as if life was fated—that it was out of their hands. Among the few monistic mystics, human freedom was lost in the divine nature.

ULTIMATE REALITY

Islam is perhaps the most *theocentric* of the major religions. Before Muhammad, some Arabs had spoken of a high god "Allah" who was above the numerous idols. The divine name itself seems to fuse two words: *al-Ilah* ("the God"). It was an attempt to designate an ultimate divinity, a God who was beyond all demigods. From his visionary experience, Muhammad recognized that God is the only divinity, and that his primary designations are "Creator" and "Judge." As such, God leaves no place for other deities to function

When we considered the life cycle rituals, the annual rituals, and the weekly rituals of Yoruba Muslims, we glimpsed Islam's accommodation to the West African religious traditions that predated it. We get another glimpse of such cross-cultural accommodation by studying the different ways the different Muslim ethnic groups have conceived sainthood, the peak achievement of Muslim selfhood. For example, the Indonesian Muslims, who have been greatly influenced by Indian culture, have focused their religious imagination on saints whose style is markedly quieter than the style of the saints Moroccan Muslims have venerated. Since Islam starts to come into focus only when one begins to find the unity underlying such differences, let us attempt a comparative study of the Indonesian and Moroccan Muslim saints.

In Indonesian Muslim lore, Sunan Kalidjaga is the most important of the group of nine "apostles" considered to be the founders of Indonesian Islam. Legend has it that he was born the son of a high royal official of Madjapahit, one of the greatest and last of the Indonesian Hindu-Buddhist kingdoms, which dominated most of Eastern Java during the fourteenth and fifteenth centuries. In the sixteenth century Madjapahit declined, caught between the old Hindu-Buddhist order and the new Muslim order that was emerging. Pressured by this change, Kalidjaga moved to the new harbor state of Djapara, where he met another of the early apostles, Sunan Bonang, and was converted to Islam. Later Kalidjaga so greatly influenced Javanese politics that he is credited with Java's having become solidly Muslim. Symbolically, therefore, Kalidjaga serves as a bridge between the old Indic world of god-kings, ritual priests, and Indian shrines and the new Islamic world of pious sultans, Qur'anic scholars, and austere mosques. Indonesians love to contemplate the story of his conversion, for it recapitulates their good fortune in having gained access to the world of God, and it drives home the conviction that Islam is the best flower of the new phase of their history.

When Kalidjaga arrived in Djapara, he was a ne'er-do-well, accomplished in stealing, drinking, whoring, and gambling. So deep were his vices, he stole all his own mother's money, and when he had dissipated this he set out to steal from the public at large. Eventually he became a highwayman of such renown that people were afraid to go to the Djapara market lest they encounter him and lose all their goods. Into this scene strolled Sunan Bonang, a Muslim (probably an Arab) dressed in gorgeous clothes and expensive jewels, and carrying a cane of solid gold. Naturally he attracted the attention of Kalidjaga, who put a knife to his throat and demanded all his finery. But, to Kalidjaga's amazement, Bonang laughed in his face. Calling Kalidjaga by his name (though he had never met Kalidjaga before), Bonang chided him as though he were a little boy: "Don't always be wanting this thing and that thing. Such material desires are pointless. We live but a moment. It is foolish to be attached to worldly goods. Look: there is a whole tree full of money." Kalidjaga turned and saw a banyan tree transformed to gold and hung with jewels. At a stroke, he realized that material things were nothing compared with Bonang's power. What sort of a man must Bonang be, to be able to turn trees into gold and jewels and yet not care about gold and jewels at all? With this thought, Kalidjaga's life of vice repulsed him, and he begged Bonang to teach him spiritual power. Bonang agreed, but he warned Kalidjaga that such teaching was very difficult. Kalidjaga vowed he would persist until death, but Bonang merely told him, "Wait here, by the side of the river, until I return." Then he took his leave.

Kalidjaga waited by the side of the river for forty years, lost in thought. Great trees grew up around him, floods arose and receded, crowds jostled him back and forth, buildings went up and were torn down. Still he waited, lost in thought. Finally Bonang returned, and he saw that Kalidjaga had indeed been steadfast. So instead of teaching Kalidjaga the doctrines of Islam, Bonang simply told him that he had been a good pupil—indeed, that he had come to surpass Bonang himself. To demonstrate this, Bonang asked Kalidjaga difficult questions about religious matters, and Kalidjaga answered them all correctly. Then Bonang told him to go forth and spread Islam, which Kalidjaga did with unsurpassed effectiveness.

Because he had reformed his life, and penetrated the implications of his reform, Kalidjaga had become a Muslim. When he walked the meditative way that Indian culture had been impressing on Indonesia for centuries, he came out a Muslim— the new holy man forged in the fires of Indonesia's cultural transformation. So the message that was trumpeted whenever the legend of Java's greatest saint was told was that Islam is the obvious expression of the reformed, converted, highly developed religious personality. If one finds the depths of human authenticity, one eventually realizes that the Qur'an, the mosques, and the Muslim scholars are human authenticity's best expressions.

The Moroccan saint Sidi Lahsen Lyusi is quite a contrast to Kalidjaga. Lyusi was born into an obscure tribe of shepherds in the Middle Atlas Mountains of Morocco in 1631. Although he probably was of Berber descent, he claimed to be a *sherif,* or direct descendant of Muhammad. Lyusi died in 1691, so the sixty years of his life coincided with the rise of the Alawite dynasty (which still rules today in Rabat, the capital of Morocco) from the chaos of a preceding sectarian strife. Like Kalidjaga's, therefore, Lyusi's sainthood was intimately tied to a difficult time of transition, when people were looking for models of a new social order. However, where Kalidjaga functioned as a miniature of the new harmony that Indonesia sought, Lyusi directly opposed the power he saw rising in his times. Thus Clifford Geertz, whose description of these two saints we are following, characterizes Lyusi's approach as moralistic, in contrast to the aesthetic approach of Kalidjaga.

The chaos of Lyusi's lifetime is sometimes called the Maraboutic Crisis, and it arose after the collapse of the last of the Berber dynasties, the Merinid. A *marabout* is a holy man, and during the Maraboutic Crisis Morocco splintered into different political groups clustered around different holy men. Lyusi wandered from political group to political group, always restless and on the move. When he arrived in Tamgrut, a desert oasis, he encountered the famous Muslim saint Ahmed ben Nasir. Ben Nasir was sick with smallpox, and so he asked his disciples, one by one, to wash out his loathsome nightshirt. Each disciple refused, repelled by the disgusting garment and afraid for his health. Lyusi, who had just arrived and was not known to ben Nasir, approached the saint and volunteered for the job. He took the shirt to a spring, rinsed it, wrung it out, and then drank the foul water it produced. When he returned to the master his eyes were aflame, not with sickness but with what Moroccans call *baraka:* the supernatural power that makes a *marabout.*

The story summarizes the Moroccan notion of sainthood. The main forces at work in Lyusi's transformation into a man of *baraka* were his extraordinary physical courage, his absolute personal loyalty to his "teacher," his moral intensity, and an almost physical passage of sainthood from teacher to disciple. Thus the Moroccan notion of Muslim sainthood seems more energetic than the Indonesian. Whereas Kalidjaga was transformed by forty years of meditation near a river, Lyusi was transformed by a single act of heroic courage. Thirty years after this event, Lyusi had a momentous confrontation with Sultan Mulay Ismail, the great consolidator of the Alawite dynasty. In 1668, the Alawites had put an end to the Maraboutic Crisis and gained power in Morocco. The confrontation took place in the Sultan's new capital of Meknes, and it reveals the delicate relation between strongman politics and Maraboutism that has dominated Moroccan history. The warrior and the saint have been the two basic forms of heroism in Morocco, and this epic confrontation pitted a great warrior against a greater saint.

When Lyusi arrived in Meknes, Mulay Ismail received him as an honored guest. Indeed, he brought Lyusi to the court and made him his spiritual adviser. The sultan was building a large wall around the city and treating the men working on the wall cruelly. When one of the workmen fell from exhaustion and was sealed into the wall, some of the other workers came to Lyusi secretly to complain. Lyusi said nothing, but that night, when his supper was brought to his chamber, he broke all the dishes. He continued to do this, night after night, until all the dishes in the palace were broken.

Eventually the sultan learned what was happening and ordered Lyusi brought to him. When he asked the saint why he was acting so outrageously, the saint asked in return whether it was better to break pottery of clay or the pottery of God (human beings). Then he proceeded to upbraid the sultan for his cruelty to the workers. The sultan was not moved. Lyusi had abused his hospitality (a high crime in Moroccan culture), so he ordered Lyusi out of the city.

Lyusi left the palace and pitched his tent near the wall that was being built. When the sultan asked why the saint had not obeyed the royal order, Lyusi said that he had left the sultan's city and taken up residence in God's city. At this answer the sultan was so enraged that he charged out on horseback. Interrupting the saint's prayers (another high crime), he again asked why the royal order had been disobeyed. Again he received the answer that Lyusi was now in the city of God. Wild with fury, the sultan advanced to kill the saint. But the saint drew a line on the ground, and when the sultan's horse crossed the line, the horse's legs began to sink into the earth. Terrified, the sultan begged mercy and promised that he would reform. Lyusi said he only wanted a decree acknowledging that he was a *sherif,* entitled to the honors of a direct descendant of the Prophet. The sultan gave him this decree and Lyusi left Meknes (fearing for his life) to preach to the Berbers in the Middle Atlas forests.

After his death a great cult developed at his tomb, and he has since been revered as a most powerful *marabout.* In Lyusi Moroccan Islam has found an ideal embodiment of its moral passion, just as in Kalidjaga Indonesian Islam has found an ideal embodiment of its meditative passion.

in either the world's creation or in the destiny of humankind. Islam polished its theocentricity through controversy with polytheistic Arabs and then with Christians committed to the Incarnation and the Trinity.

The Creator made the world in six days (or in a single moment, according to *Sura* 54:50). Muslims trust that he guides the world wisely and unfailingly. God's knowledge of all creatures is total, and his mercy extends to all who acknowledge him. It is God in whose name every work is being begun and upon whose name will every future action depend. Thus, one has to add *"insha Allah"* ("if God wills") to every sentence that refers to a future act or a new direction of thought. To try to indicate God's fullness, the Qur'an encircles him with "most beautiful names." He is the First and the Last, the Inward and the Outward. Above all, he is Merciful and Compassionate. He is the All Holy, the Peace, the Light of Heaven and Earth. Transcendent though he be, he is also as near as the jugular pulse. Wherever one turns, there is his Face (the Qur'anic expression for God's essence).

Angels are also essential objects of Muslim doctrine. According to tradition, God created them from light. The Qur'an stresses that they are neither children of God nor female beings. They are intelligent and can become visible. From the Qur'an, Muslims know Gabriel as the angel of revelation. Israfil will blow the trumpet at Doomsday, and Azrael is the angel of death. Iblis is the fallen angel. Like Harut and Marut, he is a source of evil. Harut and Marut taught humankind witchcraft, but a beautiful woman seduced them and then imprisoned them in a well in Babylonia. Thus, the sacred space between the creature and the Creator has been abuzz with personages of interest.

Many scholars find the negative portion of the creed ("no God but God") very important, since it unequivocally rejects other peoples' gods. As well, it determined that the greatest sin in the Muslim code would be *shirk*—**idolatry** or "association" (of other objects of worship with God). The mystics sometimes took this to mean that nothing but God exists—that God alone is real. Among modern Muslims, anti-idolatry on occasion has worked against ideologies such as Marxism, capitalism, and nationalism, which some orthodox Muslims find incompatible with pure monotheism. Insofar as such ideologies gain the

COMPARISON			
DIMENSION	ISLAM	CHRISTIANITY	JUDAISM
Name of followers	Muslims	Christians	Jews
Began	7th century C.E.	1st century C.E.	2nd millennium B.C.E.
Originated in	Middle East	Middle East	Middle East
Founder	Muhammad	Jesus	Abraham
Monotheistic?	yes	yes	yes
Trinity?	no	yes	no
Jesus is	prophet	God the Son	teacher
Proselytizing?	yes	yes	no
Also spread by	conquest	conquest	diaspora
Adam and Eve?	yes	yes	yes
Old Testament prophets?	yes	yes	yes
Priests	no	some sects	before 70 C.E.
Congregated worship	weekly	weekly	weekly
Place of worship	mosque	church	temple before 70 C.E.; synagogue
Statues	no	in Roman Catholic	no
Angels	yes	yes	yes
Resurrection and apocalypse	early Islam	early Christians and some sects	Daniel, Pharisees, some messianic sects
Emphasis on heaven and hell	major	major in most sects	minor

ultimate concern of many human beings, they amount to new kinds of idolatry.

After Muhammad's death, debates arose about God's nature. At the beginning, the orthodox clung to the letter and imagery of the received text. That meant accepting descriptions of God that gave him a face, hands, and the like. The Mutazilites, who had contact with Hellenistic rationalism, pointed out the dangers latent in such anthropomorphism: When we think of God in human terms, we think of him as finite. Thus, the Mutazilites clung to the absolute unity of God,

accepting as a consequence that God cannot be imagined. In other words, they prized God's difference—the gulf that lies between the Creator and everything created. Indeed, to safeguard God's unity, the Mutazilites even questioned the doctrine of the divine attributes (that God has speech, sight, and so on). For that reason, the orthodox described the Mutazilites as "those who deny the attributes," a charge of heresy. In these debates, Muslims shared with Jews and Christians the consequences of an exposure to Greek reason. They had to ask whether their descriptions of

DIMENSION	ISLAM	CHRISTIANITY	JUDAISM
Salvation	from works	from Grace	from works
Scripture	Qur'an	Bible	Torah
Days of fasting	yes	in some sects	yes
Charity for poor	yes	yes	yes
Ten Commandments as ethical foundation	yes	yes	yes
Polygamy sanctioned	yes, but limited	in some sects	in some periods
Celibacy	never	in some sects	rarely (Essenes)
Male circumcision	puberty	medical option	infant
Pork	prohibited	allowed	prohibited
Alcohol	prohibited	allowed by most sects	allowed
Role of pilgrimage	major	minor	minor
Abraham seen as	ancestor through Ishmael	example of commitment	ancestor through Isaac
Mystics	Sufis	Monastics	Kabbalah Hasidim
Had to flee	Hegira from Mecca	persecution from other Christians	exodus from Egypt, persecution from Christians
Theocratic	when in majority	when in majority	when in majority
Prefer secular society	when in minority	when in minority	when in minority

God could be reconciled with what they could infer from the divine transcendence. For instance, they could infer that a Creator would be independent of the world, unlimited, unimaginable in created terms. From that it followed that any picture of God would be at best a useful fiction that might help some people's understanding. As a further extension of such rationalism, the Mutazilites denied that the Qur'an is God's uncreated word. To them that would have made it a coeternal attribute, something ever existent with God. However, calling the Qur'an "created" deeply offended the orthodox, for whom the Arabic text expressed a heavenly prototype. The human Qur'an was unalterable (which led the orthodox to resist all attempts to translate it from Arabic), because it derived from eternity. Thus, the Mutazilites and the orthodox clashed in their theologies of revelation.

In contrast, the Sufis tended to forego philosophical speculation, favoring instead a personal experience of the divine. For them the profitable way was not reasoning but intuition. Furthermore, the Sufis opposed Qur'anic fundamentalists by proposing that we should obey God out of love. To the fundamentalists, such a personal relationship seemed novel, for they admitted only a relationship of obedience: the Creator commanded and the creature obeyed.

FOLK RELIGION. On the folk level, magical practices mixed with worship. The Qur'an gave such practices some foundation by saying that the (bad) angels Harut and Marut taught the Babylonians magic (2:96). Ordinarily, the magician knew formulas that could conjure up the *jinns* or the angels. This has led to an expansion of the ways in which one can imagine the spirits and call them to one's aid. Amulets, reproductions of verses from the Qur'an, reproductions of God's names, and so on, are popular expressions of Muslim interest in attaining good luck. Similarly, Muslims continue to dread the "evil eye." To ward off its malignant influence, people constantly intersperse their conversation with "as God wills," and they wear amulets or give their children ugly names to keep the evil ones away. Popular religion also retains a considerable interest in astrology and fortune telling. A favorite technique for divining the future is to open the Qur'an at random and take the first verse that one's eye falls on as a cipher for what is to come. Other popular methods are reading palms or coffee grounds.

Sacrifice also has a place in Muslim worship of God. Those who can afford it immolate a sheep on the Day of Slaughtering during the annual pilgrimage to Mecca. This sacrifice is in memory of Abraham, who was willing to sacrifice his son Ishmael. People also make votive offerings—cocks, sheep, and so on—at holy places such as the tombs of saints. The animal should be slaughtered ritually, by cutting its jugular vein and its trachea in one stroke; tradition

recommends giving it to the poor. Finally, sacrifice is appropriate on almost any important occasion, such as starting construction of a house, celebrating a child's birthday, or expiating an offense.

God is certainly the Muslim center, and because the Qur'an is the definite expression of God, the Qur'an is the central place where the invisible Muslim God has become visible. How, then, does the Qur'an portray the Lord of the Worlds, the most ultimate and holy Muslim reality? It portrays him majestically, as a sovereign beyond compare, a power nothing earthly can approach. When God commands, the heavens thunder and the earth quakes. When God consoles, the winds quiet and the soul feels bliss. Were God not compassionate, merciful, life would be utterly terrifying. He is a severe judge, and none can abide the day of his coming. Yet he has sent prophets to warn humanity of his coming, has reset the strict boundaries of his laws. Muhammad is the seal of these prophets, in whom their work has come to complete fulfillment. As there is no God but God, so there is no final prophet but Muhammad.

flashcards and matching games
http://www.quia.com/jg/52826.html

jumbled words game
http://www.quia.com/jw/8708.html

millionaire game
http://www.quia.com/rr/41406.html

paragraph game
http://www.quia.com/cz/13526.html

Now take an online practice quiz at
http://www.quia.com/session.html

For session enter
relquiz13

download multiple-choice, true-false, and fill-in drills from
http://www.ureach.com/tlbrink
click on the public filing cabinet and folder rel13 and download *m13.exe, h13.htm, t13.exe,* and *f13.exe* and crossword puzzle *CW13.html*

MODERN TIMES

MILESTONES IN CONTEMPORARY RELIGION: KEY DATES		
When?	**Where?**	**What?**
1600	Italy	Galileo's heliocentric model
1740s	New England	Great Awakening
1776	Pennsylvania	Declaration of Independence
1783	New York	Shakers arrive in U.S.
1790s	U.S.	Bill of Rights, disestablishment of churches
1800	Ohio Valley	Great Revival
1830	New York	Church of Jesus Christ of Latter Day Saints
1844	New York	Second Coming predicted by William Miller
1859	England	Darwin's *The Origin of Species*
1875	Boston	Eddy's *Science and Health with a Key to the Scriptures*
1900	Los Angeles	Pentecostalism begins
1914	New York	Second Coming predicted by C.T. Russell
1922	Turkey	Attaturk establishes secular government
1925	Dayton, TN	Scopes "Monkey Trial"
1927	Vienna	Freud's *The Future of an Illusion*
1948	Amsterdam	World Council of Churches
1960s	Rome	Vatican II
1978	Guyana	People's Temple mass suicide
1973	Washington, DC	Roe vs. Wade abortion decision mobilizes Evangelicals
1979	Iran	ayatollahs declare Islamic Republic
1990s	Afghanistan	Taliban imposes strict theocracy
1993	Waco, TX	Koreshian siege
1997	San Diego, CA	Heaven's Gate comet suicides
1999	worldwide	heightened expectations of Y2K end of world
2001	New York City, Washington, DC	Al Qaeda 9/11 attacks
2004	U.S.	renewed efforts by A.C.L.U. to limit city logos, pledge of allegiance

In this chapter we concentrate on the last three hundred years, though aspects of modernity were present in the seventeenth century and still persist today. From the myriad events and thinkers who shaped the eighteenth and nineteenth centuries, we must select the most crucial. Clearly, the Enlightenment was crucial, as were the political revolutions in France and America, which were related to it. As well, the Industrial Revolution and the European colonization of large parts of the Americas, Africa and Asia play in the background. Of the thinkers, the line from Descartes to Marx that passes through Hume, Kant, and Hegel is perhaps the most significant.

The religious life of the West changed dramatically in the modern period. It had to contend with new political, philosophical, and scientific thought. More profoundly, for the first time it met a passionate counterfaith. As a movement or cause, modernity, as opposed to reliance on God, professes a deep commitment to humanity's own powers. (It has been argued that the delay of this process in Islam may account for the persistence of fundamentalist movements seeking theocracy.)

> *Joseph Smith, Jr., Mormon prophet, viewed the Indians as descendants of the lost tribes of Israel.*

ENLIGHTENMENT

The **Enlightenment** was the period in Western history, roughly corresponding to the eighteenth century, emphasizing such themes as reason, science, humanism and secularism, and these were bound to have an impact on religion. The Enlightenment began in the Netherlands and England in the mid-seventeenth century, but its most outstanding expressions arose in France and Germany. French rationalistic and materialistic philosophy (such as that of Voltaire, Helvetius, and Comte) and French revolutionary political action both derived from the Enlightenment. In Germany, Leibniz, Lessing, and Kant were its first philosophical offspring, while the "enlightened despotism" of Frederick the Great and Joseph II was a political result.

The Enlightenment thinkers saw themselves as part of a movement for progress, the watchword of which was criticism. They took as their enemies ignorance, intolerance, and repression, vowing to attack all such manifestations in national culture. To power this critical warfare, they drew on the model of the new physical science (especially that of Newton). That meant setting goals of clarity, precision, and rational order. Thus, the Enlightenment was a tremendous affirmation of humanity's rational capacities. Furthermore, it assumed that both creation and human nature were essentially good, thus producing an expectation of great progress. Things would improve and freedom would increase as trustworthy critical reason expressed trustworthy human nature situated in a quite trustworthy natural order. Here we see the key feature of **humanism** (the assumption that human beings are basically good and capable of working out their own salvation).

Quite obviously, the Enlightenment view of human nature clashed with that of traditional Christianity. Although reason held an important place in the medieval scholastic synthesis, the medieval mind never doubted that human nature is only perfectible through divine grace. In Reformation thought, Protestant and Catholic alike, both human reason and human love suffer the grievous effects of sin, with the result that only God can give the fulfillment they seek.

Real humanist concerns did not begin until after the Medieval period, with the period we know as the Renaissance. The Reformation (especially Calvin) was not humanistic, but it too weakened the power of tradition and authority and emphasized the role of the individual in salvation. Drawing on Renaissance humanism as well as on Reformation individualism, the Enlightenment thinkers concluded that things outside the province of human experience are of marginal concern. Enlightenment leaders tended to distrust both mystical experience and pure reason (Hegel was an exception), preferring instead **empiricism** (the observational method of science). Thus, David Hume (1711–1776) made a deep impression by limiting human thought to what sensation can verify.

For Kant and Hegel, the great innovators in the modern philosophy of consciousness, the reason that was to secure "the system" would not be subordinate to traditional religious doctrine. Thus, biblical, conciliar, and even Reformation notions of how things are in the world, were rejected during the Enlightenment. By a turn to the thinking subject, reality became the domain that we now call the secular world. The transcendent domain, the holy world of past ages, now had no place in the new worldview. Only as a manifestation of human self-expression, individual or social, did religion merit attention.

A great many factors were at work here, and not all of them sprang from human pride. A general disgust with religion—well deserved after a century of religious wars—certainly made a new humanistic beginning attractive. The overbearing weight of ecclesiastical institutions, which regularly stomped on individual rights and opposed free scientific inquiry, make anti-clericalism rather healthy. (The Spanish Inquisition and Oliver Cromwell's massacre of the Irish are heinous instances of religion used to desecrate human beings.)

In the sciences, the excitement of empirical discoveries and the slow differentiation of canons of critical judgment were forces that seemed to oppose traditional doctrine and religious authority over knowledge. Under the banner of religion huddled so much superstition and anti-intellectualism that simple integrity drove many educated people away from the Church. The best and the brightest frequently found themselves forced to choose between their love of human culture (the intelligence, sober judgment, and compassionate love that represent humanity at its best) and religion, Christianity, or even God.

However, applying Enlightenment's approaches of reason and humanism produced horrors that quite challenged those of the religious witch hunts and inquisitions. For instance, the bloodbaths of the French Revolution differed little from those of the religious wars, showing that not all fanaticism trumpeted about God. The American Constitution, despite its debt to Enlightenment humanism and its expression of democratic freedoms, was the framework of a culture that often treated nonwhites and women as less than human.

DEMYTHOLOGIZATION

Demythologizing is the effort to replace a storied, rather imaginative or magical view of reality with something more critical, more insistent on hard facts and rigorous logic. *Rationalization,* as social scientists such as Max Weber have used the term, is the effort to organize social institutions and culture generally in more reasoned—detached, disciplined, objective—ways. For example, when groups move from somewhat hit-or-miss family (clan) sources of help for the poor to government agencies operating according to clear laws or public policies, one can speak of welfare efforts being rationalized. Insofar as such rationalization can mean that the welfare efforts become more efficient, that they reach more people and distribute a group's resources more fairly, one can praise rationalization. Insofar as aid becomes depersonalized, cold, and hampered by bureaucratic details, one can long for the less rationalistic, more spontaneous old days.

Reason can clear up a lot of untidiness that irritated the thoughtful in the group. It can bring the focus back on important things—love of God, love of neighbor—and away from devotion to the saints or concern with cures that had taken center stage. Moreover, it can aid the reform of religious institutions and the lives of religious professionals, lessening the impact of unthinking custom, longtime systems of patronage, longtime assumptions of autocratic powers. Once again, however, people subjected to too sweeping or sudden a demythologizing or reform can fear that they have lost precious old friends. If they were used to praying to the saints or reverencing the clergy as presences of supernatural power, they may find the reformed religion unsatisfying.

To be sure, it is a far distance from religious reforms to secularism. Most of those who seek to make religious traditions more rational, less mythological in the pejorative sense, have no desire to oust divinity

INGREDIENTS OF MODERN ALTERNATIVES TO TRADITIONAL RELIGION	
APPROACH	DESCRIPTION
Science	empirical approach to knowledge; requires freedom to explore physical world beyond limitations of religious doctrine
Political liberalism	focus on individual rights; assumes that individuals can choose their own values
Secularism	separation of church and state; allows all denominations to exist, but prohibits any from exerting power on the general society
Humanism	doctrine that people are basically good, can work out their own salvation; celebration of human potential, this-worldly affairs
Historical criticism	realization that texts, institutions are historically conditioned
Global exploration	European theism is but one of many cultural options
Evolution	human beings are merely part of nature, more advanced animal forms; modern society is more advanced than the era of Christendom
Marxism	traditional religion a source of alienation and oppression; refocus on revolution and socialist order; alternative apocalyptic vision; totalitarian values; good and evil determined by interests of social class
Nazism	traditional religion a source of weakness; refocus on racist social order; alternative apocalyptic vision; totalitarian values; good and evil determined by interests of ethnic groupings

and make the world (*saeculum*) seem the be-all and end-all. But whenever one focuses the powers of reason, starts to ask the old myths to make logical sense, and wonders whether new ways being tried outside the tribe wouldn't be worth testing, one begins to tinker with the machinery that up to that point had kept people relatively content and secure. Certainly that should not make people refuse to initiate any innovations, but it suggests why older people tend to become conservative. With experience, they have realized that change often is more radical in its implications than those proposing it realize.

MODERN SCIENCE

Modern science developed mainly in the Christian West. Historians of science debate the whys and wherefores of this phenomenon, but it seems clear that neither Greece, India, nor China was fully hospitable to the blend of empirical observation and rigorous analysis that developed in the medieval West and flowered with such early moderns as Francis Bacon and Isaac Newton. Greece and India seem to have been inhibited by their sense that the cosmos went through endless cycles, repeating over and over again the same constant trends. True enough, the investigations of nature one finds in the pre-Socratics and the naturalistic works of Aristotle display many of the intellectual characteristics one associates with modern science. But in fact Greece apparently did not generate sufficient commitment to investigate the intelligibility of empirical nature to launch the audacious enterprise begun in the later medieval to early modern West. Similarly, while India and Islam came to house considerable mathematical talent, as well as interesting technologies, their science never became the systematic investigation of nature intrinsic to the institutions of modern science. China certainly developed great technological ingenuity, but again one finds that the worldview apparently could not undergird the modern patterns of detailed observation, bold hypotheses, and rigorous verifications. Modern science may in fact have reached in recent years a postmodern phase, in which it requires a more nuanced and less mechanistic philosophy of nature than that which empowered it in the seventeenth, eighteenth, nineteenth, and early twentieth centuries. But it gained its present shape in significant part because its cultural underpinnings included a doctrine that nature was the creative work of an omniscient deity and human beings were images of that deity through their powerful faculties of reason and will. Modern scientists have treated nature as a somewhat autonomous realm possessing laws that human reason (relatively or completely unaided by special divine graces) could master.

Such mastery had a twofold significance. On one hand, there was the pure desire to know how nature was constituted—to understand how the planets moved, how peas changed genetically, how the blood circulated through the human body. On the other hand, there was the desire to bring nature more fully under human control. Francis Bacon, especially, proposed the thesis that scientific knowledge amounted to power. Modern technology owes much of its origin to this thesis, since everything from modern medicine to modern engineering could be promoted as research and application geared to increasing humanity's power to bend nature to its service.

In the controversy between the astronomer **Galileo** and the authorities of the Catholic church early in the seventeenth century, the old theological ways clashed with the new scientific ways quite dramatically. The Church's main theologians contended that the old *geocentric* view (placing the earth at the center of the solar system) was the most consistent with the idea that God had created the earth as a special abode for his creatures, and that the planets, sun and moon were mere lights or adornments. Galileo's *heliocentric* view (placing the sun in the center, with the earth and other planets revolving around the sun) was seen as a threat to the centrality of God's creation, and hence to God himself. Galileo has been vindicated and made a champion by later modernity, but it is important to realize that in his own day his proposals were bound to seem impious. God then was thought much more immediately involved in the running of the natural world, and the priority of divine revelation (necessary for salvation from sin) was considered much more important than any understanding or practical benefits the investigation of nature might bring. Certainly most present-day theologians would say the Catholic authorities were unwise to connect a geocentric view of the solar system with Christian orthodoxy, but traditional peoples have tied their sense of how the cosmos came into being and was structured with their doctrinal and ethical systems. The heliocentric view may have forced theologians to redefine God and de-mythologize some of the Old Testament stories (e.g., how Joshua commanded the sun to stand still), but it did not weaken the teleological argument for God's existence (indeed, the complicated nature of the heliocentric theory seemed to require a divine mathematical mind to create it).

A more severe threat was posed in 1859 by Charles **Darwin's** formulation of the theory of **evolution.** If different species are merely the product of natural selection of randomly occurring genetic mutations, then the complexity of individual organs can be explained in a way other than that of a divinely conscious designer. Evolution was immediately attacked by the more fundamentalist Christians of Darwin's time, who saw that this new scientific theory challenged the historical validity of the description in *Genesis*. In some localities governments have passed laws limiting the teaching of evolution, while in other localities fundamentalist parents may have responded by taking their children out of the public school system. In 1925, the famous Scopes "monkey trial" in Tennessee featured William Jennings Bryan (who prosecuted a teacher accused of teaching evolution) and Clarence Darrow (who defended the teacher by attacking literal interpretations of *Genesis* as an account of creation). The prosecution won the verdict at the trial, but Darrow carried public opinion, promoting evolution and secular education in America ever since.

Interestingly, it was the Catholic Church that resolved not to fall again into the trap of arguing theology with science. The Church's position is that God could have created the world and humans through the process of evolution. God may have given our ancestors the story of *Genesis* to convey to humans in the most vivid manner that humans are creatures who must obey God. Adam and Eve remain relevant, even if their existence cannot be verified historically.

Science steadily developed its own canons of procedure, indeed its own orthodoxies. The success of this development, combined with the greater wealth and health people came to enjoy from the labors of scientists and engineers, made the reservations of religious professionals seem either sour grapes or sheer timidity. Not until recent decades, when nuclear power burst on the scene with terrifying prospects of annihilation, chemistry and biology revealed horrible possibilities for polluting the earth, and military weaponry

Humanism is the perspective that people are basically good and can work out their own salvation. Many atheists and secularists and deists are humanists (but not all are, and certainly Freud was not humanistic). Most denominations are not humanistic, finding some problem with human nature (e.g., original sin), which requires divine intervention as a solution. However, some theologians (e.g., Pelagius) and some denominations (e.g., Unitarians) have a more humanistic orientation. One of the most powerful arguments for the humanists is that religion can be no better than humans, because

1. People wrote scripture
2. People decided which scripture to canonize
3. People interpret scripture

Respond to that argument or to other assumptions of humanism.

Contribute to this discussion at
http://forums.delphiforums.com/rel101

became unimaginably lethal, did confidence in modern science and technology take a significant body blow. Even now, huge portions of Western culture continue to cope with these and vast other problems (hunger, homelessness, drugs, economic dysfunctions, widespread criminality) as though physical science, technology, and behavioral science were the best sources for remedies. Some religious fundamentalists may oppose such an assumption, but it remains to be seen whether anti-scientific religion proves itself to be any more effective than anti-religious scientism and secularity. Religion that affirms the independence and value of science, and science that honors the mystery at the core of religion, could be good neighbors.

LIBERALISM

There are many words and movements one could use to describe the political turn away from traditional, supposedly divine norms to rights defined by human beings themselves, but *liberalism* can stand duty for a goodly number of them. Probably the most influential liberal thinker was the Englishman John Locke (1632–1704), but other thinkers in England, France, Germany, and the United States both drew upon his thought and advanced it in new directions. Locke studied the classics, lectured on moral philosophy, and then took training as a physician. His political philosophy espoused a constitutional monarchy, a parliamentary government, and an enumeration of human rights. Life, liberty, and property summarized much of his platform, which had great influence in the eighteenth-century revolutions in both the United States and France. Although Locke wrote treatises in defense of the reasonableness of Christianity, his understanding of human nature in fact was considerably more empiricist (considerably less mythological) than that of traditional Christianity. Although raised as a Puritan, he tended to treat theological themes (the existence of God, revelation) in a rather restrained way, separating doctrine from what one can determine by empirical reason. This perspective helped undergird his position that true religion is tolerant of others' religious opinions. Relatedly, Locke was skeptical of the claims of any one church or religious group to know with certainty the way to salvation. In the tradeoff between institutional authority and the rights of individual conscience, he opted for individual conscience.

One can see, then, that while Locke kept ties to traditional religious views and the priority of the divine, he paved the way for the later liberal stress on humanism. As science seemed to place more and more of the natural world under the influence of human beings, and as religious institutions showed themselves conservatively opposed to progress in either the physical sciences or political efforts to emancipate people from the destructive control of kings or the aristocratic classes, Lockean principles justified emphasizing the (empirically valid) truth human beings could discover on their own and the political freedoms that ought to flow from considering the individual conscience something precious—indeed, something sacred.

Many liberals in fact assumed that social morality would continue to follow patterns indebted to Christian culture, but liberalism itself tended to erode the doctrinal bases of that morality. Two centuries after Locke, John Stuart Mill advanced the liberal outlook, writing persuasively about individual liberties (which included the emancipation of women). In France, Jean Jacques Rousseau had brought forward romantic notions of the benefits that would accrue were human beings left free to have their unspoiled (relatively unsocialized) natures develop. In the economic sphere, Adam Smith, the Scottish economist (or moral philosopher), had advocated laissez-faire policies that would give maximum play to individual initiative, trusting that a free market would somehow manage the best possible development and distribution of wealth.

What these various "liberal" thinkers held in common was a stress on the freedom of individual human beings to run their own lives. Often they assumed social agreements and controls that their later successors did not assume, but in general they wanted to move away from strict controls by either church or state that would inhibit people from choosing to become what they thought best. Theological traditionalists tended to criticize such liberalism by arguing that sin made human beings much less trustworthy than the liberals assumed, while traditional political conservatives argued that power was well handled by only a few and liberalism opened the door to anarchy. On the whole, the religious and political establishments supported one another in offering cautions against liberal views.

Whether or not they explicitly cast aside traditional religious guidance and traditional religious views of God and human nature, liberals tended to put divinity in the shade. They were more interested in such this-worldly questions as political freedoms, educational reforms, and license to develop entrepreneurial projects. The Industrial Revolution was an ambiguous phenomenon, for on one hand it brought this-worldly expertise and drive to bear on creating previously unknown disbursements of wealth, while on the other hand it severely limited the actual liberty of thousands of workers. Behind the liberal stress on individual conscience lay the stress of the Protestant reformers on the rights of individual conscience in religious matters, but the reformers and their heirs certainly had assumed the priority of divine revelation (i.e., revelation given to individuals rather than to the Church as an institution).

Insofar as liberalism meant being free of oppressive authorities, it ran in tandem with many themes of the eighteenth-century Enlightenment. Both movements were excited at the prospect of human beings coming of age sufficiently to think for themselves, depend on their own resources, and solve their main political, economic, and technological tasks with energy and confidence. For both, traditional religion often seemed a source of ignorance and repression, so both contrasted human autonomy with an older, religiously based heteronomy, arguing that it was more honest, profitable, and fitting that human beings look to themselves.

As one can easily imagine, such a call to self-reliance tended to produce both fits of enthusiasm and fits of depression. While people who had chafed under what they took to be repressive theological or political regimes found the humanistic message emancipating, people who found human ingenuity or human goodness unequal to the tasks of producing wealth in which all might share and developing a fully inclusive political system could despair of life apart from divine assurances and controls. The freedom to which the liberal thinkers called their fellow human beings held both terrors and joys. To those who felt strong enough to depend on themselves, it was good news, pressed down and overflowing. To those who longed for a tidy sense of reality, a map through time that would lay things out quite neatly, the liberal call could seem a siren song portending disaster.

Nonetheless, liberal thought gained sufficient influence in modern Europe and modern America to become a dominant political outlook. For example, the common assumption of the typical citizen of the United States that one has the right to run one's own life with little outside interference owes much to this classical liberal tradition. Through history, of course, many notions originally associated with the liberal thinkers have been transferred to latter-day "conservatives" or "libertarians," this passion for individual autonomy primary among them. Under whatever label, however, originally liberal ideas have challenged the traditional religious systems that made God's laws the major determinant of everyday behavior and that gave religious institutions the main say in determining what was real or how people ought to live.

THE U.S. SITUATION

The American constitution became the embodiment of liberalism, secularism, and humanism. Seventeenth-century America became a refuge for Protestants who opposed what they considered oppressive practices in their native lands and who stressed individual rights of conscience. The Church of England was strong in Virginia, Georgia, and the Carolinas. The Dutch Reformed Church dominated New York and New Jersey. Germans and Dutch flocked to Pennsylvania,

where they were joined by the Quakers. Congregationalists dominated New England, except for Rhode Island (which was founded by a group of Baptists). Catholics were an important group in Maryland. A major force inspiring James Madison's theory of balanced factions was the religious diversity within and between the separate states. The solution was the First Amendment: no single denomination would be allowed to dominate the federal (or state) governments. All religions were to be tolerated, not because religious institutions had rights, but because individuals had rights to choose their own denominational affiliation, in their generally secular quest for life, liberty, and the pursuit of happiness.

MARXISM

In the nineteenth century, Karl **Marx** (1818–1883) was the main influence in shifting liberal ideas into the sphere of economics. For Marx, atheism was a necessary postulate of human freedom, while the principal subjugation human beings suffered came from the exploitation of the working classes by their capitalist bosses. Marx saw history as a dialectical interplay of such forces as evolutionary matter and class conflicts. Although he borrowed considerably from the German idealistic philosopher G. W. F. Hegel (1770–1831), Marx had little patience with Hegel's interests in the operations of the divine Spirit. To his mind, the worlds of politics and economics, which mutually determined one another, were the things upon which to concentrate.

Marxist groups became the leading representatives of a wider socialist movement that regularly targeted religious bodies as props of an oppressive status quo. In the name of human progress toward justice and prosperity, they regularly denounced old religious doctrines and practices. For some, God and Jesus were not great problems, because they could be interpreted as champions of the poor. But for others, anything religious, otherworldly, dealing with spirituality and the sacred was atavistic—a throwback to the days of superstition and degenerate myth. Now that human beings had come of age, as modern science and technology surely showed they had, such backwardness was immoral. Those who indulged in it were either hopeless fools or knowing manipulators of forces designed to keep the common people in thrall to the owners who were so handsomely profiting from their sweat.

Although Marxist groups often have been better at rhetoric than hard analysis, and although often their own accession to power has brought worse repressions than those they had promised to end, much of the Marxist vision has entered into the liberal humanistic tradition, as a sort of further transfusion of energy and idealism. Whereas the original liberals were rather individualistic and did not criticize the socioeconomic construction of reality with great penetration, Marx and his followers studied labor and capitalism with considerable acumen. In line with many of the ideas of the biblical prophets, they denounced piety that did not pay off in justice, indeed did not produce mercy and helpfulness toward society's least well-off. In their critiques of religion, they tended to demonstrate how religion could be an ideology: a scaffolding of ideas that supported current economic and political arrangements and so went hand in glove with the interests of the wealthy classes.

Marxism of course has changed shape considerably in the twentieth century, but what has remained constant in its many incarnations as the inspiration of political revolutions has been its assurances that history is on the side of the lower working classes, who have only to rise up and fight their oppressors to advance the day when there will be a classless, egalitarian society. The Soviet and Chinese communist regimes have been the two outstanding examples of wholesale efforts to remake states by Marxist principles, and the successes and failures of both have proved highly illuminating. On one hand both may have improved the material lot of their lowest level of society, but on the other neither has scrupled in shedding rivers of blood to put down any individuals or groups they felt threatened their dogmatic programs.

In these two Marxist regimes, the twentieth century had object lessons in the assets and liabilities of a humanism defined as a break with traditional recourse to divine laws about human behavior. The third great object lesson, the German Nazi regime (1933–1945) certainly stemmed from different philosophical (or mythical) foundations, but it furnished an equally powerful lesson. The wrath of the movement was particularly directed against the Jews, whom the Nazis blamed for all modern evils, but Christians soon realized that

Give a definition of religion and then show how Soviet-style communism (or the Nazism of the Third Reich) did (or did not) meet that definition of religion.

Contribute to this discussion at
http://forums.delphiforums.com/rel101

Nazism was equally antithetical to their own views, requiring them to choose between Christ and the Fuhrer.

On occasion, both liberals and evangelicals (people rooted in the Christian gospel) pressed for social change. The Industrial Revolution produced some abysmal working conditions, and late-nineteenth-century Christian exponents of the **social gospel** agreed with Karl Marx that such conditions destroyed human dignity. In Latin American Catholicism of recent decades, **liberation theology** has had an even more explicit kinship with radical movements. Some liberation theologians combined Marxist economic analyses with Christian doctrine. The most eloquent are Latin Americans, but thought like theirs has penetrated the counsels of both Protestant Geneva and Catholic Rome.

EXISTENTIALISM

The experience of war and political unrest in the first half of the twentieth century convinced many moderns that ultimate relevance was nowhere to be found. The result was the great wasteland dramatized somewhat self-indulgently by the literature of **Existentialism** that flourished after World War II. Human beings, in the phrase of Jean-Paul Sartre, were nothing but useless passions. They had no definite essence, nothing by way of a nature fashioned by God (which might have given them guidance). Their burden was to be completely free and so completely responsible for what they made of themselves.

In contrast, much psychology and sociology was deterministic, teaching that early family life or social conditioning left people little if any freedom. Religion therefore found itself disregarded on two sides: Existentialists said that human freedom was incompatible with the existence of God, while much social science said that freedom, and so choice about ultimate destiny, was largely illusory.

WORLDVIEW

NATURE AND DIVINITY IN HUMANISTIC PERSPECTIVE

At its core, humanism declares that the human experience is ultimately relevant. Some religious humanists qualify this by saying that God so loved humankind that He gave them the divine capacities for reason and love, but most humanists are secular and take the position that religious phenomena are to be evaluated according to human criteria, rather than the other way around. Since the Italian Renaissance, humanism has connoted a turn to the human figure in art, a return to the classical literature of Greece and Rome that celebrated human pathos, and an assertion that human experience is worthy of interest and concern (in contrast to theological tendencies to deprecate human experience as disfigured by sin and overshadowed by the death and judgment soon to terminate one's passage through this vale of tears). One can connect humanism with religious views, as Christian humanists especially have done, in which case it tends to mean celebrating the grandeur of what God has done in making men and women of flesh and spirit. In recent years, humanism has become the bugbear of religious fundamentalists, who have contrasted it with acceptance of the primacy of God. Where religion has said life ought to be God-centered, arrogant humanists have said that human beings ought to be the measure and interest of all our doings. Thus humanism (or more specifically, this "secular humanism") has been taken to be atheistic, in fact if not in outright profession.

Secularization is the process by which this-worldly things have become more important and heavenly things have faded into the background. Industrialization, urbanization, and the demythologizing effects of scientific and critical thinking usually are nominated as major reasons why secularization has occurred in the modern West (and, through the cultural exports of the modern West, in other parts of the globe). Secularization is ethically neutral—whether it has been good or bad depends on further premises and judgments. Secularism is the viewpoint, the philosophical position, that secularization has been good because other-worldliness was a distraction or a vitiation of human development. In other words, secularism assumes or argues that God, grace, salvation, sin, and the other staples of the religious worldviews that have urged people to look beyond the here and now for their ultimate relevance have all been misguided notions.

SOCIETY AND SELF IN HUMANISTIC PERSPECTIVE

Humanism may exalt society as the proper focus of human interest and endeavor, or it may view society as the source of most human corruption. By and large, the modern totalitarian "isms" have taken the first option, making "the people" the justification for their policies, whether benign or murderous. What has tended to suffer in modern humanistic social thought is the notion that "community" itself is a mysterious creation, a whole much greater than the sum of its parts and so a wonder suggesting divine aid. To be sure, people who share military, political, or cultural ventures usually experience bonding. The question remains, however, what makes such bonding sacred—valuable enough to warrant reverence and sacrifice? Much the same question attends human love, as we shall see when we come to humanistic perspectives on the self. On their own terms, most humanists do not raise such further questions. A few reflective humanists do not raise them as a matter of principle, having judged or postulated that such questions bring no profit or deal with a transcendent realm about which we can at best be agnostic. The majority of secular humanists, however, simply don't have the spiritual interest, need, or drive to press their first views of community toward something foundational. In this they are like the majority of adherents of any religion, whose acceptance of doctrine is equally uncritical. Nonetheless, secular humanism certainly can be developed into an impressive view of human community, if only by a logic such as the following.

Assume that there is no God demanding to be set at the center of one's system. Then survey what remains of human experience for what seems most valuable. You may decide that nature is the most valuable portion of reality and so dedicate yourself to understanding, conserving, or developing nature. You may decide that personal freedom, individual autonomy, is the most precious thing you know and so hymn the life of the artist, or the entrepreneur, or any other species of self that relies mainly on its own resources and tries to create relevance through its work or its love. If you choose either of these two courses, you certainly will not be alone. But probably you will find yourself with more company if you decide that helping suffering fellow human beings, or trying to create peaceful and beautiful human communities, best expresses your sense of how a godless world seems most worth inhabiting. So one finds dedicated but humanistic doctors, lawyers, teachers, social workers, politicians, and the like, who give their lives to helping other people or trying to bring peace and justice to a given portion of global society. One finds internationalists, even diplomats and soldiers, who have made their own the cause of trying to stay the forces of evil that ruin life for so many. Certainly it is rare to find someone both completely dedicated and fully convinced that all such social effort in no way reaches beyond the grave, but it is not unknown, perhaps not even extraordinary.

In a brave sort of agnosticism, many good people place brackets around ultimate questions and content themselves with doing here and now something they can be sure will make a positive difference. So they set broken bones, try to repair broken marriages, arbitrate grievances between owners and workers, try to smooth relations between alienated or warring nations. Realizing that most societies are much less just and enjoyable than they might be, such humanists decide they will spend themselves playing midwife to the birth of a somewhat better world. However slight their success, it will justify their time spent as police, firefighters, nurses, ministers of a gospel they contend centers on brother- and sisterhood.

The self emerges in humanistic perspective no less mysteriously than it does in religious perspective, because any probing of the self—psychological, artistic, or medical—runs into reams of unknown factors. We have learned a great deal about the physical and psychological mechanisms that go into a human identity, yet we are so far from understanding the whole that what we have learned clearly is but a fraction of all there is to know. How our brains work, how our hormones interact with our brains, whether we have souls, how our nerves quicken our bodies, what causes some people to have brilliant memories or imaginations or computational skills, what causes other people to suffer severe depression or schizophrenia or to be savants—these and hundreds of other aspects of selfhood await full understanding. Although genetic

Is the Darwinian theory of evolution (that the human species evolved from earlier, apelike species) incompatible with your understanding of Christianity? What should be the response of Christians to the claims of evolution? Should they seek to find evidence to disprove evolution? Should they concede that if enough scientific evidence supports evolution, then God becomes irrelevant? Should Christians opt for more symbolic interpretations of *Genesis* that would not be vulnerable to scientific evidence? (*Hint:* Make sure that you use these terms correctly.)

Validity (relating to the truth of scientific statements)

Value (relating to the truth of religious statements)

Verification (relating to proof of scientific statements)

Vindication (relating to proof of religious statements)

Belief (relating to faith of scientific statements)

Commitment (relating to faith of religious statements)

Contribute to this discussion at http://forums.delphiforums.com/rel101

research continues to pinpoint connections between our genes and certain illnesses and behaviors, we still don't know exactly why some people are shy and other people are extroverted. We don't understand how children acquire language so easily, so naturally.

But perhaps the greatest of the self's mysteries continues to be the encounters with other selves that bring the healing and fulfillment associated with "love." Love is so common a phenomenon, and yet so precious a flower, that we understandably find it bruited about everywhere, advertised in the cheapest of bookstores, collapsed into sex to sell automobiles. Romantic love, the love of friendship, parental love, love of nature, love of God, love of creative work, the love that arises when two or three gather in the name of a common cause, suffering love, self-love—on and on the varieties go. Love is the foremost energy of the self, not to be divorced from the self's eros for knowledge but more central and profound. Children who are not loved do not thrive. Adults who are not loved and do not love in return do not thrive. Love naturally overflows into teaching, guiding, caring for, trying to heal, trying to help make amends. It takes form as forgiveness, reconciliation, peacemaking. And all of these forms of love, all of these facets of the self's adventure in search of love, of course intrigue humanists as much as religious people—sometimes more.

The humanistic self may be in special danger of turning narcissistic, but the religious self is in special danger of alienation—prematurely surrendering the self to "God" and so never maturing, becoming responsible, developing a healthy self-esteem. The humanistic self may be in special danger of despairing, since its philosophy offers it no ultimate explanation for its brief time in the sun. On the other hand, the religious self can be repulsively full of answers, a know-it-all confusing the mystery of God with the doctrines of its little church, synagogue, mosque, or sect. On its own terms, the humanistic self has to consider the religious self liable to the same anxieties it is and so a fit object for compassion. On its own terms, the religious self has to say that the divine mystery plays in all people's lives, humanistic and religious selves alike, wooing them at the center where they occasionally go still and wonder about the whole. Neither humanistic wholeness nor religious grace can rightly be considered the exclusive preserve of a favored few.

Everywhere, people who enter into themselves, center down, and face both their terrors and their joys,

How could we use the terms in this course to understand the political differences between Republicans and Democrats? Have the Democrats merely assumed the position of humanistic theologians (e.g., Pelagius) that people are basically good, and therefore we must spend more on education and to help the poor? Have the Republicans merely assumed a Calvinist-Freudian perspective: people are driven by sexual and aggressive drives, and therefore we need harsh punishments and a strong military to protect us?

Contribute to this discussion at
http://forums.delphiforums.com/rel101

find an ambiguous darkness. Is it the blank nothingness of nature's muteness, the near side of a cosmic and personal irrelevance? Or is it the cloud of unknowing about which the mystics speak, the presence of a God who can never be understood and always must be accepted in trust? Positioned this way, the two selves, humanistic and religious, seem more alike than different. The honest humanist who does not know about ultimacy and fears that religious commitment would be hypocritical seems little different from the religious person who confesses that God or the Buddha-nature can never be mastered and will always force human hearts to abide in mute hope.

SUMMARY: THE HUMANISTIC CENTER

Although there are many varieties of humanists (people who do not configure reality in terms of God or a transcendent ultimate reality), they all qualify as humanists because they make humankind the main treasure or focus of their lives. A few think that the natural world onto which human intelligence opens is the most important consequence of there being a species that can understand and reflect, but more are preoccupied with social and personal questions. Indeed, probably the most typical center in a humanistic worldview is the border between society and the self, where the group and the individual interact to construct "reality."

In traditional, premodern societies, most people gained their personal identity and sense of the world through dramatic rites of passage. At puberty and marriage, they appropriated their people's sense of

how reality was configured, of what the ultimate powers expected of a man or a woman. With the demise of the great, guiding myths typical of premodern societies, the social shaping of personal identities has become more diffuse and confused. Indeed, at times it seems that young people are the main targets in a war for influence over the future generation. Certainly parents, teachers, coaches, and friends continue to exert major influences, but the lack of heroic role models means that many young people will have only middling confidence that they know what they would like to become.

What is it that the typical secular humanist wants to become? Our estimate is someone self-reliant, realistic, and free. There being no privileged revelation in the humanistic worldview, one has to make do with the best wisdom one can glean from either past humanistic traditions or personal experience. The best educated of humanists working with these tools soon find that little has changed in their project since the time that Plato or the Buddha ventured forth. Drop the few trappings of myth and divinity one finds in the Platonic dialogues or the sutras of the Buddha and you have two interesting models of the effort to find relevance without recourse to religious institutions. In fact, both Plato and the Buddha ended with visions of transcendent reality, but their methods seem quite amenable to adaptation by modern humanists.

In creating the literary identity of Socrates, Plato described a man bent on wringing wisdom from his experience, deflating the pompous fools who trumpeted unthinkingly about tradition, and listening to the inner voice of conscience, which he called his *daimon*. Socrates became the wisest man in Athens because he learned how much he didn't know—most of his wisdom was negative. For Plato the death of Socrates was a telling judgment on Athenian society. If the polis could not see the worth of the one man who might have saved its culture, it was blind unto spiritual death. The Platonic notion that one would only have a decent polis if one gained a philosopher-king extrapolated from the death of Socrates: the chance that a truly wise person would come to secular power was slim indeed.

The Buddha was humanistic in not relying on past Indian tradition but basing his teaching on his personal experience. Certainly he was formed by Indian meditation techniques and philosophical assumptions, but the crucial aspects of his own program drew their

authority from his own enlightenment experience. Above all, the proposition that the way to escape suffering is to eliminate desire went to the heart of every person's existence, presenting itself as something anyone might test at home.

In latter days, humanists have been most true to their own principles when they have followed Socrates and the Buddha in focusing on personal experience. In arguing that religious tradition was folly, they were most persuasive when they challenged religious institutions to show how religious doctrines formed people who were happy, productive, and left the world better for their having passed through it. In the light of such a challenge, the religions that had been responsible for slaughter in warfare, repression in sexual life, poverty in subjugation to wealthy upper classes, and crippling fear of divine wrath, stood revealed as inhumane, perhaps even antihuman. On the other hand, the religions that could point to mystics rapt in love of a good God, to men and women spending themselves in caring for the poor, the sick, and the uneducated, and to thinkers who took away some of the sting of death and injustice, stood up to the humanists' challenge. Usually they had already accepted a pragmatism such as that of Jesus and agreed that one could know any group or intellectual position by the fruits it grew.

In all such experientially focused studies, one of course would run smack into evil, destruction, the dark side of human existence. The pessimistic humanisms pay such heed to this admittedly gigantic side that they come away with little hope that peace or justice will ever prevail. Perhaps the best question then becomes why light has continued to shine in the midst of such darkness, why the darkness has failed to snuff it out. For the metaphysician, the thrust of this question is toward the roots of existence, where one must wonder why there is something rather than nothing. For the anthropologist, the question becomes why creativity, goodness, and even holiness continue to emerge, generation after generation.

RESPONSES TO SECULARISM

Although Americans have generally endorsed secularism as public policy, this does not mean that they perceived a diminishing spiritual need. If anything, the fact that public and communal displays of the spirit were limited meant that people had to direct their spiritual needs even more to private denominations. The fact that no one denomination received the support of the government meant that there would be an extreme competition among denominations to market their own brands of doctrines, ethics, and rituals. For these reasons, America has been the most fertile soil of new religious movements in the last three hundred years.

THE GREAT AWAKENING AND THE GREAT REVIVAL

In the early part of the eighteenth century a religious revival took place that was known as the **Great Awakening.** The hallmark of this revival was dedicated and inspirational preachers. In North America, the movement began around 1725 and was eclipsed by the American Revolution. It was strongest in the Calvinistic churches: Presbyterian, Dutch Reformed, Congregationalist, but later the Baptists and Methodists also got into the act. The most famous of these preachers was Jonathan **Edwards** (1703–1758), who revitalized Calvinist theology, and demanded a purified church of regenerate members.

The **Great Revival** occurred in the early days of the new American Republic, and mostly on (what was then) the western frontier. This meant the western part of the original thirteen colonies (e.g., New York, Pennsylvania) and in the Ohio Valley. Whereas the Great Awakening a generation earlier had emphasized theology and church organization, the Great Revival in the west emphasized ritual. In order to understand the psychological and sociological dynamics of this movement, we must start with the westering Yankee family. If they had a book in the log cabin, it was the Bible. Yet the rush into the Appalachian mountains and Ohio Valley had outstripped the organizational structure of the established denominations. The Great Revival was more like a series of Woodstock concerts than a campaign to build local churches. The Baptists, Methodists, and Presbyterians all participated despite disagreements about Calvinist theology and rituals such as infant baptism. Perhaps it would be more appropriate to say that all of these denominations competed for souls who were ripe for communal religious activity.

Perhaps the most famous of the events of the Great Revival occurred in 1800 in Kane Ridge, Kentucky, where an estimated 100,000 persons arrived and were treated to dozens of preachers on the tops of rolling hills, each trying to outdo the others, using metaphors drawn from frontier life. One would describe the power of the Holy Spirit coming upon you as the power of the cracking of a whip. Upon hearing this, some of the audience in attendance developed the "jerks" in which their limbs (and women's long hair) would behave like the end of a whip, jerking violently, apparently beyond conscious control. Other preachers talked about the Holy Spirit hitting you like the power of an Indian's arrow, and some in the audience grabbed their chests and keeled over, having been slain by the power of the spirit. Other preachers said that Satan was as wily as a raccoon and that God wanted Christians to be as loyal and brave as hound dogs. Some of the audience then got down on all fours, barked, and ran around as if treeing the devil.

PENTECOSTALISM

About a hundred years later, another time of emotional revivalism swept the United States. The movement, known as **Pentecostalism,** started in Los Angeles and spread throughout the country. The primary audience was rural Americans who were moving to the large cities, which were typically dominated by the culture of Catholic and Jewish immigrants and secular governments. Pentecostal revivals appealed primarily to the poor—whether white, Hispanic, or African American. Many of these early revivals were racially integrated. The emotional experiences that could be found at Pentecostal revivals included "faith" healings of physical illness, testimonials of miraculous financial blessings that removed poverty, and occasional exorcisms of demons. The emotionalism became excessive at times, with spirit-filled individuals falling onto the floor and rolling around (thus the somewhat pejorative nickname "Holy Rollers").

Perhaps the most distinctive, and controversial, feature of the Pentecostal movement has been speaking in **tongues (glossolalia).** This was described in the New Testament (e.g., *Luke 4*, *Acts*) as a spiritual gift given to the apostles: they were overcome by the Holy Spirit and could then could speak in a strange language (tongue) that they had not previously known. This experience has been interpreted as foreign languages (in order to facilitate proselytizing to a polyglot

Glossolalia, the speaking in tongues, was a spiritual gift during apostolic times. How do you understand this spiritual gift: ecstatic utterances in an altered state of consciousness? the language of angels? a sign of spiritual favor? self-delusion? What is the proper role of speaking in tongues in today's church? Cite scripture to back up your position.

Contribute to this discussion at
http://forums.delphiforums.com/rel101

Prayer tower at Oral Roberts University

world); the language of the angels (for praising God); or, from a modern psychological perspective, a dissociative altered state of consciousness in which an individual experiences ecstasy while uttering unintelligible sounds. In his first epistle to the Corinthians (chapter 12) Paul indicated a concern that this practice was becoming excessive. Although he acknowledged tongues as a genuine spiritual gift, he urged the Corinthian Christians not to value tongues higher than other gifts or to allow the pursuit of tongues to distract Christians from more important concerns, such as charity. Some of the more extreme modern Pentecostals have ignored Paul's cautions and have claimed that speaking in tongues is essential, a sign of the "second baptism," implying that one who lacks this experience is a second-class Christian.

The Pentecostal (also known as Holiness) movement led to the establishment of many different denominations: United Pentecostal, Assembly of God, and Church of God in Christ, among others. These were the preachers who came to dominate the mass media. Aimee Semple McPherson (1890–1944), who founded the Foursquare Church, became the first radio broadcast evangelist in the 1920s. Oral Roberts, of the Assembly of God, was a tent "faith healer" in Oklahoma, but when he demonstrated his powerful "faith healing" rituals on television in the 1950s, he raised millions of dollars and established Oral Roberts University in Tulsa. In the 1970s, "Reverend Ike" used radio and TV to market his "blessing plan" for financial success to the urban ghettoes. In the 1980s Jim Bakker and (then) wife Tammy Faye, produced emotion-filled television broadcasts but finally ran afoul of federal law when they sold timeshares for a Christian resort. In the 1990s, Creflo Dollar, Benny Hinn, Carlton Pearson, and Kenneth Hagan were just some of the many televangelists preaching "word faith" formulas for health and wealth as one's rightful inheritance as a child of God.

CHRISTIAN SCIENCE

While many Pentecostals preach that God has the power to heal people today, just as Jesus (and the apostles) had worked healing miracles on earth in the first century, few of the Pentecostal "faith healers" maintain that Christians should only turn to God for healing. Indeed, many of the people giving testimonials about their healings report that they first went to a physician for a diagnosis and treatment; when that failed, they came to the "faith healer"; and afterward they returned to the physician to confirm that the miraculous healing had actually been complete. Oral Roberts built a hospital at his university (complete with a prayer tower where members of his team pray over requests sent in from all over the world).

The demand to rely exclusively upon God for healing was advanced by Mary Baker **Eddy** (1821–1910) and the denomination she founded, **Christian Science.** (Its detractors have quipped that it is neither "Christian" nor "scientific.") Mrs. Eddy's early life was plagued with physical suffering of vague etiologies. In 1862 she came into contact with a "magnetizer" (i.e., mesmerist or hypnotist) named Phineas Quimby, who gave her some relief from her symptoms. A few years later, she began to develop her theological doctrine of the nature of health and illness: that disease is only an illusion brought about by lack of right thinking. The church she founded—officially called Church of Christ, Scientist—rejected medical treatment for physical illness and urged reliance upon prayer alone for healing. Her approach to healing is based less upon emotional public ritual (akin to the Pentecostals) and more to sober study of her doctrine. Sometimes her writings come close to the monism of the Upanishads: "Nothing is real and eternal . . . but God and His ideal; evil has no reality." After the 1875 publication of her book, *Science and Health with a Key to the Scriptures,* the movement grew rapidly, despite low-pressure proselytizing, although it has had a steady decline since her death in 1910. The movement's newspaper, the *Christian Science Monitor,* is well regarded for its high standards of journalism and does not slant news stories to fit a particular doctrinal agenda.

APOCALYPTICISM

The expectation of a forthcoming end to the world as we know it, brought about by the second coming of Christ, has been a recurrent doctrine throughout the history of Christianity. In the middle part of the first century, Paul had to preach against this expectation in his epistles because many Christians did not give sufficient attention to doing the work of the Church in the meantime. In the second century Montanus had claimed the ability to determine the date of the Second Coming. If the rise of secularism and humanism is viewed as something evil, it may be seen as fulfilling the New Testament prophecies about troubled times just before the Second Coming. One solution to the state of the secular order is for Jesus to come with a divine order.

In the United States, one of the greatest apocalyptic movements was that of William **Miller** (1782–1849) and his Adventists. Miller argued that when Christians died, they would not immediately go to heaven or hell but would "soul sleep" in the earth until the second coming of Jesus, at which time they would be resurrected and judged. Starting in 1831, Miller claimed that he had the mathematical key to understanding the books of *Daniel* and *Revelation* and that he had calculated the end to be coming around 1844. By that time, he had attracted thousands of followers, many of whom sold their property or stopped working their fields in expectation of the end of the world.

JEHOVAH'S WITNESSES

Charles Taze **Russell** (1852–1916) was raised a Congregationalist, but he challenged the doctrine of eternal punishment. Russell took interest in reading the writings of Miller, exploring the concept of soul sleep, and calculating the date of the Second Coming. He concluded that the second coming of the invisible Christ had already occurred (1874) and that the great apocalyptic battle with Satan would be in 1896, a date that he then postponed, recalculating it as 1914. When that date came and went, 1914 was declared the beginning of the end, and the generation alive then would not pass away before all was fulfilled. Russell's organization became known as the Russellites, then, alternatively, as the Millennial Dawn, the International Bible Students Association, the Watch Tower Society, Kingdom Hall, and finally *Jehovah's Witnesses.* Originally, the Russellites claimed that only 144,000 would be saved, but now that their membership is several million, that doctrine has been modified: only 144,000 get a special position with God, but the rest of the followers will enjoy life on a restored earthly paradise after the resurrection.

What most contemporary Americans find most controversial about the Jehovah's Witnesses is not their apocalypticism but their doctrines, which diverge from those of mainline Christianity. Russell was convinced that early in the second century the Church became too eager to please pagans and incorporated Roman holidays, Greek philosophy, and later, Celtic and Teutonic symbols. So, the Jehovah's Witnesses rejected the early Church councils (except for the canon of scripture). For the Jehovah's Witnesses, there is no Trinity, just God the Father, Jehovah. The status of Jesus is reduced to that of an angel; indeed, he is often identified with the angel Michael. The Jehovah's Witnesses emphasize works, as opposed to reliance upon God's grace, which means that the more time you spend knocking on doors and standing on street corners distributing *Watch Tower* or *Awake,* the greater your reward after the resurrection. The followers are discouraged from participating in civic life: no military service, no voting, no saluting the flag. (In Germany under the Third Reich, this refusal by Jehovah's Witnesses to pledge allegiance to Hitler or serve in the army led to their being some of the first Germans sent to the concentration camps, where many died rather than comply with Nazi demands.) Followers are not supposed to celebrate holidays tainted by paganism (e.g., Easter, Halloween) or even birthday parties.

Following in the tradition of Russell, the Jehovah's Witness organization is authoritarian, with the leadership having the sole right to interpret scripture. (Indeed, their New World Bible is more of a paraphrase than a translation, with renderings of some verses slanted to defend certain doctrines. For example, the prohibition against drinking animal blood in the Old Testament is interpreted to mean that you should not get a medical blood transfusion in a hospital.)

Dedicated proselytizing is a feature of this denomination, leading to a rapid growth in the United States and Mexico, especially among the poor, who find the prospect of a better life on this planet quite attractive.

SEVENTH DAY ADVENTISTS

Ellen Gould Harmon **White** (1826–1915) became one of the most prolific writers in all of religious history. As a child she suffered from infirmity: an accident at age 10 left her unconscious for several weeks. She was a semi-invalid for some time, then had a host of illnesses. Although originally a Methodist, she fell in with the Millerite Adventists in 1844. When Christ failed to appear on the designated date, she went into a trance and came up with the answer: Jesus had assumed the throne in heaven, and judgment had commenced. In subsequent visions, she emphasized the importance of the return to the Saturday Sabbath (hence the name **Seventh Day Adventists**) and physical health. She moved to Battle Creek, Michigan, and became associated with vegetarianism and the water cure as well as shunning alcohol and caffeine. Her denomination has built several colleges and universities (among them Loma Linda University, with schools of medicine, dentistry, physical therapy, and public health). It is this emphasis on taking realistic steps to assuring health that distinguished Ellen White from Mary Baker Eddy. It is this emphasis on building institutions for betterment before the millennium that distinguished White from Russell. What distinguishes the Seventh Day Adventists from most Protestants (in addition to the Millerite doctrine of soul sleep) would be the emphasis on the Old Testament rules. For example, the debate about whether to hold the Eucharist on the Jewish Sabbath (Saturday) or the day that Jesus rose from the tomb (Sunday) was present in the first century. Gradually, Sunday became more popular, which Ellen White attributed to the early corruption of Christianity by Roman influences.

COMMUNITARIAN SOCIETIES

Many secular utopian societies were attempted in the United States in the first half of the nineteenth century. Several American religious movements of the nineteenth century also tried to redefine the family, and started communitarian settlements. The first came to the United States under Ann Lee (1736–1784). In England she had joined a splinter group of Quakers who had been influenced by French Camisards. Lee later claimed that she was a prophet, and later, the female incarnation of the second coming of Christ. In 1774 the group came to New York, where they established a farming community. Since these were the end times, the community was to live as celibate brothers and sisters. This sect came to be called the **Shakers** because of their vigorous dancing rituals. They grew rapidly from converts and orphans. They established about two dozen farming communities throughout the northeast. With their motto of "hearts to God, hands to work" they invented several labor-saving devices that they produced and marketed, along with furniture, seeds, and herbal medicines. "Shaker" became a well-respected brand name, a sign of quality. Their movement peaked just before the Civil War and had a steady period of decline in the twentieth century. Now, their idle farm buildings are but museums.

The opposite end of the sexuality pole was advocated by the **Oneida** community in New York, also known as the **Perfectionists.** The community lasted from 1848 to 1880. Its founder was John Humphrey **Noyes,** who, after training for the Congregationalist ministry, had a revelation that the second coming of Christ occurred with the destruction of the Jerusalem temple in 70 C.E. We were therefore now living in the age of the spirit and must live without the sin of selfishness. This led to the doctrine of economic communism and changed the definition of the family to one of "complex marriage," in which every male was married to every female. In other words, it would be selfish of a man to say that his wife was his mate only: he had to share her with all the other men of the community. The children who were born were considered children of the entire community. Noyes developed an innovative technique for controlling his followers, a ritual of mutual criticism in which a member would have to sit silently while the others would disclose his or her shortcomings. This community was well disciplined and prosperous (thanks to the success of its high-quality manufactured items, especially silverware). But internal strife eventually led to the abolition of complex marriage. Later, the community reorganized (the current manufacturers of the silverware have no connection with the former denomination).

MORMONISM

Another denomination that toyed with communism and the family structure was the Church of Jesus Christ of **Latter Day Saints** (LDS), better known as the **Mormons.** In terms of membership growth, they have become the most successful denomination of purely American origin. This denomination has come up with major innovations in doctrine, ritual, symbols, myth, ethics, and church organization that can be traced to its founder, Joseph **Smith,** Jr. (1805–1844). Smith was born in Vermont but grew up on the frontier in western New York. His family was typical of the westering Yankees: religious but unchurched. The Smith family considered their nocturnal dreams as divinely inspired visits from angels. When young Joseph had a dream about an angel telling him about golden plates buried on the Hill Cumorah, his family encouraged him. He then claimed to find those plates as well as the prophetic gift to translate them. The result was the *Book of Mormon* (published in 1830), which purported to be a history of the prophets of the Nephites, a branch of Israelites who had come to the New World. The book has the style of the Old Testament and records that the resurrected Christ appeared on this continent.

There is very little in the Book of Mormon that would directly contradict mainline Christian doctrine (which is why Mormon missionaries distribute the Book of Mormon and the King James Version of the Bible and encourage people to read both, compare, and pray about it). The Mormon canon of scripture includes the Book of Mormon, the Bible (specifically, the translation inspired by Joseph Smith, in which new explanatory verses are added), the *Pearl of Great Price* (which includes an inspired translation that Smith made of an Egyptian papyrus he saw in a frontier traveling show), and the *Doctrine and Covenants* (the most important of all LDS scripture).

Smith's role as prophet began with the Book of Mormon, but certainly did not end there. He then

COMPARISON OF JUDAISM AND MORMONISM

DIMENSION	JUDAISM	MORMONISM
Followers known as	Jews	Mormons
Referred to themselves as	The Chosen	Latter Day Saints
Referred to outsiders as	Gentiles	Gentiles
Writings	Torah Old Testament Prophets Apocrypha Talmud	Torah, Old Testament Prophets, New Testament, Book of Mormon, *Pearl of Great Price, Doctrine and Covenants*
Lost Hebrew Tribes	Lost with fall of northern Kingdom of Israel	went to New World, ancestors of Nephites
Promised land	Israel	first Ohio, then Missouri, then Illinois, then Utah
Referred to as	Zion	Zion
Built temple	yes	yes
Temple rituals	until 70 C.E.	After 1833 C.E.
Revelations from	prophets	prophets
Purpose	to restore true religion	to restore true religion
Proselytizing?	no	yes
Government	initially a theocracy	initially a theocracy
Had to flee	Egypt	New York, Ohio, Missouri, Illinois
Prophet of Exodus	Moses	Joseph Smith, Jr.
Prophet leading them into Promised Land	Joshua	Brigham Young
Apocalyptic?	400 B.C.E.–200 C.E.	1830–850 C.E.
Required fasting?	yes	yes
Contributions	tithing	tithing
Social organization	patriarchal	patriarchal
Child's mother determines status	as a Jew	in celestial kingdom
Polygamy	1000 B.C.E.–400 B.C.E.	1843–1890 C.E.
Restrictions on what may be consumed	kosher	no alcohol, tobacco, tea, coffee
Priesthood of	Aaron	Aaron, Melchizedek
Priesthood for	tribe of Levi	all males
Racial equality	not initially	not initially

received regular revelations (recorded as the *Doctrine and Covenants*) to found his new church and on how to guide it. In this document we can see the development of a denomination with its distinctions. The Mormons left western New York for Ohio, where they established a common property scheme and designed a temple. It was here that Smith received the "word of wisdom" that prohibited the use of alcohol, tobacco, tea, and coffee. Local mob actions forced them to leave, and they headed for western Missouri, where they abolished common property but once again had problems with the local people. They went back across the Mississippi River to Illinois, where they established the city of Nauvoo. Here a great temple was constructed and Smith received revelations about the temple rituals of sealing for eternity (marriage) and baptism for deceased ancestors (hence the later interest in genealogy).

These temple rituals tied in with Smith's evolving doctrine. The family is eternal, not ended by death on this planet. Smith and his wife Emma loved children, but many of their biological children died in infancy. Smith responded by adopting dozens. Smith envisioned an afterlife in which those men who held the priesthood (e.g., Mormon adult males in good standing) would become godlike and have their own celestial kingdoms populated by their wives and children. In 1843 he received a revelation about plural marriage. In Nauvoo, this was practiced secretly by Smith and only the highest levels of leadership. These additional wives were sealed for eternity so that they would be wives in the afterlife (and in some cases there is doubt about whether any physical consummation of the marriage took place on earth). What was most controversial was that some of the plural wives had already been married to other earthly husbands. When a local Nauvoo newspaper leaked the story, Smith was furious and destroyed the print shop. The governor of Illinois called out the state militia and sent it to Nauvoo to arrest Smith, who surrendered, along with his elder brother Hyrum. The two were taken to nearby Carthage, where an angry mob tried to lynch them. In the resulting fight, Joseph and Hyrum were killed.

Phase two of Mormonism began with the death of Smith. Many splinter groups formed at this time, but the majority of Mormons recognized Brigham **Young** as the new prophet. (The largest remaining splinter group was called the Reorganized LDS church, which held that the son of Joseph Smith was the next rightful heir to the presidency. This sect changed its name to the Community Christian Church and denies that Joseph Smith, Jr., ever authorized polygamy.) The majority of Nauvoo Mormons followed Brigham Young when he received a revelation to move west. The Mormons settled in the valley of the Great Salt Lake in Utah. During that phase of Mormon history, polygamy was practiced openly. A middle-class farmer might have two or three wives in the same farm house, while a wealthier man might have several houses, a wife in each. This phase lasted until 1890, when the U.S. government put pressure on Utah to cease polygamy, and the fourth president (prophet) of the church, Wilford Woodruff, received a revelation that polygamy was to cease. Some of the Mormons rejected this new teaching and moved to Mexico, where they still thrive and practice polygamy openly. Others continued to practice polygamy in secret in Utah, but most Mormons obey the 1890 revelation.

During the twentieth century, Mormonism moved into the American mainstream, at least in the sense of affirming common values such as patriotism, industry, and taking care of the poor within the church. Their missionaries are cleancut, polite, and better informed (and less persistent) than the Jehovah's Witnesses. Over the past twenty years, the prophets have received revelations eliminating any racist tinge, declaring that the priesthood (and the hereafter) can be attained by good men of all races. The great success of Mormonism did not come from the clarity of its doctrines or the writing style of the Book of Mormon, but despite these factors. Mormonism is a case study of the victory of values: personal purity, family integrity, and community concern.

Joseph Smith was both charismatic and a shrewd organizer. He created an administrative structure, with an office for every task and gave his followers august titles as he assigned them mundane tasks. Every boy gets the priesthood of Aaron at age twelve, and the higher priesthood of Melchizedek at age eighteen. At age nineteen, this "elder" can be sent on a two-year mission (for which he or his family have saved to pay the expenses). Local congregations (wards) are run by bishops (who are usually local businessmen with families of their own) who serve without pay for a term of a few years. All families are supposed to contribute a tithe of at least 10 percent to the church,

DIMENSION	ISLAM	MORMONISM
Official name	Islam	Church of Jesus Christ of Latter Day Saints
Followers known as	Muslims	Mormons
Referred to outsiders as	Infidels	Gentiles
Began	610 C.E.	1830 C.E.
Place of origin	Arabia	New York, U.S.A.
Founded by	Muhammad	Joseph Smith, Jr.
Title	The Prophet	The Prophet
Motive	to restore true religion	to restore true religion
Proselytizing?	yes	yes
Childhood	orphaned	illness
First revelation	came in a cave	was about a mountain
Was probably	a dream	a dream
Revelation brought by	Angel Gabriel	Angel Moroni
Support for initial quest	wife	parents, brothers
Later revelations	settled disputes	settled disputes
Acceptance of Old and New Testament	if interpreted correctly	if interpreted correctly

which funds not only the building of its elegant temples, but also its massive welfare program for the poor.

EVANGELICALISM

Reacting against both secularism and the newer religious movements just discussed have been America's **fundamentalist Christians.** They are also known as **Evangelicals** or **born-again Christians.** We will use these three terms interchangeably, although not every fundamentalist considers himself born again, and vice versa. We have defined fundamentalists as those who put a great reliance upon the literal interpretation and daily application of scripture. However, even though this may also characterize some Catholics, Mormons,

and Jehovah's Witnesses, the term *fundamentalist Christian* is usually reserved for Protestants, especially those Protestants who may belong to mainline denominations such as Baptist, Church of Christ, even Presbyterian or Pentecostal, or the newer megachurches like Calvary Chapel or Harvest Crusade. For them, denominational affiliation is not the key, but personal commitment and having the "correct" doctrine (i.e, what Paul said in the book of *Romans*: that people are saved by God's grace, not by their works). Sometimes they simply call themselves "Christians" (especially when comparing themselves to Catholics, Mormons, and Jehovah's Witnesses). Sometimes they refer to their own churches as "nondenominational" (implying that other denominations are "manmade"

DIMENSION	ISLAM	MORMONISM
Revelations formed the basis for new scripture	Qur'an	Book of Mormon, *Doctrine and Covenants*
Prophet led people	politically and militarily	politically and militarily
Government	initially a theocracy	initially a theocracy
Had to flee	Mecca	New York, Ohio, Missouri, Illinois
Apocalyptic?	in early years	in early years
Required fasting?	yes	yes
Contributions	alms	tithing
Social organization	patriarchal	patriarchal
Polygamy	sanctioned but limited	1843–1890 C.E.
Prohibited	alcohol, pork, gambling	alcohol, tobacco, tea, coffee
Ritual based upon sacred place	pilgrimage	temple rites
Reverence for Adam	first prophet	earthly patriarch
Reverence for Abraham	pilgrimage to his shrine	translated his lost book
Should man aspire to be God?	no, greatest sin	yes, greatest hope
Racial equality	from the beginning	not initially
Basis of later sectification	descent from founder	descent from founder

and therefore inferior). Some will even say, "I'm not religious, I just love Jesus" (implying that organized other religions have forgotten the central focus).

Part of Buddhist, Christian, and Islamic ethics is that followers should spread the teachings of the founder's word and seek to make converts. Today, Hare Krishnas, Jehovah's Witnesses, Mormons, and evangelical Christians are very active proselytizers. However, at what point do efforts of proselytization become counterproductive or inappropriate within a secular society? What would be a reasonable and equitable policy?

Contribute to this discussion at
http://forums.delphiforums.com/rel101

The foremost Evangelical for the past fifty years has been the Baptist Billy Graham, who eloquently and powerfully preaches a simple message of salvation by grace. Other leaders who have expressed a greater interest in politics include Jerry Falwell (Liberty University), Ralph Reed (Christian Coalition), and past presidential candidates such as Pat Robertson, Gary Bauer, and Alan Keyes. These fundamentalists have been at the forefront of movements to stem the tide of secularism and liberalism. Some of the positions they have taken include demanding the right to home-school their children, prohibiting gay marriage, and upholding the "right to life" (i.e., banning or at least limiting abortions). On political issues such as abortion, Evangelicals often cooperate with Orthodox Jews, Roman Catholics, and Mormons.

ECUMENISM

A broader realm of trans-denominational cooperation
is **ecumenical.** Hallmarks of the ecumenical movement
are toleration for other denominations and cooperation with other denominations. During the Great
Depression of the 1930s, many urban churches and
synagogues cooperated in dispensing relief services.
In World War II, most American denominations cooperated in the war effort. These experiences led to
tolerance for other denominations and a commitment
to work together on common issues, such as helping
the poor and ending war, through local efforts as well
as larger organizations such as the National Council
of Churches and World Council of Churches. Most
mainline denominations have embraced some degree
of ecumenism: Episcopalians, Lutherans, Methodists,
Congregationals, even some Baptist denominations.
In general, embracing ecumenism implies that a
denomination is giving up its right to consider itself
as the sole representative of Christianity on earth.

Ecumenism may be the first step to denominational merging. Some Lutherans and Episcopalians
are considering cooperation if not unification. So far,
ecumenism has been resisted by most Evangelicals,
Jehovah's Witnesses, and Mormons, who cling to their
notion of superiority compared to other denominations. These nonecumenical denominations are the
ones who are still growing because of their dedicated
proselytizing, viewing the Catholic populations of Latin
America as ripe for conversion to "real Christianity."

A good example of how a denomination can become
more ecumenical is presented by the Roman Catholic
Church. As late as 1960, that church claimed that it was
the sole Christian church and that Protestants were going to hell. In the 1960s, a series of councils of bishops
known as Vatican II set about reforming doctrine and
ritual. The results ranged from saying mass in the local
language (instead of Latin) to the demotion of saints (to
reemphasize the focus on Christ) and a complete revision of the catechism in 1994. Now Protestants are referred to as "separated brethren." Anti-Semitism is seen
as a grave sin. Muslims are seen as fellow monotheists.
The Catholics would like to see all religious people of
the world rise above their differences (hopefully unifying under the leadership of the Pope).

The Catholics have focused much of their social
and political agenda on **social justice** issues. The Church
does not define itself solely by what it is against (e.g.,
abortion) but by what it is for: promoting international peace and protecting the rights of immigrants,
the poor, and prisoners around the world. Pope John
Paul II has been one of the last quarter century's most
articulate spokespersons against the excesses of both
communism and multinational capitalism. Looking
forward in this new millennium, the focus on social
justice might be a unifying theme for a broader ecumenical movement that brings together not just progressive Christians but Jews, Muslims, Buddhists,
Hindus, and secular humanists. The key for successful ecumenism is looking beyond the differences in
doctrines, myths, symbols, and rituals, and celebrating common values expressed in social justice ethics.

CULTS

New religious movements (NRMs), often called *New
Age* in their modern form, have sprouted up throughout the course of American religious history, including some of the ones just mentioned. The process is

COMPARISON OF CHRISTIAN DENOMINATIONS

COMPARISON	ROMAN CATHOLIC	MAINLINE PROTESTANT	JEHOVAH'S WITNESS	L.D.S. MORMON
God is	Trinity	Trinity	Jehovah alone	three distinct personages
Jesus is	God the Son	God the Son	Angel of God	a god
Afterlife	heaven, limbo, hell, purgatory	heaven, hell	new kingdom on this earth	celestial kingdoms
Apocalyptic?	no	varies	yes	yes
Setting dates?	no	no	yes	no
Proselytizing?	low key	varies	yes	yes
Salvation	open to all	varies	144,000	open to all
Priests	celibate	no	no	all males
Canon	Bible, *Apocrypha*	Bible	Bible	Bible Book of Mormon, *Doctrine and Covenants, Pearl of Great Price*
Preferred translations	Vulgate, Douay, New Jerusalem, New American	King James, Revised Standard, New International	New World	King James, Inspired
Authority to interpret Scripture	leaders	individual	leaders	leaders
Baptism	infant	varies	adult	adult and for dead
Marriage	for life	varies	until leaves	for eternity
Holy communion	yes	yes	yes	yes
Rituals for dying and dead	last rites, prayers for dead	none	none	baptism for dead
Peculiar prohibitions	artificial contraception	varies (e.g., Disneyland)	blood transfusions	alcohol, tobacco, tea and coffee
Participation in secular government	yes	yes	no	yes

ongoing and may accelerate as many individuals find secularist material values unfulfilling. Many of these NRMs are labeled cults. There are three definitions (or criteria) by which a denomination may be called a **cult**. The first is the popular criterion: you probably regard a denomination as a cult if you would be embarrassed if your children converted to it. The second criterion is doctrine or theology, which differs from mainline religions. While cults are generally new religious movements, they frequently manage to resurrect Gnostic doctrine or Celtic ritual (e.g., **Wicca**) in new variations. Any movement that claims that Jesus was only a man or only a spirit would run afoul of the orthodox Trinitarian doctrine. So, never try to label a fundamentalist group as a cult, or vice versa. Fundamentalism looks backward to tradition and accepted scripture, whereas cults are founded by people who bring forth a new doctrine not found in the old scripture.

Most social scientists prefer a third criterion for expressing concern about a denomination: churches that abuse their followers (or society in general). This abusive behavior frequently occurs because the cult's founder is charismatic and claims new revelation (a prophet) or even to be divinity incarnate. A cult might be a movement that stockpiles weapons in preparation for an apocalyptic battle (e.g., the Branch Davidians under David Koresh, in Waco) or urges its followers to commit mass suicide (e.g., Heaven's Gate in San Diego, People's Temple under Jim Jones in Guyana). **Scientology** (the organizational branch of Dianetics) has been labeled a cult by some because it seems to demand quite a bit of the follower's money to go through the various "clearing" rituals. Indeed, some denominations that may have very traditional doctrine and rituals (e.g., International Churches of Christ) are sometimes seen as cults because of their claims of exclusive salvation and the great authority placed over individuals by their "shepherding" leaders.

Some Evangelicals regard Mormons and Jehovah's Witnesses as cults. Certainly, these denominations embrace a theology out of step with Trinitarian Christianity and have authoritarian leadership. Both probably fall short on the criterion of "abuse of members" unless you consider required missionary work and tithing to be abusive. Mormonism in the nineteenth century would have come closer to the social science definition of cult, since the followers were told to give up their property (in the Ohio period), take more than one wife (in the Nauvoo period), and then go back to one wife (in 1890).

Of course, it could be argued that first-century Christianity met all three definitions of a cult. Romans would be embarrassed to have their children join it, its doctrines (particularly that forbidding emperor worship) were certainly out of step with mainline theology, and it could be considered abusive, if not for its common property scheme, then for the risk of martyrdom.

It is not just within North America that new religious movements arise. Throughout the Americas, wherever slaves were brought, there was a syncretism between African religion, native American tribal practices, and Catholicism. These forms have included Voodoo (Haiti), Hoodoo (southern U.S.), Macumba (Brazil), Espiritualismo (Mexico), and Santaria, Lukumi, and Regla de Ochoa (Cuba, Puerto Rico, Dominican Republic). It is Santaria and related Hispanic Caribbean forms which bear the most obvious ties to the West African Yoruba pantheon of deities (orishas), now cast in a role similar to that of Catholic saints (i.e., God's helpers).

Historically, these religious forms arose when the slave masters forbade the open practice of Yoruba religion, but the slaves were allowed to devote themselves to the saints, whom the slaves concluded were just manifestations of their deities. Some of the rituals of vigorous dancing, exorcisms, communication with ancestors, and animal sacrifice still had to be conducted in secret, and unorthodox doctrines had to be transmitted orally. In 1993 some practitioners of Santeria in Florida were brought to court by animal rights activists, but the United States Supreme Court ruled that this ritual was protected by the first amendment (*Church of the Lukumi Babalu Aye, Inc. v. City of Hialeah*) at least in this case because the local law seemed to be targeting that denomination.

One hotbed of new religious activity is the slums around Lima, Peru. One can see a variety of Catholic sects, especially those devoted to the local saints of St. Rose and St. Martin. Tune into AM radio and you will hear a variety of Pentecostal preachers (many speaking Spanish with Brazilian accents) talking about exorcisms, miraculous healings, and *prosperidad* (blessings of miraculous wealth).

Perhaps the most interesting phenomenon of Peruvian syncretism is that several Indian tribes in the

APOCALYPTIC MOVEMENTS				
NAME	WHEN	WHERE	MESSAGE	RESULT
Teutons	Before 1000 C.E.	Germany Scandinavia	fight alongside of gods	converted to Christianity
Zoroaster	600 B.C.E.	Iran	obey one God	conquering religion, but later most followers converted to Islam
Old Testament Prophets	600–400 B.C.E.	Palestine Babylonia	obey one God	Jews maintained community
Pharisees	1st century	Palestine	obey one God	Jewish diaspora
Jesus	1st century	Palestine	obey one God	crucifixion, proselytizing success
Montanus	2nd century	Asia Minor (Phrygia)	get ready for Second Coming	declared heretical by the Church
Muhammad	7th century	Arabia	obey one God	proselytizing success
Nichiren	13th century	Japan	build temple	proselytizing success
Aztecs	15th century	Mexico	a god will return	conquered by Cortez
"Old Believers"	17th century	Russia	traditionalism	died out
Ann Lee and Shakers	18th and 19th century	England and U.S.	celibate communism	died out
Joseph Smith and Mormons	19th and 20th century	U.S.	obey new revelations	proselytizing success
William Miller and Adventists	1844	U.S.	get ready for Second Coming	died out
Ellen White and Seventh Day Adventists	19th and 20th century	U.S.	obey Old Testament	proselytizing success
Charles Taze Russell and Jehovah's Witnesses	19th and 20th centuries	U.S.	obey new interpretations	proselytizing success
Jim Jones and People's Temple	1978	U.S., Guyana	socialist utopia	mass suicide
David Koresh and Branch Davidians	1993	U.S. (Waco)	Koresh is Jesus	killed in battle with government
Applewhite and Heaven's Gate	1997	U.S. (San Diego)	travel to the comet	mass suicide

Andes have had leaders who received revelations that their tribe was really one of the lost tribes of Israel and that they were supposed to go back to the ancient Hebrew rituals (including animal sacrifice). One such case began with a man named Villanueva, a devout Catholic, who after immersing himself in the Old Testament, concluded that the covenants of Abraham and Moses were to be practiced. Villanueva began criticizing the local priest and urged his village to convert to Judaism. His neighbors initially responded by disconnecting his electricity and plumbing. He continued preaching and eventually had a flock of five hundred. When he came to Lima to ask the local rabbi to formally convert his followers, they were not received warmly by this congregation of mostly post–World War II refugees of Polish and Hungarian descent.

In 1985 Villanueva made contact with the Lubavitcher orthodox Jewish movement in the U.S. When a rabbi arrived, he was thoroughly impressed with the Indians' attempts to follow Jewish ethics and rituals. (They had even become vegetarian because they did not know how to perform kosher slaughter.) A rabbi then performed the rite of circumcision on the men. Eventually, the majority of this new community chose to immigrate to Israel, where the Israeli government resettled them on the West Bank.

It is not just within the New World that syncretism occurs. Previous chapters have looked at some offshoots of Islam (e.g., Bahai, Sikhs, Nation of Islam). Perhaps there is no better example of syncretism than in Southeast Asia. The **Cao Dai** movement began in Vietnam by Ngo Van Chieu, an official in the French colonial government. In 1926 he claimed to receive a commandment from God ordering him to combine the religions of the world. Cao Dai acknowledges the creator deity of Christianity and Islam, symbolized by a painting of the Divine Eye of God. This doctrine is combined with a Theravada Buddhist understanding of the ephemeral nature of physical reality, as well as karma and transmigration. Ethics consist of a combination of a vegetarian diet with a Confucian respect for family and community duties. Drawing on indigenous animism and ancestor worship, Cao Dai also involves communication with these spirits.

Cao Dai, which is centered in Vietnam's Tay Ninh province, may claim up to 10 million adherents worldwide. The denomination has been generally tolerated by the communist government of Hanoi. Cao Dai has a hierarchical structure modeled after the Roman Catholic Church: a pope, cardinals, bishops and priests; however, both males and females may be ordained. Additionally, there are spiritual mediums and channelers who offer guidance from wise spirits; the latter include not only ancestors but also Joan of Arc, Victor Hugo, Rene Descartes, Louis Pasteur, Lenin, and Sun Yat-sen (founder of the 1911 Chinese Republic).

A different kind of East Asian syncretism has developed in North Korea. **Juche** literally means "self-reliance" in Korean, but it is an ideology and system of ritual practice that the communist government itself sponsored in the wake of the Korean War. The doctrines and ethics are applied Marxism (as interpreted by communist founder Kim Il Sung, father of current dictator Kim Jong Il): the proletariat is the great body of the country, the leader is like the brain, and the party is the nervous system that communicates between the brain and the body. Followers attain immortality to the extent that they serve the immortal state. The massive celebratory rituals are geared to reinforce social cohesion.

Perhaps the greatest confusion surrounding new religious movements is the tendency of even the media to equate them with fundamentalists ("after all, they are both religious fanatics, right?") In the 1990s, cults such as the Branch Davidians and Heaven's Gate were sometimes described as "fundamentalists," but the greatest misunderstanding has occurred since September 11, 2001, with the characterization of Osama Bin Ladin and al-Zarqawi as Islamic fundamentalists. To be sure, the leaders of **al-Qaeda** and related organizations want to be thought of as defending Islamic traditions of strict doctrines and ethics.

However, most new religious movements selectively appropriate some old traditions, claiming that the movement is about returning to an original and pure form of religion. (The Mormons sought "Restored Christianity" and the Jehovah's Witnesses wanted to return to pre-Trinitarian conceptions of the Deity.) The main reason why al-Qaeda should not be given the title of fundamentalist is that its leaders have rejected some of the key traditions of Islam: the *Futuwwat* Muslim chivalry code, with its injunctions to protect the innocent women and children from battle and bestow kindness to the vanquished. (The medieval European code of chivalry might have been influenced by the Christian Crusaders coming back from the Holy Land after having contact with Muslim troops).

A better characterization of al-Qaeda would be that of a cult. Leaders are charismatic. Doctrinal and ethical positions may not be challenged. Most important, these terrorist organizations are highly abusive of members, turning them into suicide bombers. Previous suicide cults (e.g., People's Temple in 1978, Branch Davidians in 1993) only killed outsiders when they approached the compound. In 2004 alone, al-Zarqawi's forces in Iraq used suicide bombers to attack U.S. troops, Iraqi police, the Jordanian embassy, the U.N. mission in Baghdad, and even a holy Shi'ite shrine. The targets of these terrorist movements include other cults, true Islamic fundamentalists (e.g., the Saudi government), but the primary enemy is secularism. The goal of these terrorist leaders seems to be power, and this goal has been well served by these terrorist tactics, which destabilize and demoral-

Since the end of World War II the ecumenical movement has sought to foster interdenominational toleration and cooperation. Most "mainline" denominations have participated. For example, Pope John Paul II went to Damascus, Syria, and prayed at some sites holy to both Muslims and Christians. Are you in favor of the ecumenical movement, or do you worry that it might lead to a "watering down" of doctrine, myth, ritual, or ethical positions? (*Hint:* Do an exegesis of one passage of scripture.)

Contribute to this discussion at
http://forums.delphiforums.com/rel101

ize established secular powers. When the United States and other secular nations attempt to ignore these terrorist acts or respond ineffectively, the terrorists gloat in their accomplishments. When the U.S.-led coalition overreacts and bombs insurgent strongholds, creating "collateral damage" of dead civilians, the outrage may draw new recruits to the terrorist movement.

UNITY AND DIVERSITY

The unity of the phenomena we have studied is *religion*—the common quest for a way to the center. The diversity of the phenomena makes *religions*—the distinctive traditional ways in which sizable numbers of people have worked at this quest together.

We contend that Frazer, Marx, and Freud were wrong: we have not seen science or political liberalism

DIMENSIONS OF CULTIC TENDENCIES		
THEOLOGICALLY*	ABUSIVE OF FOLLOWERS**	NONABUSIVE
Orthodox	International Churches of Christ, Snake Handlers	Calvary Chapel, Lutherans, Presbyterians, Catholics, Seventh Day Adventists, Pentecostals
Heterodox	Al Qaeda, Moonies, Scientology, Hare Krishna, People's Temple, Branch Davidians, Heaven's Gate, Satanism	Mormons, Jehovah's Witnesses, Christian Science, Religious Science, Wicca
*According to mainline Christianity as defined by concilar creedal statements **As alleged by former members		

New religious movements that get the label of a "cult" usually have several, if not all, of the following characteristics:

1. The founder is a charismatic person who claims to be a prophet of God (or God himself).

2. Some of the doctrines, rituals, and ethical practices introduced are far from the mainstream of the predominant religion of the society.

3. Cult authorities may abuse or exploit their followers (e.g., by confiscating individual wealth).

4. Members are discouraged from maintaining contacts with family members who are not in the cult.

5. The actions of the cult leaders often set up violent confrontations between the cult and the authorities of the secular world or mainline denomination.

6. Members who leave the cult may be persecuted by the cult.

Take a particular denomination and indicate how many of these cultlike characteristics it seems to possess.

EXAMPLE: First-century Christianity meets all but one of the above characteristics.

1. Jesus was viewed as Son of God, God the Son, an equal and co-eternal part of the developing doctrine of the Trinity (*Matthew* 19:17; *John* 1:1).

2. The Eucharist implemented at the Last Supper involved eating a body and drinking blood, and even when seen as mere symbolism, that would be pretty far from Jewish ritual (*Mark* 14:12-24). Also, on several occasions, Jesus and His disciples did not strictly observe the Sabbath (*Mark* 2:27).

3. Jesus told his followers to go and proselytize and not to worry about where their next meal would come from (*Luke* 12:22)and he told a young rich man to sell all of his possessions and give the money to the poor (*Mark* 10:21). The early Christians were told to sell all of their possessions and then the apostles would distribute to all according to each one's needs. (*Acts* 2:44-46; 4:32-35).

4. Jesus told his followers to leave parents, siblings, spouses, and even children in order to follow Him (*Matthew* 10:37; *Mark* 10:29), and early Christians were discouraged by the Apostle Paul from marrying non-Christians (*II Corinthians* 6:14 "Be ye not unequally yoked. . . ").

5. Jesus' actions throwing the moneychangers out of the temple would clearly rile secular and religious authorities in Jerusalem (*Matthew* 21:22). His followers were told to take up their crosses and follow Him (*Matthew* 10:38; 16:24). Many early Christians were martyred by being crucified or thrown to the lions.

6. Persecution by the cult of those who leave it may be the only cultlike characteristic lacking in early Christianity.

Contribute to this discussion at
http://forums.delphiforums.com/rel101

---

or secularism eradicate religion. What we have seen is that these intellectual and political movements of the last three hundred years have challenged religion, and the result has been religious diversity: ecumenism, fundamentalism, and new religious movements.

Relatedly, we suggest that the empiricism that misses such unity and mystery is at least an unwitting **reductionism**—an insistence that humanity is no more than what can be explained by biology, psychology, sociology, and so forth. The student of religion must develop a peculiar balance. One who is blind to the unity behind all religions will miss the deep humanity that the traditions can offer us. On the other hand a student of religion who sweeps all the information together, making all Buddhists anonymous Christians or all Christians renegade Jews, will miss the grainy texture that religion always has in people's lives. As is often the case, the ideal involves a duality: both cutting to the heart of the matter, where all human beings are siblings, and respecting the idiosyncrasies that differentiate people as nations, tribes, sexes, individuals, and traditional religionists.

We do not want to imply that ecumenism alone is good, nor are we calling for the defeat of all fundamentalists, secularists, and new religious movements. Ecumenism can become a bland, boring mixture of watered-down and inoffensively "politically correct" compromises unless it is held up by the simultaneous pulls from the three sides of secularism, fundamentalism, and new religious movements.

Although we are aware that reductionism thrives on facile generalizations, we will accept the risk of offering seven generalizations about religion. As we saw in Chapter 1, first (by *definition*), religion is

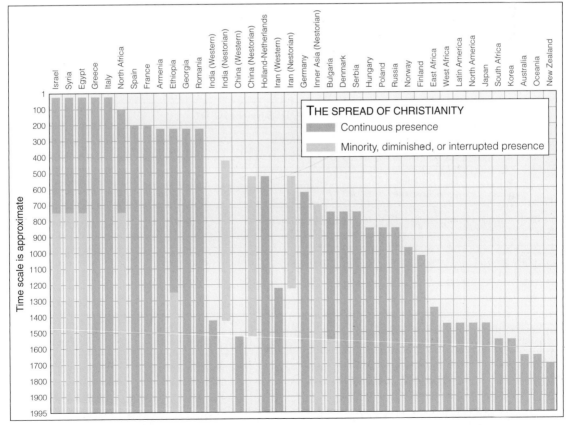

THE SPREAD OF CHRISTIANITY

- Continuous presence
- Minority, diminished, or interrupted presence

Current distribution of major religions

Forces within Twenty-first-Century Christianity

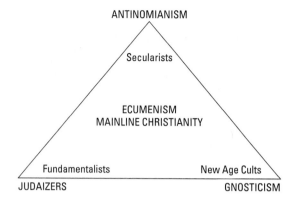

described by its components, and each religion is an answer to some basic questions:

- What is sacred? = *symbols*
- When was sacred? = *myths*
- Where is sacred? = *ritual* sites
- Why is something sacred? = *doctrine*
- How to live a life consistent with the sacred? = *ethics*
- Who functions in the sacred? = *roles*

Perhaps it is more appropriate to view religion as a series of choices that individuals and communities make:

- Which doctrines to accept?
- Which ethics to follow?
- Which rituals to practice?
- Which myths to retell?
- Which symbols to revere?
- Which persons will lead us?

Of course, all decisions are influenced by both the push of the past, the weight of present situations, and the pull of future aspirations.

Second (*predominance of action*), the behavioral components of religion (ritual, ethics) are more important than doctrine. Although it is doctrine that gives us the cognitive reframing that enables religion to bring new understanding of ourselves and our conditions, it is the dozens of daily inspired acts of self-restraint (ethics) and communal celebration (ritual) that enable people to grow in their commitments. Religion is more action than thought, more process than product.

Third (*relevance*), religions thrive or die according to their relevance. Religions are like families: even the most dysfunctional ones may sustain the enduring

FORCES IN MODERN RELIGION				
	ECUMENISM	SECULARISM	FUNDAMENTALISM	NEW RELIGIOUS MOVEMENTS
1st-century parallel	mainline Christianity	antinomianism	Judaizers	Gnostics
Pulls toward	toleration, unity, cooperation	individual freedom	tradition	separatism
Pulls away from	every extreme	religiosity	innovation	immersion in broader society
Syncretism	celebrates	ignores	resists	incorporates
Catholicism in this period	since Vatican II	never	4th through 20th centuries	1st through 4th centuries
Islam	some Muslims living in Western countries	Turkey since 1920s	Saudi Arabia, Iran since 1979, Afghanistan under Taliban	offshoots of Sikhs, Bahai, Sufis, Druses, nation of Islam

What are appropriate justifications for someone to change religious affiliation? When should someone stay with his or her religion of upbringing and when is a rejection of that tradition called for?

Contribute to this discussion at
http://forums.delphiforums.com/rel101

commitment of their members. External observers who are outside of a given religion can easily find fault with it, but those who follow a religion will ignore the defects as long as it satisfies emotional needs. No matter how ridiculous or superstitious a religion's doctrines, no matter how farfetched a religion's myths, no matter how incomprehensible a religion's symbols, no matter how difficult a religion's rituals, no matter how severe a religion's ethics, no matter how corrupt a religion's institutional leadership, the majority of a religion's practitioners have found some degree of satisfaction in terms of ability to express relevance.

Fourth (*morphology*), no enduring religious tradition is static. Religious traditions endure because they are dynamic. Religions can and must adapt to the shifting physical and social environments in which humans find themselves. Some religious will change by embracing syncretism (e.g., Buddhism), while others will change by their resistance to syncretism (e.g., Judaism). The atheists may be disappointed, for religion will endure. The fundamentalists may be disappointed, for the relevance of specific traditions of the past may not endure. But the greatest disappointment will be found by some of the new religious movements, for the verdict of history is that highly abusive cults do not long survive.

Fifth (*independence from science*), science does not directly impact religion. The advance of scientific knowledge or its technological applications is not a direct assault on religious doctrine or ethics, let alone the more evocative components of myth, symbol, and ritual. It is when scientific and technological change sets in motion a challenge to the values held by an individual or a society that religion must respond. Thus, religious breakthroughs come about, not when new evidence surfaces but when new values are called for.

Sixth (*syncretism*), whenever there is a mass conversion by the people of one culture to an incoming proselytizing religion, these converts do not lose their culture, though it may be greatly transformed.

In some cases (e.g., Buddhism) it can be said that the incoming religion is more transformed than the culture that has newly embraced it, while in other cases (e.g., Islam) the culture is more transformed than is the religion.

Seventh (*homology and diversity*), the major religions have more similarities than differences. There is more diversity within any major religious tradition than there are real differences between major religious traditions. (In other words, a Roman Catholic monk may share more similarities of ritual and ethical practice with his Buddhist counterpart than he shares with some merely nominal Catholics.) Ecumenists will choose to emphasize and celebrate these similarities, while showing a respectful tolerance of the differences.

For ecumenists, genuine differences about the implications of symbols and ethics for civil legislation become topics of empathic dialogue rather than rallying points for culture wars. Adherents of fundamentalism and cultic movements will choose to emphasize their own peculiarities, even at the expense of civil cohesion.

ANNOTATED

BIBLIOGRAPHY

CHAPTER 1: INTRODUCTION TO RELIGIONS

Bell, Catherine M. *Ritual Theory, Ritual Practice.* New York: Oxford University Press, 1992. This is one of the most profound and articulate statements of the position that the core of religion is not doctrine, but ritual.

Bishop, Donald H., ed. *Mysticism and the Mystical Experience: East and West.* Selinsgrove, PA: Susquehanna University Press, 1995. Individual chapters consider the role of mystics and mysticism within different religious traditions.

Bonnefoy, Yves. *Mythologies,* 2 vols. Chicago: University of Chicago Press, 1991. A comprehensive survey of the mythologies of the world's leading cultures.

Brink, T. L. "Belief vs. Commitment, Validity vs. Value: A Response to Ward Goodenough." *Zygon* 28, no. 2(1993): 283–286. A detailed description of religious versus scientific perspectives on reality.

———. "Depression and Spiritual Formation." *Studies in Formative Spirituality* 14, no. 3 (1993): 381–394. A detailed description of religion as a quest for ultimate relevance. Views the epidemic of depression in contemporary society as due to a loss of reliance upon religion.

———. "Quantitative and/or Qualitative Methods in the Scientific Study of Religion." *Zygon* 30 (1995): 461–475. Argues that social scientists studying religious phenomena should use both quantitative (e.g., correlational data

analysis) and qualitative (e.g., biographies, focus groups) research methods.

Buckley, Michael J. *At the Origins of Modern Atheism.* New Haven, CT: Yale University Press, 1987. A demanding study of the origins of modern atheism.

Carmody, Denise Lardner. *Responses to 101 Questions about Feminism.* Mahwah, NJ: Paulist Press, 1994. Places the rise of feminism in proper perspective within religion.

———. *Women and World Religions,* 2nd ed. Englewood Cliffs, NJ: Prentice Hall, 1988. A survey of female images and roles in the major religious traditions that describes what being religious as a female has meant in the past and means today.

Carmody, Denise Lardner, and Carmody, John T. *Religion: The Great Questions.* San Francisco: Harper and Row, 1983. A comparative study of the major traditions in terms of their positions on the central existential questions of life, such as evil, the good life, and so on.

Eliade, Mircea. *The Sacred and the Profane.* New York: Harcourt, Brace and World, 1959. A concise statement of Eliade's view that human beings try to find relevance by making sacred the primary reality of their lives.

Harner, Michael. *The Way of the Shaman.* San Francisco: Harper and Row, 1980. A clear presentation of the nonordinary reality used by shamans, with many tips on how to adapt shamanic techniques to current Western life.

Hick, John. *Disputed Questions in Theology and the Philosophy of Religion.* New Haven: Yale University Press, 1993. A good survey of the main problems and concepts involved in the theological aspects of the study of religion.

Jonte-Pace, Diane, ed. *Teaching in Religious Studies.* New York: Oxford University Press, 2003. Part of the American Academy of Religion teaching series, this book is one of the best collections on teaching social science models of religious phenomena, specifically, the psychoanalytic approach.

Jonte-Pace, Diane, and Parsons, William. *Religion and Psychology: Mapping the Terrain.* New York: Routledge, 2001. A broader introduction to social science models of religious phenomena.

Marty, Martin E.; Appleby, R.; and Scott, R. *Fundamentalisms and the State: Remaking Polities, Economies, and Militance.* Chicago: University of Chicago Press, 1993. A comprehensive review of fundamentalist approaches in different religious traditions.

Penaskovic, Richard. *Critical Thinking and the Academic Study of Religion.* Atlanta: Scholars Press, 1997. The study of religion involves three levels of knowledge: declarative (the facts), procedural (methods of approach), metacognition (the big picture).

Schmidt, Roger. *Exploring Religion.* Belmont, CA: Wadsworth, 2000. A conceptual introduction to the different components of religion: myth, ritual, and so forth.

Schmidt, Roger, et al. *Patterns of Religion.* Belmont, CA: Wadsworth, 2000. A high-level introduction to the study of world religions.

Sharma, Arvind, and Young, Katherine T., eds. *Feminism and World Religions.* Albany: State University of New York Press, 1999. Individual chapters cover the position of women in different Asian religious traditions.

Smith, Huston. *Forgotten Truth: The Common Vision of the World's Religions.* San Francisco: HarperSanFrancisco, 1992. Smith is a classic author in this field, and this is one of his most readable introductions.

Stackhouse, John G., Jr. *Can God Be Trusted?* Oxford: Oxford University Press, 1998. This contemporary exploration of theodicy is quite readable.

Stewart, David, ed. *Exploring the Philosophy of Religion.* Englewood Cliffs, NJ: Prentice Hall, 1988. A reader of selections from primary sources in the history of Western thought about religious experience, God, religious language, evil, and death.

Van Voorst, Robert E. *Anthology of World Scriptures,* 5th ed. Belmont, CA: Wadsworth, 2004. One of the best collections of scripture for Hinduism, Buddhism, Jainism, Sikhism, Confucianism, Daoism, Shinto, Zoroastrianism, Judaism, Christianity, Islam. A helpful index allows the student to search by topic (e.g., marriage).

Wulff, David M. *Psychology of Religion: Classic and Contemporary Views.* New York: Wiley, 1991. Probably the most comprehensive introduction to psychological studies of, and perspectives on, religious phenomena.

CHAPTER 2: TRIBAL RELIGIONS

Auel, Jean M. *The Clan of the Cave Bear.* New York: Bantam, 1981. A persuasive novel about Neanderthal life that focuses on women's roles.

Brancatelli, Paul. *Pilgrimage as a Rite of Passage for Youth.* Mahwah, NJ: Paulist Press, 1998. Although geared less to tribal religions per se, this book describes the importance of rites of passage, especially Catholic pilgrimage.

Carmody, Denise Lardner. *The Oldest God: Archaic Religion Yesterday and Today.* Nashville: Abingdon, 1981. A study of the ancient religious mentality from prehistoric times to the present.

Dickson, D. Bruce. *The Dawn of Belief: Religion in the Upper Paleolithic of Southwestern Europe.* Tucson, AZ: University of Arizona Press, 1990. This archeological book makes inferences about the probable religious practices of the "cavemen" of Europe.

Eliade, Mircea. *Australian Religions.* Ithaca, NY: Cornell University Press, 1973. A somewhat demanding application of Eliade's theories to the data available on Australian Aborigines.

Fienup-Riordan, Ann. *Boundaries and Passages: Rule and Ritual in Yup'ik Eskimo Oral Tradition.* Norman: University of Oklahoma Press, 1994. Examines ethical and ritual dimensions of Inuit society.

Gill, Sam D. *Beyond the Primitive: The Religions of Non-Literate Peoples.* Englewood Cliffs, NJ: Prentice Hall, 1982. A good theoretical orientation to the study of non-literate peoples, informed by recent cultural anthropology and laced with many examples.

Gimbutas, Marija. *The Goddesses and Gods of Old Europe: 6500–3500 B.C.E.* Berkeley: University of California Press, 1982. Reports and guarded speculation about the findings of archeological excavations of prehistoric sites in Eastern Europe. Primary focus is on the varieties of goddesses and fertility figures found.

Hilger, Mary Inez. *Together with the Ainu: A Vanishing People.* Norman: University of Oklahoma Press, 1971. Focuses on Ainu history and social conditions as well as religion.

Hirschfelder, Arlene B. *The Encyclopedia of Native American Religions: An Introduction.* New York: Facts on File, 1992. Probably the most comprehensive assemblage of information about religion among Native American tribes.

Hultkrantz, Ake. *The Religions of the American Indians.* Berkeley: University of California Press, 1979. A topical study of the main ideas, institutions, and ritual concerns of both the tribes of North and South America and the high cultures of the Incas, Mayas, and Aztecs.

Loftin, John D. *Religion and Hopi Life in the Twentieth Century.* Bloomington: Indiana University Press, 1991. Focuses on one Indian tribe and their experience on the reservation.

Osterreich, Shelley Anne. *The American Indian Ghost Dance, 1870 and 1890: An Annotated Bibliography.* New York: Greenwood Press, 1991. A comprehensive guide to sources about this movement.

———. *Native North American Shamanism: An Annotated Bibliography.* Westport, CT: Greenwood Press, 1998. A guide to sources about shamanism among Native American tribes.

Swain, Tony. *A Place for Strangers: Towards a History of Australian Aboriginal Being.* New York: Cambridge University Press, 1993. Focuses on the rituals and doctrines of the Australian Aborigines.

Trompf, G. W. *Payback: The Logic of Retribution in Melanesian Religions.* New York: Cambridge University Press, 1994. Examines the doctrinal, ritual, and societal aspects of practices such as head hunting and cannibalism.

Turlington, Shannon R. *The Complete Idiot's Guide to Voodoo.* New York: Alpha, 2002. A thorough introduction to the historical and cultural aspects of Voodoo that clearly distinguishes the living syncretistic tradition from what has been portrayed by Hollywood.

Turnbull, Colin M. *The Forest People.* New York: Simon and Schuster, 1962. A study of the pygmies of the Congo by an anthropologist who came to know and love them well enough to be adopted into their tribe.

———. *The Human Cycle.* New York: Simon and Schuster, 1983. Studies illuminating the key moments of the human life cycle from the author's anthropological experience among several African tribes.

Underhill, Ruth M. *Red Man's Religion.* Chicago: University of Chicago Press, 1965. A readable introduction, rich in details, to the principal myths and rituals of Indians north of Mexico.

Wall, Steve. *Shadowcatchers: A Journey in Search of the Teachings of Native American Healers.* New York: HarperCollins, 1994. Focuses on doctrinal and mystical aspects of medicine men.

Zahan, Dominique. *The Religion, Spirituality and Thought of Traditional Africa.* Chicago: University of Chicago Press, 1979. An interesting attempt to sketch the general doctrinal system and ritualistic world views of Africans not greatly influenced by Islam or Christianity.

CHAPTER 3: ANCIENT CIVILIZATIONS

Baldwin, Neil. *Legends of the Plumed Serpent: Biography of a Mexican God.* New York: Public Affairs, 1998. Considers myths of Quetzalcoatl and Kulkulcan in pre-Columbian Aztec society.

Broda, Johanna. *The Great Temple of Tenochtitlan: Center and Periphery in the Aztec World.* Berkeley: University of California Press, 1988. Starting from an archeological investigation of a Meso-American temple, the author attempts to infer Aztec theology.

Choksy, Jamsheed K. (Jamsheed Kairshasp). *Purity and pollution in Zoroastrianism: Triumph over Evil.* Austin, TX: University of Texas Press, 1989. A review of the dualistic doctrine behind Parsi ritual.

Eliade, Mircea. *A History of Religious Ideas,* Vols. 1–3. Chicago: University of Chicago Press, 1978, 1982, 1985. Chapters on Greece, Iran, and Egypt place these countries in the overall history of religious ideas.

Jacobsen, Thorkild. *The Treasures of Darkness: A History of Mesopotamian Religion.* New Haven, CT: Yale University Press, 1976. A solid overview by one of the leading scholars and interpreters of Mesopotamian mythology.

Lattimore, Deborah Nourse. *Why There Is No Arguing in Heaven: A Mayan Myth.* New York: HarperCollins, 1989. A clever presentation of a Mayan myth in order to illustrate a point of doctrine.

Leca, Ange Pierre. *The Egyptian Way of Death: Mummies and the Cult of the Immortal.* Garden City, NY: Doubleday, 1981.

Leon Portilla, Miguel. *The Aztec Image of Self and Society: An Introduction to Nahua Culture.* Salt Lake City: University of Utah Press, 1992. Doctrinal aspects of Aztec religion are inferred from social norms and rituals.

Longhena, Maria. *Ancient Mexico: The History and Culture of the Maya, Aztecs, and Other Pre-Columbian Peoples.* New York: Stewart, Tabori and Chang, 1998. A readable account of Meso-American society prior to the arrival of the Spanish.

Lopez Lujan, Leonardo. *The Offerings of the Templo Mayor of Tenochtitlan.* Niwot: University Press of Colorado, 1994. Based on archeology, this book examines human sacrifice and other Aztec ritual.

Mercatante, Anthony S. *Who's Who in Egyptian Mythology.* Lanham, MD: Scarecrow Press, 1995. This is an introduction to Egyptian mythology and pantheon.

O'Brien, Joan V. *In the Beginning: Creation Myths from Ancient Mesopotamia, Israel, and Greece.* Chico, CA: Scholars Press, 1982.

Pangborn, Cyrus R. *Zoroastrianism: A Beleaguered Faith.* New York: Advent Books, 1983. Considers the social context of contemporary Zoroastrian communities around the world.

Pritchard, James B., ed. *Ancient Near Eastern Texts Relating to the Old Testament,* 3rd ed. Princeton, NJ: Princeton University Press, 1969. The standard source for key Mesopotamian and Egyptian texts, arranged according to genres for easy comparison.

Redford, Donald B., ed. *The Oxford Encyclopedia of Ancient Egypt.* New York: Oxford University Press, 2001.

Ringgren, Helmer. *Religions of the Ancient Near East.* Philadelphia: Westminster, 1973. A good introduction to Mesopotamian religions.

Shlain, Leonard. *The Alphabet vs. the Goddess.* New York: Penguin Putnam, 1998. Argues that the rise of writing rewired the human brain (left/masculine hemisphere) away from the tribal (right/feminine hemisphere).

Stierlin, Henri. *The Maya: Palaces and Pyramids of the Rainforest.* New York: Taschen, 1997. A vivid pictorial introduction to Mayan geography, architecture, society, and religion.

CHAPTER 4: INDIA

Basham, A. L. *The Wonder That Was India.* New York: Grove Press, 1959. A readable and comprehensive study of Indian life before the coming of the Muslims.

Coward, Harold G.; Lipner, Julius J.; and Young, Katherine K. *Hindu Ethics: Purity, Abortion, and Euthanasia.* Albany: State University of New York Press, 1989. An attempt is made to apply the ethical foundations of the Hindu classics to these contemporary moral issues.

Eliade, Mircea. *Yoga: Immortality and Freedom.* Princeton, NJ: Princeton University Press, 1970. A classical study of the presuppositions and main features of the various yogic quests to defeat space and time.

Erikson, Erik H. *Gandhi's Truth.* New York: Norton, 1969. A psychoanalytic study of the modern founder of militant nonviolence.

Garg, Ganga Ram, ed. *Encyclopaedia of the Hindu World.* New Delhi: Concept, 1992.

Hardy, Friedhelm. *The Religious Culture of India: Power, Love, and Wisdom.* New York: Cambridge University Press, 1996. Synthesizes the doctrines of Hinduism into some central themes.

Huntington, Susan L. *The Art of Ancient India: Buddhist, Hindu, Jain.* New York: Weatherhill, 1985.

Lender, Lilia. *The Choice is Yours: Ethics in Vedanta.* Bombay: Central Chinmaya Mission Trust, 1991. Gives the ethical implications of Upanishadic monism.

Leslie, Julia. *Roles and Rituals for Hindu Women.* Rutherford: Fairleigh Dickinson University Press, 1991. This readable

book considers both the historical and contemporary place of women in India.

O'Flaherty, Wendy Doniger. *Women, Androgynes and Other Mythical Beasts.* Chicago: University of Chicago Press, 1980. Studies in Hindu symbolism associated with fertility, vitality, and sacredness.

Pintchman, Tracy. *The Rise of the Goddess in the Hindu Tradition.* Albany: State University of New York Press, 1994. Views goddess worship as a historical development that blends pre-Aryan fertility worship and post-Mahabharata responses to Upanishadic monism.

Possehl, Gregory L. *The Indus Civilization: A Contemporary Perspective.* Walnut Creek, CA: AltaMira Press, 2002.

Renard, John. *Responses to 101 Questions on Hinduism.* Mahwah, NJ: Paulist Press, 1999. A readable introduction to Hindu doctrine and rituals.

Stanford, Anne, trans. *The Bhagavad Gita.* New York: Seabury, 1970. A fairly readable verse translation of Hinduism's most influential book.

Stierlin, Henri. *Hindu India: From Khajuraho to the Temple City of Madurai.* New York: Taschen, 1998. A geographic study of holy places in India (nice photographs).

CHAPTER 5: JUDAISM

Armstrong, Karen. *A History of God: The 4000-Year Quest of Judaism, Christianity, and Islam.* New York: Knopf, 1993. A very readable book tracing the growth of monotheistic thought in the Western religious traditions.

Baker, Cynthia M. *Rebuilding the House of Israel: Architectures of Gender in Jewish Antiquity.* Stanford, CA: Stanford University Press, 2002.

Borowitz, Eugene B. *Renewing the Covenant: A Theology for the Postmodern Jew.* Philadelphia: Jewish Publication Society, 1991.

Brook, Kevin Alan. *Jews of Khazaria.* Northvale, NJ: Jason Aronson, 1999. An important historical link in the understanding of the origins of the Jews of Eastern Europe.

Cantor, Norman F. *The Sacred Chain: The History of the Jews.* New York: HarperCollins, 1994. A readable introduction to the Jewish people.

Carmody, John; Carmody, Denise Lardner; and Cohn, Robert L. *Exploring the Hebrew Bible.* Englewood Cliffs, NJ: Prentice Hall, 1988. A basic text that analyzes all the books and suggests their lasting significance.

Cohen, A. *Everyman's Talmud.* New York: Schocken, 1975. A topical presentation of rabbinic Judaism's main teachings, rich in quotations and details.

———. *The Tremendum.* New York: Crossroad, 1981. A theological reflection on the significance of the Holocaust.

Cohen, Shaye J. D. *The Beginnings of Jewishness: Boundaries, Varieties, Uncertainties.* Berkeley: University of California Press, 1999. Attempts to define philosophically, psychologically, sociologically, and historically, the essence of Jewish society.

Cohn-Sherbok, Dan. *Jewish and Christian Mysticism: An Introduction.* New York: Continuum, 1994. A good comparison of these monotheistic mystical traditions.

———. *The Crucified Jew: Twenty Centuries of Christian Anti-Semitism.* Grand Rapids, MI: Eerdmans, 1997.

Cook, Stephen L. *Prophecy and Apocalypticism: The Postexilic Social Setting.* Minneapolis: Fortress Press, 1995. Examines ancient Judaism under the Persians, Greeks, and Romans.

Dearman, John Andrew. *Religion and Culture in Ancient Israel.* Peabody, MA: Hendrickson, 1992. An important work for setting the historical context for both Judaism and Christianity.

Dershowitz, Alan. *Genesis of Justice.* New York: Warner, 2000. Explores how the first book of the Bible records the Hebrews' perception of injustice and their attempts to develop a more just society.

Elcott, David M. *A Sacred Journey: The Jewish Quest for a Perfect World.* Northvale, NJ: Jason Aronson, 1995. A review of Jewish philosophy and theology with an emphasis on the modern.

Encyclopedia Judaica. 16 vols. Jerusalem: Keter, 1971. The standard comprehensive reference work, with articles on all aspects of Jewish history, doctrine, ethics, and ritual.

Feldman, Louis H. *Jew and Gentile in the Ancient World: Attitudes and Interactions from Alexander to Justinian.* Princeton, NJ: Princeton University Press, 1993. Examines the position of the Jews in the Hellenistic and early common era.

Finkelstein, Israel, and Silberman, Neil Asher. *The Bible Unearthed.* New York: Free Press, 2000. Raises some questions about the Bible's depiction of the Israelite kingdoms of David and Solomon, a single Exodus, and a unified conquest of Canaan.

Gerber, Jane S. *The Jews of Spain: A History of the Sephardic Experience.* New York: Free Press, 1992.

Gillman, Neil. *Sacred Fragments: Recovering Theology for the Modern Jew.* Philadelphia: Jewish Publication Society, 1990.

Greenberg, Melanie Hope. *Celebrations: Our Jewish Holidays.* Philadelphia: Jewish Publication Society, 1991.

Gribetz, Judah; Greenstein, Edward L.; and Stein, Regina. *The Timetables of Jewish History: A Chronology of the Most Important People and Events in Jewish History.* New York: Simon and Schuster, 1993. A clear presentation of chronology in Jewish history.

Hanson, Kenneth C. *Palestine in the Time of Jesus: Social Structures and Social Conflicts.* Minneapolis: Fortress Press, 1998. A good source for understanding the sociohistorical context provided by first-century Palestine.

Heilman, Samuel C. *Synagogue Life.* Chicago: University of Chicago Press, 1976. A sociological study of the interactions among Jews at synagogue gatherings.

Idel, Moshe. *Hasidism: Between Ecstasy and Magic.* Albany: State University of New York Press, 1995. A scholarly consideration of the role of these Jewish mystics.

Jacobs, Louis. *The Jewish Religion: A Companion.* New York: Oxford University Press, 1995. A comprehensive introduction.

Kaufman, Debra R. *Rachel's Daughters: Newly Orthodox Jewish Women.* New Brunswick: Rutgers University Press, 1991. Reflects upon Jewish women who decide to embrace orthodoxy.

Matthews, Victor Harold. *Social World of Ancient Israel, 1250–587 B.C.E.* Peabody, MA: Hendrickson, 1993. This is a clear and readable introduction to social structure and customs of the Israelites between the Exodus and the Exile.

Murphy, Catherine M. *Wealth in the Dead Sea Scrolls and in the Qumran Community.* Leiden: Brill, 2002.

Neusner, Jacob. *The Life of Torah.* Encino, CA: Dickenson, 1974. A selection of readings that illustrate basic aspects of Jewish religion, both traditional and modern.

———. *The Way of Torah,* 2nd ed. Encino, CA: Dickenson, 1974. A readable introduction to Judaism that delineates its classical structure, the Torah, and the modern situation.

Ostriker, Alicia. *The Nakedness of the Fathers: Biblical Visions and Revisions.* New Brunswick, NJ: Rutgers University Press, 1994. Investigates the possibility of new roles for women within Judaism.

Pagels, Elaine H. *The Origin of Satan.* New York: Random House, 1995. An exploration of the development of Persian, Jewish, and Christian doctrine.

Pleins, J. David. *The Social Visions of the Hebrew Bible: A Theological Introduction.* Nashville, TN: Westminster/John Knox, 2001.

———. *When the Great Abyss Opened: Classic and Contemporary Readings of Noah's Flood.* New York: Oxford University Press, 2003.

Raphael, Marc Lee. *Judaism in America.* New York: Columbia University Press, 2003.

Rubenstein, Richard L. *After Auschwitz.* Indianapolis: Bobbs-Merrill, 1966. One of the first and most radical interpretations of the implications of the Nazi Holocaust for Jewish religion.

Samuelson, Norbert Max. *Judaism and the Doctrine of Creation.* New York: Cambridge University Press,

1994. Reflects upon the theory of evolution and Jewish doctrine.

Scholem, Gershom. *Major Trends in Jewish Mysticism*. New York: Schocken, 1961. A classical brief treatment of the evolution of Jewish mysticism stressing Cabalistic and Hasidic developments.

Seeskin, Kenneth. *Jewish Philosophy in A Secular Age*. Albany: State University of New York Press, 1990. A consideration of contemporary Jewish worldviews.

Shanks, Hershel, ed. *Christianity and Rabbinic Judaism: A Parallel History of Their Origins and Early Development*. Washington, DC: Biblical Archaeology Society, 1992. Examines the demise of temple Judaism in Palestine and how both Christianity and the rabbinic tradition competed for the leadership of post-Diaspora Judaism.

Zborowski, Mark, and Herzog, Elizabeth. *Life Is with People*. New York: Schocken, 1962. An absorbing portrait of shtetl life before World War II, based on interviews and personal reminiscences.

Zwi Werblowsky, R. J., and Wigoder, Geoffrey. *The Oxford Dictionary of the Jewish Religion*. New York: Oxford University Press, 1997.

CHAPTER 6: CHINA AND JAPAN

Ben-Ari, Eyal; Moeran, Brian; and Valentine, James. *Unwrapping Japan: Society and Culture in Anthropological Perspective*. Honolulu: University of Hawaii Press, 1994. An anthropological and historical view of Japanese society and religion.

Chan, Wing-Tsit, ed. *A Sourcebook in Chinese Philosophy*. Princeton, NJ: Princeton University Press, 1963. Remains the standard one-volume anthology of translated texts, covering the full historical range of precommunist Chinese culture.

Chow, Kai-wing. *The Rise of Confucian Ritualism in Late Imperial China: Ethics, Classics, and Lineage Discourse*. Stanford, CA: Stanford University Press, 1994. Examines how pre-Confucian Chinese classics paved the way for Confucianism.

Davis, Winston Bradley. *Japanese Religion and Society: Paradigms of Structure and Change*. Albany: State University of New York Press, 1992. A historical and sociological view of the role of religion in Japanese society and history.

Dawson, Raymond Stanley. *Confucius*. New York: Hill and Wang, 1982. Remains one of the best biographies of Confucius.

Ebrey, Patricia Buckley. *Confucianism and Family Rituals in Imperial China: A Social History of Writing about Rites*.

Princeton, NJ: Princeton University Press, 1991. Considers the interaction of Chinese tradition and Confucianism in family-centered rituals.

Henderson, John B. *Scripture, Canon, and Commentary: A Comparison of Confucian and Western Exegesis*. Princeton, NJ: Princeton University Press, 1991. A scholarly analysis of how the Chinese and Europeans have interpreted Confucius.

Huang, Al Chung-liang, and Lynch, Jerry. *Mentoring: The Tao of Giving and Receiving Wisdom*. San Francisco, CA: HarperSanFrancisco, 1995. Looks at the relationship of teacher and student in Chinese society, especially within Confucian and Zen traditions.

Jordan, David K., and Overmyer, Daniel L. *The Flying Phoenix: Aspects of Chinese Sectarianism in Taiwan*. Princeton, NJ: Princeton University Press, 1986. A systematic study of modern Chinese popular sects that brings out the shamanic and folk-religious motifs.

Kato, Genchi. *A Historical Study of the Religious Development of Shinto*. New York: Greenwood Press, 1988. A classic study of Shinto assembled for the United Nations information agency.

Lagerwey, John. *Taoist Ritualism in Chinese Society and History*. New York: Macmillan, 1987. A study of the roots and intricacies of Daoist ritual.

Loewe, Michael. *Divination, Mythology and Monarchy in Han China*. New York, NY: Cambridge University Press, 1994. A scholarly work that considers the historical context of divination in Chinese society.

Maspero, Henri. *Taoism and Chinese Religion*. Amherst: University of Massachusetts Press, 1981. A thorough look at the different elements of the Daoist tradition and how they contributed to Chinese society.

Reader, Ian. *Religion in Contemporary Japan*. Honolulu: University of Hawaii Press, 1991. A look at the role of religion in modern Japan.

Reader, Ian; Andreasen, Esban; and Stefansson, Finn. *Japanese Religions: Past and Present*. Honolulu: University of Hawaii Press, 1993. Attempts to present the diversity of the Japanese religious tradition: Ainu, Shinto, and Buddhist.

Sommer, Deborah. *Chinese Religion: An Anthology of Sources*. New York: Oxford University Press, 1995. A reader of well-translated Chinese treatises.

Weiming, Tu; Hejtmanek, Milan; and Wachman, Alan. *The Confucian World Observed: A Contemporary Discussion of Confucian Humanism in East Asia*. Honolulu, HI: Institute of Culture and Communication, East-West Center, 1992. Examines the historical and contemporary context of Confucian ethics and ritualism in China and other countries.

CHAPTER 7: GREEK AND HELLENISTIC RELIGION

Burkert, Walter. *Structure and History in Greek Mythology and Ritual.* Berkeley: University of California Press, 1979. An historical investigation that finds a continuous tradition evolving from Paleolithic to Hellenistic times.

Eliade, Mircea. *A History of Religious Ideas,* Vols. 1–3. Chicago: University of Chicago Press, 1978, 1982, 1985. Chapters on Greece, Iran, and Egypt in these volumes place these countries in the overall history of religious ideas.

Frankfurter, David. *Religion in Roman Egypt: Assimilation and Resistance.* Princeton, NJ: Princeton University Press, 1998. A good example of the syncretism of Egyptian and Greek traditions in the Hellenistic and Roman era.

Garland, Robert. *Introducing New Gods: The Politics of Athens.* Ithaca, NY: Cornell University Press, 1992. Considers the political and historical context of the Olympian and mystery religions in ancient Athens.

Goff, Barbara E. *Citizen Bacchae: Women's Ritual Practice in Ancient Greece.* Berkeley: University of California Press, 2004.

Green, Tamara M. *The City of the Moon God: Religious Traditions of Harran.* New York: Brill, 1992. A good archeological and historical investigation of a Hellenistic religion of Asia Minor.

Guthrie, W. K. C. *The Greeks and Their Gods.* Boston: Beacon Press, 1955. A thorough commentary on the religion of classical Greece.

O'Brien, Joan V. *In the Beginning: Creation Myths from Ancient Mesopotamia, Israel, and Greece.* Chico, CA: Scholars Press, 1982. A good comparative introduction to Greek and Mesopotamian creation myths.

Pomeroy, Sarah B. *Ancient Greece: A Political, Social, and Cultural History.* New York: Oxford University Press, 1999. A recent and comprehensive introduction to ancient Greece.

CHAPTER 8: BUDDHISM

Conze, Edward, et al., eds. *Buddhist Texts through the Ages.* New York: Harper Torchbooks, 1964. A good selection of representative primary sources, dealing with most of the major Buddhist sects.

Conze, Edward. *Buddhist Thought in India.* Ann Arbor: University of Michigan Press, 1967. A fairly demanding study of the origin of Buddhist philosophy in Indian dialectics.

Fischer-Schreiber, Ingrid, et al., eds. *The Encyclopedia of Eastern Philosophy and Religion: Buddhism, Hinduism,* *Taoism, Zen.* Boston: Shambhala, 1989. A translation of a German language encyclopedia.

Franck, Frederick, ed. *The Buddha Eye.* New York: Crossroad, 1982. An anthology of writings by members of the recent Kyoto school, one of the most influential modern circles of Buddhist philosophy.

Hoover, Thomas. *The Zen Experience.* New York: New American Library, 1980. Studies in the thought of major Chinese and Japanese Buddhist masters.

Huntington, Susan L. *The Art of Ancient India: Buddhist, Hindu, Jain.* New York: Weatherhill, 1985.

Johnston, William. *The Inner Eye of Love.* New York: Harper and Row, 1978. Shows the contemplative foundations of religion, with special reference to Christianity and Buddhism.

Kapleau, Philip, ed. *The Three Pillars of Zen.* Boston: Beacon Press, 1967. A clear view of the practice of Zen in modern Japan.

King, Winston. *In the Hope of Nibbana: Theravada Buddhist Ethics.* La Salle, IL: Open Court, 1964. A solid survey of the framework and content of Theravada ethics, both individual and social.

Nyanaponika, Thera. *The Heart of Buddhist Meditation.* London: Rider, 1969. A thorough study of the Buddha's way of mindfulness that reflects Theravada traditions.

Rahula, Walpola. *What the Buddha Taught.* New York: Grove Press, 1974. A fine exposition, focusing especially on the Four Noble Truths, with selected important texts.

Renard, John. *Responses to 101 Questions on Buddhism.* Mahwah, NJ: Paulist Press, 1999. A brief, readable introduction to Buddhism, organized conceptually.

Robinson, Richard H., and Johnson, Willard L. *The Buddhist Religion.* Encino, CA: Dickenson, 1977. A comprehensive survey of Buddhist religion throughout the world.

Suzuki, Shunryu. *Zen Mind, Beginner's Mind.* New York: Weatherhill, 1970. A lovely and penetrating vision of Zen by a contemporary master.

Swearer, Donald K. *Buddhism.* Niles, IL: Argus, 1977. A good brief sketch of the teachings, history, and practice of Buddhism. Well illustrated.

Tucci, Giuseppe. *The Religions of Tibet.* Berkeley: University of California Press, 1980. A well-regarded investigation of both pre-Buddhist and Buddhist religious thought and practices in Tibet.

Welch, Holmes. *The Practice of Chinese Buddhism, 1900–1950.* Cambridge, MA: Harvard University Press, 1967. A valuable window onto the state of Chinese Buddhism (especially monastic life) prior to the antireligious crackdown of the Maoists.

Wright, Arthur F. *Buddhism in Chinese History.* Stanford, CA: Stanford University Press, 1959. A straightforward survey of Buddhism's fortunes in the major historical periods.

Zwolf, W., ed. *Buddhism: Art and Faith*. New York: Macmillan, 1986. A lavishly illustrated study based on collections in the British Museum.

CHAPTER 9: CHRISTIANITY

Brading, D. A. *Mexican Phoenix, Our Lady of Guadalupe: Image and Tradition across Five Centuries*. Washington, DC: Catholic University Press, 2001. An excellent study of images of syncretism (blending of religious traditions) and morphology (the historical developments of religious traditions) using the central symbol of Mexican Catholicism as an example.

Carmody, Denise Lardner, and Carmody, John Tully. *Christianity: An Introduction,* 2nd ed. Belmont, CA: Wadsworth, 1988. A basic text that offers an analysis of the Christian worldview, a succinct history, and sketches of current schools of Christian religious thought.

————. *Jesus: An Introduction*. Belmont, CA: Wadsworth, 1987. New Testament, historical, recent theological, and comparative studies of Jesus that situate him in both Church history and the full spectrum of the founders of the world religions.

Carmody, John; Carmody, Denise Lardner; and Robbins, Gregory A. *Exploring the New Testament*. Englewood Cliffs, NJ: Prentice Hall, 1986. A comprehensive introduction to the New Testament stressing the ideas on which later Christian tradition built.

Carroll, James. *Constantine's Sword: The Church and the Jews*. Boston: Houghton Mifflin, 2001. A riveting history of the Catholic Church's relationship with the Jews. The author urges a Vatican III for the redress of the Church's past errors.

Cohn-Sherbok, Dan, and Cohn-Sherbok, Lavinia. *Jewish and Christian Mysticism: An Introduction*. New York: Continuum, 1994.

Cook, Michael L. *Responses to 101 Questions about Jesus*. Mahwah, NJ: Paulist Press, 1993. Presents a readable, moderate Catholic view, organized conceptually.

Crowley, Paul. *In Ten Thousand Places: Dogma in a Pluralistic Church*. New York: Crossroad/Herder, 1997. The Catholic Church today can be viewed as a balance between a top-down authoritative church and one that is a conglomeration of divergent local congregations.

Elliott, Dyan. *Proving Woman: Female Spirituality and Inquisitional Culture in the Later Middle Ages*. Princeton: Princeton University Press, 2003. Examines the role of female monastics during medieval Christianity: how the mystics were honored as living saints but later persecuted as potential heretics.

Farmer, David Hugh. *The Oxford Dictionary of Saints,* 2nd ed. New York: Oxford University Press, 1987. A handy reference to many of the great personalities who shaped Christian doctrine and piety.

Freed, Edwin D. *The Apostle Paul, Christian Jew*. Lanham, MD: University Press of America, 1994. Places Paul in his context, pulled by the forces of his Pharisaic past, and his revelatory attraction to the Christian movement.

Fredriksen, Paula. *From Jesus to Christ*. New Haven, CT: Yale University Press, 1988. A thorough study of the origins of the New Testament's images of Jesus that served as the foundation for a 1998 PBS series of the same name.

Grassi, Joseph A. *The Hidden Heroes of the Gospels: Female Counterparts of Jesus*. Collegeville: Liturgical Press, 1995.

————. *Rediscovering the Jesus Story: A Participatory Guide*. Mahwah, NJ: Paulist Press, 1995.

Jenkins, Philip. *Hidden Gospels: How the Search for Jesus Lost Its Way*. Oxford: Oxford University Press, 2001. Reviews not only some of the noncanonical gospels (e.g., Thomas) but examines the impact of the "discovery" of such texts on contemporary American society.

Jones, Cheslyn; Wainwright, Geoffrey; and Yarnold, Edward, eds. *The Study of Spirituality*. New York: Oxford University Press, 1986. An excellent handbook guiding readers through the historical development of the major Christian schools of devotion.

Koester, Helmut. *Ancient Christian Gospels: Their History and Development*. Philadelphia: Trinity Press International, 1990. One of the most scholarly introductions to the Gospels.

Maguire, Daniel C. *Sacred Choices*. A Catholic theologian opens up new perspectives on the Church's positions on birth control and abortion through a comparison with the perspectives offered by other religions.

Meissner, William W. *Ignatius of Loyola: The Psychology of a Saint*. New Haven: Yale University Press, 1992. One of America's foremost Jesuit scholars, who is also a psychoanalyst, provides an in-depth understanding of the founder of the Jesuit order.

Murphy, Catherine M. *John the Baptist: Prophet of Purity for a New Age*. Collegeville, MN: Liturgical Press, 2003.

Pagels, Elaine. *Beyond Belief*. New York, Random House, 2003. A thorough, yet readable, investigation of the Gospel of Thomas and how it portrays some of the Gnostic influences in first-century Christianity.

Pelikan, Jaroslav. *Jesus through the Centuries*. New Haven, CT: Yale University Press, 1985. A good survey of how Christian views of Jesus developed through interaction with succeeding historical cultures.

Prothero, Stephen. *American Jesus: How the Son of God Became a National Icon*. New York: Farrar, Straus and Giroux, 2003. Different secular as well as religious movements in the United States have recast Jesus in their own image.

Sanders, E. P. *The Historical Figure of Jesus*. New York: Pelican, 1993. One of the most thorough and objective approaches to the life of Jesus, taking great pains to establish historical sources and context.

Shanks, Hershel, ed. *Christianity and Rabbinic Judaism: A Parallel History of Their Origins and Early Development*. Washington, DC: Biblical Archaeology Society, 1992. Examines the demise of temple Judaism in Palestine and how both Christianity and the rabbinic tradition competed for the leadership of post-Diaspora Judaism.

Sloyan, Gerard Stephen. *The Crucifixion of Jesus*. Minneapolis: Fortress Press, 1995. Examines historical and doctrinal aspects of the crucifixion.

Spohn, William C. *Go and Do Likewise: Jesus and Ethics*. New York: Continuum, 2000. A reflection upon the ethical foundations of Christianity.

———. *What Are They Saying About Scripture and Ethics*. Mahwah, NJ: Paulist Press, 1995. A very readable introduction to the biblical foundations of ethics and contemporary ethical perspectives.

Stark, Rodney. *The Rise of Christianity: A Sociologist Reconsiders History*. Princeton, NJ: Princeton University Press, 1996. A sociological and historical analysis of the first two centuries of Christianity examines issues of social cohesion and social class.

Vermes, Geza. *The Religion of Jesus the Jew*. Minneapolis: Fortress, 1993. Vermes argues convincingly that Jesus must be considered in his historical context, as an observant Jew.

———. *The Changing Faces of Jesus*. New York: Viking, 2000. Vermes systematically explores the thesis that the different writers of the gospels and epistles held divergent views of Jesus.

Walker, Williston, et al. *A History of the Christian Church*, 4th ed. New York: Scribner's, 1985. A standard text that has the advantage of offering all the major chronological periods roughly equal space.

Wittberg, Patricia. *The Rise and Decline of Catholic Religious Orders: A Social Movement Perspective*. Albany: State University of New York Press, 1994. Sociological analysis that focuses on celibate orders of monks and nuns, their important social role, and their recent decline.

CHAPTER 10: ISLAM

Al Faruqi, I. *Islam*. Niles, IL.: Argus, 1979. A simple introduction that offers an overview of Islamic thought and practice. Well illustrated.

Al Faruqi, I., and Al Faruqi, Lois L. *The Cultural Atlas of Islam*. New York: Macmillan, 1986. A large, comprehensive work stressing institutional and cultural themes more than history or theology.

Arberry, A. J. *Aspects of Islamic Civilization*. Ann Arbor: University of Michigan Press, 1971. Selections that illumine major themes of Muslim culture, including science, law, poetry, and mysticism.

Arkoun, Mohammed. *Rethinking Islam: Common Questions, Uncommon Answers*. Boulder: Westview Press, 1994. One of Islam's formost theologians attempts to demonstrate the relevance of this tradition for contemporary society.

Bosworth, C. E., and Schacht, Joseph, eds. *The Legacy of Islam*, 2nd ed. New York: Oxford University Press, 1974. Studies of such major cultural areas as Islamic art and architecture by leading scholars of the previous generation.

Ernst, Carl W. *Following Muhammad: Rethinking Islam in the Contemporary World*. Chapel Hill, NC: University of North Carolina Press, 2003.

Fawzi El-Solh, Camillia, and Mahro, Judy, eds. *Muslim Women's Choices*. Providence, RI: Berg, 1994. Analyzes Islamic doctrine and history and its interaction with contemporary society.

Hick, John, and Meltzer, Edmund S. *Three Faiths—One God: A Jewish, Christian, Muslim*. Albany: State University of New York Press, 1989. A brief comparison of the doctrine and history of these three religions.

Inamdar, Subhash C. *Muhammad and the Rise of Islam: The Creation of Group Identity*. New York: International Universities Press, 2001. A psychoanalytic and sociological model is presented to explain the growth of Islam.

Kandiyoti, Deniz, ed. *Women, Islam, and the State*. Philadelphia: Temple University Press, 1991. Looks at contemporary governments in Islamic nations and the interaction between modern secularizing forces and tradition.

Khalidi, Tarif, ed. *The Muslim Jesus*. Cambridge, MA: Harvard University Press, 2001. A collection of Quranic suras and hadiths about Jesus, portraying him as resisting his followers' view of his divinity.

Lewis, Bernard. *What Went Wrong?* New York: Oxford University Press, 2002. In comparing the Western World and contemporary Islamic nations, Lewis contends that the latter's lack of secularism goes back to some of the original features of Islam.

McLeod, W. H. *The Sikhs*. New York: Columbia University Press, 1989. A historical study of Sikh traditions and culture.

Pinault, David. *The Shiites: Ritual and Popular Piety in a Muslim Community*. New York: St. Martin's, 1993. One of the most scholarly, yet readable, presentations of one Islamic sect.

———. *Horse of Karbala: Studies in South Asian Muslim Devotionalism*. New York: Palgrave/St. Martin's Press, 2000. This case study of a Shiite ritual demonstrates the role of complex interactions of history and culture.

Rahman, Fazlur. *Islam,* 2nd ed. Chicago: University of Chicago Press, 1979. A solid, fact-filled history of Islam from Muhammad to the present.

———. *Major Themes of the Qur'an.* Chicago: University of Chicago Press, 1980. Systematic presentations of the view of the Qur'an on such themes as God, human nature, and revelation.

Renard, John. *Responses to 101 Questions on Islam.* Mahwah, NJ: Paulist Press, 1998. A highly readable introduction to Islam, noting similarities with Christianity.

Sells, Michael A., ed. *Early Islamic Mysticism: Sufi, Qur'an, Miraj, Poetic and Theological Writings.* New York: Paulist Press, 1996. The editor has provided the introduction and the translation, but much of what is here is from the original Sufi sources.

White, Vilbert. *Inside the Nation of Islam.* Gainesville, FL: University of Florida Press, 2001. The author is a member and was a major figure in organizing the Million Man March. The book is thorough, balanced, objective, and scholarly. The author views the movement as being primarily a reaction to white racism rather than spirituality. He raises serious questions about internal corruption.

Wolfe, Michael, ed. *Taking Back Islam: American Muslims Reclaim their Faith.* New York: Rodale, 2002. A series of popular articles written after 9/11 by American Muslims, addressing such issues as terrorism, democracy, race and gender in Islam.

CHAPTER 11: CONTEMPORARY RELIGION

Baer, Hans A., and Singer, Merrill. *African-American Religion in the Twentieth Century: Varieties of Protest and Accommodation.* Knoxville: University of Tennessee Press, 1992. A good historical introduction to the socio-political context of African American religion.

Bellah, Robert N.; Madsen, Richard; Sullivan, William M.; Swidler, Ann; and Tipton, Steven M. *Habits of the Heart: Individualism and Commitment in American Life.* Berkeley: University of California Press, 1985. A team of sociologists looks at contemporary, secular America and finds that many Americans turn to government and other "nonreligious" sources for myth, symbol, and ritual.

Beaudoin, Thomas. *Consuming Faith: Integrating Who We Are With What We Buy.* Chicago: Sheed and Ward, 2004.

———. *Virtual Faith: The Irreverent Spiritual Quest of Generation X.* San Francisco: Jossey-Bass, 1998.

Bloom, Harold. *The American Religion: The Emergence of the Post-Christian Nation.* New York: Simon and Schuster, 1993. The author contends that traditional Christianity has been largely eclipsed by materialist, secular culture.

Collins, John J., ed. *The Encyclopedia of Apocalypticism.* New York: Continuum, 2000.

Douglas, Kelly Brown. *The Black Christ.* Maryknoll, NY: Orbis, 1994. The syncretism of Christian symbolism and ethics with African American culture.

Fontenot, Wonda L. *Secret Doctors: Ethnomedicine of African Americans.* Westport, CT: Bergin and Garvey, 1994. Looks at folk medicine and its relation to culture and religion.

Hammond, Phillip, ed. *The Sacred in a Secular Age.* Berkeley: University of California Press, 1985. Studies civil religion as the background for the recent contest between secularity and sacrality.

Haught, John F. *Responses to 101 Questions on God and Evolution.* Mahwah, NJ: Paulist Press, 2001. A readable introduction to the impact of evolution on religion that takes a moderate, Catholic perspective.

———. *Deeper than Darwin: The Prospect for Religion in the Age of Evolution.* Boulder, CO: Westview Press, 2003.

Hoge, Dean R. *Vanishing Boundaries: The Religion of Mainline Protestant Baby Boomers.* Louisville, KY: Westminster/John Knox Press, 1994.

Jenkins, Philip. *Hidden Gospels: How the Search for Jesus Lost Its Way.* New York: Oxford University Press, 2001. Reviews the noncanonical gospels (later, frequently Gnostic texts) and the historical role that they and their frequent "rediscoveries" have played in the history of Christianity.

Kuhn, Thomas S. *The Structure of Scientific Revolutions,* 2nd ed. Chicago: University of Chicago Press, 1970. Kuhn's thesis that science proceeds by observing normative paradigms until something revolutionary creates a new paradigm (which then becomes normative) aroused great controversy among historians and philosophers of science. As well, historians of other disciplines, theology among them, soon adapted the notion of paradigms and normal science to study the evolution of their own fields.

Kung, Hans. *The Catholic Church: A Short History.* New York: Modern Library, 2001. One of the most progressive voices within the Catholic Church presents a critical review, admitting past mistakes and calling for a more ecumenical focus in the future.

Leon, Luis D. *La Llorona's Children: Religion, Life and Death in the U.S.-Mexican Borderlands.* Berkeley: University of California Press, 2004.

McDermott, Gerald. *Can Evangelicals Learn from World Religions?* Downers Grove, IL: Inter-Varsity Press, 2000. Targeting contemporary American evangelical Christians, the author contends that they can respect and learn from non-Christian traditions.

ANNOTATED BIBLIOGRAPHY

Mason, Michael Atwood. *Living Santería: Rituals and Experiences in an Afro-Cuban Religion.* Washington, DC: Smithsonian Institution Press, 2002.

Melton, J. Gordon. *Encyclopedic Handbook of Cults in America.* New York: Garland, 1992. A comprehensive collection of different new religious movements.

Moore, R. Lawrence. *Religious Outsiders and the Making of Americans.* New York: Oxford University Press, 1986. Chapters on the history of the process by which many groups, either sectarian or marginal to the cultural mainstream, were Americanized.

Myers, David. *The American Paradox: Spiritual Hunger in an Age of Plenty.* New Haven: Yale University Press, 2000. This social psychologist indicts contemporary American culture for overemphasis on individualism and materialism. He argues that the key element of religion is behavior (ritual and ethics) and that happiness is directly associated with religious participation.

Nelson-Pallmeyer, Jack. *Is Religion Killing Us? Violence in the Bible and the Quran.* Harrisburg, PA: Trinity Press International, 2003.

Peacock, Arthur. *Paths from Science to God.* New York: Oxford, 2001. A pantheist approach is developed as a foundation for ecumenism today.

Powers, Tom. *The Call of God: Women Doing Theology in Peru.* Albany, NY: State University of New York Press, 2003.

Richardson, James T.; Best, Joel; and Bromley, David G., eds. *The Satanism Scare.* New York: Aldine de Gruyter, 1991. A sociological perspective on charges of satanic ritual child abuse.

Sawyer, Mary R. *Black Ecumenism: Implementing the Demands of Justice.* Valley Forge, PA: Trinity Press International, 1994. A view of African American churches as being at the forefront of the ecumenical movement, overlooking doctrinal and ethical differences in the quest for solidarity.

Sered, Susan Starr. *Priestess, Mother, Sacred Sister: Religions Dominated by Women.* New York: Oxford University Press, 1994.

West, Cornel; Glaude, Eddie S., Jr., eds. *African American Religious Thought: An Anthology.* Louisville, KY: Westminster/John Knox Press, 2003.

Williams, Juan, and Dixie, Quentin. *This Far by Faith : Stories from the African-American Religious Experience.* New York: William Morrow, 2003.

Wright, Robert. *Nonzero: The Logic of Human Destiny.* New York: Pantheon, 2002. Looks at the process of evolution of human consciousness, which is getting ever closer to the understanding of God and freedom.

Zabilka, Ivan L. *Scientific Malpractice: The Creation/Evolution Debate.* Lexington, KY: Bristol Books, 1992. Considers the weakness of some of the claims made on behalf of evolution.

INDEX AND GLOSSARY

This glossary serves also as an index. The page numbers in parentheses at the end of the entries refer to the major text discussion.

Amaterasu: Japanese sun goddess; ancestor of the Emperor (189)

Amish: pacifist Protestant sect committed to living a simple, 19th century life style, found in rural Pennsylvania

Anabaptist: original Baptist churches of the European Reformation; associated with peasant rebellions of the 16th century (287)

angel: a resident of heaven, a spiritual being who mediates between man and God; important in Islam and some Christian denominations (133, 265, 331, 332, 356)

Anglican: the Church of England, established by Henry VIII; known as Episcopalian in the U.S.; more ritually oriented than most Protestants; call their ministers "priests," but abolished celibacy (288)

animism: "all objects have a spirit"; this view is common in many tribal religions (10–11, 30–31, 53, 59)

anoint: a ritual in which oil is put on someone as a sign of God's favor in Judaism and Christianity

Anselm (1033–1109): medieval Catholic theologian, developed ontological argument (19, 283)

antediluvian: before the flood of Noah

anthropomorphic: a deity having human form (e.g., some Greek Olympian deities) (10–11, 66, 80, 204)

Antichrist: final opponent of God in apocalyptic times

anticlerical: governmental policies which try to limit the role of religious leaders in a society (13)

antinomianism: "Since we are saved, we do not have to obey any morals or rules"; this heresy has recurred throughout Christian history, and was one of Paul's opponents in Corinth (266, 273, 366)

anti-Semitism: prejudice against Jews; this has a long history in the actions of the early Church and later western civilization (142, 145)

apocalypse: world-ending battle; doctrine found in Teutons, Christians, Pharisees, Muslims, Zoroastrians (48, 74, 128–133, 265, 271, 273, 332, 351–354, 359–362)

apocryphal: religious writings not a part of canon; the book known as the Apocrypha would be fourteen inter-testamental books from 400 B.C.E. on that are now part of Catholic but not Protestant canon of the Old Testament (15, 359)

Apollo: Greek Olympian deity representing reason, moderation (204, 208)

Apologetics: theology defending a specific denomination's doctrines (19)

apostasy: renouncing one's denomination for another; a person who does this is an apostate (273)

apostles: major figures in the early Church, (e.g., the disciples chosen by Jesus in Galilee, then later, Paul) (261–263, 270)

Aquinas, St. Thomas (1225–1274): Catholic theologian; synthesized Aristotle with Catholicism (19, 212, 283)

Arianism: early Christian heresy of Arius; "the Father is greater than the Son" (274)

Aristotle (384–322 B.C.E.): Greek philosopher: emphasized reason, observation, moderation; influenced Aquinas (Catholic), Averroes (Muslim), and Maimonides (Jewish) (19, 212, 214, 218)

Arminianism: position of Arminius: "use your free will to Accept God; you can lose your salvation by losing your commitment to God"; 17th century opponent of Calvin; influenced Wesley and Methodism (286–287)

Aryan: nomadic Eurasian tribes; especially those who invaded Persia and India 2,000–1,500 B.C.E. (84, 156)

asceticism: self-denial of pleasure, self-imposition of hardship to achieve spiritual advancement (Jainism, Hinduism, monastic Christianity) (32–33, 96, 105, 209, 211, 214, 224, 275)

Ashkenazim: Jews of Northern European extraction (138–139, 149)

Asoka (270–270 B.C.E.): Emperor who spread Buddhism in southeast Asia (239)

astrology: observation of stars and planets for divination (Babylonian roots) (63)

Athanasius: formulator of Athanasian Creed, affirming Trinity (274)

atheism: "no deity or deities exist" (11, 14, 19, 20, 95, 105, 224)

Atman: Upanishad concept of the human soul, which at its core is equivalent to Brahman (90, 103)

atonement: expiation or propitiation to escape punishment for sins (Judaism, Christianity)

attitude: a learned habit to respond to a social stimulus; there are cognitive, affective and behavioral components

Augustine (354–430): Catholic theologian who synthesized Plato and Christianity; the Church administers the sacraments; major opponent of Pelagius and Donatus (19, 212, 271, 274, 275)

austerities: asceticism: self-denial of pleasure, self-imposition of hardship to achieve spiritual advancement (Jainism, Hinduism, Christian monasticism)

avatar: an incarnation of a Hindu deity (e.g., Krishna appears as an avatar in the Bhagavad Gita) (97)

Averroes, Ibn Rushd (1126–1198): Islamic theologian synthesizing Aristotle with Islam (212, 310)

Awakening, Great: 18th century American revival of interest in religion, led by Congregationalist preachers such as Jonathan Edwards

Axial, Axis Age: period of great religious and philosophical speculation, 600 B.C.E.–200 C.E. (18, 159, 164, 222)

Aztec: 14th–15th century Mexican civilization; emphasis on priests, theriomorphic polytheism, multiple creation, human sacrifice, calendar-based divination (78–80, 361)

Babylonia: a major empire in Mesopotamia; Hammurabi was the Babylonian king who gave the written code of laws (62–68)

Bachofen, J. J. (1815–1887): Swiss anthropologist: "Society evolved from promiscuity to matriarchy to patriarchy; this was paralleled by a shift from female to male deities" (23)

Bacon, Francis (1521–1626): "Use the scientific method in gaining knowledge." (340)

Bahai: modern syncretistic religion, originally from Persia: "All denominations lead to the one God." (324, 325)

baptism: initiation/conversion rite of water immersion (Hellenistic, Christian) (276)

Baptist: large Protestant denomination; emphasizes adult Baptism by full immersion (287, 359)

Baptist, John the: 1st century C.E. Jewish prophet, foretold of the Coming Messiah, baptized Jesus

bar mitzvah: Jewish puberty rite: at age thirteen the boy is accepted as an adult in this religion (132, 150)

B.C.E.: before the common era; historical times and dates before the birth of Jesus (4)

beatify: the pope declares that a deceased person was blessed; the first step to becoming a saint (278)

Behaviorism: Watson/Skinner school: "behavior is learned from experience with environment; religion is superstition"

belief: an intellectual credence, especially a purely cognitive assertion as to the validity of a fact; in general, it is best not to use this term in a religious context with the acceptance of doctrines, performance of rituals, following of ethics, reverence for symbols, or retelling of myths (4, 7)

Bellah, R.: "We have a civil religion in America, with national rituals, symbols transcending denominations"

beneficent: deity who is completely good (20)

Bhagavad Gita: Hindu book written by 200 C.E. in the wake of the Upanishads, Buddhism, and Jainism; it accepted karma and transmigration, but discouraged the mystical approach to salvation, defending instead devotion to caste duties and theistic devotion to specific deities (96–99, 105, 156, 224)

Bhakti: the Hindu path emphasizing theism, personal devotion to a specific deity; a main theme of the Bhagavad Gita (106–107, 115, 117)

Bible: the basic Christian canon, the books of the Old and New Testaments (6–7, 261–263)

bishop: a member of the clergy having direct authority over other priests or ministers

Black Muslims: Nation of Islam; African-American movement with prejudicial views against whites and Jews (324–325)

blasphemy: verbal offenses against the sacred doctrine

bless: to invoke divine favor for spiritual or material benefit

bodhisattva: a Buddha who decides to stay in this world to help the rest of us; a personal savior or role model in Mahayana Buddhism (231, 232)

Bonism: the indigenous religion of Tibet, before Buddhism (237)

born again: a Christian who has had a profound personal experience of Jesus; born again Christians tend to be Protestants who have re-affirmed, as adults, their commitment to their religion; also known as Evangelicals, Fundamentalists (356)

Booth, William (1829–1913): founder of Salvation Army

Brahma: Hindu creator deity (87)

Brahman: absolute reality, the pantheistic deity of Upanishads and Vedanta Hinduism (90, 92, 97, 105, 117, 125, 224)

Brahmin: the highest caste (priests) in India (88, 100–102, 156)

Buber, Martin (1878–1965): Jewish theologian who urged a theistic approach: "God is a thou, not an it"

Bucke, Richard M. (1832–1802): Canadian psychiatrist; "Mystic experience is due to growth of human consciousness"

Buddha: "enlightened one"; mystic Siddharta Gautama Sayka was the original Buddha around 500 B.C.E. (220–225)

Buddhism: monastic, soteriological religion; founded by Gautama; proselytizing, spread from India to east Asia (90, 218–258, 295)

Bultmann, Rudolf (1884–1976): existentialist theologian: "We must demythologize Christianity from its 1st century terminology to make it relevant for us today"

bushido: Japanese code of knights' chivalry; blends Confucian ethics, Shinto ritual, Zen self-discipline (190–193, 196)

Cabala, Cabbala, Kabbala: esoteric Jewish mysticism, arose in Spain in Middle Ages; influenced numerology, searched for a mathematical code in the Torah (140–146, 156, 298–301, 333)

Calvin, John (1509–1564): Protestant reformer; preached predestination; influenced Reformed Churches, Puritans (285–286)

cannibalism: eating of one's own species; usually done as a puberty or funeral ritual (Melanesia) (53)

canon: an official list, especially of scripture that religious leaders accept as authoritative (15, 274, 295, 359)

canonize: to declare someone a saint in the Catholic church; to declare writings to be authoritative scripture (278)

Cao Dai: a 20th century Vietnamese sect synthesizing Buddhism, Confucianism, Christianity, and indigenous animistic traditions (362)

cardinal: a member of a powerful council in the Catholic Church that selects the new pope; the pope can name new cardinals (17)

cargo cults: 20th century Melanesian movement; hope for ancestral gifts coming by plane and ship; influenced by contact with Europeans (53)

Carlyle, Thomas (1795–1881): Scottish essayist: "Muhammad was not an impostor, but sincerely considered himself to be a prophet" (21)

carnival: festival characterized by indulgent behavior before a prescribed period of abstinence (e.g., Mardi Gras)

caste: Hindu rigid system of heredity social class: 1, Brahmin priests; 2, warriors and nobles; 3, merchants and artisans; 4, peasants and workers (88–89, 105, 156, 169, 224, 253)

catechism: systematic instruction in doctrine (Catholic)

Cathari: heretical medieval European cult, some Gnostic influences: ascetic, dualist (282)

cathedral: the main church in a Catholic diocese

Catholic: Holy Roman Catholic Apostolic Church; largest Christian denomination, syncretistic, follows the Pope (276, 283, 287, 288, 290, 295, 359, 366)

C.E.: common era, history after the birth of Jesus (also known as A.D.) (4)

celibacy: abstinence from sexual relations and marriage (Catholic priests, monks, nuns; Buddhist monks, nuns, all members of the Shakers) (18, 32, 333)

Celts: original inhabitants of British isles, emphasis on priests (Druids), megaliths (Stonehenge), tricksters (53–55)

Ceres (Demeter): a Greek and Roman goddess of grain, mother of Kore (Persephone) and important in the Eleusinian mysteries (204, 208–209)

channeling: achieving contact with disembodied spirits

charismatic: modern Christian sects (e.g., Pentecostals) emphasizing spiritual gifts (e.g., tongues); also Weber's term for religions lead by a dynamic personality

Christ: Greek term, "anointed one," given to Jesus of Galilee, founder of Christianity

Christian: a member of any denomination of Christianity; sometimes held to apply only to people who have had a personal encounter with the resurrected Jesus (260–296, 332–333, 359, 364)

Christian Science: a denomination founded by Mary Baker Eddy; emphasizes spiritual healing (350–351)

Christianity: all those churches accepting the role of Jesus as Son of God

Christology: theological speculation about the role of Jesus with God (275)

chthonic: deities representing powers of the earth (Greek) (202–203, 214)

church: a building for Christian worship; a denomination, especially the Roman Catholic or an established sect

circumcision: male initiation rite: removal of foreskin (Judaism, Islam, Africa, Aborigines) (41–42, 50, 73, 132, 150, 333)

civilization: societies organized around cities (Egypt, Mesopotamia, Aztec, Maya, Inca) (60)

clairvoyance: perceiving objects despite great distance or obstacles (17)

clergy: a minister of the church, religious leadership (283)

clerical: pertaining to the religious leadership as opposed to the laity

clitoridectomy: removal of the female clitoris, usually as part of a puberty rite (50)

cloistered: monastic orders shunning contact with outside world

cognitive: relating to concepts, beliefs, logic; rather than emotions or values (affect) (4, 21, 22)

cognitive dissonance: describes how people change their beliefs to match their behavior when the components of an attitude are internally inconsistent

commitment: faith in the realm of relevance; religious faith is to be understood as commitment rather than a contingent belief in a set of facts (4, 7)

common era: history after the birth of Jesus (previously known as A.D.) (4)

communion, Holy: Eucharist, Lord's Supper; Christian ritual partaking of bread and wine in remembrance of Christ (277, 359)

compassion: a central Buddhist virtue exemplified by Bodhisattvas (232)

Comte, Auguste (1798–1857): French positivist; influenced humanism: "progress from religion to philosophy to science." (338)

confession: to proclaim one's adherence to a religion (e.g., Islam); also to recount one's sins (e.g., Catholic, Inca) (277, 279)

confirmation: sacrament of full initiation into the Church (277)

Confucius (552–469 B.C.E.): Chinese philosopher, teacher; emphasized duty to family, unequal relationships, moderation (158–159, 161, 166–172, 177–178, 218)

conscience: the part of the mind that sustains guilt

conscious: the part of the mind which is awake and aware of the material world; other levels of consciousness are altered states of consciousness

consecrate: to associate objects or places with ultimate relevance, to make them symbols

Conservative Judaism: accommodate to the modern world, but try to keep Jewish traditions; large in U.S. (145)

Constantine: 4th century Roman Emperor, Christian convert (274)

contrition: penance

conversion: forming an affiliation to a religion; many sects proselytize in hopes of gaining converts

Copernicus (1473–1543): Polish Renaissance astronomer: "the earth circles the sun" (heliocentric); upset pope

Coptic: North African church founded by Mark, later blended with indigenous and Gnostic traditions

cosmogony: story of the creation of the world (Mesopotamian myth) (183)

cosmological argument: "All that exists must have been caused by something else; God must be the first cause; therefore, He exists" (19, 20)

councils: bishops assemble and agree on what is canon or doctrine (e.g., Trinity) vs. heresy; councils were important in the ongoing development of Christian and Buddhist traditions

covenant: contract between people or between God and His people (especially ancient Israel); symbolized by circumcision (127, 128, 132)

creed: a denomination's doctrinal system

cross: method of execution used by Romans on Jesus, now a symbol of Christianity

crucifix: model of Jesus on a cross (Catholicism)

Crusades (1095–1291): wars launched by the popes in order to re-conquer Palestine from Muslims (282)

cult: a small sect with devoted followers; a pejorative term for a new religious movement denomination (especially one which has doctrines or rituals outside of the mainstream, or is abusive of followers) (358–366)

curia: a small group of Catholic clerics assigned to advise the pope

curse: an expression of disapproval, call for divine intervention to create earthly misfortune or damnation

Cybele: mother goddess from Asia Minor, popular in Rome in the early common era; self-castration ritual (213–215, 218)

Cynics: Greek philosophy influenced by Socrates: reject all social conventions; asceticism, members were hermits (e.g., Diogenes) (211, 214)

Cyrenaics: Greek philosophy influenced by Socrates: reject all social convention; pursue pleasure (211–214, 218)

Dalai Lama: spiritual head of Tibetan Buddhism (239, 245)

damnation: when one has offended God and does not receive salvation

Daoism: Taoism; Chinese religion; emphasis on nature mysticism (Laozi), alchemy, hermits, hedonism (Yang Zhu) (160–163, 168–176, 178, 185–186, 240, 295)

Darwin, Charles (1809–1882): theory of evolution: "higher species evolved from lower species"; initially perceived as heresy because it could challenge the teleological argument and a literal interpretation of Genesis (341, 346)

data: facts, information derived empirically from observations

deacon: a low level position of leadership in church, still considered laity

Deism: view popular in 18th century: "God can be known without revelation, He created the world but does not intervene" (10–11)

deity: term for a god

Delphi: a Greek oracle where divination was practiced (204)

Demeter (Ceres): a Greek and Roman goddess of grain, mother of Kore (Persephone) and important in the Eleusinian mysteries (204, 208–209)

Democritus (460–370 B.C.E.): Greek philosopher: "Atoms are the material from which everything is made"; no afterlife, hedonistic

demon: a spiritual being that can communicate with humans, usually evil

demythologization: removal of supernatural content from myths (Bultmann) (339)

denomination: a sect or religious group, especially one having some status of legitimacy, though not necessarily state support (7)

deontological: an approach to ethics based upon determination of duties (rather than utilitarian, results based approach) (8)

dervish: Islamic mystic who attempts to gain ecstasy by dancing (another name for Sufi) (316)

Descartes, René (1596–1650): French mathematician, philosopher; advanced the ontological argument (19)

Design Argument: also known as the teleological argument: "There is order in the world, therefore God must exist to have ordered it"

Detachment: a central Buddhist virtue of the Theravada school: do not get too concerned about the world's suffering (232)

determinism: people's actions are not due to free choice, but are determined by factors beyond their control (e.g., predestination, heredity, environment); Calvinism argues that people's salvation is due to God's predestination

deus otiosus: a "high" creator god, who has retired; not now active in the world's affairs (Aborigines, African)

devil: an evil spirit, especially Satan, the prime evil spirit in Christianity, Islam

devotion: piety, worship and adherence to the doctrine

devout: people who are very committed to their religion (opposite of nominal or lapsed)

dharma: Hindu and Buddhist term for doctrine (99, 224, 226)

Diaspora: Rome's forcible dispersion of the Jews from Palestine after 70 C.E. (133)

dietary restrictions: certain foods are taboo (Jews, Muslims, Jains, Hindus, Seventh Day Adventists)

Dilthey, Wilhelm (1833–1911): "the study of cultures requires an intuitive approach: verstehen"

diocese: a bishop's geographic and administrative unit in the Catholic Church

Dionysus: Greek god of wine and ecstatic rites, son of Zeus; his mystery cult involved devouring live animals (204, 208, 214)

disciple: one of the twelve apostles selected by Jesus in Galilee, also the name of an American Protestant sect

disfellowship: expulsion from the denomination (Jehovah's Witnesses), or loss of privileges (Mormon)

dissonance, cognitive: describes how people change their beliefs to match their behavior when the components of an attitude are internally inconsistent

divination: attempting to foretell the future through various rituals (Africa, Mesopotamia, China, Greece) (17, 31, 34–35, 52, 59, 62, 165–166, 178, 206–208, 214, 218)

divine: as an adjective it means pertaining to God; as a verb it means to predict the future

diviner: one who predicts the future through the practice of divination

Docetism: heretical Gnostic doctrine: "Christ's incarnation and suffering on the cross was illusory, not real" (272)

doctrine: the specific teachings of a denomination on the nature of the Deity, sin, salvation, and/or afterlife (9)

dogma: core of authoritative doctrine of a denomination, which must be accepted by the adherent

Dominicans: order of Roman Catholic priests devoted to apologetics (Aquinas) (282)

Donatism: early Christian heresy: "if the priest is a sinner, his sacraments are no good"; Augustine opposed this doctrine, arguing that the Church is Holy, and so are its sacraments regardless of the priest (273)

Douay: early 17th century Roman Catholic translation of Bible from Vulgate to English

Dravidian: early Indus Valley civilization (84)

Dreamtime: primordial paradise on earth (Aborigines, Melanesians) (40–41, 53)

Druids: members of the Celtic priestly caste (55)

Druses, Druze: Islamic, apocalyptic, exclusivistic, nonproselytizing sect found largely in Lebanon (324–325)

dualism: doctrine of two forces or realms (Zoroastrianism, Jainism, Gnosticism, Plato, Yin/Yang) (74, 76, 77, 95, 105, 163, 211–214, 224,271–273)

Durkheim, Emile (1858–1917): "Religion celebrates the unity of society, group cohesion" (22–23, 58–59, 147, 273)

Easter: Christian spring holiday celebrating the last days of Jesus, his crucifixion, and resurrection; many Teutonic and Celtic symbols (eggs, rabbits) become part of this holiday

Eastern Orthodox: form of Christianity predominant in Eastern Europe, North Africa, Middle East (Greek, Russian, Syrian, Coptic, Maronite, Ethiopian, Armenian) (279–282)

ecclesiastic: relating to the organized Church

Eckhart, Meister (1260–1328): medieval Christian mystic

eclectic: drawing from many different theoretical perspectives

ecumenical: attempts to achieve unity (or at least cooperation between) and tolerance for other denominations (358, 364, 366, 368)

Eddy, Mary Baker (1821–1910): founder of Christian Science church (350–351)

Edwards, Jonathan (1703–1758): American Calvinist revivalist emphasizing sin and damnation, major Great Awakening preacher (348)

Egypt: Nile civilization starting 4,000 B.C.E., emphasis on priests, theriomorphs, mummies, pyramids, afterlife (64–73, 80)

eightfold path: Buddhist formula for spiritual life on earth (223, 227)

Eleatics: Greek monistic philosophers who denied the existence of change (Parmenides, Zeno) (210, 214)

Eleusinian Mysteries: Greek, Hellenistic cult; mother-daughter goddesses; secret initiation rites (208–209, 214)

Eliade, Mircea (1907–1986): advocated phenomenological approach (22–23)

Elijah Muhammad (1897–1975): leader of U.S. Black Muslims, Nation of Islam

Elohim: a Hebrew name used for God in the Old Testament

empiricism: gaining knowledge through sense experience of the material world; the method of science; not religion (3, 338–339)

enlightenment: in Buddhism, the mental & spiritual state of salvation; also an 18th century European movement emphasizing science, secularism, humanism (21,223,338–339)

Epicureanism: Greek philosophy, materialist, hedonist: "We free man from fear of death and religion" (212–214, 218)

Episcopalian: what Church of England is called in the U.S.; rituals similar to Catholicism; priests can marry (288)

epistles: books of the New Testament that are letters by the apostles (e.g., Paul, Peter, Jude, James) (263–265)

Erasmus, Desiderius (1469–1536): Dutch Renaissance philosopher, emphasized humanism and free will

Erikson, Erik (1902–1994): psychoanalyst who theorized eight stages of human development; contended that religious rituals were helpful for individual maturation (22, 23)

eschatology: discourse on last things: judgment, afterlife (Zoroastrianism, Islam, Christianity, Judaism) (74, 132)

Eskimo: old name for Inuit; Arctic peoples, emphasis on shamanism (42–44, 53)

esoteric: doctrines taught to, or understood by, only a few in the inner circle of adherents

ESP: extra-sensory perception: perceiving in ways not dependent upon the senses: telepathy, clairvoyance, precognition

Essenes: 1st century pietistic, apocalyptic Jewish sect; initiation rites, shared wealth, Dead Sea settlements (132–133, 265)

ethics: theoretical perspectives on rules governing human conduct (8–9)

ethnic: related to particular cultural, national, or racial groups

Eucharist: Holy communion, Lord's Supper: a Christian ritual of bread & wine in remembrance of Christ (277, 359)

Evangelical: modern born-again Christians who emphasize Bible's authority; proselytizing, Fundamentalist Protestants (356–357)

evangelist: a preacher, especially a revivalist or missionary; also a term for the gospel authors Mark, Matthew, Luke, John

evolution: Darwin's 1859 theory that humans developed from ape-like animal ancestors; seen by some Fundamentalists as a threat to literal interpretation of Genesis (339, 341, 346)

ex-cathedra: official pronouncement of a doctrinal statement by the pope so that it has infallibility

excommunication: when someone is kicked out of a denomination or order (Catholicism)

exegesis: a thorough attempt to interpret a passage of scripture (15, 139)

Exile: period when Jews were carried off to Babylon in 586 B.C.E. (131)

Existentialism: 20th century philosophy: "Existence is prior to essence; there are no absolute values, commitment vindicates values." (344)

Exodus: when Moses led Hebrews out of Egypt (124)

exorcism: rituals to drive out evil spirits; performed by shamans, priests, sorcerers, witch doctors (31–34, 59, 164)

expiation: placating angry deity or spirits with penance or sacrifice

extra-sensory perception (ESP): perceiving in ways not dependent upon the senses: telepathy, clairvoyance, precognition

extreme unction: the Catholic sacrament of last rites, given to a dying person (277)

faith: a vague term that can refer to (1) a specific denomination, (2) a doctrine, or (3) strength of commitment (3–7)

faith healing: reliance upon prayer for miraculous healing (Christian Science, Pentecostal) (350–351)

Fall, the: myth explaining how Adam or Lucifer fell from grace (Judaism, Christianity)

fasting: going without food, or restricting one's diet, often used as a religious penance or devotion (Islam) (303, 333)

Father: reverential title for God and Christian priests

Feng-shui: Chinese system of geomancy (166, 183)

Fertile Crescent: the Middle East, especially the part running from Asia Minor through Palestine; originally characterized by mother-earth goddesses

fertility: rites and cults associated with sexuality, reproduction, and agriculture

fetish: a charm or amulet seen as having magical power against evil spirits (44)

Feuerbach, Ludwig (1804–1872): "Religion is the product of wish, but a necessary stage in human development"

filial piety: devotion, respect, ritual performance for one's family and ancestors (Confucius)

Five Pillars: the main points of Islam: monotheistic doctrine, pilgrimage, almsgiving, fasting, and prayer (303)

Four Noble Truths: basic Buddhist doctrine: life is suffering, due to desire, and only the eightfold path can remove this desire (223–227, 256–258)

Fox, George (1624–1691): Englishman who founded Quakers (Society of Friends)

Francis of Assisi (1182–1226): Christian mystic, founder of Franciscan Order of Catholic priests and monks (282, 290)

Frazer, James (1854–1941): "Humanity is evolving from magic, then to religion, then to science to control the world" (21–22)

free will: "people can make decisions free from the determinism of heredity or environment or from God's predestination"

Freud, Sigmund (1856–1939): psychoanalyst, atheist; "Religion is a neurotic childish obsession which mankind will outgrow" (21–22, 229)

Friends: formal name for Quakers, a denomination founded by Fox; minimizes ritual

Fromm, Erich (1902–1980): psychoanalyst who viewed religion as a means of social transformation

Functionalism: perspective that emphasizes the social and psychological function of religious phenomena (E. T. Parsons, Malinowski, James) (22)

Fundamentalism: "literal interpretation of scripture," combats modern secularizing trends (Iran, some U.S. Protestants) (15, 356, 366, 368)

Gabriel: angel who announced birth of Jesus to Mary and brought the Quran to Muhammad (300, 302, 306)

Galilee: nominally Jewish district in northern Palestine, from which Christianity sprang (264)

Galileo (1564–1642): Italian Renaissance scientist: "The earth moves around the sun" (heliocentric); his views upset the Pope (340)

Gandhi, Mohandas (1869–1948): nonviolent leader of political independence in India (107–109)

Ganeesh, Ganesh, Ganesha: Hindu deity with elephant head, "the remover of obstacles" (89)

Gautama: 6th century B.C.E. Indian prince who became the Buddha, a mystic who proselytized, developed monasteries (222–224)

Gentile: Jewish and Christian term for people who are not of Jewish origin (123, 266, 356)

geocentric: "the sun orbits the earth"; idea of ancient Greeks, challenged by Galileo and Copernicus (340)

geomancy: rituals that consult spirits in order to determine the proper site for a building or activity (China) (166)

ghost dance: apocalyptic 19th century American Indian religion: "rituals will bring forth the ancestors, better world" (48, 53)

Gilgamesh: Mesopotamian mythic figure, culture hero, survivor of the flood (56–57, 67–68, 80)

glossolalia: ecstatic speaking in unusual languages ("tongues"); held to be a charismatic gift (e.g., Pentecostals) (349–350)

Gnosticism: 1st century movement emphasizing secret knowledge about dualism of matter/spirit; foundation of many heresies (214, 271–272, 295, 366)

gospel: one of the first four books of the New Testament; the "good news" about Jesus and salvation (263, 269, 270, 349)

Grace: God's beneficence which saves sinners; Augustine: "Grace is dispensed through sacraments"

Graham, Billy: a Protestant Evangelical, effective preacher with simple message: salvation by grace (357)

Great Mother: fertility goddess prevalent in Hellenistic times (e.g., Isis, Cybele) (28, 59)

Great Revival: an 1800 upsurge of religious activity on the American frontier (349)

guru: a Hindu, Jain, or Sikh spiritual leader or teacher (236)

hadith: informal, apocryphal teachings of Muhammad (312–315)

hagiography: an inspirational biography of a saint or martyr (e.g., Christianity)

Hainuwele: Melanesian myth of primordial murder as the origin of tuberous plant agriculture (52)

Hajj: the Islamic pilgrimage to Mecca (304)

halal: food prepared in accordance with Muslim dietary rules (322)

Hammurabi: Babylonian king who got first written code of laws as revelation from a deity, around 1850 B.C.E. (63)

Hanukkah: December Jewish festival commemorating the Maccabee liberation of the temple (138)

Harappan: pre-Aryan early civilization in northwest India (84)

Hare Krishna: proselytizing new religious movement, a spin off from Hinduism (167)

Hasidic, Hasidim: mysticism of contemporary pietistic orthodox Jews; emphasis on singing (141–146, 156, 333)

heathen: derogatory term for people who are not Christians, Jews or Muslims

heaven: state of spiritual bliss in the afterlife, dwelling place of God and angels (Islam, Christianity) (133, 265, 332, 359)

Heaven's Gate: 1990s cult that committed mass suicide in order to join extra-terrestials on a comet

Hebrew: the language in which the Old Testament was written; also, the people who left Egypt with Moses (124)

hedonism: philosophical doctrine that pleasure is the sole or highest value (Yang Zhu, Cyrenaics, Epicureans) (168–169, 211, 212)

heliocentrism: "the earth goes around the sun"; advocated by Galileo, Copernicus, Kepler; theory that upset the medieval Church (340)

hell: place of afterlife and punishment for the wicked (133, 332, 359, 365)

Hellenistic: Greek culture in the time after Alexander (300 B.C.E.) (213, 340)

henotheism: "There are many gods, but some are more important" (11, 59, 61)

Henry VIII (1491–1547): English king who declared himself head of the Church in order to get a divorce (288)

Heraclitus: 6–5th century B.C.E. Greek philosopher "All is flux, change"; attacked popular religion as superstition (210, 214)

hermeneutics: methodological principles underlying interpretation of texts (15, 124)

heresy: a statement not in accord with a church's doctrine is declared a heresy by that church

Hermetic Tradition: esoteric Europeans mystery cult from 5th century; influenced Masonry, alchemy

Heterodox: heresy, not in accord with mainline doctrine (e.g., Buddhism is a heterodox offshoot of Hinduism)

heuristic: an idea or method that can stimulate further thought or research

hexagrams: a symbolic coding system used in Chinese divination (e.g., Yi Jing) (163–166, 178)

hierophany: a place where the sacred has happened (59, 62)

high god: a father, creator god has withdrawn from active intervention in the world; a feature of many tribal religions (31, 36, 48)

Hillel: 1st century rabbi, silver rule, provided guidelines for interpretation and commentary on Torah (135)

Hinayana Buddhism: also known as Theravada; predominant in Southeast Asia; emphasizes individual salvation of small raft

Hinduism: syncretism of Aryans and indigenous peoples of India; emphasis on caste and Vedas; both polytheism and pantheism (82–120, 156, 169, 308)

history: an objective recount of past events (contrast with myth) (6)

Holocaust: the Nazi attempt to exterminate the Jews in concentration camps (145, 151–152)

holy: the emotional experience of beholding the sacred (Otto) (22)

holy communion: Lord's Supper, Eucharist: Christian ritual of partaking bread and wine in remembrance of Christ (277, 359)

Holy Ghost: third person of Trinity; indwelling spirit of God in Christians, also known as Holy Spirit

Holy Roller: derogatory term for 20th century Pentecostals or Charismatic Christians who sway or fall down in ecstasy

Holy Spirit: third person of Trinity; indwelling spirit of God in Christians, also known as Holy Ghost

homiletics: the art of preaching

homily: an informal discourse on doctrine (Christianity); a sermon

homology: looking for similarities between different religions (9, 367)

Hubbard, L. Ron: 20th century science fiction writer who founded Scientology, Dianetics

human sacrifice: killing human victims as part of a ritual (Celts, Maya, Aztecs) (79–80)

Humanism: humanity is good, can save itself, (e.g., Renaissance, Enlightenment) (11–12, 338–339, 344–348, 358)

Hume, David (1711–1776): Scottish philosopher, empiricist, determinist, hedonist; "problem of evil cannot be solved"

Hus, Jan (1369–1415): Czech reformer burned at the stake for heresy (284)

I Ching: Yi Jing, a handbook for ancient Chinese divination using hexagrams (161, 165, 178, 183)

icon: a religious image or object, suitable for devotion; very common in Eastern Orthodox Christianity (281)

iconoclasm: opposition to the veneration of images; opposition to tradition in general

idolatry: excessive devotion to the images of the deity, a serious sin in Judaism, Islam, Protestant Christianity (301, 331)

Ignatius of Loyola (1491–1556): founder of Jesuit Order of Priests, the Society of Jesus (288)

imam: an Islamic leader of prayer; in Shi'a, a divinely inspired successor to Muhammad (309)

immaculate conception: the doctrine that Mary was conceived in her mother's womb without original sin

immanence: "God is within" vs. transcendence "God is beyond"

Inca: South American civilization 13–15th centuries; emphasis on priests, sin, confession, afterlife (80–81)

incarnation: when a spirit, soul or god assumes human flesh (e.g., Christ, Krisna) (296)

indoctrination: authoritative teaching of doctrines to the young or to converts

indulgences: medieval Catholic practice of letting people give money to the Church to escape (or lessen time in) purgatory (285)

ineffable: a characteristic of the mystical; inexpressible in words; too sacred to be spoken

infallibility: Vatican Council of 1870 declared "The Pope speaking ex-cathedra on doctrine or morals is infallible"

inference: the process of reasoning from something known to something else not already known (2–3)

infidel: derogatory Muslim term for a non-Muslim

initiation rites: rituals of puberty, marriage, conversion, confirmation (e.g., Africans, Aborigines, Melanesians, North American Indians)

Inquisition: Catholic persecution of heretics and witches, starting in 12th century (338)

instrumental: values which are merely utilitarian, serving as a means to produce a desired end (6)

International Churches of Christ: a new religious movement sometimes labeled as a cult because of allegedly harsh treatment of followers (363)

intrinsic: things valuable in and of themselves, not just because they are instrumental as means (5–6)

introspection: looking within, searching one's own thoughts, feelings, soul, as spiritual exercise or research

Inuit: previously known as Eskimo; Arctic peoples, emphasis on shamanism (42–44, 53)

Iran: Persia, the region in which Zoroastrianism, Sufism, and Bahai arose; now a theocratic center of Shi'ite Islam (73–77, 80, 318–319, 325)

Ishtar: Near Eastern mother goddess

Isis: Egyptian and Hellenistic mother goddess, theistic, answered prayer (72, 213–215, 218)

Islam: monotheistic, soteriological, apocalyptic, proselytizing religion founded by Muhammad: "submit to Allah" (298–335, 356, 357, 366)

Israel: biblical kingdom founded by ancient Hebrews (Israelites); modern nation created by U.N. as Jewish homeland (Israelis) (124, 125)

Jainism: a very ascetic Indian religion, atheist, dualist, noninjury to animals; Mahavira was its major proponent in the 6th century B.C.E. (95–96, 105, 156, 224, 272)

James, William (1842–1910): psychologist, pragmatist: "Judge religions by their fruits, not their roots" (21, 22, 262)

Jansen, Cornelius: 17th century Catholic theologian who advocated predestination, this doctrine was later declared heretical (286)

Jaspers, Karl: German psychiatrist, existentialist: "Myths make contact with the ultimate"; emphasized the concept of the axial age (600–200 B.C.E.)

Jehovah: Hebrew and Christian name for God

Jehovah's Witnesses: proselytizing denomination founded by C. T. Russell; set apocalyptic dates, deny the trinity, refuse participation in civil affairs (351–352, 359, 361, 363)

Jesuit: Catholic order of priests founded by Ignatius Loyola in 16th century, the Society of Jesus (20, 287, 288)

Jesus: 1st century Galilean, worshipped as Son of God by Christians; accepted as prophet by Muslims; life described in New Testament (260–269, 305, 332, 359, 361)

Jew: an adherent of Judaism; a person of Jewish ethnicity (123, 332, 361–362)

jihad: Islamic holy war against infidels; also includes ethics about treatment of innocent in warfare; can refer to an inward struggle (323–324)

Joachim of Fiore (1135–1202): apocalyptic Italian monk: "Old Testament was time of Father, New Testament was time of Son, now is the time of the Holy Spirit"

John: 1st century Christian apostle; credited with writing a logos-based gospel, three epistles, and book of Revelation (262, 263)

John the Baptist: 1st century Jewish prophet; foretold of coming Messiah; baptized Jesus, executed by Herod (263)

Jones, Jim: founder of People's Temple, a cult that committed Mass suicide in Guyana in 1978

Juche: the state sponsored religion of North Korea (362)

Judaism: religion developed by Abraham, Moses, Hebrews, Israelites and Jews; monotheistic, nonproselytizing (122–157, 354)

Judaizers: 1st century Christians who advocated adherence to Jewish law (e.g., circumcision, kosher) (272–273, 366)

Judea: Roman province which included Jerusalem (264)

Jung, Carl G. (1875–1961): Swiss psychiatrist: "Religion offers symbolic keys to the collective unconscious, mental health" (21, 22)

Justification: the subjective experience of redemptive salvation; Augustine: "Justification by grace"; Luther: "justification by faith"

Kabbala, Cabala, Cabbala: esoteric Jewish mysticism, arose in Spain in Middle Ages, inspired numerology, search for a mathematical code of the Torah (140–146, 156, 298–301, 333)

Kachinas: Native American spirits (47, 48)

Kali: Hindu goddess, consort of Shiva, demands sacrifice (118)

Kami: Shinto mythical spirits (187–197)

Kant, Immanuel (1724–1804): German philosopher: "We must postulate free will, God and immortality of the soul" (19, 20)

karma: doctrine of the good or bad consequences of deeds, impacts one's reincarnation (Hindu, Buddhist, Jain) (89–90, 98, 105, 156, 224, 257)

Khadijah: first wife of Muhammad; supported his religious quest (300)

Khomeini, Ayatollah: theocratic leader of the 1979 Islamic revolution in Iran (318–319)

Kierkegaard, Søren A. (1813–1855): Danish philosopher: "Religious faith is not the result of proof, but of choice"

King James version: 17th century English translation of the Bible, still used by many Protestants

King, Martin Luther, Jr. (1929–1968): Baptist minister, nonviolent civil rights leader of African-Americans

Kingdom Hall: a building for Jehovah's Witness meetings

koan: Zen riddle or mental puzzle, designed to produce enlightenment (241)

Koran: Islamic scripture, revelations received by the prophet Muhammad, usually transliterated as Qu'ran

Kore: Greek goddess, also known as Persephone, daughter of Demeter (Ceres); a figure in the Eleusinian mysteries (208–209)

Koresh, David: self-proclaimed second Jesus who led the Waco group of Branch Davidians into a 1993 battle with federal agents

kosher: Jewish rules of propriety (especially dietary rules, e.g., abstinence from pork, rules for meal preparation) (30, 135, 156)

Krishna: Hindu avatar of Visnu, hero of Bhagavad Gita (96–97, 103, 110, 117, 120)

laity: adherents of a religion who are not clergy (15–17, 230–231, 278)

Lakshmi: Hindu goddess of prosperity, consort of Vishnu (103)

lama: Tibetan Buddhist head monk (239, 245)

Lao (Laozi, Lao Tse, Taotze, Lao Tsu, Lao Tzu): 6th century B.C.E. Chinese, mystical Daoist; opposed social conventions; "Follow nature, unite with the Dao"; advocated perfect government of minimal structure (161, 169–178, 218)

lapsed: someone who is no longer an active member of the denomination (e.g., Catholics who do not attend mass)

last rites: sacrament given to those close to death (Catholic); extreme unction, now changed to sacrament for the sick (277)

Latter Day Saints: formal name for Mormon church (335–336, 353–356, 359, 361, 363)

lay: a person who does not have a leadership position in the denomination (15–17, 230–231, 278)

Lee, Anne: 18th century founder of Shakers, claimed to be feminine incarnation of Christ (353, 361)

Legalism: the Chinese axial age school emphasizing strict laws and harsh punishments; opposed by Mencius (161, 176–178)

lent: ascetic period from Ash Wednesday until Easter (Catholic, Eastern Orthodox)

Levi-Strauss, Claude (1908–): French anthropologist: "The religion, language and society of a people have a similar structure" (21, 22)

Levite: ancient Jewish hereditary priesthood who performed temple sacrifices (127, 156)

Lévy-Bruhl, Lucien (1857–1939): "Primitives have a completely different mentality, a participation mystique" (21, 22)

Liberalism: movement starting in the Enlightenment and emphasizing individual rights and participatory government (339–343)

Liberation Theology: Latin American Catholic theology emphasizing radical, quasi-Marxist social justice (344)

limbo: eternal resting place of souls of the unbaptized innocents (Catholic doctrine) (276)

liturgy: public ritual (Catholicism)

logos: divine reason incarnated in Christ and His word; theology influenced by Stoics and basis of the Gospel of John (213)

Lollard: 15th century English reform movement, followers of Wycliffe, anti-Church hierarchy, popular among poor (284)

Lonergan, Bernard (1904–1984): Jesuit process theologian: "Each religion has its own language"

Lord: Jewish and Christian title for God

Lord's Supper: holy communion, Eucharist: Christian ritual of partaking bread and wine in remembrance of Christ (277, 359)

Loyola, Ignatius (1491–1556): Spanish founder of Jesuit order of Catholic priests, Society of Jesus (288)

Lucifer: synonym for Satan, especially before the Fall

Luther, Martin: 16th century German Protestant reformer: "Salvation is by faith (commitment), not works" (284–285)

Lutheran: Christian denomination based upon Luther's teachings; prominent in northern Germany, Scandinavia, upper Midwestern United States

Maccabbees: 2nd century B.C.E. Jews who fought against Romans (138)

Macumba: Brazilian popular religion with African roots

magic: the use of ritual to manipulate spirits or natural phenomena for utilitarian or ulterior relevance (8, 31, 33)

Mahavira 6th century B.C.E.: title given to a major figure in Jainism; emphasis on meditation, asceticism, noninjury (95, 96, 105, 224)

Mahayana: "big ferryboat" Buddhism common in China, Japan; emphasizes bodhisattvas, "Worship Buddha as savior" (232–235, 245, 258, 259)

Maimonides (1135–1204): medieval Spanish Jew who synthesized Greek philosophy and Judaism (139–140, 212)

Maitreya: Buddhist messiah who will come in the future to save us (according to some Japanese sects) (242)

Malcolm X: African-American spokesman for Nation of Islam who later challenged its doctrine of racial prejudice (324)

Malinowski, Bronislaw (1884–1942): "Primitives distinguish between magic and science, and use the best technology available; Religion is consolation for tragedy" (21, 22)

Manicheanism: 3rd century Christian heresy, Gnostic, dualistic; Augustine was once in that sect (76, 271, 272)

Marcionism: 2nd century Christian heresy, ascetic, Gnostic, dualist, rejected God of Old Testament (272)

Marduk: Babylonian war deity (65–66)

margas: Hindu pathways suggested by the Bhagavad Gita (97–98, 115)

marginalized: people who are not in the mainstream of a society; these groups tend to join messianic, millenarian cults

Maronite: a Uniate Christian church found in Lebanon, Syria

martyr: someone who suffers and dies willingly to defend one's religion

Marx, Karl (1818–1883): communist, atheist; "Religion is a tool of exploitation, opiate of the masses" (22–23, 111, 339, 343, 344)

Mary: mother of Jesus, Catholics give her special veneration (278–279, 283, 305–306)

Maslow, Abraham (1908–1970): American psychologist who viewed mysticism as peak experiences of self-actualized individuals (23)

mass: Church service culminating in Eucharist (Catholic)

materialism: "Matter is all there is" (e.g., Democritus, Epicureans, Marx)

Mauss, Marcel (1872–1950): French sociologist: "Ritualized gift exchange reinforces social order" (22, 23)

Maya: Central American civilization 3rd–8th century C.E., emphasis on priests, calendars, pyramids, myths of multiple creations, human sacrifice (77–80)

McPherson, Aimee Semple: early 20th century founder of Foursquare denomination; first radio preacher

mean: Aristotle and Confucius argued that it was best to seek a mean between extremes (167–168)

Mecca: Islamic city of obligatory pilgrimage; Muslims face Mecca when praying (288, 289, 300–301, 304, 333)

mechanical solidarity: Durkheim's model of tribal society in which individuals assumed non-specialized roles (58–59)

medicine man: shamanic figure using folk medicine (North American Indians)

meditation: focusing of attention, used as means for attaining mystical experience (Hinduism, Buddhism) (175, 231–232)

medium: one claiming psychic abilities (17)

megaliths: stone monument centers for rituals (e.g., Stonehenge for the Celts) (31, 37, 38, 59)

Melanesia: western Pacific (e.g., New Guinea); emphasized puberty rites, dream time, ritual cannibalism, head hunting, Hainuwele myth; cargo cults came in the mid 20th century (52–54)

Mencius: (371–289 B.C.E.): Chinese Confucian theologian (161, 177–178, 218)

Mennonites: pacifist Anabaptists, one splinter group became the Amish

Mesopotamia: region of civilizations arising between Tigris & Euphrates rivers (Iraq), emphasis on divination, creation myths (62–64, 80)

Messiah: expected Jewish savior king; Christians accept Jesus as the Messiah (132, 133, 139, 265)

metaphysics: philosophical inquiry into the nature of reality

Methodism: Christian denomination split off from Episcopalian Church in 19th century; emphasizing individual piety, free will, founded by John Wesley (287)

metropolitan: title given to a bishop in the Eastern Orthodox Church

Middle Way: Buddhism was seen as avoiding the extremes of asceticism (Jainism) and hedonism (Tantrism)

millenarian, millennialism: "the end of the present order is at hand, God's kingdom will be established soon on this earth"

Miller, William: 19th century apocalyptic preacher, predicted the second coming in 1844; Adventist, Millerite movement (351, 361)

minister: title for church leader, especially Protestant clergy

miracle: when supernatural power upsets the natural order; in myths, some religious leaders have miraculous powers

mission: proselytizing in order to gain converts (Christianity, Buddhism, Islam)

Mithra (Mitra): Iranian son god who became an important cult among Roman soldiers; secret rituals, bull sacrifice (75, 214, 215, 218)

Mo (Mohism, Moism): Chinese religion that taught love and a personal heaven; founder Mo Ti (Mozi) 475–395 B.C.E. (161, 177–178, 218, 269)

Mohammad (570–632 C.E.): Arab founder of Islam, "the prophet" who recited the Qur'an, preached theistic monotheism (300–304, 306, 321, 322, 328, 332)

Mohenjo-Daro: pre-Aryan civilization in northwest India (84)

monastery, monasticism: life of monks, nuns committed to celibacy, meditation (Buddhism, Christianity) (229–230, 255–256, 275, 282, 284, 295, 333)

monism: "all reality is of a single thing" (Vedanta, Parmenides) (94, 105, 117, 156, 175, 210, 214, 224)

monk: a male living a monastic life of celibacy and contemplation

monolatry: worshipping only one deity (11, 59, 61)

monotheism: acceptance of one deity (Islam, Christianity, Judaism, Sikhism, Zoroastrianism) (10–11, 59, 61, 70, 132, 156, 332)

Montanism: 2nd century charismatic, apocalyptic sect, claimed glossolalia and prophecy, declared a heresy by Pope (273, 361)

Moon, Sun Myung: Korean founder of Unification Church, considered a cult by many

morals: guidelines for ethical conduct of human affairs: interpersonal relations, and avoidance of sin

Mormon: Christian denomination started in 19th century by Joseph Smith; emphasizes family, temple rituals, no smoking/coffee (335–336, 353–356, 359, 361, 363)

morphology: the structure/development of a religion over time (10, 367)

mortification: overcoming the desires of the flesh, also self-inflicted privation and pain (Hinduism, Jainism)

Moses (1200 B.C.E.): prophet who led Hebrews out of Egypt: received ten commandments, Torah (122–126, 149, 305)

Moslem: an adherent of Islam

mosque: building for Islamic worship (148, 307, 310, 314, 332)

mother superior: honorific title given to head nun (Catholic)

Muhammad (570–632 C.E.): Arab founder of Islam, "the prophet" who recited the Qur'an, preached theistic monotheism (300–306, 332, 335, 361)

Müller, Max: 19th century philologist: "Religion began as confused speech" (21, 22)

mummification: preservation of corpses for afterlife (Egypt, Inca) (69, 81)

Muslim (Moslem): an adherent of Islam, "one who submits to God" (299, 300, 332, 335)

mystery cults: Hellenistic religions having secret myths or rituals known only to the initiated (e.g., Mithra, Cybele, Isis, Dionysian, Eleusinian)

mystic, mysticism: contemplation to achieve union with God; the experience is ecstatic and ineffable (Laozi, Buddha, Hasidim, Sufis, Upanishads, Sufis, early Christian monastics) (17–19, 105, 115, 140–141, 146, 156, 169–175, 218, 223, 224, 281, 289–290, 295, 333)

myth: sacred narrative of past events, retold to express values; not necessarily objective history (6–9, 68, 126, 132)

Names: axial age Chinese school emphasizing idle disputation of metaphysical questions (177–178, 218)

Nanak (1469–1539): founder of Sikh religion, he was originally a Muslim in India (106, 324)

Nataputta Vardhamana 6th century B.C.E.: founder of Jain religion, known by his title, Mahavira; ascetic, meditation, noninjury (95, 96, 105, 224)

Nation of Islam: "Black Muslims"; African-American movement with prejudicial views against whites and Jews (324–325)

Nazis: Hitler's National Socialist German Workers Party, governing Germany 1933–1945 (339, 344)

necromancy: conjuring up souls of the dead in séances

neo- : prefix indicating "new"

Nestorianism: 5th century heresy: "Jesus had two separate natures: human and divine" (doctrine popular from Middle East to China) (275)

New Age: term applied to recent religious movements offering a syncretism of the occult and pre-Christian doctrine, ritual

Newman, John H. (1801–1890): convert Catholic cardinal: "Faith is both objective (dogma), and subjective (acceptance of dogma)"; universities should be open to competing ideas

New Testament: part of the Bible describing Jesus and Apostles; it is composed of the four gospels, the Book of Acts, and many epistles by Paul, Peter, John, James, Jude (262)

Nicene: creed adopted by Council of Nicea, Trinitarian (274, 280)

Nichiren: 13th century Japanese Buddhist prophet, demanded a national shrine; emphasized chanting, inspired Soka Gakkai (245–247, 361, 295)

Nietzsche, Friedrich: 19th century German philosopher: "Christianity is a slave morality, people must create their own values."

nihilism: doctrine that nothing is relevant

nirvana: Buddhist concept of salvation; liberation from the cycle of suffering and reincarnation (222, 252–253)

noble eightfold path: Buddhist formula for spiritual life on earth (223, 227)

noble truths: basic Buddhist doctrine: life is suffering, due to desire, and only the eightfold path can remove this desire (223–227, 256–258)

nominal: a member "in name only" of a denomination, someone who is not devout

nonliterate: tribal peoples of hunter, gatherers, herders (e.g., Aborigines); pre-literate, relying upon oral passage of tradition rather than writing

nonsectarian: not tied to any particular denomination (13)

North American Indians: emphasis on shamans, tricksters, male initiation rites; Ghost Dance & Peyotism in 19th century

Noyes, John H.: 19th century founder of Oneida Perfectionists; advocated complex marriage (multiple husbands and wives) (353)

nun: pious, celibate female monastic (e.g., Catholic, Buddhist)

occult: inclusive term for astrology, alchemy, divination, sorcery, necromancy, magic, parapsychology, spiritual healing

Old Testament: part of Bible written before Jesus, including the Jewish Torah, and writings of the Hebrew and Israelite prophets

Olympian: ancient Greek pantheon that included anthropomorphic deities such as Zeus (203–205, 214)

omnipotent: deity who is all-powerful (20)

omniscient: deity who is all-knowing (20)

Oneida community: the 19th century Perfectionists established by J. H. Noyes; practiced communism and complex marriage (353)

ontological argument: "the definition of 'perfect being' proves God" (Anselm, Descartes) (19,20)

oracles: Greek shrines for divination (206–208, 214, 218)

oral: preservation of myth by retelling stories (before they were written down as scripture); oral (pre-literate) societies are tribal, hunter-gatherers (25, 59)

orders: established communities of priests, monks, nuns

ordination: sacrament of initiation into an order (Catholic priesthood) (278)

organic solidarity: Durkheim's model of tribal society in which individuals assumed specialized roles (58–59)

Origen (185–255): Christian mystic, incorporated Neoplatonism (274)

original sin: when Adam sinned, the entire human race fell from grace

orishas: African deities appearing in a Roman Catholic pantheon in Santeria

Orphics 6th century B.C.E.: ancient Greek mystery cult, emphasized afterlife, vegetarianism, asceticism, secret rituals, music (209, 214)

Orthodox Church: predominant form of Christianity in East Europe, North Africa, Middle East (279–282)

Orthodox Judaism: strict form of modern Judaism adhering to teachings of Torah, Fundamentalist (144–146)

Osiris: Egyptian and Hellenistic god; dying and rising, judge of the dead (71)

Otto, Rudolf (1869–1937): German scholar: "the emotional experience of the 'holy' underlies all religions" (21, 22, 302, 333)

pacifism: nonviolence, especially refusal to participate in organized warfare (e.g., Quakers, Amish)

pagan: derogatory term for primitive religion (27)

pagoda: Buddhist temple or shrine used for ritual activity (242)

Palestine: geographical area in which ancient and modern Israel have been established; also, a proposed Arab nation in that region (124, 125, 149, 264)

Paley, William (1743–1805): Anglican theologian emphasizing teleological argument (19)

pantheism: "all is god" doctrine found in Upanishads (10–11, 91, 169, 175)

pantheon: a structured relationship between polytheistic deities (Greeks, Teutons, Mesopotamians, Aztecs) (10–11, 59, 61, 80, 203, 204)

papal: pertaining to the Pope (279)

parables: symbolic stories used by Jesus (267–269)

parapsychology: study of psychic phenomena such as channeling, psychokinesis, extra-sensory perception (ESP)

Parmenides: ancient Greek Eleatic philosopher who advocated monism (210, 214)

Parsis, Parsees: modern remnants of Zoroastrianism, found in India, Pakistan, Iran (77)

parson: title given to Protestant clergy

Parsons, E. T.: sociologist: "The key to understanding religious phenomena is their social function"

passion: suffering of Jesus on the cross

Pascal, Blaise (1623–1662): French philosopher offering the wager argument for accepting the existence of God (19)

pastor: title given to Christian clergy, especially head of a local church

pastoral: term relating to societies emphasizing herding animals, or to Christian clergy who herd their flocks

patriarch: an historical figure (e.g., Abraham); also, title given to archbishop (Eastern Orthodox) (59, 61)

patristics: the study of the history of the early Church

Paul: 1st century Christian convert Apostle; wrote many of the New Testament epistles; opponent of Judaizers, Gnostics, Anti-nomians (19, 262, 266, 273)

peak experience: psychologist A. Maslow's description of the mystical experience (23)

Pelagianism: 4th–5th century heresy, minimized importance of grace, emphasized free will and salvation by one's one efforts (276)

penance: ritual punishment in order to expiation of sin

Pentateuch: Greek term for first five books of Bible (124)

Pentecostal: 20th century American denomination; emphasizes presence of the Holy Spirit; speaking in tongues (349–350)

Perfectionists: 19th century Oneida community founded by J.H. Noyes; practiced communism and complex marriage (353)

Persephone: Greek goddess, also known as Kore, daughter of Demeter (Ceres); a figure in the Eleusinian mysteries (208–209)

Persia: Iran, the region in which Zoroastrianism, Sufism, and Bahai arose; now a theocratic center of Shi'ite Islam (73–77, 80, 318–319, 325)

Peter: Galilean fisherman disciple of Jesus; became apostle and first pope (also known as Simon, Cephas) (262)

peyotism: American Indian movement emphasizing eating of a hallucinogenic cactus, spread after 19th century on reservations (48, 53)

phallic, phallus: referring to symbols of the male organ, fertility rites

pharaoh: Egyptian king; seen as a descendent of the sun god

Pharisees: 1st century Jewish lay movement emphasizing rigid adherence to Torah traditions; apocalyptic, resurrection, angels (132, 133, 265, 361)

phenomenology: a descriptive, rather than evaluative, approach to comparative religion; "appreciate each in own context" (e.g., M. Eliade) (22, 23)

Philo Judaeus (30 B.C.E. – 50 C.E.): Hellenistic Jewish apologist "God is Being itself; His Logos created the world"

philology: semantics, linguistics

Pietism: 17th–18th century German devotional movement within Lutheranism; influenced Kant, Schleiermacher

piety: noun form of pious

pilgrimage: a journey to attend a shrine; pilgrimage to Mecca is obligatory in Islam (304)

pious: devout, people who are very committed to their religion (opposite of nominal or lapsed)

Plato (429–347 B.C.E.): Greek philosopher: "The physical world is but a physical manifestation of ideal forms"; dualist, reincarnation, ideal controlled society (211–212, 214, 218)

Plotinus (205–270): Neoplatonist mystic in Hellenistic world; influenced Origen (212)

pluralistic: a society in which several power bases are active and none predominates; not theocratic, not totalitarian

polemic: arguments designed to defend one's doctrine and refute that of opponents (like apologetics)

polygamy: the doctrine that one man may have several wives (e.g., early Hebrews, Muslims, Mormons) (333)

Polynesia: Pacific islands, emphasis on taboo; puberty rites (53–54)

polytheism: acceptance of several deities (Hindus, Teutons, Greeks, Egyptians, Aztecs, Mesopotamia) (10–11, 59, 80, 87, 169, 300, 323, 354)

pope: Bishop of Rome, head of Catholic Church; may issue ex-cathedra, infallible statements (17, 279)

Positivism: Comte: "Human knowledge has progressed from reliance on religion to philosophy to science"

Pragmatism: philosophy: "If it works, it is good" (Dewey, James)

prayer: attempt at human communication with the divine, may be a petition or adoration

precognition: form of ESP that predicts the future

predestination: doctrine that God has already determined whom will be saved, before they are born (Calvin, Jansen) (285–287)

preliterate: tribal peoples of hunter, gatherers, herders (e.g., Aborigines); rely upon oral tradition, not writing (25)

Presbyterianism: Protestant denomination growing out of Puritans; emphasizes governance by councils over local churches; influenced by Calvinist doctrine (287)

priest: religious leaders who perform scheduled rituals in post-tribal societies (Catholics, Brahmins) (16–17, 59, 62, 80, 87, 156, 332, 354, 355, 359)

primitive: religions of pre-civilized, tribal peoples (e.g., Aborigines); also known as pre-literate (27)

profane: not sacred; may be unclean (30, 31)

proof: something used to vindicate a commitment or verify a belief; see Ontological, Cosmological, Teleological (3–6)

prophecy, prophet: proclaiming the will of God (Zarathustra, Muhammad, J. Smith, Moses) (17, 18, 73, 123, 124, 127–128, 139, 149, 156, 295, 305, 328, 335–336, 354–357)

propitiation: atonement for one's sins via sacrifice, asceticism or good works; rites often performed by priests

proselytize: to seek converts (Christianity, Buddhism, Islam) (156, 221, 295, 332, 355–359)

Protestant: Christian denominations growing out of Europe's Reformation of the 16th century (284–288, 295, 359)

psychic: a person who claims parapsychological abilities (e.g., channeling, psychokinesis, telepathy, clairvoyance) (17)

psychokinesis: ability to influence physical objects with mental powers alone (17)

puberty rite: rituals for coming of age, initiation into adulthood (e.g., Aborigines, Africans, American Indians) (32, 53, 59)

purgatory: afterlife in which sins are expiated, prior to resurrection or entrance into heaven (Catholic doctrine) (276, 279, 280, 359)

Puritanism: 16th–17th century Calvinist movement in English Protestantism (287)

pyramid: monument used as tomb or sacrificial site (Egypt, Mayans) (69)

Pythagoras (570–500 B.C.E.): Greek mathematician and cult leader: reincarnation, vegetarianism, secret rituals, ascetic (209, 214)

Quaker: pacifistic religion founded by G. Fox; no clergy, no sacraments; also known as the Society of Friends

quasi: prefix meaning "in the form of . . . almost"

Quetzalcoatl: Aztec theriomorphic deity (79–80)

Qu'ran: sacred book of Islam, dictated by angel through Muhammad (300–303, 310, 320, 333, 357)

rabbi: member of clergy in modern Judaism; more of a teacher than priest or prophet (16, 132–137)

Ramadan: month long Muslim festival involving daytime fasting (304)

Rauschenbusch, W. (1861–1917): American Protestant clergy "social gospel" of political reform (344)

reconciliation: new name for sacrament of confession (Catholicism)

Reconstructionist Judaism: 20th century movement to revitalize Jewish culture (145)

reductionism: attempt to reduce religion to social, psychological or biological influences, with no ultimate relevance; opposed by phenomenologists (23, 364)

redemption: salvation from sin (Christianity)

Reformation: 16th–17th century northern European formation of Protestant denominations (Lutheranism, Puritanism) (284–288)

Reform Judaism: least strict branch of contemporary Judaism, largest in the United States (142–146)

reincarnation: transmigration doctrine that "souls are recycled into new bodies" (Hinduism, Buddhism, Jainism, Plato, Orphics, Pythagoras) (37, 105, 156, 209, 212, 214, 222)

relevance: realm in which human mind encounters or creates values: ultimate, utilitarian or ulterior (4–6)

religion: system of doctrines, ethics, myths, symbols, and rituals expressing ultimate relevance (1–2, 8)

Renaissance: 15th–16th century C.E. intellectual and aesthetic awakening in Western Europe; promoted science, humanism

repentance: to regret one's sins

resurrection: revivification of one's physical body after death (Christianity, Islam, Pharisees, Zoroastrianism) (133, 156, 265, 332)

revelation: disclosure of the will of God; a method of gaining knowledge different from the empirical approach of science (356–357)

revival: proselytizing aimed primarily at lapsed or nominal adherents in order to make them more devout

Revival, Great: movement around 1800 on American frontier; characterized by emotional excesses and lack of organization (349)

rishi: Hindu title for a guru, inspired writer

rites of passage: initiation, mourning, funeral rituals at times of life transitions (Van Gennep, Turner) (22–23, 31–32, 59)

Ritschl, A. (1822–1889): German Protestant theologian: "The religious experience cannot be comprehended by science" (21–22)

ritual: ceremonies undertaken to express or achieve ultimate or ulterior relevance, often re-enact myths (6, 7, 9, 366)

Roberts, Oral: Assembly of God minister, spiritual healer, founder of Oral Roberts University in Tulsa (350)

Robertson-Smith, William: 19th century British anthropologist studying Semites, emphasized the role of ritual in religion (22, 23)

Roman Catholic: formal name of Catholic Church, which is centered in Rome, Holy Roman Catholic Apostolic Church (276)

roshi: Japanese title for Buddhist master teacher, a guru

Russell, Bertrand (1875–1970): British mathematician and agnostic

Russell, Charles T. (1852–1916): millenarian preacher, founder of Jehovah's Witnesses (351–352, 361)

Sabaean-Mandean: an ancient monotheistic religion of the Middle East; practices baptism

sabbath: holy day of rest in Judaism, Saturday, begins Friday evening

sacerdotal: pertaining to priestly roles or powers

sacrament: rituals, especially those of Catholic Church (275–278, 289–290)

sacred: that which is valued in the realm of ultimate relevance (29–31)

sacrifice: a ritual offering of something to deity human sacrifice practiced by some religions (Aztecs, Mayas) (31–33, 59, 79–80, 87–88, 216)

Sadducees: a 1st century C.E. Jewish sect representing higher socio-economic classes, wanted stable society and accommodation with Greek culture and Roman law; denied resurrection, angels; suppressed Jesus (133, 265)

saint: honorific title given to persons who led exemplary lives, and as angels can intercede for people (Catholic); Paul used the term to describe early Christians in general (278–279)

Sakya: clan to which Gautama Buddha was born (222)

Sakyamuni: a term used especially in Japan to describe Siddhartha Gautama Sakya, in order to distinguish him from other Buddhas (222)

salvation: a promise of liberation from the human problem; heaven, resurrection or a new world order on this planet

Salvation Army: 19th and 20th century Protestant sect targeting poor and alcoholics; offshoot of Methodists

Santeria: a syncretistic religion of Catholic and African themes found in the Hispanic islands of the Caribbean

Satan: chief evil spirit, the devil, God's opponent (Christianity, Islam, Zoroastrianism, Judaism) (128, 131)

satori: Zen Buddhists term for mystical experience (240)

schism: split between segments of a church, such as the one in 1054 between Roman Catholics and Eastern Orthodox (279–281)

Schleiermacher, Friedrich D. E. (1768–1834): "Religion is in a different sphere from science; a feeling of dependence" (21, 22)

Schmidt, W.: "All peoples originally had a monotheistic, father-deity"

scholasticism: medieval theology emphasizing logic and Greek philosophical traditions (Anselm, Aquinas) (282–283)

science: approach to knowledge based upon empiricism; the belief we have in scientific claims is contingent upon the process of empirical verification: we may change our minds when new data are discovered (3–5, 338–341, 367)

Science, Christian: 19th century sect founded by Mary Baker Eddy, emphasizes "faith" healing (350–351)

Scientology: 20th century denomination founded by L. Ron Hubbard; opponents consider it to be a mere front for the Dianetics Movement and to have cultish tendencies (363)

scripture: religious writings included in the sacred canon (15)

seance: ceremony that attempts to contact souls of dead, necromancy

sect: religious group with common doctrine and leadership; can also refer to a splinter group within a denomination

sectarian: pertaining to particular sects; the opposite of secular (13)

secular: this-worldly orientation; refers to cultural phenomena not related to religion; opposing theocracy; refers to a society in which no denomination has undue influence; non-sectarian (13, 59, 333, 339, 345, 348, 359, 366)

Sephardic: Jews of Spanish or North African origin (138, 149)

sermon: an oral religious discourse, especially one delivered at a worship service

Seventh Day Adventist: 19th century Protestant sect founded by Ellen White: apocalyptic, vegetarian, worship on Saturday (352, 361)

Shakers: 19th century American sect founded by Ann Lee, famous for rigorous dancing; celibate, communitarian; now extinct (353, 361)

Shakti: Hindu goddess serving as a consort (e.g., Kali is the consort of Shiva) (104–105)

shaman: medicine man figure prominent in religion of tribal cultures, performs variety of rituals such as exorcisms (16–17, 31, 38–40, 53, 59)

Shi'a, Shiite: sect of Islam predominant in Iran; has present day living prophet (imam) (309, 325)

Shinto: indigenous Japanese religion; emphasizes nature, spirits, clan, ancestors, nation (187–190)

Shiva: Hindu destroyer deity (87, 98, 104)

shrine: sacred place for religious worship or pilgrimage, sometimes associated with miracles

Siddharta (Gautama): 6th century B.C.E. Indian prince who became the Buddha, a mystic; formed monasteries, proselytized (222)

Sikh: religion blending some elements of Islam and Hinduism, founded by Nanak in 15th century in Northern India (106, 324, 325)

sin: falling out of relationship with the deity, specific acts which offend the deity (Islam, Judaism, Christianity)

sister: honorific title given to Catholic nuns

skeptic: doubter of religious claims, hesitant to form religious commitments

Smith, Joseph Jr. (1805–1844): founder of Latter Day Saints, "the prophet" who translated Book of Mormon, had other revelations (295, 335–336, 353–355, 361)

social gospel: 19th century U.S. Protestant political activism (344)

Society of Jesus: Jesuit order founded by Ignatius Loyola of Spain in the 16th century (288)

sociobiology: theory that humans have evolved religion because it helps their societies survive; a reductionistic perspective

Socrates 470–399 B.C.E.: Greek philosopher, executed for allegedly challenging traditional religion (211, 214, 218)

Soka Gakkai: modern Japanese Buddhist sect stressing chanting for financial success, political power; inspired by 13th century prophet Nichiren

solipsism: doctrine that only the individual's mind exists

sophists: morally relativistic Greek philosophers who sought self-gain (210–211, 214, 218)

sorcery: magic, witchcraft, especially for evil purposes

soteriology: emphasis on salvation from doom or damnation (e.g., Buddhism, Islam, Christianity, Hellenistic mystery)

sphinx: a theriomorphic figure in Greek and Egyptian mythology (69)

Spinoza, Baruch (1632–1677): Jewish pantheist (142)

Stoicism: Greek philosophy, sought brotherly love under natural law; self-control; influenced Christian doctrine (212–214, 218)

Stonehenge: English megalith used in pre-Christian rituals (37)

Structuralism: the structure of language, society, and religion has parallels (Levi-Strauss) (22)

Stupa: a Buddhist burial site that has become a shrine (231)

Sufis: Islamic mystic sect originated in Persia, some are dancing dervishes, influenced Al Ghazzali (316–317, 325)

Sunni: sect of Islam predominant outside of Iran; based upon consensus agreement on Qu'ran; Muhammad was the last prophet (309, 325)

superstition: a belief that cannot be verified by either logical or empirical methods

Swami: honorific title given to Hindu sage

symbol: a word or image that expresses or establishes contact with the realm of ultimate relevance (6, 7)

synagogue: the building for worship in modern Judaism (133, 134, 137, 147)

syncretism: fusion, blending, or combination of parts of different religions (Greece, China, Catholicism) (9, 59, 61, 165, 186–187, 201, 208, 366, 367)

synod: a council or ongoing group of bishops for church government or formulation of doctrine

synoptic gospels: New Testament books of Mark, Matthew, Luke; record the life and ministry of Jesus (263)

taboo: something forbidden for ordinary use (Polynesians) (30–31, 44, 53)

Talmud: Jewish commentary on the Torah, completed about 500 C.E. (132–137, 156)

Tanak: the Old Testament; Pentateuch plus the writings of the prophets (126)

tantric: Buddhist and Hindu cults emphasizing salvation by sinful ecstasy (e.g., sex, alcohol) (105, 224, 235–236, 245, 252–253, 256–257, 277, 295)

Taoism: Daoism; Chinese religion; emphasis on nature mysticism (Laozi), alchemy, hermits, hedonism (Yang Ju) (160–163, 168–176, 178, 185–186, 240, 295)

Teilhard de Chardin, Pierre (1881–1955): French Jesuit paleontologist: "Mind is evolving into new consciousness"

telekinesis: influencing physical objects with mental powers, also known as psychokinesis

teleological argument: "the natural world's order proves existence of God" (design argument) (19, 20)

telepathy: reading another person's mind; thought transference (17)

temple: building for performance of rituals (ancient Israelites, Mormons) (148, 354–357)

Tertullian (155–222): urged Christians to separate from pagan cultural practices (291)

Teutons: northern European tribes, raiders; polytheistic pantheon, apocalyptic, megaliths (53–55, 361)

Thales: 6th century B.C.E. Greek philosopher" "everything is water" (210)

theism: view of God as all-powerful, all-knowing transcendent Creator Deity, usually capable of personal contact and answering prayer (10–11, 103, 105, 224)

theocracy: government by religious leaders (12–13, 62, 333)

theodicy: theological speculation dealing with the problem of evil (19, 20, 117–118)

theology: rational elaborations of religious doctrine (17–18)

theophany: a manifestation of a god in human form; incarnation, avatar

Theosophy: 19th century esoteric cult founded by H. Blavatsky; blend of mysticism and the occult

Theravada: Hinayana Buddhism; predominant in southeast Asia; emphasizes individual salvation (233, 245)

theriomorphic: deities in animal form (Egypt, Aztec, Maya) (10, 11, 78, 80, 202)

Tillich, Paul (1886–1965): German Protestant theologian: "Religion is ultimate concern"

toleration: of various religions by state (e.g., Edict of Nantes in France in 1598)

tongues: glossolalia, ecstatic utterances discussed by Paul in his epistle to the Corinthians and advocated by present day Pentecostals (349–350)

Torah: Jewish canon: first five books of Old Testament; the Pentateuch (124, 132, 133, 156, 265, 273)

totem: animal symbols to represent ancestral or tribal relationships (Aborigines, North American Indians) (31, 36, 53, 59)

transcendence: "God is beyond" vs. immanence "God is within"

transmigration of souls: reincarnation of soul into other bodies after death (e.g., Hinduism, Jainism, Pythagorus, Orphics, Buddha, Plato, Upanishads) (37, 105, 156, 209, 212, 214, 222)

transubstantiation: Roman Catholic doctrine that the bread and wine of the Eucharist become body and blood of Christ

Trent: 16th century Catholic council which affirmed Catholic doctrine and ritual, and expanded the canon of scripture (290)

tribal: religions of hunting-gathering peoples (Aborigines, Ainu, Melanesians, Celts, Teutons, North American Indians)

trickster: clever deity, demon or human who teases or uses cunning to succeed (North American Indians, Africa, Celts, Japan, Teutons) (31, 35–37, 53, 59)

Trinity: Christian doctrine of one God as three persons: the Father, the Son (Jesus), and the Holy Spirit (274–275, 332)

truth: the validity of a statement (scientific or logical truth) or the value of a thing; religious truth deals with values (3–6)

Turner, Victor: anthropologist "rites of passage involve a liminal phase" (22–23)

Tylor, E. B. (1832–1917): "Religion is an attempt to understand death and ghosts; emphasizes animism" (21–22)

Tyndale, William: 16th century translator of Bible

ulterior: refers to values whose relevance is illusory or inhibitory; people pursue these values irrationally, because of obsessive-compulsive tendencies (5)

ultimate: values relevant to the creative source of all values; religion concerns the ultimate (1, 5, 29)

Uniate: former Eastern Orthodox Churches now under Roman Catholic jurisdiction; they get to keep their rituals and married priests

Unification Church: 20th century sect founded by S. M. Moon

Unitarian: 18th century U.S. denomination, very non-dogmatic, "Jesus is human"

United Church of Christ: new name for Congregational Church

Upanishads: Hindu writings 800–200 B.C.E.: mystical, pantheistic, monist; concept of Brahman (87, 90–95, 102–105, 156, 175, 224)

utilitarian: instrumental values whose relevance deals with survival or pleasure; practical, functional; an ethical approach based upon practical outcomes rather than duties or commandments (5, 8–9)

Vaihinger, H. (1852–1933): German philosopher of science, distinguished between verification and vindication (21, 22)

validity: truth in the realm of scientific and mathematical statements (4)

value: truth in the realm of relevance, including religious truth) (4)

Van Gennep, Arnold (1873–1957): "Rituals have liminality: separation, transformation, return" (22, 23, 32)

Vardhamana 6th century B.C.E.: major figure in Jainism, also known as Mahavira, advocated meditation, asceticism, noninjury (95, 96, 105, 224)

Vatican: location of Catholic Church leadership in Rome (277)

Vedanta: Hindu sect emphasizing pantheism, mysticism, asceticism; (see Upanishads) (102–103, 156)

Vedas: earliest and most sacred of all Hindu literature; describe Aryan conquest, castes, polytheistic (86, 156)

vegetarianism: abstinence from meat (e.g., Hinduism, Jainism, Seventh Day Adventists)

verification: proof based upon empirical observation or logical reasoning; may not prove doctrinal or ethical claims (3–5)

Vikings: see Teutons

vindication: proof in the realm of relevance; establishes the value of a doctrine, myth, symbol, ritual, or moral behavior

Vishnu: Hindu preserver deity (87, 98)

vision quest: puberty rite of American Indians; young man is sent into wilderness for communion with spirits (47)

voodoo: Haitian syncretism of African religion, Catholicism and sorcery

vulgate: Roman Catholic, Latin version of Bible completed 400 C.E.

Wahabi: 19th century fundamentalist religious and theocratic movement in sunni Islam (317–320)

Waldensians: 12th century French pious reformers: translated Bible, lay preaching, became heretical

Watch Tower: publication of Jehovah's Witnesses; emphasizes apocalyptic themes

Weber, Max (1864–1920): German sociologist: "Religion impacts economic attitudes" (22, 23, 339)

Wesley, John (1703–1791): pious Anglican priest who founded Methodists

Wheel: Buddhist and Jain symbol for life as suffering and transmigration (224)

White, Ellen (1826–1915): founder of Seventh Day Adventists (352, 361)

Wicca: recent movement incorporating old Celtic pre-Christian myths, rituals, and symbols (360, 363)

witch: someone claiming the power of sorcery, may be related to pre-Christian deities or Satanic worship (33)

witch doctor: sorcerer, especially in African religion (53)

Wittgenstein, Ludwig (1889–1951): linguistic philosopher: "Religion is a realm in which fact and logic do not apply"

worship: adoration of the divine by participation in ritual or prayer

Wycliffe, John (1320–1384): British reformer, founder of Lollards (284)

Yahweh: a Hebrew name for God in the Torah (126)

yang: male cosmic energy principle in ancient China (162–163, 178)

Yang Zhu, Yang Ju, Yang Chu: ancient Chinese hedonistic Daoist (161, 168–169, 218)

Yi Jing: I Ching a handbook for ancient Chinese divination using hexagrams (161, 165, 178, 183)

yin: female cosmic energy principle in ancient China (162–163, 178)

Yin Yang school: Chinese school of folk medicine, divination (165–166)

yoga: Hindu bodily exercises for mystical experience (90)

Young, Brigham: 19th century Mormon leader; took over after Smith's assassination and led Mormons to Utah

Zarathustra, Zoroaster: 7th century B.C.E.: Persian prophet, founder of Zoroastrianism (73)

Zealots: 1st century Jews seeking military rebellion against Rome (132–133, 265)

Zen: a meditative, mystical sect of Buddhism in China, Japan (240–248)

Zeno: several ancient Greek philosophers had this name, including a major cynic and also the Eleatic who presented logical paradoxes (210–214)

Zeitgeist: "spirit of the times"; intellectual concept found among many thinkers during the same period of time

Zeus: head deity of thunderbolt in Greek Pantheon; known as Jupiter in Rome; anthropomorphic (204–206)

Zhuangzi, Chuang Tsu: axial age mystical Daoist (161, 172–173)

Zionism: 19th–20th century movement to return Jews to Palestine (145–147)

Zoroastrianism: Persian religion: dualist, apocalyptic; angels, resurrection (73–77, 80, 308, 322, 361)